Handbook on Product Standards and International Trade

Global Trade Law Series

VOLUME 55

Series Editors

Introduction and Contents/Subjects

The *Global Trade Law Series* addresses key issues in international trade law. It covers a broad range of topics, including WTO dispute settlement, free trade agreements, investment law and arbitration, export control, and compliance with international trade obligations.

Objective & Readership

The volumes published in this series are aimed at offering high-quality analytical information and practical solutions, for practitioners, policy makers and academics.

Frequency of Publication

2-3 new volumes published each year.

The titles published in this series are listed at the end of this volume.

Handbook on Product Standards and International Trade

Navigating the Regulatory Landscape in India

Edited by

James J. Nedumpara
Satwik Shekhar
Akshaya Venkataraman

Wolters Kluwer

Published by:
Kluwer Law International B.V.
PO Box 316
2400 AH Alphen aan den Rijn
The Netherlands
E-mail: international-sales@wolterskluwer.com
Website: lrus.wolterskluwer.com

Sold and distributed by:
Wolters Kluwer Legal & Regulatory U.S.
7201 McKinney Circle
Frederick, MD 21704
United States of America
E-mail: customer.service@wolterskluwer.com

ISBN 978-94-035-3413-8

e-Book: ISBN 978-94-035-3414-5
web-PDF: ISBN 978-94-035-3415-2

Editors

James J. Nedumpara, Head and Professor, Centre for Trade and Investment Law, New Delhi.

Satwik Shekhar, Consultant (Legal) | Assistant Professor, Centre for Trade and Investment Law, New Delhi.

Akshaya Venkataraman, Senior Research Fellow, Centre for Trade and Investment Law, New Delhi.

Contributors

Arthur Appleton, Partner, Appleton Luff – International Lawyers; Adjunct Professor Johns Hopkins School of Advanced International Studies (SAIS Europe); Principal, TCube Consulting (India).

Amandeep Kaur Bajwa, Research Fellow, Centre for Trade and Investment Law, New Delhi.

Smrithi Bhaskar, Research Fellow, Centre for Trade and Investment Law, New Delhi.

Aparna Bhattacharya, Senior Research Fellow, Centre for Trade and Investment Law, New Delhi.

Ashish Chandra, Partner, International Trade/WTO Law Practice group at L&L Partners, New Delhi.

Anupal Dasgupta, Senior Associate, International Trade/ WTO Law Practice group at L&L Partners, New Delhi.

Manya Gupta, Senior Research Fellow, Centre for Trade and Investment Law, New Delhi.

Hari Maya Gurung, Senior Research Fellow (Economics), Centre for WTO Studies, New Delhi.

Murali Kallummal, Professor, Centre for WTO Studies, New Delhi.

Sreelakshmi S. Kurup, Research Fellow, Centre for Trade and Investment Law, New Delhi.

Rishabha Meena, Research Fellow, Centre for Trade and Investment Law, New Delhi.

Trishna Menon, Senior Research Fellow, Centre for Trade and Investment Law, New Delhi.

Shiny Pradeep, Assistant Professor (Legal), Centre for Trade and Investment Law, New Delhi.

Ridhish Rajvanshi, Research Fellow, Centre for Trade and Investment Law, New Delhi

Malvika Shetty, former Research Fellow (Legal), Centre for WTO Studies, New Delhi.

Shailja Singh, Legal Consultant (Associate Professor), Centre for WTO Studies, Indian Institute of Foreign Trade, New Delhi.

Rita Teaotia, Chairperson, Food Safety and Standards Authority of India (FSSAI).

Sunanda Tewari, Senior Research Fellow, Centre for Trade and Investment Law, New Delhi.

Apoorva Singh Vishnoi, Research Fellow, Centre for Trade and Investment Law, New Delhi.

Summary of Contents

Table of Contents

List of Figures

List of Tables

Foreword

The setting, development, implementation, monitoring and enforcement of standards have assumed critical importance in recent times. With progressively increasing global trade in goods and services, and with India coming to play a vital and increasingly noticeable role in global trade, standards have become indispensable to Indian businesses and firms. In order to keep up with these developments, the regulatory environment governing standards has been undergoing a sea-change in the past decade. The Indian National Strategy for Standards envisioned first in 2014 and the new Bureau of Indian Standards Act brought into force in 2016 marked the beginning of a new era for standardisation in India. The BIS Act led to establishment of a national standards body for the harmonious development of the activities of standardisation, conformity assessment and quality assurance of goods, articles, processes, systems and services.

Given these developments, this Handbook – a collection of essays on standardisation encompassing international and India specific issues – is a timely publication on a subject of crucial importance to the modern Indian economy. Touching upon broad areas of discussions as well as specific issues within focused industries, this book presents informed and critical perspectives on the evolution and development of standards in India. The first part of this book serves as a useful guide on the international perspectives and issues in standard setting. It provides valuable discussions on the international rules on standard-setting while at the same time, critiquing the shortcomings in these rules and providing a roadmap for the negotiation of agreements in the future. The second part of this Handbook delves into the Indian standardisation regime. It provides insights on the workings of institutions such as the Food Safety and Standards Authority of India (FSSAI) and the Bureau of Indian Standards (BIS), historical analyses of issues such as compliance with the Sanitary and Phytosanitary (SPS) and Technical Barriers to Trade (TBT) Agreements and discussions on standardisation in industries of the future, for instance, services and digital trade.

Collectively, the essays of this Handbook offer a comprehensive and lucid account of the contemporary issues for the benefit of the stakeholders involved in standardisation activities in India and their role in enhancing India's trading capabilities. These essays highlight the increase in standardisation activities in India across sectors and the enhanced participation of the Indian industry and Indian regulators internationally.

The Department of Commerce, Ministry of Commerce and Industry in India has been organizing the National Standards Conclave since 2014 to generate awareness and enhance preparedness among the various stakeholders concerning the entire gamut of standards – from preparation to enforcement. The effort is to help the industry, the users and the standards bodies to work in tandem to create a standards ecosystem in India built on the edifice of quality, safety and sound regulatory principles while ensuring that unnecessary barriers to trade are eliminated. The Department of Commerce along with BIS and other partner agencies has organized National and Regional Standards Conclaves since 2014, to spread awareness and discuss policy and operational issues with regulators/stakeholders on various aspects related to standardization of goods and services. As a result of these Standards Conclaves, a strategy document viz. Indian National Strategy for Standardization (INSS) was prepared and adopted at the 5th National Standards Conclave (18-19 June 2018, New Delhi). The strategy provides a key to standards and allied activities related to goods and services.

The publication of this book by Centre for Trade and Investment Law (CTIL) professional staff complements the goals and objectives of the Department of Commerce. The editors of this book have put together a collection which takes the reader – both the technical reader and the non-technical, non-expert reader – through the regulation of standardisation internationally as well as in India. There is a compelling need to disseminate the commendable work carried out by various standards bodies and product regulators in India. Contributions from FSSAI Chairperson Ms Rita Teaotia and international experts such as Dr Arthur Appleton contribute to the richness of the book. The collection of essays is comprehensive, detailed and meticulous in its approach and contents.

Several of the contributors of this Handbook as well as the editors of this Handbook, are affiliated with either CTIL or the Centre for WTO Studies (CWS), two centres that the Department of Commerce, Government of India, has created. It is matter of pride and satisfaction that these research centres have taken up the challenge to produce valuable research outputs which can cater to the demands of the industry, standards bodies and the government in relation to a host of trade and regulatory issues. I would like to place on record my appreciation for the efforts of Professor James Nedumpara and his colleagues Mr Satwik Shekhar and Ms Akshaya Venkataraman for coming up with this Handbook. I am confident that this Handbook will serve as a useful primer for a large target audience – regulators, policy officials, industry experts, exporters, importers, lawyers and other stakeholders in the international trade of goods and services.

Amit Yadav, IAS
Additional Secretary and Director General of Foreign Trade,
Department of Commerce,
Ministry of Commerce and Industry

Preface and Acknowledgement

A substantial amount of the work that we carry out at the Centre for Trade and Investment Law pertains to non-tariff barriers to trade. These barriers are complex and they manifest in different forms. The World Trade Organization SPS Agreement and the TBT Agreement succeeded in many ways in dealing with these non-tariff barriers. Being parties to these agreements and related international standard-setting organizations and bodies entailed that most WTO Members are required to build institutions and devote resources for capacity building in standard-setting and enforcement. We felt that a comprehensive book on standards including views and perspectives from diverse experts and practitioners catering to the needs of the global standards community is timely and relevant.

We are truly grateful to Mr Jeff Snyder, Partner at Crowell and Moring LLP and the General Editor of Global Trade and Customs Journal for directing us to the key contacts at Wolters Kluwer. We also grateful to Kiran Gore, the Acquisition Manager at Wolters Kluwer for considering our proposal. We are also grateful to Simon Bellamy, Acquisition Manager at Wolters Kluwer for fast-tracking the publication. We are particularly delighted that this Handbook on Standards is released as part of the prestigious Global Trade Law Series edited by Professors Andreas Ziegler and Ross Buckley.

Most chapters of this Handbook reflect the experience that the authors have gained from working on standards specific work relating to India and other jurisdictions. Our participation in the Standards Conclave during the past few years, organized by the Department of Commerce with other industry associations have been a particularly enriching experience. We are grateful to the Honourable Union Minister for Commerce and Industry Mr Piyush Goyal and the current Commerce Secretary Mr B V R Subrahmanyam for the inspiration they provide. We would also like to thank the past Commerce Secretaries including Ms Rita Teaotia and Dr Anup Wadhawan. We are also indebted to Mr Sudhanshu Pandey, Secretary (DFPD), Mr Darpan Jain, Joint Secretary, Ms Jyoti Yadav, Deputy Secretary and Ms Tanu Singh, Deputy DGFT for the opportunities they have provided us to work on standard-related issues.

In writing and editing this Handbook we are grateful to the authors for their prompt response and cooperation. We would also like to place on record our appreciation for the work of Ms Pradhiba and her team at Newgen Knowledge Works.

James J. Nedumpara, Satwik Shekhar and Akshaya Venkataraman

Editors' Introduction: Handbook on Product Standard and International Trade – Navigating the Regulatory Landscape in India

James J. Nedumpara, Satwik Shekhar & Akshaya Venkataraman

When we plug our laptop's charging chord into a power socket, we are confident that the pins of the chord will fit into the socket and that there will be no damaging electrical outage. This sense of a product being suitable and safe for use by way of its size, shape, quality and operability is a consequence of the applicable product 'standards'. In India, there are three plug types – types C, D and M. Only chords suitable for these three plug types will fit into power sockets in India. A chord/cable suitable for type J plug outlet, for example, will not be useful. Likewise, all the electrical products sold in India are set up to function smoothly and safely when connected to a 230V supply voltage – because that is the voltage of supply of household electricity in India. Any electrical product or its chord which does not suit the above 'standards', will either be of no use or a cause of safety concern to the user. In addition, the product could be irreparably damaged. The same is true when we choose pencil cell batteries for use in a clock or a home appliance; we know the appropriate type (AA or AAA) of battery that can ensure performance, quality and safety. To choose another example, when we choose airbags for passenger cars, we would like to ensure that the airbags get deployed on time and that they can withstand the crash. Examples are aplenty.

Standards apply to almost every product we come across in our daily lives – from the clothes we wear to the houses we live in, from the packaged juice we drink to the food served in a restaurant, and so on. Standards ensure safety, quality and functionality in virtually every aspect of our lives. The objective of the creators and developers of standards is typically to build a 'norm' of quality and safety to ensure the protection of human life and health, animal life and health and the preservation of environment. The prevalence of these norms is intended to facilitate trust among consumers and induce confidence in the products that they buy. Product standards also ensure greater product liability. Conversely, manufacturers/traders are also able to assure product specification, performance and stated operability of their products.

While it is easy to discuss the importance of standards for ensuring the quality of modern life, the origins of these standards - who develops them, who tests them and who enforces them - is somewhat complicated. Standards are generally set by governments, autonomous standard-setting bodies or private industries. Standards take the form of government regulations, voluntary certifications, practices enforced by industry associations or guidelines and rules issued by technical bodies. Across the world, standards are a result of extensive consultations and deliberations. Given the interconnectedness of the various processes involved in standard-setting and conformity assessment[1] and the number of entities operating in a field, it is crucial for industries, exporters, manufacturers, policy makers and regulators to be aware of these standards and the policy framework in which various standard-setting bodies function.

In the World Trade Report for the year 2012 (WTR12), the World Trade Organization (WTO) observed the proliferation and impact of non-tariff measures such as standards, technical regulations and sanitary and phytosanitary (SPS) measures on global trade. The WTR12 notes that due to the diversity and complexity of such non-tariff measures in services and goods trade, a deeper understanding of the standards and their effects is 'crucial not only for a sound policy strategy but also from the perspective of international cooperation'.[2] The United Nations Economic and Social Commission for Asia and the Pacific (UNESCAP) in its Asia-Pacific Trade and Investment Report of 2019 has also made similar observations on the proliferation of such measures and the need to understand their impact and effects on global trade.[3]

There is a complex network of bodies involved in standards and conformity assessment processes in most countries. Their primary interlinkages and relationships with international and regional organizations are seemingly complex. The aim of this book is to explore the nature of this relationship. While numerous governmental agencies in India such as the Ministry of Science and Technology, the Ministry of Agriculture, Ministry of Health and Family Welfare, and the Ministry of Consumer Affairs, Food and Public Distribution (and their relevant departments) at the federal level are responsible for setting standards, statutory bodies like the Bureau of Indian Standards (BIS) and Food Safety and Standards Authority of India (FSSAI) create standards drawing their powers from their parent legislations. While India has several national accreditation and registration boards (e.g., NABL, NABCB, NRBPT housed under the Quality Council of India [QCI])), there are also a number of private certification bodies registered under these boards. Any product which is placed in the Indian territory for either commercial use or final consumption is required to meet the

1. The process of checking conformity with a standard - *See* Chapter 6for a detailed discussion on Conformity Assessment Processes.
2. WTO, *World Trade Report 2012 Trade and Public Policies: A Closer Look at Non-Tariff Measures in the 21st Century,* at p. 37, available at https://www.wto.org/english/res_e/booksp_e/anrep_e/world_trade_report12_e.pdf.
3. UNESCAP, *Asia-Pacific Trade and Investment Report,* 2019, at p. 13, available at https://www.unescap.org/sites/default/d8files/APTIR2019_Introduction.pdf.

technical regulations and standards as set by the above stakeholders. These requirements may be mandatory or voluntary. Finally, several private companies also develop their testing capabilities which can be accepted, provided they meet the legitimate policy objectives of consumer interests, public health, safety, environment, plant and animal life, among others.

The aforesaid discussion merely provides a snapshot of the various bodies involved in the process of standard-setting in India. A detailed examination raises questions such as: - How do BIS and FSSAI interact while formulating standards in the food industry? What is the role of the Agricultural and Processed Food Products Export Development Authority (APEDA) in this? What is the difference between certification and accreditation? How does the QCI coordinate with its constituent bodies such as NABL, NABCB, NRBPT, etc.? There are several questions at the heart of the standard-setting process. Given the ever-expanding relevance of standards to international trade, there is critical need for a holistic examination of the functions, responsibilities and the nature of tasks assigned to these bodies. Given the broad ambitions of this book, details of the processes as well as the various bodies involved is a vital piece of information necessary for all stakeholders - from policy makers to manufacturers and traders. This Handbook is intended to serve this purpose.

This Handbook features a detailed enquiry into multifaceted dimensions of standards -setting, implementation and compliance, with specific reference to India. With contributions from practitioners, academicians, experts and regulators, the Handbook attempts to simplify complex concepts, processes and regulations, and aims to be a one-stop-shop for the key stakeholders in the standards ecosystem - industry and businesses as well as policy makers and academia. Keeping in mind that consumers are becoming more aware of standards and quality of products they use, the Handbook has been drafted with the hope that consumers and other non-technical readers are also able to gain fruitful insights into the standards development and implementation systems. Consequently, the Handbook is structured in the form of an easy-to-read guide with extensive use of tables, figures and charts to suit the non-expert reader. The overall objective of the Handbook is to develop an up-to-date guide about the creation of technical regulations, standard-setting and conformity assessment, including testing, quality checks and related processes. The Handbook examines the meaning of these concepts as well as provides analysis on how these concepts are interpreted and applied from a legal perspective. The Handbook also aims to examine and lay out the functions, powers, mandates and relationships between Central/State Governments, regulatory bodies, certification agencies, non-governmental entities and other stakeholders in the standard-setting process. This Handbook identifies the relevant legislations from which the above entities draw their powers, and attempts to provide clarity on the overlaps in the functions of different entities, the regulatory gaps and uncertainty in laws, and the coordination and cooperation among various entities in creation of technical regulations (TR) and standard-setting.

With the first Indian National Standards Conclave in 2014, India began the mammoth task of harmonizing, modernizing and streamlining its legal regime for standardization. Since then, the Indian regulatory regime has grown leaps and bounds - with the implementation of the Bureau of Indian Standards Act of 2016 and the introduction of the Indian National Strategy for Standardization. India's WTO 7th Trade Policy Review of 2021 (India TPR 2021) notes that as of 2018, of the 19,294 Indian Standards in force, over 27% have already been harmonized with International Standards. In addition to the revamped role of the BIS, the regulatory regime has also seen a push toward the formal recognition of specialized regulators and private institutions that prepare sector-specific standards. The BIS operates a scheme for the recognition of such standards development organization (SDOs) bringing them within the fold of the 'One Nation One Standard' paradigm identified by the Indian Government, and ensuring that these SDOs follow the WTO's Code of Good Practices for standardization. This period has also seen marked increase in India's engagement with the WTO transparency and accountability system for standards and technical regulation. While India's Trade Policy Review of 2015 (India TPR 2015) noted that between 2011 and 2015 India notified 11 new technical regulations, the India TPR 2021 notes that between 2015and 2020, 102 new technical regulations were notified to the WTO by India – a nearly tenfold increase.

All of these statistics and developments point to a change in the Indian landscape – a change toward integrating better with the global economy, and toward facilitating trade and ease of doing business. With contributions from academicians, practitioners and experts in various legal and practical domains of standards development, this Handbook attempts to contextualize the Indian standardization framework within the global governance of this process and identify potential areas of growth and further development. While some chapters lay the groundwork on the processes, explaining the network of rules and regulations and regulators in distinct sectors of standardization, some other chapters take a critical look at some of the persisting issues in harmonizing Indian Standards globally and how these challenges may be addressed.

The Handbook is organized to introduce the reader to the broad contours of the process of standard-setting and enforcement. The Handbook begins with outlining the international perspectives relevant to standards development. The first chapter 'Trade Regulation of Product Standards: An Overview', from the editors' desk, introduces how broad concepts such as standards, technical regulations and allied terms are legally and internationally understood. This chapter explains the key legal principles of the Agreements of the WTO which govern the creation and implementation of standards in a global setting. With this introduction, Chapter 2 by Arthur Appleton on 'Technical Regulations and Standards: Lessons Learnt from TBT Disputes' critically examines the jurisprudence of the WTO Agreement on Technical Barriers to Trade. It provides an easy-to-comprehend roadmap for policy makers and other standards developing organizations on the rules and principles to be kept in consideration. The chapter also provides an insightful commentary on the ability of the TBT Agreement, in its current form, to meaningfully govern the vastly expanding and changing landscape of standards and technical regulations. Chapter 3 of the Handbook looks at the role of free trade agreements in product regulation. In this chapter on 'Product Regulations: Designing a Development-Friendly FTA – An Indian Perspective', Shailja Singh explores four issues relating to standards and technical regulations, i.e., international standardizing bodies, sectoral annexes, trans-governmental network of regulators, and language barriers faced by developing countries in particular. This chapter provides key insights into the role that FTAs have played in these issues, and how India in its future trade engagements could leverage the instrument of FTAs to design more development-friendly and equitable norms. Chapter 4 of the Handbook titled 'Standards and the WTO Agreement on Import Licensing Procedures' by Aparna Bhattacharya and Trishna Menon, examines the intersection of standards and the WTO Agreement on Import Licensing. The chapter explores the procedures for grant of SPS and TBT approvals and whether they are subject to the rules contained in the WTO Agreement on Import Licensing in light of the absence of a clear definition of 'import license', limited jurisprudence on the intersection of standards and the rules contained in the Import Licensing Agreement, and the ambiguous notification practice of Members.

With these comments on the developments and rules in standard-setting internationally the Handbook shifts focus and explores the regulatory regime in India. Chapters 5 and 6 of the Handbook again provide the broad contours of the process of standard-setting and implementation, but this time with a specific focus on India. Chapter 5 'Standards Ecosystem and Standardization Activities in India', also from the editors' desk, explains how standards are developed in India. It looks at the history of standard-setting, and unravels the web of regulatory bodies involved in this process of standard-setting. Chapter 6 on 'Conformity Assessment Practices and Procedures' by Smrithi Bhaskar and Apoorva Singh Vishnoi follows this overview with a detailed examination on the regulatory landscape for conformity assessment procedures. In this chapter, the authors paint a thorough account of the concept of conformity assessment procedures (CAP), the various elements involved in CAPs, and the multitude of bodies in India which are a part of the CAP ecosystem. Subsequently, in Chapter 7 on 'Mutual Recognition Agreements: An International and Indian Perspective', Manya Gupta and Rishabha Meena analyse the WTO norms applicable to bilateral MRAs (a critical tool for harmonization of CAPs) and the trends seen internationally on the proliferation and utility of MRAs. Thereafter, they provide a comprehensive view of the various MRAs entered into by India, the bodies involved in this process and the various gaps to be addressed. Collectively these three chapters are intended to serve as the framework within which the reader has the opportunity to understand the mechanism of the standards ecosystem in India.

With these broad perspectives, the Handbook shifts toward examining specific issues and sectors within the Indian Standards framework. In particular, the food, agriculture and food products sector which is governed internationally by the SPS Agreement of the WTO, provides excellent case studies to examine the issues that crop-up at the intersection of domestic and international standard-setting processes. The Handbook proceeds to examine India's relationship with standard-setting in the food and agriculture sector in three parts. First, Chapter 8 on the 'Food Safety Ecosystem in India' elaborates on the role and functions of the apex regulator for food standards in India – the FSSAI. Written by Rita Teaotia, India's former Commerce Secretary and the incumbent Chairperson of the FSSAI, the chapter succinctly lays out the statutory scheme, the responsibilities and the instrumental role of FSSAI in developing and shaping the food standards in India. With the benefit of this introduction, the next Chapter 9 on 'Understanding the SPS Regulatory Framework in the Indian

Context' looks at the evolution and current state of India's legal framework for Sanitary and Phytosanitary measures. This chapter, authored by Ashish Chandra and Anupal Dasgupta, provides practitioners' perspectives on the relationship of the FSSAI with various other food regulatory bodies in India and the systemic issues involved in the standard-setting processes. Finally, Murali Kallummal and his team - Malvika Shetty and Hari Maya Gurung, throw rich insights on the sensitive topic of pesticide residue in food products. In their chapter on 'India's Initiatives in Addressing Food Safety: The Concerns with Maximum Residue Levels', the authors provide a comprehensive review and analysis of the evolution of MRLs internationally and within India, and examine the various concerns which have plagued the implementation of MRLs.

Both specific and broad at the same time, these three chapters provide a snapshot of the scale at which standard-setting processes operate, their impact on essential goods and the various regulatory and practical hurdles in introducing standards for ensuring the quality and safety of food products.

With these insights on the history of standard-setting and its current status in India, the Handbook thereafter veers course to examine the emerging sectors on the horizon. In the following chapters, the Handbook focuses on two specific sectors where standards are just emerging. Chapter 11 of the Handbook by Shiny Pradeep, Trishna Menon and Sreelakshmi S. Kurup focuses on 'Services Standards: Trends, Gaps and Future Directions'. While product standards are already ubiquitous, the massive growth of the services sector globally has warranted the development of standards in this sector as well. Chapter 11 introduces these trends internationally and thereafter focuses on the emergence of standards in this sector in India. It provides guidance for the service sectors where such standards are already becoming prevalent and also outlines the areas where the reader can expect standards in the near future. Closely connected to services, yet occupying a universe of its own, is the digital sector. Chapter 12 of the Handbook on 'Standardization of the Digital Economy: An Indian Perspective' unpacks the complex variables involved in the standardization of digital services. With a particular focus on India, this chapter by Sunanda Tewari, Amandeep Kaur Bajwa and Ridhish Rajvanshi, explores the intricacies of why and how standard-setting for digital services is unique, and how various concerns such as privacy, security and interoperability are accounted for in this process.

Given the critical importance of services trade in the future of the global economy, these two chapters shed fresh light on a valuable component of the global economy.

In the following chapters, this Handbook attempts to undertake the herculean task of untangling and explaining both the broad and specific concepts of standard-setting in all the key sectors of the economy. This challenging task is made further complex and exciting because of the fast-evolving developments in this legal ecosystem in India. Between the commencement and completion of this Handbook, for instance, BIS formally implemented its recognition scheme for standards development organizations (the 'SDO Recognition Scheme') by recognizing Indian Railways' Research Design and Standards Organization (RDSO) as India's first BIS recognized sectoral SDO and in the process, streamlined RDSO's working to bring it in conformity with WTO

Code of Good Practice. In other words, standards are bound to emerge and proliferate in various sectors of the economy.

It is the editors' hope that the readers gain fruitful insights from the chapters, and that this Handbook serves as a useful *vade mecum* for the stakeholders involved in the Indian Standards ecosystem or those who would like to know more about India's standards administration.

CHAPTER 1

Trade Regulation of Product Standards: An Overview

James J. Nedumpara, Satwik Shekhar & Akshaya Venkataraman

Trade agreements have an important role in regulating product standards. As a starting point, this chapter provides a clear understanding of how international trade agreements, in particular, the WTO Agreements, address product standards. In addition to explaining how trade treaties regulate standards, the chapter unpacks through a discussion of the case law, the nature and contours of the basic obligations under the specialised agreements, viz., the Agreement on Technical Barriers to Trade and the Agreement on Sanitary and Phytosanitary Measures under the WTO. The chapter critically explains the differences between mandatory and voluntary standards and the legal obligation they entail. Finally, the authors trace how standardisation activities, conformity assessment procedures, and standard-setting processes are governed under the WTO and under the preferential trade agreements. The chapter concludes with an attempt to provide a macro view encompassing the various issues in the legal governance of standards internationally and sets the background for a more detailed and focussed discussion of the intricate issues relating to standard-setting, standards recognition, and standards enforcement in the subsequent chapters.

1.1 INTRODUCTION

Standards have become ubiquitous in the contemporary economy. Consumer goods of all forms (e.g., food, textiles, industrial equipment, fuel and electronic devices) are subject to standards. In 2016, for instance, the Food Safety and Standards Authority of India (FSSAI) announced that it would be developing standards specifically for instant noodles, in response to a year-long public outcry in India over the presence of high levels of MSG in certain instant noodle brands.[1] One of the earliest disputes to come up before the World Trade Organization (WTO) Dispute Settlement Body, the *US – Gasoline Dispute*,[2] dealt with the imposition of mandatory standards for gasoline. Standards are proliferating in the services sector as well. Standardisation in the field of healthcare and education are becoming more common. The pressing concerns raised by climate change have given rise to 'sustainability' or energy efficiency standards, an example of which is the ecolabels displayed in everyday electronic goods such as refrigerators and air-conditioners.

In essence, standards are rules, guidelines or recommendations which identify or specify characteristics for products or their process and production means. Characteristics can include design, size, texture, weight, safety, energy and environmental performance, interoperability, materials used, and other attributes relating to physical and chemical composition; it may be embodied in marking, labelling, packaging, testing, inspection and quarantine, and information requirements.

Standards are capable of furthering critical domestic public policy goals while also facilitating trade, commerce and ease of doing business. Standards can ensure access to safe and reliable goods, minimise health hazards to consumers, develop safeguards for the protection of the environment and facilitate the growth of exports. Standards can serve as public policy tools for achieving outcomes such as product safety, consumer protection, food safety, environment protection and safe infrastructure.

Standards create the basis for mutual understanding between manufacturers, traders, distributers and consumers, and are critical to ensuring the ease of quantification, communication, manufacture and trade of goods. Standards, *inter alia*, facilitate business interaction, enable businesses to comply with relevant laws and regulations, accelerate the introduction of innovative products to the market and promote interoperability between new and existing products, services and processes. Product standards also act as a platform for the transmission of information and knowledge across various stages of a supply chain and between different interactive industries.

In recent years, the number of technical regulations and standards adopted by countries has grown significantly. The WTO Information Management System for the Agreement on Technical Barriers to Trade (TBT Agreement) and the Agreement on Sanitary and Phytosanitary Measures (SPS Agreement) notes that in 1995, only 364 TBT notifications and 189 SPS notifications were made. That number has significantly increased as of 2020. The number of TBT notifications made in 2020 was 2043[3] and the

---

1. *Maggi effect: FSSAI plans specific regulations for noodles*, The Economic Times (18 May 2016, 05:57 PM IST), https://economictimes.indiatimes.com/industry/cons-products/food/maggi-effect-fssai-plans-specific-regulations-for-noodles/articleshow/52327460.cms?utm_source = con tentofinterest&utm_medium = text&utm_campaign = cppst.
2. Appellate Body Report on *United States – Standards for Reformulated and Conventional Gasoline*, (hereinafter '*US – Gasoline*'), WT/DS2/AB/R, adopted 20 May 1996.
3. *Technical Barriers to Trade: Information Management System*, WTO, http://tbtims.wto.org/en/Notifications/Search (from 'Date of Distribution', select 1 January 2020 to 31 December 2020, from 'Type of Notification', select 'Regular notification') (last visited 1 February 2021).

number of SPS notifications in 2020 was 1,942.[4] The WTO, in a report, notes that as of May 2020, over two-thirds of all notifications submitted by Member States in response to the COVID-19 pandemic are related to standards and technical regulations.[5]

A study of standards and technical regulations is, therefore, essential to understand global trade in in the twenty-first century. Inasmuch as standards facilitate cooperation, they also demonstrate diversity in ideologies, moral values and perceptions of safety across jurisdictions. Standards and technical regulations are influenced by (a) difference in levels of development and technology, (b) varied level of risk posed by the same goods in different countries, and (c) geographical, climatic and social-cultural differences. This diversity of motivation and factors behind the development of standards has prompted the creation of rules and agreements between countries, international bodies and industry players on how standards may be developed. The WTO has recognised that while it may be difficult to identify a precise monetary estimate of their impact on international trade, standards, particularly when they vary in different jurisdictions, result in significant costs to producers and exporters. In globalised supply chains, even minor differences in legal standards among countries can be significant barriers to trade. With a view to ensuring that standards achieve their intended objective of facilitating trade, and that they do not instead operate as disguised barriers to international trade, rules governing standard-setting have been developed.

This Handbook on Standards tracks not just the development of standards in India but also how Indian Standards interact with international standards as well as a detailed examination of the application of international trade rules on standards. The chapter locates the various types of standards in an international context and sets out the best practices and rules (both at the WTO and otherwise) which impact the creation, implementation and enforcement of standards.

1.2 DEVELOPMENT AND ENFORCEMENT OF STANDARDS

Public welfare, health concerns and mitigation of environmental risks are some of the most common bases upon which standards are developed by regulatory bodies and standard-setting organisations.

There are many ways to categorise standards - on the basis of how they are developed, the kind of functions they serve, or the sectors they operate in, etc. These different perspectives of categorising standards provide the framework for understanding how standards are developed and applied. In particular, this section curates some of the different categorisations of standards and introduces the process of development of standards (i.e., standard-setting) and implementation of standards (i.e., conformity assessment procedures). A fuller examination of these concepts – standard-setting and

4. *Sanitary and Phytosanitary: Information Management System*, WTO, http://spsims.wto.org/en/Notifications/Search from 'Date of Distribution', select 1 January 2020 to 31 December 2020, from 'Type of Notification', select 'Regular and emergency notification') (Last visited 1 February 2021).
5. *Standards, Regulations and Covid-19 – What Actions Taken By WTO Members?*, WTO (4 December 2020), https://www.wto.org/english/tratop_e/covid19_e/standards_report_e.pdf.

conformity assessment procedures, from an Indian as well as an international perspective, is presented across the various chapters of this Handbook.

1.2.1 Types of Standards

One way to categorise standards is to look at its geographic scope of application. From this perspective, standards can be international, regional or national. Bodies like the International Standards Organisation (ISO) and the Codex Alimentarius Commission (Codex) are responsible for the preparation of standards internationally. There is a wide scholarship on what truly constitutes an 'international' standard, particularly within the interpretation of the WTO rules. Chapter 2 of this Handbook takes a focused look at the lessons learn from this jurisprudence of the WTO rules on international standards and technical regulations. When international or global cooperation is difficult to achieve, geographically or socio-politically aligned countries have cooperated to set up organisations to develop standards for the identified regions. The European Committee for Standardisation (CEN), the ASEAN Consultative Committee for Standards and Quality (the ACCSQ), and the African Regional Organisation for Standardization (ARSO) are examples of bodies that develop or provide guidance on the development of regional standards. The proliferation of preferential trade agreements (PTAs) in the past two decades has helped foster common trade rules applicable to such regional bodies. Section 1.3.3 of this chapter examines in some more detail the approach that PTAs take toward governing the development and implementation of standards regionally.

The Organisation for Economic Co-operation and Development (OECD) in a publication in 2011 categorised standards on the basis of the functions that they served.[6] Acknowledging the existence of a degree of overlap between these categories, the OECD presented the following categories of standards: (a) quality standards; (b) informational standards; (c) uniformity standards; (d) professional conduct and certification standards; and (e) interoperability standards (Figure 1.1).

6. Directorate for Financial and Enterprise Affairs – Competition Committee, *Standard Setting*, Organisation for Economic Co-operation and Development 21 (8 March 2011) https://www.oecd.org/daf/competition/47381304.pdf.

Figure 1.1 Types of Standards as per OECD

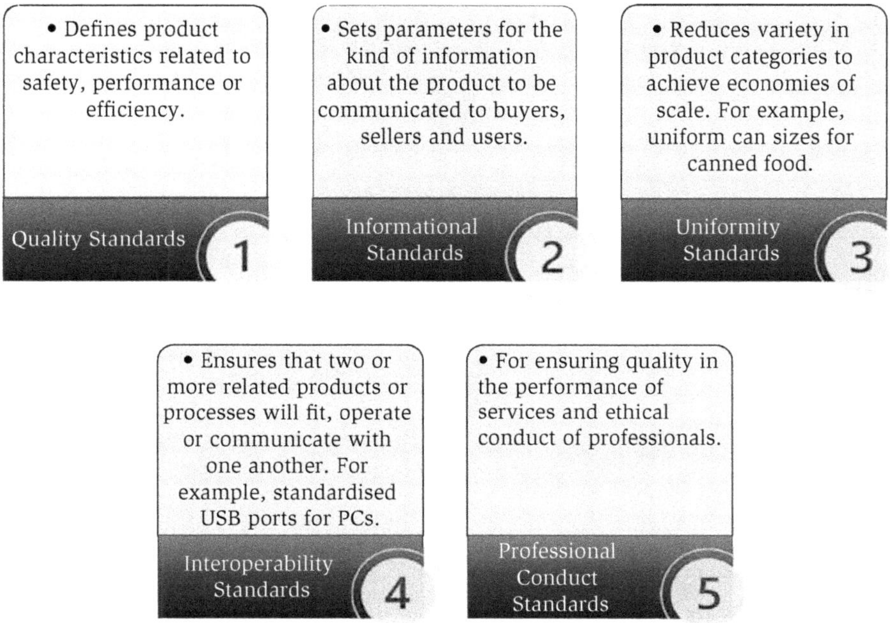

There are many more methods of categorising standards on the basis of the roles and functions they serve. For instance, Europe's CEN catalogues its standards on the basis of the following four criteria (Figure 1.2).[7]

7. *Types of Standards*, European Committee for Standardisation, https://www.cencenelec.eu/research/innovation/standardstypes/Pages/default.aspx (last visited 11 December 2020).

Figure 1.2 Types of Standards as per CEN

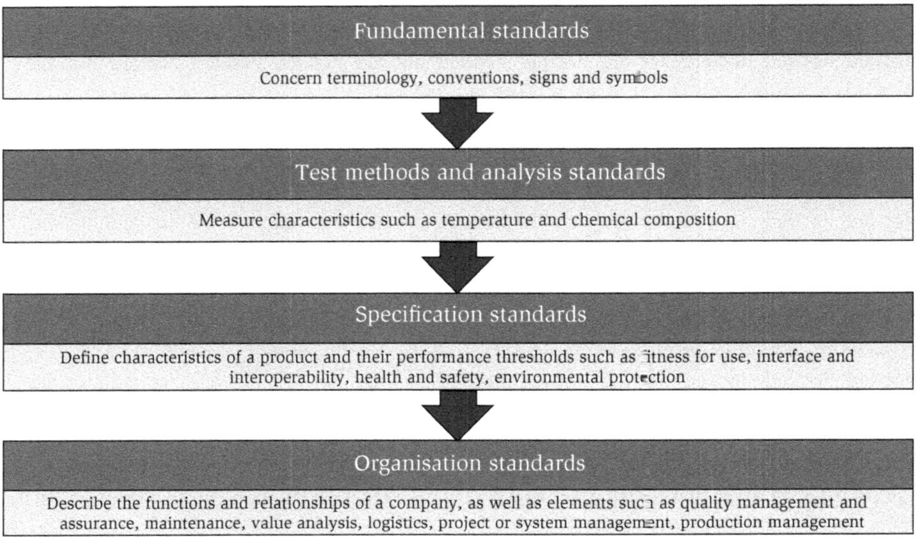

Source: European Committee of Standardisation.

Standards can also be categorised on the basis of the types of bodies that develop them, i.e., whether they are developed by private bodies, government bodies, industry associations or international organisations.

1.2.2 Standard-Setting Bodies

As noted previously, standards are developed at international, regional and national levels. Standards are largely developed either by (a) governments, (b) industry associations, (c) international organisations, or (d) private bodies. For national standards, governments typically set up a national standard-setting body, standards developed by which will usually have legal or statutory sanction. For example, in India, the Bureau of Indian Standards (BIS) acts as the national standard-setting body. At the national level, there are often other non-governmental bodies which may be recognised for specific sectors as standards developing organisations (SDOs). The FSSAI is one such SDO in India. Chapter 5 of this Handbook examines national standard-setting in India in detail.

The WTO SPS Agreement refers to intergovernmental standard-setting bodies such as the Codex Alimentarius Commission, World Organization of Animal Health and the International Plant Protection Council. In addition, bodies such as the ISO, the International Electrotechnical Commission, ASTM International and the International Telecommunication Union operate as international non-governmental organisations where national standard-setting bodies participate and develop internationally applicable standards.

Beyond such organisations, standards are also privately developed either by industry associations or non-governmental bodies for profit-making as well as non-profit entities. Where government standards may be either mandatory (in which case they are called technical regulations in the parlance of the WTO, *see* section 1.3.1.1) or voluntary, private standards are by definition always voluntary.

1.2.3 Conformity Assessment Procedures

Once a standard has been developed, the next step is referred to as 'conformity assessment'. Conformity assessment involves a set of processes that show that a product, service or system meets the requirements of a particular set/prescribed standard. Conformity assessment typically involves three processes – certification, testing and inspection. Figure 1.3 examines these three processes.

Figure 1.3 Conformity Assessment Procedures

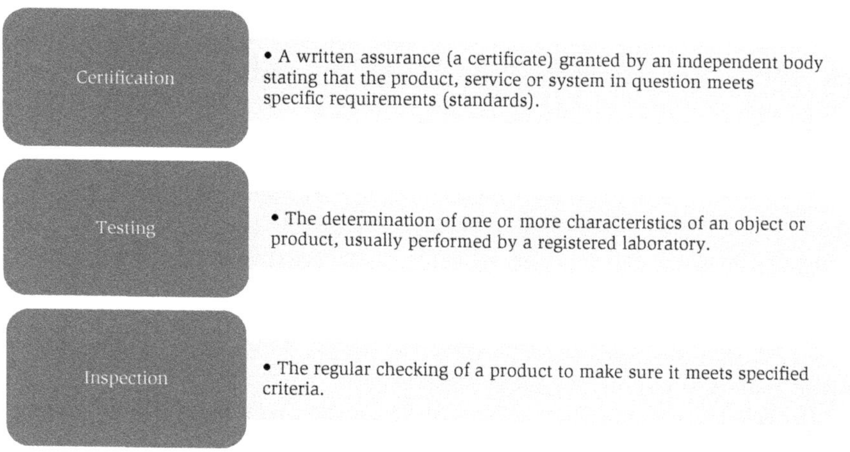

Once a standard is developed, conformity assessment processes ensure the implementation of such a standard. Typically, at the international level, conformity assessment bodies are distinct from standards developing bodies. For instance, while the ISO publishes criteria and guidelines through its Committee for Conformity Assessment (CASCO) for conformity assessment procedures for ISO Standards, it does not, by itself, conduct any certification, testing or inspection. At national levels, standard-setting bodies are often significantly more involved in conformity assessment processes. The BIS has published the BIS (Conformity Assessment) Regulations, 2018 and also has surveillance operations to conduct regular inspections and testing of bodies certified under BIS standards.[8] Generally, where conformity assessment procedures are conducted by third-party conformity assessment bodies, such bodies are 'accredited'. Accreditation recognises and provides legitimacy to third parties who are conducting conformity assessment against published standards. The International Accreditation Forum is an example of an organisation that aims to bring about international consensus and recognition to accredited bodies. Similarly, in India, several accreditation boards, housed under the Quality Council of India, accredit and recognise various conformity assessment bodies (for example, testing labs and certification bodies). Chapter 6 of this Handbook provides a detailed account of the various processes involved in conformity assessment and the types of bodies that carry out these functions. The chapter also looks closely at how conformity assessment bodies are accredited, and the role that Quality Council of India plays in accreditation.

1.3 INTERNATIONAL TRADE REGULATION AND STANDARDS

Standards are undoubtedly recognised as an important tool for the realisation of domestic policy concerns, but they also play a crucial role in the international trade of goods and services. When standards are deployed harmoniously world over, it ensures smooth and efficient interoperability and trade. However, given vast differences between countries in levels of development, climatic and geographical factors and socio-cultural values, complete international harmonisation may be difficult. International trade rules permit certain flexibility for redress of safety and quality related concerns while encouraging the harmonisation of standards globally.

As part of the WTO system, the TBT Agreement[9] and the SPS Agreement[10], both explicitly permit the use of national standards. These Agreements regulate the manner in which standards and technical regulations are implemented by WTO Members and set out obligations and rights in a manner that allow the benefits of standards (such as efficiency, product awareness, etc.) to flourish while limiting the negative impact of divergent standards on international trade.

This chapter, therefore, introduces the TBT Agreement and the SPS Agreement, both of which govern standards across different sectors, and their key principles.

8. Rule 3, Bureau of Indian Standards (Conformity Assessment) Regulations, 2018, F. No. BS/11/11/2018, 4 June 2018.
9. Agreement on the Technical Barriers to Trade (Marrakesh, Morocco, 15 April 1994), Marrakesh Agreement Establishing the World Trade Organization, Annex 1A, *The Legal Texts: The Results of the Uruguay Round of Multilateral Trade Negotiations* 121 (1999), 1868 U.N.T.S. 120 (hereinafter TBT Agreement).
10. Agreement on the Application of Sanitary and Phytosanitary Measures (Marrakesh, Morocco, 15 April 1994), Marrakesh Agreement Establishing the World Trade Organization, Annex 1A, *The Legal Texts: The Results of the Uruguay Round of Multilateral Trade Negotiations* 59 (1999), 1867 U.N.T.S. 493 (hereinafter SPS Agreement).

1.3.1 Agreement on Technical Barriers to Trade

The TBT Agreement aims to balance the public policy goals of Members of 'improving efficiency in production and facilitating the conduct of international trade'. Nevertheless, standards may also be implemented in a manner which has trade distorting effects by increasing cost of production and compliance, especially to the detriment of foreign manufacturers and exporters. These costs may be a result of hiring experts to understand the regulations, or changes to the manufacturing process to account for the regulations, or the cost of proving that the requirements provided under the regulations have been met.

Transparency, certainty and reasonableness are crucial elements to ensuring that public policy purpose of measures is met without causing unnecessary barriers to trade. The TBT Agreement ensures that if a regulator bans the use of a chemical in an imported toy (on health grounds), or requires energy efficiency labels on imported appliances (on environmental grounds), then the implementing regulations are clear, based on relevant international standards if such standards are available, and not discriminatory or arbitrary. Although the TBT Agreement recognises that each Member may require its own measures to ensure the protection of human, plant, animal health, the environment, national security, and to protect the quality of goods that are traded, the Agreement places an emphasis on the creation and adoption of international standards and conformity assessment procedures.

1.3.1.1 Scope of Application

Scope of TBT Agreement

The TBT Agreement applies to trade in goods. It does not apply to:

1. Services trade (Preamble, TBT Agreement)
2. Government procurement (Article 1.4, TBT Agreement)
3. Measures covered under the SPS Agreement (Article 1.5, TBT Agreement)

Measures under the TBT Agreement may relate to the finished good that is being traded, or it may relate to the process or production method that is used to manufacture that good. It may also extend to cover labelling and packaging requirements.

The TBT Agreement deals with technical measures that affect trade in goods, including measures on aspects relating to standards, testing and certification procedures. The Agreement covers all aspects of the regulation of goods – from the preparation of a regulation to its adoption, application as well as conformity assessment. It is relevant to note that the TBT Agreement does not apply to 'sanitary and phytosanitary measures' (SPS measures) as defined under Annex 1A of the SPS Agreement. SPS measures aim to protect human, plant or animal health and life from risks that may arise from additives, contaminants, toxins or other disease-causing organisms in food, diseases carried by humans, plants or animals, pests and other disease-causing organisms, or damage caused by pests. A more detailed examination of SPS measures is set out in section 1.3.2 of this chapter.

The TBT Agreement is applicable to technical regulations, standards and conformity assessment processes. The meaning of these terms, as defined under the TBT Agreement and subsequently clarified by the WTO dispute settlement body, are set out in Figure 1.4.

Figure 1.4 Difference Between Technical Regulations, Standards and Conformity Assessment Procedures

Technical Regulation

- A **document** that lays down (positive or negative) product *characteristics*, for which compliance is **mandatory** (AB, *EC-Asbestos*, 69).
- The products must be identifiable, either by express mention within the measure or implied by way of the prescribed characteristic (Clausel, Annex 1, TBT Agreement).
- Market access must be contingent on the presence or the absence of a prescribed characteristic of the product.
- Technical Regulations may also be measures that prescribe processes and production methods related **to** the product itself. It is unclear whether a non-product related process and production method, absent labelling, could fall within the definition of TR.
- Example: prohibitions on the use of lead paints in toys, or emission limits set for engines.

Standard

- **Rules, guidelines or characteristics** regarding products, pocesses and production methods provided by a **recognised standards setting body**, compliance with which is **non-mandatory** (Clause 2, Annex 1, TBT Agreement).
- Standards may be prescribed by governments as Technical Regulations or they may be made mandatory through prescribed Conformity Assessment Procedures.
- Voluntary standards are prepared by private bodies in response to consumer demand.
- Example: grading system for produce based on size/quality, or what products may use a particular symbol.

Conformity Assessment Procedure

- Procedures used to determine whether a particular TR or standard is fulfilled (Clause 3, Annex 1, TBT Agreement).
- They may include sampling, testing, inspecting, evaluation, verification, etc., as well as registration, accrediation and approval.

Notably, the TBT Agreement differentiates between standards and technical regulations fundamentally on the basis of whether they are mandatory or voluntary. To explain, compliance with technical regulations is mandatory whereas compliance with standards is voluntary. For example, the Indian Ministry of Electronics and Information Technology (MeitY) in 2012, notified the Electronics and Information Technology Goods (Requirement for Compulsory Registration) Order, 2012 (CRS Order). This CRS Order mandates that no person may manufacture or store the 15 product categories mentioned therein without conforming to relevant standards issued by BIS on those products.[11] As per the definitions set out in Annex 1 of the TBT Agreement, this CRS Order is a technical regulation and not just a standard. Consequently, such mandatory standards will need to be compliant with the obligations set out for technical regulations in Article 2 of the TBT Agreement. If a standard published by a national standardising body (e.g., BIS) is voluntary, then only Article 4 - which requires compliance with Annex 3 (Code of Good Practice) is applicable. The following section highlights the key obligations and principles of the TBT Agreement which are applicable to technical regulations and standards, both. The TBT Agreement also details rules applicable to conformity assessment procedures. Chapter 6, which looks more closely at conformity assessment procedures in India, provides an overview of the relevant TBT rules on conformity assessment procedures.

1.3.1.2 Key Principles of the TBT Agreement

1.3.1.2.1 Non-discrimination

Non-discrimination is at the heart of the TBT Agreement. It includes obligations on governments to ensure that their technical regulations, standards, and conformity assessment procedures are not arbitrary in nature and are not used to distort fair trade. Measures must not discriminate against foreign products (in favour of domestic like products), or between two like imported products. In other words, the treatment of like products should be no less favourable, regardless of their origin. WTO Members are required to adhere to two non-discrimination obligations under the TBT Agreement. These are the national treatment obligation and the most favoured nation obligation. Article 2.1 sets out both of these obligations:

Article 2.1, TBT Agreement

MFN and National Treatment Obligation

'In respect of technical regulations, products imported from the territory of any Member shall be accorded treatment no less favourable than that accorded to like products of national origin[1] and to like products originating in any other country[2].'

Explanation

1. National origin: enumerates the national treatment obligation, i.e., treatment accorded to products from one country should not be less favourable than that accorded to like domestic products.

11. Rule 3, Electronics and Information Technology Goods (Requirement for Compulsory Registration) Order, 2012, S.O. 2357(E), 7 September 2012.

2. Originating in any other country: enumerates the MFN obligation, i.e., treatment accorded to products from one country should not be less favourable than that accorded to like products from any other country.

The core of both obligations lies in the interpretation of the two phrases 'no less favourable treatment' and 'like products'. There is a rich jurisprudence of WTO dispute settlement panels and the Appellate Body on these terms within the specific context of the TBT Agreement. The Appellate Body has recognised that technical regulations inherently do create a distinction between products; in so far as such technical regulations create distinctions that are based exclusively on particular product characteristics or their related processes and production methods, such distinctions may not *per se* be less favourable treatment.[12] The WTO Appellate Body's decision in the *US – COOL* case revisited the jurisprudence of Article 2.1 and provided clarity on what constitutes less favourable treatment.[13]

Box 1

***US – Country of Origin Labelling* [DS 384]**

The measure under challenge was certain mandatory country of origin labelling (COOL) provisions introduced under the amended Agricultural Marketing Act in the US. The COOL obligations mandated, *inter alia*, that for a covered commodity (beef and pork) to be labelled as US origin, it had to be derived from an animal that was exclusively born, raised and slaughtered in the United States. This would exclude such a designation in respect of beef or pork derived from livestock that is exported to the United States for feed or immediate slaughter. The Panel determined that imported livestock covered by the COOL provisions was treated less favourably than like domestic livestock.

In examining the appeal, the Appellate Body while interpreting what constitutes 'less favourable treatment' noted that 'In every case, it is the effect of the measure on the competitive opportunities in the market that is relevant to an assessment of whether a challenged measure has a detrimental impact on imported products. If a panel determines that a measure has such an impact on imported products, however, this will not be dispositive of a violation of Article 2.1. This is because, not every instance of a detrimental impact amounts to the less favourable treatment of imports that is prohibited under that provision. Rather, some

12. Appellate Body Report on *United States – Measures Affecting Production and Sale of Clove Cigarettes*, (hereinafter '*US – Clove Cigarettes*'), WT/DS406/AB/R, adopted 24 April 2012, ¶ 169.
13. Appellate Body Report on *United States – Certain Country of Origin Labelling (COOL) Requirements*, (hereinafter '*US – COOL*'), WT/DS384/AB/R, adopted 23 July 2012, ¶ 271.

technical regulations that have a de facto detrimental impact on imports may not be inconsistent with Article 2.1 when such impact stems exclusively from a legitimate regulatory distinction.' (Appellate Body Report, Para 271)

1.3.1.2.2 Legitimacy of Objective and Trade Restrictiveness of the Technical Regulation

It is imperative to note that technical regulations which are applied uniformly to domestic and foreign manufacturers and/or their products may still be prohibited by the TBT Agreement if they form an unnecessary barrier to trade or are unnecessarily trade restrictive. Article 2.2 of the TBT Agreement mandates that the objective behind technical regulations must be legitimate, i.e., must relate to a public health, safety, or an environmental objective, to name a few. Countries can determine for themselves what constitutes a legitimate objective for the imposition of a technical regulation. However, to ensure that these do not create unwarranted obstacles to international trade, the Agreement prohibits measures that are more trade restrictive than necessary to achieve a given objective. There must be a degree of proportionality between a measure and the purported objective it seeks to achieve. Furthermore, all possible alternative measures must be explored and analysed based on the criteria identified in the dispute, before one of the measures is chosen as the least restrictive way to achieve a particular legitimate objective. A recent dispute at the WTO, *Australia – Plain Packaging* revisited the jurisprudence on Article 2.2 in detail.[14]

Box 2

***Australia – Plain Packaging* [DS 441/435]**

The measure at issue was the Tobacco plain packaging (TPP) rule requiring tobacco products and their retail packaging to appear in a uniform manner, with specific health labels and without prominent brand identification. One of the key claims raised in the appeal was that the TPP was more trade restrictive than necessary (contrary to the Panel's finding). The Appellate Body upheld the Panel's finding and in doing so, summarised the jurisprudence of Article 2.2 in the following terms.

'For purposes of establishing that a measure is inconsistent with Article 2.2 of the TBT Agreement, a complainant must demonstrate that a technical regulation is "more trade-restrictive than necessary to fulfil a legitimate objective, taking

14. Appellate Body Report on *Australia – Certain Measures Concerning Trademarks, Geographical Indications and Other Plain Packaging Requirements Applicable to Tobacco Products and Packaging* (hereinafter '*Australia – Plain Packaging (Honduras)*' and '*Australia – Plain Packaging (Dominican Republic)*'), WT/DS441/AB/R; WT/DS435/AB/R, adopted 29 June 2020, ¶ 6.517.

account of the risks non-fulfilment would create". The assessment of "necessity", in the context of Article 2.2, involves a relational analysis of the following factors:

(i) the trade restrictiveness of the technical regulation;

(ii) the degree of contribution that it makes to the achievement of a legitimate objective; and

(iii) the risks non-fulfilment would create.

Moreover, establishing whether a technical regulation is "more trade-restrictive than necessary" may involve a comparison between:

(i) the trade restrictiveness and the degree of contribution of the measure at issue to the legitimate objective; and

(ii) the trade restrictiveness and the degree of contribution of possible (or proposed) alternative measures that are reasonably available to the legitimate objective, taking account of the risks non-fulfilment would create.' (Appellate Body Report, Para 6.517; US – Tuna II (Mexico, Appellate Body Report, para. 322).

While arriving at this finding, the Appellate Body made observations regarding the relationship between the relational analysis and the comparative analysis involved in Article 2.2. After examining the elements of a relational analysis test, the Appellate Body went on to examine how and when a comparative analysis becomes relevant.

It noted that '[t]he phrase in the second sentence of Article 2.2 that "technical regulations shall not be more trade-restrictive than necessary" implies that "some" trade restrictiveness is allowed .... However, there are certain instances when such a comparative analysis might not be required, such as, when the measure is not trade-restrictive at all, or when a trade-restrictive measure makes no contribution to the achievement of the relevant legitimate objective. Likewise, a comparative analysis might not be required where it can be demonstrated that, by its design, a trade-restrictive measure is incapable of contributing to the achievement of the relevant legitimate objective.' (Appellate Body Report, Para 6.4).

1.3.1.2.3 Use of International Standards

The use of international standards is promoted to reduce the cost of compliance for producers/manufacturers whose products are traded across multiple countries. When standards are harmonised across countries, it eases the process of trade. This is due to the reduced costs to the manufacturers and traders in adopting same or similar production processes, conducting testing and quality checks and other requirements applicable in multiple countries (as compared to different process as per the requirements of different countries). Therefore, such regulatory convergence is promoted within the TBT Agreement. Article 2.4 of the TBT Agreement sets out this obligation.

In the interest of harmonisation, countries are encouraged under the TBT Agreement to use international standards as the basis for their own technical regulations and standards. Article 2.4 of the TBT formalises this obligation by requiring the use of relevant international standards. When there is an international standard available or its completion is imminent, WTO Members are obliged to use them, and can deviate from this only if the international standard is an ineffective or inappropriate for the identified objective. Testing compliance with this obligation requires proving three steps:[15]

When a technical regulation is based on an international standard, it creates a presumption that such a technical regulation is legitimate and does not fall foul of the TBT Agreement. While the goal of the TBT Agreement is harmonisation of international standards, it also recognises that in certain sectors, harmonisation is either impossible or not desirable, based on local circumstances. These circumstances could range from climatic, geographical to technological reasons. Therefore, though international standards may exist for a particular sector, Members may choose to create technical regulations without taking such standards into consideration. Additionally, developing country Members are given a flexibility to not use international standards that may not be appropriate to their level of development and needs.[16]

1.3.1.2.4 Transparency

Transparency is a key element of fair and free trade. In the interest of making technical regulations and standards more accessible and transparent, the TBT Agreement makes the following obligations mandatory on all Members: (a) Notification of draft technical regulations, conformity assessment procedures, etc., as well as information on the administrative bodies for implementation of the TBT Agreement; (b) establishment of enquiry points and a notification authority; and (c) publication of technical regulations, conformity assessment procedures and standards. Table 1.1 provides an overview of the transparency obligations under the TBT Agreement.

15. Panel Report on *United States – Measures Concerning the Importation, Marketing and Sale of Tuna and Tuna Products*, (hereinafter '*US – Tuna II (Mexico)*'), WT/DS381/R, adopted 13 June 2012, ¶ 7.627.
16. Article 12.4, TBT Agreement.

Table 1.1 Notification and Publication Requirements under the TBT Agreement

Standard	*Technical Regulations and Conformity Assessment Procedures*
1. Once the process of preparing a standard has started, it must be notified to the WTO Secretariat. 2. Every 6 months, a work programme detailing the standards that are being prepared and that have been adopted is to be submitted. 3. Draft standards are to be notified, and a 60-day period for comments is to be provided. 4. Once the standard has been adopted, copies of the final text should be readily provided.	1. Members must publish an early notice of their intention to introduce a particular measure. 2. Once the measure is drafted, it must be published and notified to other Members. 3. After the 60-day period of comments has ended, the measure may be adopted. 4. The adopted measure must be published before it can enter into force.

The transparency provisions of the TBT Agreement apply to the WTO Members but the Code of Good Practice under Annex 3 of the TBT Agreement applies to the international standard-setting organisations. These organisations must declare their participation in or withdrawal from international standard-setting organisations by virtue of notification in the ISO/IEC Information Centre, Geneva. Moreover, they must also publish half-yearly reports of their progress on the preparation and adoption of standards. This ensures the effective functioning of a transparent standards ecosystem using the platform of the TBT Committee. The website of the WTO includes a portal which allows the public to track, in English, French and Spanish, all notifications, enquiry points, publications and specific trade concerns raised under the TBT Agreement. This TBT Information Management System includes a specific search for all standards-related notifications.[17] Figure 1.5 provides a snapshot of the TBT IMS.

17. *Standards related notifications (Annex 3: Code of Good Practice)*, WTO Technical Barriers to Trade: Information Management System, http://tbtims.wto.org/en/CodeOfGoodPractice Notifications/Search (last accessed 11 December 2020).

Figure 1.5 Snapshot of the TBT IMS

Source: World Trade Organisation, *Technical Barriers to Trade Information Management System*, available at **http://tbtims.wto.org/** (Last accessed on 1 February 2021)

1.3.1.3 The TBT Committee

The TBT Committee was formed under the TBT Agreement to provide a platform for Members to consult and discuss standards-related issues. In the Committee, Members may raise specific trade concerns (STCs) regarding measures of other Members that affect their trade. Apart from this, the Committee also serves to improve implementation of the TBT Agreement.[18] An STC may be raised with respect to a proposed measure or a measure that is in force. Raising a concern in the TBT Committee is a way for Members to discuss measures that may otherwise become the subject of a dispute to be resolved by the WTO dispute settlement body.

1.3.2 Agreement on SPS Measures

The SPS Agreement applies to laws and regulations of WTO Members implemented to specifically limit health risks to humans and animals from food, as well as threats to flora, fauna and humans from pests and diseases. In other words, the SPS Agreement sets out basic rules for food safety and animal and plant health standards. Like the TBT Agreement, the aim of SPS Agreement is to ensure public policy goals of Member States are achieved in balance with the facilitation of trade.

18. TBT Agreement, Article 15.2.

1.3.2.1 Scope

Despite their close linkages, the application of the SPS Agreement may be distinguished from the scope and coverage of the TBT Agreement. The TBT Agreement identifies the government actions which are covered by it on the basis of the *type* of measure – standard or technical regulation.

The SPS Agreement, on the contrary, identifies government actions under its scope on the basis of the *purpose* of the measure. The two agreements have common obligations like non-discrimination and advance notification of proposed measures and the creation of information offices. However, many of the substantive rules are different. For example, though both agreements encourage the use of international standards, they differ in the rationale behind a divergence from adopting international standards. Under the SPS Agreement the only rationale for not using international standards for food safety and animal/plant health protection is scientific justification based on an assessment of the potential health risks or the appropriate level of protection which a Member has determined. In contrast, under the TBT Agreement governments may decide that international standards are not appropriate for reasons like fundamental technological problems or geographical factors. Furthermore, SPS measures may be imposed only to the extent necessary to protect human, animal or plant health, on the basis of scientific justification, as is discussed in further detail below. This contrasts with the TBT Agreement which permits the introduction of technical regulations by countries for a number of objectives, including national security and prevention of deceptive practices. Thus, to understand standards and how international trade regulations have shaped their development (both domestic and international), it is relevant to determine if a standards-related regulation falls within the scope of the TBT Agreement or the SPS Agreement.

The SPS Agreement is applicable to any 'sanitary or phytosanitary measures' which may, directly or indirectly affect international trade. There are three elements to determining if a government action falls within the scope of the SPS Agreement (Figure 1.6). These elements are set out in Annex A(1) of the SPS Agreement which provides a broad illustrative definition for 'SPS measures'.

Figure 1.6 Elements for Determining Scope of the SPS Agreement

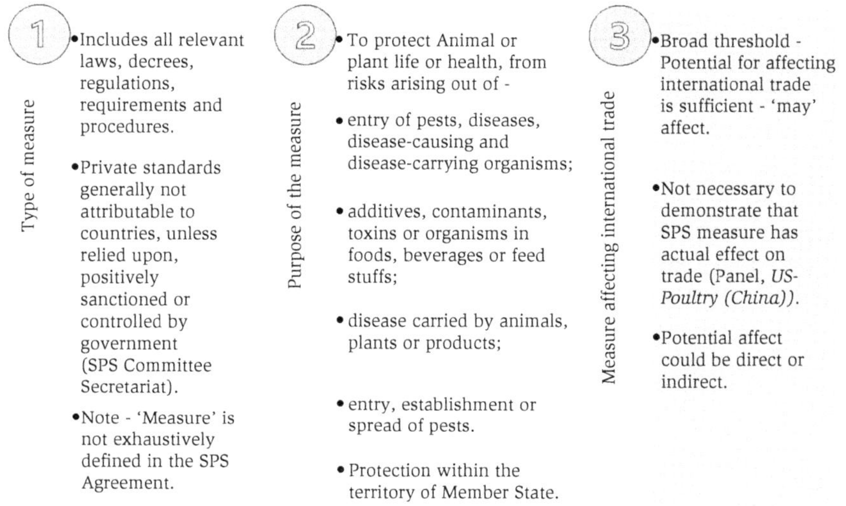

It is relevant to observe here that the first paragraph of the definition of an SPS Measure (i.e., point 2 in the above chart) sets out the purposes for which a measure, when imposed, qualifies as an SPS measure, and the second paragraph (point 1 of the above chart) is an illustrative list of the various types or forms of such SPS measures. Notably, unlike the TBT Agreement, emphasis is placed on the 'purpose' of the measure (i.e., the second element) as opposed to the type of the measure. The jurisprudence of the WTO Appellate Body and dispute settlement panels suggests that they are willing to include a 'broad scope of measures' within the SPS Agreement, provided that an 'objective nexus with the specified purpose' can be established.[19]

Box 3

***Australia – Apples* [DS 367]**

Australia adopted 16 phytosanitary measures on the importation of New Zealand apples, including eight measures adopted against the risk of fire blight, four against European canker, one against apple leaf curling midge (ALCM) and three measures applying generally to all three pests, which were challenged in the dispute. These SPS measures were based on a 'Final Import Risk Analysis Report

19. Appellate Body Report on *Australia – Measures Affecting the Importation of Apples from New Zealand*, (hereinafter '*Australia – Apples*'), WT/DS367/AB/R, adopted 17 December 2010, ¶ 173.

for Apples from New Zealand' published by the agency Biosecurity Australia. Australia put forth the argument that these 16 phytosanitary rules, individually and as a whole, were only procedural requirements and not 'phytosanitary measures' as defined under the SPS Agreement Annex A. The Appellate Body was therefore tasked with determining the meaning of the phrase 'applied to protect' as under Annex A(1)(a).

While doing so, it was held that the determination of the purpose of the measure was not only to be done by reading the objectives of the measure itself but, following the rules of treaty interpretation, and from the text and structure of the relevant measure, its surrounding regulatory context, and the way in which it is designed and applied. Further, an assessment of whether the determined purpose of the measure has an objective relationship with the purposes enlisted in Annex A(1)(a) was held to be a necessity for a measure to be deemed to be 'applied to protect' against an enlisted risk. (Appellate Body Report, Para. 173).

1.3.2.2 Key Principles

1.3.2.2.1 Basic Rights and Obligations under the SPS Agreement

Article 2 of the SPS Agreement sets out the basic rights and obligations which are applicable to all WTO Members. These rights and obligations are crucial to ascertain the interpretation of the rest of the provisions of the SPS Agreement.

Article 2 of the SPS Agreement confers two basic rights and two fundamental obligations. While Article 2.1 and 2.4 set out the rights available to WTO Members, Articles 2.3 and 2.4 set out the obligations to be complied with when implementing an SPS standard. If a government has prescribed the application of standards, for instance, in a food product, then the government must also ensure that these obligations are met. Figure 1.7 sets out the crucial elements of the rights and obligations under Article 2.

Figure 1.7 Key elements under Article 2 of the SPS Agreement

Article 2.1	Article 2.2	Article 2.3	Article 2.4
• Explicit right of Members to maintain SPS measures. • Other provisions of the SPS Agreement, given their specific nature, may limit this general right (*India-Agricultural Products*).	• Three elements to the obligation. SPS measures: • (a) are to be applied only as **necessary** to protect human, animal or plant life or health, • (b) must be based on **scientific principles**, and • (c) must not be maintained without **scientific evidence**.	• Two separate obligations under this Article - • no arbitrary or unjustifiable discrimination between Members as a result of the SPS Measure; and • measure to not be applied as a 'disguised restriction on trade'	• Conformity with the SPS Agreement deems a measure to be in conformity with GATT 1994.

Articles 2.2 and 2.3 are intricately linked to other provisions of the SPS Agreement. In particular, Article 5 on risk assessment by WTO Members assumes significant relevance in the context of the obligations under Article 2.2 and 2.3. Section 1.3.2.2.3 of this chapter examines Article 5 and the rules on risk assessment it prescribes in detail. Briefly, while Article 2.2 and Articles 5.1 and 5.2 (on the obligation of risk assessment and relevant factors) are not identical, the Appellate Body has repeatedly emphasised the importance of reading these provisions in conjunction.[20] Similarly, Articles 5.4 to Articles 5.6 (*see* Figure 1.10: Rules on risk assessment under the SPS Agreement) are considered to be specific applications of the basic obligations provided for in Article 2.2.[21]

Generally, if a WTO Member enacts an SPS measure, it is required to conform with a relevant international standard, if one exists. If there is no such relevant standard, or if there exists such a standard and the WTO Member deviates to impose a higher standard of protection through their SPS measure, such measure will have to follow the rules on risk assessment set out in Article 5. The following section examines the requirement on Member States to conform to or base their measures on international standards. The section also examines a scenario where WTO Members may choose to apply higher standards of protection than what is set out in an international standard.

1.3.2.2.2 Harmonisation

Harmonisation of standards and SPS measures is one of the key ambitions of the SPS Agreement, as stated in its Preamble. The SPS Agreement encourages the use of

20. Appellate Body Report on *Australia – Measures Affecting Importation of Salmon*, (hereinafter '*Australia – Salmon*'), WT/DS18/AB/R, adopted 6 November 1998, ¶ 138.
21. Panel Report on *European Communities – Measures Concerning Meat and Meat Products (Hormones)*, (hereinafter '*EC – Hormones (Canada)*'), WT/DS48/R, adopted 13 February 1998, ¶ 8.99.

harmonised SPS measures, based on international standards, guidelines and recommendations. This objective finds more detailed consideration in Article 3 of the SPS Agreement. Harmonisation of measures targets the prevention of 'arbitrary or unjustifiable discrimination between the Members' or a 'disguised restriction on international trade'. It must be noted that harmonisation does not intend to hinder Members from adopting SPS measures necessary to protect human, animal or plant life or health, based on scientific principles.

Even though the SPS Agreement recommends the adoption of international standards, guidelines and recommendations for harmonisation, deviation from international norms is permitted if conditions (specifically Articles 2 and 5) of the SPS Agreement are fulfilled.

In preparing SPS standards, a Member has three broad choices. The first choice for a Member, set out in Article 3.1, is 'to base' its SPS measures on international standards. The second choice, as enshrined in Article 3.2, is to 'conform' to those international standards. The third choice available to Members is to adopt a 'higher level of protection' than what is set out in the international standard. *India – Agricultural Products,* a WTO dispute, examined the distinction between the three choices in Article 3 in detail.[22] Box 4 below looks at this dispute and its identification of the distinction between Articles 3.1, 3.2 and 3.3.

Box 4

***India – Agricultural Products* (DS 430)**

India's Livestock Act, 1898 was designed to regulate import of livestock that may be infected or have contagious diseases. Under this Act, the Indian Government was empowered to regulate, restrict, and prohibit the import of possibly affected livestock or livestock products; based on their discretion. Orders were issued under the Act that prohibited the import of certain livestock and livestock products; unless a Sanitary Import Permit was issued.

When these orders were challenged before a WTO Panel, India argued that its measures 'conformed to' the relevant international standard, i.e., Chapter 10.4 of the Terrestrial Code of the OIE. Therefore, due to the 'presumption of consistency" under Article 3.2, India argued that its measure need not be tested against the remaining provisions, specifically Article 5 of the SPS Agreement. It did not need to comply with the risk assessment related provisions in Article 5 of the SPS Agreement.

The Appellate Body of the WTO, when examining this dispute, very succinctly summarised the distinction between Articles 3.1, 3.2 and 3.3 of the SPS Agreement, and their effect:

22. Appellate Body Report on *India – Measures Concerning the Importation of Certain Agricultural Goods,* (hereinafter '*India – Agricultural Products*'), WT/DS430/AB/R, adopted 19 June 2015, ¶ 5.58.

Referring to the Appellate Body report in *EC – Hormones*, the WTO panel explained that the paragraphs of Article 3 of the SPS Agreement define three separate scenarios. The first scenario is where a Member adopts an SPS measure that embodies an international standard completely. In this circumstance, the SPS measure benefits from a rebuttable presumption of compliance with the SPS Agreement and the GATT 1994. The second scenario is where the SPS measure adopts some, but not all, of the elements of that standard. The SPS measure, in this circumstance, would not "conform to" the standard but, rather, would be "based on" it, as provided in Article 3.1. The Panel stated that such a measure would not benefit from a presumption of compliance but, as clarified by the Appellate Body, the burden of proof would still rest on the complainant to make a *prima facie* case of violation of Article 3.1. Finally, as a third scenario, a Member may decide to deviate from the recommendations of an international standard and adopt an SPS measure that results in a higher level of protection than the one prescribed in the standard, as provided in Article 3.3. In order to do so, the Panel added, the Member must ensure that its measure is consistent with the other relevant provisions of the SPS Agreement, including, for instance, the requirement of having a risk assessment in accordance with Articles 5.1 and 5.2.' (Appellate Body Report Para. 5.58.)

India's measure was found to be neither 'based on' nor 'conforming to' the international standard.

'Based on', as per Article 3.1, means that if a Member chooses to 'base' their domestic SPS measures on the internationally accepted standards, it is not required to strictly comply with all elements of the international standard. The domestic standard may vary to some extent from the international standard. This is a helpful choice where WTO Members may seek to align their standards with international best practices, but also need to account for unique domestic concerns such as climatic or geographic factors. Once a WTO Member has identified the relevant international standard and based its measures on it, the burden of proof would rest *prima facie* on a complainant in a potential dispute to showcase that such a standard is non-compliant with the other provisions of the SPS Agreement.

'Conform to' on the other hand means that a WTO Member has chosen to apply an international standard as is and, therefore, the domestic standard must be strictly compliant and aligned with the international standard. This approach is encouraged to ensure consistency in global supply chains. This rule reflects the ambition of the SPS Agreement to fully harmonise international standards into municipal standards as is, for all practical purposes. If a measure under dispute is shown to conform to an international standard, there is a presumption of consistency with GATT 1994 and the

SPS Agreement.[23] Such a measure is also *prima facie*, deemed 'necessary to protect human, animal or plant life or health'.

The third choice is to apply domestic standards with higher levels of protection than what is set out in international standards. This choice comes with the caveat that the SPS measure must be based on a 'scientific justification' and must be strictly compliant with the SPS Agreement's provisions on risk assessment as set out in Article 5.[24] A scientific justification exists if a Member undertakes an examination and evaluation of available scientific information and concludes that the relevant international standards, guidelines or recommendations are insufficient for its chosen appropriate level of protection.[25] Section 1.3.2.2.3 below examines in detail the prescriptive rules on risk assessment as set out under Article 5. All three options of harmonisation under Article 3 are treated at par, and governments are not penalised for the option they choose, provided that the attached conditions with each choice are complied with. Figure 1.8 summarises the three choices briefly:

Figure 1.8 Comparison of the Harmonisation Choices

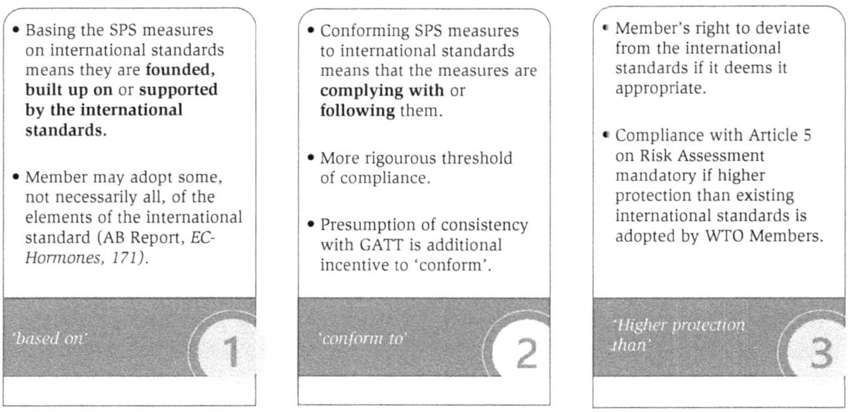

An issue that merits further consideration under Article 3 is the basis on which a 'relevant international standard' is identified. There are three international organisations whose 'international standards, guidelines and recommendations' are specifically mentioned for consideration in Annex A, paragraph 3 attached to the SPS Agreement – (a) Codex Alimentarius Commission with respect to food safety; (b) World Organisation for Animal Health (OIE) for animal health; and (c) the Secretariat of International Plant Protection Convention (IPPC) on plant health. However, international standards from other international organisations may also be relevant for matters not listed here,

23. Appellate Body Report on *European Communities – Measures Concerning Meat and Meat Products (Hormones)*, (hereinafter '*EC – Hormones*'), WT/DS26/AB/R, adopted 13 February 1998, ¶ 170.
24. SPS Agreement, Article 3.3, n.2.
25. *EC – Hormones*, WT/DS26/AB/R, ¶ 173.

if such organisations are open for membership to all WTO Member countries and are identified by the SPS Committee. There is no definition of 'standards', 'guidelines' and 'recommendations' in the SPS Agreement, thereby granting flexibility to the scope of these terms. The WTO Committee on Sanitary and Phytosanitary Measures (SPS Committee) in 1998, upon a request from the Codex Alimentarius Commission looked into these three terms. The SPS Committee noted that SPS agreement itself makes no distinction between the three terms and always uses them collectively.[26] WTO dispute settlement panels tend to take a broad view of what constitutes of 'relevant' international standard.[27]

Box 5

***Australia – Salmon* (DS18)**

The measure at issue was Australia's prohibition on the importation of fresh, chilled or frozen salmon from Canada under Quarantine Proclamation 86A ('QP86A'). As per the proclamation, the import of dead fish of the 'Salmonidae sub-order' was prohibited unless such fish was subject to appropriate treatment for infectious or contagious disease as identified by the Director of Quarantine. The Director of Quarantine identified a list of 24 diseases of concern. The applicable international standard was OIE's International Aquatic Animal Health Code. The AAHC identifies a list of 'Notifiable Diseases' which are regarded as having the potential for serious damage to aquaculture industries or wild populations of fish, molluscs and crustaceans. Of the 24 diseases listed by Australia, two were included in the AAHC list of Notifiable Diseases. Section 1.4 of the AAHC prescribed the manner in which an import risk analysis could be conducted. While determining the sequence of claims to be addressed before the Panel, Australia claimed that there existed no relevant international standard for 'some of the diseases of concern and that the measure at issue validly aims at a higher level of protection than that reflected in the international guidelines referred to by Canada.' Canada's contention, on the other hand, was that an OIE standard existed for two salmon-specific diseases, which should be the relevant international standard vis-à-vis Article 3.1.

The Panel recognised that while a relevant standard may not exist for all 24 diseases identified by Australia, that 'does not mean that an international guideline which applies to only *one* of these diseases cannot be relevant' to the challenged measure. (Panel Report Paragraph 8.46)

26. *Clarification of References to Codex Texts*, G/SPS/W/86/Rev.1, (13 March 1998), p. 2, ¶ 3.
27. Panel Report on *Australia – Salmon*, WT/DS18/R, adopted 6 November 1998, ¶ 8.46.

1.3.2.2.3 Risk Assessment under the SPS Agreement

Where a Member's SPS standard is not 'based on' nor 'conforms to' an international standard, or if no relevant international standard exists, then a Member is required to showcase that such domestic standard is based on an assessment of risk, in compliance with Article 5.1 of the SPS Agreement.[28] All SPS measures, as evident from the illustrative definition of the term, relate to the assessment and identification of risks and their subsequent management. By setting out prescriptive rules on the assessment and management of risks, the SPS Agreement attempts to ensure that the design and implementation of SPS measures do not discriminate, act as a restriction to trade and is necessary for the objectives it seeks to achieve.

Risk Assessment Definition (Annex A, 4)

The evaluation of the likelihood of entry, establishment or spread of a pest or disease within the territory of an importing Member according to the sanitary or phytosanitary measures which might be applied, and of the associated potential biological and economic consequences; or the evaluation of the potential for adverse effects on human or animal health arising from the presence of additives, contaminants, toxins or disease-causing organisms in food, beverages or feedstuffs.

The evaluation of the likelihood of entry, establishment or spread of a pest or disease within the territory of an importing Member according to the sanitary or phytosanitary measures which might be applied, and of the associated potential biological and economic consequences; or the evaluation of the potential for adverse effects on human or animal health arising from the presence of additives, contaminants, toxins or disease-causing organisms in food, beverages or feedstuffs.

This definition of risk assessment can be separated into two components. In the case of food safety related risks, it is the 'the evaluation of the *potential* for adverse effects on human or animal health arising from the presence of additives, contaminants, toxins or disease-causing organisms' (*emphasis added*). In the case of risks associated with pests or diseases, it is the 'evaluation of the *likelihood* of entry, establishment or spread of a pest or disease within the territory of an importing Member... and of the associated potential biological and *economic* consequences' (*emphasis added*). Article 5.1 of the SPS Agreement sets out the primary obligation with respect to risk assessment, i.e., that WTO Members are required to base their SPS standards and other measures based on 'assessment, as appropriate, of the risks to human, animal or plant life or health, taking into account risk assessment techniques developed by the relevant international organisations.'

28. *EC – Hormones*, WT/DS26/AB/R ¶ 175.

Article 5.2 identifies a set of factors which a WTO Member imposing an SPS standard is required to take into account. Figure 1.9 sets out the factors identified by Article 5.2 of the SPS Agreement. It is relevant to note, that Members are not required to conduct their own risk assessment if reliable risk assessment techniques have already been developed by international organisations which take into account the specified factors.

Figure 1.9 Factors Relevant to the Assessment of Risks

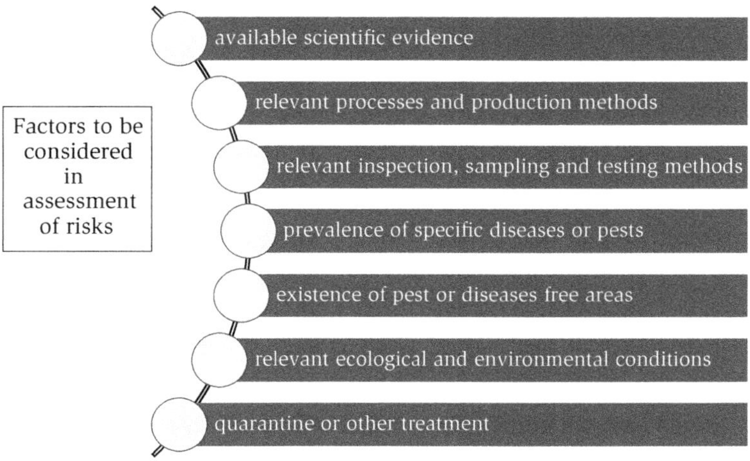

Articles 5.3 to 5.7 of the SPS Agreement detail the additional rules applicable to risk assessment conducted by Member States.

Figure 1.10 Rules on Risk Assessment under the SPS Agreement

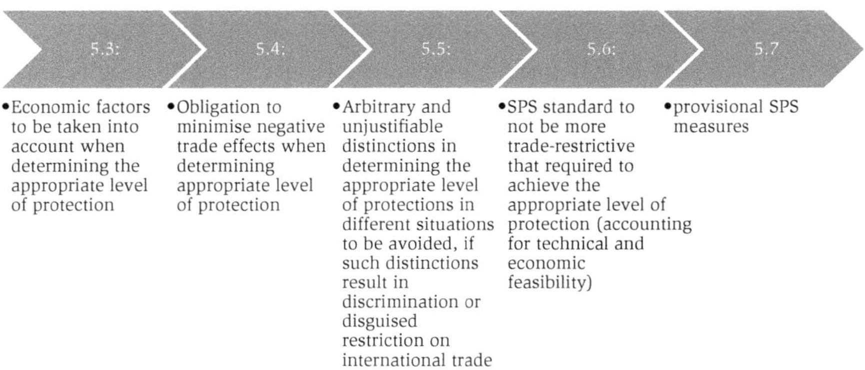

The WTO Appellate Body has noted that a risk assessment should provide a rational nexus between the risk, the underlying cause of such risk and what the SPS measure seeks to achieve. This assessment should be 'specific' to the disease and the host/vector through there is the risk of 'entry, establishment or spread' of disease. Box 6 illustrates the Appellate Body's view on what constitutes such specificity.[29]

Box 6

***Japan – Apples* (DS 245)**

Japan imposed SPS measures restricting the import of apples based on concerns about the transmission of fire blight bacterium. These measures were challenged before the WTO by the United States. One of the issues raised was that the SPS measures were not based on 'risk assessment' as required under Article 5.1. It was claimed that Japan's Pest Risk Assessment 1999 (PRA) did not specifically focus on the risk associated with a 'particular commodity, i.e., apple fruit' and therefore the PRA did not meet the requirement for specificity of risk assessment under the Article 5.1.

The Panel convened in the dispute held that it was non-compliant with Article 5.1 – that 'the conclusion of the [1999] PRA [did] not purport to relate exclusively to the introduction of the disease through apple fruit, but rather more generally, apparently, through any susceptible host/vector' (Panel Report, para 8.253).

The Appellate Body upheld the Panel's finding and made the following remarks while referring to a previous dispute *EC – Hormones* 'Under the SPS Agreement, the obligation to conduct an assessment of "risk" is not satisfied merely by a general discussion of the disease sought to be avoided by the imposition of a phytosanitary measure'. '[W]hen discussing the risk to be specified in the risk assessment in *EC – Hormones*, the Appellate Body referred in general to the harm concerned (cancer or genetic damage) as well as to the precise agent that may possibly cause the harm (that is, the specific hormones when used in a specific manner and for specific purposes).' (Appellate Body Report, Para 202).

The Appellate Body further noted that 'Members are free to consider in their risk analysis multiple agents in relation to one disease, provided that the risk assessment attribute a likelihood of entry, establishment or spread of the disease to each agent specifically.' (Appellate Body Report, Para 204).

It is relevant to note that in the case of pests or diseases-related risk (i.e., not food related), the SPS Agreement allows economic factors to be considered as well. Potential damage from entry, establishment or spread in the form of loss of production or sales, costs of control or eradication, and cost effectiveness of alternative approaches to

29. Appellate Body Report on *Japan – Measures Affecting Importation of Apples*, (hereinafter '*Japan – Apples*'), WT/DS245/AB/R, adopted 10 December 2003, ¶¶ 202-204.

limiting risk are all elements that can be considered as a part of the risk assessment when designing and implementing an SPS measure.

1.3.2.2.4 Transparency and Notification of SPS Measures

Article 7 and Annex B of the SPS Agreement contend with transparency obligations and procedures vis-à-vis SPS Measures. Annex B requires publication of all SPS Regulations which have been adopted. All notifications are published in a searchable format on the WTO's SPS Information Management System portal. The Figure 1.11 provides a snapshot of the SPS IMS and the number of notifications made to the system.

Figure 1.11 Snapshot of SPS IMS

Source: World Trade Organisation, *Sanitary and Phytosanitary Information Management System*, available at http://spsims.wto.org/ (last accessed on 1 February 2021).

1.3.2.3 The SPS Committee

The SPS Committee is the forum actively enforcing transparency and notification requirements. In 2002, the Committee adopted the 'Recommended Procedures for Implementing the Transparency Obligations of the SPS Agreement' detailing and elaborating the procedures that all Members must follow. This has created a massive database of SPS Measures with text available in the three official languages of the WTO – English, French and Spanish.

Through these notifications, Members remain updated about any new or changed regulations of their trading partners which may affect them. It also serves as a forum for discussion on the meaning and implications of new SPS regulations.

1.3.3 PTAs and Other Arrangements

WTO Agreements are not the only source of rules on international trade which apply to standards. PTAs are popular tools used by countries to negotiate bilateral or plurilateral trade rules and benefits. Particularly with the increase in the number of mega-regional trade agreements,[30] the scale and scope of rules set out in such agreements has also expanded significantly. Many PTAs thus include rules on the preparation and adoption of technical regulation and standards.

Another type of bilateral agreement that countries enter into in relation to standards are mutual recognition agreements (MRAs). MRAs are executed to facilitate the interoperability of domestic standards between international trade partners.

This section briefly looks at both PTAs and MRAs and the role they play in governing and facilitating the adoption of standards.

1.3.3.1 Different Approaches Within PTAs

Article XXIV of the General Agreement on Tariffs and Trade, 1994[31] (GATT) recognises the right of Member States to enter into regional trade arrangements. The WTO's Regional Trade Database notes that there are currently 305 PTAs in force, of which 271 deal directly with trade in goods.[32] Broadly, in the context of SPS and TBT measures, it is possible to identify two distinct approaches that PTAs take toward setting out rules on such measures. While many PTAs directly incorporate the WTO Agreements governing standards, some agreements, particularly mega-regional PTAs also enumerate their own detailed provisions on technical regulations and conformity assessment procedures that apply in addition to the obligations under the WTO Agreements. This section briefly looks at these two approaches.

Approach 1: PTAs with this approach directly incorporate or refer back to commitments under the TBT Agreement and SPS Agreement. Some PTAs which primarily adopt Approach 1 may also include one or two additional provisions (such as the setting up of a TBT Committee within the framework of the PTA). For instance, Article 8(2) of the ASEAN – India Trade in Goods Agreement takes Approach 1:

30. Such as the RECP – Regional Comprehensive Economic Partnership; and CPTPP - Comprehensive and Progressive Agreement for Trans-Pacific Partnership.
31. General Agreement on Tariffs and Trade 1994, (Marrakesh, Morocco, 15 April 1994), Marrakesh Agreement Establishing the World Trade Organization, Annex 1A, The Legal Texts: The Results of the Uruguay Round of Multilateral Trade Negotiations 17 (1999), 1867 U.N.T.S. 190, 33 I.L.M. 1153 (1994) (hereinafter GATT 1994).
32. *Regional Trade Agreements: Database*, WTO, https://rtais.wto.org/UI/PublicMaintainRTAHome.aspx (last accessed 11 December 2020).

> The Parties reaffirm their rights and obligations under the Agreement on Technical Barriers to Trade in Annex 1A to the WTO Agreement and the Agreement on the Application of Sanitary and Phytosanitary Measures in Annex 1A to the WTO Agreement, including notification procedures on the preparation of relevant regulations to reduce their negative effect on trade as well as to protect human, animal or plant life or health.

Approach 2: PTAs adopting this approach typically incorporate some provisions of the WTO Agreements but also include separate substantive provisions on a number of rules relating to technical regulation, standards, and SPS measures. Oftentimes, PTAs which take this approach incorporate either definition provisions or non-discrimination obligations as is from the WTO Agreements, and then set out separate substantive provisions on conformity assessment procedures, harmonisation etc. The India - Malaysia Comprehensive Economic Cooperation Agreement, for instance, follows the Approach 2. Article 6.3 of Chapter 6 (on SPS Measures) states '[f]or purposes of this Chapter, the definitions in Annex A to the SPS Agreement shall apply'. Similarly, Article 6.4 states 'The Parties reaffirm their existing rights and obligations with respect to each other under the SPS Agreement.' However, the Articles 6.5 to 6.9 set out detailed provisions with respect to harmonisation, adoption of international standards, equivalence, certification and verification.

A third, less common approach, is when PTAs do not make a direct reference to obligations under the TBT Agreement or SPS Agreement but instead formulate separate detailed rules vis-à-vis technical regulations, conformity assessment procedures or Standards. For instance, Chapter 5 of the India - Singapore Comprehensive Economic Cooperation Agreement (India - Singapore CECA) on 'Standards and Technical Regulations, Sanitary and Phytosanitary Measures' does not directly incorporate the TBT or SPS Agreement but instead includes detailed rules on mutual recognition of conformity assessment bodies.

Of course, these approaches only provide a broad snapshot of how PTA rules on TBT and SPS measures are formulated, but they are assistive in providing context to the governance of such measures globally.

Table 1.2 looks at a few sample regional agreements and FTAs and maps the kind of approach such FTAs take to regulating standards.

Table 1.2 Table of PTA Provisions and Their Approach to Regulating Standards

Sr. No.	*FTA Name*	*Provision Reference*
1	India-Chile Preferential Trade Agreement	Approach 1 for both TBT and SPS + reference to recognising international standards of IOE, IPPC and Codex Alimentarius.
2.	ASEAN-India Trade in Goods Agreement	Approach 1 for both TBT and SPS measures.

Sr. No.	*FTA Name*	*Provision Reference*
3.	SAFTA	Approach 3. No provision on the WTO Agreements; obligation to progressively harmonise standards between the parties.
4	India-MERCOSUR	Approach 1 for both TBT and SPS Measures.
5	India-Japan CEPA	Approach 1 for both TBT and SPS + creation of oversight committee for conformity.
6	India-Malaysia FTA	Approach 2 for both TBT and SPS. Definitions incorporated from the TBT Agreement and the SPS Agreement with distinct substantive provisions in the FTA.
7	India-Singapore CECA	Approach 3: Extensive guidelines on application of Singapore's CAPs regarding Telecommunication products on Indian borders due to the existence of a mutual recognition Agreement between the two Members.
9	India-South Korea	Approach 2 for both TBT and SPS Measures. Additional transparency provisions
10	CPTPP	Approach 3 for both TBT and SPS Measures.
11	USMCA	Approach 3 for SPS Measures but some parts of TBT Agreement incorporated along with new provisions.
12	Canada-EU CETA	Approach 2. Reaffirms the SPS Agreement and incorporates some provisions of the TBT Agreement. Separate provisions on *inter alia*, equivalence, transparency, mutual acceptance of CAPs and emergency SPS measures.

1.3.3.2 MRAs and the Principle of Equivalence

The principle of equivalence is another tool available under the TBT Agreement and the SPS Agreement to allow Members to realise the ambition of harmonisation of standards. The equivalence principle allows different measures developed and applied by different Members for the same objective, to be assessed and accepted as being equivalent to one another. As a result, compliance by the manufacturers/traders with measure of a Member would ensure deemed compliance with the measure of another Member and would allow market access without actual compliance requirements.

For illustration purposes, assume that country A requires automobiles to be equipped with catalytic converters for the protection of the environment from high carbon emission levels. If other countries are able to achieve the same objective to address the same concern through other methods (for example through the use of diesel engines instead of catalytic converters) then they could seek the recognition of equivalence of their measures to country A's measure.[33]

One of the methods employed by countries to recognise equivalence is through Mutual Recognition Agreement (MRAs). MRAs are cooperative arrangements between countries which aim to resolve impediments and increase cooperation in standards-related conformity assessment procedures.[34] MRAs are typically entered in to between countries, and recognise each other's conformity assessment procedures as being equivalent. MRAs may be entered into between various certification bodies, accreditation bodies etc. of countries as well, with their counterparts in another country. They are recognised under the TBT Agreement[35] as a way for Members to ensure that conformity assessment procedures of other countries are accepted as long as they can ensure conformity with applicable technical regulations. These are mostly bilateral sector-specific agreements. It is notable that regional agreements or FTAs entered into between trading partners also often encourage the signing of MRAs. For instance, the India–Singapore CECA details the rules on mutual recognition of conformity assessment procedures. The Telecommunications Engineering Centre, India has an MRA with the Infocomm Development Authority, Singapore for the recognition of conformity assessment bodies, telecom specifications and test procedures.[36] Similarly, in the year 2018, the Indian Nursing Council and the Singapore Nursing Board formalised an MRA on nursing services through the India–Singapore MRA on Nursing Services, 2005. MRAs in relation to product certification are also signed by accreditation bodies. NABCB has signed an MRA with the Asia Pacific Accreditation Cooperation (APAC), and the International Laboratory Accreditation Cooperation (ILAC) for quality management systems, environmental management systems, product certification, food safety management systems, energy management systems, etc. NABCB also has an MRA with the Asia Pacific Accreditation Cooperation for occupational health and safety management systems.[37] Several Indian export certifications are also recognised by regulators of other countries. These are, however, typically not a mutually reciprocal arrangement. For instance, in 2006, the US Department of Agriculture's Agricultural Marketing Service (AMS) recognised the conformity assessment procedures of the Indian Agricultural and Processed Food Products Export Development Authority (APEDA) for USDA's National Organic Program Standards. The European Union has also recognised the Indian Export Inspection Council's conformity assessment procedures regarding certain fishery and aquaculture products.[38] Examples of MRAs are

33. *Technical Information on Technical Barriers to Trade*, WTO, https://www.wto.org/english/tratop_e/tbt_e/tbt_info_e.htm (last visited 11 December 2020).
34. Mahesh Sugathan, *Mutual Recognition Agreement on Conformity Assessment*, ICTSD, 17 (May 2016), https://seors.unfccc.int/applications/seors/attachments/get_attachment?code=8BETGK3Z4HK8V64AX9BNMX7N9X3TBFA3.
35. TBT Agreement, Article 6.1.
36. Telecommunications Engineering Centre, India Standards Portal, http://indiastandardsportal.org/standardbodiecontent.aspx?StandardBodyId=22 (last visited 1 February 2021).
37. 'About NABCB', National Accreditation BCB, http://nabcb.qci.org.in/about.php (last visited 1 February 2021).
38. Commission Decision of 23 December 1997 laying down special conditions governing imports of fishery and aquaculture products originating in India, 97/876/EC, Article 1.

common in the practice of other countries as well. Japan has entered into MRAs with Philippines, European Community, and the United States. The United States also has MRAs on conformity assessment procedures with the European Union and EEA-EFTA States.[39] Chapter 7 of this Handbook delves deeper into MRAs and the role they play in harmonising conformity assessment procedures globally.

1.4 CONCLUSION

This chapter seeks to provide an introduction to the complex rules governing the promulgation of mandatory standards by Members. Each of the following chapters of this Handbook addresses different aspects of the process of developing and implementing standards with a particular focus on India. Chapter 1, thus, provides the context and framework of international rules within which each of the various aspects of standards development may be understood. To appreciate the complexity of framing and implementing domestic standards -be they private, governmental, voluntary or mandatory - it is crucial to keep in consideration the international obligations and the impact on international trade which drives the domestic regulatory space. According to the WTO database, at the end of 2020, 56 disputes relating to the TBT Agreement and another 49 relating to the SPS Agreement have been submitted to the WTO dispute settlement body.[40] Consequently, the rules of international trade framed under these agreements play a critical role in shaping the functioning of domestic regulatory processes that develop technical regulations and standards. This chapter, accordingly, lays out the background for the readers of this Handbook to understand and appreciate the key processes and issues relating to standards and technical regulations addressed in the following chapters, through the lens of the relevant international law principles.

39. The EEA EFTA states in this Agreement refer to the Republic of Iceland, the Principality of Liechtenstein, and the Kingdom of Norway.
40. Disputes by Agreement (as cited in request for consultations), WTO, https://www.wto.org/english/tratop_e/dispu_e/dispu_agreements_index_e.htm (under 'Agreement', click 'TBT Agreement' and 'SPS Agreement') (last visited 11 December 2020).

CHAPTER 2

Technical Regulations and Standards: Lessons Learnt from TBT Disputes

Arthur Appleton

This chapter examines the role of the World Trade Organization (WTO) dispute resolution system, specifically the Appellate Body, in interpreting and clarifying various aspects of the Agreement on Technical Barriers to Trade (TBT Agreement). The chapter identifies key findings of panels and the Appellate Body related to various aspects of the agreement, such as scope and nomenclature, key TBT disciplines of non-discrimination and necessity, harmonization and transparency. The chapter analyses whether the Panel and Appellate Body have constructively filled the gaps and repaired the poor and imprecise drafting of the agreement. This chapter aims to clarify some of the questions that may arise for Members, especially India, on issues such as the retroactive application of the agreement, its applicability to private standards, import bans, labelling measures and so on. The chapter demonstrates how interpretative clarity can render other provisions in the TBT Agreements such as equivalence and mutual recognition provisions, which are more in the nature of soft obligations, more effective and meaningful.

2.1 INTRODUCTION

The World Trade Organization (WTO) Agreement on Technical Barriers to Trade ('TBT Agreement') is poorly drafted – no surprise as negotiators compromised on wording to achieve a consensus. As a result, the Appellate Body has played an outsized role in interpreting the TBT Agreement and there are lessons that India and other Members can learn from its decisions – even if India has never participated as a complainant or respondent in a TBT dispute.[1] This chapter is not intended to describe the operation of the TBT Agreement, but instead to discuss some of the more important lessons learnt from panel and Appellate Body reports. Before proceeding, some preliminary observations are in order:

(1) The definitions of major terms are contained in Annex 1 of the TBT Agreement and not in Article 1, meaning that in order to understand the TBT Agreement, one must start with Annex 1. This inconvenience also appears in the Sanitary and Phytosanitary (SPS) Agreement.
(2) Technical regulations, standards, and conformity assessment procedures are largely subject to the same TBT disciplines. The provisions dealing with technical regulations have a greater effect on Members with strong central regulatory bodies, such as the European Union. The provisions governing standards have a stronger effect on Members, like the United States, which rely on private standardization companies that operate under government auspices. Some Members, including India, rely on a large number of voluntary standards promulgated by government entities such as the Bureau of Indian Standards (BIS).[2] As a result, TBT provisions governing standards are of considerable importance.
(3) There is a tendency to use the term *standards* imprecisely and this can lead to confusion. One must distinguish between standards developed by recognized international standardization bodies, and the work of regional, central government, local government and non-governmental standardization bodies.[3]
(4) Negotiators did not define the meaning of *non-discrimination* in Article 2.1, Annex 3:D, and Article 5.1.1 of the TBT Agreement, as incorporated by reference in Articles 7-9 of the Agreement. The Appellate Body 'explored' the meaning of 'non-discrimination' in the Trilogy Cases – *US – Clove Cigarettes*, *US – Tuna II*, and *US – COOL*, creating the doctrine of a 'legitimate regulatory distinction' to justify discriminatory regulations.[4] The TBT non-discrimination requirement is based in part on Appellate Body decisions

1. India has participated as a Third Party/Third Participant in TBT disputes. *See, e.g.*, Appellate Body Report on *US – Certain Country of Origin Labelling (COOL) Requirements*, (hereinafter '*US – COOL*'), WT/DS384,386/AB/R, adopted 23 July 2012, and Appellate Body Report on *Russia – Measures Affecting the Importation of Railway Equipment and Parts Thereof* (hereinafter '*Russia – Railway Equipment*'), WT/DS499/AB/R, adopted 5 March 2020.
2. The BIS has formulated over 19,500 standards. *See Overview of Standards*, Bureau of Indian Standards, https://www.services.bis.gov.in:8071/php/BIS_2.0/eBIS/about-standards (last visited 12 February 2020). These standards far outnumber India's technical regulations which usually take the form of Quality Control Orders (QCOs) and Compulsory Registration Orders (CRO). Although the rules governing technical regulations and standards are similar, India will need to be aware that some measures presently viewed as standards may in fact be technical regulations based on Appellate Body jurisprudence.
3. *See* the definitions in the Explanatory Note to Annex 1, Agreement on the Technical Barriers to Trade (Marrakesh, Morocco, 15 April 1994), Marrakesh Agreement Establishing the World Trade Organization, Annex 1A (hereinafter 'TBT Agreement'), *The Legal Texts: The Results of the Uruguay Round of Multilateral Trade Negotiations* 121 (1999), 1868 U.N.T.S. 120.
4. Appellate Body Report on *United States – Measures Affecting the Production and Sale of Clove Cigarettes* (hereinafter '*US – Clove Cigarettes*'), WT/DS406/AB/R, adopted 24 April 2012;

interpreting Articles I and III of the General Agreement on Tariffs and Trade 1994 ('GATT 1994'), and Appellate Body jurisprudence interpreting the chapeau of Article XX. This is consistent with the Appellate Body's approach in *US – Clove Cigarettes*:

> The balance set out in the preamble of the *TBT Agreement* between, on the one hand, the desire to avoid creating unnecessary obstacles to international trade and, on the other hand, the recognition of Members' right to regulate, is not, in principle, different from the balance set out in the GATT 1994, where obligations such as national treatment in Article III are qualified by the general exceptions provision of Article XX.[5]

(5) The Appellate Body weakened the application of the 'necessity' test that appears in Article 2.2 of the TBT Agreement consistent with its decisions interpreting various Article XX GATT exceptions that employ this term.[6] To do otherwise would make it difficult to promulgate a regulation that meets the requirements of the TBT Agreement as less trade-restrictive measures are almost always available. The Appellate Body opted to apply a slightly different test in the *Russia – Railway Equipment* case,[7] which involved conformity assessment and the application of the necessity test set forth in Article 5.1.2 of the TBT Agreement.

(6) The definition of a 'recognized' standardization body is unclear from the text of the TBT Agreement. One must refer to a Decision[8] of the Members to better understand the meaning that Members have ascribed to this term.

(7) With the exception of cases involving the TBT Agreement's harmonization and transparency provisions, which differ from the requirements of GATT 1994, it is unlikely that the results of TBT cases will differ much from cases involving GATT 1994. In other words, in most cases the TBT Agreement does not advance the treatment of regulations, standards and conformity assessment procedures much beyond GATT practice.

2.2 LESSONS LEARNT: SCOPE AND NOMENCLATURE

Because the TBT Agreement is poorly drafted, the lessons learnt stem largely from important Appellate Body decisions interpreting the problematic provisions of the

---

Appellate Body Report on *United States – Measures Concerning the Importation, Marketing and Sale of Tuna and Tuna Products* (hereinafter '*US – Tuna II (Mexico)*'), WT/DS381/AB/R, adopted 13 June 2012; *US – COOL*, WT/DS384,386/AB/R; Article 21.5 Appellate Body Report on *US – COOL*, WT/DS384,386/AB/RW, adopted 29 May 2015.

5. *US – Clove Cigarettes*, WT/DS406/AB/R, ¶ 96.
6. *See infra* section 2.3.2.
7. *Russia – Railway Equipment*, WT/DS499/AB/R.
8. *Decision of the Committee on Principles for the Development of International Standards, Guides and Recommendations with Relation to Articles 2, 5, and Annex 3 to the Agreement*, (hereinafter '*the Decision*'), G/TBT/I/Rev.14 (Annex 2) (24 September 2019), p. 62.

Agreement, in particular the *EC – Seals*[9] and the Trilogy Cases. The Appellate Body's TBT decisions have helped to clarify both scope and nomenclature – including the applicability of the TBT Agreement to various trade measures and the difference between a technical regulation and a standard.

2.2.1 Scope

2.2.1.1 The TBT Agreement Has Retroactive Application

In the *EC – Sardines* decision, the Appellate Body found that the TBT Agreement has retroactive application. A Member's obligation to use international standards as a basis for its technical regulations applies to technical regulations that entered into effect before the WTO Agreement entered into force, provided that the regulation remains in effect.[10] The result is that Members must review pre-1995 regulations that are still in effect for compliance with the TBT Agreement.

2.2.1.2 The TBT Agreement Does Not Apply to Private Standards

Purely private standards, for example purchasing standards established by a supermarket chain which relate to the size, quality and production methods of products acquired for sale, are outside the scope of the TBT Agreement. This is evident from the Appellate Body's decision in *US – Tuna II (Mexico)* which determined that an international standardization body is a recognized standardization body that is open to the relevant bodies of at least all WTO Members on a non-discriminatory basis at every stage of standard development.[11] Supermarket purchasing standards, and other private standardization programmes, do not meet this test and are outside the scope of the TBT Agreement.

2.2.1.3 The TBT Agreement Is Unlikely to Apply to Many Import Bans

A threshold question concerning the scope of the TBT Agreement arose in *EC – Asbestos*[12] and *EC – Seals*: Does the TBT Agreement apply to a general import ban, or is GATT 1994 the only applicable agreement? In *EC – Asbestos*, the Appellate Body took a broad approach, finding that the European Communities ('EC') ban on the import of asbestos and products containing asbestos fibres met the requirements set forth in

9. Appellate Body Report on *European Communities – Measures Prohibiting the Importation and Marketing of Seal Products*, (hereinafter '*EC – Seal Products*' or '*EC – Seals*'), WT/DS400, DS401/AB/R, adopted 18 June 2014.
10. Appellate Body Report on *European Communities – Trade Description of Sardines*, (hereinafter '*EC – Sardines*'), WT/DS231/AB/R, adopted 23 October 2002, ¶ 216.
11. *US – Tuna II (Mexico)*, WT/DS381/AB/R, ¶¶ 378, 382 and 392. For further discussion, *see infra* section 2.3.3.
12. Appellate Body Report on *European Communities – Measures Affecting Asbestos and Products Containing Asbestos* (hereinafter '*EC – Asbestos*'), WT/DS135/AB/R, adopted 5 April 2001.

Annex 1.1 of the Agreement for the measure to be considered a 'technical regulation'. The Appellate Body based its decision on its view that the trade measure was a document that laid 'down "characteristics" for all products that might contain asbestos'; that it laid 'down the "applicable administrative provisions" for certain products containing chrysotile asbestos fibres which are excluded from the prohibitions in the measure'; and that compliance was mandatory. Based on these findings, the Appellate Body concluded that the EC measure was a technical regulation.[13]

In *EC – Seals,* a more recent decision, the Appellate Body took a narrower and seemingly contradictory approach with respect to a similar import ban, finding that the TBT Agreement did not apply to the EC ban on the import of seals *and* products made from seals. The Appellate Body based its decision on its finding that the general ban on pure seal products did not lay down the product characteristics required to satisfy the definition of a technical regulation. Although the more specific ban on '*seal-containing products*' did lay down product characteristics, the Appellate Body deemed that this portion of the regulation was not the main feature of the trade measure:

> For example, to the extent that the measure *regulates* the placing on the EU market of pure seal products, which is a part of the integral and essential aspects of the measure, it does *not* prescribe or impose any 'characteristics' on the products themselves. To the extent the measure prohibits the placing on the EU market of seal-containing products, it could be seen as imposing certain 'objective features, qualities or characteristics' on all products by providing that they may not contain seal. However, as stated above, we are not persuaded that this part of the Regulation constitutes the main feature of the measure at issue. [...] we do not consider that the measure as a whole lays down product characteristics.[14]

These contradictory decisions are difficult to reconcile. Based on the Appellate Body's reasoning in *EC – Asbestos*, an import ban based entirely on a product's vital and detectable product characteristics would fall within the TBT Agreement (for example whether a product contains a cancer-causing substance such as asbestos). If this remains the case, it is difficult to understand why an import ban on products made from seals would fall outside the TBT Agreement since such a regulation deals with objective features, including product-related qualities and characteristics that are detectable in the final product. Of course, from a practical viewpoint, this distinction is likely to be unimportant given the Appellate Body's proclivity to interpret TBT and GATT obligations congruently. From a historical and academic perspective, these decisions continue to raise interesting questions.[15]

Much of the discussion surrounding the regulation of foreign processes and production methods is due to the controversial interpretation of Article III and Note Ad

13. *Ibid.* ¶ 75.
14. *EC – Seals,* WT/DS400, DS401/AB/R, ¶ 5.58.
15. There are also practical questions that will interest non-lawyers: (i) If import bans are largely outside the TBT Agreement, does it make a difference if the import ban is based on characteristics undetectable in the final product – for example the importer's production-related environmental or labour requirements? (ii) If TBT and GATT disciplines are largely the same, does it matter which agreement applies when a Member seeks to ban the import of a product?

Article III in the 1991 US dispute (*Tuna/Dolphin I*).[16] This unadopted GATT report involved a US ban on the domestic production and importation of tuna, including Mexican tuna, caught in a manner that resulted in dolphin deaths. The Panel ruled that Article III dealt with regulations that affected 'products as such' (characteristics detectable in the final product). While the US measure was arguably in accord with Article III, as US producers were subject to the same regulation, the Panel instead applied GATT Article XI (General Elimination of Quantitative Restrictions) finding that the US trade measure violated this provision. This unadopted report crystallized the view that Article III only applies to trade measures 'related to' characteristics detectable in a final product or relating to its sale.[17] For the environmental community this was a controversial finding, as was the Panel's conclusion that the US measure was not justified pursuant to the exceptions set forth in Article XX(b) and (g) of GATT 1947.[18]

The WTO Appellate Body revisited a similar question in a case involving India, the 1998 *US – Shrimp* dispute. This dispute dealt with a US ban on the importation of shrimp caught using fishing methods that resulted in the death of endangered sea turtles (another process not detectable in the final product – in other words not 'product-related'). The Panel again found a violation of Article XI.[19] On appeal, the Appellate Body determined that the US measure satisfied the GATT exception set forth in Article XX(g), but not the conditions set forth in GATT Article XX's chapeau.[20] Although the measure failed to meet the conditions of the chapeau, the Appellate Body set forth what the United States would need to do to satisfy its obligations under this provision: (i) adopt a flexible approach to Members that used different means to protect sea turtles, (ii) seek an international cooperative solution before resulting to unilateral action, (iii) negotiate seriously with all countries where similar conditions prevail, and (iv) deliver the same level of effort when providing assistance to Members seeking to meet US environmental requirements.[21]

In a subsequent case, *US – Shrimp (Article 21.5 – Malaysia)* involving two of the original parties and a similar fact situation, the US position prevailed.[22] The Appellate Body found that the US import ban on Malaysian shrimp did not cause arbitrary or unjustifiable discrimination or a disguised restriction on international trade, despite the fact that the United States was unsuccessful in its effort to negotiate a cooperative agreement with Malaysia to protect sea turtles.[23]

16. GATT Panel Report on *United States – Restrictions on Imports of Tuna* (hereinafter '*Tuna/Dolphin I*'), DS21/R-39S/155, 3 Sept. 1991, unadopted.
17. *Ibid.* ¶¶ 5.10-5.14.
18. *Ibid.* ¶¶ 5.24-5.34 (dealing with the protection of human animal or plant life and health and the conservation of exhaustible natural resources).
19. Panel Report on *United States – Import Prohibition of Certain Shrimp and Shrimp Products* (hereinafter '*US – Shrimp*'), WT/DS58/R, adopted 6 November 1998, ¶¶ 713-715.
20. *US – Shrimp,* WT/DS58/AB/R. (dealing with the prohibition of arbitrary or unjustifiable discrimination and disguised restrictions on international trade.)
21. *Ibid.* ¶¶ 163-181.
22. *See generally US – Shrimp* (Recourse to Article 21.5 of the DSU by Malaysia), WT/DS58/AB/RW, adopted 21 November 2001, ¶¶134, 136, 145-150.
23. *Ibid.*

The *US – Shrimp* decision supports a Member's right to ban the import of a product not manufactured in accordance with its environmental standards, provided the Member does not apply the ban in a manner that results in arbitrary or unjustifiable discrimination or a disguised restriction on international trade. Members may condition market access on satisfaction of a discriminatory process or production method not detectable in the final product – such as environmental measures, and perhaps human rights, labour and other norms, provided that a measure meets the requirements of GATT Article XX, in particular the chapeau's cooperation and flexibility requirements. The *US – Shrimp* decision is important to help understand the Appellate Body's TBT decisions, not least because the language found in Article XX's chapeau appears in Recital 6 of the TBT Agreement's preamble, but also because the Appellate Body appears to be harmonizing its interpretation of relevant GATT and TBT provisions.

The term 'technical regulation' is defined in Annex 1.1 of the TBT Agreement in part 'as a measure which lays down product characteristics or their related processes and production methods…'. The word 'related' has historical importance. A narrow reading of this term, rooted in the GATT *Tuna/Dolphin I* report and subsequent legislative history,[24] could be interpreted to mean that technical regulations do not include processes or production methods not 'related' to a product (i.e., not detectable in the final product).[25] Appellate Body decisions have avoided discussion of the meaning of the term 'related'. For example, the Appellate Body's Article XX decision in *US – Shrimp*, which gained the WTO considerable environmental goodwill, moves in the opposite direction. Avoiding the 'product-related' debate is in accord with the WTO Agreement's preamble, which favours both the environment and sustainable development, and which influenced the *US – Shrimp* decision. Avoiding the product-related debate also allows Members some latitude to influence foreign production practices. This is evidenced by the Appellate Body's decision in *US – Tuna II*, discussed below, which also avoided the 'product-related' debate and eventually allowed the United States to exercise some influence over Mexican fishing practices.

2.2.1.4 The TBT Agreement Applies to Labelling Measures

Both the Panel and the Appellate Body's decision in *US – Tuna II (Mexico)* dealt with the labelling of production characteristics undetectable in the final product – more specifically whether tuna was harvested in a manner that avoided dolphin deaths. Both decisions agreed that a US programme that established criteria, which if met allowed a manufacturer to affix a 'dolphin-safe' label on canned tuna was a technical regulation *within* the meaning of the TBT Agreement.[26]

24. *See* Ming Du, *The Regulation of Product Standards in World Trade Law* 16 (Hart 2020). Mexico, the victor in *Tuna/Dolphin I* (unadopted) sought inclusion of the word 'related' in both the first and second paragraphs of Annex 1.1. The negotiators agreed to place the word 'related' in the first paragraph, but not the second (which deals with labelling).
25. *Tuna/Dolphin I* (unadopted), DS21/R-39S/155.
26. *US – Tuna II (Mexico)*, WT/DS381/R, ¶¶ 7.100-145; *US – Tuna II (Mexico)*, WT/DS381/AB/R, ¶¶ 190-199. Note, the term labelling appears in Annex 1.1, para. 2.

On the basis of *US – Tuna II (Mexico)*, a WTO Member may regulate the use of a label indicating product characteristics not detectable in the final product, such as fishing techniques. This far-reaching decision opens the door for many forms of social and environmental labelling. The reasoning of *Tuna II* is applicable to labelling programmes that flag compliance with production-related environmental, human rights or labour norms, including satisfaction of core labour standards. Of course, the labelling programme must meet the requirements of the TBT Agreement, in particular Article 2.1 (non-discrimination) and those of GATT 1994.

2.2.2. Nomenclature

2.2.2.1 Technical Regulations Versus Standards

Appellate Body decisions provide important lessons as to which trade measures are technical regulations and which are standards. As defined in Annex 1.1 of the Agreement, *technical regulations* are mandatory, written rules that apply to identifiable products and which set out product characteristics or their related processes and production methods. They include rules dealing with terminology, symbols, packaging, marking and labelling requirements (but not bans…). The definition of a *standard* is similar, with one important difference – 'compliance' with a standard is 'not mandatory'.

In the *US – Tuna II* decision the Appellate Body clarified this distinction, which is not as clear-cut as the definitions suggest. *US – Tuna II* dealt with a US measure regulating the use of a label certifying that tuna is 'dolphin-safe' – i.e., that tuna was fished in a manner that protected dolphins. The US regulation at issue did not require that the dolphin-safe label be affixed to a tin of tuna, but it did establish the *conditions* for use of the label.

The Appellate Body affirmed the Panel's ruling in *US – Tuna II,* finding that the labelling programme at issue is a technical regulation and not a standard as it is composed of governmental legislative and regulatory acts that (i) set out 'a single and legally mandated definition of a "dolphin-safe" tuna product and disallows the use of other labels on tuna products that do not satisfy this definition', (ii) 'prescribes in a broad and exhaustive manner the conditions that apply' for asserting dolphin-safety, and (iii) 'covers the entire field of what "dolphin-safe" means in relation to tuna products.'[27] This finding has general applicability to government regulations applicable to labelling programmes.

27. *US – Tuna II (Mexico)*, WT/DS381/AB/R, ¶ 199. (Although the Appellate Body *US – Tuna II* found that the US trade measure was technical regulation that fell within Articles 2 and 3 of the TBT Agreement, the United States relies largely on standards developed by private standardization companies that operate under government auspices. Such standards will usually fall within Article 4 and Annex 3 of the TBT Agreement (The Code of Good Practice for the Preparation, Adoption and Application of Standards)).

2.2.2.2 *International Standardization Body*

In *US – Tuna II* the Appellate Body examined whether, pursuant to Article 2.4 of the TBT Agreement, the Agreement on the International Dolphin Conservation Program (AIDCP) is a body with recognized activities in standardization whose work should be used as a basis for a Member's technical regulations. If the answer had been yes, Mexico would have continued to pressure the United States to use AIDCP standards as a basis for its dolphin-safe labelling programme (assuming that AIDCP standards were effective and appropriate). In answering no, the Appellate Body concluded that 'the AIDCP is not open to the relevant bodies of at least all Members and thus not an "international standardizing body" for purposes of the TBT Agreement.'[28] As a result, the AIDCP's dolphin-safe definition and certification did not constitute a relevant international standard for purposes of the TBT Agreement.[29] In the words of the Appellate Body, 'not all transnational standardizing bodies are "international"' for TBT purposes.[30] The question of harmonization based on international standards is discussed further in section 2.3.3.

2.3 LESSONS LEARNT: TBT DISCIPLINES

TBT decisions have dealt with technical regulations and more recently conformity assessment procedures. However, with minor exceptions the underlying TBT disciplines are similar for technical regulations, standards and conformity assessment procedures.

The TBT Agreement requires that technical regulations, standards and conformity assessment procedures: (i) are not discriminatory,[31] (ii) do not create unnecessary obstacles to international trade;[32] (iii) be based on existing international standards when effective and appropriate ('harmonization');[33] and (iv) be transparent.[34] Other than the harmonization requirement, analogous obligations are found in GATT 1994. Appellate Body decisions have interpreted all four of these requirements.

2.3.1 Non-discrimination

Article 2.1 of the TBT Agreement contains both national treatment and most-favoured-nation obligations, as do provisions of the TBT Agreement governing standards and conformity assessment procedures. These are the most important disciplines of the

28. *Ibid.* ¶ 399. (The activities of AIDCP are pursued through the Inter-American Tropical Tuna Commission (IATTC) which is largely concerned with tuna fishing in the Eastern Tropical Pacific region. With the exception of the United States and the European Union, the states that have ratified AIDCP are from Central and South America.)
29. *Ibid.* ¶ 401.
30. *Ibid.* ¶ 365.
31. TBT Agreement, Articles 2.1, 5.1.1 and Annex 3:D.
32. TBT Agreement, Articles 2.2, 5.1.2 and Annex 3:E.
33. TBT Agreement, Articles 2.4, 5.2.2 and Annex 3:G.
34. TBT Agreement, Articles 2.9, 5.6 and Annex 3:J-Q.

TBT Agreement, and most Appellate Body TBT decisions have dealt with non-discrimination.

Non-discrimination is not defined in the TBT Agreement. Nor does the TBT Agreement provide explicit exceptions that would justify a discriminatory regulation designed to fulfil a legitimate objective. This oversight is a major difference between the TBT Agreement and GATT 1994 which establishes a clear rule and exception relationship. As a result, the Appellate Body had to reconcile the Members' need to regulate to fulfil a legitimate regulatory objective with the need of Members to prevent technical regulations, standards and conformity assessment procedures from being used for purely protectionist purposes. It did so by referencing language present in Recital 6 of the TBT Agreement's preamble which is drawn partially from GATT Article XX – specifically the obligation not to apply exceptions that would result in arbitrary or unjustifiable discrimination. In summary:

(1) GATT 1994 creates a rule and exception relationship. For example, if a Member's regulation violates the non-discrimination provisions of the GATT Articles I or III, the Member can seek to justify the violation based on the general exceptions contained in Article XX.
(2) The TBT drafters intended that the Members be permitted to regulate to fulfil a legitimate objective. Unlike GATT 1994, the TBT Agreement does not set forth a rule and exception relationship, making it unclear how a Member should justify a discriminatory, but even-handedly applied regulation designed to fulfil a legitimate objective.
(3) The Appellate Body addressed this oversight in the Trilogy cases by formulating a test for non-discrimination that draws from its decisions interpreting GATT Articles I and III and the chapeau of Article XX.
(4) The Trilogy cases apply a four-part test that permits discriminatory regulations if they are applied even-handedly based on a legitimate regulatory distinction – concepts that do not appear in the TBT Agreement.

The Four-Part Test[35]

(1) Are the products like products? If not, a Member may subject the products to different regulatory treatment. The traditional like product test applies.[36]

(2) If the products are like products, does the imported product(s) receive less favourable treatment (i.e., does the measure alter the conditions of competition),

35. Adapted from Arthur Appleton and Patrick Macrory, *Non-Tariff Barriers – The Agreements on Sanitary and Phytosanitary Measures and Technical Barriers to Trade*, in BUSINESS GUIDE TO TRADE AND INVESTMENT, VOLUME 1, INTERNATIONAL TRADE 105 (Arthur Appleton and Patrick Macrory eds, ICC, 2017).

36. Look to (i) the physical characteristics of the product (its properties, nature & qualities), (ii) its customs classification based on the Harmonized System, (iii) the end uses of the product, and (iv) consumer preferences.

either when compared to domestic like products (national treatment), or as between imported like products (MFN treatment)?

(3) If a given product is subject to less favourable treatment, is the less favourable treatment based on a 'legitimate regulatory distinction' (LRD)? For example, assuming for the sake of argument that all automobiles are like products, a regulation stating that all automobiles operating within a particular Member must be zero emission vehicles discriminates in favour of electric and hydrogen cars and against gasoline-powered cars, but appears to be based on an LRD - protection of the environment.

(4) Is the LRD applied even-handedly? Examine the regulation's design, architecture, revealing structure, operation, and application. If the above measure only authorizes zero emission electric automobiles to the exclusion of zero emission hydrogen vehicles and the regulating state is an efficient producer of such electric vehicles, this would suggest that it is not even-handed as there would not appear to be an LRD between the treatment of electric and hydrogen vehicles.[37] The measure as applied would appear designed to discriminate de facto in favour of domestically produced electric automobiles.

In each of the Trilogy cases, the Appellate Body found that there was not a legitimate regulatory distinction that justified discriminatory technical regulations, with the result that the US trade measures at issue violated the non-discrimination obligation set forth in Article 2.1 of the TBT Agreement:[38]

- *US – COOL:* The US 'country of origin labelling' (COOL) programme was purportedly designed to provide US consumers with information as to the origin of the beef they purchased (where the livestock were born, raised and slaughtered). The Appellate Body found that the COOL programme discriminated impermissibly against Canadian and Mexican livestock producers by imposing higher costs on their livestock in the slaughtering process and through the collection of administrative information that was never provided to retail consumers. There was no LRD as retail consumers did not necessarily benefit from the labelling programme.
- *US – Clove Cigarettes:* The Appellate Body struck down as discriminatory a US ban on the sale of clove cigarettes on the grounds that the ban did not apply to a like product, menthol cigarettes, which are popular in the United States. The ban resulted in less favourable treatment for Indonesian clove cigarettes (which were not permitted to be sold) as opposed to US-produced menthol cigarettes (whose sale was permitted) thereby discriminating against Indonesian clove cigarettes. There was no LRD as the stated objective of the US

37. Assuming that both are like products.
38. *See* Appleton and Macrory, *supra* note 35, at 106, from which this explanation is adapted.

regulation was to reduce youth smoking, but both clove and menthol cigarettes are attractive to young smokers.
- *US – Tuna II (Mexico):* Dolphins swim with tuna in certain tropical regions of the eastern and western Pacific Ocean. The United States regulates the use of a 'dolphin-safe' label that manufacturers can apply to tuna products to indicate that the tuna is caught in a manner that avoids dolphin deaths. The Appellate Body found that there was no LRD justifying the discriminatory measure. The US labelling regulations discriminated against Mexico as stricter rules were applied in the eastern tropical Pacific Ocean where both the US and Mexico fish for tuna, but laxer rules were applied in the western tropical Pacific Ocean where Mexico does not fish for tuna.

The Trilogy cases demonstrate the importance of the TBT Agreement's non-discrimination obligation, which is likely to be the obligation most at issue in TBT cases. Due to the similarity of discrimination obligations under the TBT and GATT Agreements, had the Appellate Body adjudicated the same trade measures under GATT 1994, it would have ruled against the United States on similar grounds in each of the three cases.

In its subsequent *US – Tuna II (Mexico)* compliance decision, the Appellate Body acknowledged the similarity of the calibration analysis applied by the Panel to uphold the legality of the amended US trade measure, stating 'where the difference between Article 2.1 and Article XX are taken into account, it may be permissible to rely on reasoning developed in the context of one agreement for the purpose of conducting an analysis under the other.'[39]

2.3.2 Necessity

The terms 'necessary' and 'unnecessary' appear throughout the TBT Agreement, among the most important provisions being the following:[40]

Preamble – Recital 6: *Recognizing* that no country should be prevented from taking measures **necessary** to ensure the quality of its exports, or for the protection of human, animal or plant life or health, of the environment, or for the prevention of deceptive practices, **at the levels it considers appropriate**, subject to the requirement that they are not applied in a manner which would constitute a means of arbitrary or unjustifiable discrimination between countries where the same conditions prevail or a disguised restriction on international trade, and are otherwise in accordance with the provisions of this Agreement;

39. Appellate Body Report on *United States – Measures Concerning the Importation, Marketing and Sale of Tuna and Tuna Products Recourse to Article 21.5 of the DSU by the United States, United States – Measures Concerning the Importation, Marketing and Sale of Tuna and Tuna Products, Second Recourse to Article 21.5 of the DSU by Mexico*, WT/DS381/AB/RW/USA, WT/DS381/AB/RW2, adopted 11 January 2019, ¶ 7.12.
40. Emphasis added throughout this table.

Technical Regulations – Article 2.2: Members shall ensure that technical regulations are not prepared, adopted or applied with a view to or with the effect of creating **unnecessary** obstacles to international trade. For this purpose, technical regulations **shall not be more trade-restrictive than necessary** to fulfil a legitimate objective, taking account of the risks non-fulfilment would create.

Standards – Annex 3(E): The standardizing body shall ensure that standards are not prepared, adopted or applied with a view to, or with the effect of, creating **unnecessary** obstacles to international trade.

Conformity Assessment Procedures – Article 5.1.2: Conformity assessment procedures are not prepared, adopted or applied with a view to or with the effect of creating **unnecessary** obstacles to international trade. This means, *inter alia*, that conformity assessment procedures **shall not be more strict or be applied more strictly than is necessary to give the importing Member adequate confidence** that products conform with the applicable technical regulations or standards, taking account of the risks non-conformity would create.

The language in these provisions is no accident. The interpretation of the term 'necessary' has a history, albeit controversial, in GATT 1947 panel reports interpreting Article XX(b) and (d). These panels understood the term to mean that a trade measure is necessary if there is no alternative measure consistent with the GATT, or less inconsistent with it, which a contracting party could reasonably be expected to employ to achieve its policy objectives.[41] The language from these GATT-era Panel reports found its way into TBT Articles 2.2 and 5.1.2.

The problem with these GATT 1947 decisions is that they made it easier to protect exhaustible natural resources, like oil and coal, under Article XX(g), which only requires that a trade measure be 'related to conservation of an exhaustible natural resource',[42] than to protect human life under Article XX(b) which applied the necessity

41. *See* GATT Panel Report on *Thailand – Restrictions on Importation of and Internal Taxes on Cigarettes*, DS10/R, 37S/200, adopted 7 November 1990, ¶ 74. (where the Panel found necessity existed if there were no alternative measure consistent with the General Agreement, or less inconsistent with it, which a contracting party could reasonably be expected to employ to achieve its policy objectives.) The Panel cited GATT Panel Report on *United States - Section 337 of the Tariff Act of 1930*, L/6439, adopted on 7 November 1989, ¶ 5.26. This interpretation was also supported in the GATT Panel Report on *United States - Measures Affecting Alcoholic and Malt Beverages*, DS23/R - 39S/206, adopted 19 June 1992, ¶ 5.41.
42. Article XX(g) was invoked with success in Appellate Body Report on *United States – Standards for Reformulated and Conventional Gasoline* (hereinafter '*US – Gasoline*'), WT/DS2/AB/R, adopted 20 May 1996, p. 19.; *US – Shrimp*, WT/DS58/AB/R, ¶¶ 141-142.; Appellate Body Report on *China – Measures Related to the Exportation of Rare Earths – Tungsten and Molybdenum* (hereinafter '*China – Rare Earths*'), WT/DS431/AB/R, adopted 29 August 2014, ¶ 5.94.

test.[43] Consequently, the Appellate Body was compelled to relax the meaning of the term necessary in Article XX(b).[44]

For example, in *Brazil – Retreaded Tyres,* the Appellate Body found that 'In order to determine whether a measure is "necessary" within the meaning of Article XX(b) of the GATT 1994, a panel must assess all the relevant factors, particularly the extent of the contribution to the achievement of a measure's objective and its trade restrictiveness, in the light of the importance of the interests or values at stake.'[45] In effect, the Appellate Body established a continuum. The test is easier to satisfy if the legitimate objective at issue is more important – in such cases, the trade measure need only be apt to make a material contribution. If the objective at issue is not vital, the measure must be the least trade-restrictive measure reasonably available. In reality, many cases fall between the two poles.

2.3.2.1 Technical Regulations

Although TBT Article 2.2 draws some of its language from GATT 1947 Panel reports, the Trilogy cases and *Australia – Plain Packaging*[46] aligned the Appellate Body interpretation of the term 'necessary' in Article 2.2 with its interpretation of the same term in GATT Article XX. The Appellate Body found that the assessment of 'necessity', in the context of Article 2.2, involves a 'relational analysis' of the following factors: (i) the trade restrictiveness of the technical regulation; (ii) the degree of contribution that the technical regulation makes to the achievement of a legitimate objective; and (iii) the risks non-fulfilment would create.[47]

These cases suggest that a technical regulation is likely to satisfy Article 2.2 if it is apt to make a meaningful contribution to a legitimate objective. While this may depend on the relative importance of the legitimate objective at issue, this distinction is not apparent from the TBT cases. Perhaps this is because Recital 6 of the TBT Agreement's preamble, which sets forth the 'necessity' requirement, contains language similar to Article 5.6 of the SPS Agreement – both agreements appear to grant the regulating Member some discretion to determine whether a particular trade measure is necessary. In conclusion, TBT cases involving technical regulations are more likely to

43. *See* Arthur E. Appleton, *GATT Article XX's Chapeau: A Disguised 'Necessary' Test? The WTO Appellate Body Ruling in United States – Standards for Reformulated and Conventional Gasoline,* 6 REV. EUROPEAN COMMUNITY AND INT'L ENVTL. L. 131 (1997).
44. *See generally* Appellate Body Report on *Korea – Measures Affecting Imports of Fresh, Chilled and Frozen Beef* (hereinafter '*Korea – Beef*') WT/DS161,169/AB/R, adopted 10 January 2001, and Appellate Body Report on *Brazil – Measures Affecting Imports of Retreaded Tyres* (hereinafter '*Brazil – Retreaded Tyres*'), WT/DS332/AB/R, adopted 17 December 2007.
45. *Brazil – Retreaded Tyres,* WT/DS332/AB/R, ¶ 156.
46. Appellate Body Report on *Australia – Certain Measures Concerning Trademarks, Geographical Indications and Other Plain Packaging Requirements Applicable to Tobacco Products and Packaging* (hereinafter '*Australia – Plain Packaging (Honduras)*' and '*Australia – Plain Packaging (Dominican Republic)*'), WT/DS441,435/AB/R, adopted 29 June 2020, ¶ 6.3.
47. *Ibid. citing US – COOL,* WT/DS384,386/AB/R, ¶ 374 (referring to Appellate Body Report, *US – Tuna II (Mexico),* WT/DS381/AB/R, ¶ 318).

turn on whether the non-discrimination obligation in Article 2.1 is fulfilled, as opposed to whether a particular trade measure is necessary.

2.3.2.2 *Conformity Assessment Procedures: Article 5.1.2*

The legal situation with respect to conformity assessment procedures is similar to that of technical regulations, but not exactly the same. In the *Russia – Railway Equipment* case, the Appellate Body compared Article 2.2 and Article 5.1.2 to determine whether Russian conformity assessment procedures were prepared, adopted or applied with a view to or with the effect of creating unnecessary obstacles to international trade. The Appellate Body found:

> As we see it, both Articles 2.2 and 5.1.2 set out obligations for WTO Members not to create unnecessary obstacles to international trade with regard to technical regulations and conformity assessment procedures, respectively, and identify certain factors to be considered in a necessity analysis. In particular, the factors relevant to the analysis under Article 2.2 include the legitimate objective of the technical regulation, its trade restrictiveness, and the risks non-fulfilment of the objective would create. Under Article 5.1.2, relevant factors include the function of the conformity assessment procedure, its strictness, and the risks non-conformity with the underlying technical regulation or standard would create.[48]
>
> Based on these considerations, the existence of an 'unnecessary obstacle[] to international trade' under the first and second sentences of Article 5.1.2 of the TBT Agreement, read together, may be established on the basis of an analysis of the following factors: (i) whether the conformity assessment procedure provides adequate confidence of conformity with the underlying technical regulation or standard; (ii) the strictness of the conformity assessment procedure or of the way in which it is applied; and (iii) the nature of the risks and the gravity of the consequences that would arise from non-conformity with the technical regulation or standard.[49]

Both the *Russia – Railway Equipment* decision and Annex (C)(1)(h) of the SPS Agreement speak of establishing 'adequate confidence' that a product meets the applicable regulation.[50] Nevertheless, panels are not bound by a Member's view. Although both the TBT and the SPS Agreements grant some latitude to the importing Member to determine whether a conformity assessment procedure provides such confidence, this is not to be mistaken for complete deference to the importing Member's opinion. The Panel will be the ultimate arbitrator of this question of fact.

48. *Russia – Railway Equipment,* WT/DS499/AB/R, ¶ 5.185.
49. *Ibid.* ¶ 5.186.
50. Annex (C)(1)(h) provides: 'whenever specifications of a product are changed subsequent to its control and inspection in light of the applicable regulations, the procedure for the modified product is limited to what is necessary to determine whether adequate confidence exists that the product still meets the regulations concerned'.

2.3.2.3 Standards

There are no WTO cases interpreting the meaning of 'necessary' as applicable to standards.[51]

2.3.3 Harmonization

An important innovation in the TBT Agreement is the obligation for Members to use international standards as a basis for their technical regulations and standards when effective and appropriate,[52] or in the case of conformity assessment procedures when appropriate,[53] to achieve a legitimate objective. These provisions were a source of confusion, and the Members intervened to address certain deficiencies through the Decision of the Committee on Principles for the Development of International Standards, Guides and Recommendations with Relation to Articles 2, 5, and Annex 3 to the Agreement.[54] This Decision played an important part in the resolution of the *US – Tuna II (Mexico)* dispute, in particular with respect to the definition of a recognized standardization body.[55]

As noted previously, in *US – Tuna II* the Appellate Body determined that an international standardization body is a recognized standardization body that is open to the relevant bodies of at least all WTO Members on a non-discriminatory basis at every stage of standards development.[56] It further found that 'recognition of a body's standardization activities may "be inferred from the recognition of the resulting standard, i.e., when its existence, legality and validity [have] been acknowledged".'[57] An international organization that develops a single standard could have recognized activities in standardization if the evidence suggests that the body's standardization activities are recognized by a large number of WTO Members that participated in the development of the standard and acknowledge the standard's validity and legality.[58]

The framework which the negotiators established in the TBT Agreement and the Decision for Harmonization has shortcomings. First, the carve-out for standards that are ineffective or inappropriate is broad in nature and leaves considerable discretion (subject to review under the Dispute Settlement Understanding) to the regulating Member. Article 2.4 provides three examples of ineffective or inappropriate means for fulfilment of a legitimate objective: (i) fundamental climatic factors, (ii) fundamental geographic factors, and (iii) fundamental technological problems. Unfortunately, the third is unclear. Second, recognized international standardization bodies are generally

51. *See* Paragraph E of the Code of Good Practice (Annex 3, TBT Agreement).
52. Article 2.4 (Technical Regulations) and Annex 3:F (Standards), TBT Agreement.
53. Article 5.4, TBT Agreement.
54. *See* the Decision, *supra* note 8.
55. The list of recognized international standardization bodies is open-ended in the TBT Agreement. The Agreement only mentions the International Standardization Organization and the International Electrotechnical Commission in passing.
56. *US – Tuna II (Mexico)*, WT/DS381/AB/R, ¶¶ 378, 382 and 392.
57. *Ibid.* ¶ 392.
58. *Ibid.* ¶ 394.

inter-governmental in nature, meaning that businesses that want to participate in the activities of these international organizations must usually work through a friendly government. These governmental organizations are often slow-moving in nature, and businesses in high-tech sectors have frequently found that it is better to establish their own private standards. Third, the rebuttable presumption in TBT Article 2.5 has little value. If a Member's technical regulation is in accordance with relevant international standards, it is presumed not to create an unnecessary obstacle to international trade. However, the 'necessity' test has been watered down so it is unlikely in most cases that a technical regulation will be found to create such an obstacle. Fourth, not all international standardization organizations are open to all WTO Members.[59]

2.3.4 Transparency

Transparency is a cornerstone principle in the WTO Agreement, and enjoys a prominent position in the TBT Agreement. Of particular importance are the requirements set forth in Article 2.9 dealing with notification preceding adoption of a technical regulation.[60] Article 2.9.2 requires that a Member notify other Members through the WTO Secretariat of the products to be covered by a proposed technical regulation. This notification must take place at an early appropriate stage so that comments from Members can be considered and amendments introduced. The Panel in *US – Clove Cigarettes* found that the United States acted inconsistently with Article 2.9.2 by failing to notify the technical regulation at issue.[61]

The Appellate Body in *US – Clove Cigarettes* also commented on a transparency-related provision. Article 2.12 of the TBT Agreement requires that Members allow a 'reasonable interval' after publication of a technical regulation before it enters into force so that producers can adapt to the new regulation. Article 5.2 of the Doha Decision on Implementation-related Issues and Concerns defines 'reasonable interval' to be at least six months.[62] Importantly, the Appellate Body determined that the Doha Ministerial Decision constitutes a subsequent agreement between the parties on how to interpret the phrase 'reasonable interval' pursuant to Article 31(3)(a) of the Vienna Convention on the Law of Treaties.[63]

2.4 CONCLUSION

Perhaps the most important lesson to be learnt from the Appellate Body's TBT decisions is that 'the more things change, the more they stay the same.'[64] In short, the

59. Taiwan is a case in point.
60. Similar obligations exist in Article 5.6 (Conformity Assessment), and related but slightly different obligations applicable to standards exist in paragraphs J, L, M, N and O of the Code of Good Practice (Annex 3).
61. *US – Clove Cigarettes*, WT/DS406/R, ¶ 7.542.
62. *Implementation-related Issues and Concerns, Decision of 14 November 2001*, WT/MIN(01)/17 (20 November 2001).
63. *US – Clove Cigarettes*, WT/DS406/AB/R, ¶ 268.
64. Jean-Baptiste Alphonse Karr.

TBT Agreement demonstrates limited ambition. Decisions interpreting the TBT Agreement seldom go further than decisions interpreting GATT 1994.

A review of TBT decisions concerning non-discrimination demonstrates overall consistency with GATT decisions interpreting Article XX's chapeau. The TBT non-discrimination requirement allows Members to pursue legitimate objectives whilst limiting the potential for Members to apply technical regulations, standards, and conformity assessment procedures for protectionist purposes. It prevents justification of technical regulations that result in arbitrary or unjustifiable discrimination.

The TBT decisions examining the necessity requirement are also aligned with the Appellate Body decisions interpreting Article XX (a), (b) and (d) of GATT 1994. WTO jurisprudence has interpreted this provision in a manner that makes it easier for Members to fulfil legitimate objectives. The Article 2.2 necessity requirement cannot be relied upon as an effective buttress against protectionism.

As with the necessity requirement, Members should not view the harmonization requirement as either a strong means to facilitate the achievement of legitimate objectives or as a bulwark against protectionism. International harmonization moves gradually, with the slowest boat in the convoy setting the pace. As a result, international standards will frequently be lower than regional and national standards. Furthermore, the existence of an international standard may make it easier for Members with higher standards to argue that they have used the international standard 'as a basis' for their technical regulations, standards and conformity assessment procedures. In instances when this argument is rebuttable, a Member is likely to rely on the escape clause – arguing that a particular international standard is ineffective or inappropriate to achieve its desired level of protection, and that a tougher measure is warranted. Members thus have some discretion under the TBT Agreement to pursue legitimate objectives.

Likewise, while the transparency provisions of the TBT Agreement are important, they do not impose the disciplines necessary to minimize non-tariff barriers. They only require notification of a regulation's first draft, and not subsequent drafts. While this allows reasonable time for initial comment and minimizes delay, the transparency provisions do not address instances when a regulating Member makes substantial changes to its original draft.

The TBT Agreement's most interesting provisions are those that deal with equivalence of technical regulations and mutual recognition of conformity assessment procedures.[65] These provisions are soft law and, as such neither bind Members nor are likely to be a source of important Appellate Body decisions. Having never been interpreted by the Appellate Body, they are beyond the scope of this chapter. However, they merit a passing mention as soft law often indicates the direction of future negotiations and agreements. Just as the plurilateral Tokyo Round Standards Code evolved into the TBT Agreement, these soft law provisions may indicate the evolution of TBT disciplines. Actualization of the existing TBT provisions on equivalence and mutual recognition will require Members to have the human and technical resources to

65. *See, e.g.*, Articles 2.7 and 6.1, TBT Agreement.

draft quality technical regulations, and confidence in foreign conformity assessment procedures. Not all WTO Members possess the required expertise. When they do, the value of this relatively shallow and unambitious Agreement may increase and benefit more WTO Members.

CHAPTER 3

Product Regulations: Designing a Development-Friendly FTA – An Indian Perspective

*Shailja Singh**

Rules relating to technical barriers to trade (TBT) and sanitary and phytosanitary (SPS) measures are increasingly constituting a crucial core of modern free trade agreements (FTAs). The FTAs can, thus, serve as an important medium to address the developmental concerns on these issues. This chapter sets out to examine four key SPS and TBT issues that need to be considered in designing a development-friendly FTA for India. These relate to (i) international standardising bodies (ISBs); (ii) sectoral annexes; (iii) trans-governmental network of regulators; and (iv) language barriers. The chapter highlights the challenges associated with the ISB standard-setting process; the past experience of incorporating SPS and TBT sectoral arrangements in FTAs, particularly for India; issues associated with referencing select trans-governmental network of regulators in FTAs; and, finally, the role FTAs can play in reducing language barriers in product regulations. The chapter recommends a possible 'India approach' on these issues for future trade engagements, from a developmental perspective.

'It makes a difference, doesn't it, whether we [fully] fence ourselves in,
or whether we are fenced out by the barriers of others?'

– E. M. Forster, *A Room with a View*

* Views expressed are personal.

3.1 INTRODUCTION

Non-tariff measures (NTMs) in the form of technical barriers to trade (TBT) and sanitary and phytosanitary (SPS) measures are neither new nor rare. In fact, the World Trade Report, 2012, recognises it as one of the most frequently encountered NTMs in international trade.[1] Thus, while the WTO regulates these measures through its TBT and SPS agreements, it is not surprising that free trade agreements (FTAs) are the latest frontiers where the rules are being further elaborated and built upon. At the core of regulating TBT and SPS measures, whether at the WTO or the FTAs, lies the fundamental question – *how can countries pursue their legitimate objectives without creating undue barriers to international trade?* Maintaining a delicate balance between the two goals, which can often appear to be at odds with each other, becomes particularly challenging within FTAs, where the aim is to agree upon WTO-Plus rules. The challenge is amplified in case the trading partner is a developing country whose developmental needs are to be (and should be) taken into account within the FTA framework.

India is no stranger to exploring the FTA route for regulating SPS and TBT measures (used interchangeably here with national product regulations). With SPS and TBT obligations ranging widely from being absent,[2] to a few paragraphs,[3] to having their own dedicated chapters and annexes,[4] the Indian approach toward SPS/TBT issues in its FTAs has evolved over time. While there is a variety of issues where the developmental challenges need to be accounted for in the FTA text on product regulations, this chapter attempts to highlight four such essential issues from an Indian perspective. These relate to the approach India should adopt toward (i) *international standardising bodies (ISBs); (ii) sectoral annexes; (iii) trans-governmental network of regulators; and (iv) language barriers in its FTAs*. To explore the possible options for India, each issue has been examined by studying the relevant background, recent FTA practice and the Indian position on the same. An attempt has been made to undertake a holistic qualitative as well as quantitative (where possible) analysis of the issues to arrive at a possible 'India approach'. To this end, sections 3.2 to 3.5 examine each of the four issues in detail, which is followed by the conclusion in section 3.6.

---

1. *World Trade Report, 2012 – Trade and Public Policies: A closer look at non-tariff measures in the 21st century*, World Trade Organization, p. 43 (available online at https://www.wto.org/english/res_e/booksp_e/anrep_e/world_trade_report12_e.pdf).
2. *See*, *Agreement on South Asia Free Trade Area* (SAFTA), available at https://commerce.gov.in/wp-content/uploads/2020/05/safta.pdf.
3. *See*, Article 2.28, *India – Korea Comprehensive Economic Partnership Agreement.*
4. *See* Chapter 5 and related Sectoral Annexes, *India – Singapore Comprehensive Economic Cooperation Agreement.*

3.2 INTERNATIONAL STANDARDISING BODIES AND STANDARDS

3.2.1 Background

The TBT and SPS agreements attach great importance to international standards and perceive them as a means to attain international regulatory convergence. WTO Members are required to broadly base their domestic product regulations on international standards, with the international standards acting as the 'de facto mandatory normative technical material'[5] in standard-setting. Such a high level of deference to a non-WTO instrument has been included within the texts of these agreements to ensure that the adoption of domestic SPS and TBT measures minimize the negative effects on trade,[6] and do not create unnecessary obstacles to international trade.[7] The SPS Agreement, for example, requires that Members 'shall base' their SPS measures on international standards, guidelines or recommendations, where they exist, unless covered by one of the permitted grounds.[8] The aim is to attain as wide a harmonisation as possible. Along similar lines, the TBT Agreement, which regulates technical regulations, standards and conformity assessment procedures (CAPs) for goods, imposes obligations to base these on international standards[9] issued by ISBs.[10] However, where these two agreements significantly diverge is the identification of ISBs that issue the relevant international standards.

The SPS Agreement clearly identifies the three ISBs developing international standards, guidelines and recommendations on food safety, animal health and plant health for its purposes.[11] Though not exhaustive, the list covers the primary SPS-related ISBs, namely, the Codex Alimentarius Commission (Codex), International Office of Epizootics (OIE) and the International Plant Protection Convention (IPPC). The TBT Agreement, on the other hand, does not elaborate what these bodies are, despite referring to ISBs twelve times in the text. There are, of course, signposts in the agreement that appear to point the direction to be taken. For instance, the Explanatory Note to the definition of 'standards' in Annex 1 of the TBT Agreement states that '[s]tandards prepared by the international standardization community are based on consensus', and '[t]his Agreement covers also documents that are not based on consensus.'[12] Similarly, 'international body' is defined as a body whose membership is open to the relevant bodies of at least all Members.[13]

5. *See* Delimatsis, Panagiotis, '*Into the Abyss of Standard-Setting: An Analysis of Procedural and Substantive Guarantees within the International Organization for Standardization (ISO)*', (2015) RSCAS 2015/35 European University Institute Working Paper, p. 5.
6. *See* para. 4, Preamble to the SPS Agreement.
7. *See* para. 6, Preamble to the TBT Agreement.
8. Article 3.1 of the SPS Agreement. Also *see* Articles 3.2 and 3.3.
9. With varying degree of strictness, depending on the nature of the measure as well as the entity formulating it. For instance, stricter for central government bodies formulating TRs and CAPs.
10. *See* Articles 2.4 and 5.4, and Article 4.1, read with the para. F, Code of Good Practice, TBT Agreement.
11. *See* Annex A, para. 3 of the SPS Agreement.
12. Paragraph 1.2 of Annex 1 of the TBT Agreement.
13. Paragraph 1.4 of Annex 1 of the TBT Agreement.

However, all is not crystal clear, as these textual signposts could also allow for differing interpretational positions. For instance, the Explanatory Note continues to linger the debate on whether the TBT Agreement intends to legitimise non-consensus based standard-setting for international standards. While the Appellate Body in *EC – Sardines* found the absence of consensus as not determinative in the identification of a relevant international standard, subsequent development in *US- Tuna II* points otherwise.[14]

A 2000 TBT Committee Decision (or Decision) on the principles for development of international standards, guides or recommendations has prescribed six principles and procedures that need to be observed by international standardising bodies in their standards development process.[15] These include – transparency, openness, impartiality and consensus, effectiveness and relevance, coherence as well as development considerations in the standards development process. While the interpretative approach and finding of the Appellate Body in *EC – Sardines* runs contrary to the consensus principle in the Decision that predated it, interestingly, the Appellate Body in *US – Tuna II* considered the TBT Committee Decision to be a 'subsequent agreement' within the meaning of Article 31(3)(a) of the Vienna Convention on the Law of Treaties.[16] Thus, according to the Appellate Body, the Decision is to inform the interpretation and application of a term or provision of the TBT Agreement, pursuant to Article 3.2 of the Dispute Settlement Understanding (DSU).[17] This has laid down the groundwork for the WTO dispute panels and Appellate Body increasingly adopting a more scrutinising approach toward the international standard-setting processes.

3.2.2 Recent FTA Practice

Given the TBT Agreement's restraint in naming the relevant ISBs in its text, several FTAs have attempted to tackle this lacuna. Two approaches have been observed.[18] The first one comprises FTAs referencing the TBT Committee Decision for determining the relevant international standard. In a study conducted on 200 FTAs that cover TBT issues till 2017, it was observed that almost 27% of the FTAs used the TBT Committee

14. Appellate Body Report, *EC – Sardines*, para. 227, *See also* Delimatsis, Panagiotis, Relevant International Standards' and 'Recognized Standardization Bodies' under the TBT Agreement, 2014, TILEC Discussion Paper, DP 2014-031, pp. 18-19; Du, Ming & Deng, Fei, *International Standards as Global Public Goods in the World Trading System*, Legal Issues of Economic Integration 43, no. 2 (2016): 113-144.
15. Decision of The Committee on Principles for the Development of International Standards, Guides and Recommendations with Relation to Articles 2, 5 and Annex 3 of the Agreement; G/TBT/1/Rev.14, p. 62.
16. Appellate Body Report, *US – Tuna II*, WT/DS381/AB/R, paras 372-401. Cf. Panel Report, EC-Sardines, para. 7.91.
17. As per Article 3.2 of the DSU, panels and the Appellate Body are to 'clarify' the provisions of the covered agreements 'in accordance with customary rules of interpretation of public international law'.
18. For a detailed examination of FTAs till 2017, *see* McDaniels, Devin; Molina, Ana Cristina; Wijkström, Erik (2018): *How Does the Regular Work of WTO Influence Regional Trade Agreements?*, WTO Staff Working Paper, No. ERSD-2018-06, World Trade Organization (WTO), Geneva.

Decision as a means to identify international standards.[19] The second, *albeit,* a minority approach (observed in 5% of the FTAs till 2017),[20] goes a step further, with the FTAs also naming the relevant ISBs. The ISBs listed in these FTAs include ISO, IEC, ITU, Codex, OIML, WHO and FAO.[21] This could be done in the main chapter dealing with TBT issues or as part of an annex for a specific sector.

A cursory examination of some of the prominent FTAs entered into *after* 2017 also broadly confirms this approach. With some minor differences, reliance on the TBT Committee Decision in the determination of ISBs can be seen in these FTAs, as provided in Table 3.1. By obligating countries to follow the principles laid down in the TBT Committee Decision, the FTAs have adopted a WTO-Plus approach. As per *US – Tuna II*, the Decision was relevant for interpreting the TBT Agreement.

Table 3.1 Recent FTAs Referencing the TBT Committee Decision

Name of the FTA	*Reference to the TBT Committee Decision*	*Provision*	*Level of Obligation w.r.t the Decisions*
Comprehensive and Progressive Agreement for Trans-Pacific Partnership (CPTPP)	Yes	Article 8.5.2	To determine whether an international standard – obligation to 'shall apply' the Decision
Agreement between the United States of America, the United Mexican States, and Canada (USMCA)	Yes	Article 11.2 Article 11.4.2	'international standard *means a standard* that is consistent with the TBT Committee Decision' To determine whether an international standard - obligation to 'shall apply' the Decision
Regional Comprehensive Economic Partnership Agreement (RCEP)	Yes	Article 6.5.2	Each Party 'takes into account' the TBT Committee Decision
EU – Vietnam Free Trade Agreement (EU – Vietnam FTA)	Yes	Article 5.5.1	Parties 'affirm their adherence' to the Decision

Source: Author's compilation

19. *Ibid.*, p. 8.
20. *Ibid.*, pp. 10-11.
21. *Ibid.*, p. 10.

Additionally, some FTAs also deem it fit to name what the relevant ISBs are, as provided in Table 3.2.

Table 3.2 Recent FTAs Mentioning Specific ISBs

Name of the FTA	*Provision*	*ISBs Mentioned*	*Purpose*
CPTPP	Annex 8A on Wine and Distilled Spirits	Codex Alimentarius Commission ('shall consider' Codex Alimentarius Guidelines for Design, Production, Issuance and Use of Generic Official Certificates)	If certification of wine is necessary to protect human health or safety or to achieve other legitimate objectives.
EU-Vietnam FTA	Article 5.4.1.	a) International Organization for Standardization (ISO) b) International Electrotechnical Commission (IEC) c) International Telecommunication Union (ITU) d) Codex Alimentarius Commission (Codex)	Use these international standards as a basis for technical regulations.
	Annex 2-C Pharmaceutical /Medicinal Products and Medical Devices	a) World Health Organization (WHO), b) Organisation for Economic Co-operation and Development (OECD) c) International Council for Harmonisation of Technical Requirements for Pharmaceuticals for Human Use (ICH) d) Pharmaceutical Inspection Convention and Pharmaceutical Inspection Co-operation Scheme (PIC/S) for pharmaceutical products e) International Medical Device Regulators Forum (IMDRF) for medical device	'shall base' technical regulations on international standards, practices and guidelines for pharmaceutical/ medicinal products or medical devices (3), including the ones listed in the previous column.

Source: Author's compilation

3.2.3 The Developmental Perspective: Special Focus on India

Harmonisation with international standards, while desirable for efficiency and for reducing transaction costs, can in no way guarantee positive outcomes if the common standard is 'too stringent or poorly designed'.[22] It is also problematic if the international standards favour those existing in a particular market. As this, in turn, will be advantageous for firms operating in such a market, and detrimental to others, particularly those from developing countries lacking in technical and financial capacity. Importantly, the international standard-setting process at the ISBs can also be plagued with substantive and procedural issues. Although the TBT Committee has attempted to streamline the standard-setting processes at the ISBs, it is not devoid of problems. For instance, though the six principles laid down by the Committee includes impartiality and consensus, consensus in this context is different from the way it is understood at the WTO and does not imply a lack of objection or opposition. The ISBs are to merely lay down procedures to take into account views of all concerned parties and to reconcile conflicting arguments.[23] As India submitted at the WTO in 2011, many ISBs have the provision of voting in case consensus is not achieved.[24] Therefore, it would have been prudent to define consensus in the same manner as prevalent at the WTO 'where even a single negative vote would defeat this principle' or at the very least to require that 'whenever voting is used, consensus would be achieved only when a significant number of participants (not less than 90 per cent of those voting) give a positive vote'.[25] This, was however, not accepted at the WTO. As a result, ISBs such as the ISO, specifically provide that 'consensus need not imply unanimity'.[26]

The pitfalls of such an approach were experienced by India in the development of ISO 14067, which relates to the guidelines for quantification and communication of greenhouse gas footprints of products. In 2013, ISO/TS 14067 was published as a technical specification, having failed to gain consensus for adoption as a standard, to be reviewed and upgraded by 2018. As recorded in the minutes of the 2017 meeting of the Committee on Trade and Environment, India had, on several occasions, expressed concern regarding the reliance on uncertain and selective science in making standards as in the draft ISO 14067.[27] There were apprehensions that carbon footprints analysis on a lifecycle basis would create barriers to trade for firms in developing countries. Concerns were also raised regarding the neutrality of ISO's approach in standard

22. Charan Devereaux, Robert Z. Lawrence and Michael D. Watkins September, 2006, Chapter 7, *The US-EU Mutual Recognition Agreements in Case Studies in US Trade Negotiation: Making the Rules*, Peterson Institute for International Economics, available at https://www.piie.com/publications/chapters_preview/392/07iie3624.pdf.
23. *Decision of the Committee on Principles for the Development of International Standards, Guides and Recommendations with Relation to Articles 2, 5 and Annex 3 of the Agreement*; G/TBT/1/Rev.14, p. 63.
24. As noted in *EC – Sardines* for instance, the Codex standard, considered an international standard by the panel, was adopted by 18 countries, of which only 4 accepted it fully, at the time of the dispute; See Panel Report, *EC – Sardines*, para. 6.5.
25. Communication from India, Principles of International Standard-Setting, G/TBT/W/345, 10 November 2011.
26. *See* Clause 2.5.6, ISO/IEC Directive, Part 1, available at https://www.iso.org/sites/directives/current/consolidated/index.xhtml.
27. Report of the Meeting Held on 20 June 2017, Note by The Secretariat, Section 1.1.3, Committee on Trade and Environment – WT/CTE/M/63.

development. India's concerns, supported by other developing countries, were dismissed at the ISO, with the ISO 14067 getting adopted as standards in 2018, replacing the 2013 technical specifications.[28]

The challenges faced by developing countries is also evident in the manner in which the membership at the ISBs such as the ISO may operate. The ISO recognises three kinds of Members – full members that influence the standard development and can vote at the meetings; correspondent members, that can observe the meetings; and subscriber members that cannot participate but keep up to date with the organisation's work.[29] The ISO has 165 members in the form of national standards bodies. A look at the members' participation clearly points toward a lop-sided standards development process. The technical committee (TCs) participation (where much of the technical work on standards takes place) of even the full members varies widely from 5 TCs for Afghanistan to 742 TCs for the UK, with India participating in 669 such committees (Figure 3.1). This divergence in TC participation is also evident in Table 3.3, which demonstrates that around 37 ISO full members participate in 50 or less TCs only, with 22 ISO full members at the upper end of the spectrum, with participation in more than 500 TCs.

*Table 3.3 Participation of ISO Members in Technical Committees (TCs)**

No. of ISO Members Participating in 100 or Less TCs		*No. of ISO Members Participating in 500 or More TCs*	
No. of TCs	*No. of Full Members*	*No. of TCs*	*No. of Full Members*
0-10	6	501-550	1
11-20	9	551-600	5
21-30	12	601-650	3
31-40	7	651-700	7
41-50	3	701-750	6

Source: Author's compilation.[30]

28. https://www.iso.org/standard/71206.html.
29. https://www.iso.org/members.html.
30. Based on data available at https://www.iso.org/members.html.

*Figure 3.1 Select Country Participation at the ISO Technical Committee**

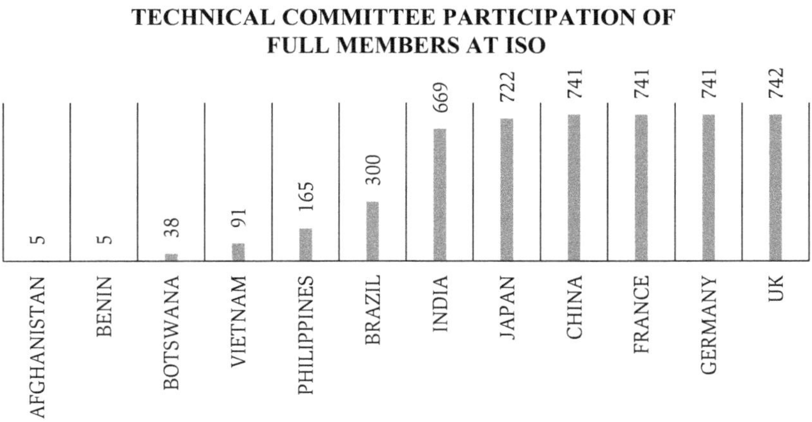

Source: Author's compilation.[31]

While India's participation at the ISO TCs has steadily increased over the years, the effectiveness of such a participation remains to be seen. A more robust barometer for measuring the influence of an ISO member to standards-setting can perhaps be perceived from the number of secretariats held by it.[32] In 2020, for instance, a substantive portion of the secretarial work was divided among a handful of developed countries, namely, US, UK, France, Germany and Japan; as well as China - the only developing country in the group.[33] India held 11 secretariats, compared to 135 held by Germany, the highest at ISO (Figure 3.2).

Figure 3.2 Number of Active Secretariats Held by Select ISO Member Bodies

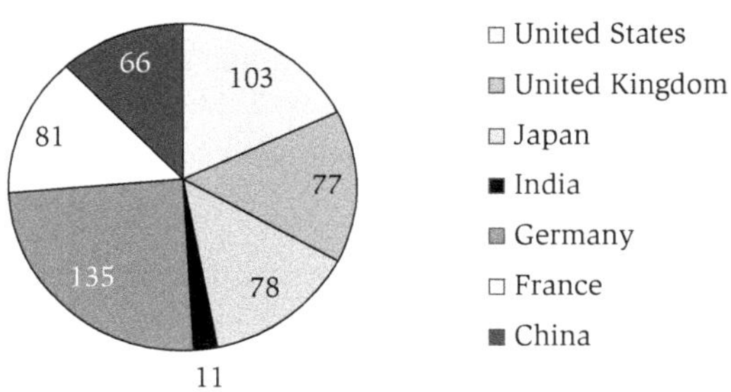

* Author's compilation.[34]

31. Based on data available at https://www.iso.org/members.html
32. *See also* Delimatsis, Panagiotis, *Global Standard-Setting 2.0: How the WTO Spotlights ISO and Impacts the Transnational Standard-Setting Process*, Duke Journal of Comparative & International Law, Vol. 28, 2018, 273, p. 292.
33. ISO - Detailed Figures, available at https://www.iso.org/iso-in-figures.html.
34. Based on data available at https://www.iso.org/iso-in-figures.html.

This asymmetry is exacerbated by the generally opaque and inadequate reporting on standard development and the views and objections submitted by the members in the process.[35] The ISO, of course, is just one example. There are several ISBs promulgating standards in different spheres.[36] Hence, it becomes imperative for countries such as India to have a coherent policy on how to approach ISBs in their FTAs. Notwithstanding the inadequacies in the TBT Committee Decision on international standards, it appears best in the Indian interest to refer to the same in its FTAs, in the event a WTO-Plus approach is to be adopted. This would ensure there is an applicable benchmark against which the ISB standard-setting process could be evaluated on a case-by-case basis. The second approach, i.e., accepting the standards of a particular ISB as an 'international standard' in the FTA for all times and purposes would be tantamount to fully recognising the standard-setting bodies in respect of every standard adopted or to be adopted by them. A snapshot of the Indian practice in select FTAs is provided in Table 3.4.

Table 3.4 Select Indian FTAs and Approach Towards 'International Standards'

FTA	*Approach Towards 'International Standards'*
India – Mauritius Comprehensive Economic Cooperation and Partnership Agreement (CECPA), 2021	TBT Committee Decision to be taken into account when determining whether an international standard exists (Article 5.5.1)
India – Singapore Comprehensive Economic Cooperation Agreement (CECA), 2005	No general reference to ISBs or the TBT Committee Decision. Sectoral Annex 5A for Telecommunications Equipment) refers to ISO/IEC standards and guides in respect of conformity assessment. Sectoral Annex 5C for Electrical and Electronic Equipment refers to ISO/IEC as well IEC standards.
India – Japan Comprehensive Economic Partnership Agreement (CEPA), 2011	No reference.

35. Vitaliy Pogoretskyy & Tatiana Yanguas, *From 'Standard-Takers' to 'Standard-Makers': Developing Countries and Least-Developed Countries' Perspectives in the Harmonization of Technical Regulations Through International Standards*, Global Trade and Customs Journal, Vol. 11:9, 2016, p. 386.

36. *See*, for instance, International Trade Centre UNCTAD/WTO, Commonwealth Secretariat, *Influencing and Meeting International Standards: Challenges for Developing Countries*, Geneva: ITC/CS, 2004; ITC/P181.E/TSS/BAS/04-XII.

FTA	*Approach Towards 'International Standards'*
India – Malaysia Comprehensive Economic Cooperation Agreement (CECA), 2010	No reference.
India – Korea Comprehensive Economic Partnership Agreement (CEPA), 2009	No reference.

Source: Author's compilation

While referring an adopted international standard for a specific sector may be desirable in an FTA (and can be incorporated by taking into account its standard-setting process), a sweeping reference may have its own risks and should be approached cautiously. Alternatively, India could propose the inclusion of certain additional safeguards in its FTAs for determining the relevant international standard for the TBT measures. This would, of course, have to be agreed upon by its trading partner, and may be an uphill task, given the lack of available precedence supporting it.

3.3 SECTORAL ANNEXES, EQUIVALENCE AND MUTUAL RECOGNITION

3.3.1 Background

Sector-specific commitments can constitute an important component of the TBT and SPS commitments in FTAs. Dedicated rules and arrangements in a particular sector, as part of an annex or a side-letter, have the potential to spur cooperation and enhance regulatory alignment across trading partners. Tying the conclusion of these sector-specific rules with the FTA can also provide the impetus for their timely finalisation, as stand-alone agreements may be difficult to arrive at and negotiations on these may drag on and remain inconclusive. These also provide a useful platform to record countries' agreement on equivalence and mutual recognition and should be utilised for the same.

At the WTO, although harmonisation with international standards remains the primary mode of attaining international regulatory coherence, the SPS and TBT Agreements also recognise other means of attaining this objective. This is especially evident in the provisions relating to equivalence and mutual recognition. The TBT Agreement, for instance, in Article 2.7 requires Members to give 'positive consideration' to accepting as equivalent technical regulations of other Members if they are satisfied that these regulations adequately fulfil the objectives of their own regulations. In contrast, the SPS Agreement adopts a more stringent approach toward equivalence in Article 4, mandating that Members 'shall accept' the SPS measures of other Members as equivalent if the exporting Member is able to objectively demonstrate to the importing Member that its measures achieve the importing Member's appropriate level of SPS protection.[37] This demonstration has to be on the basis of appropriate science-based and objective information.[38] Reasonable access is to be provided to the importing country for inspection, testing, and other relevant procedures for the recognition of equivalence.

Additionally, in the SPS Agreement, the Members are mandated to enter into consultations, if so requested, with the aim of arriving at a bilateral or multilateral recognition agreement with respect to equivalence.[39] This is the only limited reference to mutual recognition observed in the SPS Agreement. When it comes to the TBT Agreement, the concept of mutual recognition is used for the purpose of encouraging Members to enter into negotiations for mutual recognition of results of each other's conformity assessment procedures.[40]

In practice, however, mutual recognition can take various forms and shapes. They can be in the form of an 'enhanced' mutual recognition agreement (MRA) where mutual recognition is based on 'equivalence or full alignment of regulatory requirements'.[41] The EU's internal market and the Trans-Tasman MRA between Australia and New Zealand are two prime examples of this.[42] Alternatively, the more traditional approach to MRAs is restricted to merely recognising the certificates, testing/lab reports of the exporting country for the purpose of meeting the requirements of the importing country. In this case, both the exporting and importing countries continue with their respective technical requirements, without any regulatory convergence.

Further, an MRA can be entered into between the governments directly through a free trade agreement or a stand-alone agreement,[43] or between the respective conformity assessment bodies, including the accreditation bodies.[44,45] However, while the former benefits from the overall protection and dispute settlement provisions of the

37. Article 4.1 of the SPS Agreement.
38. Paragraph 4, Decision on the Implementation of Article 4 of the Agreement on the Application of Sanitary and Phytosanitary Measures, G/SPS/19/Rev.2, 23 July 2004.
39. Article 4.2 of the SPS Agreement.
40. Article 6.3 of the TBT Agreement.
41. Correia de Brito, A., C. Kauffmann and J. Pelkmans (2016), *The Contribution of Mutual Recognition to International Regulatory Co-operation*, OECD Regulatory Policy Working Papers, No. 2, OECD Publishing, Paris, p. 17.
42. Marianna B. Karttunen, International Regulatory Co-operation under the SPS and TBT Agreements in, *Transparency in the WTO SPS and TBT Agreements – The Real Jewel in the Crown*, Cambridge University Press (2020), 110-128, at 113. For the text of Trans-Tasman MRA, *see* https://www.legislation.gov.au/Details/C2020C00304.
43. The TBT Agreement under Article 10.7 requires Members to notify any agreement relating to technical regulations, standards and conformity assessment procedures which may have a significant effect on trade.
44. The CPTPP tries to distinguish between the two by referring the government to government agreements as MRAs, whereas by referring to the mutual recognition between accreditation or conformity assessment bodies as 'mutual recognition arrangement'. *See* Article 8.2, Definitions, CPTPP.
45. It may be noted that TBT Committee classifies 'Cooperative (Voluntary) Arrangements Between Domestic and Foreign Conformity Assessment Bodies' as distinct from an MRA. *See Indicative List of Approaches to Facilitate Acceptance of the Results of Conformity Assessment* in the Decisions and Recommendations Adopted by The WTO Committee on Technical Barriers to Trade Since 1 January 1995, G/TBT/1/Rev.14, p. 60.

FTAs (if applicable), the latter is largely dependent on the good efforts of the respective agencies and are non-enforceable.

As of 2019, out of the 153 bilateral or plurilateral agreements entered into between Members on TBT issues and notified under Article 10.7 of the TBT Agreement, MRAs (38%) outnumbered equivalence agreements (4%) considerably, with the remaining majority of agreements (58%) being in the nature of cooperation agreements.[46] The notified MRAs are primarily in relation to conformity assessment procedures, relating to (in descending order of popularity), conformity assessment procedures and results; recognition of test reports; certification and certificates; acceptance of inspection reports; acceptance of marking; recognition of the operation of quality management systems;[47] accreditation procedures; recognition of testing laboratories; acceptance attestation of authorisations and mutual acceptance of data in the assessment.

3.3.2 Recent FTA Practice

Countries are progressively entering into FTAs with dedicated sector-specific commitments in annexes or side-letters. These can relate to authorisation requirements, labelling, production processes, product identity requirements, product quality and performance requirements, TBT product registration requirement, conformity assessment related to TBT and testing, certification and inspection.[48] Further, while empirical evidence on the benefits of MRAs continues to be questionable - primarily due to lack of robust data on the difference in costs relating to conformity assessment, both with and without an MRA - economic gain through increased trade flow appears to be the primary driver for entering into them.[49] And this is evidenced by the inclusion of mutual recognition in some of these sectoral annexes. The recent trend in important FTAs on this is provided in Table 3.5.

46. Chapter 5, OECD/WTO (2019), *Facilitating trade through regulatory cooperation: The case of the WTO's TBT/SPS Agreements and Committees,* WTO, Geneva/OECD Publishing, Paris, p. 84.
47. Quality management systems or QMS is understood to be a formalized system that documents processes, procedures and responsibilities for achieving quality policy and objectives. 'A QMS helps coordinate and direct an organization's activities to meet customer and regulatory requirements and improve its effectiveness and efficiency on a continuous basis.' *See* https://asq.org/quality-resources/quality-management-system.
48. Based on CPTPP annexes as classified in UNCTAD, *How to Encode Non-Tariff Measures in Regional Trade Agreements? The case of the Comprehensive and Progressive Agreement for Trans-Pacific Partnership (CPTPP)*, 2020, UNCTAD/DITC/TAB/2020/2.
49. Correia de Brito, A., C. Kauffmann and J. Pelkmans (2016), '*The contribution of mutual recognition to international regulatory co-operation*', OECD Regulatory Policy Working Papers, No. 2, OECD Publishing, Paris, p. 12.

Table 3.5 Recent FTAs and Sectoral Annexes

Name of the FTA	*Annexes*	*Key Commitments*
CPTPP	Wines and Distilled Spirits (Annex 8-A)	Relates to product identity requirements, labelling, certification (harmonisation with relevant Codex guidelines encouraged)
	Information and Communication Technology (ICT) Products that Use Cryptography (Annex 8-B)	Limits the types of technical regulations and CAPs that can be introduced, testing/SDOC, encouraged to implement APEC Mutual Recognition Arrangement for Conformity Assessment of Telecommunications Equipment and the APEC Mutual Recognition Arrangement for Equivalence of Technical Requirements
	Pharmaceuticals (Annex 8-C)	Relates to marketing authorisation, collaboration on pharmaceutical inspection
	Cosmetics (Annex 8-D)	Relates to marketing authorisation, labelling
	Medical Devices (Annex 8-E)	Relates to product identity requirements, marketing authorisation
	Proprietary Formulas for Prepackaged Foods And Food Additives (Annex 8-F)	Relates to labelling consistent with Codex standards
	Organic Products (Annex 8-G)	Relates to cooperation and equivalence grant process
USMCA	Chemical Substances (Annex 12-A)	Relates to enhancing regulatory compatibility, and data and information exchange
	Cosmetic Products (Annex 12-B)	Relates to enhancing regulatory compatibility, regulatory controls, labelling
	Information and Communication Technology (Annex 12-C)	Relates to product identity requirements, regional cooperation activities, including encouraged to implement APEC Mutual Recognition Arrangement for Conformity

Name of the FTA	*Annexes*	*Key Commitments*
		Assessment of Telecommunications Equipment and the APEC Mutual Recognition Arrangement for Equivalence of Technical Requirements
	Energy Performance Standards (Annex 12-D)	Relates to enhancing regulatory compatibility and voluntary approaches
	Medical Devices (Annex 12-E)	Relates to enhancing regulatory compatibility, regulatory controls and marketing authorisations
	Pharmaceuticals (Annex 12-F)	Relates to enhancing regulatory compatibility, regulatory controls and marketing authorisations
RCEP	No sectoral annex	
EU-Vietnam FTA	Motor Vehicles and Motor Vehicles Parts and Equipment (Annex 2-B)	Relates to regulatory convergence (refrain from diverging from UNECE Regulations in new domestic technical regulations)
	Pharmaceutical/Medicinal Products and Medical Devices	Relates to harmonisation with international standards, transparency and country of origin marking

Source: Author's compilation

As is evident, the sectoral annexes can cover a variety of issues pertaining to regulatory convergence and presents the best opportunity for FTA partners to identify the SPS and TBT barriers in their priority sectors and use the FTA framework to take targeted actions toward reducing the same. Interestingly, none of the sample FTAs above have included mutual recognition or equivalence as part of these annexes.

3.3.3 The Developmental Perspective: Special Focus on India

Sector-specific commitments have tremendous potential in ironing out issues in international trade for priority goods and sectors. Conducting stand-alone negotiations, particularly on equivalence and mutual recognition can be challenging for developing countries. Difference in regulatory systems, particularly weak technical infrastructure and administrative challenges in developing countries can make the process daunting for most of them.[50] Another hurdle before any sectoral arrangement, particularly MRAs, between trading partners at different levels of development is the issue of trust. Any successful outcome will depend on trust in each other's regulatory systems and conformity assessment procedures in place.[51] While India has attempted to use the sectoral annex route in the past, not all of them appear to have come to fruition. An overview of India's sector-specific annexes is provided in Table 3.6.

Table 3.6 Select Indian FTAs and Their Approach Towards Sectoral Annexes

FTA	*Sectoral Annex*	*Description*
India – Mauritius CECPA	No sectoral annex	–
India – Singapore CECA	*Sectoral Annex for Telecommunications Equipment (Annex 5 A)*	Phase I: mutual recognition of test reports – within one year of entry into force of the Agreement Phase II: mutual recognition of equipment certification – no specified timeline
	Sectoral Annex for Food Products (Annex 5B)	Relevant regulatory authorities designated by the *Parties shall enter into discussion* to identify food products that may be covered by this Sectoral Annex and thereafter enter into conformity assessment arrangements. *Already contains arrangements for egg products, milk products and packaged drinking water.*
	Sectoral Annex for Electrical and Electronic Equipment (Annex 5C)	Mutual recognition of certification of the results of conformity assessment activities.
India – Japan CEPA	No sectoral annex.	The Parties shall, through the Sub-Committee, discuss the feasibility of MRAs in such sectors as electrical products, telecommunications terminal equipment and radio equipment and other sectors as may be mutually agreed by the Parties.

50. Frode Veggeland and Christel Elvestad, *Equivalence and Mutual Recognition in Trade Arrangements – Relevance for the WTO and the Codex Alimentarius Commission*, 2004, Norwegian Agricultural Economics Research Institute, Oslo, p. 65.
51. Correia de Brito, A., C. Kauffmann and J. Pelkmans (2016), *The Contribution of Mutual Recognition To International Regulatory Co-operation*, OECD Regulatory Policy Working Papers, No. 2, OECD Publishing, Paris, p. 12.

FTA	*Sectoral Annex*	*Description*
India – Malaysia CECA	No sectoral annex at the time of conclusion.	TBT: Article 7.9: The Parties shall, within sixty days upon the request of the other Party, enter into negotiations for possible MRAs on the results of conformity assessment procedures in the sectors which both Parties agree upon. Article 7.7: The list of products for which the technical regulations of the exporting Party is accepted by the importing Party as equivalent shall be recorded and attached as Annex 7-1 SPS: Article 6.6: Both Parties to agree to an initial list of products or sectors in respect of which decision on equivalence to be undertaken (to be included as an Annex to the FTA).
India – Korea CEPA	No sectoral annex.	Article 2.28: Parties to undertake consultation no later than one year from the date of entry into force of this Agreement with a view to arriving at mutual recognition agreements or arrangements for conformity assessment within three years after the start of the consultation, for 1. Telecommunication equipment 2. Electrical and Electronic equipment

Source: Author's compilation

An examination of the Indian FTAs indicates that apart from *India–Singapore CECA*, none of the FTAs has been successful in achieving the conclusion of sector-specific MRAs/Equivalence as part of these agreements (*see* Table 3.6). Rather, these have been addressed through a built-in agenda to launch discussions at a later date. It is pertinent to note that as per the author's discussions with government officials, none of these sector-specific negotiations envisaged appear to have been concluded once the FTAs entered into force. This clearly indicates that the strategy of relegating these critical discussions to commence after the entry into force of the parent FTAs has not been successful. Therefore, going forward, it is essential for India to ensure that sector-specific negotiations in priority areas are conducted in parallel with the main treaty text, and that these enter into force with the FTAs. Otherwise the possibility of these negotiations losing steam after the FTA conclusion is not unlikely.

3.4 TRANS-GOVERNMENTAL NETWORK OF REGULATORS

3.4.1 Background

Trans-governmental network of regulators has been identified as one of the significant means of attaining international regulatory cooperation. The OECD describes such networks as 'co-operation based on loosely structured, peer to peer ties developed through frequent interaction rather than formal negotiation involving specialised officials (typically regulators) directly interacting with each other (through structured dialogues, MoUs), often with minimal supervision by foreign ministries'.[52] These networks can play an important role in not just learning from each other's experiences but also developing strategies for challenges that may be common across jurisdictions. Trans-governmental networks provide for a flexible and trust-building approach toward attaining regulatory coherence and understanding. However, given the lack of enforcement and monitoring and their informal nature, they may also be susceptible to geo-political power dynamics.[53] Limited public accountability can be a major downside of these networks.[54] While such networks are fairly prominent in competition[55] and banking,[56] they are gaining importance in areas relating to product regulations as well, particularly accreditation. Important multilateral trans-governmental regulators networks[57] include the International Council for Harmonization of Technical Requirements for Registration of Pharmaceuticals for Human Use (ICH),[58] International Medical Device Regulators Forum (IMDRF),[59] International Pharmaceutical Regulators Programme (IPRP),[60] and International Cooperation on Cosmetics Regulation (ICCR).[61] Interestingly, these appear to have a limited membership, with India only participating as an Observer at one of these forums, namely the ICH.

The two accreditation networks, on the other hand, have a much wider participation. These are ILAC (International Laboratory Accreditation Cooperation)[62] and IAF

52. OECD (2013), *International Regulatory Co-operation: Addressing Global Challenges*, OECD Publishing, p. 24. For the purpose of the current paper, this does not include regional standard-setting organisations such as the GCC Standardization Organization.
53. Kauffmann, Céline and Nikolai Malyshev, *International Regulatory Co-operation: The Menu of Approaches. E15Initiative*, Geneva: International Centre for Trade and Sustainable Development (ICTSD) and World Economic Forum, 2015, p. 6.
54. Abbott, K., C. Kauffmann and J. Lee (2018), The *contribution of trans-governmental networks of regulators to international regulatory co-operation*, OECD Regulatory Policy Working Papers, No. 10, OECD Publishing, Paris, p. 43.
55. International Competition Network, an in informal network of competition law authorities globally (https://www.internationalcompetitionnetwork.org/).
56. The Basel Committee on Banking Supervision, a forum for regulatory cooperation on banking supervisory matters (https://www.bis.org/bcbs/).
57. For a detailed list, *see* Abbott, K., C. Kauffmann and J. Lee (2018), The *contribution of trans-governmental networks of regulators to international regulatory co-operation*, OECD Regulatory Policy Working Papers, No. 10, OECD Publishing, Paris p. 49.
58. https://www.ich.org/.
59. http://www.imdrf.org/index.asp.
60. http://www.iprp.global/home.
61. https://www.iccr-cosmetics.org/.
62. Established in 1977; https://ilac.org/.

(International Accreditation Forum).[63] ILAC and IAF are global networks of accreditation bodies and organizations involved in conformity assessment activities. In particular, ILAC and IAF signatories that are also party to the ILAC MRA or the IAF Multilateral Recognition Agreement (IAF MLA) respectively agree to recognise certificates, results and reports issued by organisations accredited by other members of these arrangements.[64] While the ILAC has more than 120 accreditation bodies as members, the IAF has around 87 such bodies. Similar networks also operate at the regional level.[65]

Despite ILAC and IAF's wider reach, they are yet to be granted the observer status at the WTO.[66]

3.4.2 Recent FTA Practice

Although these transnational regulatory networks are typically a cooperative venture and not enforceable, they can be granted acceptability and legitimacy through the FTAs, as provided in Table 3.7.

Table 3.7 Recent FTAs Referring to the Trans-Governmental Regulatory Networks for SPS/TBT

Name of the FTA	*Main Text/Annexes*	*Key Reference*
CPTPP	Pharmaceuticals (Annex 8-C)	Marketing authorisation request to be in the format consistent with the principles of ICH.
USMCA	Article 11.7.7: Parties to consider approving or recognising accredited conformity assessment bodies for its technical regulations or standards, by an accreditation body that is a signatory to a mutual or multilateral recognition arrangement, for example, the ILAC and IAF.	
	Pharmaceuticals (Annex 12-F)	Marketing authorisation in a format that is consistent with the specifications set forth in the Common Technical Document (CTD) of ICH.
RCEP	-	

63. Established in 1993; https://www.iaf.nu/.
64. *See Benefits of the ILAC & IAF Multilateral Mutual Recognition Arrangements*, G/TBT/GEN/117, 28 June 2011, p. 6.
65. *See* for instance, the Asia Pacific Accreditation Cooperation (APAC) (https://www.apac-accreditation.org/).
66. *See* International Intergovernmental Organization: Observer Status in the Committee on Technical Barriers To Trade, Note by The Secretariat, G/TBT/GEN/2/Rev.1523, February 2021.

Name of the FTA	*Main Text/Annexes*	*Key Reference*
EU-Vietnam FTA	Article 5.6(c): exchange information on accreditation policy and to consider how to best make use of international standards for accreditation and of international agreements involving the Parties' accreditation bodies, for example, through the mechanisms of the ILAC and IAF.	
	Pharmaceutical/ Medicinal Products and Medical Devices (Annex 2-C)	Parties shall base their technical regulations on international standards, including those by...ICH...and the IMDRF for medical devices

Source: Author's compilation

Albeit small in size, the sample above indicates that countries are more willing to bind themselves with standards set by some of these trans-governmental regulatory networks like the ICH than granting recognition to conformity assessment bodies accredited by ILAC/IAF Members, despite the latter's broader participation. With respect to ILAC and IAF, the commitments appear to be more softly worded.

3.4.3 The Developmental Perspective: Special Focus on India

Given that India is not a party to several of these trans-governmental regulatory frameworks, it needs to adopt a vigilant strategy toward incorporating them in its FTAs by reference. This becomes especially critical since some of these FTA obligations may also be subject to the dispute settlement provisions. Further, participation in some of these networks may particularly be challenging for developing countries' regulators on account of costs and lower capacity.[67] Perhaps this underscores India's reluctance or inability to participate at several of these forums. Trans-governmental networks like the ICH have also been found to set demanding standards (e.g., for clinical trials on new medicines), which firms in developing countries find difficult to meet.[68] Therefore, it is not surprising that India has largely adopted a restrained approach in referencing these in its FTAs.

An exception to this can be found in the *India–Singapore Comprehensive Economic Cooperation Agreement*, where the Parties have agreed that for telecommunication equipment, and electrical and electronic equipment, the basis for designing test facilities would be that the accreditation body participates in mutual recognition arrangements, such as the Asia Pacific Laboratory Accreditation Cooperation (APLAC)

67. Abbott, K., C. Kauffmann and J. Lee (2018), The *contribution of trans-governmental networks of regulators to international regulatory co-operation*, OECD Regulatory Policy Working Papers, No. 10, OECD Publishing, Paris, p. 42.
68. Abbott, K., C. Kauffmann and J. Lee (2018), The *contribution of trans-governmental networks of regulators to international regulatory co-operation*, OECD Regulatory Policy Working Papers, No. 10, OECD Publishing, Paris, p. 42.

Mutual Recognition Arrangement, where they are subject to peer evaluation of the competence of accreditation bodies and the test facilities accredited by them.[69]

The *India-Korea Comprehensive Economic Cooperation Agreement* also adopts a softer general obligation where it requires the Parties to consider accepting results of conformity assessment procedures by conformity assessment bodies accredited by the national accreditation body of the other Party, which is a member of the ILAC Mutual Recognition Arrangement or IAF Multilateral Arrangement.[70]

Thus, while the Indian approach has been relatively favourable toward ILAC and IAF, perhaps on account of its own participation in these forums, the same cannot be said for some of the other trans-governmental networks such as the ICH. Going forward too, India should determine the desirability of referring these trans-regulatory networks only if it participates there, its developmental interests are adequately addressed at the network, and importantly the Indian entities are able to meet the requirements set by the network. Otherwise, it may not be overall beneficial for India to bind itself with rules in respect of which its domestic entities are not adequately prepared to meet and compete globally.

3.5 LANGUAGE AS A BARRIER TO TRADE

3.5.1 Background

The importance of language in the context of SPS and TBT measures was noted in the WTO's 2012 World Trade Report which stated that 'sharing a common regulatory language increases transparency and predictability of SPS/TBT measures and provides common criteria against which to judge measures.'[71] Recent economic studies, as highlighted below, have further supported this position. Language barriers have now been empirically proven to be a significant deterrent to bilateral trade between countries, with trade and language seen to be having a symbiotic relationship. Languages can either facilitate or impede trade among nations.[72] The newly constructed Language Barrier Index (LBI) quantifies international language barriers by measuring the dissimilarity between the main languages of the trading partners (the LBI increases with decreasing similarity of the languages of two countries). It has been seen that a 10% increase in the Language Barrier Index can cause a 7% to 10% decrease in trade flows between two countries.[73] While sharing an official or native language is generally found to facilitate trade (in fact, a study shows that a common

69. Paragraph 5.6, Annex 5A.
70. Article 7.8.8.
71. *World Trade Report, 2012 – Trade and Public Policies: A closer look at non-tariff measures in the 21st century*, World Trade Organization, p. 176 (available online at https://www.wto.org/english/res_e/booksp_e/anrep_e/world_trade_report12_e.pdf).
72. E. Kwan Choi, *Trade and the Adoption of a Universal Language*, International Review of Economics and Finance, Vol. 11:3, 2002, pp. 265-275.
73. *See* Johannes Lohmann, *Do Language Barriers Affect Trade?*, Economics Letters, Vol. 110:2, 2011, pp. 159-162.

language increases trade flows directly by 44%),[74] it has been observed that trade partners with no common native language can overcome the language barrier by communicating in a non-native language. Empirical results demonstrate that an acquired proficiency in English can mitigate the impact of historically determined language barriers.[75]

Understanding the product regulations is the first challenge faced by market operators when navigating the myriad regulatory systems While the WTO notification of these measures are available in the three official languages, namely, English, French and Spanish, the notifications merely contain the bare-bones of regulatory intent and requirements. These notifications provide the reference to the underlying regulations, usually in the form of the web link. However, as would be expected, these lead to regulations in the official language of the notifying Member. Such a language barrier can also reduce the effectiveness of the comment process envisaged in the SPS and TBT Agreements.

Appreciating the difficulties faced on account of language, the TBT Agreement negotiators attempted to address this issue as part of 'Information and Assistance' under Article 10 of the TBT Agreement. Article 10.5 specifically states that the developed country Members shall, if requested by other Members, provide, in English, French or Spanish, translations of the documents covered by a specific notification or, in case of voluminous documents, of summaries of such documents. A similar obligation is also contained in Annex B, paragraph 8 of the SPS Agreement, indirectly acknowledging the important role of language in international trade.

3.5.2 Recent FTA Practice

Trade agreements can serve as a useful medium to eliminate language-related challenges emanating from international trade, particularly from SPS and TBT measures. Governments should hence utilize the platform of FTAs to address this issue,[76] if needed, particularly if they wish to go beyond the contours of what is provided in the TBT and SPS Agreements. Given that the ultimate compliance with these measures lies in the hands of market operators, committing to provide these in a mutually agreed language can help facilitate trade.

A recent example at addressing the language barrier can be seen in Article 11.7.20 of the TBT Chapter of the USMCA, where a conditional best endeavour obligation has been included. The provision provides that if a Party obtains a translation of a measure notified to the WTO TBT Committee, whether official or unofficial, in an official WTO

74. Peter H. Egger and Andrea Lassmann, *The Language Effect in International Trade: A Meta-analysis*, Economics Letters, Vol. 116, 2012, pp. 221-224.
75. Hyejin Ku and Asaf Zussman, *Lingua franca: The Role of English in International Trade*, Journal of Economic Behaviour & Organisation, Vol. 75:2, 2010, pp. 250-260.
76. Sarkodie and Awuni, *Economic Value of International Language(s) in International Trade, a Case Study of Traders (GhanaTogo-Ghana) in Central Business District of Kumasi*, Ghana, Journal of Economics, Management and Trade, Vol. 21:5, 2018, 1-7; Article no. JEMT.39651, p. 4.

language other than the language of the notification, it shall endeavour to send the translation to the Parties' contact points.

The issue of language becomes particularly important in the case of mega-regionals where multiple countries may be participating with different official languages. To ensure that the relevant technical and legal information percolates to all those benefitting from the operation of such an agreement, language gains critical importance. RCEP is one such agreement, where the Parties have attempted to tackle this issue.

For instance, in Article 6.11.2 of the Standards, Technical Regulations and Conformity Assessment Procedures chapter of RCEP, the parties have undertaken to provide upon written request, the full text or summary of its notified technical regulations and conformity assessment procedures in the English language, if already available. If unavailable, a summary in English has to be made available within a reasonable period of time. As can be seen, this is a WTO-Plus commitment, as it is not linked to the developmental status of the Parties. Further, English is the identified language for this purpose. Similarly, Articles 5.12.7 and 5.12.8 of the SPS chapter contain a similar obligation in respect of draft as well as adopted notified SPS measures. While providing translations of regulatory requirements may impose an extra cost on the translating country, the overall benefits in international trade from removing the language barrier may outweigh any such costs.

3.5.3 The Developmental Perspective: Special Focus on India

The *India–Malaysia CECA* contains provisions aimed at tackling the language barrier in a limited manner. Other FTAs, for example, the *India –Japan CEPA* do not contain any similar provision. This is presumably because Japan is already governed by the relevant TBT and SPS Agreement provisions that require it to provide the English translation of regulations, by virtue of being a developed country. Interestingly, India and Korea have not agreed upon any language-related commitment in respect of SPS/TBT measures despite the language differences between the two countries. A tabular representation of language provisions in major Indian FTAs is provided in Table 3.8.

Table 3.8 Select Indian FTAs and the Language Requirements Therein

FTA	*Description*
India – Singapore CECA	Nil.
India – Japan CEPA	Nil.
India – Malaysia CECA	SPS: Article 6.8.1 (c) – certificates to be drawn up in English.

FTA	*Description*
	Article 6.9.2 (c) – verification and audit report to be conducted in English
India – Korea CEPA	Nil.

Source: Author's compilation

As of June 2021, India is currently engaged in FTA negotiations with Chile, Peru, MERCOSUR, Thailand and Indonesia.[77] Several of these countries and groupings have a different working language compared to India. Further, on account of their developmental status, these countries would also not be bound by the obligation to provide translations under the TBT and SPS Agreements. Thus, it would be imperative and beneficial for both sides to agree on basic language parameters for SPS and TBT measures, including other relevant underlying documents within the FTAs. This would go a long way in facilitating international trade.

3.6 CONCLUSION

FTAs provide a critical regulatory framework to address SPS and TBT concerns of trading partner countries. While aiming to facilitate international trade by reducing non-tariff barriers, the FTAs can also play an important role in addressing the developmental concerns and challenges faced by developing countries. With India as the focus, this chapter has attempted to highlight four important issues and the possible Indian approach toward them in future trade engagements.

The first issue relates to the approach India should adopt in respect of ISBs and international standards as part of its FTA's TBT commitments, given that the TBT Agreement is silent on ISBs. As demonstrated through the example of ISO, the international standard-setting sphere is far from perfect and despite efforts to make it more development-friendly, it continues to be plagued by asymmetric participation of its members. Therefore, a reasonable approach for India would be to not bestow perpetual credibility on any such ISB by recognising their standards as 'international standards' for all intent and purposes of the FTAs. The TBT Committee Decision on international standards, despite its problems, provides a more useful benchmark for conducting a case-by-case evaluation of what constitutes an international standard, and hence may be relied upon instead in the FTA text.

Second, India should explore undertaking and concluding sector-specific commitments as part of its FTA to ease trade in priority sectors and goods. As the Indian experience demonstrates, a built-in FTA agenda to conduct these negotiations after the FTA has entered into force has not been successful for India in the past. Thus, this should be avoided. Third, trans-governmental networks of regulators have again

77. https://commerce.gov.in/international-trade/trade-agreements/indias-current-engagements-in-rtas/ (last accessed on 20 June 2021).

gained prominence, particularly in the case of accreditation. Given that Indian regulators are not a member to many of these networks, it needs to adopt a cautious approach and avoid referencing such networks in its FTAs for the purpose of creating new and elevated obligations. In light of India's active participation at ILAC and IAF, these could be relied upon in its FTAs to ease the process of conformity assessment.

Finally, language barriers have the potential to derail projected benefits from international trade. Taking into account the technical and scientific complexity of several SPS and TBT measures, it becomes especially essential to address the language barrier issues within the confines of an FTA. It is, thus, recommended that India arrives at a mutually agreed solution on the issue of language in its future FTAs with its trading partners (particularly those not covered by the relevant provisions of the TBT and SPS agreements).

CHAPTER 4

Standards and the WTO Agreement on Import Licensing Procedures

Aparna Bhattacharya & Trishna Menon[*]

Standards are an important part of a country's trade toolkit and hence, are strictly regulated at the World Trade Organization (WTO). It is well known that Members' domestic policies on standards are subject to the stipulations under the Technical Barriers to Trade (TBT) and Sanitary and Phytosanitary (SPS) Agreements. However, an issue that is underexplored is whether the procedures for grant of SPS and TBT approvals, like other import controls, are subject to the rules contained in the WTO Agreement on Import Licensing Procedures (Import Licensing Agreement). This chapter confronts this question in the absence of a clear definition of 'import license', limited jurisprudence on the intersection of standards and the rules contained in the Import Licensing Agreement as well as the ambiguous notification practice of Members. In conclusion, the chapter notes that there is need for a closer examination of the meaning and types of 'import licenses' and a clarification as to whether approvals from standards authorities will be subject to the disciplines of the Import Licensing Agreement.

4.1 INTRODUCTION

Standards serve as a tool to regulate the quality and the safety of products that are traded internationally, and hence constitute an important part of a country's trade policy. Countries maintain a mix of technical regulations and sanitary and phytosanitary (SPS) measures to give effect to policy objectives such as improving the efficiency

* All opinions and errors in this chapter are the authors' own.

of production, ensuring the quality of imports, ensuring protection of human, animal or plant life or health, protection of the environment, prevention of deceptive practices, etc.

While standards achieve an important policy objective, these controls, if allowed to operate unchecked, may also adversely affect international trade by creating unnecessary obstacles. As a result, the World Trade Organization (WTO) prescribes rules to govern and monitor the Members' implementation of standards. The Agreement on Technical Barriers to Trade[1] (TBT Agreement) and the Agreement on the Application of Sanitary and Phytosanitary Measures[2] (SPS Agreement) provide the rules applicable to Members' policy on standards.

The pertinence of TBT and SPS agreements to a Member's domestic policy on standards is widely established. However, an area that has not received much academic attention is the relevance of the WTO Agreement on Import Licensing Procedures (Import Licensing Agreement) to import controls related to standards. This short chapter attempts to unravel the convergence, if any, between standards and the Import Licensing Agreement. It provides an overview of the disciplines contained in the Import Licensing Agreement and then proceeds to examine whether the procedures to obtain approvals from regulatory authorities on standards will be subject to such rules.

4.2 OVERVIEW OF DISCIPLINES CONTAINED IN THE WTO AGREEMENT ON IMPORT LICENSING PROCEDURES

The movement of goods across international borders may either be free or regulated. For instance, India maintains four categories of imports as part of its Foreign Trade Policy: first, prohibited items, import of which are not allowed; second, those items, which can be imported freely; third, restricted items, imports of which are allowed against an authorisation and subject to conditions under which the items can be imported; and last, canalised items, the imports of which are permitted only through the designated state trading enterprises.[3] Regulated trade entails multiple levels of scrutiny and authorisations prior to entry of goods into national boundaries.

Import licenses and approvals may be the most prominent measures used in trade policy for the regulation of the volume and movement of imported goods. For instance,

1. Agreement on the Technical Barriers to Trade (Marrakesh, Morocco, 15 April 1994), Marrakesh Agreement Establishing the World Trade Organization, Annex 1A *The Legal Texts: The Results of the Uruguay Round of Multilateral Trade Negotiations* 121 (1999), 1868 U.N.T.S. 120 (hereinafter TBT Agreement).
2. Agreement on the Application of Sanitary and Phytosanitary Measures (Marrakesh, Morocco, 15 April 1994), Marrakesh Agreement Establishing the World Trade Organization, Annex 1A, *The Legal Texts: The Results of the Uruguay Round of Multilateral Trade Negotiations* 59 (1999), 1867 U.N.T.S. 493 (hereinafter SPS Agreement).
3. The Foreign Trade (Development and Regulation) Act, 1992, as amended and Foreign Trade (Regulation) Rules, 1993; See also The Foreign Trade Policy.

in 2020, 362 non-automatic import licensing measures were notified by WTO Members.[4] The import licensing procedures adopted may be aimed at administering quantitative restrictions, such as quotas, on the importation of products.[5] Members may also apply import licenses with a view to achieving other policy objectives, such as to protect human and animal health, to safeguard the environment, or to protect national security, etc.[6] Certain licenses are maintained to keep track of imports for statistical purposes.

In India, the Directorate General of Foreign Trade (DGFT) or its regional authorities grant authorisation for the import of restricted items.[7] The conditions for import are collated together in Schedule 1 of ITC (HS) 2017. For instance, an importer seeking to import livestock products must be granted a 'sanitary import permit' by the Department of Animal Husbandry, Dairying and Fisheries of the Government of India as per section 3A of the Livestock Importation Act, 1898.[8] Likewise, with respect to vegetable products, the seeds of cabbage, cauliflower, onion, radish and tomato are permitted to be imported freely in accordance with an import permit granted under the Plant Quarantine (Regulation of Imports into India) Order, 2003.[9] Both these measures have been notified to the Committee on Sanitary and Phytosanitary Measures.[10] These permit requirements have also been notified to the WTO's Committee on Import Licensing as part of India's licensing procedure relating to these products.[11]

The Import Licensing Agreement is designed to minimise the undesirable consequences of GATT-compatible import licensing.[12] It recognises the inevitability of some form of import licenses forming part of the Members' trade policy.[13] The Import Licensing Agreement, therefore, focuses on the administration of the import licensing

4. *Quantitative Restrictions Database*, WTO, https://qr.wto.org/en#/explore/types_of_measures.
5. General Agreement on Tariffs and Trade 1994, (Marrakesh, Morocco, 15 April 1994), Marrakesh Agreement Establishing the World Trade Organization, Annex 1A, *The Legal Texts: The Results of the Uruguay Round of Multilateral Trade Negotiations* 17 (1999), 1867 U.N.T.S. 190, 33 I.L.M. 1153 (1994) (hereinafter GATT 1994), Article XI.
6. Overview of the Agreement on Import Licensing Procedures, https://importlicensing.wto.org/content/introduction-agreement.
7. India's Notification to the WTO Committee on Import Licensing, WTO Doc. G/LIC/N/3/IND/20 dated 28 May 2021, para. 2. Some of the items presently under restriction include live animals, including fish, planting material (seeds), stones, metal waste, plastic waste, certain new pneumatic tyres, sandalwood, security printing paper, radio and television broadcast transmitters, palm oil, power tiller and components, colour television sets, communication jamming equipment, aircraft, including helicopters and items covered under the Convention on International Trade in Endangered Species of Wild Fauna and Flora (CITES), Chemical Weapons Convention (CWC) or other similar domestic/international legislation.
8. ITC (HS), 2017, Schedule 1, Chapter 2, policy condition (3).
9. ITC (HS), 2017, Schedule 1, Chapter 12.
10. WTO Committee on Sanitary and Phytosanitary Measures, Notification (11 April 2002), G/SPS/N/IND/9; WTO Committee on Sanitary and Phytosanitary Measures, Notification (4 March 2004), G/SPS/N/IND/12.
11. WTO Committee on Import Licensing, Agreement on Import Licensing Procedures: Notification under Article 1.4(a) and/or 8.2(b) of the Agreement (15 May 2018), G/LIC/N/1/IND/14.
12. Michael Trebilcock et al., *The Regulation of International Trade*, 235 (Routledge, 4th edn. 2013).
13. Agreement on Import Licensing Procedures (Marrakesh, Morocco, 15 April 1994), Marrakesh Agreement Establishing the World Trade Organization, Annex 1A, *The Legal Texts: The Results of the Uruguay Round of Multilateral Trade Negotiations* (1999), 1869 U.N.T.S. 436 (hereinafter Import Licensing Agreement), Preamble.

measures adopted pursuant to provisions of the GATT 1994 with a view to simplify, and bring transparency to these administrative procedures.[14] It aims to ensure the fair and equitable application and administration of such procedures and practices.

Article 1.1 delineates the scope of the Import Licensing Agreement, and defines 'import licensing' as:[15]

> administrative procedures used for the operation of import licensing regimes requiring the submission of an application or other documentation (other than that required for customs purposes) to the relevant administrative body as a prior condition for importation into the customs territory of the importing Member.
>
> (Original footnotes omitted)

The agreement mandates that the administrative procedures for obtaining such licences are applied neutrally and administered in a fair and equitable manner.[16] It categorises licenses into 'automatic' and 'non-automatic' licenses, and prescribes rules to govern their procedures.

The agreement defines 'automatic import licensing' as when the application for an import license is granted in all cases. These are to be implemented in accordance with certain requirements provided in Article 2 of the Import Licensing Agreement.[17] Automatic import licensing procedures must not be administered in a way that will have restricting effects on imports subject to such license.[18] In order to ensure that such automatic import licensing do not have a trade-restrictive effect on imports, Members must (a) ensure that any person, firm or institution fulfilling the legal requirements of the importing Member is equally eligible to apply for and to obtain import licences; (b) allow application for license to be submitted on any day prior to customs clearance; and (c) approve applications (in appropriate and complete form) within a maximum of ten working days.[19]

Licensing which is not automatic is called non-automatic licensing,[20] and Article 3.2 of the Import Licensing Agreement entails an obligation to ensure that such licensing does not have trade-restrictive or trade-distortive effects on imports additional to those caused by the imposition of the restriction. Further non-automatic licenses shall be no more administratively burdensome than absolutely necessary to administer the measure.[21]

In the case of non-automatic licensing requirements, for purposes other than implementing quantitative restrictions, Members must publish sufficient information for other Members and traders to know the basis for granting and allocating licences. If exceptions or derogations from a licensing requirement are to be requested, Members must include this fact, along with information on how to make such a request and, as

14. *Ibid.*
15. *Ibid.*, Article 1.1.
16. *Ibid.*, Article 1.3.
17. *Ibid.*, Article 2.1.
18. *Ibid.*, Article 2.2(a).
19. *Ibid.*
20. *Ibid.*, Article 3.1.
21. *Ibid.*

far as possible, an indication of the circumstances under which such requests would be considered, in the information notified to the Committee on Import Licensing.[22] Besides this, Members must comply with detailed provisions on the administration of non-automatic import licensing.[23] This includes the provision of relevant information to other Members upon request, and the publication of information on quotas being administered through import licenses.

The Import Licensing Agreement also prescribes notification requirements with respect to Members' procedures on import licensing. Members are required to publish rules and all relevant information concerning procedures for the submission of applications.[24] Members must also comply with certain notification requirements: (i) they must notify to the Committee on Import Licensing, the sources or publications in which information concerning import licensing procedures are published,[25] (ii) they must respond to a Questionnaire on Import Licensing Procedure on an annual basis,[26] which seeks information on import licensing and similar administrative procedures maintained by a Member, and (iii) detailed notification requirements are also provided for members which institute licensing procedures or changes in their procedures.[27]

4.3 WTO JURISPRUDENCE ON THE INTERSECTION BETWEEN STANDARDS AND THE IMPORT LICENSING AGREEMENT

Having provided a background to the disciplines on import licensing procedures, it is important to address the fundamental question that arises on the intersection of standards and import licensing - whether the licenses granted under SPS and TBT measures are subject to the rules contained in the Import Licensing Agreement.

As noted above, Article 1.1 of the Import Licensing Agreement defines 'import licensing' as 'administrative procedures used for the operation of import licensing regimes'.[28] The definition indicates that the administration of import licensing rules which entail authorisation as prior condition for importation is the subject-matter of the Import Licensing Agreement. Such procedures include requiring the submission of an application or other documentation, except those related to customs, to competent authorities to obtain necessary import licenses.

The Import Licensing Agreement defines 'import licensing'; no definition is provided for an 'import license'. A license is simply a permit to do something.[29] While

22. *Ibid.*, Article 3.3.
23. *Ibid.*, Article 3.5.
24. *Ibid.*, Article 1.4(a).
25. *Ibid.*, Article 1.4(a).
26. Procedures for Notification and Review under the Agreement on Import Licensing Procedures, Note by Secretariat, WTO Committee on Import Licensing, G/LIC/3, 7 November 1995. Import Licensing Agreement, *supra* note 13, Article 7.3.
27. Technical Cooperation Handbook on Notification Requirements, Agreement on Import Licensing Procedures, WTO, https://www.wto.org/english/tratop_e/implic_e/implic_handbook_on_notifications_e.pdf; Import Licensing Agreement, *supra* note 13, Article 5.
28. *Ibid.*, Article 1.1.
29. 'License', Definition, Oxford Learner's Dictionaries, https://www.oxfordlearnersdictionaries.com/definition/english/licence.

SPS and TBT approvals may be necessary for obtaining an import authorisation, do these approvals constitute an 'import license' in themselves for the purpose of the Import Licensing Agreement?

The Panel in *Turkey – Rice* suggests they do not. In this dispute, the United States challenged Turkey's import restrictions on rice.[30] The Panel examined whether Turkey's import licensing regime that required importers to obtain a Certificate of Control from its domestic authority constituted discretionary import licensing. In the course of its analysis, the Panel noted that:

> [N]ot all documents giving the permission to import may be necessarily considered to be 'import licences'. As noted by the parties, the importation process is often a complex procedure during which a number of steps must be completed in order to obtain the permission to import certain products. Throughout this process, governments may require that written documents be obtained and then produced to certify the completion of certain steps and thus the compliance with certain legal requirements, in order to allow the importation of goods and their final entry into the importing market. Each of these steps and documents may serve particular objectives. *Strictly speaking, these special documents, when used for purposes such as sanitary and phytosanitary control, customs clearance, payment of taxes or duties, are not to be considered as 'import licences.'*[31]
>
> (Emphasis supplied)

Therefore, procedures involved in obtaining SPS approvals are not be considered as 'import licenses' according to the Panel.

Further, the jurisprudence on Article 1 of the Import Licensing Agreement has drawn a very clear distinction between import licensing rules *per se* and their administration. A combined reading of the Preamble and Article 1 of the Import Licensing Agreement indicates that the Agreement relates to import licensing procedures and their administration, and not to import licensing rules.

In *EC – Bananas III*, the Appellate Body distinguished between licensing rules *per se*, and their application and administration, in the context of Article 1.3 of the Import Licensing Agreement. Importantly, the Appellate Body observed that none of the provisions of the Import Licensing Agreement governed import licensing rules. The preamble and Article 1.1 of the Import Licensing Agreement sufficiently clarifies that the agreement relates to import licensing procedures and their administration, not to import licensing rules.[32]

Korea – Various Measures on Beef reiterated that substantive rules on import policy, are not relevant to the Import Licensing Agreement, which is actually concerned with the administrative rules of import licensing systems.[33]

---

30. Panel Report, *Turkey – Measures Affecting the Importation of Rice*, WT/DS334/R, adopted on 22 October 2007 at para. 2.1.
31. *Ibid.*, at para. 7.127.
32. Appellate Body Report, *European Communities – Regime for the Importation, Sale and Distribution of Bananas*, WT/DS27/AB/R, adopted on 25 September 1997, paras 197-198.
33. See Panel Report, *Korea – Measures Affecting Imports of Fresh, Chilled and Frozen Beef*, WT/DS161/R, adopted 10 January 2001, paras 784-785. In this dispute, US' claims regarding alleged violations of the Import Licensing Agreement were concerned with the substantive provisions of Korea's import (and distribution) regime (by the LPMO or SBS super-groups). The

In *Indonesia-Chicken*, Brazil had challenged Indonesia's 'positive list' requirements and 'intended use' requirements in its import licensing system for chicken meat and chicken products as being restrictive rules and procedures that effectively prohibited Brazilian imports into the Indonesian market.[34] Brazil claimed that these measures were implemented in a manner inconsistent with disciplines on non-automatic licenses prescribed in Article 3 of the Import Licensing Agreement.

Indonesia's 'positive list' requirement allowed importation of only the products listed in the positive list, effectively prohibiting any imports of outside not so listed which included chicken cuts and other prepared or preserved chicken meat.[35] Similarly, the 'intended use' requirement operated as a condition on the importation of chicken meat and chicken products. The importer was required commit to not selling in modern (chicken meat) and in traditional markets (chicken meat and processed chicken) to obtain the necessary approvals for import.[36] The Panel found that these conditions had the effect of restricting imports within the meaning of Article XI:1 of GATT.[37] However, the Panel opined that the positive list requirement and the intended use requirement challenged by Brazil were in the nature of an import licensing rule, and consequently, did not fall within the purview of the Import Licensing Agreement.[38]

Therefore, jurisprudence on the scope of the Import Licensing Agreement suggests that the substantive provisions which regulate import policy, which may include SPS and TBT controls, do not fall within the ambit of the Import Licensing Agreement. Rules for the implementation of SPS measures are instead contained in Article 8 read together with Annex C of the SPS Agreement. It requires, *inter alia*, that procedures for sampling, testing and certification are undertaken and completed without undue delay; such procedures are implemented in a manner that does not discriminate between domestic and foreign products; processing of applications for

---

Panel noted that these claims related to import licensing rules, and were therefore, outside the purview of the Agreement on Import Licensing Procedures.

34. Panel Report, *Indonesia – Measures Concerning the Importation of Chicken Meat and Chicken Products*, WT/DS484/R adopted on 22 November 2017; paras 2.1-2.7. Brazil made claims against two categories of measures: (i) general prohibition on importation of chicken meat and chicken products on account of a combination of measures including, positive list requirement, intended us requirement of imported products, restrictive import licensing regime etc.; and (ii) specific restrictions and prohibitions on such import due to the (a) non-inclusion of certain chicken products in the list of products that may be imported; (b) the limitation of imports of chicken meat and chicken products to certain intended uses; (c) Indonesia's alleged undue delay in the approval of health certificates for chicken products; and (d) Indonesia's import licensing regime.
35. *Ibid.*, para. 7.118.
36. *Ibid.*, paras 7.196-7.202.
37. *Ibid.*, para. 7.202.
38. *Ibid.*, para. 7.360. In this dispute, Indonesia's licensing system contained certain provisions of the Ministry of Agriculture (MoA) and Ministry of Trade Regulations governing the importation of meat that prescribed the type of carcass for which an importer may obtain an MoA Import Recommendation and an MoA Approval. Chicken cuts and other chicken products could not be subject to the above requirements since they were not listed in the relevant appendices and regulations (para. 7.103). The Intended Use requirement was contained in the MoA Regulation and limited the use of imported chicken meat products to specific 'intended uses' (para. 7.176).

certifications are done in a transparent manner; a procedure exists to review complaints concerning the operation of such procedures, etc.[39] Similarly, the TBT Agreement prescribes rules governing conformity assessment procedures under Articles 5 to 8. These provisions too require that procedures for sampling, testing and inspection, evaluation, verification and assurance of conformity, and registration, accreditation and approval, etc. to be conducted expeditiously, ensuring that not prepared, adopted or applied with a view to or with the effect of creating unnecessary obstacles to international trade.[40]

Notwithstanding, several disputes have raised claims against the adoption and implementation of standards inconsistently with relevant WTO rules on SPS and TBT, together with claims against restrictive import licensing procedures. A case in point is the *Ukraine – Measures Relating to Trade in Goods and Services*.[41] In 2017, Russia initiated consultations with Ukraine regarding multiple measures that had the effect of restricting bilateral trade. The Russian Federation claimed that the restrictions, prohibitions, requirements and procedures in respect of trade in goods between the Russian Federation and Ukraine, covering a broad range of food products (including certain meat products, dairy products, fish products, etc.), spirits and beer, cigarettes, diesel-electric locomotives, certain plant products, etc., were inconsistent with, *inter alia*, provisions of the SPS Agreement and the Import Licensing Agreement. This dispute did not proceed beyond the consultations stage.[42]

Other disputes which involved claims under the SPS and TBT Agreements as well as the Import Licensing Agreement include *Indonesia – Measures Concerning the Importation of Bovine Meat*[43] and *Australia – Fresh Fruit and Vegetables*.[44] In *Indonesia – Measures Concerning the Importation of Bovine Meat*, Brazil requested consultations on Indonesia's 'positive list' measure (described earlier in this chapter), and other specific measures which, according to Brazil, unduly restrict access to its market of bovine meat through a non-transparent and intricate import-licensing regime. In *Australia – Fresh Fruit and Vegetables*, the Philippines challenged measures under Australia's *Quarantine Proclamation 1998*, which was an SPS measure that required that 'the importation into Australia of a fresh fruit or vegetable is prohibited unless the Director of Quarantine has granted the person a permit to import it into Australia.'[45]

39. SPS Agreement, *supra* note 2, Annex C.
40. TBT Agreement, *supra* note 1, Article 5.
41. Request for Consultation by the Russian Federation, *Ukraine – Measures relating to Trade in Goods and Services*, G/L/1179 G/LIC/D/52 G/SPS/GEN/1549 G/TBT/D/50 S/L/414 WT/DS525/1 dated 1 June 2017.
42. This dispute has not progressed beyond the consultation stage.
43. See Request for Consultation by Brazil, *Indonesia – Measures Concerning the Importation of Bovine Meat*, WT/DS506/1, G/L/1145, G/SPS/GEN/1486, G/LIC/D/50, G/TBT/D/49, G/AG/GEN/130 dated 7 April 2016. This dispute has not progressed beyond the consultation stage.
44. See Request for Consultation by the Philippines, *Australia – Certain Measures Affecting the Importation of Fresh Fruits and Vegetables*, WT/DS270/1, G/L/575, G/SPS/GEN/345, G/LIC/D/34 dated 23 October 2002. This dispute has not progressed beyond the panel being established.
45. J. Javelosa and A. Schmitz, *Cost-Benefit Analysis of a WTO Dispute*, WPTC 04-03 (University of Florida IFAS, July 2004), p. 7.

The Philippines' challenged this measure on the basis of both the SPS and Import Licensing Agreements. While a panel was established for this dispute, it was not composed, and there have been no further developments since 2003.

In addition to this, Members have been found to notify import controls aimed at the protection of human, animal or plant life and health, and protection of the environment to the Committee on Import Licensing.[46] In the latest Biennial Review of the Implementation and Operation of the Agreement on Import Licensing Procedures, the Committee on Import Licensing noted that with respect to the administrative purposes of the import licensing measures being implemented, among all those reported, 47% concerned the protection of human, animal or plant life and health, and protection of the environment.[47]

In fact, the Secretariat has noted that Members have frequently raised the question whether administrative procedures for issuing technical visas for SPS and TBT purposes, which is a prior condition of importation and involves submission of an application and other documentation to relevant administrative bodies, constitute import licensing procedures.[48] In the Secretariat's view, this issue requires clarification and discussion by the Committee.[49] Therefore, there exists significant ambiguity on this issue despite the Panel's observations in *Turkey – Rice*.

4.4 CONCLUSION

While the TBT and SPS Agreements prescribe the rules applicable to Members' policies on standards, this chapter has sought to explore the question of whether standards may also be subject to the Import Licensing Agreement. The authors have reviewed the role of import licenses in trade policy, disciplines under the Import Licensing Agreement, and WTO jurisprudence relevant to this question.

Given the fact that the Import Licensing Agreement does not define an 'import license', the question of whether SPS and TBT approvals qualified as import licenses remained open. Although this issue was considered very briefly in *Turkey – Rice*, where the Panel suggested that all documents giving permission to import may not necessarily be considered as 'import licences', the precise scope of the term 'import license' remains unclear. The ambiguity regarding whether SPS and TBT approvals form part of import licenses is compounded given the overlap in notification practice at the WTO. As discussed earlier, the administrative purposes of import licensing measures reported to the Committee on Import Licensing remains overwhelmingly concerned with the protection of human, animal or plant life and health, and protection of the environment.

46. *See* WTO Committee on Import Licensing, Thirteenth Biennial Review of the Implementation and Operation of The Agreement on Import Licensing Procedures, WTO Doc. G/LIC/W/54 dated 1 October 2020 at para. 5.6.
47. *Ibid.*
48. See WTO Committee on Import Licensing, Twelfth Biennial Review of the Implementation and Operation of The Agreement on Import Licensing Procedures, WTO Doc. G/LIC/27 dated 26 October 2018 at para. 2.10.
49. *Ibid.*

While at present, the limited jurisprudence emerging from *Turkey – Rice* dispute offers some guidance on the issue of the applicability of the Import Licensing Agreement to implementation of standards, there is scope for clear and reasoned elaboration on the meaning of 'import licenses', the types of approvals that will constitute such license, and consequently, be subject to the disciplines of the Import Licensing Agreement. If the pending disputes highlighted above proceed to adjudication, or if any future disputes arise challenging SPS/TBT measures that have implications under the Import Licensing Agreement, it is possible that this may lead to further development of the jurisprudence on a possible convergence of standards and import licensing procedures.

CHAPTER 5

Standards Ecosystem and Standardization Activities in India

James J. Nedumpara, Satwik Shekhar & Akshaya Venkataraman

The process of standard-setting in India involves a complex mesh of multiple bodies/entities (governmental as well as non-governmental) which operate individually as well as jointly in formulating and implementing standards in the country. Agencies such as the Bureau of Indian Standards (BIS), the Food Safety and Standards Authority of India (FSSAI), Research Design and Standards Organisation (RDSO), the Telecommunication Engineering Centre of India, the Central Drugs Standard Control Organisation, the Petroleum and Explosives Safety Organisation and Agricultural and Processed Food Products Export Development Authority are examples of such bodies that set standards in specialized products and sectors and fields in India. Since 2014, India has undertaken a targeted exercise to modernize and harmonize its standard-setting activities and the revamped BIS Act 2016 was the first major milestone in this process. With the adoption of the Indian National Strategy for Standardization (INSS), India's systems and institutions for standards and standardization are increasingly aligned with international best practices. This chapter recounts the evolution of a new regulatory landscape, and the various strategies and initiatives that the governments (both at the central and state levels) have adopted to streamline and build India's standardization activities. The chapter proceeds to lay out the broad contours and structures of the legal regime governing and implementing standards in India. This chapter is intended to serve as the context within which the specific issues discussed in other chapters can be understood.

5.1 INTRODUCTION

As the Indian economy continues to grow, the demand for safe and high-quality products and services has increased, with consumer preference being primarily driven by performance, quality and reliability of products. To ensure that India becomes a hub for the global manufacturing industry, the safety of consumers and workers has become increasingly relevant. India has committed itself to the sustainable development goals (SDGs) and is on a path toward meeting its targets by protecting its environment, flora and fauna, natural resources and wildlife.

Standards are tools to achieve these goals while also facilitating business interactions. They enable companies to comply with relevant laws and regulations, accelerate the introduction of innovative products in the market and provide interoperability between new and existing products, services and processes. The World Trade Organization (WTO) Secretariat noted in its report as part of 7th Trade Policy Review of India that as of March 2018 there were 19,294 Indian standards, 27.3% of which were harmonized with international standards.[1] WTO Members recognize the need to develop a harmonized, effective, dynamic and robust standards framework. India too has realized the importance of developing a well-functioning regime for administering standards and conformity assessment procedures. Since 2018, there has been a further push toward creating, harmonizing and consolidating Indian standards through policy proposals such as the Indian National Strategy for Standardization (INSS) and the Standards National Action Plan (SNAP). While countries may adopt different types of standards, increasing globalization and closer economic ties underline the need to harmonize these standards and thereby reduce the barriers to international trade. India's standards landscape currently, however, is a complex mesh of multiple bodies and entities (governmental as well as non-governmental) which operate individually as well as jointly.

The purpose of this chapter is to provide an overview of this landscape and lay out how different standard-setting bodies with similar roles, overlapping scope of functions and driven by the same essential public policy motivations, come together to cohesively create quality standards for the Indian economy. This chapter first looks at a historical evolution of standards in India to understand how this multi-agency process of standard-setting came into being. A review of history also provides valuable insights into the policy rationales that drive the multitude of laws and regulations governing standards in India. Thereafter, the chapter examines the INSS to understand the Government of India's approach toward standardization and standard-setting. The remaining sections of this chapter trace the functions of the foundational pillars of the process of standard-setting in India – the entities and organizations that develop standards. By identifying the structure and functions of these entities, this chapter hopes to provide the reader with a clearer picture of how to navigate the Indian regulatory landscape for product standards.

1. Report by the Secretariat, *Trade Policy Review of India*, WT/TPR/S/403, 25 November 2020.

5.1.1 History of Standard-Setting in India

By the time India joined the WTO, nearly 3,500 Indian standards had already been harmonized with international standards (namely, International Organization of Standards (ISO) and International Electrotechnical Commission (IEC) standards or regulations). This development of standards ecosystem in the 1990s occurred through several phases of Indian economic history. What is now considered an 'Indian Standard',[2] is the result of several changes in regulatory framework and progressive integration with the world economy. The creation of standards began through the Institutions of Engineers which created the first draft of a constitution for a formal entity with a responsibility to set up standards at a national level.[3] This led to the creation of Indian Standards Institution (ISI) in 1947. To provide the advantages of standardization to common consumers, the ISI started operating the Certification Marks Scheme under the Indian Standards Institution (Certification Marks) Act, 1952. Under this Scheme, ISI granted licences to manufacturers who produced goods in conformity with Indian Standards and applied the 'ISI Mark' on their products. Despite the certification process being undertaken by ISI under the Scheme, ISI's process of standard-setting and other relevant processes on creation of standards remained unregulated. On 26 November 1986, a bill was brought in the Indian Parliament to create an organization, namely, the Bureau of Indian Standards (BIS) to achieve the above objectives.[4] Since then, the BIS has operated as India's national standards body which creates, recognizes, and adopts product standards that are applied at the national level. With the promulgation of a new BIS Act in 2016, the BIS was recognized as the National Standards Body and its functions expanded. The structure, powers, functions, and standardization process of the BIS, and its role within India's standards ecosystem are covered under section 5.3 of this chapter.

India's standards ecosystem that developed gradually since India's independence in 1947 can be broadly classified under four economic phases.[5] A study of this historical evolution provides key insights into the existing regulatory landscape on standards. In particular, this changing approach to standardization, as witnessed

2. Section 2(17), Bureau of Indian Standards Act, 2016 defines 'Indian Standards' as: the standard including any tentative or provisional standard established and published by the Bureau, in relation to any goods, article, process, system or service, indicative of the quality and specification of such goods, article, process, system or service and includes –

    (i) any standard adopted by the Bureau under sub-section (2) of section 10; and any standard established and published, or recognized, by the Bureau of Indian Standards which was in force immediately before the commencement of this Act.

3. *Origin of BIS*, Bureau of Indian Standards, https://bis.gov.in/index.php/the-bureau/origin-of-bis/ (last visited 14 October 2020).
4. *Id.*
5. Indo-German Working Group on Quality Infrastructure, *Overview of India's Quality Infrastructure – A Guide to Standardisation, Conformity Assessment, Accreditation, Market Surveillance, and Metrology*, Knowledge Series 1, 14 (2018), https://www.gpqi.org/preview_studies/overview-of-india-s-qualityinfrastructure.html?file=files/upload/india/documents/2018-12_Overview%20of%20the%20Indian%20Quality%20Infrastructure_GPQI-India.pdf [hereinafter *Overview of India's Quality Infrastructure*].

through India's economic history, provides necessary context to the decentralized system of standard-setting prevalent in India and how that is now being harmonized under umbrella policy frameworks.

Table 5.1 presents the economic phases and the key developments in the standards ecosystem.

Table 5.1 The Four Phases in Evolution of Standards Ecosystem in India

Economic Phase	Key Developments in Standards Ecosystem
1947-1965 Phase 1: Establishment of institutions and legal frameworks	State-owned institutions established to cater to standards development, metrology, testing, export quality, essential technical regulations enacted.
1965-1980 Phase 2: Era of licensing and low economic growth	Spread of government supported product certification, setting standards in food and agriculture.
1980-1991 Phase 3: Partial liberalization and decontrol	Introduction of global standards through automotive tie-ups, adoption of quality management systems by industry.
1991-present Phase 4: Institutional reforms and integration into the world economy	Setting up of national accreditation boards, setting up operations by foreign certification bodies, increase in technical regulations.

Source: Indo-German Working Group on Quality Infrastructure. *Overview of India's Quality Infrastructure*, Knowledge Series 1 (New Delhi: Deutsche Gesellschaft für Internationale Zusammenarbeit (GIZ) GmbH, 2018).

5.1.1.1 Phase 1: 1947-1965

The first phase of evolution of standards ecosystem coincided with the creation of a strong public sector, especially in iron and steel, capital goods and heavy industry, and basic physical infrastructure sectors. The creation of the ISI was swiftly followed by the establishment of the National Physical Laboratory (NPL) in 1950 as India's National Metrology Institute.[6] NPL, which continues to be one of the 'premiere research labs in the field of physical sciences in India' as CSIR-NPL (under the parent agency Council of Scientific and Industrial Research), was responsible at that time for the 'realization, establishment, upgradation, maintenance and dissemination of standards at par with international level through R&D and latest technology.'[7] NPL aided the development of a testing infrastructure across sectors. One of India's earliest technical regulations, the

6. *Id.* at 14.
7. *National Metrology*, CSIR-National Physical Laboratory, https://www.nplindia.in/national-metrology (last visited 19 December 2020).

Prevention of Food Adulteration Act was enacted in 1954 and is now subsumed within the Food Safety and Standards Act, 2006. In 1956, India passed the Standards of Weights and Measures Act, which incrementally introduced the metric system, making metric weights and measures mandatory in the country.[8]

5.1.1.2 Phase 2: 1965-1980

During the second phase of economic growth, the government took greater control of industrial activities through tools like licensing of private enterprises. This era of government control on private industries, often termed the 'license raj', required private enterprises to obtain licenses and permits for almost all industrial activities, including starting new businesses, expanding existing businesses, producing now products, expanding production capacity, etc. State-owned institutions such as the ISI and NPL operated within a controlled environment, leading to developmental stagnation in the standardization ecosystem.[9] The abovementioned Certification Mark Scheme ('ISI Mark') is regarded as the only noteworthy progress of this phase. Another significant development was the creation of a 'food and agriculture division' at ISI to facilitate growth in the agriculture sector through standardization of equipment, machinery, and processed foods. This complimented the growth in agriculture sector which was backed by the 'Green Revolution' of the late 1960s.

5.1.1.3 Phase 3: 1980-1991

Reforms in the direction of liberalization by relaxing government control over industrial activities began during the third phase. Foreign investments, primarily from Japan in the automobile sector saw technical collaborations with their Indian counterparts. The advent of technology and expansion of telecommunications sectors steered the introduction of high standards in automotive and telecommunication industries, two major sectors of the economy.[10] The creation of the BIS in 1986 marked the advent of a more centralized mechanism for standard-setting. Through this Act, the Indian government laid a robust legal framework regulating standards development and product certification.[11] A key objective was to enable the adoption of international standards and promote certification. The growth of the automotive and engineering sectors, coupled with the development of the ISO 9001 series[12] of standards influenced the introduction of overseas conformity assessment bodies and launch of certifications beyond product certification.[13]

8. *Overview of India's Quality Infrastructure, supra* note 5, at 14.
9. *Id.*, at 15.
10. *Id.*
11. *Id.*
12. First introduced in 1987 by the International Standards Organization and subsequently updated in 2015.
13. *Id.*

5.1.1.4 *Phase 4: 1991-Present*

In the year 1991, India initiated its major macroeconomic reforms, opening the economy to trade and foreign direct investment. India's economic reforms were in line with the mantra of 'liberalization, privatization and globalization' which signalled India's broad acceptance of neo-liberal economic policies and its slow integration with the global markets. Important policies were introduced which led to relaxation of the licensing requirements, reduced regulation of foreign investment and technology importation, and introduction of floating exchange rates.[14] India's Information Technology (IT) sector developed at a fast pace and India became an important player in the global economy. India also became a powerhouse in providing various categories of skilled services, especially IT services.

This phase saw an accelerated push toward creation of a robust standards regulatory regime primarily since India became more engaged in the global trading network. The introduction of the 'Compulsory Registration Scheme (CRS) for Electronic and IT Products' in 2012 is believed to be a 'turning point' in the use of technical regulations in India.[15] The scheme regulates products such as video games, wireless keyboards, mobile phones and laptops.[16] In addition to the advent of electronic and IT products, the increase in importance of steel, specifically in the defence sector led to a sudden rise in formulation of standards for these products since 2012.[17] One of the main developments during this phase was the unprecedented collaboration between the Central Government and the three main national industry associations in India – the Confederation of Indian Industry (CII), the Federation of Indian Chambers of Commerce and Industry (FICCI), and the Associated Chambers of Commerce and Industry of India (ASSOCHAM). These industry associations jointly set up the Quality Council of India (QCI) in 1997.[18] This development was a critical milestone in India's progress toward creating a formalized structure of accreditation and conformity assessment in the country. The National Accreditation Board of Certification Bodies (NABCB) became the first agency to be set up under the QCI. Two more boards were set up in 2007, the National Accreditation Board for Education and Training (NABET), and the National Accreditation Board for Hospitals (NABH).

The National Accreditation Board for Testing and Calibration Laboratories (NABL) (formerly National Coordination of Testing and Calibration Facilities) and NABCB signed Mutual Recognition Agreements (MRAs) and Multilateral Recognition Agreements (MLAs) with regional accreditation bodies like the Asia Pacific Laboratory

---

14. *Overview of India's Quality Infrastructure*, *supra* note 5, at 16.
15. Observer Research Foundation. *Quality Rules in India: Trade, Technical Regulations and Consumer Protection*, Issue No. 245 4 (June 2018) https://www.orfonline.org/wp-content/uploads/2018/06/ORF_IssueBrief_245_Trade_Regulations.pdf [hereinafter *Quality Rules in India*].
16. *Id.*
17. *Id.*, at 4.
18. *About QCI*, Quality Council of India, https://www.qcin.org/qci.php (last visited 19 December 2020).

Accreditation Cooperation (APLAC), the International Laboratory Accreditation Cooperation (ILAC), Pacific Accreditation Cooperation (PAC), and the International Accreditation Forum (IAF).[19] NABCB began accrediting certification bodies in India since the year 2000. The Central Government also provided various incentives for promoting certification bodies. The Ministry of Micro, Small and Medium Enterprises (MSMEs) announced subsidies for ISO 9001[20] certification to MSMEs that was backed by NABCB accreditation. QCI's National Board for Quality Promotion (NBQP) promotes application of quality management standards and statistical quality tools with an objective of enabling industry to improve their competitiveness with a specific focus on the MSME sector.

In 2016, the Government of India enacted a new BIS Act by replacing the BIS Act of 1986. The new legislation revised and expanded the functions of the BIS, specifically in relation to development of product standards and conformity assessment procedures. Most notably, the 2016 Act positions the role of BIS as the national standards body of India. The scope of the new Act applies to articles, processes, and services as well, (and not just products) and includes conformity assessment procedures within the functions of the BIS. The new Act also includes provisions to ensure that the BIS is the only body vested with the ability to recognize and issue 'Indian national standards'. Section 5.3 of this chapter examines the standard-setting processes of the BIS in further detail. Separately, Chapter 6 also introduces the distinct functions of the BIS in relation to conformity assessment procedures.

The Food Safety and Standards Authority of India (FSSAI) was established in 2006 to create food standards, grant certification for food safety, control food-based hazards such as adulteration, presence of the toxic substances, limit the use of food additives, crop contaminants, pesticide residues, 'pharmacological active' substances, develop food-labelling standards, promote and coordinate guidelines for risk assessment, provide training in food safety and standards, etc.[21] This was a major step in the direction of ensuring high nutrition diet, improved public health and protection of public morals by adopting not just product standards, but also standards for proper treatment of environment and plant and animal life. The role of the FSSAI in the creation of standards based on scientific analysis, and certification of organic food led to a consistent increase in the number of food and related products to be mandatorily certified since 2010.[22] The FSSAI and the BIS today share a complementary relationship in the development and enforcement of Indian Standards related to food and food products. While both are statutory bodies independent of each other, they operate in tandem for the creation of food standards and their certification. Since the recognition

19. *Overview of India's Quality Infrastructure, supra* note 5, at 16.
20. ISO 9001 belongs to the ISO 9000 family of standards of quality management. ISO 9001 sets out the criteria for a quality management system and companies, organizations, their products and processes are certified to ISO 9001. It can be used by any organization, large or small, regardless of its field of activity. This standard is based on a number of quality management principles including a strong customer focus, the motivation and implication of top management, the process approach and continual improvement.
21. *See* section 16 of the Food Safety and Standards Act, 2006.
22. *Quality Rules in India, supra* note 15, at 4.

of BIS as the national standardization body, it has been vested with Food Safety Management Scheme, and the power to conduct audits for certain food standards developed by the FSSAI. These schemes are examined in section 5.5.7. Given the important role of food standards in consumer welfare and public interest, Chapter 8 of this Handbook covers the role, functions, and operations of the FSSAI in detail.

During this Phase 4, there has also been a marked attempt at harmonising the standards regime with international trade rules developed on standards. The establishment of the WTO in 1995 facilitated the existence of a common platform for countries to harmonize their standards and technical regulations. As Chapter 1 of this Handbook examined, the Agreement on Technical Barriers to Trade (TBT) and the Agreement on Sanitary and Phytosanitary (SPS) Measures of the WTO require Members to, regularly and promptly, notify their domestic standards and technical regulations.

Between 1995 and 2020, India's has made 226 TBT notifications.[23] Table 5.2 shows the periodic increase in these notifications. A closer look at the sectors regulated show that at the beginning, the notifications predominantly dealt with the primary sectors relating to essential goods. Most of the notifications made during 1995-2008 concerned with four categories of industries: the food and beverage industry (pre-packaged foods, food ingredients, materials in contact with food and beverages), medical equipment (stents, protective gear, thermometers and medical tools), vehicles (petrol, vehicle parts, machinery, nuts and bolts, electric vehicles), and daily use commodities (plastics, protective equipment, housing parts and iron and steel products). Since then, the focus has shifted to products and goods broadly related to the maintenance of human health and safety, related quality requirements, environmental protection, prevention of deceptive trade practices and reducing barriers to trade (specifications for the usage of metals, IT products, technological products, chemicals and medical equipment and tools). However, specifications relating to food and articles of food as well as the medical sector have attracted greater focus than other sectors in the last twenty years of implementation of the TBT Agreement.

Table 5.2 Number of Notifications by India to the WTO TBT Committee

Years	*No. of Notifications*
1995-2000	45
2001-2005	11
2006-2010	30
2011-2015	11
2016-2020	129

Source: Author's representation

23. *Search TBT Notifications*, Technical Barriers to Trade Information Management System, http://tbtims.wto.org/en/Notifications/Search?page = 9&sortBy = DistributionDate&sortDirection = desc&NotifyingMember = India&DoSearch = True (last visited 1 February 2021); *WTO Information Centre*, Bureau of Indian Standards, https://bis.gov.in/other/WTOTBTEnquiryPoint.htm (last visited 23 October 2020).

India's notifications during the 2016-2020 period show a clear indication of the Indian Government to address the previously prevalent problem of under-notification. With 129 notifications during 2016-2020, India has notified more measures during the past five years than it had notified in the preceding twenty years (1995-2015).

India has also increased the number of WTO notifications of its measures under the SPS Agreement. Table 5.3 shows that there has been a steep rise in notifications in the last five years – almost three times when compared to the previous corresponding period and roughly twice that of the last decade. The notifications during 1996–2005 have broadly dealt with agricultural products such as plant products, animals and animal products including livestock, poultry, bovine and ovine and processed foods.[24] A more scientific focus can be seen by way of notifications on Biological agents and other beneficial organisms (since 2006), food additives and its limits (since 2006) and usage of pesticides and maximum limits (since 2008). Since 2015 however, a more specific approach was taken with notifications dealing with specific products and goods such as pulses, honey, caffeine, additives, carbonated drinks, chocolates, milk and milk products, frozen foods and rice bran and other oils. Few notifications have also exclusively dealt with Carbide gas, additives, metal residue levels and healthy dietary levels for children – all dealing with restrictions and quantities that are considered to be accepted levels.

Table 5.3 Number of Notifications by India to the WTO SPS Committee

Years	*No. of Notifications*
1996-2000	8
2001-2005	30
2006-2009	43
2010-2015	57
2016-2020	140

Source: Author's representation

The sharp rise in the number of TBT and SPS notifications by India can be said to be a result of notifying measures which were earlier not notified as well as continuous push toward creation of new standards and revising obsolete ones. The following sections of this chapter attempt to provide a snapshot of how these new standards are created.

24. *Search Notifications*, Sanitary and Phytosanitary Information Management System, http://spsims.wto.org/en/Notifications/Search?DoSearch = True&NotifyingMember = India&NotificationFormats = 1&NotificationFormats = 7&NotificationFormats = 200&NotificationFormats = 201&NotificationFormats = 202&NotificationFormats = 203&NotificationFormats = 8&NotificationFormats = 9&DisplayChildren = true (last visited 18 December 2020).

5.1.2 Overview of India's Standards Regulatory Landscape

The process of standard-setting in India involves a complex mesh of multiple bodies/entities (governmental as well as non-governmental) which operate individually as well as jointly in formulating and implementing standards in the country. Agencies such as the BIS, the FSSAI, Research Design and Standards Organisation (RDSO), the Telecommunication Engineering Centre of India, the Central Drugs Standard Control Organisation, the Petroleum and Explosives Safety Organisation, Agricultural and Processed Food Products Export Development Authority, etc., are examples of such bodies that set standards in different sectors and fields in India. Once the standards have been laid down, the role of accreditation bodies becomes relevant. The setting up of QCI in 1997 and bringing NABCB, NABET, NABH and NBQP under its oversight led to a formalized structure for testing, certification and conformity assessment within the quality ecosystem. Chapter 6 of this Handbook examines the role of accreditation bodies in conformity assessment procedures and certification in further detail. Figure 5.1 provides a snapshot of some of the key bodies involved in standard-setting in India.

Figure 5.1 Snapshot of Some of the Standard-Setting, Conformity Assessment and Accreditation Bodies in India

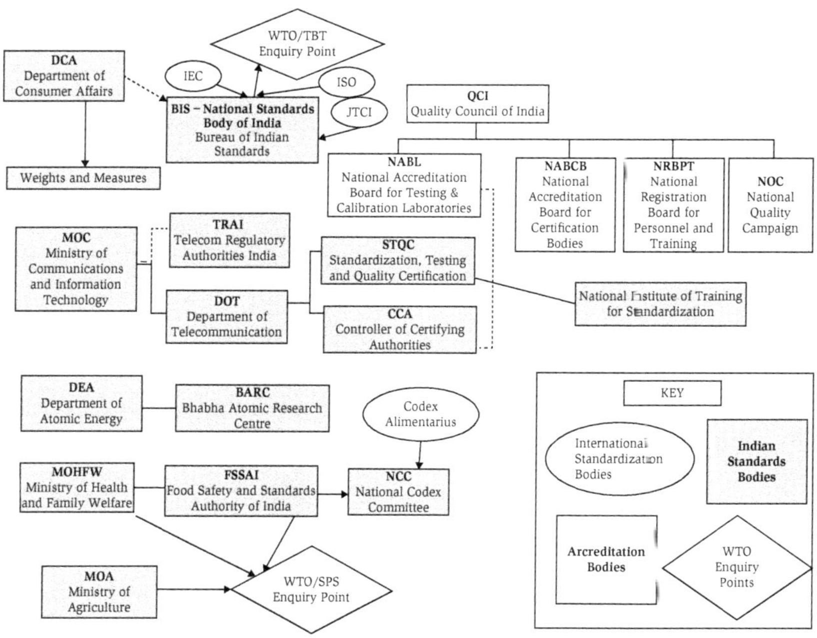

Source: Author's representation based on information on the American National Standards Institute website at https://share.ansi.org/shared%20documents/standards%20activities/country%20charts%20-%20standards%20and%20conformity%20assessment%20systems/india.ppt.

In the context of India, the process of standard-setting involves three different types of approaches:

(a) standard-setting by the government;
(b) standard-setting bodies; and
(c) industry standards.

At first glance, these three approaches would indicate the existence of a clear delineation between standards that are set by government departments, those set by agencies or organizations vested with this specific purpose, and those developed by the industry. However, a deeper look into the actual mechanisms employed in development of standards in these three approaches shows that there is extensive consultation among different entities and bodies, including government entities, regulatory bodies, autonomous bodies, industry representatives and experts. While government departments, standards developing organizations (SDOs) and industry bodies are capable and empowered to develop standards independently, the process typically requires collaboration.

For example, a government department like the Ministry of Road Transport and Highways (MRTH) can specify standards through an order published in the Official Gazette under the Motor Vehicles Act, 1988 or by submitting a proposal to a standard-setting body. A standard-setting body like the BIS on the other hand, may receive a proposal for standard development either from the government (such as the MRTH) or may receive a proposal from an interested party/stakeholder. The process of adoption of that standard by the standard-setting body, regardless of who makes the first proposal, would depend on the process set out in the governing law of such body (for example, the BIS creates standards under BIS Act, 2016). Distinct from the government and the standard-setting bodies approach, an industry standard is adopted through collaboration among the industry, manufacturers, processors and trade associations. A recent example is the Indian Standards for Soybean being drafted by the Soybean Processors' Association (SOPA), the apex body of soybean processors units, along with the Indian Institute of Soybean Research and Solidaridad Regional Expertise Centre.[25] While several industrial standards exist in the Indian market, such standards will be considered an 'Indian standard' and have national application, only if they are recognized under section 10(2)(b) of the BIS Act, 2016.[26]

Unpacking this complex mesh of regulations, processes and approaches to standards development in India, therefore, requires a study of the entities that are responsible for the development of standards. In other words, understanding *who* sets the standard is crucial for understanding *how* these standards are set. The following

25. *SOPA Developing Industry Norms for Sustainable Soya*, Financial Express (17 December 2019 1:23 AM), https://www.financialexpress.com/market/commodities/sopa-developing-industry-norms-for-sustainable-soya/1795771/.
26. Section 10(2)(b), The BIS Act, 2016, which states that –

> (2) The Bureau may [...] adopt as Indian Standard, any standard, established by any other Institution in India or elsewhere, in relation to any goods, article, process, system or service in such manner as may be prescribed.

sections of this chapter attempt to create a map to navigate the regulatory processes for standards in India. Despite the differences in the governing legislations and everyday-processes that are involved in standard-setting as carried out by different entities in India, common motivations and public policy goals drive and underpin the work of these bodies. Section 5.1.2.1 below first attempts to locate and highlight the various policy rationales that drive the creation of standards in India. Subsequently, section 5.1.2.2 provides a bird's eye view of the various legislations, borne out of these policy ambitions, which ultimately form the backbone of standard-setting in India.

5.1.2.1 *Policy Rationale for Standards*

The standardization process in India follows a set of central Acts, rules, regulations and orders. Although the Constitution of India does not expressly mention product standards and the standardization process, the objectives laid down under the Constitution – promotion of public health, nutrition levels, standard of living, protection of environment, flora and fauna, etc. – remain the key policy objectives which the Central Government aims to realize through setting up standards under various laws, Acts, rules and regulations.

Any policy step toward improving public health and preserving plant, animal and human life should ensure the safe consumption of products. Regulation of the chemical content in food items or residue limits in fertilizers or food products is important to ensure safe consumption. Food safety has a direct effect on public health and India has recognized its duties as a welfare state to provide improved levels of nutrition and standard of living to its people. Article 47 of the Constitution expressly directs the State (India) to fulfil this duty. Standards mandating certain quality and safety parameters of various food products and health supplements, including concentration of additives and preservatives in foods, fall under this duty of the government to protect public health.

Protection of environment is another major policy goal. India is a signatory to the Paris Agreement (21st Conference of the Parties to the UN Framework Convention on Climate Change, or UNFCCC, held at Paris in 2015) or COP21 and endeavours to meet the targets thereunder for creation of a sustainable environment by reducing greenhouse emissions and protecting/preserving its forests and wildlife. However, prior to COP21, India had resorted to standards to regulate industry activities and production processes in favour of protecting environment and public health. Article 48A of the Constitution lays down the principle of safeguarding forests and wildlife of the country. Protection of environment directly affects human health and any industrial activity in India must not be detrimental to the environment, forests, plants and wildlife. An example of a standard formulated to achieve this aim is the Eco Mark Scheme of the BIS which was introduced for labelling of environment friendly products.[27]

27. *Operation of Eco Mark Scheme,* Bureau of Indian Standards, https://bis.gov.in/index.php/product-certification/operation-of-eco-mark-scheme/ (last visited 19 December 2020).

India has also a legislative and administrative framework to regulate the trading of any product which is deemed to be harmful to public health or against public interest. For example, manufacture or import of drugs like amidopyrine, phenacetin and fixed combinations of vitamins with anti-inflammatory agents and tranquilizers, and certain other chemicals is either banned or restricted on strict approval basis in India.[28] Likewise, in order to protect wildlife, import of wild animals (including their parts and products) as defined in the Wild Life (Protection) Act, 1972 is prohibited and the list of such animals and their products is maintained and notified by the Directorate General of Foreign Trade. These powers of the Central Government to restrict trade of certain products and impose high levels of standards for their suitability for public interests and morals can be said to be derived from Article 302 of the Constitution of India.

5.1.2.2 Regulations on Product Standards

Product standards in India have been regulated since the creation of Indian Standards Institution (ISI) in 1947. ISI carried out standard-setting as well as certification processes in India, the functions which have now been expanded through the BIS Act 2016. As the national standards body, the BIS formulates Indian Standards covering all areas *other than* those mentioned in Agricultural Produce (Grading and Marking) Act, 1937 and the Drugs and Cosmetics Act, 1940. While the Agricultural Produce Act of 1937 empowers the Central Government for fixing and marking grades on agricultural and other produce, the Drugs and Cosmetics Act of 1940 prescribes laying of standards for drugs to be done by the Central Drugs Standards Control Organization (CDSCO), which is the central drugs authority under the Ministry of Health and Family Welfare. All the rules and regulations under these Acts also form an integral part of the standardization process in India.

The Ministry of Consumer Affairs, Food and Public Distribution is the main central government department dealing with product standards, although each ministry or department also has its own system of framing and publishing product standards. There are several legislations (sector-specific as well as general) which govern standard-setting processes. A list of the key legislation, rules and regulations that have contributed to evolution of the standards regulatory framework in India include, but are not limited to:

(a) The BIS Act, 2016;
(b) Agricultural Produce (Grading and Marking) Act, 1937;
(c) Drugs and Cosmetics Act, 1940;
(d) Prevention of Food Adulteration Act, 1954;
(e) Export (Quality Control and Inspection) Act, 1963;

28. *See* Notification No. GSR NO. 578(E), 3 July 1983; Notification No. GSR NO. 578(E), 23 July 1983.

(f) The Cigarettes and Other Tobacco Products (Prohibition of Advertisement and Regulation of Trade and Commerce, Production, Supply and Distribution) Act, 2003;
(g) The Petroleum and Natural Gas Regulatory Board Act, 2006;
(h) The Food Safety and Standards Act, 2006;
(i) Explosives Act, 1984;
(j) Environment Protection Act, 1986; and
(k) All the rules and regulations framed under these Acts, including the BIS Act.

In recent times, India has introduced a number of mandatory certification requirements for the electronics and IT sector, steel, and agro-based industries. These mandatory certification requirements are implemented through various BIS schemes. For instance, the ISI Mark Scheme includes products ranging from Sulphate Resisting Portland Cement,[29] Electric Irons and Stoves,[30] skimmed milk-powder,[31] tubes for pneumatic tyres[32] to LPG gas containers for automotive use.[33] These standards under the ISI Mark Scheme, being mandatory standards, are notified in the Gazette of India – either through quality control orders, sectoral legislations, or rules under such legislation (*e.g., see footnotes 30 – 34*). The most regulated sectors, until at least a decade ago, were cement and electronics, presumably in view of consumer safety objectives.[34]

The existence of several such laws, rules and quality control orders governing standards development has meant that there is a need to harmonize these regulations domestically. The adoption of the INSS by India's Ministry of Commerce and Industry in 2018 is the latest attempt to build an effective standards-setting process and harmonize the standards framework.[35] The INSS notes that in the seventy years that preceded its introduction, more than 20,000 Indian Standards were developed, half of which were product standards.[36] Despite these efforts, the INSS observed that standards in India did not often account for unique domestic requirements and were typically adopted as is from international standards, or there were large product and sectoral gaps where standards were absent. The INSS sought to address the gaps in standard-setting, as well as other pressing needs such as the development of service sector standards.

29. Notified through Cement (Quality Control) Order, 2003 S.O. No. 191(E), 17 February 2003.
30. Electrical Wires, Cables, Appliances and Protection Devices and Accessories (Quality Control) Order, 2003 No. 189(E), 17 Feb 2003 (amended several times subsequently, and most recently through S.O. 2604 (E), dated 19 October 2010).
31. Food Safety and Standards (Prohibition and Restrictions on Sales) Regulations, 2011 under the Food Safety and Standards Act 2006.
32. Pneumatic Tyres and Tubes for Automotive Vehicles (Quality Control) Order, 2009 S.O. No. 2953(E), 19 November 2009.
33. Gas Cylinder Rules, 2016 under the Explosive Act, 1884.
34. *Quality Rules in India, supra* note 15, at 3.
35. *Indian National Strategy for Standardization*, (2018) Ministry of Commerce and Industry, Government of India https://commerce.gov.in/wp-content/uploads/2020/02/MOC_636655449469105249_INSS_Booklet_2018.pdf [hereinafter INSS].
36. *Id.* at 9.

5.2 INDIAN NATIONAL STRATEGY FOR STANDARDIZATION

The INSS was prepared by the Department of Commerce, Ministry of Commerce and Industry after undertaking consultations from 2014 through 2017 through national and regional standards conclaves and dialogues. The INSS sought to represent the 'broad consensus' arrived at as a result of these consultations with government bodies, industry, regulatory bodies, other standard-setting and conformity assessment bodies, academia.[37]

The INSS 'provides direction for India's political and executive leadership on how best to use standardization, technical regulations, quality infrastructure and related activities to advance the interests and well-being of Indians in a global economy.'[38] The INSS is based on considerations around positioning standards as a key driver of all economic activities relating to goods and services. In other words, the INSS is an attempt to develop a comprehensive network of standardization in India. As mentioned in the previous section of this chapter, harmonization of standards, adopting best practices of conformity assessment and accreditation makes the quality ecosystem of a country effective and benefits the manufacturers and traders. INSS lays down a roadmap to create an integrated quality infrastructure at par with the international best practices.

By the creation of a robust standardization system in India and improving the applicable standards, INSS envisions India to play an active role and take leadership positions in international and regional fora in standard-setting. Conformity assessment bodies under QCI (like NABL and NABCB) are members of international and regional accreditation bodies such as International Laboratory Accreditation Cooperation (ILAC) and Asia-Pacific Accreditation Cooperation (APAC). An important aim of INSS is to create a response mechanism to global developments on standards, technical regulations and conformity assessment that impact market access of Indian goods and services in other countries.

The INSS proposes an implementation plan to undertake the strategy over a five-year period (2018-2023).[39] The plan is being monitored by a high-level committee (with quarterly reviews). The importance of INSS lies in the fact that it is a strategy adopted by the Government of India which would shape the standard-setting processes in the country, which have so far remained scattered.

5.2.1 Standards Development

The INSS aims to develop 'a dynamic, relevant and priority-driven standards ecosystem that will drive development across sectors, promote competitiveness of Indian products and services, and foster India's eminence among the global leaders in

37. *National Policy*, Directorate of Standardisation, Department of Defence Production, https://ddpdos.gov.in/standards/national-policy (last visited 19 December 2020).
38. INSS, *supra* note 35, at 7.
39. *Id.*

standardization'.[40] With this mission statement, the Government of India has highlighted eight goals which it aims to achieve by 2023, thereby creating a robust and an organized approach to development of standards. The eight goals which have been envisioned under the INSS are mentioned in Figure 5.2.

Figure 5.2 Goals under the 'Standards Development' Pillar of the INSS

Source: INSS Document

Converging standards developing activities in India is a priority target that INSS aims to achieve by 2023. This goal takes particular precedence to address systemic issues in the fragmentation of standard -setting activities in India. Streamlining the various regulations and bodies which form a part of the Indian standards ecosystem and setting up a mechanism which accommodates these diverse functions, is critical for the future that INSS envisages. As noted earlier in this chapter, the standard-setting process in India involves extensive consultation among the various standard-setting bodies and stakeholders. The INSS sets out ambitions for furthering and streamlining participation of all stakeholders (including MSMEs) in the standard-making process and leveraging India's role in standard-setting process globally.

It is expected that the INSS will govern all future standard-setting processes in India, whether the standards are formulated by the government, the standard-setting bodies or industry associations. India's standards-setting process has been led thus far by the BIS. The role of BIS as the apex national standards body in India has been reaffirmed in the INSS. The BIS will continue to oversee harmonious development of

40. INSS, *supra* note 35, at 8.

standardization activities under its own umbrella as well as through memoranda of understanding with the other SDOs.[41]

The following sections of this chapter provides a detailed explanation of the functioning of various standard-setting agencies in India.

5.3 BUREAU OF INDIAN STANDARDS

The central objective of the BIS as noted in BIS Act of 2016 is the 'harmonious development of activities of standardization, marking and quality certification of goods and for matters connected therewith or incidental thereto'.[42] The BIS is headquartered in New Delhi and its five Regional Offices (ROs) are at Kolkata (Eastern), Chennai (Southern), Mumbai (Western), Chandigarh (Northern) and Delhi (Central). The BIS has also various branch offices in several other cities in India.[43]

The BIS has been established to cater to the interest of consumers as well as the industry stakeholders. Table 5.4 lays out the various activities which the BIS has been involved in.

Table 5.4 Key Activities Undertaken by the BIS

Standards Formulation	*Product Certification Scheme*
Compulsory Registration Scheme	Foreign Manufacturers Certification Scheme
Hall Marking Scheme	Laboratory Services
Laboratory Recognition Scheme	Sale of Indian Standards
Consumer Affairs Activities	Promotional Activities
Training Services (National and International)	Information Services

Source: *About BIS*, Bureau of Indian Standards, https://bis.gov.in/index.php/the-bureau/about-bis/.

5.3.1 Members of the BIS

The BIS consists of 25 members representing both Central and State governments, Members of Parliament, industry, scientific and research institutions, consumer organizations and professional bodies; with Union Minister of Consumer Affairs, Food and Public Distribution as its President and with Minister of State for Consumer Affairs, Food and Public Distribution as its Vice-President. The representatives from industry

41. *Id.*
42. *About BIS*, Bureau of Indian Standards, https://bis.gov.in/index.php/the-bureau/about-bis/ (last visited 19 December 2020).
43. *Id.*

associations or federations, namely the Confederation of Indian Industry (CII), Federation of Indian Chambers of Commerce and Industry (FICCI) and the Associated Chambers of Commerce and Industry of India (ASSOCHAM) are also members of the BIS.[44] In addition, the scientific and research institutions, technical, educational and professional organizations, regulatory authorities or bodies and national accreditation boards or bodies are also represented at the BIS.

5.3.2 Divisions of the BIS

Once a proposal to formulate a standard is received, the BIS utilizes its impressive organization setup of Technical Departments, Division Councils, Technical Committees, Sectional Committees and Standardization Cells (in other organizations). Several consultation and coordination among all the stakeholders, including government bodies, private entities, industry associations, consumer organizations and experts. The BIS prepares and updates detailed Work Programme for each Division Council and Sectional Committee. While the Work Programme provides scope of the Division Council and Sectional Committees, it also contains details of status of enforced standards and the stage of preparation at which draft standards have reached (like preliminary, wide circulation and finalized draft standards).[45]

At present, there are 335 Sectional Committees functioning within the BIS. These consist of over a thousand experts from government bodies, regulatory bodies, industries, consumer boards, scientists, technologists and testing agencies.[46] These committees work to develop consensus based voluntary National standards with stakeholder consultations.

Table 5.5 enlists the sectors, each of which has a Technical Department and a Division Council.[47] In addition, each Technical Department consists of Technical Committees which operate within the mandate of the Technical Department they fall under. The sectors are:

Table 5.5 Sectors in Which the BIS Engages in Formulation of Indian Standards

Chemicals	Metallurgical Engineering	Mechanical Engineering
Civil Engineering	Petroleum Coal and Related Products	Management and Systems

44. *Bureau Members*, Bureau of Indian Standards, https://bis.gov.in/index.php/the-bureau/organization-2/bureau-members/ (last visited 23 December 2020).
45. *Process of Standards Formulation*, Bureau of Indian Standards, https://bis.gov.in/index.php/standards/standard-formulation/process-of-setting-standards/ (last visited 19 December 2020).
46. *Review of BIS Annual Report 2018-19*, Bureau of Indian Standards, https://bis.gov.in/wp-content/uploads/2020/03/ReviewStatementofBISAR201819.pdf (last visited 13 October 2020).
47. *Technical Departments*, Bureau of Indian Standards, https://www.services.bis.gov.in:8071/php/BIS_2.0/dgdashboard/committee_sso (last visited 7 October 2020).

Electronics and Information Technology	Production and General Engineering	Medical Equipment and Hospital Planning
Electrotechnical	Services Sector Department	Textile
Food and Agriculture	Transport Engineering	Water Resources

Source: *Technical Departments*, Bureau of Indian Standards, https://www.services.bis.gov.in:8071/php/BIS_2.0/dgdashboard/committee_sso

The structure of Technical Departments for each of the above sectors includes Technical Committees, Sub-Committees, Working Groups and Panels.[48] Each of these teams has a defined scope with respect to products and sectors and experts (including scientists) are members of these teams. Depending on the primacy and priority of the products and sectors, the number of Technical Committees under the Technical Departments could be as high as 45.

5.3.3 Standards Formulation Process of the BIS

The process of standards formulation at the BIS may include establishing a new standard or revising, amending or cancelling an established standard. Written proposals are accepted by the BIS from stakeholders and interested parties, which could be either government entities or private corporations. In addition to external proposals, members of the BIS as well as members of the Technical Committees also submit proposals for the BIS to take requisite action.[49] Once the proposal is received, the proposal is analysed in a structured manner with these steps followed meticulously:

The Figure 5.3 lays out the steps the BIS adopts for formulation of standards.

48. *Id.*
49. *Process of Standards Formulation*, *supra* note 45.

Figure 5.3 Process of Standard Formulation by the BIS

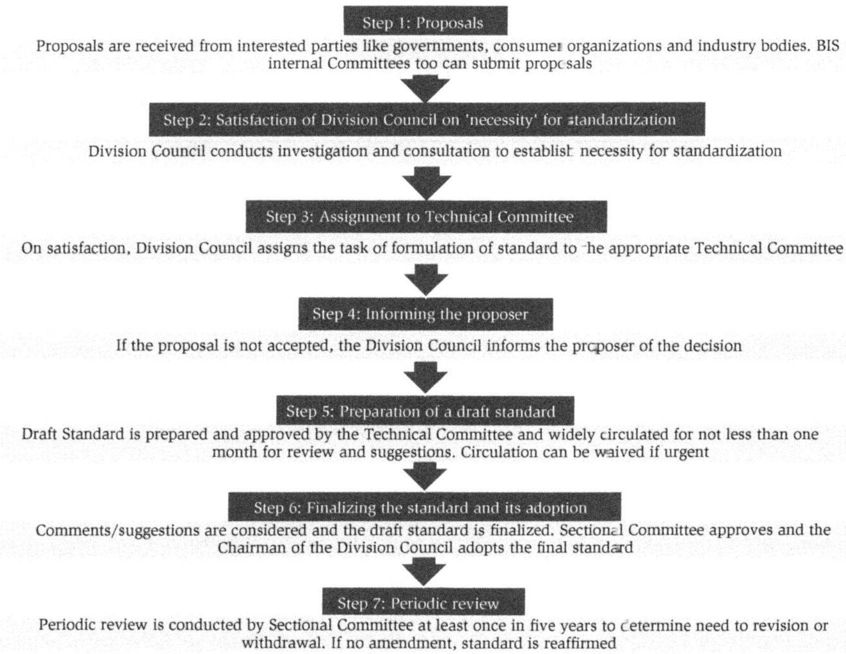

Source: Process of Standards Formulation, Bureau of Indian Standards, https://bis.gov.in/index.php/standards/standard-formulation/process-of-setting-standards/

It must be noted that while deliberating and consulting over the proposed standard, the BIS gives special attention to multidisciplinary areas such as energy conservation, environmental protection, rural development and safety.

The process of formulation of standards is documented on the BIS website. Details of proposals received, and their status are publicly available.

The BIS follows internationally accepted good standardization practices while continuing to comply with the WTO-TBT Code of Good Practice for preparation, adoption and application of standards.[50] As seen from above, the BIS provides all interested stakeholders with a neutral platform to come together and work toward common agreements to develop national standards. It must be noted that the fifteen Division Councils of the BIS formulate Indian Standards covering all areas under the scope of the BIS Act. Though the BIS is the national standard-setting body in India, there are other industries and professional bodies which formulate sector-specific standards. These bodies are referred to as SDOs. The standards developed by the SDOs are recognized by the BIS as relevant standards to be applicable at a national level. The statutory provisions under section 10(2)(c) of the BIS Act and section 30 of the BIS

50. *Review of BIS Annual Report, supra* note 46, at 1.

Rules, 2018 (enforced under the BIS Act) confer upon the BIS, powers to recognize any SDO in India for development of standards. Section 5.5 of this chapter looks at certain key SDOs in India and how they operate.

Standard-Setting by SDOs

Standards Developing Organizations (SDOs) are bodies recognized by the BIS as having sector-specific knowledge and serve an important function of formulating sector-specific standards. When an SDO develops a standard, it is required to then get it recognized as an Indian Standard by the BIS[51] in line with India's 'One Nation, One Standard' policy.

The BIS specifies certain criteria that must be met when SDOs develop standards, such as a mandatory public consultation. Once an SDO standard is prepared, it must apply for the recognition of the standard, and must provide details to the BIS regarding the standard and its formulation process, the technical committee involved in formulation, details of consultations, etc. If the BIS is satisfied that its requirements for standards formulation have been met, the appropriate BIS Technical Committee must consent to the SDO Standard being formulated as an Indian Standard. The draft is then published on the BIS website for public comment for at least a month, and any comments received are directed back to the SDO. Once resolved, the SDO standard is adopted as an Indian Standard by the BIS.

Being the national standards body in India, the BIS had a responsibility to further the aims and objectives of the INSS. The Bureau, therefore, released the Standards National Action Plan (SNAP) in 2019 which provides a framework of actionable and measurable standardization priorities in India.

5.4 STANDARDS NATIONAL ACTION PLAN

Recognizing that standardization supports economic growth, enhances competitiveness, fosters technological development and supports innovation, the BIS developed the 2019 SNAP.[52] The SNAP is a direct result of the strategies and goals identified under the INSS with an emphasis on standardization activities. Through the SNAP, the BIS intends to ensure a synergy of the standardization activities taking place in India such that national standards development is aligned with the technological, economic and social priorities of the country. The Action Plan notes that:

51. Rule 8, Bureau of Indian Standards' Scheme for Recognition of Standards Developing Organizations (SDOs), available at https://www.services.bis.gov.in:8071/php/BIS_2.0/sdo/sdonew/SDO-recognition-scheme-document.pdf.
52. *Standards National Action Plan, 2019*, Bureau of Indian Standards (2019) https://bis.gov.in/wp-content/uploads/2019/03/SNAP-Documents.pdf.

> Standardization activities in the BIS are to be based on strong foundation and systems that are aligned to meet the current and anticipated standardization needs and priorities, coordinated to remain effective and to be able to address emerging standardization issues.[53]

The five key issues identified by the BIS, in consultation with stakeholders like regulators, industry associations and research bodies, are:

(a) Gap between the products needed to be standardized and the actual number of products covered by standards and subjects/topics to be taken up for future standards development;
(b) Evolving mechanism for regular feedback on standards and standardization needs;
(c) Constraints faced in participation in standardization work both at national and international level;
(d) Difficulties faced in implementation of standards; and
(e) Capacity building needs of stakeholders for effective participation in standards development.

On the basis of inputs from policymakers, regulators and industry and industry associations, the BIS assessed national socio-economic requirements through a process of secondary research against the ISO guidelines. With these considerations, SNAP was developed with the objectives as highlighted in Figure 5.4.

53. *Id.*, at 18.

Figure 5.4 Objectives of Standards National Action Plan

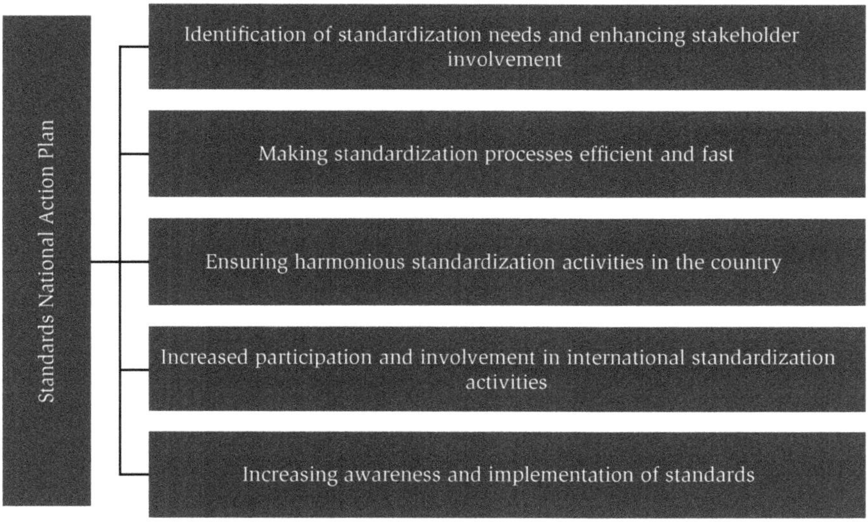

Source: SNAP Document

The SNAP details multiple action plans which the BIS has indicated to undertake to achieve the above objectives. The actions proposed to be undertaken will be implemented within defined timeless set by the BIS by 2022. The progress will be monitored periodically in terms of the measures identified against each action.[54] The BIS has earmarked certain measures which it intends to assume to realize the five broad objectives. To implement this action, the BIS intends to conduct at least six sector-wise programmes held every year.

5.4.1 Actions and Measures under SNAP

The SNAP establishes the intention, purpose, actions and timelines for the BIS to follow in its standardization process with an emphasis on widespread stakeholder consultation, capacity building, sector-wise awareness programmes and UN Sustainable Development Goals. The SNAP consists of 42 'actions' which the BIS intends to perform to fulfil its five objectives.[55] As mentioned earlier, the BIS proposes a measure to adopt or enact for each of the 42 action points. Few of the select important actions (and their respective measures) under SNAP have been enlisted in Table 5.6.

54. *Id.*, at 34.
55. *Id.*, Annex 1 at 35.

Table 5.6 Actions and Measures under SNAP

Objective	*Action*	*Measure*	*Targeted Benefit*
1. Identification of standardization needs and enhancing stakeholder involvement	Regular and planned interaction with Ministries or Regulators or Industry Associations to assess standardization needs, promote use of standards through govt. policies and regulations and identify experts for participation in standardization (national and international)	One interaction every quarter	- Availability of timely inputs on standardization - Identification of new subjects for standardization. - Identification of relevant experts. - Enhance the implementation of standards
2. Making standardization processes efficient and fast	Create National Commenting Platform - online commenting/ feedback mechanism on existing standards/ draft documents	Online commenting platform made operational	- Increased participation of stakeholders and technical committee members. - Faster standards development processes.
3. Ensuring harmonious standardization activities in the country	Introduce a Scheme for accreditation or recognition of Standards Developing Organizations (SDOs)	Policy framed and scheme launched	- Coordinated efforts in national standardization. - Harmonized standard development in the country. - International good standardization practices followed in the country.

Objective	*Action*	*Measure*	*Targeted Benefit*
4. Increased participation and involvement in international standardization activities	Identify priority areas of participation in ISO and IEC that are of strategic importance for India, identify relevant experts who would participate and draw an annual delegation plan	- Strategic plan developed for participation in ISO/IEC technical work. - Relevant guidelines for participation in international meetings framed and implemented. - Relevant Technical committees/Working Groups of International Standardization Bodies along with the relevant experts identified. - Annual delegation plan developed.	Focused and effective participation in international standardization.
5. Increasing awareness and implementation of standards	Carry out sector-wise awareness programme for Industry with focus on MSME	At least six sector-wise programmes held every year	Increased awareness and implementation of standards

Source: Annex 1 of SNAP Document

5.4.2 Key Standardization Areas

The SNAP intends for sustainability, smartness and service standardization to be the key aspects that will define the future national standardization work of the BIS.[56] In this regard, in order to create an extensive action plan for the standardization process, the BIS has also identified 'key standardization areas' and ranked them on the basis of their priority. Few of the standardization areas with a high priority are enlisted in Table 5.7.

Table 5.7 'Priority' Subject Areas for Standardization under SNAP

Sector	*Field*	*Subject Area*
Agriculture	Agriculture - Soil	Soil Health
Health and Safety	Occupational health, safety and management practices	Safety guidelines for laboratories

56. *Id.*, at 49.

Sector	Field	Subject Area
Manufacturing	Industrial Production	Anthropometric data for Indian population
Water Resources	Water management	Water quality management

Source: Author's representation based on Annex 2 of SNAP Document

The areas listed in the above table are those which have been marked with the highest priority for standardization. However, with varying priority, a total of 176 subject areas under 64 fields spanning across 26 sectors have been identified in which standardization process under SNAP will be undertaken. Reviewing the standards development process is an essential part of SNAP. Periodic review of areas in which standards are developed is expected to be conducted and the requirements in this regard are proposed to be updated as necessary.[57]

5.5 STANDARDS DEVELOPING ORGANIZATIONS

In addition to the BIS, there are other regulators, ministerial departments, industries and professional bodies in India which formulate sector-specific standards, generally referred to as SDOs. At present, the BIS maintains a list of 48 SDOs which formulate standards and technical regulations.[58] This list consists of ministries/department of the Government of India, autonomous regulatory bodies, statutory organizations, industry bodies, professional bodies, export promotion councils/bodies/authorities and research and technical institutions. The statutory provisions under section 10(2)(c) of the BIS Act and Rule 30 of the BIS Rules, 2018 confer upon the BIS, powers to recognize any SDO in India for development of standards. Accordingly, the BIS launched the scheme for Recognition of SDOs as a part of the 'One Nation One Standard' Mission. In June 2021 the BIS gave formal 'recognition' to the first SDO as a part of this Scheme – the RDSO of the Indian Railways. This recognition will allow the BIS to adopt RDSO standards as 'Indian National Standards' if it deems fit, and will give RDSO the acknowledgement and recognition that it is compliant with the TBT Agreement Code of Good Practice.

The QCI has also independently developed criteria for formal accreditation of other bodies as SDOs though no organization has been granted such accreditation yet.[59]

India's institutional framework, with a plethora of governmental, non-governmental and autonomous bodies working individually and collectively in

57. *Id.*, at 34.
58. *Organisations/Departments of Government of India Formulating Standards and Technical Regulations and their area of Activity*, Bureau of Indian Standards, https://bis.gov.in/wp-content/uploads/2018/11/SDOs_information_for_BIS_Website_09-11-18_1704_h-1.pdf (last visited 10 October 2020) [hereinafter *List of SDOs*].
59. *Accreditation Program for standards Development Organisation*, Quality Council of India, available at https://qcin.org/SDOS.

standard-setting, carries a possibility of duplication of standards if there is no well-integrated information system. India has created such an integrated system around greater harmonization of standards along the lines of national (Indian Standards) as well as international standards. The TBT Agreement requires every WTO Member State to designate an 'enquiry point' for all TBT-related issues. Article 10.1 of the TBT Agreement states:

> Each member shall ensure that an enquiry point exists which is able to answer all reasonable enquiries from other members and interested parties in other member countries as well as to provide the relevant documents.

Since the BIS is the national standards body, it has been identified as the enquiry point of all TBT measures/standards notified by other Member States and for notifying India's standards.[60] Whenever a standard is created and enforced, it must be notified to the WTO. In addition to the BIS standards, standards which are formulated by other SDOs are also notified at the WTO. India's TBT notifications (226 as of 2020) and SPS notifications (278 as of 2020) include BIS standards and standards developed by other SDOs. The BIS maintains and updates the list of SDOs it recognizes for formulating standards in India, and this makes communication related to standardization between the BIS and other SDOs convenient. The following section provides an examination of select SDOs and their roles in India's standardization process.

5.5.1 Agricultural and Processed Food Products Export Development Authority (APEDA)

The APEDA was established by the Government of India under the Agricultural and Processed Food Products Export Development Authority Act, 1985. It has been set up as an autonomous body under the Department of Commerce (part of the Ministry of Commerce and Industry). APEDA undertakes the task of export promotion activities and development of 14 agricultural and processed food product groups listed in the Schedule to the APEDA Act.[61] In addition to this, APEDA has been entrusted with the responsibility to monitor the import of sugar as well. The key function areas of APEDA include standards-setting and formulation of specifications for exports, inspection of meat and meat products in processing plants, storage premises, conveyances, organic production and systems.

Since the BIS does not formulate standards under the Agricultural Produce (Grading and Marking) Act, 1937, the standards made under this Act (popularly called AGMARK standards) are referred to by APEDA. Standards of Export Inspection Councils are also referred to by APEDA. APEDA has published and regularly updated the National Programme for Organic Production (NPOP) that lays down standards for

60. More specifically, the 'International Relations & Technical Information Services' Department of the BIS is the designated enquiry point of India for all queries except Telecom Sector. The enquiry point for the Telecom Sector is the Telecommunication Engineering Centre (TEC).
61. *Agricultural and Processed Food Products Export Development Authority*, Department of Commerce, https://commerce.gov.in/about-us/autonomous-bodies/agricultural-and-processed-food-products-export-development-authority-apeda/ (last visited 25 October 2020).

organic production, systems, criteria and procedure for accreditation of certification bodies, the National (India Organic) Logo and the regulations governing its use.[62]

The NPOP formulates standards and procedures keeping into consideration harmonization of national standards with other international standards which regulate trading of organic products.

In another instance of cooperation between different standard-setting organizations, APEDA and the FSSAI have collaborated to develop standards for organic food. The aim behind these standards is to create products of holistic agricultural practices focusing on biodiversity, soil health, chemical-free inputs, etc., with an environmentally and socially responsible approach. Organic food products which comply with these standards are labelled 'organic' and conformity with these standards is conducted through the Food Safety and Standards (Organic Foods) Regulations, 2017, which are based on the NPOP standard and Participatory Guarantee System (PGS-India).

The European Commission and Switzerland have recognized the NPOP standards as equivalent to their national standards for production and accreditation system. Likewise, the NPOP CAPs have been granted equivalence by the United States Department of Agriculture (USDA). Such coordination, recognition and cooperation with these countries eases the burden of certification for Indian exporters of agricultural and food products. With these recognitions, Indian organic products duly certified by the accredited certification bodies of India are accepted by the importing countries. Mutual recognition of equivalent standards is an area of study which presents different facets of the process of international harmonization of standards. Chapter 7 of this Handbook takes a deeper look into the various prospects for such equivalency of standards through mutual recognition agreements.

APEDA also undertakes collection of statistics from the owners of factories or establishments engaged in the production, processing, packaging, marketing or export of the scheduled products and publication of these statistics. This helps in the creation of a system of information readily available to any stakeholder who wishes to access such information. Clean and hygienic processing and storage of food products (especially meat and meat products) is also important to ensure food safety and quality. APEDA ensures this by carrying out inspection of meat and meat products in slaughter-houses, processing plants, storage premises, conveyances or other places where such products are kept or handled for the purpose of ensuring the quality of such products. Inspection of meat processing plants is carried out by a committee of experts. This committee is inter-departmental in nature, and has members from EPC, the FSSAI, Dept. of Animal Husbandry and Dairying, APEDA and the veterinary department of state governments. There is a separate expert committee for red meats, with a similar composition.

---

62. *National Programme for Organic Production*, Agricultural and Processed Food Products Export Development Authority, http://www.apeda.gov.in/apedawebsite/organic/ORGANIC_CONTENTS/National_Programme_for_Organic_Production.htm (last visited 25 October 2020).

5.5.2 Automotive Research Association of India (ARAI)

The ARAI plays a crucial role in assuring that safe, less polluting and more efficient vehicles run on the Indian roads. ARAI is an autonomous body - however, it is affiliated to the Ministry of Heavy Industries and Public Enterprises and is administered by the Department of Heavy Industries. It finds place under this department's allotted business in the Government of India (Allocation of Business) Rules.

The protection of environment and prevention of health risks and diseases are at the heart of ARAI's operations. It provides technical expertise in R&D, testing, certification, homologation and framing of vehicle regulations.[63] ARAI functions in coordination with its members, consumers and the Central Government. It has been granted ISO 9001, ISO 14001, OHSAS 18001 and NABL accreditations.[64] ARAI is recognized by the international certification authorities of Singapore, Netherlands, and Australia for carrying out tests as per their standards and regulations.[65]

The Automotive Industry Standards Committee (AISC) was set up under Central Motor Vehicles Rules –Technical Standing Committee (CMVR - TSC) by Ministry of Road Transport and Highways (formerly Dept. of Road Transport and Highways, MoRT&H) in the year 1997 within ARAI to review safety in the design, construction, operation and maintenance of motor vehicles in India. ARAI also represents India on WP29 - World Forum for Harmonization of Vehicle Regulations under UNECE.

5.5.3 Building Materials and Technology Promotion Council (BMTPC)

The erstwhile Ministry of Urban Development (presently Ministry of Housing and Urban Affairs) had established the Building Materials and Technology Promotion Council (BMTPC) in 1990 to create a nexus between R&D and large scale application of new building material technologies.[66] It is one of the only two entities which have an understanding with the BIS for adoption of its standards as Indian Standards.

BMTPC has worked closely to create Indian Standards on cost effective technologies such as fly-ash bricks, RCC planks and joist, bamboo mat corrugated roofing sheets, etc. The Council prepares and submits draft standards on innovative technologies to the BIS for formulation of Indian Standards. BMTPC is in consultation with the BIS for preparation of two draft standards on Rat Trap Bond in Bricks and Filler Slabs.[67] Through Performance Appraisal Certification Scheme (PACS), the Council is carrying out performance evaluation of new and emerging materials, technologies and construction systems, on which there are no standards available. In the process so far twenty

63. *Certification and Standardization*, Automotive Research Association of India, https://www.araiindia.com/services/certification-and-standardisation (last visited 25 October 2020). [hereinafter *Certification and Standardization*].
64. *List of SDOs*, *supra* note 58, at 25.
65. *Certification and Standardization*, *supra* note 63.
66. *About Us*, Building Materials and Technology Promotion Council, https://bmtpc.org/topics.aspx?type=sub&mid=19 (last visited 25 October 2020).
67. *Building Materials and Construction Technologies*, Materials and Technology Promotion Council, https://bmtpc.org/topics.aspx?mid=43&Mid1=55 (last visited 25 October 2020).

Performance Appraisal Certificates (PACs) have been issued on various innovative systems and products.

5.5.4 Central Drugs Standard Control Organization (CDSCO)

The CDSCO is the Central Drug Authority for discharging functions assigned to the Central Government under the Drugs and Cosmetics Act (DCA). CDSCO has six zonal offices, four sub-zonal offices, thirteen port offices and seven laboratories under its control. It oversees regulatory control over the import of drugs, 'approval of new drugs and clinical trials, meetings of Drugs Consultative Committee (DCC) and Drugs Technical Advisory Board (DTAB), approval of certain licenses as Central License Approving Authority is exercised by the CDSCO headquarters'.[68] CDSCO lays down the standards for Drugs and health care devices or technologies and approve new drugs under the Drugs and Cosmetics Act.

The Ministry of Health and Family Welfare (MHFW), through Gazette notifications, has notified certain medical devices to be considered as drugs under section 3 of DCS.[69] At present, 14 medical device and 8 substances are notified and accordingly the standards of these 14 medical devices are formulated/updated and controlled by CDSCO through the different provisions of the DCA as given below:

(a) GMP Requirements are specified under Schedule M III of the DCA.
(b) Requirements on Labelling of Medical Devices specified in Rule 109-A of the DCA.
(c) Standards for Medical Devices are prescribed in Rule 125-A of the DCA.

CDSCO follows a general structure of adoption of product standards for medical devices. At first, a medical device shall conform to the standards laid down by the BIS or as may be notified by the MHFW, from time to time. Where no relevant standards of any medical device have been laid down by the BIS or MHFW, such devices shall conform to the standards laid down by the International Organization for Standardization (ISO) or the International Electrotechnical Commission (IEC), or by any other pharmacopoeial standards. Last, in case there are no standards specified by the BIS, MHFW or international standards bodies, the device shall conform to the validated manufacturer's standards.[70]

68. *Introduction*, Central Drugs Standard Control Organization, https://cdsco.gov.in/opencms/opencms/en/About-us/Introduction/ (last visited 25 October 2020).
69. *Central Drugs Standards Control Organization*, India Standards Portal, http://indiastandardsportal.org/standardbodiecontent.aspx?StandardBodyId=5 (last visited 25 October 2020).
70. R. 7, Medical Devices Rules, 2017.

5.5.5 Directorate of Marketing and Inspection (DMI)

The Directorate of Marketing and Inspection (DMI) was set up in 1935 to implement the agricultural marketing policies and programmes for integrated development of marketing of agricultural and other allied produce in India.[71] Later, it became an attached office of the Department of Agriculture, Cooperation and Farmers Welfare under Ministry of Agriculture and Farmers Welfare. Safeguarding the interests of farmers and consumers is at the heart of DMI's functions.

DMI undertakes standardization, grading and quality control of agricultural and allied produce. It develops and publishes its 'AGMARK standards' in the form of Grading and Marking Rules of the commodities under the scheme for Promotion of Standardization and Grading of Agricultural and Allied Produce.[72] So far 222 commodities have been formulated and notified under the Agricultural Produce (G&M) Act 1937.[73]

Standard-setting in agricultural and allied produce requires consideration of wide variations in physical and chemical parameters. Standards of agricultural commodities are framed on the basis of scientific evidence.[74] The standards are set on the agricultural commodities which are of national 'priority, necessity and demand'. The physical and chemical parameters to formulate the standard are decided to determine the quality and purity of the commodity. It is worth noting that the samples are analysed after being collected from the growing areas. Analytical data is obtained on statistical analysis on the basis of quality parameters. Since standards harmonization is the constant aim of standardization process, international standard bodies like Codex Alimentarius Commission and ISO are also consulted by the DMI. Once the draft rules are framed and Preliminary Grading and Marking Rules are drafted, these are vetted by the Ministry of Law and Justice, translated into Hindi and published in the Gazette of India.

DMI is also implementing the scheme of certification of agricultural commodities for domestic trade as well as export. It is a voluntary scheme.

5.5.6 Directorate of Standardization (DoS)

DoS determines standards for defence purchases and codification of defence inventories. The DoS was established in 1962 while the Defence Cataloguing Authority was merged with it in 1965. At present, it operates within the Department of Defence Production under the Ministry of Defence. DoS coordinates the standardization

71. *List of SDOs*, *supra* note 58, at 3.
72. *Directorate of Marketing and Inspection (DMI) – AGMARK*, India Standards Portal, http://www.indiastandardsportal.org/standardbodiecontent.aspx?StandardBodyId=7 (last visited 25 October 2020).
73. List of all products is maintained by the DMI and available at https://dmi.gov.in/Documents/listcommodity1937.pdf.
74. Ananta Saikia, *AGMARK Grades and Standards*, 2 (EEI-NER, Working Paper), http://www.eei-ner.org/wp-content/uploads/2019/09/AGMARK-Grades-and-Standards.pdf.

activities in Defence PSUs viz., BEML, BEL, HAL and shipyards, etc.[75] It is the nodal agency for all the Defence Standards. The DoS constantly undertakes harmonization of Defence Standards with the Indian Standards.

DoS has endorsed the INSS published by the Ministry of Commerce and Industry and the SNAP as formulated by the BIS. It defines 'Defence Standardization' as 'a means to provide the use of minimum number of parts to serve the maximum number of purposes consistent with economical manufacture, minimum whole life cost and the quality/reliability necessary to ensure maximum fighting effectiveness'.[76]

The Directorate has adopted two methods of implementing standardization – Entry control and Variety reduction.

'**Entry Control'** through standardization is planned and implemented for preventing variations in items from entering the Defence supply system. It is primarily achieved through 'Codification' and screening of proposals for availability of similar/related standards/specifications. When one service wishes to introduce any item, it shall first refer to the Joint Services Preferred Ranges (JSPR) or Joint Services Specifications (JSS) issued on similar items. Introduction of the items to the service are to be selected from the JSPR of the items so that proliferation of the items is checked. It is always intended to codify the entire current Defence inventory for effective Entry Control.[77]

'**Variety reduction**' is a form of standardization consisting of the reduction of the number of types of products, or materials or parts within a definite range to a lesser number which is adequate to meet prevailing needs at a given time. Variety reduction is a preferred method from a logistical and economic point of view. It is believed that for better war preparedness and fighting fitness, the variety of items purchased, stocked, transported and used by the Defence Services are intended to be less.[78] The Variety Reduction is achieved through preparation of Joint Services Rationalised List (JSRL)[79] for commodities/equipment/assemblies/sub-assemblies/items for Defence Services.

In addition to the above documents, Standardization Sub-Committees also prepare Joint Services Guides (JSG) and Approved Notification (AN) to ensure Standardization of products and processes. The Standardization Committee generally adopts BIS Standards where practicable in preference to making departmental specifications to avoid duplicity and exercise economy of effort. If, it is adopted in full without any modification, an Approval Notification would be issued by the Directorate.

To sum up, the DoS prepares five types of Standardization documents in respect of components, assemblies, sub-assemblies, equipment and other Defence Stores:

75. *About Us*, Directorate of Standardization, https://ddpdos.gov.in/about/about-us (last visited 25 October 2020).
76. *Organization Brief*, Directorate of Standardization, https://ddpdos.gov.in/about/standardisation-profile (last visited 25 October 2020).
77. *Id.*
78. *Id.*
79. Joint Services Rationalized List is a list of existing inventory items, arrived at after elimination of superfluous variety from existing inventory, which is adequate to meet the present requirement of users.

(a) Joint Services Specification (JSS)
(b) Joint Services Preferred Range (JSPR)
(c) Joint Services Rationalised List (JSRL)
(d) Joint Service Guide (JSG)
(e) Approved Notification (AN) for adoption of Indian Standards

These 5 types of standards prepared by the DoS are available for purchase by private vendors, firms and traders on the basis of an RFI (Request-for-Information), RFP (request-for-proposal), a supply order, a development order, or a referral letter from defence organizations or defence related PSUs. Upon submission of the reason for purchase, the standards can be purchased.

Therefore, while primarily for non-commercial use, there do appear to be a wide range of situations, including fairly preliminary stages such as RFIs, in which these standards might prove valuable for private players as well.

5.5.7 Food Safety and Standards Authority of India (FSSAI)

The FSSAI is governed by the Food Safety and Standard Act, 2006. It has been set up to create food standards, grant certification for food safety and controls the food-based hazards like adulteration, presence of the toxic substances. Food Safety Standards are developed/reviewed taking into account the latest developments in food science, food consumption pattern, new products and additives, advancement in the processing technology and food analytical methods, and identification of new risks.[80] The development of standards is undertaken by twenty-one Scientific Panels and a Scientific Committee comprising more than 250 subject independent experts/scientists of eminence. These divisions function under the supervision of the Food Authority which has been entrusted with setting standards, policy making and advising the Central Government on health goals for India. The FSSAI lays down 'science-based standards for articles of food and to regulate their manufacture, storage, distribution, sale and import to ensure availability of safe and wholesome food for human consumption'.[81] There are seven regulations under the Food Safety and Standards Act which deal with quality and safety parameters of various food products:

- Food Safety and Standards (Food Products Standards and Food Additives) Regulations, 2011.
- Food Safety and Standards (Contaminants, Toxins and Residues) Regulations, 2011.
- Food Safety and Standards (Packaging and Labelling) Regulations, 2011.

80. *Food Safety and Standards Authority of India (FSSAI)*, India Standards Portal, http://www.indiastandardsportal.org/standardbodiecontent.aspx?StandardBodyId=10 (last visited 25 October 2020).
81. *About FSSAI*, Food Safety and Standards Authority of India, https://www.fssai.gov.in/cms/about-fssai.php (last visited 25 October 2020).

- Food Safety and Standards (Food or Health Supplements, Nutraceuticals, Foods for Special Dietary Uses, Foods for Special Medical Purpose, Functional Foods and Novel Food) Regulations, 2016.
- Food Safety and Standards (Organic Foods) Regulations, 2017.
- Food Safety and Standards (Alcoholic Beverages) Regulations, 2018.
- Food Safety and Standards (Fortification of Food) Regulation, 2018.

The FSSAI has currently over 500 standards published for food and food products. The FSSAI also prescribes standards for health supplements and nutraceuticals. It has also developed standards for food businesses and processes. The Food Safety Management System (FSMS) has been adopted as a tool for ensuring food safety. FSMS is a systematic approach to controlling food safety hazards within a food business to assure that food is safe to eat. All businesses are expected to put in place, execute and maintain an FSMS based on the principles of 'Hazard Analysis Critical Control Point' (HACCP). HACCP is a management system in which food safety is addressed through the analysis and control of biological, chemical and physical hazards from raw material production, procurement and handling, to manufacturing, distribution and consumption of the finished product. It is a preventive approach to food safety from biological, chemical, physical hazards and more recently radiological hazards in production processes that can cause the finished product to be unsafe and designs measures to reduce these risks to a safe level. HACCP has been recognized internationally as a logical tool for adapting traditional inspection methods to a modern, science-based, food safety system.[82]

Under the Food Safety and Standards (Licensing and registration of Food Businesses), Regulations 2011, while prescribing hygiene and sanitary conditions as a prerequisite to both registration and licensing of Food Business Operators (FBOs), it is also stated that the FBOs are encouraged to go for implementation an HACCP based system. The Regulation states that:

> These are the basic – compulsory requirements for ensuring safety of the food manufactured in ay premise and FBOs shall continuously try to improve the sanitary and hygiene conditions at the premises with a goal of attaining India HACCP standards within a – previously determined period ... .

Codex Alimentarius (Codex) Commission had published a 'Recommended International Code of Practice – General Principles of Food Hygiene'[83] describing the controls recognized internationally as essential for safety and suitability of food. In addition, HACCP is recommended for ensuring enhanced food safety. The Codex General Practice of Food Hygiene (GPFH) is applicable across the food chain. Since the Codex GPFH and HACCP are guidance documents and hence, not amenable to auditing

82. Hazard Analysis Critical Control Point (HACCP) Principles & Application Guidelines, available at https://www.fda.gov/food/hazard-analysis-critical-control-point-haccp/haccp-principles-application-guidelines; *See also* Food and Agricultural Organization, *Hazard Analysis And Critical Control Point (HACCP) System And Guidelines For Its Application*, Annex to CAC/RCP 1-1969, Rev. 3 (1997) available at http://www.fao.org/3/Y1579E/y1579e03.htm.
83. Recommended International Code of Practice – General Principles of Food Hygiene, Codex Alimentarius, CAC/RCP 1-1969, Rev. 4-2003.

or certification, the Quality Council of India (QCI), with multi-stakeholder participation and consultation, has developed an IndiaHACCP Certification Scheme, for enabling third-party verification of compliance by FBOs through voluntary certification initiative.

IndiaHACCP certification, which can be obtained under the Voluntary Certification Scheme for Food Safety operated by Quality Council of India (QCI), is based on international best practices and global standards to ensure internationally acceptable certification. This Scheme is intended to provide assurance that food is suitable for human consumption but also maintain confidence in internationally traded food. The IndiaHACCP Scheme provides Indian FBOs an alternative to foreign certifications and outgo of foreign exchange. Thus, FBOs are encouraged to implement IndiaHACCP in their operations and take certification from certification bodies approved under this Scheme. On compliance with the requisite conditions, the certification can be obtained under the IndiaHACCP Scheme which ensures internationally acceptable certification as the Scheme is based on international best practices and global standards such as DutchHACCP, Codex General Principle of Food Hygiene and ISO 22000:2005.

The FSSAI develops guidance documents, codes of practices, etc., which are used for upgrading the level of food safety implementation by food business, especially in the SME sector across the country. A Risk Assessment Cell develops framework for carrying out risk assessment-based studies. A Scheme of Research and Development/Food Quality and Safety has also been developed by the FSSAI. The FSSAI also houses a Quality Assurance Division (QA Division). The QA Division notifies food laboratories and research institutions accredited by NABL for the purposes of carrying out analysis of samples by the Food Analysts. Notification of food testing laboratories/referral laboratories including recognition, renewal, suspension, de-recognition, etc. is also conducted by the QA Division. As per Chapter VIII, section 43 of the Food Safety and Standards Act, 2006, the FSSAI fosters an ecosystem for testing of food at food laboratories for compliance with the food safety standards.

A Scientific Committee framed under the FSS Act is also engaged in constantly updating the standards either through revision or amendment with the help of 8 Scientific Panels working under it.

The FSSAI has had a central role to play in the development of India's standards ecosystem in the food sector. In addition to being the domestic regulator for the food sector, the FSSAI is also the enquiry point notified by India under the SPS Agreement. In view of its role as a key driver of standard-setting in India, Chapter 8 of this Handbook is dedicated to tracing the history, functions and operations of the FSSAI within India's standards ecosystem.

5.5.8 Ministry of Environment, Forest and Climate Change (MoEFCC)

The MoEFCC is the nodal agency of the Central Government for planning, promotion, coordination and overseeing of implementation of India's environmental and forestry policies and programmes.[84] These policies and programmes are guided by the principle of sustainable development and enhancement of human well-being. MoEFCC creates standards which are formulated to conserve India's natural resources including rivers and lakes, biodiversity, forests and wildlife, ensuring animal welfare, and the prevention and abatement of pollution.[85]

The Central Pollution Control Board (CPCB), established as a statutory organization under the Water Act 1974, acts as a technical support organization for the MoEFCC. Environmental standards of emission and discharge for different industrial activities, ambient air quality and noise standards developed by the CPCB are notified by MoEFCC in the respective rules and regulations framed under the Environmental Protection Act, 1986 (EPA) for mandatory compliance.[86] CPCB is entrusted with the task of development and revision of Environmental Standards. The Board maintains, revises and upgrades the Comprehensive Industrial Document (COINDS) and guidelines for environmental management in various industrial sectors.[87] The CPCB has developed National Standards for Effluents and Emission under the statutory powers of the Water (Prevention and Control of Pollution) Act, 1974 and the Air (Prevention and Control of Pollution) Act, 1981. These standards were approved and notified by the MoEFCC under section 25 of EPA. The environmental standards which have been notified by CPCB include effluent standards (for 37 categories of industries), emission standards (for 31 categories of industries), standards for ambient air quality, ambient noise, automobile and fuels quality specifications for petrol and diesel. Guidelines have also developed separately for hospital waste management.[88] The CPCB has also established and is operating the National Air Monitoring Programme (NAMP) to 'determine the present air quality status and trends and to control and regulate pollution from industries and other source to meet the air quality standards'.[89] The NAMP also provides background air quality data needed for industrial siting and towns planning.

The CPCB creates standards in the following areas:

(a) Air Quality Standards;
(b) Water Quality Standards;
(c) Vehicular Exhaust;

84. *About the Ministry*, Ministry of Environment, Forest and Climate Change, http://moef.gov.in/about-the-ministry/introduction-8/ (last visited 25 October 2020).
85. *List of SDOs, supra* note 58, at 28.
86. *Ministry of Environment, Forest and Climate Change (MoEFCC)*, Ind a Standards Portal http://www.indiastandardsportal.org/standardbodiecontent.aspx?StandardBodyId = 13 (last visited 25 October 2020).
87. *Central Pollution Control Board (CPCB)*, India Standards Portal, http://indiastandardsportal.org/standardbodiecontent.aspx?StandardBodyId = 6 (last visited 26 October 2020).
88. *Environment Standards in India*, EnviroCare Labs, http://envirocare.co.in/environmental-standards-in-india.htm (last visited 26 October 2020).
89. *Central Pollution Control Board (CPCB)*, Ministry of Environment, Forest and Climate Change http://moef.gov.in/about-the-ministry/organisations-institutions/boards/central-pollution-control-board/ (last visited 26 October 2020).

(d) Noise Standards – Noise Limits for Vehicles and Airports and Noise Limits for Generator Sets;
(e) Bio-Medical Incinerators;
(f) Auto Fuel Quality;
(g) Common HW Incinerators;
(h) Generator Set; and
(i) Industry specific standards.

The NAMP has set up a network of operating stations across various cities, towns and villages in India to constantly monitor identified air pollutants such as SO_2 and CO_2, and particulate matter. The aim is to use this data to determine trends in air quality, and to determine if standards of air quality are being followed. These standards are the National Ambient Air Quality Standards (NAAQS), notified by CPCB under the Air (Prevention and Control of Pollution Act, 1981. These standards focus on prescribing air quality levels that are required for protection of health, and to provide 'a uniform yardstick' for assessment of air quality across the country.[90] These are in addition to air pollution reduction measures such as the prescription of advanced vehicle emission and fuel quality standards such as Bharat Stage-VI (BS-VI). BS-VI refers to Indian standards for petrol and diesel, released by the BIS.[91]

CPCB also prepares manuals, codes and guidelines relating to treatment and disposal of sewage and trade effluents as well as for stack gas cleaning devices, stacks and ducts. CPCB lays down standards for stream or well in consultation with the State Governments, and also lays down standards for the quality of air.

Some examples of the key standards prepared by CPCB are:

(a) National Ambient Air Quality Standards (NAAQ);
(b) Water Quality Criteria;
(c) Standards for Emission or Discharge of Environmental Pollutants from various industries (Industry specific standards);
(d) Standards for Treatment and Disposal of Bio-Medical Waste by Incineration;
(e) Emission Standards and Noise Limits for Diesel Engines; and
(f) Emission and Noise Limit of LPG and CNG Generator Sets.

CPCB also formulates the Minimal National Standards (MINAS) for various categories of industries with regards to their effluent discharge (water pollutants), emissions (air pollutants), noise levels and solid waste.[92] The majority of MINAS were published under the Environment (Protection) Rules of 1986, while some were developed or revised thereafter. In addition to having developed a MINAS for the textiles sector, CPCB has also issued a regulation aiming for facilities to attain a zero

90. *National Clean Air Programme Report*, Ministry of Environment, Forest and Climate Change, 10, 11, (2019) http://moef.gov.in/wp-content/uploads/2019/05/NCAP_Report.pdf.
91. *See* Indian Standards on Petrol (IS 2796) and Diesel (IS 1460); *Sale of BS-VI Norm Vehicles*, PIB, (9 December 2019, 2:25 P.M), https://pib.gov.in/Pressreleaseshare.aspx?PRID=1595507.
92. *Charter on Corporate Responsibility for Environmental Protection*, Central Pollution Control Board, https://cpcb.nic.in/crep/ (last visited 11 September 2021).

liquid discharge target, i.e., that no effluents are discharged into environment by the industries.[93] The driving force behind the development of a new MINAS or the revision of an existing one can be the availability of new technologies for improvement in prevention, control, and abatement of pollution. The public pressure generated by civil society organizations or NGOs also plays an important role in raising environmental issues which could be addressed by revised or new MINAS. The CPCB and MoEFCC work together to create MINAS standards where the former provides expertise and recommendations and the latter reviews the work done by CPCB before notifying these standards. These standards are required to be adopted by State Governments and Union Territory administrations as minimal standards.

5.5.9 Oil Industry Safety Directorate (OISD)

OISD is a technical directorate under the Ministry of Petroleum and Natural Gas. It 'formulates and coordinates the implementation of a series of self-regulatory measures aimed at enhancing the safety in the oil and gas industry in India'.[94] Standardization is one of its major activities. OISD observes and monitors the latest design and operating practices in the areas of safety and fire fighting in the hydrocarbon processing industry in the developed countries.[95] This is done so as to develop standards and codes that would be suitable for the conditions prevailing in India. These OISD standards are periodically reviewed to incorporate the latest technological developments and experiences gained in their implementation to keep them in line with the current international practices.

All the activities related to standardization such as framing of new OISD standards, revision or amendment of existing OISD standards are carried out as per the requirement of the industry members. Such requirements are duly recorded in the meetings of the steering committee of the OISD, which are held at least once in a year. Alternatively, OISD may also take up revision/amendment/reaffirmation with the approval of Executive Director, OISD.

The OISD had released a document titled 'Guidelines for Preparation of OISD Standards' which directs and provides instructions for preparation of technical safety standards as well as procedure for updating the standards. The process of standard-setting under these guidelines starts with identification of topics for standardization and through a process of consultation with members of a Functional Committee and panellists, and review of public comments, OISD standards are printed by the Safety Council of OISD following the approval by the Steering Committee.

93. OECD, *India: Procedures to develop comprehensive industry documents and national emission standards, in Report on Best Available Techniques for Preventing and Controlling Industrial Pollution: Activity 2 – Approaches to Establishing BAT Around the World*, 74, 76 (2018).
94. *List of SDOs, supra* note 58, at 6.
95. *About Us*, Oil Industry Safety Directorate, https://www.oisd.gov.in/about-us (last visited 26 October 2020).

5.5.10 Petroleum and Explosives Safety Organization (PESO)

PESO is a statutory authority, entrusted with the responsibilities under Explosives Act, 1884; Petroleum Act, 1934; Inflammable Substances Act, 1952, Environment (Protection Act), 1986 and the rules framed under these Acts.[96] PESO is under the auspices of the Department for Promotion of Industry and Internal Trade. Presently, PESO is dealing with the administration of the rules under Explosive Act, 1884 and Petroleum Act, 1934 as mentioned in Table 5.8.[97]

Table 5.8 Rules under Explosives Act, 1884 and Petroleum Act, 1934

Rules under Explosives Act, 1884	Rules under Petroleum Act, 1934
Explosives Rules, 2008	Petroleum Rules, 2002
Gas Cylinders Rules, 2016	Calcium Carbide Rules, 1987
Static & Mobile Pressure Vessels (Unfired) Rules 1981	Cinematographic Film Rules, 1948
Ammonium Nitrate Rules, 2012. Notification No. GSR 625 (E) dated 07.08.1983 regarding Acetylene	Inflammable Substance Act, 1952
Notification No. GSR 625 (E) dated 07.08.1983 regarding Acetylene	

Source: *Objectives PESO*, Petroleum and Explosives Safety Organization, https://peso.gov.in/web/objective

PESO lays down the technical standards and specifications including safety standards in activities related to explosives, petroleum and petroleum products, pipelines, gases, gas cylinders, safety fittings, special electric equipment that have been specified in relevant section of various rules framed under the Explosives Act, 1884 and Petroleum Act, 1934.[98]

Since the Indian Standards formulated by the BIS and the standards developed by OISD cover the products under its scope, PESO takes a leading role in their formulation and revision. These standards are related to manufacture, refining, processing, storage, transportation, handling, testing and quality specification of explosives, petroleum, flammable and non-flammable compressed gases and other hazardous substances and referred various Indian Standards it its regulations making them mandatory.[99] PESO also undertakes the grant of approval, licences for manufacture, authorization, storage,

96. *Annual Report 2017-2018*, Petroleum and Explosives Safety Organization 5 (2018) http://www.peso.gov.in/web/sites/default/files/2019-12/AR2017_18.pdf.
97. *Objectives PESO*, Petroleum and Explosives Safety Organization, https://peso.gov.in/web/objective (last visited 27 October 2020).
98. *Petroleum and Explosives Safety Organization (PESO)*, India Standards Portal http://www.indiastandardsportal.org/standardbodiecontent.aspx?StandardBodyId=17 (last visited 26 October 2020).
99. *Id.*

import/export, transport by road and packaging for explosives, petroleum, calcium carbide, gas cylinders, pressure vessels and other hazardous substances.

5.5.11 Telecommunication Engineering Centre (TEC)

TEC is a technical body under the Department of Telecommunications of the Ministry of Communications. It is the WTO-TBT Enquiry Point for India in the Telecommunication Sector. TEC develops standards and specifications for modern technologies in telecommunication and related ICT systems to be deployed in India. Specifications which are published by TEC are categorized into three types – Generic Requirements (GRs), Interface Requirements (IRs) and Service Requirements (SR). The Centre promotes development and upgradation of ubiquitous, resilient and state-of-the-art quality infrastructure by testing and certification.[100] At the end of 2020, a total of 624 Technical Specifications have been formulated that includes 523 on GRs, 65 on IRs, 13 on SRs, and 23 Standards.[101] TEC has also been associated with international standardization bodies like International Telecommunications Union (ITU) in respect of developing global standards. National Working Groups in TEC corresponding to various study Groups of ITU contribute to global standards-making process.

TEC has been entrusted with the power to implement the standard-adoption process with the help of an institutional framework consisting of Telecom Standards Advisory Committee (TSCA), Consultative Committee(s)(CC) and task force(s) setup for the purpose. The standard adopted by TEC is regarded as the National Standard in India. In this regard, a Standardization Guide was formulated for ratification or adoption of TSDSI/International Telecom Standards.[102]

The **Standardization Guide** has underlined the standards ratification/adoption process as follows:

(a) *Proposal*: On receipt of a proposal for ratification/adoption in TEC, the same is examined to see whether the standard proposed for adoption is duly approved by General Body/governing body of Telecommunications Standards Development Society (TSDSI) or Telecom Standards Development Organization (TSDO) concerned and whether the national requirements have been represented or taken care of during standardization or transposition.

(b) *Telecommunication Standards Advisory Committee (TSAC)*: The proposal is then put up to TSAC for examination whether the standard can be adopted as national standard.

100. *Quality Policy and Objectives*, Telecommunications Engineering Centre, https://www.tec.gov.in/quality-policy-and-objectives/ (last visited 27 October 2020).

101. *Telecommunications Engineering Centre (TEC)*, India Standards Portal, http://www.indiastandardsportal.org/standardbodiecontent.aspx?StandardBodyId = 22 (last visited 27 October 2020).

102. Telecom Engineering Centre. *Standardization Guide: Adoption of TSDSI/International Telecom Standards*, Version 1.0.0 (2019) https://www.tec.gov.in/pdf/PMI/Final%20Standardization%20Guide.pdf.

(c) *Draft TEC standard*: Proposed standard once agreed for adoption as national standard, becomes draft TEC standard for circulation.
(d) *Circulation of draft*: The draft standard is thereafter circulated electronically for inviting public comments.
(e) *Public comments*: The draft standard is normally available for public comments irrespective of its national or international origin. Further, only technical content or the amendments affecting the technical content of standard are open for public comments.
(f) *Rejection of proposal*: If the proposal is not agreed/approved for adoption as national standards, TSDSI or the source of the proposal may be intimated accordingly.
(g) *Resolution of comments*: The comments are compiled and reviewed. If no comments other than the editorials are received, the draft shall be recommended for 'identical adoption' after making editorial changes. If comments or deviations related to incorporation of national requirements/ parameters/levels are received, the standard is modified accordingly in a manner consistent with 'ISO/IEC guide 21' and submitted for approval as 'modified adoption'. Process of seeking comments and discussion are repeated to resolve all the issues.
(h) *Finalization of draft*: After completion of the process, the draft is finalized by the Consultative Committee and submitted for approval.
(i) *Notification*: Whether the proposal is approved for adoption or not, information on the decision is notified and in case of any discrepancy in comments, procedure is followed for the same.

It is important to note that it is the TSDSI which either develops its own standards or transposes International Standards to India. However, for these standards to apply nationally in India, they must be formally adopted by the TEC.

As we can see, SDOs prepare standards in their specific areas or sectors. However, SDOs cannot claim their standards to be Indian standards. Only the BIS is empowered to set Indian standards. As highlighted above, standards set by SDOs attain national implementation once the BIS recognizes standards set by these SDOs as Indian Standards. So far, only two of these bodies - the Building Materials and Technology Promotion Council (BMTPC), and the Automotive Research Association of India (ARAI) - have an understanding with the BIS to get their standards adopted as Indian Standards.[103]

5.6 CONCLUSION

The current regulatory regime for standardization in India is the culmination of several decades of phased development of law-making. Since the establishment of the ISI in

103. *Overview of India's Quality Infrastructure, supra* note 5, at 23.

1947, the approach to standard-setting and the processes and entities involved in standard-setting have undergone significant changes.

Today, at the helm of this regulatory landscape sits the BIS which is the apex national standardization body in India. It creates and enforces standards across several sectors and classes of products and is responsible for handing the official designation of 'Indian standards'. The BIS's work is complemented by the SDOs which operate in specific sectors. SDOs are important actors in the standard-setting process in India and contribute to the development of modern technology, science, research and development, and technical expertise. SDOs may be statutory bodies such as the FSSAI and CDSO, or in other cases, ministries such as MoEFCC. The process of standard-setting in the BIS as well as SDOs involves extensive stakeholder consultations. The development of a standard in a specific sector may be initiated either by a stakeholder, a regulator, any interested party or the SDOs. Technical and expert committees within the SDOs work on such proposals to develop standards for use. Depending on the mandate and scope of powers of the SDO, such standards are then published and adopted for use in the sector either mandatorily or on a best practices basis. For national application and for recognition as an Indian Standard, a proposal may be submitted to the BIS. BIS's technical divisions will evaluate these standards and accordingly adopt them as 'Indian standards'. While standards may generally be published and notified by an SDO or the BIS in any such manner as prescribed in their governing laws, mandatory standards must be notified in the Gazette of India to acquire the legal force necessary to ensure their mandatory application. This is done through quality control orders or rules and regulations under parent statutes. The BIS consolidates mandatory standards under one of its four compulsory registration schemes.

The complexity of legislation, processes and interaction among these bodies has led the Government of India to push for a drive to harmonize and house standard-setting under a single umbrella framework. The government released the INSS in 2018 to 'provide direction for India's political and executive leadership on how best to use standardization, technical regulations, quality infrastructure and related activities to advance the interests and well-being of Indians in a global economy.' The INSS enlists the aims, roles and functions of a robust quality ecosystem by providing strategies to be considered in the standardization process. The strategies, aims and priorities formulated under the INSS have been widely accepted as guidelines for standard-setting process by the BIS as well as the SDOs. The INSS brings all the stakeholders, their experiences, their legislations/rules/regulations under a single guiding document to find uncomplicated pathways through the complex regulatory network of standardization in India.

The BIS was prompt to release its own action plan under the guidance provided by the INSS. The SNAP released in 2019 seeks to ensure synergy of the standardization activities taking place in India. A key issue identified in the INSS is the gap in the product coverage of the existing regulatory framework on standards in India. Though there has been a push in favour of standardization and harmonization of India's standards with international standards, the BIS has acknowledged the further need to enforce standards on priority products which are critical for India's domestic industry and public health and safety. In this regard, the SNAP details certain actions and measures which are intended to be adopted by the BIS to meet its targets under the Action Plan. Through SNAP, the BIS lays out a systematic path which it aims to cover, giving a clear and extensive picture of its standardization process in the future. This provides a much-needed understanding and clarity to the businesses in India about the BIS's standard-setting process and the relevant divisions of the Bureau which have specified functions in the standardization process.

This chapter is intended to provide an overview of the landscape of standard-setting in India. The subsequent chapters provide a comprehensive account of the individual aspects of standard-setting and implementation in India.

CHAPTER 6

Conformity Assessment Practices and Procedures

Smrithi Bhaskar & Apoorva Singh Vishnoi

Conformity assessment procedures (CAPs) are used to ensure compliance with set standards and technical regulations. CAPs include within their umbrella a wide range of activities, ranging from testing to inspections, and self-certification, that are selected on the basis of the products or services involved, as well as the risk non-compliance with the standard will pose. CAPs are administered nationally by a variety of governmental and non-governmental agencies, forming a complex ecosystem for ensuring that products and services meet requisite standards. This chapter provides an overview of the various types of CAPs, as well as an introduction to the law governing them at the World Trade Organization (WTO). The chapter also discusses in detail the various bodies, global, as well as in India, that manage and administer CAPs. Understanding the function and disciplinary structure of CAPs at the international level provides the necessary context for them at the Indian level. In examining the use of CAPs in India, the chapter details how the Bureau of Indian Standards (BIS) and Quality Council of India (QCI) serve as focal points for certification and accreditation respectively. The bodies in charge of CAPs in India have a complex but interrelated structure and this is reflected in the processes they are in charge of. This chapter presents an overview of these bodies and their working. Through this, the chapter ensures a clear understanding of what CAPs are, their role in international trade, and their application in India.

6.1 INTRODUCTION TO CONFORMITY ASSESSMENT PROCEDURES

Any quality assurance infrastructure comprises standards, technical regulations (TRs), and conformity assessment procedures (CAPs). The development and use of standards and technical regulations have been covered in detail in previous chapters.[1] Standards and TRs are indispensable in ensuring consumer protection, improving competition, enhancing public welfare and so on. However, the use of TRs and standards is insufficient to meet these goals. Once standards and TRs are developed, procedures need to be put in place to ensure compliance, in order for them to have their intended effect. CAPs refer to these processes that demonstrate that a product, service or system meets the conditions prescribed in a standard or a TR.[2] CAPs are crucial for all stakeholders. They help regulators ensure that carefully crafted standards and TRs are actually effective and help consumers have trust in the safety and utility of products. Well-crafted CAPs are also crucial for trade since cumbersome CAPs may be expensive and time-consuming for manufacturers and exporters. CAPs that are not effectively administered may hinder market-access commitments.[3] Therefore, CAPs form a crucial step in the standards ecosystem.

Conformity assessment is a broad term that covers a wide variety of processes. It may refer to mandatory or voluntary practices, carried out by manufacturers, importers, independent third parties or regulators.[4] There may also be a wide variety of processes used to determine conformity, such as testing, inspection, certification, evaluation, verification and accreditation.[5] Generally, anybody that performs a CAP is a conformity assessment body (CAB). Goods, processes and services may all be subject to CAPs. In effect, anything that has a standard or a TR may have a corresponding CAP.

CABs may be accredited by accreditation bodies. Accreditation refers to an attestation or the formal recognition of the ability of a body to carry out specific conformity assessment tasks.[6] This formal recognition of competency is based on standards that are specified for particular kinds of CABs and is provided only by specific accreditation bodies.[7] In effect, accreditation is a kind of CAP, but is done in the limited context of recognising a CAB. The difference between a CAP and accreditation is illustrated in Table 6.1.

1. *See* Chapters 1 and 5, *supra.*
2. *Certification & Conformity,* International Organisation for Standardization, https://www.iso.org/conformity-assessment.html.
3. Panel Report on *Russia – Measures Affecting the Importation of Railway Equipment and Parts Thereof* (hereinafter 'Russia – Railway Equipment'), WT/DS499/R, adopted 5 March 2020, para. 7.374.
4. *U.S Conformity Assessment System: Introduction,* American National Standards Institute, https://www.standardsportal.org/usa_en/conformity_assessment/introduction.aspx#: ~ :text=Conformity%20assessment%20is%20a%20term,identified%20in%20a%20specified%20standard.
5. *See* Agreement on the Technical Barriers to Trade (Marrakesh, Morocco, 15 April 1994), Marrakesh Agreement Establishing the World Trade Organization, Annex 1A, The Legal Texts: The Results of the Uruguay Round of Multilateral Trade Negotiations 121 (1999), 1868 U.N.T.S. 120 [hereinafter TBT Agreement], para. 3, Annex 1.
6. *What is Accreditation?, Frequently Asked Questions,* National Accreditation Board for Testing and Calibration Laboratories, https://nabl-india.org/faq/#4.
7. *See ISO/IEC 17025: Testing and Calibration Laboratories,* International Organization for Standardization, https://www.iso.org/ISO-IEC-17025-testing-and-calibration-laboratories.html.

Table 6.1 Difference between CAP and Accreditation

Conformity Assessment Procedure	*Accreditation*
- Process to determine whether requirements prescribed in standards and technical regulations have been complied with - Carried out by CAB	- Attestation of the competence of a CAB to carry out a CAP - Provided by accreditation bodies based on standards

Source: Author's representation

The application of CAPs and their chronology may be best understood with an example, as detailed in Box 6.1.

Box 6.1: Chronology of CAPs

Taking for instance electronic goods such as laptops, tablets or notebooks, the process of development of a TR or standard, until the application of the CAP, may be understood.

1. Development of TR or Standard: The Bureau of Indian Standards (BIS) develops and adopts, IS 13252:2010 that inter alia covers laptops, notebooks and tablets.

2. Selection of a CAP: The Ministry of Electronics and Information Technology notifies the Electronics and Information Technology Goods (Requirement for Compulsory Registration) Order, 2012, stating that laptops, notebooks and tablets must conform to the IS. Manufacturers are required to apply for BIS registration, after getting their products tested in BIS recognised labs.

3. Accreditation of requisite CABs: The CABs, being the recognised labs, must be accredited to the Laboratory Quality Management System (IS 17025). One such accreditation body is the National Accreditation Board for Testing and Calibration of Laboratories (NABL). Following this accreditation, the labs must be recognised by BIS.

4. Conformity assessment by accredited CAB: Manufacturers must obtain requisite test reports from accredited labs, and submit them to BIS for registration.

5. Certification/Declaration of Conformity Assessment: Once registered with the BIS, the manufacturers may self-declare that the products are in conformity with IS 13252:2010.

6. Goods may then be placed on the market.

6.1.1 Types of Conformity Assessment Procedures (CAPs) and Conformity Assessment Bodies (CABs)

6.1.1.1 Types of CAPs

CAPs generally include any procedure or process prescribed to determine the conformity with any standard or TR. Certain common types of CAPs may be found in Table 6.2. Each type of CAP has its own benefits and disadvantages based on the level of risk of the particular product or sector, level of compliance that can be secured, the risk and costs of non-compliance and so on.[8] It must be noted that CAPs are usually developed as a mix of procedures, based on the TR or standard. For instance, a CAP may require inspection of production plants as well as testing of products and materials used in processing, prior to being granted a certificate of conformity. Therefore, the classifications used in Table 6.2 are not to be read as exclusionary, but as explanatory.

Table 6.2 Classification of CAPs

Based on Assessor[9]	*Based on Procedures*
First-Party Assessment Unilateral declaration or self-declaration by a supplier. This is also known as Supplier's Declaration of Conformity. This has a low level of trustworthiness.	**Certification** Written document from a CAB that states that the product, process or system meets the relevant standard or TR.
Second-Party Assessment Assessment by importer/purchaser or on the insistence of importer/purchaser. Thus, has a mid-level of trustworthiness.	**Testing** Any process used to determine the characteristics of a product, to see if the characteristics prescribed in the standard or TR are satisfied.
Third-Party Assessment Assessment by institution independent from supplier and purchaser, either voluntarily or mandatorily. This has a high level of trustworthiness, and is suitable for high-risk products and sectors.	**Inspection** The checking of products to ensure they satisfy prescribed criteria. In India, inspection is done by Inspection Bodies (IBs)

8. For a detailed discussion on weighing different CAPs, *see Preparation of the Fourth Triennial Review: Conformity Assessment Procedures, Background Note by the Secretariat,* JOB(05)/XX (26 October 2005).
9. *Types of Conformity Assessment,* IEC, https://www.iec.ch/conformity-assessment/types-conformity-assessment.

Based on Assessor[9]	Based on Procedures
	Accreditation Attestation that a CAB meets the requisite standards to carry out CAPs such as testing.

Source: Author's representation

6.1.1.1.1 Certification

Certification refers to a written assurance (known as a certificate of conformity) that the products in question meet the standards or TRs. This certification has to be provided by an independent third party and, therefore, is a kind of third-party conformity assessment.[10] Self-certification or Supplier's Declaration of Conformity refers to a written declaration of a supplier stating that the products meet the requisite standards. This may be with the involvement of a third-party or a regulator. For instance, regulatory authorities may require that the supplier obtain a mark in order to market their products or involve third parties prior to making a self-declaration.

6.1.1.1.2 Testing

Testing refers to the determination of the characteristics of a product and is usually performed by laboratories. There are various kinds of testing, with specific laboratories for each kind of test, for instance, medical laboratories (such as pathology, molecular testing, medical imaging, etc.) and calibration laboratories (mechanical, thermal, radiological, etc.). Taking the example of auto emission standards, testing would require a laboratory to conduct tests to calculate the amount of emissions emitted by a vehicle in different conditions (such as when the vehicle is idling, or when it starts) and compare it to permissible emission amounts listed in the standard or TR. The protocol for testing (such as the requirements of the test area, how a test vehicle is to be selected, etc.) will be provided in the standard.[11]

6.1.1.1.3 Inspection

Inspection refers to the examination of a product, process or service, to determine its conformity with specific requirements or, on the basis of professional judgement, with

10. International Organisation for Standardization, *supra* note 2.
11. Automotive Industry Standard: Test Method, Testing Equipment and Related Procedures for Type Approval and Conformity of Production Testing of LS Category Vehicles for Bharat Stage VI Emission Norms as per CMV Rules 115, 116 and 126, AIS0137 (Part2), Central Motor Vehicles Rules - Technical Standards Committee, Ministry of Road Transport and Highways.

general requirements.[12] Inspection may include inspection of personnel, facilities, the technology used, and methodology by an independent and impartial third-party (i.e., an Inspection Body). Inspection is done so as to compare existing characteristics of the product, or service, against the requirements in the standard or TR. The inspections may be carried out by a third party, or by a governmental agency depending on the nature of the standard. The costs are usually borne by the manufacturer or the supplier/importer.

6.1.1.2 Types of CABs

Since the nature and type of CAPs are wide-ranging, the bodies that may perform them are equally diverse. CABs may be government-owned or private, national standardisation bodies, industry bodies, consumer organisations, companies or firms.[13] They may be limited to particular sectors or to certain types of tests or procedures alone. Largely, CABs are divided into laboratories (testing, calibration, medical), proficiency testing producers, reference material producers, and systems certifiers. In India, a list of all accredited CABs is maintained by the National Accreditation Board for Testing and Calibration Laboratories and is discussed in detail below.

6.2 WTO DISCIPLINES

6.2.1 CAPs in International Trade

In order to effectively implement TRs and standards, CAPs are crucial, and therefore, play an important role in international trade. Described as a 'passport to trade',[14] CAPs ensure that foreign regulators and foreign customers are confident that imported products meet their TRs and standards. International, harmonised and simple CAPs ensure ease of international trade. However, the converse is also true, wherein complex CAPs with duplication of tests and certification requirements increase costs for suppliers and may significantly hamper market-access commitments. When complex CAPs that differ across jurisdictions exist, exporters either have to bear the costs of multiple certification requirements (which may include payments made to multiple testing laboratories to carry out the same tests, or multiple inspection bodies that may inspect the same aspects of the goods), or use the services of multinational certification

12. *For instance, see* QCI Scheme for Approval of Inspection Bodies for Infrastructure Projects, Quality Council of India,https://qcin.org/documents/Infrastructure_Projects/documents.php, para. A.2.2.; *see also* para. 3.1, *ISO/IEC 17020:2012 Conformity Assessment – Requirements for the Operation of Various Types of Bodies Performing Inspection*, International Organization for Standardization, https://www.iso.org/obp/ui/#iso:std:iso-iec:17020:ed-2:v1:en.
13. *What Types of CABs can Seek Accreditation? Frequently Asked Questions*, National Accreditation Board for Testing and Calibration Laboratories, https://nabl-india.org/faq/#9.
14. *Passport to Trade*, International Organization for Standardization, https://www.iso.org/news/ref2429.html.

companies, which may prove to be expensive.[15] This may serve as a trade barrier or even exclude certain firms from the market entirely. Therefore, it has consistently been a goal of WTO Members to remove duplicity in CAPs worldwide and have transparent information exchange regarding CAPs.[16]

The importance of CAPs to world trade is also underscored by its inclusion in both the Agreement on Technical Barriers to Trade and the Agreement on Sanitary and Phytosanitary Measures. Both these agreements include obligations that the Member States must comply with when introducing CAPs, prescribing *inter alia*, non-discrimination, transparency and harmonisation.

6.2.2 TBT Agreement

The Agreement on Technical Barriers to Trade (hereinafter the 'TBT Agreement') covers technical regulations and standards, as well as CAPs. As is the norm for definitions under the TBT Agreement, the definition of CAPs is found in Annex I of the Agreement.

CAPs are a specific category of technical barriers to trade recognised and governed by the TBT Agreement, following standards and technical regulations. A CAP is the step following the adoption of a standard or technical regulation.

Recital 3 of the TBT Agreement's Preamble recognises the importance of international standards and CAPs in improving the efficiency of production and facilitating the conduct of international trade.[17] Recital 4 states that Members desire to encourage the development of these systems. International standards and CAPs are seen within the WTO framework as 'vehicles of integration.' As has been noted, the TBT Agreement places a strong emphasis on harmonisation of standards, with integration and cooperation of WTO Members. International standards are seen as the best way to achieve this harmonisation, though it is not mandated under the TBT Agreement.[18]

It is important to note the differences in the aims of TRs and standards on the one hand and CAPs on the other. TRs and standards may have various legitimate objectives, whereas, CAPs have the singular objective of ensuring compliance with TRs or standards, to ensure confidence that the products conform.[19]

6.2.2.1 Definition of CAPs in the TBT Agreement

As per the definition in Annex 1.3, a CAP is any procedure used to determine that a TR or standard is fulfilled. This must be read broadly and, as per the explanatory note,

15. *First Triennial Review of the Operation and Implementation of the TBT Agreement, Mexico*, G/TBT/W/50 (5 August 1997), para. 21.
16. *First Triennial Review of the Operation and Implementation of the Agreement on Technical Barriers to Trade*, G/TBT/5 (19 November 1997), para. 13.
17. TBT Agreement, Recital. 3, Preamble.
18. TBT Agreement, Articles 2.4 and 9.
19. *Russia – Railway Equipment*, WT/DS499/AB/R, fn. 337.

includes a wide range of procedures, such as sampling, testing, inspection and verification. The definition is reproduced in Box 6.2.

Box 6.2: Conformity assessment procedures[20]

Any procedure used, directly or indirectly, to determine that relevant requirements in technical regulations or standards are fulfilled.

Explanatory note

Conformity assessment procedures include, *inter alia*, procedures for sampling, testing and inspection; evaluation, verification and assurance of conformity; registration, accreditation and approval as well as their combinations.

Given that the definition of CAPs in the Agreement is so broad, there has been some confusion regarding its overlap with TRs or standards. This question arose before the panel in the case of *EC – Trademarks and Geographical Indications* where it was examined whether inspection structures read together with product specifications, can form a TR within the definition of the TBT Agreement. The Panel found that since the definition of CAP referred to the *assessment of conformity* with TRs and standards, necessarily, CAPs and TRs would have to be understood to be distinct from each other and mutually exclusive.[21] While they may both be part of the same measure, a measure may not simultaneously be a TR and a CAP. The Panel categorically stated that 'procedures for inspection' are not technical regulations. This provides some clarity when reading government regulations, as often a measure may include a TR and a CAP within the same document. In such an instance, it is essential to differentiate the prescribed product characteristics from the procedures for inspection that are prescribed, so as to ensure adequate compliance.

6.2.2.2 *Substantive Provisions of the TBT Agreement*

One-third of the articles in the TBT Agreement exclusively deal with obligations of Member States with respect to CAPs.[22] The TBT Agreement is comprehensive and covers CAPs by central government bodies, local government bodies and non-governmental bodies, as well as international and regional systems. While a Member's obligations differ slightly for each of these bodies and systems, the core principles of the TBT Agreement as applied to CAPs remain the same and can be found in Articles 5 and 6. Figure 6.1 furnishes an overview of Articles 5, 6, 7, 8 and 9 of the TBT Agreement.

20. TBT Agreement, Annex 1, para. 3.
21. Panel Report on *European Communities – Protection of Trademarks and Geographical Indications for Agricultural Products and Foodstuffs* (hereinafter '*EC – Trademarks and Geographical Indications*'), WT/DS290/R, adopted 20 April 2005, para. 7.512.
22. TBT Agreement, Arts. 5-9.

Figure 6.1 Overview of TBT Provisions on CAPS

Articles 5 and 6

- TBT disciplines related to Central Government Bodies
- Provides for non-discrimination and prevention of unnecessary obstacles to trade
- Harmonisation and transparency
- Technical assistance
- Recognition of CAPs of other Member States

Article 7

- TBT Disciplines related to local government bodies
- Provisions of Articles 5 and 6 apply to local government bodies as well
- Members are not to take measures which require or encourage local government bodies to act in a manner inconsistent with Articles 5 and 6

Article 8

- TBT Disciplines related to non-governmental bodies within Member's territories
- Members are to take reasonable measures to ensure that non-governmental bodies comply with Articles 5 and 6
- Central Government Bodies may only rely on CAPs operated by non-governmental bodies if they comply with Articles 5 and 6

Article 9

- International and regional systems for CAPs, in which bodies within Member's territories are members or participants
- Where possible, Members must formulate and adopt international systems for CAPs
- Members to take reasonable measures to ensure that international and regional systems for CAPs are in compliance with Articles 5 and 6, when bodies in their territories are Members

Source: Author's representation from Articles 5-9, TBT Agreement.

6.2.2.2.1 Non-discrimination

Non-discrimination principles, i.e., the most-favoured-nation (MFN) and national treatment (NT) principles,[23] are the core principles of the WTO Agreements.[24] They are present in the TBT Agreement as well and are applied to mandatory CAPs by virtue of Article 5.1. Article 5.1.1 provides for non-discrimination of access and states that CAPs must be prepared, adopted and applied so as to grant **no less favourable access** to CAPs for suppliers of like products.

While the principles of MFN and NT are found in most WTO Agreements, there has been some confusion as to the phrase 'no less favourable access'. This article does not relate to the treatment of imported products, and focuses rather only on suppliers and the conditions of their access to a CAP.[25] This was decided in a recent, and only, dispute to consider Article 5.1.1., *Russia – Railway Equipment*. Box 6.3 sheds further light on the case.

Box 6.3: Russia – Measures Affecting the Importation of Railway Equipment and Parts Thereof

In 2015, Ukraine challenged three Russian measures related to CAPs for railway products such as railroad switches and rolling stock. The three measures were: *first*, the suspension of conformity certificates given by the Russian certification

23. Most-Favoured Nation principle refers to the obligation for states to treat all WTO Member countries similarly, and to not provide less favourable treatment in like circumstances to imports from any one Member country. National Treatment refers to the obligation of a Member to provide the same treatment to imports as it does to its domestically produced products.
24. Appellate Body Report on *European Communities – Conditions for the Granting of Tariff Preferences to Developing Countries* (hereinafter '*EC – Tariff Preferences*'), WT/DS246/AB/R, adopted 20 September 2004, para. 101.
25. *Russia – Railway* Equipment, WT/DS499/R, para. 7.260; *see also*, *Russia – Railway* Equipment, WT/DS499/AB/RABR, para. 5.122, which draws a contrast between the non-discrimination obligations under other WTO Agreements, and under Article 5.1.1.

body to Ukrainian railway products due to the impossibility of conducting required yearly inspections of Ukrainian suppliers; *second*, rejection of applications for new certificates; and *third*, the non-recognition of conformity certifications issued by other Customs Union (CU) countries for railway equipment produced in a non-CU country. Ukraine also alleged systematic prevention of Ukrainian railway products imports into Russia by way of the above three measures.

Russia had a mandatory certification system for conformity with operational safety, labour safety, environmental safety, etc. This included certification (including testing of samples and inspection of production sites) as well as inspection post-certification. Annual inspections were mandatory. Ukrainian supplier's certificates were suspended, as Russia stated that the security risks in Ukraine made it impossible to carry out on-site inspections. Ukraine alleged that Ukrainian suppliers had access to Russian CAPs in less favourable conditions, compared to Russian and other European suppliers.

The Panel found that there was less favourable treatment provided to Ukrainian suppliers. However, the Panel concluded that the security situation in Ukraine made it such that it was not comparable to suppliers from other countries and, therefore, Ukrainian suppliers were denied no less favourable access in a situation not comparable to a situation wherein Russia granted access to suppliers from Russia and other countries.[26]

The Appellate Body clarified that the term access in Article 5.1.1 refers to a supplier's right to an assessment of conformity under the rules of the CAP, including, when foreseen by this procedure, the possibility to have conformity assessment activities undertaken at the site of facilities and to receive the mark of the system.[27] Therefore, Article 5.1.1 focuses on a supplier's rights to access CAPs and the modalities of their access.[28] The AB ultimately held that although the Panel's interpretation of Article 5.1.1 was correct, it had erred in its application to these facts, since it did not focus on circumstances specific to the suppliers who claimed to have been granted access in less favourable conditions.

The Panel noted the following three elements for a determination of discrimination under Article 5.1.1:

Paragraph 7.251:

'a. The suppliers of another Member who have been granted less favourable access are suppliers of products that are like the products of domestic suppliers or suppliers from any other country who have been granted more favourable access;

26. *Russia – Railway Equipment*, WT/DS499/R, para. 7.387.
27. *Russia – Railway Equipment*, WT/DS499/AB/R, para. 5.121.
28. *Russia – Railway Equipment*, WT/DS499/AB/R, para. 5.126.

b. the importing Member (through the preparation, adoption or application of a covered conformity assessment procedure) grants access for suppliers of products from another Member under conditions less favourable than those accorded to suppliers of domestic products or products from any other country; and

c. the importing Member grants access under conditions less favourable for suppliers of like products in a comparable situation.'

The Appellate Body, while discussing whether access was granted under conditions no less favourable, in a comparable situation, held:

Paragraph 5.128:

'In light of the above, the assessment of whether access is granted under conditions no less favourable "in a comparable situation" within the meaning of Article 5.1.1 of the TBT Agreement should focus on factors with a bearing on the conditions for granting access to conformity assessment in that specific case and the ability of the regulating Member to ensure compliance with the requirements in the underlying technical regulation or standard. ... Nevertheless, the relevant factors for determining the existence of a "comparable situation" should ultimately relate to the Member's ability to make a positive assurance of conformity with respect to the specific suppliers of like products at issue, such that if no comparable situation existed for these suppliers, the obligation to grant non-discriminatory access to conformity assessment would not apply to them. In all instances, this analysis has to be made on a case-by-case basis in light of the measure at issue and the particular circumstances of the case.'

6.2.2.2.2 Unnecessary Obstacles to International Trade

Article 5.1.2 requires that CAPs are not prepared, adopted or applied so as to create unnecessary obstacles to international trade. This means that CAPs shall not be 'more strict' than is necessary to provide adequate confidence of conformity, keeping in mind the risk of non-conformity. This determines the necessity of CAPs.[29] Figure 6.2 sheds further light on analysis by the AB of the factors that determine whether a CAP is an unnecessary obstacle to trade.

29. *Russia – Railway Equipment*, WT/DS499/AB/R, para. 5.184.

Figure 6.2 Article 5.1.2. Analysis by the AB

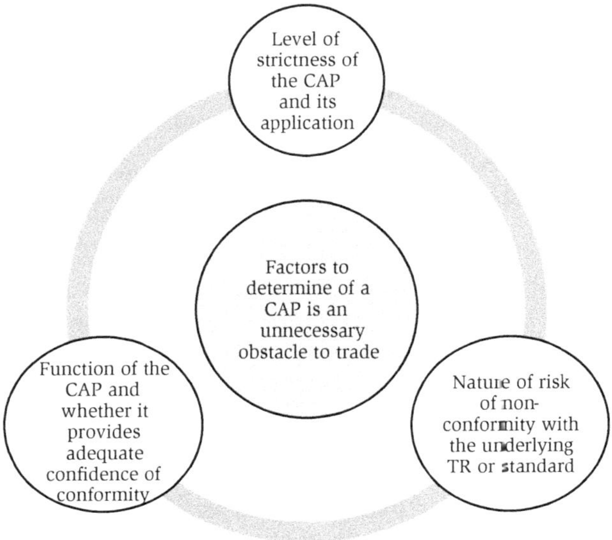

Source: Author's representation based on Russia – Railway Equipment, WT/DS499/AB/R, para. 5.184.

Russia – Railway Equipment also included a claim that the suspension of conformity certificates was inconsistent with Article 5.1.2. Ukraine alleged that the application of the Russian CAPs was stricter than necessary to give Russia confidence that the Ukrainian products conformed to the relevant TRs. Ukraine also argued that there were less-trade-restrictive methods to check conformity, such as additional communication to Ukrainian producers, entrusting on-site inspection to authorities of Kazakhstan and Belarus, or accrediting non-Russian inspectors and off-site inspections. The Appellate Body, in considering who has the burden of proof to show the existence of an unnecessary obstacle to international trade, held that a Complainant must identify an alternative measure and establish that such measure is less trade-restrictive, makes an equivalent contribution to the objective and is reasonably available.[30]

6.2.2.2.3 Other Procedural Requirements

Article 5.2 outlines various obligations that Members must adhere to while implementing the provisions of Article 5.1, i.e., in relation to preparing, adopting and applying mandatory CAPs. These obligations cover all aspects of a CAP such as fees, confidentiality of information, duration and information requirements. A brief overview of all obligations is provided in Table 6.3. Together, Articles 5.1 and 5.2 provide procedural

30. *Russia – Railway Equipment*, WT/DS499/AB/R, para. 5.195.

requirements that CAPs must comply with. Article 5.3 clarifies that Members are permitted to carry out spot checks within their territories.

Table 6.3 Overview of Key Provisions of Article 5.2

Article	**Provision**
5.2.1	CAPs are undertaken and completed as expeditiously as possible, in a non-discriminatory manner.
5.2.2	Standard processing period for each CAP is published or communicated to applicants on request. Applications received to be immediately examined for completeness and results to be informed to applicants as soon as possible, in a precise and complete manner.
5.2.3	Information requirements are limited to what is necessary to assess conformity.
5.2.4	Confidentiality of information is to be protected.
5.2.5	Fees charged is to be equitable in relation to fees charged for national suppliers
5.2.6	Sitting of facilities and selection of samples not to cause unnecessary inconvenience to applicants.
5.2.7	If product specifications are changed post determination of conformity, the CAP for the revised specification must be limited to what is necessary to determine whether adequate confidence exists that the product still meets the revised TR or standard.
5.2.8	Procedures must exist to review complaints concerning operations of CAPs and to take corrective action if needed.

Source: Author's representation

6.2.2.2.4 Harmonisation

Harmonisation is a crucial part of the TBT Agreement, with obligations on Members to participate in international standardising bodies, as well as to use relevant guides or recommendations issued by such bodies as a basis for their CAPs. These requirements are contained in Articles 5.4 and 5.5, and provide the basis for harmonisation of CAPs by focusing on guidelines of international standardising bodies and their recommendations.

Members are required under Article 5.5 to participate in international standardising bodies to the extent possible. Article 5.4 requires that when Members prescribe a mandatory CAP, they must use relevant guides or recommendations prescribed by international standardising bodies as a basis for the CAPs. Similar obligations are also prescribed under Article 9.1, by virtue of which Members must, when possible, formulate and adopt international systems for CAPs, and become members of, and participate in, such systems. Guides and recommendations issued by international standardising bodies may also be useful in ensuring that Members recognise CAPs carried out by other Members are equivalent to their own, as required by Article 6.1.1. Members are permitted to derogate from these guides if they are inappropriate for the Member, for the reasons of national security, protection of human health or safety, animal or plant life or health, environment, geographical factors, technological or infrastructural problems, etc.

6.2.2.2.5 Transparency and Notification Requirements

Notification requirements for CAPs are prescribed in Articles 5.6 and 5.7. Article 5.6 requires Members not basing their CAP on a guide or recommendation of an international standardising body, and if the CAP may have a significant effect on trade of other Members, to notify interested parties that a new procedure is proposed, and notify other Members of the products to be covered in the proposed CAP along with its objective and rationale. Members are also required to provide copies of the proposed CAP to other Members on request and allow Members time to make comments in writing and discuss these comments if needed. Article 5.8 requires members to publish all CAPs promptly, while Article 5.9 requires Members to provide a reasonable period between the publication of a CAP and its entry into force, so as to allow other Members to adapt to the new procedures.

Article 5.7 contemplates a situation where there are urgent issues related to health, safety, environmental protection or national security. In such a situation, Members are permitted to derogate from the obligations under Article 5.6, provided that once such a CAP to address these urgencies is adopted, it is immediately notified to other Members, copies are provided upon request, and Members are permitted to make comments and request discussions. In such urgent situations, the requirements of Article 5.9 are also waived.

6.2.3 The SPS Agreement

Similar to the TBT Agreement, the Agreement on Sanitary and Phytosanitary Measures[31] (hereinafter the 'SPS Agreement') also deals with CAPs. Though the terms 'conformity assessment procedure' is not used within the SPS Agreement, the Agreement does contain certain provisions regarding control, inspection and approval procedures (Article 8 and Annex C).[32] However, these provisions are much more limited than the TBT Agreement, though in effect covering the same substantive obligations.

31. Agreement on the Application of Sanitary and Phytosanitary Measures (Marrakesh, Morocco, 15 April 1994), Marrakesh Agreement Establishing the World Trade Organization, Annex 1A, The Legal Texts: The Results of the Uruguay Round of Multilateral Trade Negotiations 59 (1999), 1867 U.N.T.S. 493 [hereinafter SPS Agreement].
32. SPS Agreement, Article 8, Annex C.

Annex A (Definitions) to the SPS Agreement states that a SPS measure includes 'testing, inspection, certification and approval procedures'.[33] Therefore, a preliminary question arises as to whether in effect testing, inspection and approval procedures are subject to all provisions of the SPS Agreement. However, it is crucial to differentiate between SPS measures that have substantive SPS requirements and control, inspection, and approval procedures that are applied to check and ensure the fulfilment of these substantive requirements.[34] Therefore, though the general definition of an SPS measure does include control and approval procedures, this is not to be read mechanically and, importantly, control, inspection and approval procedures are to be judged against the requirements of Article 8 and Annex C alone.[35] Therefore, the provisions of Article 8 will apply specifically to all control, inspection and approval procedures. Article 8 is reproduced below in the Box 6.4.

Box 6.4: Article 8 of the SPS Agreement

Control, Inspection and Approval Procedures

Members shall observe the provisions of Annex C in the operation of control, inspection and approval procedures, including national systems for approving the use of additives or for establishing tolerances for contaminants in foods, beverages or feedstuffs, and otherwise ensure that their procedures are not inconsistent with the provisions of this Agreement.

6.2.3.1 Scope of Article 8 and Annex C

Annex C applies to 'any procedure to check and ensure the fulfilment of a sanitary or phytosanitary measure.' The footnote to the heading of Annex C notes that Control, Inspection and Approval Procedures include, inter alia, procedures for sampling, testing and certification. A failure to follow the provisions of Annex C(1) implies a breach of Article 8, SPS Agreement.[36] The substantive Provisions of Annex C are discussed in detail.

The Panel in *US – Poultry (China)* clarified that Article 8 and Annex C(1) applies to procedures dealing with control, inspection and approval aimed at checking and ensuring fulfilment of SPS measures.[37] Annex C(1) places an obligation on Members to ensure that 'any procedure' aiming to check and ensure fulfilment with SPS measures complies with the Annex. In considering specifically whether equivalence procedures

33. SPS Agreement, Annex A, para. 1.
34. Panel Report, *European Communities – Measures Affecting the Approval and Marketing of Biotech Products* (hereinafter '*EC – Approval and Marketing of Biotech Products*'), adopted 21 November 2006, WT/DS291/R, para. 7.424.
35. *EC – Approval and Marketing of Biotech Products*, WT/DS291/R, para. 7.1337.
36. *EC – Approval and Marketing of Biotech Products*, WT/DS291/R, para. 7.1569.
37. Panel Report, *United States – Certain Measures Affecting Imports of Poultry from* China (hereinafter '*US – Poultry (China)*'), adopted 25 October 2010, WT/DS392/R, para. 7.356.

fall under the scope of Article 8 and Annex C of the SPS Agreement, the Panel noted that since the equivalence requirement operated as a market-access barrier, it was, in fact, an approval procedure within the scope of Annex C.[38]

6.2.3.2 Undue Delay and Non-discrimination

Paragraph 1(a) of Annex C requires that procedures to check and ensure fulfilment of any SPS measure is undertaken without undue delay and in no less favourable manner for imported products than for like domestic products. Undue delay as used in paragraph 1(a) does not refer to a particular time period, but rather whether there is a legitimate reason or lack of justification for any delays that are faced. Annex C (1) (a) is to prevent Members from not reaching approval decisions. Annex C(1)(b) states that the standard processing times for each procedure is to be published or that it is communicated to the applicant on request, and goes on to prescribe how bodies must process applications, including placing an obligation on them to promptly inform applicants of defects in applications, delays, and results. These are similar to the obligations contained in Article 5.2 of the TBT Agreement. The Panel in *EC – Biotech* noted that the requirement for not causing undue delay applies to both initiating approval processes, as well as completing them (that is to say, the entire process beginning to end must be carried out without undue delay).[39] This dispute revolved around a general moratorium placed by the EC on the approval of biotech products. The Panel found that this general moratorium was a violation of the Agreement. The Panel noted that this is a good faith obligation, requiring Members to proceed with their procedures 'as promptly as possible, taking account of the need to check and ensure the fulfilment of their relevant SPS requirements.'[40] As a result, delays that are required in order to check the fulfilment of SPS requirements cannot be considered undue.

The non-discrimination requirement under Annex C(1)(a)[41] is the same as the requirement under Article III of the GATT and requires that the procedures are undertaken in a non-discriminatory manner. Non-discrimination in other aspects such as confidentiality of information,[42] fees[43] and sitting of facilities[44] are also prescribed, similar again to the provisions of Article 5.2, TBT. It is important to note that the non-discrimination requirement under this paragraph is worded differently from that under the TBT Agreement and does not refer to access of a supplier to the CAP, and instead only focuses on the procedure being undertaken in no less favourable manner for imported and domestic products.

38. *US – Poultry (China)*, WT/DS392/R, para. 7.370.
39. *EC – Approval and Marketing of Biotech Products*, WT/DS291/R, para. 7.1495.
40. *EC – Approval and Marketing of Biotech Products*, WT/DS291/R, para. 7.1498.
41. SPS Agreement, Annex C(1)(a).
42. SPS Agreement, Annex C(1)(d).
43. SPS Agreement, Annex C(1)(f).
44. SPS Agreement, Annex C(1)(g).

6.2.3.3 Necessity

The concept of necessity of a procedure is introduced in three paragraphs of Paragraph 1, namely, in (c), (h) and (e). Paragraph 1(c) of Annex C prescribes that information requirements are limited to what is necessary for the procedure, while (e) prescribes that the requirements for control, inspection and approval of individual specimens are limited to what is reasonable and necessary.

6.2.3.4 Other Obligations

Similar to the TBT Agreement, Annex C also requires Members to have a mechanism for review of complaints.[45] Paragraph 2 details that when the SPS measure specifies control at the level of production, the Member in whose territory the production takes place (i.e., the exporting Member) must provide assistance to facilitate such control. Last, Paragraph 3 retains the authority of Members to carry out inspections within their own territories.

6.3 CONFORMITY ASSESSMENT IN INDIA

6.3.1 BIS and Conformity Assessment

The scope of conformity assessment is wide in India, as elsewhere. As discussed above, a whole range of activities come under the umbrella of this term, such as certification, testing and accreditation, whether made mandatory or voluntary. These activities are managed usually by public bodies overseen by the Government of India, but also sometimes by private bodies, and they may cover a whole system at times or have a narrow focus on a specific sector or a product. In this section, we will focus on the major framework of conformity assessment procedures in India, with an overview of product certification activities of BIS and an illustrative example of non-BIS conformity assessment schemes by the MeitY.

The Bureau of Indian Standards ('BIS'), the largest certification body in India, is the focal point of conformity assessment activities in India by virtue of the BIS Act, 2016 ('BIS Act')[46] and the various rules and regulations promulgated under it. The BIS is the centre of a variety of CAPs undertaken independently or in collaboration with the Department of Consumer Affairs and other branches of the government.[47] The BIS Act empowers BIS to bring about various conformity assessment schemes as well as lays down certain requirements and powers regarding the conformity assessment activities of the BIS.[48] It should be noted that while the BIS has a number of responsibilities and

45. SPS Agreement, Annex C(1)(i).
46. BIS Act, Act No. 11 of 2016.
47. Product Certification Overview, BIS, https://bis.gov.in/index.php/product-certification/product-certification-overivews/.
48. Frequently Asked Questions, Product Certification, https://bis.gov.in/index.php/product-certification/product-certification-faq/.

powers, such as managing voluntary certification schemes,[49] systems certification,[50] recognition and accreditation of standards developing organisations (SDOs),[51] etc., this section will explore mainly the compulsory product certification schemes of BIS.

6.3.1.1 Structure of BIS Conformity Assessment Activities

The BIS Act is the point of origin for many of the powers and responsibilities regarding the conformity assessment that the BIS is charged with. The Rules issued by the Department of Consumer Affairs and regulations promulgated by BIS provide the next level of structure for the conformity assessment activities. The BIS (Conformity Assessment) Regulations, 2018 and some other regulations provide for the schemes for various Standard Marks and conformity assessment certificates. The schemes themselves then regulate the use of Standard Marks or grant of certificate of conformity. This hierarchical framework can be viewed in Figure 6.3.

Figure 6.3 Hierarchy of CAP Activities of BIS

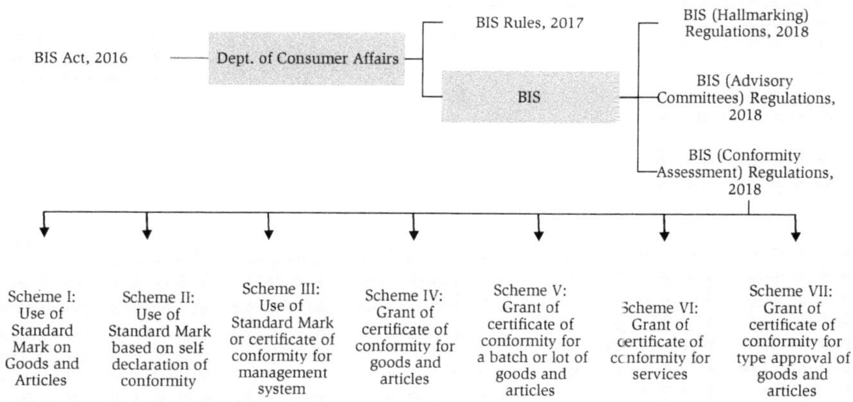

Sources: BIS Act, Rules & Regulations, BIS, https://bis.gov.in/index.php/the-bureau/bis-act-rules-and-regulations/.

This structure interacts with the ISO standards and other international organisations governing CAP on one hand, and the various ministries, department, institution,

49. E.g., Scheme- III under BIS (Conformity Assessment) Regulations 2018.
50. Features of BIS Management Systems Certification Scheme (BIS MSCS), BIS (2020), https://bis.gov.in/wp-content/uploads/2020/04/Features-of-BIS-MSCS.pdf.
51. Bureau of Indian Standards' Scheme for Recognition of Standards Developing Organizations (SDOs), BIS (2021), https://www.services.bis.gov.in:8071/php/BIS_2.0/sdo/sdonew/SDO-recognition-scheme-document.pdf.

etc. on the other hand to create a whole ecosystem of conformity assessment, both voluntary and mandatory in nature, depending on the goods, service or system concerned. This system interacts with the product owners and the wider public through tools such as 'license', 'Standard Mark' and 'Certificate of Conformity' that are defined in Box 6.5.

Box 6.5: Definitions

'License' is used to refer to a license granted under section 13 of BIS Act to use a specified Standard Mark in relation to any good, article, process, system or service, which conforms to a standard.[52]

'Standard Mark' is defined as the mark specified by BIS, including Hallmark, to 'represent conformity of goods, articles, processes, systems or services to a particular Indian Standard' and is 'marked on the article or goods as a Standard Mark or on its covering or label attached to such goods or article.'[53]

The BIS Rules define 'certificate of conformity' as a certificate granted by the BIS or designated authority demonstrating compliance with a standard or specified requirements, following assessment of conformity.[54]

6.3.1.2 BIS Act, 2016

The BIS Act is the key legislation providing the main conformity assessment structure for the Department of Consumer Affairs as well as BIS. Section 12 of the BIS Act allows the BIS to notify 'a specific or different conformity assessment scheme for any goods, article, process, system or service or for a group of goods, articles, processes, systems or services' with respect to any Indian Standard or any other standard.[55] Under the same section, the BIS is also empowered to 'establish a Standard Mark in relation to each of its conformity assessment schemes' with design and particulars as specified by regulations.[56]

Consequently, the Act allows a person to apply for a license or certificate of conformity if the goods, article, process, system or service to an Indian Standard.[57] Further, where any goods, service, etc. conforms to a standard, the Director General of the BIS is empowered to 'grant a certificate of conformity in a manner as may be specified by regulations' or 'a license to use or apply a Standard Mark in a manner as may be specified by regulations'.[58] While granting such a certificate of conformity or

52. Section 2(20), BIS Act.
53. Section 2(40), BIS Act.
54. Rule 1(c), BIS Rules 2018.
55. Section 12(1), BIS Act.
56. Section 12(2), BIS Act.
57. Section 13(1), BIS Act.
58. Section 13(2), BIS Act.

license for Standard Mark, the BIS can also specify marking or labelling requirements that are required to be affixed. In addition, the BIS is given the power to establish, maintain or recognise testing laboratories for the purposes of conformity assessment and quality assurance.[59] In addition, there is a special provision empowering BIS to notify precious metal articles or other goods or articles to be marked with a Hallmark or Standard Mark.[60]

While all this may be voluntary, the Act also specifically allows the BIS and the government to make conformity assessment activities compulsory if it considers necessary.[61] In order to declare a CAP compulsory, the Central Government must consider such a step necessary or expedient 'in the public interest or for the protection of human, animal or plant health, safety of the environment, or prevention of unfair trade practices, or national security'.[62]

6.3.1.3 BIS Rules and Regulations

6.3.1.3.1 BIS Rules, 2018

These rules were promulgated by the Department of Consumer Affairs in suppression of Chapter IV A titled 'Registration' in the BIS Rules, 1987.[63] These rules lay down the institutional structure of BIS and the functions of its various constituent bodies. Rule 32 of the BIS Rules is related to the establishment, maintenance and recognition of laboratories to test samples in relation to conformity assessment schemes. They further empower the BIS to inspect goods, article, process, system or service when Standard Mark or conformity to Indian Standards is required by the BIS Act or under any other law.[64] These inspections can be carried out through its certification officers or agents.[65] In the other functions of the BIS, it may 'promote harmonious development' of conformity assessment and matters connected to this, both within the country and at the international level.[66] It may, if authorised, carry out inspections and testing of goods and articles or may conduct audits of process, system or service for conformity to any other standard.[67] In addition, BIS has been given the power to 'formulate, implement and coordinate activities of conformity assessment to the relevant Indian Standards on *voluntary* or *compulsory* basis of goods, article, process, system or service as may be considered expedient in public interest'.[68] This basically gives it wide-ranging powers for carrying out any conformity assessment activities. Certification

59. Section 13(3), BIS Act.
60. Section 14(1), BIS Act.
61. BIS lists 'Products under Compulsory Certification' on its website under various schemes and Quality Control Orders. *See* Products under Compulsory Certification, BIS, https://bis.gov.in/index.php/product-certification/products-under-compulsory-certification/.
62. Section 16(1), BIS Act.
63. Notification No. G.S.R. 584(E) dated 25 June 2018 from the Department of Consumer Affairs.
64. Rule 34(1), BIS Rules 2018.
65. Rule 34(1), BIS Rules 2018.
66. Rule35(b), BIS Rules 2018.
67. Rule35(f), BIS Rules 2018.
68. Rule 35(g), BIS Rules 2018.

Officers, appointed under the BIS Act,[69] are also provided with the power to 'enter upon any premises in which any goods, article, process, system or service, in respect of which a license or certificate of conformity has been granted'.[70]

6.3.1.3.2 BIS (Advisory Committees) Regulations, 2018

The regulation provide for the constitution of Conformity Assessment Advisory Committee by the Governing Council of the BIS.[71] The Conformity Assessment Advisory Committee is mandated to advise on:[72]

(i) policy matters relating to conformity assessment procedures;
(ii) development of conformity assessment activities of the Bureau in the country and abroad;
(iii) coordination of conformity assessment activity with other organisations in the country and abroad;
(iv) surveys and surveillance;
(v) review conformity assessment schemes and suggest improvements;
(vi) other matters regarding conformity assessment.

6.3.1.3.3 BIS (Conformity Assessment) Regulations, 2018

One of the major responsibilities of the BIS relating to conformity assessment under the Act is product certification. The conformity assessment schemes for product certification by the BIS are laid down in BIS (Conformity Assessment) Regulations, 2018. These regulations are based on the principles laid down in IS/ISO/IEC 17067:2013 titled 'Conformity assessment - Fundamentals of product certification and guidelines for product certification schemes'.[73] The 2018 regulations provide for conformity assessment schemes in Schedule II.[74] The schemes are:

69. They are appointed by the BIS for 'the purpose of inspection whether any goods, article, process, system or service in relation to which the Standard Mark has been used conforms to the relevant standard or whether the Standard Mark has been properly used in relation to any goods, article, process, system or service with or without licence, and for performing such other functions as may be assigned to them.' *See* section 27 of BIS Act 2016 and Rules 47 and 48 of BIS Rules 2018.
70. Rule 48, BIS Rules 2018.
71. Notification No. F. No. BS/11/04/2018 dated 7 June 2018. *See* Regulation 3(b), BIS (Hallmarking) Regulations, 2018.
72. Regulation 5(2), BIS (Hallmarking) Regulations, 2018.
73. It describes the 'fundamentals of product certification and provides guidelines for understanding, developing, operating or maintaining certification schemes for products, processes and services'. It is intended for anybody with that has an interest in product certification. But the certification scheme owners will find it especially useful, whether governmental or private. ISO/IEC 17067:2013 Conformity assessment – Fundamentals of product certification and guidelines for product certification schemes, ISO, https://www.iso.org/standard/55087.html.
74. Schedule II, BIS (Conformity Assessment) Rules 2018.

(1) Scheme – I: Conformity assessment scheme for Grant of license to use or apply Standard Mark on goods and articles as per Indian Standards.

This scheme regulates the use of ISI Mark, and can be called ISI Mark Scheme. It is the most important of all the schemes due to its widespread use and the long list of products for which it is compulsory.[75] There are 371 products covered under this part under various categories. For example, 'Sulphate Resisting Portland Cement' and 'Low heat Portland Cement' are both categories of 'Cement' that have to comply with ISI Mark Scheme as per Cement (Quality Control) Order, 2003.[76] The BIS Mark has been reproduced below in Figure 6.4.

Figure 6.4 BIS Standard Mark

Sources: BIS Standard Mark, BIS, https://bis.gov.in/index.php/fmcs/certification-process/bis-standard-mark/.

(2) Scheme – II: Conformity assessment scheme for Grant of licence to use or apply Standard Mark through registration based on self-declaration of conformity for goods and articles as per Indian Standards.[77]

Under this Scheme, also known as the Registration Scheme, license to use or apply a Registration Mark that is reproduced in Figure 6.5, is granted by the BIS through registration, when based on self-declaration of conformity, for goods or articles when manufactured in manufacturing premises and conforming to all the requirements of the relevant Indian Standard. It is also compulsory for 76 products,[78] in the following categories:

(a) Electronics and IT Goods under 'Compulsory Registration Scheme' for Self-Declaration of conformity-Notified by Ministry Of Electronics And Information Technology,

(b) Solar Photovoltaics, Systems, Devices and Components under Compulsory Registration Scheme: Notified by Ministry of New and Renewable Energy and

75. Scheme - I (ISI Mark Scheme), BIS, https://bis.gov.in/index.php/product-certification/products-under-compulsory-certification/scheme-i-mark-scheme/.
76. S.O. No. 191(E) dated 17 February 2003.
77. Scheme - II (Registration Scheme), BIS, https://bis.gov.in/index.php/product-certification/products-under-compulsory-certification/scheme-ii-registration-scheme/.
78. *Ibid.*

(c) Low – Voltage switchgear and control gear: Notified by Ministry Of Heavy Industries And Public Enterprises

Figure 6.5 BIS Registration Mark

Sources: Central Marks Department-3, CMD 3/8:1/6975, MeitY, https://www.meity.gov.in/writereaddata/files/Circular-Mark_Registration.pdf.

(3) Scheme – III: Conformity assessment scheme for Grant of licence to use Standard Mark or certificate of conformity for management system as per Indian Standard

This scheme is limited to the management systems and is completely voluntary.[79] This scheme grants licence to use Standard Mark and certificate of conformity if conformity of system to all requirements of the relevant Indian Standard is demonstrated by a person. The Standard Mark for Medical Device Management System (standard IS/ISO 13485) is reproduced in Figure 6.6.

Figure 6.6 BIS Standard Mark for Management System

Sources: Standard Marks, BIS, https://bis.gov.in/index.php/system-certification-overview/system-certification-licence/view-standard-mark/.

79. *See* Schedule II, BIS (Conformity Assessment) Regulations, 2018.

(4) Scheme - IV Conformity assessment scheme for grant of certificate of conformity for goods and articles as per any standard

This scheme is also compulsory for two categories of products and deals with certificate of conformity for goods and articles. These are:

(a) Stampings/laminations/cores of transformers (with or without winding) and

(b) Retro-Reflective Devices for Bicycles.[80]

(5) Scheme - V Conformity assessment scheme for Grant of certificate of conformity for a batch or lot of goods and articles as per any standard

Under this Scheme, certificate of conformity may be granted by BIS to a person for batch or lot of goods or articles, conforming to specified requirements given in standard or part of standard or essential requirements, as applicable.[81] This, as well as Schemes VI and VII, are voluntary.

(6) Scheme - VI Conformity assessment scheme for Grant of certificate of conformity for services as per any standard

Under this Scheme, certificate of conformity may be granted by the BIS to an organisation providing service to a person or an organisation on demonstration of conformity of service and provision of services to the specified requirements.[82]

(7) Scheme - VII Conformity assessment scheme for grant of certificate of conformity for type approval of goods and articles

Under this Scheme, certificate of conformity may be granted by the Bureau to a person for type approval of goods or articles based on design review or type testing.[83]

The regulations also specify in Schedule I the categories of processes for which schemes can be made, the activities covered under each process and the type of certification provided in each scheme.[84] These processes include:

(a) selection (activities such as sampling or application falling under it),

(b) determination (testing or audit of product are examples of activities under it),

(c) review (examination of the evidence of conformity),

(d) decision (grant or cancel),

(e) attestation and

(f) surveillance (market surveillance or factory surveillance).

80. Scheme – IV (Grant of Certificate of Conformity), https://bis.gov.in/index.php/product-certification/products-under-compulsory-certification/scheme-4/.
81. *See* Schedule II, BIS (Conformity Assessment) Regulations, 2018.
82. *Ibid.*
83. *Ibid.*
84. Regulation 3(a) and Schedule I, BIS (Conformity Assessment) Regulations 2018.

6.3.1.3.4 BIS (Hallmarking) Regulations, 2018

These regulations lay down the conditions for the use of hallmarking goods such as gold, silver or any other product notified. Hallmarking is the process of certifying the purity or fineness of precious metals, with the hallmark acting as a form of guarantee to the consumer.[85] Since 2021, it is compulsory for the gold jewellery and gold artefacts and the silver jewellery and silver artefacts.[86] The regulations deal with the procedures and requirements for grant of certificate of registration, terms and conditions of certificate of registration and conditions for renewal and cancellation of certificate of registration.[87]

A jeweller has to apply for grant of certificate of registration to sell precious metal articles notified under section 14 of the BIS Act.[88] This has to be accompanied by fees and other documents. If the application is in order and fees paid, the registration is granted which is valid for a five-year period.[89] There are certain terms and conditions the jeweller has to follow.[90] Jeweller is responsible for the purity and fineness of the notified metal he sells.[91] If there is any shortage in purity, the jeweller has to pay compensation to the customer. If the terms and conditions are violated, then the registration can be cancelled.[92] Once registered, the jeweller submits the gold or silver jewellery to Assaying and Hallmarking (A&H) centres recognised by the BIS. These A&H centres are where the jewellery is actually tested.[93] Once testing is done, if the given requirements are fulfilled, the A&H centre will apply a hallmark on the submitted jewellery.[94] Hallmarked Jewellery consists of these four marks:[95]

(a) BIS Mark (as reproduced in Figure 6.7)
(b) Purity in carat and fineness of gold (22, 18 or 14 carats) and only fineness of silver
(c) A&H centre's identification mark or number
(d) Jewellers identification mark or number.

85. Overview of Hallmarking, BIS, https://abis.gov.in/index.php/hallmarking-overview/overview-of-hallmarking/; Hallmarking of gold jewellery mandatory now, The Economic Times, 17 Jan. 2020.
86. Notification F. No. 6/1/2017-BIS dated 14 Jun. 2018.
87. *See* Regulations 3-7, BIS (Hallmarking) Regulations, 2018.
88. Regulation 3, BIS (Hallmarking) Regulations, 2018.
89. Regulation 4, BIS (Hallmarking) Regulations, 2018.
90. Regulation 5, BIS (Hallmarking) Regulations, 2018.
91. *Ibid.*
92. *Ibid.*
93. Regulation 5, BIS (Hallmarking) Regulations, 2018.
94. Brief on Hallmarking Scheme, https://www.bis.gov.in/wp-content/uploads/2020/12/brief-on-Hallmarking.pdfBIS.
95. *Ibid.*

Figure 6.7 BIS Mark

Sources: Hallmarking, BIS, https://bis.gov.in/index.php/hallmarking-overview/.

6.3.2 Non-BIS Scheme

While BIS remains the source for most of the conformity assessment activities and schemes in India, there are certification schemes that are undertaken by other government bodies for certain products. S-Mark Scheme is an example of a conformity assessment scheme that has been pursued by Standardisation Testing and Quality Certification Directorate (STQC), an attached office of the Ministry of Electronics and Information Technology ('MeitY') based on international standards by the IEC. STQC undertakes certification of products through schemes such as the S-Mark Scheme, as well as testing (in its own NABL-accredited laboratories), systems certification, calibration, etc. for software products and systems.[96]

6.3.2.1 S-Mark Scheme

The Safety Certification (also known as the 'S' Mark) scheme is an example of a third-party certification scheme. It is prescribed for the electronics sector and promoted by the STQC Certification Services under the MeitY.[97] It is based on the ISO/IEC 17067, just like the BIS (Conformity Assessment) Regulations 2018.[98] This scheme aims to provide confidence that the product conforms to the requirements of relevant safety standards published by IEC.[99] For example, in case of 'information technology equipment',[100] the presence of S-Mark shows it is consistent with IEC 60950-1.[101] This level of confidence is secured using system assessment, product testing and subsequent

96. About STQC, STQC, https://www.stqc.gov.in/about-stqc.
97. STQC Division provides 'quality assurance services in the area of Electronics and IT through countrywide network of laboratories and centres.' About STQC, STQC, https://www.stqc.gov.in/about-stqc.
98. ISO/IEC 17067:2013, Conformity assessment – Fundamentals of product certification and guidelines for product certification schemes, ISO.
99. Safety Certification Scheme (S -Mark), STQC, https://www.stqc.gov.in/safety-certification-scheme-s-mark.
100. *See* STQC Certification Services, NABCB, nabcb.qci.org.in/accreditation/prdt/prdt006.php.
101. IEC 60950-1:2005, Information technology equipment - Safety - Part 1: General requirements (2005), https://www.iecee.org/dyn/www/f?p=106:49:0::::FSP_STD_ID:4020.

surveillance. It enhances the export capability of the products and makes it easy to get international safety approvals such as Verband der Elektrotechnik or VDE,[102] Underwriters Laboratories,[103] etc. The process is shown in a simplified manner in Figure 6.8.

Figure 6.8 Process of Receiving Safety Inspection Certification

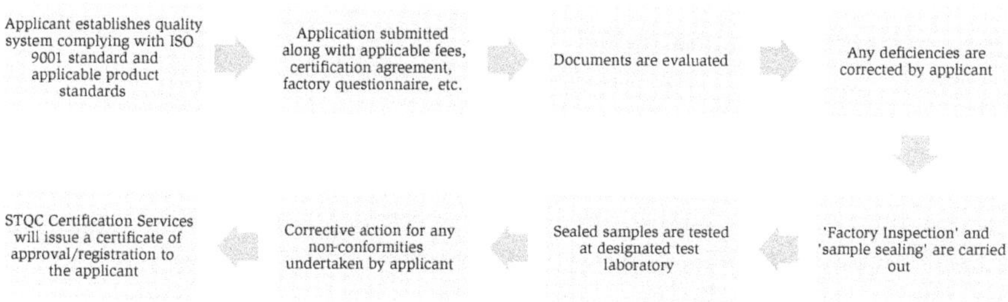

Source: Author's representation from STQC Certification Services, NABCB, nabcb.qci.org.in/accreditation/prdt/prdt006.php and Safety Certification Scheme (S -Mark), STQC, https://www.stqc.gov.in/safety-certification-scheme-s-mark.

A business interested in receiving a certificate of approval under the 'Safety Certification scheme' has to fulfil certain pre-certification requirements. The applicant business should establish a well-documented quality system that is in compliance with the requirements the ISO 9001 standard, the international standard for Quality Management Systems.[104]

If everything is consistent and completed satisfactorily, a Certificate of Approval is issued by the STQC Certification Services for three years. Surveillance is undertaken by the STQC during the period of certification validity. In case, the certified business fails to accept surveillance, is found to have major non-conformities, fails to take timely corrective actions or fails to fulfil financial obligations then the certificate can be suspended or withdrawn. For renewal, the quality system of the certified business is re-assessed and samples from factories are retested.[105]

6.4 ACCREDITATION IN INDIA

Accreditation in India is governed by the Quality Council of India ('QCI'), a body set up in the 1990s through the joint efforts of the Government of India and industry

102. Verband der Elektrotechnik or VED is one of the largest technology organisations in Europe granting marks and certifications. About Us, VDE, https://www.vde.com/tic-en/about-us.
103. Underwriters Laboratories or UL is one of the largest and oldest product certification companies in the world. History, UL, https://www.ul.com/about/history. *See also* About Us, UL, https://www.ul.com/about.
104. Safety Certification Scheme (S -Mark), STQC, https://www.stqc.gov.in/safety-certification-scheme-s-mark.
105. Safety Certification Scheme (S -Mark), STQC, https://www.stqc.gov.in/safety-certification-scheme-s-mark.

associations.[106] QCI runs independent certification schemes and oversees the functioning of the five constituent boards responsible for granting accreditation.[107] These accreditation schemes cover a variety of sectors, and cover the entire universe of CABs, being open to public as well as private players. The following section provides an overall view of the accreditation infrastructure as running with the close collaboration of the government and private bodies, centred around QCI.

6.4.1 Quality Council of India

In the early 1990s, a need for a national accreditation body was identified.[108] The effort to establish a new accreditation body that had a wider scope was spearheaded by the Department of Industrial Policy & Promotion (renamed Department for Promotion of Industries and Internal Trade or 'DPIIT'). It was recommended that the organisation should be set up as the joint efforts of the Government and industry and should be self-sustaining and autonomous. On the acceptance of these recommendations,[109] the Ministry of Commerce under the Government of India set up the QCI in 1997 as an autonomous body jointly with three leading industry associations, namely the Federation of Indian Chambers of Commerce and Industry (FICCI), Associated Chambers of Commerce and Industry of India (ASSOCHAM) and Confederation of Indian Industry (CII).[110]

The goal of the QCI is to promote quality through establishing a national accreditation and certification structure and provide a reliable mechanism for third-party assessment of products, services and processes acceptable at a global level.[111] It promotes quality standards in the infrastructure sector, environmental protection, healthcare, education and governance, among others.[112] Its objectives are shown in Figure 6.9.

106. History, QCI, https://qcin.org/history.
107. QCI PADD Schemes, https://qcin.org/padd-schemes.
108. History, QCI, https://qcin.org/history.
109. *Ibid.*; *see also* Extract of Minutes of the meeting of the Cabinet held on 9 February 1996 conveyed vide Cabinet Secretariat's Letter No. 6/CM/96(i) dated 14 February 1996, https://qcin.org/public/uploads/ck-docs/1609751215.Extract%20of%20minutes%20of%20meeting%20of%20Cabinet.pdf.
110. About Us, QCI, https://qcin.org/about-us.
111. *Ibid.*; Guidebook for AB PMJAY Quality Certification, National Health Authority and QCI, https://www.pmjay.gov.in/sites/default/files/2019-09/Quality%20Certification%20Process%20Guidebook.pdf.
112. About Us, QCI, https://qcin.org/about-us.

Figure 6.9 Objectives of QCI

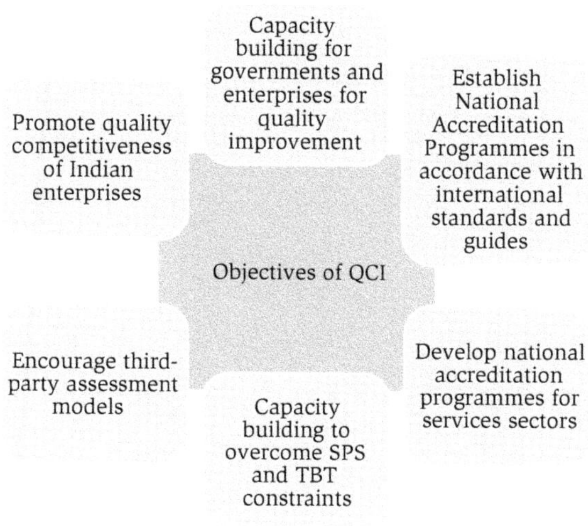

Sources: Key Objectives, QCI, https://qcin.org/key-objectives/.

Starting as an experiment in public-private partnership, today QCI operates as a non-profit society registered under the Societies Registration Act, 1860,[113] and has equal representation from the government officials, industry members and consumers. The QCI relies on its five executive boards to operate accreditation schemes.[114] These boards, depicted in Figure 6.10, are the accreditation boards – National Accreditation Board for Testing and Calibration Laboratories (NABL), National Accreditation Board for Hospitals and Healthcare Providers (NABH), National Accreditation Board for Certification Bodies (NABCB), National Accreditation Board for Education and Training (NABET) – and the quality promotion board – National Board for Quality Promotion (NBQP) – each headed by a CEO.[115]

113. Act XXI of 1860.
114. Guidebook for AB PMJAY Quality Certification, National Health Authority and QCI, https://www.pmjay.gov.in/sites/default/files/2019-09/Quality%20Certification%20Process%20Guidebook.pdf.
115. Boards, QCI, https://qcin.org/boards.

Figure 6.10 Constituent Boards of QCI

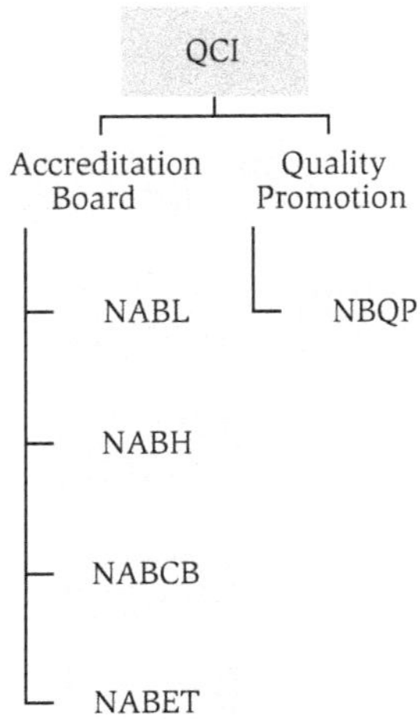

Sources: Governance structure, QCI, https://qcin.org/governance-structure/.

6.4.2 National Accreditation Board for Testing and Calibration Laboratories

National Accreditation Board for Testing and Calibration Laboratories was an independent accreditation body until 2017 when it was amalgamated into the QCI.[116] Its accreditation system is been established in accordance with ISO/IEC 17011, which is the standard for 'Conformity Assessment Requirements for Accreditation bodies accrediting conformity assessment bodies'.[117] NABL provides accreditation to testing, calibration, medical testing laboratories, as well as proficiency testing providers and reference material providers, from across various industries. Each of these classes of CABs is accredited against the relevant ISO requirement, as detailed in Figure 6.11.

116. *See* MOA, No. SDM(HQ)/C/2017/881, https://qcin.org/public/uploads/ck-docs/1609751125.MoA-2017.pdf.
117. Introduction, About NABL, https://nabl-india.org/about-nabl/introduction/.

Figure 6.11 Types of CABs and the Relevant International Standards for Conformity Assessment

Testing and Calibration Labs	Medical Labs	PTP	RMP
•ISO/IEC 17025 – General Requirements for the Competence of Testing and Calibration Laboratories	•ISO 15189 – Medical Laboratories – Requirements for Quality and Competence	•ISO/IEC 17043 – Conformity Assessment – General Requirements for Proficiency Testing	•ISO 17034 – General Requirements for the Competence of Reference Material Providers

Sources: NABL, https://nabl-india.org/.

6.4.2.1 Accreditation Services Provided by NABL

The accreditation services are provided on a voluntary basis for testing and calibration laboratories, proficiency testing providers (PTPs) and reference material providers (RMPs).[118] NABL has prescribed certain disciplines for each CAB group for which accreditation services are offered.[119] Proficiency testing providers refer to accredited providers who offer proficiency testing programmes for testing and calibration laboratories. Proficiency testing refers to the evaluation of performance by way of inter-laboratory comparisons. Reference materials are materials that have been demonstrated to fit an intended use or process, as a result of identified or specified properties, that are used in validation, calibration and quality control. Providers of these materials may be accredited by the NABL.

6.4.2.2 Accreditation Process

There are six stages of the accreditation process, as shown in Figure 6.12, including the optional stages of pre-assessment visit and resulting corrective action, before the accreditation is granted. The accreditation process begins with the application submitted by the applicant, followed by either a pre-assessment or assessment visit. A report is prepared for each one of these visits and the applicant has to take corrective actions

118. Introduction, About NABL, NABL, https://nabl-india.org/about-nabl/introduction/. Laboratories are 'give(n) formal recognition of technical competence for specific tests/ measurements, based on third party assessment and following international standards'. Proficiency Testing Providers are accredited for their competence in conducting proficiency tests, which is the evaluation of laboratories based on inter-laboratory comparisons. The 'RMP accreditation' gives 'formal recognition of competence to carry out the production of reference materials based on third party assessment and following international standards'. Why Laboratory Accreditation?, About NABL, NABL, https://nabl-india.org/about-nabl/why-laboratory-accreditation/.
119. Introduction, *ibid.*

based on them. On the basis of verification of the corrective actions as well as other reports and documents, the Accreditation Committee under the NABL makes a recommendation of approval or rejection to the CEO. Based on the recommendation, the CEO may grant accreditation to the applicant. This accreditation is valid for two years, subject to annual review, and applicant can also submit an application for renewal before the expiry of accreditation.

Figure 6.12 Procedure for NABL Accreditation

Application	•Online application via NABL website •Document detailing management system as per ISO standard to be submitted
Pre-assessment (Optional)	•NABL-appointed lead assessor visits CAB •CAB is assessed on the implementation of the quality system, the degree of preparedness for the assessment, etc., to determine the number of assessors required in various fields based on the scope of accreditation, number of key locations to be visited, etc. •Pre-assessment Report submitted to NABL Secretariat
Corrective Action	•If any non-conformities are found regarding the management system, CAB is required to take corrective action •Report on corrective action to be submitted to NABL Secretariat
Assessment	•Visit by assessment team constituted by NABL in consutlation with CAB •Assessment report detailing non-conformities prepared
Corrective Action	•CAB may take corrective action within 30 days, under monitoring and verification of NABL
Recommendation	•Assessment report, corrective actions and verification are considered by NABL Accreditation Committee •Committe makes recommendation of accreditation/non-accreditation to NABL CEO
Grant of Accreditation	•CEO may grant/reject accreditation based on Committee recommendation •If Committee recommended rejection of accreditation application, an appeal may be made to the CEO
Annual review	•Accreditations are valid for 2 years, subject to annual review
Renewal	•Application for renewal to be submitted by CAB atleast 6 months prior to expiry of accreditation

Sources: FAQ, NABL, https://nabl-india.org/faq/.

6.4.3 National Accreditation Board for Certification Bodies (NABCB)

The NABCB is the QCI constituent board responsible for providing accreditation to certification and inspection bodies. NABCB uses its own criteria, as well as international standards and guidelines in order to accredit a large variety of CABs that seek to operate various certification schemes.[120] Similar to NABL, it is a self-financing body, which helps maintain its independence.[121] NABCB is governed by eighteen members[122] including the chairman, three representatives from the industry associations (one each from ASSOCHAM, CII and FICCI), five government representatives,[123] and two representatives from national regulators.[124] The Board also has members hailing from the QCI and BIS. The NABCB provides accreditation for the schemes listed in Table 6.4.

Table 6.4 NABCB Accreditation Schemes

Scheme Type	*Certification Type*	*Accreditation Criteria/Standard CAB Has to Comply With*
Management Systems All CABs seeking to certify management systems must comply with **ISO/IEC 17021-1** - Conformity Assessment - Requirements for bodies providing audit and certification of management systems	Anti-bribery Management Systems (ABMS)	**ISO/IEC TS 17021-9** - Competence requirements for auditing and certification of Anti-bribery management systems.
	Asset Management Systems (AMS)	**ISO/IEC TS 17021-5** - Competence requirements for auditing and certification of asset management systems
	Business Continuity Management Systems (BCMS)	**ISO/IEC TS 17021-6** - Competence requirements for auditing and certification of business continuity management systems.
	Energy Management Systems (EnMS)	**ISO 50003** - Energy Management System - Requirements for bodies providing audit and certification of Energy Management Systems.
	Environmental Management Systems (EMS)	No additional criteria.
	Food Safety Management Systems (FSMS)	**ISO/TS 22003:20013** - Food safety management systems - Requirements for bodies providing audit and certification of food safety management systems.

120. About, NABCB, http://nabcb.qci.org.in/about.php.
121. Integrity, Independence, Impartiality in Certification and Inspection through Internationally Recognised Accreditation, NABCB, https://nabcb.qci.org.in/pop/NABCBBrochure.pdf.
122. Board Composition, NABCB. http://nabcb.qci.org.in/Boardcomposition.php.
123. Department for Promotion of Industry and Internal Trade, Department of Commerce, Department of Consumer Affairs, Council of Scientific and Industrial Research and Railway Board.
124. Central Drugs Standard Control Organisation (CDSCO) and Petroleum and Natural Gas Regulatory Board Regulations (PNGRB), Board Composition, NABCB, http://nabcb.qci.org.in/documents/NABCB%20Quality%20Manual_Issue%207%20Rev%2001_Jul%202020.pdf.

Scheme Type	*Certification Type*	*Accreditation Criteria/Standard CAB Has to Comply With*
	Information Security Management Systems (ISMS)	**ISO/IEC 27006** - Information technology - Security techniques - Requirements for bodies providing audit and certification of information security management systems No specific requirement to comply with **ISO/IEC 17021-1** - Conformity Assessment - Requirements for bodies providing audit and certification of management systems.
	Trustworthy Digital Repository Management Systems (TDRMS)	**ISO 16919** - Space data and information transfer systems - Requirements for bodies providing audit and certification of candidate trustworthy digital repositories.
	Quality Management Systems (QMS)	No additional criteria.
	Information Technology Service Management Systems (ITSMS)	No additional criteria.
	Road Traffic Safety Management Systems (RTSMS)	No additional criteria.
	Occupational Health and Safety Management Systems (OHSMS)	No additional criteria.
Greenhouse Gases	Greenhouse Gases Validation and Verification (GHG)	**ISO 14065:2013** - Greenhouse gases - Requirements for greenhouse gas validation and verification bodies for use in accreditation or other forms of recognition.
Inspection	Inspection Bodies (IB)	**ISO/IEC 17020:2012** -Conformity assessment - Requirements for the operation of various types of bodies performing inspection.
Personnel	Personnel Certification (PrCB)	**ISO/IEC 17024:2012**, General requirements for bodies operating certification of persons.

Scheme Type	*Certification Type*	*Accreditation Criteria/Standard CAB Has to Comply With*
Product Certification	Product Certification Bodies (PCB)	**ISO/IEC 17065:2012** Requirement for bodies certifying product, processes and services.

Sources: NABCB Website, https://nabcb.qci.org.in/.

6.4.3.1 *Process of Accreditation*

Figure 6.13 depicts the generalised stages of various processes undertaken by the CAB (in rectangular box) and the NABCB (in hexagonal box), as per NABCB's Accreditation Procedure for Management Systems Certification Bodies.

Figure 6.13 Process of Accreditation of CAB by NABCB

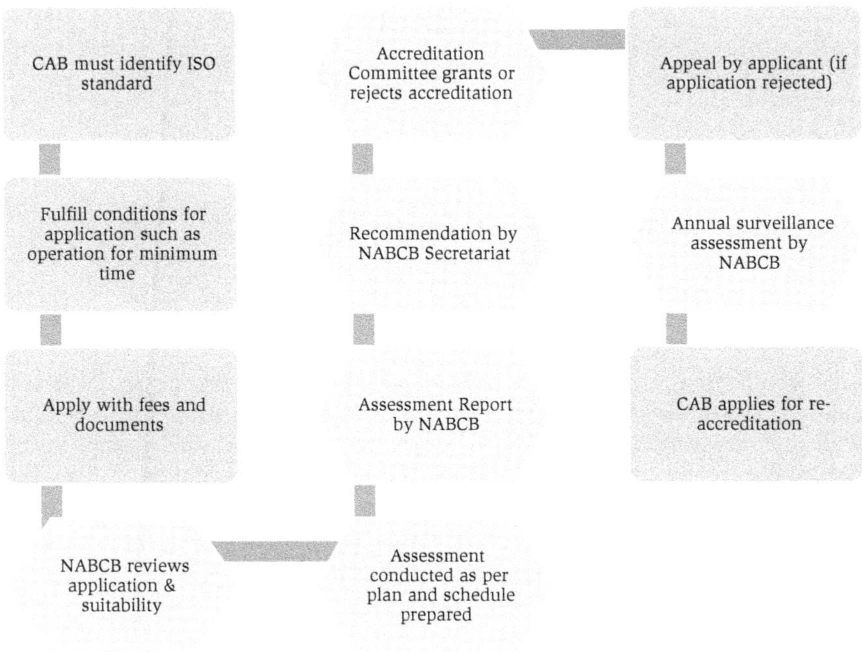

Sources: Accreditation Procedure for Management Systems Certification Bodies, BCB 201 (MS) – Mar. 2021, NABCB.

A CAB seeking accreditation from NABCB must identify the relevant ISO Standard it seeks accreditation for (listed in Table 6.4). Each accreditation scheme has its own procedure set out, but largely they remain the same across the board. A CAB seeking accreditation for their certification system must fulfil requirements such as to operate the certification process for at least 6 months.

6.4.4 National Accreditation Board for Education and Training (NABET)

The NABET is the constituent board of the QCI and provides accreditation for educational institutions, vocational training organisations and skill certification bodies.[125] NABET runs voluntary accreditation schemes for education as well as other institutes, and has the focus areas or verticals depicted in Figure 6.14.

Figure 6.14 Verticals of NABET

Formal Education Excellence Division (FEED)	Environment Division	Skills Certification	Skill Training and Services	Government Projects
• Accreditation of schools • Awareness Workshop on Schools • School assessments and quality assessments when directed by State and Government departments	• Accreditation of Environment Impact Assessment Consultant Organizations	• Personnel Certification Bodies – ISO/IEC 17024 Standard • Learning Services Providers for Non-Formal Education and Training – ISO 29990 Standard	• Accreditation of consultatnt organisations and training courses	• National monitoring of Lean Manufacturing Schemes • Zero Defect Zero Effect (ZED) Certification Scheme • Scheme for Accreditation of Prospecting/Exploration Agency (APA) and Mining Plan Preparation Agency (MPPA)

Sources: About Us, NABET, https://nabet.qci.org.in/about-us.

6.4.4.1 Environment Division

NABET conducts an accreditation scheme for Environmental Impact Assessment Consultant Organisations.[126] This scheme was launched in 2007 as a voluntary scheme, but has since been made mandatory by the MoEFCC.[127] The scheme includes initial accreditation, surveillance assessment as well as re-accreditation.[128] It covers all aspects of qualification and experience of EIA coordinators and experts, requirements for field investigations, laboratories, QMS systems and other facilities of the organisation.[129]

125. FAQs, NABET, https://nabet.qci.org.in/faqs.
126. Scheme for Accreditation of EIA Consultant Organizations: Version 3, NABET, https://nabet.qci.org.in/eiafile/Accreditation_EIA_Consultant_organizations.pdf.
127. *Ibid.*, p. 4.
128. *Ibid.*, p. 5.
129. NABET, About Environmental Impact Assessment,https://nabet.qci.org.in/about-eia-consultant-organization-scheme.

6.4.4.2 Lean Manufacturing for MSMEs

The Ministry of MSME operates a Lean Manufacturing Competitiveness Scheme under its National Manufacturing Competitiveness Programme. Under this, the QCI-NABET is a National Monitoring and Implementation Unit for the scheme.[130] Under this scheme, clusters of MSMEs work with Lean Manufacturing consultants in order to implement lean manufacturing techniques. Thereafter, the National Monitoring and Implementation Units will facilitate, implement and monitor the scheme.[131] Lean manufacturing techniques are an approach whereby activities that create waste in a manufacturing process are identified and eliminated. This means, that activities that take time, resources or space, but do not add to the value of the product or service, are eliminated.[132] NABET-QCI has empanelled Lean Consultants for this scheme.[133]

6.4.4.3 FEED Division

The most important activity under the FEED Division is the accreditation of schools. In order to get accredited, a school has to submit an application to NABET along with the requisite application fees. The application includes self-assessment by the school.[134] The school hosts 'readiness visit' by the NABET. The school submits 'Letter of Commitment' to comply with any findings requiring action by the school. This letter is submitted along with annual accreditation fees. The school then hosts an 'assessment visit' by NABET Team. The findings of this visit are communicated to the school and the school has to take corrective actions, if recommended. The Accreditation Committee reviews action by the applicant school. If everything is in order, accreditation is granted to the school by NABET. This accreditation is valid for 4 years with yearly progress review visits by NABET. The school may submit an application for continuance of accreditation after the expiry of validity period. Other activities of the FEED Division, apart from accreditation of schools, are organising awareness workshops for schools (including a 'Teacher Self Assessment Tool'),[135] assessment projects as per directions or agreement with government departments and training by the Directorate General of Employment and Training (DGE&T) Field Institutes.[136]

130. MSME Lean Manufacturing Scheme, NABET, https://nabet.qci.org.in/about-msme.
131. Scheme Operation Structure, Implementation Arrangement, NABET, https://nabet.qci.org.in/eiafile/sos.pdf.
132. Note on LMCS Scheme, NABET, https://nabet.qci.org.in/eiafile/Note%20on%20LMCS%20Scheme%20(1).pdf, p. 2.
133. Empanelment Process of Lean Consultants for MSME, NABET, https://nabet.qci.org.in/empanelment-of-lean-consultants.
134. Steps to School Accreditation, NABET, https://nabet.qci.org.in/accreditation-scheme/process.
135. *See* Table on Listing Names of Workshops, NABET, http://feed.qci.org.in/workshop/participants-list.php.
136. NABET: Introduction, NABET, https://nabet.qci.org.in/about-us; http://workshop/Webinar%20Registration,%20feed.qci.org.in/workshop/.

6.4.5 National Accreditation Board for Hospitals and Healthcare Providers (NABH)

National Accreditation Board for Hospitals and Healthcare Providers is the last of the accreditation boards of QCI, and has been operating accreditation programmes for healthcare organisations since 2006. It has full autonomy in its operation and a wide scope, including:[137]

(1) Accreditation of healthcare facilities;
(2) Quality promotion through initiatives such as nursing excellence and laboratory certification programs;
(3) Independent Ethics Committee (IEC)[138] activities such as public lectures, advertisements, workshops, and seminars;
(4) Education and training for quality and patient safety; and
(5) Recognition and endorsement of various healthcare quality courses and workshops.

NABH is composed of the Accreditation Committee, Technical Committee and NABH Secretariat (further containing the Assessor Management Committee, Risk Management and Improvement Committee and Complaints Committee). There is an independent Appeals Committee as well.[139]

6.4.5.1 NABH Accreditation Programmes

NABH offers accreditation programs for various healthcare organisations such as hospitals, blood banks and transfusion service providers, small health care organisations or nursing homes, primary and secondary health centres and Oral Substitution Therapy (OST) centres.[140] In total, NABH runs 11 accreditation programmes.[141] The flagship accreditation programme of NABH, the Hospital Accreditation Programme, is discussed in detail as an example.

6.4.5.1.1 Hospital Accreditation Programme

This programme is open for private as well as public hospitals, and is open to all healthcare organisations that have above fifty beds. The accreditation is provided for a whole organisation, and may not be sought for a single service or vertical of the hospital. The hospital seeking accreditation must also comply with NABH standards for

137. Introduction, NABH, https://nabh.co/introduction.aspx.
138. Programme on Implementation (POI) on Programme on Implementation of NABH Accreditation of Clinical Trial (Ethics Committees), NABH, https://www.nabh.co/EventDetails.aspx?id=212.
139. Introduction, NABH, https://nabh.co/introduction.aspx#a3.
140. FAQ, NABH, https://www.qcin.org/nabh/faqs.php.
141. Accreditation Schemes, QCI, https://qcin.org/looking-for-accreditation.

a minimum of three months prior to application for accreditation. Hospitals are assessed by the NABH-appointed Principal Assessor and a team of assessors for their compliance with NABH standards that have been prepared by its technical committee, and covers aspects of hospitals such as access and continuity of care, care of patients, management of medication, patient rights and education, facility management and safety, etc.[142]

Similar to other accreditation procedures discussed, accreditation applicants must be made online, along with requisite fees and self-assessment forms to NABH. There is an optional pre-assessment conducted in order for the hospital to take corrective actions if required, which must be reported duly to the NABH Secretariat. A principal assessor is appointed by the NABH, in order to conduct a pre-assessment of the healthcare organisation and to conduct an on-site assessment. An assessment report is prepared, based on the inadequacies identified during the assessment visits, detailing the results and examined by the NABH. The Accreditation Committee makes decisive recommendations based on the report, as well as documents submitted by the healthcare organisation. On the basis of the content of those recommendations, an accreditation certificate may be granted, signed by the CEO and the Chairman.[143] After accreditations are awarded, surveillance assessments are carried out two years following accreditation (if the accreditation is valid for four years), or eighteen months (if accreditation is valid for three years).[144] Six months prior to the expiry of accreditation, the hospital must apply for re-accreditation, which requires a re-assessment visit. If the results of this visit are positive, the Accreditation Committee may extend the certificate for three years.[145]

Apart from the accreditation, NABH also runs Certification Programmes such as HOPE (Healthcare Organizations Platform for Entry-Level Certification) for hospitals, as well as empanelment programs under Central Government Health Scheme (CGHS), Ex-service Men Contributory Health Scheme (ECHS) and Medical Value Travel Facilitator (MVTF). It also conducts training programmes, such as for assessors.[146]

6.4.6 National Board for Quality Promotion (NBQP)

NBQP is a constituent board of QCI set up in order to 'promote application of quality management standards and statistical quality tools with an objective of enabling industry, to improve their competitiveness, with specific focus on SME sectors' and second, to empower 'the consumers to demand quality and consequently creating a back-pressure on suppliers to ensure quality of their products and services.'[147] It has been set up in order to –

142. Hospital Accreditation Program: General Information Brochure, NABH, https://nabh.co/gib.aspx.
143. Policies & Procedures for Assessment, Surveillance and Reassessment of HCO, Issue No. 3 (2018), https://nabh.co/Images/PDF/NABH_Pol_ProcHCO_Issue4.pdf.
144. Accreditation timeline, NABH, https://nabh.co/Time-line.aspx.
145. Policies & Procedures for Assessment, Surveillance and Reassessment of HCO, *supra* note 143.
146. NABH Flyer, NABH, https://www.nabh.co/Images/PDF/NABH%20Flyer.pdf.
147. NBQP, https://nbqp.qci.org.in/>.

(1) promote quality awareness on Quality Management Systems, Quality Tools and Technology in all sectors pan India;
(2) spread quality awareness through live programs;
(3) identify and undertake projects for improving the work flow/process, and citizen centric services in Government departments;
(4) accreditation of training modules and processes related to Government schemes;
(5) develop and implement e-learning programs on cutting edge fields of quality.[148]

The NBQP Board is headed by a chairman and has twenty-nine representatives from apex industry associations, regional chambers, service sector associations, government, and education sector, etc.[149] and a secretariat headed by a CEO.[150]

64.6.1 Registration Schemes under NBQP

The NBQP currently accredits training courses or programmes pertaining to Lead Auditors and Internal Auditors. It provides accreditation under the following ISO-based schemes, such as:

(i) ISO 9001 (QMS)[151]
(ii) ISO 14001(EMS)[152]
(iii) ISO 18001 (OHSMS)[153]
(iv) ISO 22000 (FSMS)[154]
(v) ISO 27000 (ISMS)[155]
(vi) ISO 17025 (Learning Management Systems or LMS)[156]
(vii) ISO 10019 (Hospitals and Healthcare Consultants)[157]
(viii) ISO 50001 (Energy Management Systems or EnMS).[158]

---

148. Role Focus, NBQP, https://nbqp.qci.org.in/role_focus.php.
149. NBQP Board Members Constitution, About NBQP, https://nbqp.qci org.in/board-composition .php.
150. NBQP Secretariat, About NBQP, https://nbqp.qci.org.in/secretariat.php.
151. Consultant Registration Scheme for Quality Management System (QMS) ISO 9001:2015, QCI/NBQP/QMS/CON/Ver1.0.
152. Consultant Registration Scheme for Environment Management System (EMS) ISO 14001:2015, QCI/NBQP/EMS/CON/Ver1.0.
153. Consultant Registration Scheme for Occupational Health & Safety Management System (OHSMS) ISO 45001:2018, QCI/NBQP/OHSMS/CON/Ver1.0.
154. Consultant Registration Scheme for Food Safety Management System (FSMS) ISO 22000:2018, QCI/NBQP/FSMS/CON/Ver1.0.
155. Consultant Registration Scheme for Information Security Management System (ISMS) ISO 27001:2013, QCI/NBQP/ISMS/CON/Ver1.0.
156. Consultant Registration Scheme for Lab Management Systems (LMS) ISO 17025:2017/ISO 15189:2012, QCI/NBQP/LMS/CON/Ver2.0.
157. Consultant Registration Scheme For Hospitals & Healthcare, QCI/NBQP/HAH/CON/Ver1.2.
158. Consultant Registration Scheme for Energy Management System (EnMS), ISO 50001:2018, QCI/NBQP/EnMS/CON/Ver1.0.

This accreditation is offered under two types of registration schemes: Management Systems Course Registration Schemes (such as QMS and LMS)[159] and the Auditor/Consultant Registration Scheme (such as QMS Consultants, LMS Consultants and OHSMS Consultants).[160]

Each registration scheme is operated using its own procedure. For instance, under the Registration Scheme for LMS Consultant, NBQP certifies the credentials of competent consultants who have knowledge about ISO/IEC 17025: 2005 - General Requirements for the Competence of Testing and Calibration Laboratories' or of the ISO 15189: 2012 'Medical laboratories - Particular requirements for quality and competence'. The individual consultant has to go through two stages of assessment:

(i) 'Desktop Review' of documents pertaining to eligibility criteria, including 'education, experience, expertise, LMS documentation provided during consultancy etc.' This review is divide din two stages, first of documents submitted by consultant and second of LMS projects the consultant has done.[161]
(ii) Interview with the NBQP Panel of Consultant Examiners.[162]

If a consultant's application is accepted, they are required to submit an annual registration fees, and is granted a registration certificate valid for three years.[163]

6.5 INTERNATIONAL COOPERATION

As noted in section 6.2, as well as in Chapter 7 on MRAs, harmonisation and mutual recognition is a central requirement of the WTO disciplines on TBT as well as SPS measures. WTO Members have an obligation to participate in international standardising bodies, as well as to use the guides or recommendations provided by these bodies as a basis for their domestic CAPs. This section will cover international cooperation for CABs and Accreditation Bodies.

6.5.1 CASCO, International Organization for Standardization

The International Organization for Standardization (ISO) is a non-governmental organisation comprised of various national standards bodies. There is only one body from each country, recognised as the national standards body, with the Bureau of

159. Course Registration Course List, QCI, https://courseregistration.qci.org.in/course_reg.html.
160. Accreditation Schemes, QCI, https://qcin.org/looking-for-accreditation.
161. A consultant examiner is a 'person/committee designated to review the relevant documentation (laboratory's quality manual, procedures, work instruction etc.) of the LMS designed by the applicant and to verify the competence of applicant for registration.' Registration scheme for LMS Consultants, NBQP/QCI/LMS//V1.0/09-06-16, nbqp.qci.org.in/consultant/upload/Consultants/Scheme_for_Registration_of_LMS_Consultants.pdf.
162. Registration scheme for LMS Consultants, NBQP/QCI/LMS//V1.0/09-06-16, nbqp.qci.org.in/consultant/upload/Consultants/Scheme_for_Registration_of_LMS_Consultants.pdf.
163. Registration scheme for LMS Consultants, NBQP/QCI/LMS//V1.0/09-06-16, nbqp.qci.org.in/consultant/upload/Consultants/Scheme_for_Registration_of_LMS_Consultants.pdf.

Indian Standards being the ISO member from India.[164] The BIS is a founding member of the ISO.[165]

The ISO primarily focuses on the development of international standards.[166] Specifically for conformity assessment, the ISO has a separate council, the Committee on Conformity Assessment (CASCO). BIS is a member of CASCO as well.[167] CASCO has the role of developing and publishing standards related to conformity assessment. It is important to note that CASCO does not carry out any conformity assessment by itself. The Committee mainly studies CAPs in order to develop standards or technical specifications for such procedures. CASCO is also tasked with preparing guides relating to the various CAPs used globally, and promoting mutual recognition. Some examples of CAPs-related standards developed by CASCO are provided in Table 6.5.

Table 6.5 Examples of CAPs-Related Standards Developed by CASCO

ISO/IEC Guides		*ISO/IEC Standards*	
23:1982	Methods of indicating conformity with standards for third-party certification systems	17000:2020	Conformity assessment – Vocabulary and general principles
27:1983	Guidelines for corrective action to be taken by a certification body in the event of misuse of its mark of conformity	17007:2009	Conformity assessment – Guidance for drafting normative documents suitable for use for conformity assessment
60:2004	Conformity assessment – Code of good practice	17011:2017	Conformity assessment – Requirements for accreditation bodies accrediting conformity assessment bodies

Source: Author's representation

6.5.2 International Electrotechnical Commission (IEC)

The IEC is an international standards organisation that deals exclusively with standards for electrical, electronic and electrotechnology sectors. The IEC publishes

164. *Members: BIS, India*, International Organization for Standardization, https://www.iso.org/member/1794.html.
165. *International Cooperation*, Bureau of Indian Standards, https://bis.gov.in/index.php/standards/international-cooperation/.
166. *What we do*, International Organization for Standardization, https://www.iso.org/what-we-do.html.
167. *Supra* note 165.

international standards, as well as operates for CAP systems.[168] India, via the BIS, is a member of the IEC since 1929.[169] The IEC's CAP systems are:

(1) The IEC System of Conformity Assessment Schemes for Electrotechnical Equipment and Components (IECEE)
(2) The IEC System for Certification to Standards Relating to Equipment for Use in Renewable Energy Applications (IECRE)
(3) The IEC System for Certification to Standards Relating to Equipment for use in Explosive Atmospheres (IECEx)
(4) IEC Quality Assessment System for Electronic Components (IECQ).

Each of these systems operates as a global organisation that accepts members. National conformity assessment bodies may apply to be members of these systems, as long as they meet the relevant qualification criteria.[170] Membership to an IEC CAP system means that certifications issued by Members are recognised by other members of the same system, and therefore are portable.

India has some approved certification bodies recognised by each of these systems.[171] However, for instance with respect to the IECRE system, India's BIS is a member, but no Indian lab is recognised as a certification body, inspection body or testing lab.[172] Therefore, while India recognises certificates granted under the IECRE system, no Indian lab is qualified to provide this certificate.

6.5.3 International Accreditation Forum (IAF)

The IAF, an association of accreditation bodies,[173] manages agreements between various accreditation bodies, for mutual recognition.[174] The aim of the IAF is to create a single system of recognition of certificates of conformity globally, regardless of its place of issue.[175] The IAF also has regional Accreditation Group Members which are associations of ABs that cooperate at a regional level. From India, the National Accreditation Board for Certification Bodies (NABCB) is a member of the IAF.[176]

The IAF Multilateral Recognition Agreement (IAF MLA) is the mutual recognition agreement administered by the IAF. It requires signatory bodies to recognise the

168. *Who we* are, IEC, http://www.iec.ch/who-we-are.
169. *National* Committees, IEC, https://www.iec.ch/national-committees.
170. *How the global IEC conformity assessment systems operate,* IEC, https://www.iec.ch/conformity-assessment/how-global-iec-ca-systems-operate.
171. *Approved IECEx Certification Bodes (ExCBS) Certified Equipment Scheme.* IECEx, https://www.iecex.com/information/excbs/httpwww-iecex-comdirectorybodiesbodies1-aspid5/.
172. *RE Customer Test Facilities (RECTFs),* IECRE – Renewable Energy, https://www.iecre.org/dyn/www/f?p = 110:7:::::P7_ORG_TYPE:RECTF.
173. *IAF* Membership, International Accreditation Forum, https://www.iaf.nu/articles/IAF_Membership_/33.
174. *About Us,* International Accreditation Forum, https://www.iaf.nu//articles/About/2.
175. *Role of* IAF, International Accreditation Forum, https://www.iaf.nu/articles/Role/7.
176. *IAF Members and Signatories, Accreditation Body Member: India,* International Accreditation Forum, https://www.iaf.nu/articles/IAF_MEM_India/469.

certificates issued by CABs accredited by all other signatories to the MLA. The IAF MLA is structured around Regional Accreditation Groups.[177] The IAF MLA covers five main scopes. Attestations made by CABs under each scope are considered 'equally reliable' since the CAB conforms to the same standard.

These five main scopes are: management systems certification, product certification, certification of persons, greenhouse gas validation and verification, and validation and verification. India is a member of the IAF MLA for the product certification, management systems certification and certification of persons.[178]

6.5.4 Asia Pacific Accreditation Cooperation (APAC)

APAC is the regional accreditation cooperation body for the Asia-Pacific region, and was formed in 2019. It replaced two previous bodies, being the Asia Pacific Laboratory Accreditation Cooperation and the Pacific Accreditation Cooperation.[179] The APAC aims to manage and expand MRAs among ABs in the Asia-Pacific region.

The Indian members of the APAC are:[180]

(1) Federation for Development of Accreditation Services (FDAS) (associate member)
(2) Global Laboratories Accreditation Board (GLAB) (associate member)
(3) National Accreditation Board for Certification Bodies (NABCB) (full member)
(4) National Accreditation Board for Testing and Calibration Laboratories (NABL) (Full Member)
(5) Quality and Accreditation Institute Private Limited (QAI) (associate member).

Members may be full members or associate members. Full members' refers to members that have been through peer evaluation under the APAC MRA. Associate members are those members that provide accreditation of CABs, but are not recognised under the APAC MRA since they are not peer-evaluated.[181] Associate members are not APAC MRA Signatories.

APAC is a recognised regional cooperation body by the IAF, and the ILAC. As a result, most APAC MRA signatories are also recognised under the IAF MLA and the ILAC MRA.

---

177. There are five regional accreditation groups – African Accreditation Cooperation (AFRAC), the Asia Pacific Accreditation Cooperation (APAC), the Arab Accreditation Cooperation (ARAC), the European Cooperation for Accreditation (EA) and the Inter American Accreditation Cooperation (IAAC).
178. A list of India's main scopes and sub-scopes may be found at *supra* note 198.
179. *About APAC*, Asia Pacific Accreditation Cooperation, https://www.apac-accreditation.org/about/.
180. *Members*, Asia Pacific Accreditation Cooperation, https://www.apac-accreditation.org/membership/.
181. *Membership* Criteria, Asia Pacific Accreditation Cooperation, https://www.apac-accreditation.org/membership/membershipcriteria/.

APAC MRA Signatories must:[182]

(1) Recognise (within their scope) the accreditation of a CAB by other signatories as being equivalent to their own accreditation.
(2) Accept, for its purpose, a CAP result from a CAB accredited by other signatories on the same basis as it accepts results from CABs it has accredited.
(3) Recommend and promote acceptance of results provided by CABs accredited by signatory ABs.

6.5.5 International Laboratory Accreditation Cooperation

The International Laboratory Accreditation Cooperation (ILAC) is an international organisation for lab accreditation bodies. It includes all bodies involved in accrediting CABs that are calibration labs, testing labs, medical testing labs, inspection bodies, proficiency testing providers, and reference material producers.[183]

ILAC, in 2000, facilitated the signing of the ILAC Mutual Recognition Agreement (ILAC MRA or the ILAC Agreement). This MRA, originally between 25 members of laboratory accreditation bodies, agreed under the MRA to accept the technical test and calibration data produced by each other.

From India, the NABCB and the NABL are members of the ILAC MRA. NABCB is a member for the scope of inspection, while NABL is a member for the scope of calibration, testing, medical testing, proficiency testing providers, and reference material producers.[184]

ABs that are signatories of the ILAC MRA for the relevant accreditation activity are obliged to accept results of each other's accredited laboratories or IBs, programs provided by PTPS and reference materials provided by RMPs. Accreditation bodies are required to maintain a list of bodies they have accredited, and are also permitted to use the ILAC MRA Mark and Signatory Logo for their accreditation activities. Additionally, CABs that have received accreditation from signatory members may use the ILAC MRA Mark as well.

6.6 CONCLUSION

Conformity Assessment Procedures are a crucial part of a quality ecosystem, and are an important step in ensuring that standards and technical regulations fulfil their intended purpose. This chapter provided an overview of CAPs generally, as well as the certification and accreditation procedures implemented in India. The importance of

---

182. *APAC Mutual recognition Arrangement*, Asia Pacific Accreditation Cooperation, https://www.apac-accreditation.org/apac-mra/.
183. *About ILAC*, International Laboratory Accreditation Cooperation, https://ilac.org/about-ilac/; ILAC has membership of bodies that operate in accordance with ISO 17011, and accredit CABs in accordance with IS 17025, ISO 15189, ISO 17043 and ISO 17034.
184. *ILAC* Signatories, International Laboratory Accreditation Cooperation, https://ilac.org/signatory-search/.

CAPs and the benefit they provide to manufacturers or importers is underscored by the existence of numerous bodies in India focused solely on conformity assessment activities, ranging from the QCI, its constituent Boards, the BIS to private agencies such as private labs, other certification and inspection bodies and so on. This is supplemented by these bodies' participation in international organisations such as the ILAC or the IAF, as well in various MRAs.

This complex, tiered system for CAPs operates in complex ways: manufacturers are required to be certified; certification bodies are required to be accredited, and; the ecosystem should provide for a robust quality architecture ensuring adherence to processes and competencies at each stage. As noted in earlier chapters, the standardisation process in India is complex, with adequate safeguards for stakeholder consultations, regulatory inputs, and accounting for the requirements of interested stakeholders. In contrast, once a standard has been developed and implemented, the conformity assessment selection procedure, and related accreditation procedures are selected behind closed doors, with stakeholders usually not being provided with a chance to comment on the CAP that is chosen. However, the heavy participation of apex Indian industry bodies in these organisations generally ensures that selected CAPs are not unduly harsh, or detrimental to industry interests, while the participation of consumer organisations ensures that consumer interests are kept in mind. For example, the BIS invited comments from the stakeholders and then revised the Draft BIS (Conformity Assessment) Regulations, 2017, followed by another invitation for stakeholder comments on the draft.[185]

In a similar fashion, accreditation procedures are decided entirely by their respective accreditation bodies, and cover a wide variety of sectors and types of CABs. However, the accreditation procedure is almost uniform across all government-led accreditation schemes, with clearly laid out fees, procedures, timelines and the opportunity for appeal. These accreditation bodies prove to be a vital cog in the national conformity assessment system because they lend the same air of trust to the certification and testing bodies that the certification bodies lend to products, systems and services through certification and tests.

The accreditation system in India branches out from QCI into various constituent boards, all dealing with accreditation of CABs in different fields. However, what sets accreditation apart from other CAPs is that the industry is heavily involved from the inception in the case of the former, especially at the QCI level. While all the boards show different levels of activeness, their activities are coordinated effectively by the QCI. In addition, accreditation is less directed by laws and regulations, unlike the BIS where most of the structure is quite legal in its roots, beginning from the BIS Act and down to rules, regulations and notifications.

As a result of this large network of accreditation bodies and accredited certification bodies, India is able to ensure conformity with its numerous standards and technical regulations. These structures ensure consumer confidence, efficient functioning of systems and organisations, and reduced regulatory costs for manufacturers.

---

185. *See* Draft BIS (Conformity Assessment) Regulations, 2017, BIS, https://bis.gov.in/other/ConformityAssessmentRegulations_2017.pdf.

CHAPTER 7

Mutual Recognition Agreements: An International and Indian Perspective

Manya Gupta & Rishabha Meena

Apart from much-discussed tariff barriers, non-tariff barriers are increasingly becoming a regulatory barrier in the guise of standards and technical regulations. Technical regulations, standards and conformity assessment procedures may become potential trade barriers depending on the complexities of the national systems. Trade facilitation measures are being increasingly recognized through the tools of harmonization, equivalence and mutual recognition. Harmonization aims at achieving standardization of technical regulations and equivalence aims at accepting other countries' technical regulations as equivalent towards fulfilling similar objectives. Mutual Recognition Agreements (MRAs) are associated with the mutual acceptance of the conformity assessment procedures between conformity assessment bodies of two or more countries, removing the duplication of inspection and fees, thus facilitating unhindered trade without any compromise on the quality of the products. Against this background, this chapter aims at analysing the regulation of MRAs along with their benefits and drawbacks in international trade regimes including the World Trade Organization (WTO) and free trade agreements (FTAs). It highlights the rationale behind MRAs, their types and developing countries' perspectives on MRAs. Specifically, it discusses the Indian regime on the MRAs including the regulatory authorities, basic procedural nuances attached to them and India's MRAs independently as well as under its FTA regime. Finally, the authors conclude the chapter by identifying the way ahead with India-specific concerns.

7.1 INTRODUCTION

Pascal Lamy, the former World Trade Organization (WTO) Director-General, while highlighting concerns towards non-tariff barriers stated that 'the real 21st century trade issues are standards and rules in areas such as safety, health or consumer protection, rather than tariffs or quotas.'[1] Regulatory barrier is one of the many factors raising the overall cost of goods by 2%-10%,[2] and continues to impact trade by causing an inordinate surge in the price of goods and stringent trade barriers.[3] Due to the multiplicity in regulatory measures maintained by different countries coupled with their specific regulatory objectives, development status, taste, culture, income level, etc., several nations impose different non-tariff barriers with different goals. For instance, since the WTO Agreement on the Technical Barriers to Trade (TBT Agreement) came into force, the total number of notifications under the TBT Agreement rose from 364 in 1995 to 26795 as of 2020,[4] evidencing an increased number of technical barriers. Consequently, it becomes strenuous for the exporters to get access to the importing country's market due to multiple checkpoints in the form of testing, certification, accreditation, inspection, etc.

In order to facilitate trade, specifically to remove barriers caused as a result of regulations and standards placed on products, countries often resort to the tools of harmonization, equivalence and mutual recognition. These tools have the common goal to create a balance between domestic regulation and trade facilitation leading to 'economic efficiencies' and 'cost savings'.[5] A major source of the increase in cost for exporters is the duplication of testing and certification requirements – once in their home country and again in the importing country. Through mutual recognition, the duplication of conformity assessment is avoided thereby reducing the cost for exporters. Though the TBT Agreement and the Agreement on the application of Sanitary and Phytosanitary Measures (SPS Agreement) recognize the need for harmonization, equivalence and mutual recognition of norms, rules and regulations as well as conformity assessment procedures (CAPs),[6] these are non-binding obligations on WTO Members. Article 10.7 of the TBT Agreement requires the Members to notify the agreements that they enter into concerning technical regulations, standards or CAPs.[7] Despite the non-binding obligation to enter into negotiations for recognition of each other's CAPs under Article 6 of the TBT Agreement, Members have notified 163 agreements under Article 10.7 as of February 2021.

1. Enrique Aldaz Carroll, *Regional Approach to Better Standards Systems* (World Bank Policy Research Working Paper 3948, June 2006), 1, https://openknowledge.worldbank.org/bitstream/handle/10986/8426/wps3948.txt?sequence=2&isAllowed=y.
2. Alberto Amurgo-Pacheco, *Mutual Recognition Agreements and Trade Diversion: Consequences for Developing Nations*, No 20-2006, IHEID Working Papers from Economics Section, Graduate Institute of International Studies, 3 (October 2006) (hereinafter 'Pacheco').
3. Christel Elvestad, *Equivalence and Mutual Recognition Agreements in Relation to Technical Measures* (Norwegian Agricultural Economics Research Institute, 2002) 5 (hereinafter 'Elvestad').
4. *WTO Data*, WTO, https://data.wto.org/. The last available data is of 14 January 2020 (hereinafter 'WTO Data').
5. Helen Chruchman, *Mutual Recognition Agreements and Equivalence Agreements, in* Research Handbook on WTO and Technical Barriers to Trade 287, 280-314 (Tracey Epps & Michael J. Trebilcock eds, Edward Elgar 2013) (hereinafter 'Churchman').
6. *See* SPS Agreement, Article 4, Article 5. Article 6 and Annex A.
7. TBT Agreement, Article 10.7; *Technical Information on TBT*, https://www.wto.org/english/tratop_e/tbt_e/tbt_info_e.htm.

Among the three tools of trade facilitation, i.e., harmonization, equivalence and recognition, recognition as a tool is manifested in the form of Mutual Recognition Agreements (MRAs). MRAs are used as a tool by the countries to recognize each other's CAPs and conformity assessment bodies (CABs). The European Union (EU) has been adopting harmonization and mutual recognition for years. The mutual recognition in the context of its common internal market is regarded as the first MRA.[8] The EU followed the old style harmonization which tried to create mandatory and uniform community rules and aimed at producing 'Europroducts'.[9] Due to the burdensome process of negotiations for any minor legislation, the 'New Approach' shifted its focus to the concept of recognition.[10] After the shift from mandatory harmonization to recognition in the EU, most Members had two options - either seek EU-based certification or seek MRAs.[11] These MRAs can be categorized into different categories based on different criteria. In the beginning, MRAs were mostly negotiated as stand-alone agreements. However, modern-day FTAs also include trade facilitation measures as a result of their growing coverage of non-tariff barriers.[12] Consequentially, MRAs also form part of FTA negotiations in some cases.

Like any other international agreement, bilateral or multilateral, negotiations of MRAs require consideration of various factors between the parties. Among other factors like environment and health concerns, sound and effective administrative setup etc., the level of development becomes a determinative criterion for the participants to come together and recognize each other's CAPs and CABs. Since, MRAs are dependent on trust in the technical competence of the parties, developing and least developed countries are almost never considered for MRAs by the developed countries.[13] For instance, despite the progressive emergence of MRAs in the EU, it has not signed any MRAs with a developing country for CABs or CAPs recognition.[14]

Globally, India is the tenth largest importer of goods.[15] Currently, 45.52% of Indian imports are subjected to non-tariff measures,[16] out of which 13.08% of imports are subjected to certification requirements.[17] As of 2020, India has notified 215 TBT measures since joining the WTO.[18] In India, there are various bodies governing

8. Pacheco, *supra* note 2, 3.
9. Andrew McGee & Stephen Weatherill, *The Evolution of the Single Market: Harmonisation or Liberalisation* 53 Perspective on European Law 582, n. 5 (September 1990).
10. *Ibid.*
11. Kalypso Nicolaidis & Michelle Egan, *Transnational Market Governance and Regional Policy Externality: Why recognize foreign standards* 8 Journal of European Public Policy 464, n. 3 (2001).
12. Shnataro Hamanaka et al., *Trade Facilitation Measures under Free Trade Agreements: Are they discriminatory against non-members?* (ADB Working Paper Series on Regional Economic Integration No. 55, July 2010) 13 (hereinafter 'Hamanaka et al.').
13. Pacheco, *supra* note 2, 4.
14. European Commission, *List of mutual recognition agreements*, https://ec.europa.eu/growth/single-market/goods/international-aspects/mutual-recognition-agreements_en.
15. *Leading import countries worldwide in 2019*, Statista, (11 November 2020), https://www.statista.com/statistics/268184/leading-import-countries-worldwide/.
16. *India Non-Tariff Measure Summary*, World Integrated Trade Solution, https://wits.worldbank.org/tariff/non-tariff-measures/en/country/IND.
17. *Ibid.*
18. WTO Data, *supra* note 4. The data was last accessed on 14 January 2020.

standards such as the Bureau of Indian Standards (BIS), Export Inspection Council (EIC), National Accreditation Board of Calibration and Testing Laboratories (NABL) and National Accreditation Board for Certification Bodies (NABCB). These bodies aim to prevent trade restrictiveness arising out of compliances with different standards for the imported and exported goods. Another common feature of these bodies is that they all can enter into MRAs. However, these bodies differ in their scope, representation at international and regional organizations, product coverage, nature of MRAs, etc.

Against this background, this chapter brings out the regulatory landscape of MRAs internationally and in India. The chapter begins by highlighting various mechanisms such as equivalence, harmonization and mutual recognition to overcome technical barriers. It further provides a detailed understanding of MRAs under WTO laws from the perspective of trade in goods as well as trade in services. This part further examines the rationale behind entering into MRAs, their classification and the variance in FTAs. It examines the problems faced by developing countries on account of lack of trust in their technical capabilities. The second half of this chapter focuses on the regulation of MRAs in India by highlighting the roles of various Indian CABs and their membership of various international organizations having their own MRAs or multilateral recognition agreements (MLAs). It discusses the mutual recognition provisions and MRAs signed by India under its FTAs. Finally, this chapter concludes by identifying the way ahead.

7.2 INTERNATIONAL PERSPECTIVES ON MRAs

Some common elements of regulatory barriers are in the form of norms and rules which must be complied with for obtaining market access for goods and services in the importing country and the CAPs monitor the compliance with these norms and rules.[19] Content of norms or rules are typically regulations, standards, or guidelines (mandatory or voluntary) against which a product is judged. CAPs cover within their sphere the process through which the products are evaluated against these rules. Both norms and CAPs may cause hindrances in international trade. The standards or regulations or norms even when aimed at welfare enhancement, may impose high burdens on the exporters and create a favourable condition of competition for domestic producers. A similar problem can be seen in case of exports of IT equipment from the United States to EU where the US industry representatives have highlighted that the delays in conformity assessment of the IT equipment in the EU reduce the product value by 5 to 10 percent.[20] The use of international standards is encouraged to ensure uniformity and to promote trade. To overcome such barriers to competition, the Members use (i) harmonization; (ii) equivalence; and (iii) mutual recognition.

19. Richard Baldwin, *Regulatory Protectionism, Developing Nations and a Two – tier world trade system* (Discussion Paper Series No. 257, Brookings Trade Forum, October 2000) 237-293 (hereinafter 'Baldwin').
20. Mark Vancauteren, *Trade Effects of approaches intended to facilitate acceptance of results of Conformity Assessment: What is the Evidence?* (Workshop and Policy dialogue on Technical Barriers to Trade: Promoting Good Practices in support of open markets, OECD, 5-5 October 2009), para. 11.

Harmonization attempts to bring uniformity in technical regulations by requiring them to be aligned with international standards.[21] Full harmonization is not achievable due to differences in the level of protection across countries. However, WTO agreements place great emphasis on the role of harmonization.[22]

Equivalence requires that the Members accept the technical regulations of the other Members as equivalent on the condition that these regulations fulfil the objective of their own regulation.[23] Some examples of these objectives are national security, prevention of deceptive practices, protection of human health or safety, animal or plant life or health, or environmental protection.[24] An assessment of equivalence of a regulation is determined by its goal, text and contribution towards achieving that goal.

Mutual recognition entails the exchange of information and consultations between governments and relies on market competition to guide the process of international convergence.[25] MRAs can differ depending on the number of countries participating and CAPs or norms to be recognized. On the one hand, MRAs like the transatlantic MRA or traditional MRAs can be limited to countries mutually agreeing to recognize CAPs thereby reducing the cost of duplication of certification.[26] On the other hand, there are enhanced MRAs where the participating countries can include harmonization and equivalence of the norms or regulations to precede the recognition of CAPs.[27] The two methods of harmonization and equivalence are beyond the scope of this chapter. International perspectives on MRAs and their legal basis under the multilateral trading regime are discussed hereafter.

7.3 REGULATION OF MRAS UNDER WTO LAW

Since the inception of the WTO, mutual recognition is provided for in three agreements viz. SPS Agreement, TBT Agreement and General Agreement on Trade in Services (GATS). The relevant provisions under each agreement have been discussed below.

7.3.1 Agreement on the Technical Barrier to Trade

Internationally traded products are subject to multiple technical regulations or standards which may lead to barriers in trade. Further, the CAPs to verify compliance with importing country's technical regulations and standards pose additional burdens; more specifically, duplication of the CAPs in the exporting country as well as the importing

21. *See* TBT Agreement, Articles 2.4-2.6, 5.4-5.5, Annex 3(F)-(G).
22. Elvestad, *supra* note 3, 7.
23. TBT Agreement, Article 2.7; SPS Agreement, Article 4.
24. *See* TBT Agreement, Article 2.2. It provides a non-exhaustive list of legitimate objectives.
25. Alan O. Sykes, *Product standards for Internationally Integrated Goods Markets* 39 (Brookings, 1995) (hereinafter 'Sykes').
26. Akiko Suwa-Eisenmann & Thierry Verdier, *Reciprocity and Political Economy of Harmonization and Mutual Recognition of Regulatory Measures* (CEPR Discussion Papers 3147, 2002), 24; A. Correia de Brito et al., *The contribution of mutual recognition to international regulatory co-operation* (OECD Regulatory Policy Working Papers No. 2, 2016), 8, 10 (accessed 16 December 2020) (hereinafter 'Brito et al.').
27. *Ibid.* Refer to the discussion on classification of MRAs on the basis of scope under Part 2.3.1.

country remains a major concern. In this regard, Article 6 of the TBT Agreement requires Members to accept, 'whenever possible', other Members' CAPs if they are equivalent to its own CAPs. Article 6 further provides the countries to enter into a consultation to gain an understanding of each other's CAPs and their limitations.[28] However, such acceptance of CAP results is entirely at the discretion of the importing country in light of the phrase 'whenever possible' in Article 6.1. Article 6.1 takes into account the sovereignty of the Member but is unclear whether the WTO dispute settlement body can determine the meaning of phrases like 'whenever possible' and 'are satisfied'.[29]

Similarly, Article 6.3 of the TBT Agreement encourages Members to enter into negotiations for the conclusion of MRAs recognizing each other's CAPs. Members may accept CAP results if they are satisfied that the exporting country's CAPs are equivalent to their own CAPs. Article 6.4 encourages Members to follow the principle of non-discrimination in allowing participation of foreign CABs in their CAPs. Overall, the TBT Agreement makes specific reference to MRAs; however, the compliance with this obligation has been left to the discretion of the Members while the Agreement endorses its use.[30]

MRAs have been discussed very often in the Triennial Review of the TBT Agreement. For instance, in the fourth Triennial Review Meeting in 2006, the Committee on TBT highlighted the possible difficulties in government-to-government MRAs.[31] It recommended that the mutual introduction of cross-border designation systems in equivalent fields by governments can be cost-effective. It reiterated that the use of relevant international conformity assessment standards, guidelines and recommendations, as well as greater alignment of CAPs could facilitate the conclusion of MRAs.[32] The Committee on TBT noted that various voluntary MRAs have been entered into by domestic and foreign CABs, individual laboratories, certification and inspection bodies.[33] In the fourth and fifth Triennial Meeting, the Members shared their experiences with respect to the negotiations, difficulties and effectiveness of the MRAs.[34] International Laboratory Accreditation Cooperation (ILAC) and International Accreditation Forum (IAF), organizations formed on the basis of MRAs between accreditation bodies, described the role of multilateral MRAs in enhancing confidence in CAP results and

28. TBT Agreement, Article 6.1.1, Article 6.1.2.
29. Arthur E. Appleton, *Conformity Assessment Procedures in* Research Handbook on WTO and Technical Barriers to Trade 100 (Tracey Epps & Michael J. Trebilcock eds, Edward Elgar 2013).
30. Churchman, *supra* note 5.
31. Committee on TBT, Fourth Triennial Review of the Operation and Implementation of the TBT Agreement under Article 15.4, G/TBT/19, (14 November 2006) para. 39 (hereinafter 'Fourth Triennial Review').
32. *Ibid.*, para. 40.
33. Committee on TBT, Summary Report of the Workshop on the Different Approaches to Conformity Assessment, G/TBT/M/38/Add.1. (6 June 2006).
34. *See* Fourth Triennial Review, *supra* note 31; Committee on TBT, Fifth Triennial Review of the Operation and Implementation of the TBT Agreement under Article 15.4, G/TBT/26 (13 November 2009).

facilitating trade.[35] However, the results of these discussions have been by and large ineffectual.

7.3.2 Agreement on the Application of Sanitary and Phytosanitary Measures

SPS measures are a specific aspect of the technical measures which are solely concerned with the protection of human, plant and animal life and health.[36] Article 4.1 of the SPS Agreement requires the Members to accept other Members' SPS measures as equivalent even if these measures differ from their own provided that it achieves the same level of protection. Article 4.2 encourages the Members to enter into negotiations to conclude agreements on recognition of equivalence of specified SPS measures.

In this regard, the Committee on SPS Measures published a non-binding decision titled 'Decision on the implementation of Article 4 of the SPS Agreement in 2001'.[37] It provides elaborate guidelines to the Members on the implementation of Article 4.1 and acceptance of equivalence of SPS measures. It imposes obligations on the importing Members regarding the explanation of the measure, indication of the appropriate level of protection, responding to the requests of the exporting Member, etc.[38] Similarly, it imposes obligations on the exporting Members to provide scientific information to demonstrate the equivalence of their measures, to provide reasonable access to the importing Member for testing, inspection and other related procedures.[39] Further, it also encourages the Members to inform the Committee of any successful bilateral equivalence agreements or arrangements.[40]

The type of MRAs covered under the SPS Agreement go beyond the recognition of CABs and CAPs as is the case with the TBT Agreement. These MRAs require recognition of specific SPS measures for a good to be sold in any country which is a party to the MRA. Instead of only limiting them to the recognition of CAPs, these MRAs promote equivalence by the recognition of regulations.[41]

---

35. Committee on TBT, Seventh Triennial Review of the Operation and Implementation of the TBT Agreement under Article 15.4, G/TBT/37 (3 December 2015), para. 3.6 (hereinafter 'Seventh Triennial Review'). Refer to the discussion on classification of MRAs on the basis of parties in Part 2.3.2.
36. Peter Van den Bossche & Werner Zdouc, *The Law and Policy of the World Trade Organization Text, Cases and Materials* 462 (Cambridge University Press, 4th ed., 2017) (hereinafter 'Bossche & Zdouc'); *see also* TBT Agreement, Article 1.5.
37. Committee on SPS, Decision on the implementation of Article 4 of the SPS Agreement, G/SPS/19 (24 October 2001).
38. *Ibid.*, paras 2-3.
39. *Ibid.*, para. 4.
40. *Ibid.*, para. 12.
41. *See* Simonetta Zarrilli, *WTO Agreement on Sanitary and Phytosanitary Measures: Issues for Developing Countries* (UNCTAD Secretariat, July 1999).

7.3.3 General Agreement on Trade in Services

In the context of trade in services, an MRA warrants the qualifications of services suppliers, which are recognized in their home country, to be mutually recognized by a Member which is a party to the MRA.[42] Article VII of the GATS essentially allows the Members to recognize the education or experience obtained, requirements met, licenses or certifications granted in a particular country. This may be achieved through harmonization or otherwise and may be based on recognition measures such as agreements or arrangements or granted autonomously. However, Members must provide an adequate opportunity for other interested Members to negotiate their accession, and where the recognition is autonomous, the Member shall provide others an adequate opportunity to demonstrate that their criteria may be recognized.[43] Another condition for recognition is that it shall not constitute a means of discrimination between countries in the application of standards and criteria or a disguised restriction on trade.[44] Article VII:4 mandates the Members to notify pre-existing and any new recognition measures as well as any changes to the previously notified measures to the Council for Trade in Services.[45] The Members should base their recognition measures on international standards and they should work with inter-governmental and non-governmental organizations to formulate and adopt such standards.[46] In pursuance of this provision, the Council for Trade in Services agreed upon voluntary *Guidelines for Mutual Recognition Agreements or Arrangements in the Accountancy Sector* as a first attempt of standardizing these recognition measures.[47]

Although Article VII:4 imposes a notification obligation on the Members, most MRAs are concluded as a part of the FTAs and hence are often notified under Article V of GATS. Around 80 notifications have been made under Article VII:4 by Members till February 2021.[48] Due to multiple preferential trade agreements, their 'bilateralization' and division of notification under Article V and Article VII, the actual count of MRAs notified remains uncertain.[49]

42. *See* General Agreement on Trade in Services, Article VII (hereinafter 'GATS').
43. Juan A. Marchetti & Petros C. Mavroidis, *I now recognize you (and only you) as equal: an anatomy of (mutual) recognition agreements in GATS, in* Regulating Trade in Services in the EU and the WTO 422 (Ioanniz Lianos & Okeoghene Odudu eds, Cambridge University Press, 2012).
44. *Ibid.*, 422.
45. Bossche & Zdouc, *supra* note 36, 499; GATS, Article VII:4.
46. GATS, Article VII:5.
47. *See* Council for Trade in Services, Accountancy Services, See S/L/38, dated (28 May 1997); Bossche & Zdouc, *supra* note 36, 499.
48. *List of notifications filed under Article VII:4 of GATS* https://docs.wto.org/dol2fe/Pages/FE_Search/FE_S_S006.aspx?Language=English&SourcePage=FE_B_009&Context=Script&DataSource=Cat&Query=%40Symbol%3dS%2fC%2fN%2f*+AND+%40Articles%3dGATS+VII.04&languageUIChanged=true#.
49. *Ibid.*, 428-433.

7.4 RATIONALE BEHIND NEGOTIATING MRAs

MRAs serve as a suitable tool for reducing regulatory barriers and promoting trade, depending on the problems faced by exporters on a case-by-case basis. If the problem is related to the cost of adapting to the different norms and rules, a suitable solution may lie in harmonization i.e. ensuring similar norms and rules in both importing and exporting countries or equivalence i.e. at least recognition of the norms and rules to be fulfilling similar objectives.[50] Harmonization and equivalence may be difficult to achieve due to differences in the economic conditions, environmental risks, health risks, human safety, demography and institutional structure prevailing in countries. However, if the problem lies in the product approval as a result of different CAPs, the solution lies in recognizing the CAPs and CABs mutually so as to facilitate the process of conformity assessment.[51] For instance, a study on the implementation of the EU, Australia and New Zealand MRAs showed that it reduces the fixed costs for the exporters.[52] As a tool of trade facilitation, the primary objective of the MRAs is the reduction of the burden, cost and time on manufacturers by implementing transparent CAPs.[53] MRAs are a manageable example of reducing the cost arising out of regulatory barriers because they are generally sector specific, focusing on technical competence and based on a treaty model.[54] Further, they also remove the instruments available to governments to protect their domestic industry through the use of these norms and regulations.[55] However, the sectors where the major cost occur due to higher TBT requirements and complicated standards, limited scope of MRAs to recognize the CAPs and CABs may not be significantly helpful in reducing costs. For instance, pharmaceuticals exports from US to EU bear a TBT cost of 15.3% and EU exports to US bear a TBT cost of 9.5%, where major component of the cost is market approval and not the product certification requirements.[56]

From the perspective of an importing country, the concept of mutual recognition makes regulatory costs more transparent and reduces the cost advantage occurred to a foreign producer due to lesser degree of regulation.[57] On the other hand, it also prevents the domestic regulators to use regulations as a means of raising the cost of foreign producers to afford protection to their own industry.[58]

50. Elvestad, *supra* note 3, 6.
51. *Ibid.*, 6.
52. *See* S. Baller, *Trade effects of regional standards liberalization: A heterogeneous firm's approach* (World Bank Policy Working Paper 4124, 2007).
53. *Equipment Authorization – Mutual Recognition Agreements*, Federal Communications Commission, https://www.fcc.gov/general/equipment-authorization-mutual-recognition-agreements.
54. Jacques Pelkmans & Anabela Correia de Brito, *Transatlantic MRAs: Lessons for TTIP* (CEPS Special Report No. 101/ March 2015) 1.
55. Pacheco, *supra* note 2, 3.
56. Brito et al, *supra* note 26, 54.
57. Sykes, *supra* note 25, 149.
58. *Ibid.*, 149.

7.5 TYPES OF MRAs

MRAs are typically product/sector specific agreements characterized by lengthy sectoral annexes specifying the detailed list of products covered; scope of extension of the list; rules of origin; recognition of CABs; establishment of a committee for monitoring of CABs; withdrawal of recognition; suspension of CABs; confidentiality; dispute settlement etc. MRAs can be put into the following categories based on the scope of the MRAs, number or nature of parties to the MRA, and sectors covered.

7.5.1 On the Basis of Scope

As per the traditional understanding of MRAs, they are confined to the purpose of recognizing CAPs carried out in the participating countries. The two elements in such MRAs are: the product in question complies with the technical regulation of the importing country and the CAPs and CABs recognized by the importing country through MRA have conducted the conformity assessment. These types of MRAs which are limited to the recognition of CAPs and CABs are termed as *traditional MRAs*.[59] If the scope of MRAs extends beyond the recognition of CAPs and CABs, the MRAs are termed as *enhanced MRAs* (Figure 7.1).

Figure 7.1 Traditional and Enhanced MRAs

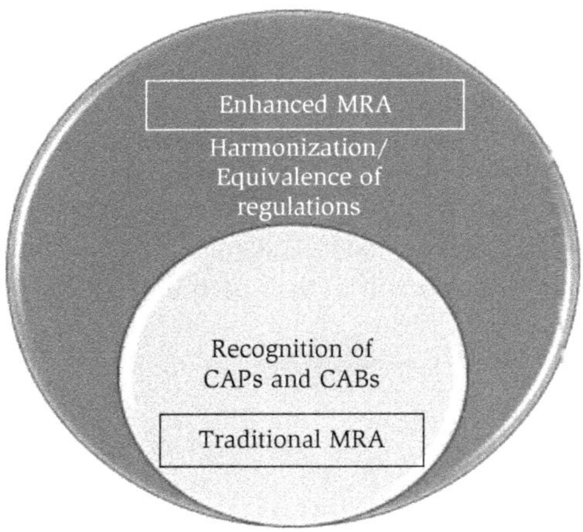

Source: Authors' rendering.

59. *International Agreements (Mutual Recognition Agreements – MRA)*, State Secretariat for Economic Affairs SECO, https://www.seco.admin.ch/seco/en/home/Aussenwirtschaftspolitik_Wirtschaftliche_Zusammenarbeit/Wirtschaftsbeziehungen/Technische_Handelshemmnisse/Mutual_Recognition_Agreement_MRA0.html.

Enhanced MRAs are characterized by prior 'equivalence' achieved through the harmonization of regulations.[60] This categorization becomes more explicit in the EU's approach of signing MRAs. The EU has signed a number of enhanced MRAs which require the candidate countries (i.e. countries which are applying for EU membership) and third countries to fully align their laws with the EU rules and requirements.[61] The EU - Switzerland Agreement is an enhanced MRA and a far more ambitious one. The CAP reports, certificate and authorizations are recognized only when Swiss and EU requirements are deemed equivalent.[62] Switzerland has aligned its relevant laws concerning each product such as RO 2007 2827 (with OJ L No 344, 27.12.2005, p. 44 as the equivalent EU law) for construction plant and equipment.[63] Alternatively, it has signed traditional MRAs with other third countries.[64]

7.5.2 On the Basis of the Parties

Most MRAs are legally binding treaties entered into by two or more governments which specify the conditions by which one party will accept or recognize the results of CAPs in assessing conformity with importing party's regulations. These kinds of MRAs may be bilateral[65] or multilateral[66] and focus extensively on the recognition of CAPs and CABs. They can make up stand-alone agreements or may feature in the free trade agreements (FTAs) entered into by the parties.[67] Such types of MRAs are called *governmental MRAs*.

MRAs entered into by CABs at a national, regional or international level are known as *non-governmental MRAs*. These agreements entered between the CABs where they recognize the quality of each other's process for testing, accreditation, certification or inspection are also known as Mutual/Multilateral Recognition Arrangements (MLAs). These agreements/arrangements do not form an obligation on the

60. Brito et al, *supra* note 26, 17.
61. *Ibid.*, 67.
62. Article 1(2), Agreement between the European Community and the Swiss Confederation on Mutual Recognition in relation to Conformity Assessment ('EU-Switzerland MRA').
63. *See* Directive 2000/14/EC of the European Parliament and of the Council of 8 May 2000 on the approximation of the laws of the Member States relating to the noise emission in the environment by equipment for use outdoors (OJ L No 162, 3.7.2000, p.1), as amended by Directive 2005/88/EC of the European Parliament and of the Council of 14 December 2005 (OJ L No 344, 27.12.2005, p. 44) and corrected by Corrigendum (OJ L 165, 17.6.2006, p. 35); *see* Ordinance of 22 May 2007 on the noise emission in the environment by equipment for use outdoors (RO 2007 2827); *see ibid.*, Annex I, EU-Switzerland MRA; *see generally ibid.*, Annex I.
64. *See also* Agreement on mutual recognition in relation to conformity assessment, certificates and markings between the European Community and Australia, Official Journal of the European Communities, L 229/3 dated 17 August 1998; Agreement on mutual recognition between the European Community and Japan, *Official Journal L 284, 29/10/2001*.
65. Agreement between the European Community and the USA on the Mutual Recognition of Certificates of Conformity for Marine Equipment, Official Journal of the European Communities L 150/46 dated 20 April 2004 https://eur-lex.europa.eu/legal-content/EN/TXT/?uri=CELEX%3A22004A0430%2803%29.
66. ASEAN Sectoral Mutual Recognition Arrangement for Electrical and Electronic Equipment, https://asean.org/?static_post=asean-sectoral-mutual-recognition-arrangement-for-electrical-and-electronic-equipment-preamble-2.
67. Churchman, *supra* note 5, 284.

associated governments. However, their contribution to trade facilitation through recognition is significant. These agreements are more often organized under the international accreditation networks (for instance ILAC and IAF) or IEC System for Conformity Assessment Schemes for Electrotechnical Equipment and Components (IECEE CB Scheme).[68] Approximately 159 CABs from a sample space of 428 CABs reported that their home country operations have formal non-governmental agreements with CABs in other countries.[69] Since such non-governmental MRAs do not put an obligation on their Members to accept each other's result, their effectiveness is disputed.

7.5.3 On the Basis of Covered Sectors

Government-to-government MRAs can be categorized further into multisectoral and single-sector MRAs. MRAs concluded by the EU and EFTA generally cover more than one sector.[70] The most common sectors which are covered in MRAs include telecommunication and electronic or electrical equipment. A possible explanation for the frequency of MRAs in these sectors is that the need of compatibility of equipment in these sectors is prominent.[71] Relative to other products, international standards developed and gained popularity quite early in these products.[72] The multisectoral MRAs heavily rely on international standards. While *multisectoral MRAs* are efficient in wider trade facilitation, there are several problems attached to it. For instance, the negotiations for amendment require a certain degree of consensus which varies according to the pace of technological and other developments in the participating countries. The difficulty in amending the MRAs with a multisectoral approach became quite prominent in the EU – Australia MRA when the parties decided to amend parts of the sectoral annexes in the Agreement. The parties had to agree to give their sectoral annexes a treatment of 'less than a treaty' due to varying degrees of consensus among them.[73]

The following table illustrates the categorization of the EU-Switzerland MRA based on the above-mentioned classifications through a checklist:

---

68. Barbara Fliess & Raymond Schonfield, *Trends in conformity assessment practices and barriers to* trade (OECD Trade Policy Papers No. 37, 2006) 20.
69. *Ibid.*, 21.
70. Agreement on mutual recognition in relation to conformity assessment, certificates and markings between the European Community and Australia, Official Journal of European Communities, L299/3, 17 August 1998;, Agreement on mutual recognition in relation to conformity assessment between the European Community and New Zealand, Official Journal of EU, L 229, 22 December 2012 2 – 18;, Agreement on mutual recognition in relation to conformity assessment between the European Community and Japan, Official Journal of EU, L 284, 29 October 2001, 3-32.
71. Brito et al., *supra* note 2, 30.
72. *See* International Electrotechnical Commission, https://www.iec.ch/technical-committees-and-subcommittees#tclist; International Telecommunication Union, https://www.itu.int/en/ITU-T/publications/Pages/recs.aspx.
73. The Agreement between the EU and Australia amending the Agreement on mutual recognition in relation to conformity assessment, certificates and markings between the European Community and Australia, Official Journal of EU, L 359/2 dated 29 December 2012.

Characteristics		*Categorization*		
Scope of MRA	Traditional MRA	✖	Enhanced MRA[74]	✔
Parties to the MRA	Governmental MRA[75]	✔	Non-Governmental MRA	✖
Sectoral Coverage	Single-sector MRA	✖	Multisectoral MRA[76]	✔

While the categorization of the MRAs differ, their intention in most cases remains centrally focused on the recognition of CABs and CAPs. In some cases, mostly MRAs concluded by the EU with its potential member countries and neighbouring countries, the MRAs also tend to include some characteristics of harmonization and equivalence.

7.6 MRAs UNDER FREE TRADE AGREEMENTS

FTAs in recent times have emerged as a tool for bilateralization of trade rules in the sense that they increasingly cover regulation of areas which are not directly dealt with under the wider multilateral framework. Apart from the liberalization of tariffs, FTAs now also focus on the liberalization of non-tariff barriers and trade facilitation. As a result, multiple FTAs now also include chapters on TBT and have MRAs annexed to the main agreement.[77] ASEAN members signed a framework for developing MRAs and later agreed upon sectoral MRAs in electrical equipment, telecommunications and cosmetics. These MRAs only require the parties to accept the test reports and certifications provided by other parties.[78]

The provision for mutual recognition in FTAs varies depending on the parties entering into these agreements and their development status. Some agreements replicate the language in Article 6.3 of the TBT Agreement and 'encourage' the parties to conclude MRAs. In some FTAs the provisions require an explanation from the parties for not concluding MRAs.[79] Some agreements provide a liberal approach of recognizing the testing process and certification if undertaken outside the members of the FTAs.[80] Some agreements contain a mandate to only recognize the accreditations and approvals taking place in the territory of the other member, hence discriminating against the non-FTA members.[81] Japan's Economic Partnership Agreements also showcase two approaches, one to only require the registration of CABs in other parties to recognize

74. *See* Article 1(2), EU-Switzerland MRA, *supra* note 62.
75. *See* Preamble, *ibid.*
76. *See* Article 3 and Annex 1, *Ibid.*
77. Churchman, *supra* note 5, 303.
78. Hamanaka et al, *supra* note 12, 19.
79. Ana Cristina Molina & Vira Khoroshavina, *TBT provisions in Regional Trade Agreements: To what extent do they go beyond the WTO TBT Agreement?* (WTO Staff Working Paper No. ERSD - 2015-09, December 2015), 13.
80. *See* ASEAN Harmonized Conformity Assessment Procedures for EEE, Appendix C, para. 1.2.
81. *See Australia-United States Free Trade Agreement*, Ch. 8; *see also* Hamanaka et al, *supra* note 12, 19.

their testing and certification procedures[82] and other where CABs are required to be accredited by the Japanese Government.[83] The first approach seems more liberal than the second one. Figure 7.2 highlights examples of recognition provisions in some of the FTAs.

Figure 7.2 Examples of Different Types of Recognition Provisions Used in FTAs

Reasons for rejection of request to negotiate	• For instance: Agreement between New Zealand and the Separate Customs Territory of Taiwan, Penghu, Kinmen and Matsu on Economic Cooperation (Article 6.11) - *Further to Article 6.3 of the TBT Agreement, where a Party declines a request of the other Party to enter into negotiations for the conclusion of agreements for mutual recognition of results of each other's conformity assessment procedures, it shall on the request of that other Party explain the reasons for its decision.*
Best endeavour clause for negotiations and reasons for rejection of request to negotiate	• For instance: Singapore - Costa Rica FTA (Article 6.6.5) *At the request of a Party, the other Party shall give favourable consideration to enter into negotiations to reach agreement on facilitating recognition in its territory of the results of conformity assessment procedures conducted by bodies in the other Party, including mutual recognition agreements, subject to the interests of both Parties. Where a Party declines a request from the other Party, it shall explain its reasons upon request.*
Territorial limitation on recognition of CAPs - exclusive to CABs located in FTA members	• For instance: Australia - United States Free Trade Agreement (Article 8.6.3) - Each Party shall accredit, approve, license, or otherwise recognise conformity assessment bodies in the territory of the other Party on terms no less favourable than those it accords to conformity assessment bodies in its territory....
Registration of CABs with the other Party to FTA	• For instance: Japan - Singapore Economic Partnership Agreement (Article 46) - *Each Party shall accept, in accordance with the provisions of this Chapter, the results of conformity assessment procedures required by the applicable laws, regulations and administrative provisions of that Party specified in the relevant Sectoral Annex, including certificates and marks of conformity, that are conducted by the registered conformity assessment bodies of the other Party.*

Source: Shintaro Hamanaka et al., *Trade Facilitation Measures under Free Trade Agreements: Are They Discriminatory Against Non-members?* (ADB Working Paper Series on Regional Economic Integration No. 55, July 2010) 13-14; Ana Cristina Molina & Vira Khoroshavina, *TBT Provisions in Regional Trade Agreements: To What Extent Do They Go Beyond the WTO TBT Agreement?* (WTO Staff Working Paper No. ERSD – 2015-09, December 2015), 13.

Among the more recent mega Regional Trade Agreements (RTAs) such as the Regional Comprehensive Economic Partnership Agreement (RCEP), recognize MRAs as a mechanism to facilitate the acceptance of CAPs. It also imposes an obligation on the importing party to explain reasons for not accepting the results of exporting party's CAPs.[84] Concerning SPS measures, similar to the SPS Agreement, it also requires

82. *See* Agreement between Japan and the Republic of Singapore for a New-Age Economic Partnership, Articles 46, 53, Ch. 6.
83. Agreement between Japan and Philippines for Economic Partnership, Article 60; Agreement between Japan and Thailand for an Economic Partnership, Article 62.
84. Regional Comprehensive Economic Partnership Agreement, Article 6.8(4), https://rcepsec.org/wp-content/uploads/2020/11/Chapter-6.pdf.

parties to enter into an agreement to bilaterally recognize their equivalence with respect to a single measure or a group.[85] Similarly, the new US-Mexico-Canada Agreement (USMCA) also imposes an obligation on the parties to explain its inability to recognize the results of a CAB which is party to the MLA and its declination to continue negotiation of the MRA.[86] It applies a similar standard for declination to accept the technical regulation of a party as equivalent to the importing party's technical regulations. This USMCA also emphasizes on the use of international standards as regulation thus also promoting harmonization.[87]

7.7 MRAs AND THE DEVELOPMENT PERSPECTIVE

Despite the provision of special and differential treatment concerning lower tariffs for imports from developing and least developed countries, these countries have still not attained the desired level of development. Among multiple reasons for the same, high non-tariff barriers such as standards, technical regulations, CAPs, etc. on imports from developing countries and LDCs poses major challenges to such countries.[88] Due to varied levels of development, both economic and technological, developing countries face several challenges while negotiating MRAs.

While MRAs are viewed as a tool for facilitating trade and removing regulatory barriers, the representation of low-income countries in the universe of MRAs remains bleak.[89] In the few developed-developing countries/LDCs agreements, the developed countries adopt different strategies while negotiating MRAs or MRA provision(s) in their FTAs with the developing and the LDCs. For instance, the EU-Algeria FTA requires Algeria to encourage the European standards and upgrade its CAB to the international standards leading to the eventual negotiations of an MRA.[90] On the other hand, the EU - Singapore FTA only stipulates that the parties should facilitate trade through the unilateral recognition of the CAP results of each other's CABs.[91] In a nutshell, the MRAs between the developed countries and the developing countries or LDCs are mostly in the nature of enhanced MRAs, whereas the MRAs among the developed countries are mostly in the nature of traditional MRAs. In other words, the conclusion of the MRA is highly guided by the development status of the parties.[92] The

85. *Ibid.*, Article 5.5(4), https://rcepsec.org/wp-content/uploads/2020/11/Chapter-5.pdf.
86. United States- Mexico-Canada Agreement, Article 11.6.4.
87. *Ibid.*, Article 11.5.
88. *Non-Tariff Measures to Trade: Economic and Policy Issues for Developing Countries*, UNCTAD, UNCTAD/DITC/TAB/2012/1 (2013), 28, https://unctad.org/en/PublicationsLibrary/ditctab20121_en.pdf.
89. Juan A. Marchetti and Petros C. Mavroidis, *I now recognize you (and only you) as equal: an anatomy of (mutual) recognition agreements in GATS* in Ioanniz Lianos and Okeoghene Odudu ed., Regulating Trade in Services in the EU and the WTO 439 (Cambridge University Press, 2012).
90. Council Decision on the signing, on behalf of the European Community, of the Euro-Mediterranean Agreement establishing an Association between the European Community and its Member States, of the one part, and the People's Democratic Republic of Algeria, of the other part, 6786/02, Article 55 (12 April 2006).
91. FTA between the EU and the Republic of Singapore, Article 4.7(1)(e).
92. Pacheco, *supra* note 2, 4, 5.

primary reason is that countries that sign agreements as technical as MRAs need a certain level of trust in the other parties' technical competence and certifying bodies that few developing nations are likely to be able to provide.[93]

This requirement of trust also excludes numerous developing countries which do not possess matching technical competence, creating a two-tier system.[94] There are several disadvantages attached to this two-tier system where the first tier is occupied by the developed countries and developing countries automatically occupy the second tier. The discriminatory effects of MRAs remain undisciplined under WTO's multilateral trading framework and on an economical level, it also harms the competitiveness of firms in the developing countries or the second-tier countries.[95] Some other concerns of developing countries have been often raised before the Committee on TBT in its Triennial Review.[96] These concerns relate to cost, transparency, exclusionary nature of MRAs, opportunities to enter into and negotiate for the conclusion of MRAs, the need to take into account qualities of CABs than the origin of the product and efficiency and effectiveness of MRAs to solve the problem of multiple testing and CAPs.[97]

7.8 INDIAN PERSPECTIVE ON MRAs

In India, the four major bodies involved in conformity assessment and international cooperation through MRAs are (i) Bureau of Indian Standards under the Ministry of Consumer Affairs, Food and Public Distribution (BIS); (ii) National Accreditation Board of Calibration and Testing Laboratories (NABL) under the Quality Council of India; (iii) National Accreditation Board for Certification Bodies (NABCB); and (iv) Export Inspection Council (EIC) under the Department of Commerce, Ministry of Commerce and Industry. Though the function, objective, and scope of these bodies differ from each other on multiple aspects, they share a common function of negotiating MRAs or MLAs. Considering high imports to India coupled with such a regulatory structure of administering MRAs, this part provides a detailed understanding of MRAs.

7.8.1 Bureau of Indian Standards

The BIS is responsible for the creation of standards for the imported and domestic goods entering into the Indian market under the BIS Act, 2016.[98] Apart from the establishment of Indian standards, the BIS play a crucial role in the *recognition of Indian Standards* outside India with any country or international institution of another

93. *Ibid.*, 4.
94. Baldwin, *supra* note 19, 276.
95. *Ibid.*, 277.
96. Committee on TBT, First Triennial Review of the Operation and Implementation of the TBT Agreement under Article 15.4, G/TBT/5 (19 November 1997) (hereinafter 'First Triennial Review'); *see* Seventh Triennial Review, *supra* note 35; Committee on TBT, Thematic session on CAPs, G/TBT/GEN/155 (29 October 2013), para. 5.
97. First Triennial Meeting under Article 15, G/TBT/5.
98. Bureau of Indian Standards Act, 2016, ss 2(17), 10(2)(a) (hereinafter 'BIS Act, 2016').

country.[99] BIS is empowered to recognize or accredit any institution,[100] in India as well as outside India, performing conformity assessment tests.[101] The BIS is delegated with the duty to promote, monitor and manage the quality of goods.[102] Altogether, these provisions evidence the authority of the BIS to enter into MRAs. Consequently, the BIS has entered into 30 Memoranda of Understanding (MOU) which are of a soft law character lacking binding force,[103] including seven (7) Bilateral Cooperation Agreements (BCA).[104] The BIS is also a member of IECEE CB Scheme on account of which the CAP results of electrotechnology equipment of the exporting country are recognized in the importing country. It is crucial to note that the BCAs entered by the BIS fulfils the purpose of mutual recognition only when the product's standards and the testing method's standards are harmonized,[105] implying the nature of enhanced MRAs. The inspection test results are recognized only if the exporting country's testing laboratories are recognized against ISO/IEC 17025. Among the 7 BCAs, the BCA between India and Israel assumes that the standards of both the parties are based on international standards, and in the event, there exist any deviations, the importing country can perform its own complementary tests.[106] The test reports of the exporting country are recognized in the importing country only if the exporting country's testing procedure is comparable to the importing country's testing procedure.[107] Such BCAs entered by India are governmental MRA because these MRAs stipulate that any dispute, controversy or claims arising under the BCA are referred to the 'respective Governments' if the negotiations and consultations fail.[108]

---

99. BIS Act, 2016, s. 9(1)(c).
100. Accreditation is a process involving an independent evaluation of CABs in light of the recognized standards and hence ensures impartiality and competence of such bodies.
101. BIS Act, 2016, s. 9(2)(f).
102. BIS, 2016, s. 9(2)(h).
103. For instance, in the case of BCAs, the countries are mandatorily required to accept each other's result. Whereas, the MOU only requires the countries to exchange information as to the rules, procedures and technical information pertaining to standardization and certification, organize training programs. In other words, the MOU do not create any obligation pertaining to the acceptance of the results.
104. *Details on MOUs signed with Countries/Organizations*, Bureau of Indian Standards, http://bis.gov.in/wp-content/uploads/2018/11/List_of_MoUs_-_MRAs.pdf.
105. The MRAs entered by the BIS are (i) Agreement between the BIS and Associação Brasileira de Normas Técnicas on Cooperation in Mutual Recognition, 2016, Article 3.1.4; (ii) Agreement between the BIS and Bhutan Standards Bureau, 2015, Article 3.1.4; (iii) Agreement between BIS and Bangladesh Standards and Testing Centre, 2015, Article 3.1.4; (iv) Bilateral Cooperation Agreement between the BIS and Sri Lanka Standards Institution, 2006, Article 3.1.4, Article 3.1.3 (hereinafter 'India-Sri Lana MRA'); (v) Agreement between the BIS and Nepal Bureau of Standards and Metrology on Cooperation in the Field of Standardization and Conformity Assessment, 2017, Article 4.1.4 (hereinafter 'India-Nepal MRA'); (vi) Agreement between the BIS and Pakistan Standards and Quality Control Authority, 2012, Article 3.1.4.
106. BCA between Bureau of Indian Standards and Standards Institution of Israel, 1994, Articles 4.1, 4.2.
107. *Ibid.*, Article 4.4.
108. *See* India – Sri Lanka MRA, Article 11; India – Nepal MRA, Article 13.

7.8.2 National Accreditation Board of Calibration and Testing Laboratories

NABL is established by the Quality Council of India, and is member of ILAC. It provides accreditation to testing laboratories,[109] calibration laboratories,[110] medical testing laboratories,[111] proficiency testing providers[112] and reference material providers[113] based on ISO/IEC 17011.[114] By being party to ILAC MRA, which is a non-governmental MRA, the CAP result by any other members of ILAC will be recognized in India, and the CAP result of any NABL accredited laboratory may be recognized outside India by such similar organizations.[115]

NABL is also a member of Asia Pacific Accreditation Cooperation (APAC). The primary role of APAC is the management and expansion of the MRAs to which accreditation bodies in Asia-Pacific regions are members. Similar to ILAC MRA, the NABL MRA also allows the recognition and hence acceptance of CAP results of the APAC members.[116] APAC is also a regional body recognized under ILAC. The scope of NABL APAC MRA is broader than ILAC as the APAC covers the conformity assessment by the CABs based on the ISO/IEC 17065,[117] ISO/IEC 17021-1,[118] ISO/IEC 17024,[119] and ISO 14065[120] standards.

It is crucial to note that the difference between the scope of the MRAs entered by the BIS and NABL lies in the fact that BIS MRAs covers only the recognition of

---

109. The testing laboratories are accredited as per ISO/IEC 17025 standards.
110. *Ibid.*
111. Medical testing laboratories are accredited as per ISO 150189. *See ISO 15189:2012 Medical laboratories – Requirements for quality and competence*, ISO, https://www.iso.org/standard/56115.html.
112. Proficiency testing providers assesses the performance of laboratories for their conduct of specific test. See *ISO/IEC 17043:2010(en) Conformity assessment – General requirements for proficiency testing*, ISO, https://www.iso.org/obp/ui/#iso:std:iso-iec:17043:ed-1:v1:en.
113. Reference materials are a fundamental instrument for the reliability of the results of tests, calibrations, inspections and verifications. *Reference materials*, Accredia, https://www.accredia.it/en/accredited-services/reference-materials/.
114. *Introduction*, NABL, https://nabl-india.org/about-nabl/introduction/; *see ISO/IEC 17011:2017 (en) Conformity assessment – Requirements for accreditation bodies accrediting conformity assessment bodies*, ISO, https://www.iso.org/obp/ui/#iso:std:iso-iec:17011:ed-2:v1:en:term:3.1.
115. ILAC Mutual Recognition Agreement, 7, https://ilac.org/?ddownload=891.
116. APAC Constitution, Articles 2.1 ((6), (9),(12),(10)) (January 2020), https://apac-production-wp.s3.ap-southeast-2.amazonaws.com/app/uploads/2019/12/31112105/APAC-GOV-001-Constitution-Ver-1.1-20200101.docx; APAC Regulations and Code, Article 3.1(17) (January 2019), https://apac-production-wp.s3.ap-southeast-2.amazonaws.com/app/uploads/2018/11/19082935/APAC-GOV-002-Regulations-Codes-Ver-1.0-20190101-1.docx; *APAC MRA*, APAC https://www.apac-accreditation.org/apac-mra/.
117. *See ISO/IEC 17065:2012(en) Conformity assessment – Requirements for bodies certifying products, processes and services*, ISO, https://www.iso.org/obp/ui/#iso std:iso-iec:17065:ed-1:v1:en.
118. *See ISO/IEC 17021-1:2015(en) Conformity assessment – Requirements for bodies providing audit and certification of management systems – Part 1: Requirements*, ISO, https://www.iso.org/obp/ui/#iso:std:iso-iec:17021:-1:ed-1:v1:en.
119. *See ISO/IEC 17024:2012(en) Conformity assessment – General requirements for bodies operating certification of persons*, ISO, https://www.iso.org/obp/ui/#iso:std:iso-iec:17024:ed-2:v1:en.
120. *See ISO 14065:2020(en) General principles and requirements for bodies validating and verifying environmental information*, ISO, https://www.iso.org/obp/ui/#iso:std:iso:14065:ed-3:v1:en.

conformity assessment test by testing laboratories and calibration laboratories due to coverage limited to ISO 17025.[121] Whereas, the MRAs entered by NABL cover the recognition of the conformity assessment tests by testing laboratories, calibration laboratories, medical testing laboratories, proficiency testing providers and reference material providers, implying wider coverage of the MRAs than BIS. The scope of CABs under NABL extend to the following:

Testing Laboratories	*Calibration Laboratories*	*Medical Laboratories*	*Proficiency Testing Providers*	*Reference Material Providers*
Biological	Fluid Flow	Clinical Biochemistry	Testing	Chemical Composition
Chemical	Mechanical	Clinical Pathology	Calibration	Physical Properties
Electrical	Radiological	Genetics	Medical	Engineering Properties
Electronics	Thermal & Optical	Cytopathology	Inspection	Miscellaneous Properties
Fluid Flow	Electro technical	Histopathology		Biological & Clinical Properties
Mechanical		Microbiology & Serology		
Non-Destructive Testing		Haematology & Immunohaematology		
Photometry		Nuclear Medicine (in-vitro tests only)		
Radiological				
Thermal				
Forensic				

Source: *Frequently Asked Questions*, NABL, https://nabl-india.org/faq/#6.

7.8.3 National Accreditation Board for Certification Bodies

NABCB accredits certification and inspection bodies after assessing their criteria based on relevant international standards. Similar to NABL, NABCB is also a member of ILAC, APAC and IAF. IAF enhances acceptance of goods and services across the borders by removing TBT in the field of *management systems, products, services,*

121. *See* ISO/IEC 17025 enables the laboratories to demonstrate that they operate competently and generate valid results, thereby promoting confidence in their work both nationally and around the world. *See ISO/IEC 17025 Testing and Calibration Laboratories*, ISO, https://www.iso.org/ISO-IEC-17025-testing-and-calibration-laboratories.html.

personnel and other similar programmes of conformity assessment.[122] Being a member of IAF,[123] NABCB covers energy management,[124] food safety management systems,[125] information security management systems,[126] occupational health, and safety management system,[127] certification of persons,[128] quality management systems,[129] and many more.[130] Similar to ILAC MRA, IAF MLA is a non-governmental MRA making it redundant as the national regulatory bodies may refuse the acceptance of the result.

7.8.4 Export Inspection Council of India

The EIC is the official certification authority for the exports of Indian products. It certifies the safety and quality of Indian exports. It was established under section 3 of the Export (Quality Control and Inspection) Act, 1963. The EIC plays a vital role in ensuring that the notified products under the Export (Quality Control and Inspection) Act 1963 fulfil the requirements pertaining to the standards of the importing country. The EIC aims to develop foreign trade in India through the exports of Indian products.[131] It creates a quality standard for the specific exports notified under the Export (Quality Control and Inspection) Act 1963.[132] EIC is also empowered to enter into MRAs, and consequently, the CAP result by the EIC or its agency is recognized in the importing country. It is crucial to note that recognition agreements entered by the EIC are different, unlike other MRAs where both the parties of the MRA or MLA recognizes each other CAP's result. These agreements stipulate that *only* the CAP result of Indian exports will be recognized in the importing country. The EIC's recognition agreements do not put any reciprocal obligation on the EIC/India to accept the CAP result of imports to India. EIC's recognition agreements are not 'mutual' in nature. The EIC provides recognition to the laboratories based on the ISO 17025 and inspection agencies based on the ISO 17020 for conformity assessment. The EIC has entered into the following recognition agreements:

---

122. *About Us*, IAF, https://www.iaf.nu//articles/About/2.
123. *The Scopes*, IAF, https://www.iaf.nu/articles/Scopes/16.
124. *See ISO 50001 Energy Management*, ISO, https://www.iso.org/iso-50001-energy-management.html.
125. *See ISO/TS 22003:2013 Food safety management systems – Requirements for bodies providing audit and certification of food safety management systems*, ISO, https://www.iso.org/standard/60605.html.
126. Information Security Management systems are based on ISO/IEC 17021-1.
127. Occupational Health and Safety Management Systems are based on 17021-1.
128. *See ISO/IEC 17024:2012 Conformity assessment – General requirements for bodies operating certification of persons*, ISO, https://www.iso.org/standard/52993.html#:~:text=ISO%2FIEC%2017024%3A2012%20contains,a%20certification%20scheme%20for%20persons.
129. Quality management systems are based on 17021-1.
130. *About: National Accreditation Board for Certification Bodies*, NABCB, http://nabcb.qci.org.in/about.php.
131. *About Us*, EIC, https://www.eicindia.gov.in/WebApp1/pages/menuInfo/aboutUs.xhtml.
132. *Ibid*.

Sl. No.	*Agreement for the recognition of Indian exports*	*Importing Country*	*Product*	*Details*
1.	Recognition of Black Pepper by the United States Food & Drug Administration (USFDA)	United States	Black Pepper	The EIC issues certification showing conformance of the black pepper export to the USA as per the US standards. However, the US FDA *will* audit such certificates issued by the EIC.[133]
2.	Commission Decision of 23 December 1997 laying down special conditions governing imports of fishery and aquaculture products originating in India	EU	Fishery and aquaculture products	The European Commission has empowered the EIC to verify and certify the compliance of the fishers to be exported from India with the EU standards.[134]
3.	Agreement for recognition of Export Inspection & Certification System of EIC of India and Import Inspection Scheme for Sri Lanka Standards Institution ('SLSI')	Sri Lanka	All products such as food, beverages, cement, steel, etc. covered in Schedule-I of the Imports (Standardization and Quality Control) Regulation 2001 (Sri Lanka).	It empowers the EIC to inspect and certify the Indian exports to Sri Lanka in accordance with SLSI's import inspection scheme, specifically the health and safety of the products.[135]

133. Summary of meeting between US FDA and Ministry of Commerce (India), 20 April 1988, https://www.eicindia.gov.in/WebApp1/resources/PDF/02_BlackPepper.pdf
134. Commission Decision of 23 December 1997 laying down special conditions governing imports of fishery and aquaculture products originating in India, 97/876/EC, Article 1.
135. Agreement for recognition of Export Inspection & Certification System of EIC of India and Import Inspection Scheme for Sri Lanka Standards Institution, Preamble, https://www.eicindia.gov.in/WebApp1/resources/PDF/05_SLSISrilanka.pdf.

Sl. No.	*Agreement for the recognition of Indian exports*	*Importing Country*	*Product*	*Details*
4.	Korea Food and Drug Administration's notice of approval of foreign authorized inspection organization	Republic of Korea	Food Products	The inspection report of certain inspection agency for the Indian food exports will be recognized in Korea.[136]
5.	Ministry of Commerce and Industry's letter TOK/COM/ 20710/2004 dated 19 October 2005	Japan	Poultry meat and its product	The hygiene certificate issued by India for the export of poultry meats and its products will be recognized in Japan.[137]
6.	Agreement on Co-operation on Inspection of Iron Ore between EIC of the Republic of India and the General Administration of Quality Supervision, Inspection and Quarantine of the Republic of China	China	Iron Ore	The inspection certificates of iron ore exports by the EIC or its recognized agencies based on Chinese standards and other relevant international standards will be accepted in China.[138]

136. Korea Food and Drug Administration's notice of approval of foreign authorized inspection organization, Article 19(3), https://www.eicindia.gov.in/WebApp1/resources/PDF/06_KFDA .pdf; Food Sanitation Act (Korea).

137. Ministry of Commerce and Industry's letter TOK/COM/ 20710/2004 dated 19 October 2005, https://www.eicindia.gov.in/WebApp1/resources/PDF/08_PoultryProductJapan.pdf.

138. Agreement on Co-operation on Inspection of Iron Ore between EIC of the Republic of India and the General Administration of Quality Supervision, Inspection and Quarantine of the Republic of China, Article 1, https://www.eicindia.gov.in/WebApp1/resources/PDF/09_IronOREChina .pdf.

Sl. No.	*Agreement for the recognition of Indian exports*	*Importing Country*	*Product*	*Details*
7.	India-Singapore Comprehensive Economic Cooperation Agreement, Annex 5B - Sectoral Annexes on Food	Singapore	Egg and egg products, dairy products, packaged drinking waters	The CAP by the EIC or its agencies for food products, especially to the Indian exports of egg products, dairy products, packaged drinking waters will be recognized in Singapore.[139]
8.	Memorandum between the Federal Service for Veterinary and Phytosanitary Surveillance (FSVPS) of the Russian Federation and EIC of India on food and biological safety of fish, fishery products and seafood to be exported to the Russian Federation from India	Russia	Sea products	The EIC ensures that the Indian exports of sea products to Russia meet the Russian requirements. FSVPS is empowered to random monitoring of such sea products.[140] Together, these stipulations imply the recognition of EC's certificate for the exports of sea products will be recognized in Russia.
9.	Embassy of India, Bangkok letter No./Ban/Comm/207/2/2012 dated 7 December 2012	Thailand	Food products	The EIC certification ensuring the compliance of Indian food exports to

139. India-Singapore Comprehensive Economic Cooperation Agreement, Annex 5B - Sectoral Annexes on Food Products, Article 3.1, 3.3, Appendix 1-3, https://www.eicindia.gov.in/WebApp1/resources/PDF/10_EggandotherSingapure.pdf.

140. Protocol on discussions held between Federal Service for Veterinary and Phytosanitary Surveillance and EIC of India, 28 July 2009, https://www.eicindia.gov.in/WebApp1/resources/PDF/12_Inter_recog_FSVPS.pdf.

Sl. No.	*Agreement for the recognition of Indian exports*	*Importing Country*	*Product*	*Details*
				Thailand will be recognized in Thailand.[141]
10.	Agreement related to the trade and safety of Feed and Feed ingredients between EIC of India, Ministry of Commerce and Industry, Government of India and the General Administration of Quality Supervision, Inspection and Quarantine of the Republic of China	China	Feed and Feed ingredients	India and China recognize each other's conformity assessment certificate ensuring the compliance of feed and feedstuffs exports with each other's safety, hygiene and plant quarantine requirements as an importing country.[142]
11.	Agreement for Recognition of Equivalence of Food Inspection and Certification Systems covering fish and fishery products exported from India to the USA	Australia	Fish and fish products	The inspection results of Indian exports of fish and fishery products will be recognized in Australia.[143]

141. Embassy of India, Bangkok letter No./Ban/Comm/207/2/2012 dated 7 December 2012, https://www.eicindia.gov.in/WebApp1/resources/PDF/EIC-Certification-Thailand.pdf.
142. Agreement related to the trade and safety of Feed and Feed ingredients between EIC of India and the General Administration of Quality Supervision, Inspection and Quarantine of the Republic of China, Article 1, https://www.eicindia.gov.in/WebApp1/resources/PDF/14-ChinaFeed.pdf.
143. Agreement for Recognition of Equivalence of Food Inspection and Certification Systems covering fish and fishery products exported from India to Australia, Article 1(5), http://115.112.238.112/eic/04_FishFisheryAustralia.pdf.

7.9 MRAs IN INDIA'S FTAs

There has been a significant shift in India's foreign trade policy as is evident from India's greater participation in regional trade agreements.[144] For improved market access, India has included provisions for co-operation in the field of MRA in the following FTAs:

Sl. No.	*Free Trade Agreement*	*Parties*	*Details of MRAs*
1.	Preferential Trade Agreement between the Republic of Chile and the Republic of India ('India - Chile PTA')	Chile and India	Article XII requires the parties to co-operate in the field of conformity assessment by recognizing and accepting the CAP results of each other to facilitate market access.[145] Article XIII imposes similar obligations pertaining to MRAs in the field of SPS measures.[146]
2.	Comprehensive Economic Partnership Agreement between Japan and the Republic of India ('India - Japan CEPA')	Japan and India	Under Article 55, India and Japan have taken the commitment to co-operate in the field of MRAs. It expressly stipulates electrical products, telecommunications terminal equipment, and radio equipment sectors requiring cooperation in MRA through a sub-committee.[147] It imposes an obligation on India and Japan to conclude upon the feasibility of MRAs, and hence the conclusion of MRA within 3 years as to the conclusion of the feasibility of the MRAs.[148]

144. Mohammed Saqib & Nisha Taneja, *Non-Tariff Barriers and India's Exports: The case of ASEAN and Sri Lanka* (Indian Council for Research on International Economic Relations Working Paper No. 165, July 2005), 1.
145. India - Chile PTA, Article XII(3).
146. *Ibid.*, Article XIII(6).
147. India - Japan CEPA, Article 55(1).
148. *Ibid.*, Article 55(2).

Sl. No.	*Free Trade Agreement*	*Parties*	*Details of MRAs*
3.	Comprehensive Economic Partnership Agreement Between India And the Republic of Korea ('India - Korea CEPA')	India and Korea	Article 2.28 requires Korea and India to enter into MRA on standards, technical regulation and conformity assessment.[149] It also requires these countries to enter into consultation for the MRAs within three years from the date the CEPA becomes effective. The priority has been given to telecommunication equipment, and electrical and electronic equipment.[150]
4.	Comprehensive Economic Cooperation Agreement between the Government of Malaysia and the Government of the Republic of India ('India - Malaysia CECA')	India and Malaysia	Article 7.8(1) requires Indian and Malaysia to facilitate recognition of CABs in each other's territories, and also facilitate the acceptance of each other's CAP results.[151] Article 7.9 requires these parties to enter into negotiations on MRAs.[152]
5.	South Asian Free Trade Agreement ('SAFTA')	Afghanistan, Bangladesh, Bhutan, India, Maldives, Nepal, Pakistan and Sri Lanka.	Article 8 of SAFTA requires its Member Parties to consider the possibility of the recognition of each conformity assessment test and the accreditation of each other's CABs.

149. India - Korea CEPA, Article 2.28(2)(a)(iii).
150. *Ibid.*, Article 2.28(2)(a)(iv), Annex 2-B.
151. India-Malaysia CECA, Article 7.8(1)(d)-(e).
152. *Ibid.*, Article 7.9.

Sl. No.	*Free Trade Agreement*	*Parties*	*Details of MRAs*
6.	Comprehensive Economic Cooperation Agreement Between The Republic of India and the Republic of Singapore ('India – Singapore CECA')	India and Singapore	Article 5.5 mandates India and Singapore to accept the results of each other's CABs provided that the CABs of one party are registered by the Designated Authority of the other party.[153]

Not all of these FTAs have resulted in trade facilitation through MRAs. However, the nature of obligations concerning MRA in these FTAs differ. For instance, India – Chile PTA and SAFTA only encourage the parties to recognize each other's CAB results. India – Singapore CECA provides for the recognition of the result of CABs through the mechanism of the Designated Authority. The other three FTAs impose soft obligations for recognition of CABs generally; however, they also impose a mandatory obligation on the parties to negotiate feasibility of MRAs. For instance, India-Japan CEPA mandates the parties to discuss the feasibility of MRA on certain sectors within three years of entry into force of the CEPA, and arrive at a conclusion about such feasibility within six months. Compared to RCEP and USMCA, Indian FTAs do not require the parties to provide reasons for the failure of negotiations. However, despite the existence of the obligations in Indian FTAs to negotiate MRAs, there has not been much progress since their conclusion.

7.10 CONCLUSION

MRAs contribute immensely as a trade facilitation tool in times when the cost for exporters is increasing due to duplicate CAP requirements such as testing, certification and inspection. While complete harmonization of product regulations and standards remain a far-fetched goal, countries have tried to come together and at least recognize the CAPs and CABs. With increasing international standardization, the scope of MRAs is widening and includes recognition as well as equivalence of product rules and standards. The divide between the developed and developing countries on account of dissimilar technical capabilities still largely exists. However, the MLAs and international standard-setting bodies have an important role to play in reducing this divide. The approach towards these MRAs and MLAs still needs to be altered to address the issues of developing and least developed countries. Some approaches that may be

153. India-Singapore CECA, Article 5.5(iii).

adopted include increased communication between the countries regarding their experiences, agreements to co-operate at a bilateral level, taking into account the feasibility of implementation before beginning the negotiations to avoid failure of agreements, increased acknowledgement of non-governmental agreements, promoting dialogues on a regulator - regulator basis and better information sharing about the implementation of current MRAs.

Considering the rise in India's trade deficit from USD 12.49 billion in 2019 to USD 15.71 billion in 2020, India's approach towards MRAs should aim at seeking market access into its export destinations while being cautious for providing the same reciprocal treatment to the imports from other countries. Such objective can be achieved by the proactive role of the EIC as the existing EIC's recognition agreements are based on such non-reciprocal arrangements. As the first stepping stone, India should focus on the products in which it seeks to achieve global competitiveness through increased market access. The key for India while negotiating MRAs must be based on the assessment of whether the additional costs incurred to its export outweighs the cost of the negotiation of MRAs.

CHAPTER 8

Food Safety Ecosystem in India: A Regulator's View

Rita Teaotia

The Food Safety and Standards Authority of India (FSSAI), set up under the Food Safety and Standards Act, 2006 (FSS Act), is the Indian national regulator responsible for the protection and promotion of public health through regulation of food safety in India. It is the enquiry point notified under the World Trade Organization's (WTO) Agreement on the Application of Sanitary and Phytosanitary Measures (SPS Agreement) for food safety and human health in India. This chapter traces the role that FSSAI plays in India's food safety ecosystem. With an overview of the historical changes that led to the creation of the FSS Act, the chapter outlines the organization structure and functions of FSSAI, providing insights into the role of different functionaries within it. Thereafter, this chapter provides insights into how food standards are developed by FSSAI, how they are enforced and how food products are tested for conformity with FSSAI standards. The chapter particularly highlights the importance of supplementing standard-setting processes with additional initiatives to build consumer awareness on food safety. In that regard, the chapter highlights the work done by FSSAI in capacity building of food business and introduces the Eat Right India initiative.

8.1 INTRODUCTION

In 2006, India enacted the Food Safety and Standards Act, 2006 (FSS Act). The introduction of this law marked a paradigm shift in the Indian approach to regulating the food sector. India transitioned from an era focusing on eliminating only food adulteration to a modern, integrated food law with a focus on voluntary compliance, with an emphasis on horizontal and process standards as well as product standards.

The Food Safety and Standards Authority of India (FSSAI or Authority) was established under this Act. Serving as the sole food regulator in India, this autonomous body is responsible for protecting and promoting public health through the regulation and supervision of food safety in India. It has established a robust architecture of scientific panels (SPs), expert groups and partner institutions to develop comprehensive science-based food standards, harmonized substantively with the Codex Alimentarius Commission, of which India is an early Member. The FSSAI has also developed many codes of practice, guidance documents and training modules to support food businesses in adopting safe food production and handling processes. Latest scientific developments inform the standard-setting work, food consumption practices, changes in processing technology and emerging risks in the area of food. The Authority plays a vital role in formulating measures to eliminate toxic and hazardous elements in food, thus providing a uniform level of assurance of food safety to every consumer.

The FSSAI also oversees the surveillance and enforcement of standards, critical in a robust regulatory environment, through the enforcement machinery of the Centre, States and Union Territories, as well as at nearly 150 ports of entry. The core elements of this enforcement mechanism include uniform licensing and registration rules; a robust network of laboratories engaged in food testing following standard testing methods and protocols; and infrastructure for capacity building of food businesses, laboratory professionals and regulatory staff. The regulatory ambit encompasses not just food production and food service but also its manufacture, storage, transport, retail, import and e-commerce. This chapter intends to lay out the framework of these elements and provide insights into their operations.

The FSSAI supplements its standards and regulatory role with food safety initiatives that target consumers directly. Promoting healthy eating habits and behavioural changes in consumers, as well as food business operators, is a critical function performed by FSSAI in order to give effect to the dictum of health, safety and sustainability in food production and consumption. The Eat Right Initiative is a key initiative in this direction that has recently received global recognition. It is designed to nudge behavioural change in India's diverse and vast landscape in response to the epidemic of lifestyle diseases. It engages with the food industry, professionals, public health organizations, civil society and various government departments in creating a common platform for improved nutritional practices in the country.

The outcomes of this multipronged approach to food safety, quality and nutrition are increasingly visible domestically as well as internationally through India's rising food exports and recognition for the regulator. This chapter recounts India's transition into its current model of food safety regulation, as implemented and effectuated by the FSSAI. It will examine the organizational framework, key functions, and scientific work of FSSAI, as well as the testing ecosystem, import regulations, the capacity building of food businesses, and consumer awareness and outreach. In conclusion, this chapter will emphasize the importance of FSSAI's role in India's efforts at ensuring safe and quality food that conforms to international standards.

8.2 TRANSITION TO 'ONE NATION, ONE FOOD LAW'

The historical importance of ensuring a safe and high-quality food ecosystem through a robust regulatory mechanism can be traced to the Constitution of India. The Constitution enshrines the state's responsibility for ensuring safe food to its citizens. Specifically, Article 21 of the Indian Constitution guarantees the 'right to life' which includes the right to live with dignity, including the right to food.[1] Article 47 of the Constitution also entrusts the state with the primary responsibility raising the nutrition level and standard of living of its people.[2] Finally, Article 246 of the Constitution provides powers to the Parliament of India and state legislatures to make laws and matters related to the adulteration of foodstuffs. These powers are listed under the Concurrent list under schedule VII, thus empowering both the Central government and the States to legislate.[3]

Until 1954, several laws governing food were in force in different states in India, which had considerable variance, leading to partial and imperfect regulation.[4] Independent India's first central legislation on food safety, namely the Prevention of Food Adulteration Act (PFA Act), was enacted by the Government of India in 1954 and it came into effect in 1955, repealing all the then existing state laws concerning food.[5] The PFA Act was the precursor to the present standardization regime in India. It included several provisions for food standards and prevention of adulteration of food. Despite the intention to integrate, the PFA Act did not remain the only legislation governing food safety. The Essential Commodities Act, 1955 was enacted to empower the government to control the production, supply, distribution, trade and commerce in certain commodities. Several orders were issued under this Act, aimed at the regulation of essential food products. These included:

- The Vegetable Oil Products (Control) Order, 1947 and 1980
- The Fruit Products Order, 1955
- The Solvent Extracted Oil, De oiled Meal, and Edible Flour (Control) Order, 1967
- The Meat Food Products Order, 1973
- The Milk and Milk Products Order, 1992 and Amendment Regulations, 2009
- The Edible Oils Packaging (Regulation) Order, 1998.

These Orders were administered by different ministries of the Government of India, and over a period of time, their implementation led to a multiplicity of (often

1. Constitution of India, 1950, Article 21.
2. *Ibid.*, Article 47.
3. *Ibid.*, Article 246.
4. *See for instance* the Assam Pure Food Act, 1932, Bengal Food Adulteration Act, 1919, the Punjab Pure Food Act 1929, the Bombay Prevention of Adulteration Act, 1925, the Madras Prevention of Adulteration Act 1919 and several other similar state/provincial legislations.
5. Section 25, Prevention of Food Adulteration Act, 1954.

overlapping and sometimes contradictory) food regulations and enforcement agencies.[6] These developments created confusion among food businesses, consumers, traders, manufacturers, and investors and hampered the growth of a modern food processing sector in the country. Realizing this inadequacy in the legal framework for food safety in India, the Prime Minister's Council of Trade and Industry in 1998 recommended the enactment of a comprehensive legislation to modernize the food sector and ensure the safety of food.[7] The Food Safety and Standards Act (FSS Act) was notified on 23 August 2006.[8] This Act repealed the PFA Act and all the six Orders mentioned above.[9] The objective of the FSS Act, 2006 as stated in its preamble, is 'to ensure the availability of safe and wholesome food for human consumption'.[10] Figure 8.1 below sets out a graphical representation of the Acts and Orders repealed by the FSS Act.

Figure 8.1 Acts and Orders Repealed by FSS Act

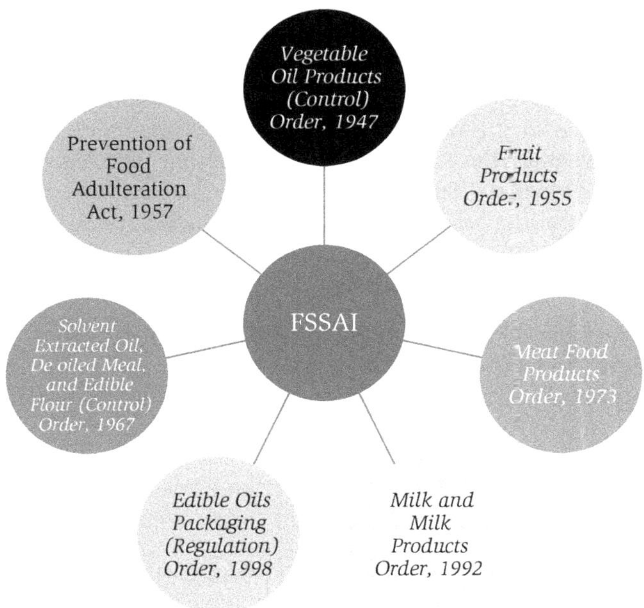

Source: Repealed Acts / Orders, *FSSAI*, https://fssai.gov.in/cms/repealed-acts-orders.php

6. *For instance*, PFA Rules allowed the use of artificial sweetener in certain products but the Fruit Products Order 1955 stipulated the contrary.
7. Standing Committee on Agriculture (2005-06), *The Food Safety and Standards Bill, 2005* (e-parliament library 2006), https://eparlib.nic.in/bitstream/123456789/66511/1/14_Agriculture_16.pdf.
8. Food Safety and Standards Act, 2006 (FSS Act).
9. *Ibid.*, section 97, Schedule II.
10. *Ibid.*, Preamble.

The FSS Act established the FSSAI in 2008[11] as the national food safety regulator, transitioning from multidepartment control to a single line of command. The FSS Act establishes the central principles for the administration of food safety in India.[12] The FSS Act, inter alia, emphasizes science-based risk assessment as the foundation of standard-setting and designates certification of food safety processes or safety audits as an integral component of the regulatory framework for ensuring food safety. The FSS Act also ensures transparency in setting standards by providing reasonable time for stakeholders to suggest proposed regulations and for Food Business Operators (FBOs) to adapt to the new regulations.

FBOs are defined under the FSS Act, and ensuring food safety is their primary statutory obligation. FBOs, in fact, have several obligations across the various stages in a food cycle that require them to adhere to applicable safety practices. The FSS Act emphasizes and adopts the contemporary practice of ensuring 'conformity assessment' to standards, as opposed to the previous practice of regulatory enforcement, making the processes more streamlined and effective. FBOs have also been provided with a legal framework for contesting adverse findings of testing laboratories through a mechanism of appeal. These changes have allowed the operation of the food regulator to be more aligned with contemporary international best practices.

8.3 ORGANIZATIONAL STRUCTURE AND FUNCTIONS

8.3.1 The Structure of FSSAI

The FSSAI comprises a Chairperson and twenty-two Members representing Ministries such as Agriculture, Commerce, Consumer Affairs, Food Processing, Health, Legislative Affairs and other stakeholders including farmers, scientists and technologists, small-scale enterprises, other food businesses and consumer bodies.[13]

The Authority is assisted by the Scientific Committee[14] and various subject-specific SPs[15] in setting standards for food products (21 SPs are currently operational).[16] These panels comprise independent scientific experts who provide scientific and technical advice for the development of food product standards. The Central Advisory Committee (CAC) is an interface between the central and the state food authorities.[17] The CAC comprises representatives of concerned central ministries, State/Union territory governments, and other stakeholders and provides the connecting bridge between the FSSAI and the States. The primary mandate of the CAC is

11. *Ibid.*, section 4.
12. *Ibid.*, section 18(1).
13. *Ibid.*, section 5.
14. *Ibid.*, section 14.
15. The panels are constituted under, section 13 of the Act. Examples of the Scientific Panels include Panel on Contaminants in Food Chains, Panel for Fish and Fisheries Products, Panel on Biological Hazards and Panel on Nutrition and Fortification. The complete list of the twenty-one Scientific Panels is set out in Figure 8.5.
16. *Committees Panels and Groups*, Food Safety and Standards Authority of India, https://fssai.gov.in/cms/committees-panels-and-groups.php.
17. FSS Act, *supra* note 8 at section 11.

advising the FSSAI on its work program, prioritization of work, identifying potential risks, and pooling of knowledge. The CAC serves to ensure uniformity of testing and enforcement throughout the country. Its work is supplemented by the State-level steering committees and District level advisory committees.

The Authority's work is also supported by a network of accredited laboratories – the National Reference Laboratories introduced in 2017, as well as referral labs and primary testing labs recognized under section 43 of the FSS Act. Figure 8.2 sets out an overview of FSSAI and its key related elements.

Figure 8.2 Structure for Standards and Enforcement

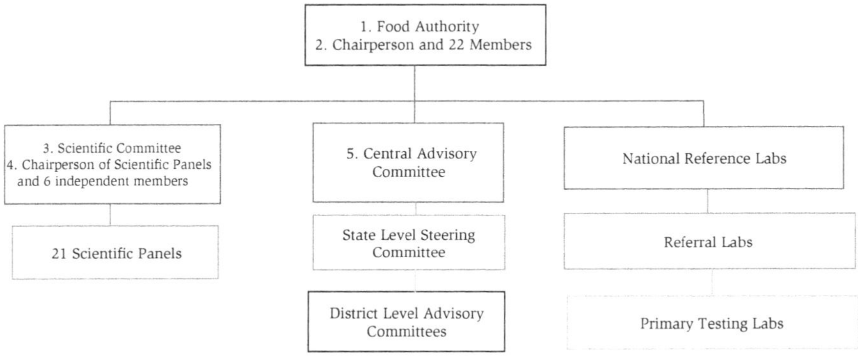

Source: FSSAI, Manual for Food Safety Officers, *Chapter 2: FSSAI, Food Safety Enforcement and State Food Authorities,* 16. 17, https://www.fssai.gov.in/upload/uploadfiles/files/Chapter2.pdf.

8.3.2 Key Functions of FSSAI

India has a federal administrative structure for the enforcement of food safety regulations. The FSSAI and State food safety departments jointly work toward the implementation of the food law in India.[18]

The role of FSSAI is prescribed under the FSS Act. The FSSAI is required to:

- Licence and regulate all food businesses.
- Specify food quality and safety standards and guidelines for food articles.
- Lay down food labelling standards such as claims on health, nutrition, special dietary uses and food categorization.
- Specify limits for additives, colours, contaminants, pesticides, veterinary drug residues, heavy metals, mycotoxins, antibiotics and irradiated foods.
- Prescribe methods of sampling, analysis, and exchange of information among enforcement agencies.

18. *Ibid.*, section 29(1).

- Recognize certification bodies engaged in Food Safety Management Systems (FSMS) auditing/certification.
- Provide scientific advice and technical support to Central/State governments in matters of framing the policy and rules in areas relating to food safety and nutrition, in the implementation of procedures relating to food safety crisis management, and for improving cooperation with international organizations.
- Provide training programs in food safety and standards for persons who are or intend to become involved in food businesses.
- Create an information network across the country to disseminate reliable and objective information on food safety and issues of concern, including the introduction of rapid alert systems to all its stakeholders.
- Contribute and promote coordination of work on food standards undertaken by international governmental and non-governmental organizations.
- Regulate the import of food products.

State Food Safety Commissioners ensure compliance with food safety standards by all food businesses at the field level. They are authorized to grant operational licenses to food businesses in addition to the ones granted at the central level by the FSSAI.[19]

The key functionaries specified under the FSS Act are the Chairperson and the CEO of the Authority at the apex level, supported by scientific and administrative teams. The Authority also has Regional Directors for North, South, West and East Zones and Designated Officers at approximately forty-six ports of entry.

The State food safety machinery comprises the Commissioner of Food Safety,[20] Designated Officers at the District level,[21] Food Safety Officers at the sub-district level,[22] Adjudicating Officers,[23] and Food Analysts.[24]

The Designated Officer (DO) is in charge of food safety administration for any food safety district and is the licensing authority who issues the license of food businesses and improvement notices; the DO also prohibits the sale of any article of food found to be substandard or unsafe, and recommends the launch of prosecutions to the Commissioner of Food Safety. The DO also supervises the actions, including all inspections made by the Food Safety Officer (FSO).

The FSO is the officer at the ground level and is the backbone of the entire food safety compliance structure. An FSO inspects all licensed units, draws samples and investigates complaints. The FSO is vested with regulatory functions and powers and is responsible for the uniform and consistent application of regulatory provisions. FSSAI has published guidance manuals that take into account the role of FSO in particular and covers the regulatory provisions, regulations, inspections, sampling, surveillance and procedures to be followed by FSOs in discharging their duties. Figure

19. *See Food Safety and Standards Regulation 2011 for State Licenses.*
20. *Ibid.*, section 30.
21. *Ibid.*, section 36.
22. *Ibid.*, section 37.
23. *Ibid.*, section 68.
24. *Ibid.*, section 45.

8.3 indicates the elements involved in the food safety enforcement machinery of FSSAI at the State level.

Figure 8.3 Food Safety Enforcement Machinery in the State

Source: FSSAI, Manual for Food Safety Officers, *Chapter 2: FSSAI, Food Safety Enforcement and State Food Authorities,* 18, https://www.fssai.gov.in/upload/uploadfiles/files/Chapter2.pdf.

8.3.3 FSSAI as the Sole Food Safety Regulator

FSSAI is the sole body responsible for establishing standards for food and regulating/enforcing them. However, it also recognizes certain other statutory bodies for specific functions relating to food safety. These statutory bodies are:

8.3.3.1 Bureau of Indian Standards (BIS)

The BIS is the national standards body of India, functioning under the aegis of the Ministry of Consumer Affairs. It is engaged in formulating Indian standards in various technology areas and service sectors, including food. The BIS has formulated over 2,150 Indian standards covering food products and equipment specifications, test methods, and hygiene codes to cover requirements from 'farm to fork'.[25] BIS standards can be voluntary or be made mandatory with the backing of a regulation. The FSSAI's Food Safety and Standards (Prohibition and Restriction of Sales) Regulations, 2011, has made BIS certification mandatory for the manufacture, sale, and distribution of some food products, food-grade equipment and packaging material.[26] Box 1 below sets out the list of such products. FSSAI thus harmonizes the standard-setting process for food products domestically by giving statutory recognition to specific BIS standards. This

25. PR Department, *BIS spearheads to make its mark on the food front,* BIS Blog (16 October 2019), https://blog.bis.gov.in:8098/BISBlog/bis-spearheads-to-make-its-mark-on-the-food-front/.
26. Sections 2, 3, 14, of Food Safety and Standards (Prohibition and Restriction of Sales) Regulations, 2011.

ensures that obtaining a BIS certification after requisite conformity assessment procedures is validly recognized and authorized under the FSS Act.

Box 8.1 List of Products for Which FSSAI Has Made BIS Certification Mandatory

Bureau of Indian Standards

BIS certification made mandatory by FSSAI

- Infant milk food
- Infant formula
- Milk cereal-based weaning food
- Processed cereal-based weaning food
- Follow up formula
- Packaged drinking water
- Mineral water

Other BIS standards recognized by FSSAI

- Potable water
- Some packaging material

Source: *FSSAI*, Manual for Food Safety Officers, *Annexure I*, 149, https://www.fssai.gov.in/upload/uploadfiles/files/Chapter15.pdf.

8.3.3.2 Agricultural Produce (Grading and Marking) Act, 1937

Commonly known as AGMARK, this is a voluntary grading standard for various agricultural commodities. This standard is implemented by the Directorate of Marketing and Inspection (DMI), an attached office of the Department of Agriculture, Cooperation and Farmers Welfare under the Ministry of Agriculture and Farmers Welfare.[27] As is the case with BIS, the FSSAI has mandated AGMARK certification for certain high-risk food products (*See Box 8.2*) instead of preparing separate standards, to ensure harmonization.

27. *Agmark Certification Scheme*, Directorate of Marketing and Inspection, https://dmi.gov.in/Documents/Final%20Text%20Matter%20related%20to%20QC%20Section.pdf.

Box 8.2 List of Mandatory AGMARK Certifications

AGMARK

AGMARK certification made mandatory by FSSAI

- Blended edible vegetable oil
- Fat spread
- Ghee with less than specified Reichert value

The requirement for some products such as Kangra tea, Carbia Callosa, Honey Dew, and Til Oil was removed recently.

Source: Food Safety and Standards (Prohibition and Restriction of Sales) Regulation, 2011.

8.3.3.3 The Export Inspection Council (EIC)

The EIC is the export–certification body of India that functions under the Ministry of Commerce and Industry. The EIC ensures the quality and safety of products exported from India.[28] The EIC provides mandatory certification for various food items, namely fish and fish products, dairy products, honey, egg and meat products, poultry products and meat by-products, feed additives, and pre-mixtures, while other food and non-food products are certified on a voluntary basis.[29] The EIC certification, however, is only for export. The FSSAI presently does not regulate exports.[30] This ensures a clear demarcation between the roles of the two regulators and avoids duplication of standardization rules and procedures.

8.3.3.4 Agricultural and Processed Food Products Export Development Authority (APEDA) and Marine Products Export Development Authority (MPEDA)

APEDA and MPEDA also function under the Ministry of Commerce and Industry, and are mandated to promote export of agriculture produce. While the APEDA is also an export related organization, its National Programme for Organic Production (NPOP)

28. *Export Inspection Council,* Ministry of Commerce, https://commerce.gov.in/about-us/autonomous-bodies/export-inspection-council-of-india-eic/#: ~ :text = The%20Export%20Inspection%20Council%20(EIC,of%20products%20exported%20from%20India.&text = The%20Export%20Inspection%20Council%20is,is%20headed%20by%20a%20Chairman.
29. *Ibid.*
30. FSSAI. *Food Safety and Standards (Amendment) Bill. 2020.* Uploaded for comments on 18.10.2020. Available at https://fssai.gov.in/notifications-archive.php?notification = notice-for-comments.

has been recognized domestically by the FSSAI as one of the schemes for certification of organic food products.[31]

Therefore, while the FSSAI is the sole and primary food safety regulator in India, it works in tandem with several other statutory organizations to ensure the quality and credibility of the food and food products sector.

8.4 DEVELOPMENT OF STANDARDS IN FSSAI

This section examines the process of standards development undertaken by the FSSAI. As noted previously, the FSSAI's major scientific arms are the Scientific Committee (SC) and the SPs. Standards development is undertaken by twenty-one SPs. The food standards are formulated taking into account scientific evidence, the latest developments in food science, including new products and additives, advancement in processing and technology, food analytical methods and identification of new risks. A complete list of the SPs is set out in Figure 8.5. The SC reviews the proposals of the SP and advises the FSSAI regarding the development of standards. The SC and SPs comprise more than 220 independent subject experts/eminent scientists.

The chronological sequencing for the development of food safety standards, from receipt of proposal to final notification, is set out in Figure 8.4.

Figure 8.4 Procedure for Development of Food Safety Standards

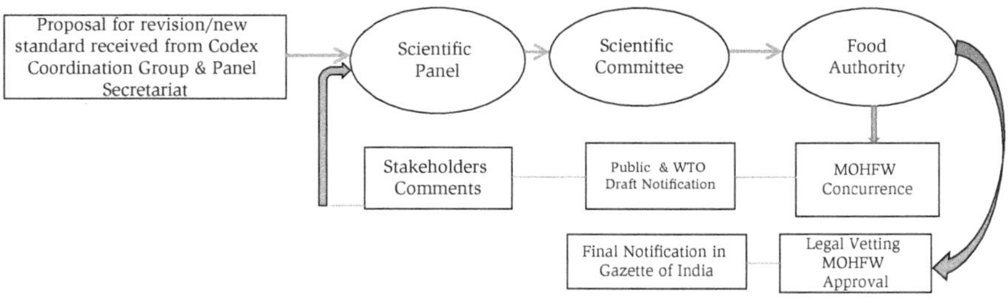

Source: FSSAI, Manual for Development of Food Regulations, *A Typical Flow Chart of Stages for Development of Standards,* 63, https://fssai.gov.in/upload/uploadfiles/files/SOP_Manual_Development_Food_Regulations_30_09_2019.pdf

After recommendation by the SP and validation by the SC, a draft standard is approved by FSSAI and concurred by the Ministry of Health and Family Welfare. Thereafter, a draft notification is issued inviting comments from domestic stakeholders/public and WTO Member Countries within a period of sixty days.[32] The comments received are then considered by the relevant SP, and after approvals of the

31. *Organic Food,* Food Safety and Standards Authority of India, <https://fssai.gov.in/cms/standards-organic-food.php>.
32. *SPAN-COM (Ver. 1.0) Handbook for Members of Scientific Panel & Scientific Committee, FSSAI (2020), Internal Publication.*

Scientific Committee, Food Authority, and the Ministry, the standard is finally notified as either an amendment to an existing regulation or a new/revised regulation. The list of horizontal and vertical panels established under the FSSAI is given in Figure 8.5.

Figure 8.5 List of Horizontal and Vertical Scientific Panels under FSSAI

HORIZONTAL	VERTICAL
SP-01: Food Additives, Flavourings, Processing Aids and Materials in Contact with Food	SP-05: Functional Foods, Nutraceuticals, Dietetic Products and Other Similar Products
SP-02: Pesticides Residues	SP-10: Fish and Fisheries Products
SP-03: Antibiotic Residues	SP-11: Cereals, Pulses & Legume and Their Products (Including Bakery)
SP-04: Genetically Modified Organisms and Foods	SP-12: Fruits & Vegetables and Their Products (Including Dried Fruits and Nuts, Salt, Spices and Condiments)
SP-06: Biological Hazards	SP-13: Meat & Meat Products, Including Poultry
SP-07: Contaminants in the Food Chain	SP:14: Milk & Milk Products
SP-08: Labelling and Claims/Advertisements	SP-15: Oils & Fats
SP-09: Method of Sampling and Analysis	SP-16: Sweets, Confectionery, Sweeteners, Sugar & Honey
SP-18: Nutrition and Fortification	SP-17: Water (Including Flavoured Water) & Beverages (Alcoholic and Non-alcoholic)
SP-20: Packaging	SP-19: Spices and Culinary Herbs
	SP-21: Alcoholic Beverages

In addition to these two statutory scientific entities, the FSSAI has also established some non-statutory bodies which interface with the SCs and SPs. Working groups are commissioned to attend specific matters which do not fall into the competence of any SPs and/or to provide opinions on the multisectoral issues falling within the competence of more than one SP.[33] FSSAI has also constituted two **Expert Committees (ECs)** to provide recommendations for approving non-specified foods/food ingredients[34] and claims related to general health benefits and disease risk reduction beyond those that are already permitted.[35]

FSSAI has recently also developed ***NetSCoFAN***, a network of research and academic institutions working in the area of food and nutrition.[36] It comprises eight groups of institutions working in different areas viz. biological, chemical, nutrition and labelling, food of animal origin, food of plant origin, water and beverages, food testing and safer and sustainable packaging. NetSCoFAN identifies research gaps in respective areas and collects, collates and develops a database on food safety issues for risk

33. *SPAN-COM (Ver. 1.0) Handbook for Members of Scientific Panel & Scientific Committee, FSSAI (2020), (Internal Publication).*
34. *Ibid.*
35. *Notice,* Food Safety and Standard Authority of India (4 September 2019), https://www.fssai.gov.in/upload/advisories/2019/09/5d7871bfd7ab9Notice_Fees_Claims_05_09_2019.pdf.
36. *'Consumers can now get food tested through consumer organizations Network of consumer organizations for food and nutrition (NetSCoFAN) created'* FSSAI, Press Note, 13 December 2019, available at https://fssai.gov.in/upload/press_release/2019/12/5df499f9a0c50Press_Release_NetCOFaN_14_12_2019.pdf.

assessment activities.[37] This scientific network also supports the SCs and SPs in the standard-setting process as needed.

The overall structure of science-related work and the bodies associated with them are schematically indicated in Figure 8.6.

Figure 8.6 Scientific Work at FSSAI

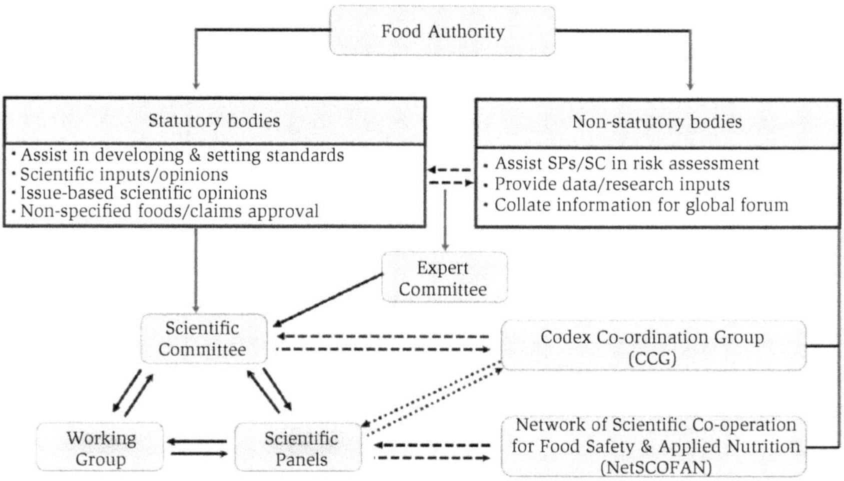

Source: SPAN-COM (Ver. 1.0) Handbook for Members of Scientific Panel & Scientific Committee, FSSAI (2020), (Internal Publication).

Harmonization of Indian food standards with global standards is one of the principles mandated under the FSS Act.[38] FSSAI sets food standards in line with the best international practices, and the domestic standards are usually harmonized with the Codex Alimentarius Commission to promote international trade and ensure high levels of food safety. The Codex Alimentarius, adopted by the Codex Alimentarius Commission, is a set of internationally recognized standards and guidelines designed to protect consumers' health worldwide and advocate fair practices in global food trade. Also referred to as the Codex by the World Health Organization (WHO) and the Food and Agriculture Organization (FAO) of the United Nations, the purpose of the Codex Alimentarius is to ensure the safety and quality of the food supply irrespective of the country of origin. Several countries use the Codex as a reference point to establish national standards, regulations and legislation, although compliance with the Codex is voluntary.

37. *FSSAI, Report on FSSAI's Participation 27th Indian Convention on Food Scientists and Technologists (ICFoST)*, 5, https://fssai.gov.in/upload/uploadfiles/files/Report_ICFoST_14_02_2020.pdf.
38. FSS Act at section 18(2)(a).

The FSSAI is the 'National Codex Contact Point' (NCCP)' for India under the Codex.[39] FSSAI has created nine subject-matter specific Codex Coordination Groups to coordinate work relating to international standard-setting bodies (such as the Codex, ISO and OIE) to review domestic standards and methods and provide inputs to scientific work at the international level. Despite its short existence, the FSSAI has achieved a considerably wide scope of work. Table 8.1 highlights the contribution of FSSAI in this regard.

Table 8.1 India's Food Standards Scorecard

S. No.	*Items*	*Codex*	*FSSAI*
1	Commodity/ General Standards	219	694
2	Method of Analysis	Manuals	**15 Manuals** for method of analysis for various foods/food additives/contaminants, etc.
3	Food Additives	4514 MLs covering 291 food additives/groups of food additives	4497 MLs covering 334 additives/groups of additive
4	Contaminants	111 MLs covering 18 contaminants	605 MLs covering 28 contaminants
5	Pesticide Residues	5437 MRLs and 63 eMRLs covering 223 pesticides	1096 MRLs covering 213 pesticides
6	Residues of Veterinary Drugs	632 MRLs covering 66 veterinary drugs and RMRs for 13 veterinary drugs	453 Tolerance Levels covering 117 veterinary drugs

Source: Author's representation

8.4.1 FSSAI: Scaling Frontiers

The FSSAI has endeavoured to innovate and formulate standards in realms usually unchartered by food safety authorities. The FSSAI is among the first regulators to have developed standards for various nutraceutical products – an emerging segment that

39. *Core Functions and Responsibilities of National Codex Committee and Its Shadow Committees*, Food Safety and Standards Authority of India, https://www.fssai.gov.in/upload/uploadfiles/files/Functions_National_Codex_Shadow_16_08_2018.pdf.

poses novel challenges for regulators.[40] The FSSAI is developing Front of Pack Labelling to declare the level of salt, sugar, and fat in a food product in relation to their Recommended Daily Allowance (RDA).[41] This labelling supports consumers in making informed choices and choosing healthier options. The FSSAI is also working on a new category 'Ayurvedic Aahar' with the AYUSH Ministry to ensure that ayurvedic food knowledge systems are brought under FSSAI's regulatory ambit and unlocked for organized businesses.[42] This regulation is intended to support scaling up the production and demand for ayurvedic food products globally.

While the focus in the early years was on product standards which can be tested and justified, FSSAI's focus has now shifted toward regulating processes. Apart from Schedule-IV which specifies process and hygiene protocols for FBOs and is mandatory, the Scheme of Testing and Inspection (STI) for milk, internal labs for oil manufacturers, audit scores, etc., are further steps in the direction of process regulation. The FSSAI's plan for the future is to build quality and safety at each step of food production and processes to ensure zero-defect quality in final food products for Indian consumers.

8.5 REGULATION AND ENFORCEMENT OF THE FOOD SAFETY STANDARDS

This section examines the conformity assessment processes and the enforcement mechanisms instituted by the FSSAI and under the FSS Act to give effect to the standardization activities undertaken.

As a preliminary step, every entity classified as an FBO under the FSS Act is mandatorily required to register with the FSSAI or obtain a license to operate.[43] The detailed criteria for such registration/license to operate are specified under FSS (Licensing and Registration) Regulations, 2011. Mandatory licensing/registration is the first step to enable food business identification and is the umbilical linkage between the food business and the regulator.

This registration requirement is universal and covers all food businesses and food handling activities including manufacturers, contract manufacturers, distributors, food storage, retailers, home-based caterers, transporters, etc.[44] To cover the entire value chain, businesses such as e-commerce food platforms and head offices are also included to ensure end-to-end traceability of food activity. A snapshot of the scope of regulation is provided in Box 8.3 below, highlighting how an e-commerce entity dealing in food is regulated by FSSAI.

40. Food Safety and Standards (Food or Health Supplements, Nutraceuticals, Foods for Special Dietary Uses, Foods for Special Medical Purpose, Functional Foods and Novel Food) Regulations, 2016. https://fssai.gov.in/upload/uploadfiles/files/Nutraceuticals_Regulations.pdf
41. 'FSSAI's new Labelling and Display regulations: Efforts to encourage consumers make healthier food choices' FSSAI (Press Release dated 25th June 2019), https://fssai.gov.in/upload/press_release/2019/06/5d144d6a64d6dPress_Release_Labelling_Regulations_27_06_2019.pdf
42. Meenakshi Verma, *FSSAI, Ayush Ministry discussing regulations for Ayurvedic Foods*, Hindu Business Line, 21 February 2019, uploaded at FSSAI website link https://fssai.gov.in/upload/media/FSSAI_News_Ayush_BusinessLine_22_02_2019.pdf.
43. FSS Act, at sections 31(1) & 31(2).
44. Food Safety and Standards (Licensing and Registration) Regulations, 2011.

Box 8.3 E-commerce Rules by FSSAI

E-Commerce operators need license to operate.

E-commerce platforms/market places act as an interface between the food business and the customer, even if there may be no direct food handling, and hence have been brought under the regulatory ambit of the FSSAI.

The requirements set out below are applicable to e-commerce entities and must be complied with during all sale of products on such platforms. This is based on the principle that that the consumer must have access to information similar to that what will be available to them while transacting at a retail store, so that they may make an informed choice when purchasing food on such platforms.

FSSAI has mandated:

- Licensing of e-commerce platforms

- Display of FSSAI license of the vendors registered on e-commerce platforms

- Display of principal display panel of the food product showing list of ingredients, Veg/Non-Veg logo, nutritional panel, etc. which help the consumer in making the right choice. (Expiry is not insisted upon owing to difficulties in tracking and tracing every package, hence only generic information is mandated.)

- FBO to ensure a minimum residuary shelf life of 30 percent or 45 days before expiry at the time of delivery to the consumer (This is to ensure consumer safety since the expiry information is not available at the time of the transaction, unlike the physical retail world).

Source: FSSAI, FSSAI Registration and Food Safety License for E-Commerce, https://fssaiindia.in/fssai-food-safety-license-registration-for/e-commerce/

The FSSAI also recognizes that each player in the food supply chain plays a crucial role in ensuring food safety. Safe food handling is a mandate at each step of the food supply chain. The FSSAI has expanded its sphere to bring crucial players in the food supply chain (such as e-commerce platforms, direct sellers, last-mile delivery agents and food vending units) under its ambit in recent years.

The registration and licensing system is online, with no need to follow up with physical documents; furthermore, all queries and responses are facilitated online and e-payments are enabled, with intimations provided via SMS and emails at each stage of processing. The aging Food Licencing and Registration System (FLRS, functional since 2011) was transitioned to the Food Safety Compliance System (FoSCoS) in 2020.[45] FoSCoS is an integrated online one-stop platform for all services to food business

45. '*FSSAI launched Food Safety Compliance System (FoSCoS)*' FSSAI, Press Release dated 01st June 2020) available at: https://fssai.gov.in/upload/press_release/2020/06/5ed4be98c59aaPress_Release_FoSCoS_01_06_2020.pdf.

operators. FoSCoS currently includes licencing, registration, inspection, hygiene rating, and audit modules. Other activities such as sample management, improvement notices, adjudications, etc. are also being integrated onto the FoSCoS platform along with laboratory testing (INFOLNET) and imports (FICS).[46] The platform is also being integrated with other platforms of the Government of India such as the GST Portal, PAN and MCA21 to ensure 360-degree profiling and validation of businesses.[47]

The integration of various portals not only promotes ease of doing business for FBOs but also enables the regulator to create an all-inclusive food safety compliance profile of FBOs, which supports the development of target-based inspections and regulatory interventions. Figure 8.7 provides a snapshot of the status of FSSAI license issued.

Figure 8.7 Status of FSSAI License/Registration (as on 30.06.2021)

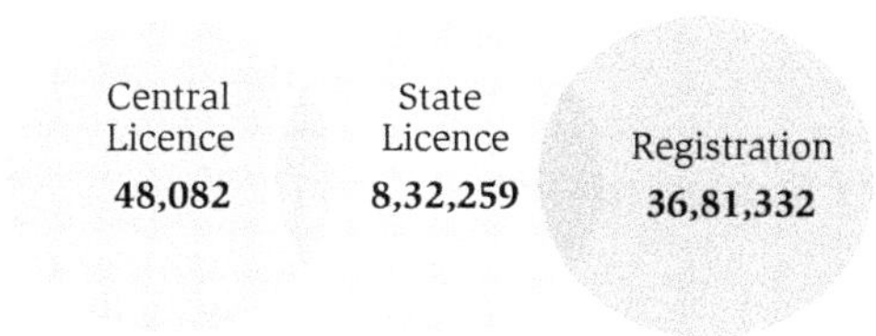

Source: FSSAI, 'Number of Central Licenses, State Licenses and Registration [Issued, Expired and Active] - FLRS/FoSCoS'.

This process of registration and licensing is supported by an oversight mechanism which involves – (a) Inspections and checks by regulatory officials, (b) Third-party certification including hygiene rating and audits, and (c) Self-regulation and compliance. Each of these mechanisms is examined in detail in the following paragraphs of this chapter.

8.5.1 Inspections and Checks by Regulatory Officials

The traditional physical oversight of food businesses continues to be the preferred oversight mechanism by FSSAI. Physical oversight can immediately be followed up with regulatory action like improvement notice and further action like suspension of license, if required. Further, it can be accompanied by sampling to ascertain the compliance of any food product with the prescribed standards. However, with only approximately 2,500 FSOs for approximately 40 lakh registrations and licenses, the scope of such checks is very limited. This has merited a need for a system of oversight which can ensure transparency, objectivity, and impartiality. Standardized operating

46. *About FoSCoS*, Food Safety and Standards Authority of India https://foscos.fssai.gov.in/about-foscos.
47. *Ibid.*

procedures and a digitized oversight mechanism appear to be the way forward, to ensure transparency and alerts for deviation if any.

Accordingly, the FSSAI has developed a Risk-Based Inspection System (RBIS) for inspection of FBOs, based on the type of business and previous history of the FBOs.[48] RBIS seeks to target FBOs as per the risk matrices, and therefore, optimizing the effort required by the regulator.

Inspection checklists have been developed by FSSAI for all kinds of business and the FSOs are required to check compliances against the given standardized checklist. Any deviation needs to be recorded in the inspection report with reasons.

FoSCoRiS, i.e., the Food Safety Compliance through Regular Inspection and Sampling is a mobile app for *real-time inspections* to be used by FSOs.[49] It serves for *monitoring, data collection and data analysis*. The results of inspection are visible to the supervisory officers for review. The database of this platform helps in identifying the key hotspots for non-compliance and supports adopting a risk-based inspection approach. It brings transparency to the system by enabling randomization of allocation of inspections, geo-tagging and time stamping of photographs.

8.5.2 Third-Party Ecosystem

Recognizing the limitation of the regulatory interface, the FSSAI has enabled a third-party food safety compliance ecosystem through Food Safety and Standards (Food Safety Auditing) Regulation, 2018.[50] FSSAI has so far recognized twenty-nine agencies that are accredited by the National Accreditation Board for Certification Bodies.[51]

Select food categories based on their risk classification have been subjected to mandatory food safety audit requirements.[52] FBOs falling under such a category are required to get their businesses audited by recognized auditing agencies at their own cost. Food businesses that are not subject to mandatory auditing can also voluntarily opt for audits of their businesses. FBOs having satisfactory audits would be subject to less frequent inspection by Central or State licensing authorities. Third-party audits reduce the burden on the regulatory inspection conducted by Central or State licensing authorities and also encourage efficient self-compliance by the food businesses.

48. *Chapter 6: Inspection of Various Food Establishments* in *FSSAI Training Manual*, Food Safety and Standards Authority of India, https://www.fssai.gov.in/upload/uploadfiles/files/Chapter6.pdf at 61.
49. *Ibid.*, 65.
50. *Food Safety Audits*, Food Safety and Standards Authority of India, https://fssai.gov.in/cms/third-party-audit.php#: ~ :text = FOOD%20SAFETY%20AUDITS&text = In%20order%20to%20cultivate%20and,August%202018%20for%20the%20same.
51. *List of agencies recognized by FSSAI as Food Safety Auditing Agencies under the Food safety and Standards (Food Safety Auditing) Regulations, 2018 as on 06.06.2020*, Food Safety and Standards Authority of India https://fssai.gov.in/upload/uploadfiles/files/Food_Audit_Agencies_Lists_26_06_2020.pdf.
52. *Order*, Food Safety and Standards Authority of India (13 August 2019) https://www.fssai.gov.in/upload/advisories/2019/08/5d53bf3b66f6cOrder_Food_Safety_Audit_14_08_2019.pdf.

Figure 8.8 Hygiene Rating Logo, FSSAI

Source: FSSAI, https://fssai.gov.in/cms/hygiene-rating.php.

In addition, FSSAI has developed the voluntary initiative 'Hygiene Rating System' (*see* Figure 8.8). This initiative encourages food service businesses to assess their own compliance through accredited hygiene-rating agencies, and further improve their food hygiene and safety levels.[53]

This initiative also supports consumers in making an informed choice while eating out. Hygiene rating reflects the standards of food hygiene found on the date of inspection by the recognized third-party audit agency. These hygiene rating agencies assess the FBOs as per the checklist and protocols developed by FSSAI, ensuring a standardized assessment.

To enable the extensive rollout and access to services for hygiene rating at affordable rates, the FSSAI has recognized twenty-six hygiene rating agencies in addition to the twenty-nine third-party agencies recognized by NABCB (as mentioned above). The Quality Council of India (QCI) at the request of the FSSAI has now evolved a scheme for approval of Hygiene Rating Audit Agencies to scale up hygiene rating by increasing the number of recognized Hygiene Rating Audit Agencies in the country.[54]

8.5.3 Self-Compliance

The FSSAI has recognized the need for FBOs to develop a culture of self-compliance voluntarily without the need for a statutory mandate to push them toward implementation of food hygiene and safety standards. FBOs are therefore made responsible for the implementation of various procedures and systems in their businesses to ensure the food safety of the product manufactured. The FSSAI encourages FBOs to be self-compliant when it comes to implementation of food hygiene and safety standards. Besides extension tools in form of guidance documents, it also provides tools such as standardized checklists, digital self-check tools like FPIVS, self-audit in case of hygiene rating, etc.

To ensure that the FBOs implement the responsibility entrusted to them, they are mandated to get their food products tested twice a year in an FSSAI-recognized lab and

53. Eat Right India, *About Hygiene Rating*, Food Safety and Standards Authority of India https://fssai.gov.in/hygieneRating.
54. FSSAI, '*QCI Launches Recognition Scheme for Hygiene Rating Audit Agencies*' Press Release (dated 15 December 2020), available at: https://fssai.gov.in/upload/press_release/2020/12/5fd8a1df0bf61Press_Release_Hygience_Rating_15_12_2020.pdf.

keep a record of the tests.[55] This self-testing ensures high compliance without any regulatory interface, cost or process, etc.

Similarly, several self-regulatory systems have been mandated such as Scheme of Testing and Inspection (STI) for dairy establishments to strengthen the internal controls through self-monitoring.[56] The scheme stipulates the minimum testing points, test methods and frequency of sampling. All records need to be maintained such that they can be checked at the time of inspection or third-party audit.

Many initiatives have also been launched which focus on FBO's self-certification. For instance, FSSAI is actively working toward the elimination of trans fat from the food supply chain by January 2022. To encourage food businesses to lower the trans-fat levels, the FSSAI has launched a 'Trans Fat Free' logo (*see* Figure 8.9).[57] Food establishments that use trans-fat-free fats/oils and do not have industrial trans-fat more than 0.2 gm per 100 gm of food can display the 'Trans Fat Free' logo in their outlets and on their food products. The logo can be used by FBOs based on self-certification.

Figure 8.9 Trans Feet Free Logo, FSSAI

Source: FSSAI Announcement, 22 July 2019, available at https://www.fssai.gov.in/upload/advisories/2019/07/5d3b01c07b950Letter_TransFat_24_07_2019.pdf.

To ensure that regulation does not become a barrier for business, FSSAI has taken several steps to promote ease of doing business. Box 8.4 sets out a snapshot of some of these steps.

Box 8.4 FSSAI promoting Ease of Doing Business

1. ***Perpetual Licensing**: FSSAI is transitioning from the present (1-5 year) licenses to a perpetual license which will require only timely e-filing of annual declaration/return and payment of fees. This will eliminate the hassle of applying for renewal of license and pursuing its approval by authorities.*

---

55. Annexure 3 of FSS (Licencing and Registration of Food Businesses) Regulations, 2011, p. 22 pt 12. Available at: https://fssai.gov.in/upload/uploadfiles/files/Compendium_Licensing_Regulations.pdf.
56. *Scheme of testing and inspection to be adopted by dairy processing plants for the purpose of self-monitoring and strengthening of internal controls,* Food Safety and Standards Authority of India (7 January 2020), https://www.fssai.gov.in/upload/advisories/2020/01/5e1c5fdf5dcd3Order_Scheme_Testing_Inspection_Diary_13_01_2020.pdf.
57. FSSAI Letter dated 22nd July 2019. Available at https://fssai.gov.in/upload/advisories/2019/07/5d3b01c07b950Letter_TransFat_24_07_2019.pdf.

2. ***Auto-generation of License/Registration**: FoSCoS provides for auto-generation of License (except in a few high-risk categories) within a prescribed period if there is no intimation of inadequacy by the regulatory body.*

3. ***E-payment** with multiple payment options has been enabled for easier payment of license fees, audit fees, fines, etc.*

4. ***Food Safety Mitra (FSM)** is a distinctive program to develop an ecosystem of low-cost facilitators (trained and certified) assisting FBOs in licensing/registration and compliance with food safety*

5. ***Food Safety Helpdesk/Helpline**: FSSAI has created helpdesk at the national, regional, and state levels to help FBOs.* A national toll-free number 1800112100 operates to provide support to FBOs across the country.

6. ***FoSCoS***: The new portal eliminates many documents by replacing them with tick-based declarations, specifies kind of business-wise document requirements, and provides an easy interpretive user interface.

8.5.4 Strengthening the State Machinery

To scale up food safety compliance, the FSSAI now enters into formal MoUs with States and Union Territories to extend support for the strengthening of their food safety machinery by providing financial assistance for laboratory infrastructure, conducting third-party and hygiene rating audits, establishment of state helpdesks for facilitating food businesses, improving IT infrastructure to ensure digital services at the field level, developing Eat Right campuses and markets, organizing camps for licensing and registration and Food Safety Training and Certification (FoSTaC) training and awareness activities.[58] State/UT Food Safety departments can submit their proposals annually and sign an MoU with FSSAI to get this support.

8.6 FOOD TESTING ECOSYSTEM

In any effective food regulatory system, a robust food testing ecosystem is critical to evaluate the quality and safety of foods, their compliance to set standards and also to identify any emerging risks from 'farm to fork'. This testing mechanism forms a critical element of the standards enforcement ecosystem. Development of infrastructure, qualified technical manpower and certified harmonized test methods are needed to make any food testing ecosystem a robust and efficient one.

58. *Memorandum of Understanding*, Food Safety and Standards Authority of India (15 March 2018), https://fssai.gov.in/upload/uploadfiles/files/MOU_FSW_15_03_2018(1).pdf.

The FSSAI has developed a robust regulatory food testing ecosystem comprising primary laboratories, referral laboratories and fourteen national reference laboratories[59] to evaluate the quality and safety of foods, their compliance to set standards, and also to identify any emerging risk in the food supply chain.

The roles and responsibilities of all laboratories notified by FSSAI follow.

8.6.1 Primary Laboratories

Any laboratory having accreditation of ISO/IEC 17025 by the National Accreditation Board for Testing and Calibration Laboratories (NABL) or other equivalent accreditation agency and having adequate capability and competence for testing of food safety and quality parameters as per the Act can apply online to be notified by FSSAI as a 'primary testing laboratories'.[60] Laboratories now undergo an integrated assessment by NABL and FSSAI. These laboratories carry out analysis of food samples taken under the FSS Act 2006 and Rules and Regulations made thereunder.[61] Currently, both government and private laboratories are notified by FSSAI.

8.6.2 Referral Food Laboratories (RFLs)

The FSSAI has also notified 'referral laboratories' which are responsible for analysis of food samples submitted by FSOs (in appeal against a finding of a primary laboratory) and for capacity building.[62]

8.6.3 National Reference Laboratories (NRLs)

The FSSAI has recognized various laboratories as NRLs, for the purpose of developing validation methods of testing, assessing the proficiency of notified food labs, providing training to the laboratory personnel and developing a repository of information for a designated product/analysis category.[63]

In addition to the above, the FSSAI has also conceptualized and built standardized mobile food testing laboratories referred to as Food Safety on Wheels (FSW).[64] These mobile labs carry out several functions, including conducting simple tests for common adulterants in milk, water, edible oil, and other items of food of daily

59. *Order*, Food Safety and Standards Authority of India (23 August 2019), https://fssai.gov.in/upload/uploadfiles/files/Order_NRL_Approval_26_08_2019.pdf.
60. *Guidelines for Recognition of Food testing Laboratories*, Food Safety and Standards Authority of India, https://old.fssai.gov.in/Portals/0/Pdf/Guidelines%20for%20Recognition%20of%20Food%20testing%20Laboratories.pdf.
61. *Food Laboratories*, Food Safety and Standards Authority of India, https://fssai.gov.in/cms/food-laboratories.php.
62. *Ibid.*
63. *Ibid.*
64. *Mobile Food Testing Laboratories: Food Safety on Wheels Scheme Guidelines 2017*, Food Safety and Standards Authority of India, https://fssai.gov.in/upload/uploadfiles/files/Scheme_Food_Safety_On_Wheels_30_08_2017(1).pdf.

consumption, building awareness around food safety and hygiene, promoting healthy eating habits in citizens at large and providing basic training. FSWs help regulatory staff and field functionaries in the states to enhance their outreach and help in conducting surveillance activities even in remote areas.

Notably, in a large country like India, with limited resources, there is a need for rapid assessment of food quality. Consequently, the FSSAI has enabled regulatory provisions for recognizing rapid testing kits by enacting the Food Safety and Standards (Laboratory and sample Analysis) First Amendment Regulations, 2020.[65] Several rapid food testing devices for the detection of food-borne pathogens and toxins have been approved. These devices ensure faster, better, and cheaper real-time testing of food. The devices are expected to become an integral part of quality assurance control programs in the food industry and also for regulatory and surveillance purposes.

Figure 8.10 sets out a graphical representation of this network of laboratories and testing ecosystem developed by the FSSAI.

Figure 8.10 Status of Food Testing Ecosystem Developed by FSSAI

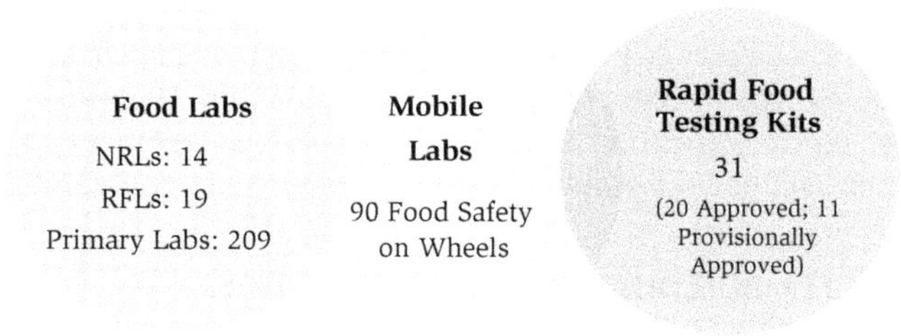

Source: Author's representation based on Food Laboratories, FSSAI, https://fssai.gov.in/cms/foodlaboratories.php; Rapid Analytical Food Testing (RAFT) Kit/Equipment/Method, *FSSAI,* https://fssai.gov.in/cms/raft.php and Mobile Labs, https://www.fssai.gov.in/cms/mobile-labs.php

8.7 IMPORT COMPLIANCE WITH FOOD SAFETY STANDARDS

The FSSAI also has the mandate to regulate the import of food into the country and ensure that it is safe and wholesome for human consumption.[66] The major food commodities being imported into India are edible oils and fats, pulses, fruits and nuts, vegetables, cereals, sugars and sugar confectionery, coffee, tea, spices and beverages. The top food exporting countries to India are Australia, Malaysia, Indonesia, Ukraine, USA, Canada, Brazil and Myanmar.

No imports of food articles are permitted to India without a valid license from the Central Licensing Authority of FSSAI.[67] Importers can apply online on Food Import

65. *Rapid Food Testing Devices and Kits set to redefine Food Safety in 2020*, Food Safety and Standards Authority of India, https://fssai.gov.in/upload/uploadfiles/files/Press_Release_Rapid_Kits_31_12_2019.pdf.
66. FSS Act, *supra* note 8, at section 16.
67. FSS Act, *supra* note 8, at section 25.

Clearance System (FICS) and after a thorough scrutiny and inspection, license is granted by the authority.[68]

The FSSAI has its presence at several locations through its own authorized officers at Chennai, Kolkata, Mumbai, Delhi, Cochin, Tuticorin, Krishnapatnam and Mundra. Offices are also being opened at Hyderabad, Bangalore, Raxaul and Wagah covering forty-six major points of entry. Further, at other points of entry throughout the country, the FSSAI has notified Customs Officials as authorized officers to regulate food imports. As of the date of writing this chapter, food products may be imported into India through any of 150 notified points of entry.[69]

FSSAI has in place an online Food Import Clearance System (FICS), integrated with the customs ICE-GATE (Indian Customs Electronic Commerce/Electronic Data interchange Gateway) under SWIFT (Single Window Interface for Facilitating Trade) which helps in quick scrutiny of applications and enables faster approvals.[70] The consignment of food articles is referred to FSSAI for clearance by customs authorities through FICS. Thereafter, the food consignments are subject to scrutiny of documents, visual inspection, sampling and testing in FSSAI notified laboratories to determine whether they conform to the safety and quality standards laid down under various FSS Regulations.

To expedite the clearance process of imports, a Risk Management System (RMS) has been introduced which subdivides every application into 'High-Risk' or 'Low-Risk' food items based on categorization of food and the previous history of import.[71] Bills of entry that are non-facilitated are subjected to mandatory sampling and processing.

8.8 CAPACITY BUILDING OF FOOD BUSINESSES

To ensure adherence to the food hygiene and safety requirements, the preliminary prerequisite is understanding by FBOs of the various food hygiene and safety principles. The FSSAI therefore employs several capacity building activities which supplement the standardization process and aim to regulate the food safety ecosystem more effectively.

FoSTaC is a large-scale training and capacity development program initiated by the FSSAI for the training of food handlers working in food businesses, to ensure that the establishments in which food is being handled, processed, manufactured, stored and distributed conform to food safety requirements.[72] Once trained, the food handlers are certified as 'Food Safety Supervisor'.

68. *Manual on Food Import Clearance System (FICS) implemented by Food Safety and Standard Authority of India (FSSAI), Ministry of Health & Family Welfare, Government of India,* Food Safety and Standards Authority of India https://old.fssai.gov.in/Portals/0/Pdf/Import_Manual %20(17.10.13).pdf.
69. *Notification,* Food Safety and Standards Authority of India (8 October 2019) https://www.fssai .gov.in/upload/advisories/2019/10/5da3ffc13176eNotification_AOs_Import_11_10_2019.pdf.
70. *Imports,* Food Safety and Standards Authority of India, https://fssai.gov.in/cms/imports.php.
71. *Food Imports,* Food Regulatory Portal, https://foodregulatory.fssai.gov.in/food-imports.
72. *Food Safety Training and Certification (FoSTaC),* Food Safety and Standards Authority of India, https://fssai.gov.in/cms/fostac.php.

Since its launch in May 2017, the training system has grown to encompass 262 Training Partners, over 2,000 trainers and nineteen courses at three levels - Basic, Advanced and Special - covering all sectors of the food business.[73] This initiative was started to enhance the availability of skilled manpower to ensure better implementation and self-compliance to FSS Regulations.

FoSTaC training focuses not only on capacity building of the organized sector but also trains smaller FBOs that are part of the unorganized sector. Such businesses are covered under the basic courses of the FoSTaC program. The FoSTaC initiative is unique in that it allows for individual tracking of each trainee (through the FoSTaC portal) with minimal cost to government.[74]

To address concerns raised as part of the COVID-19 pandemic, FoSTaC also introduced a course on *Food Hygiene and Safety Practices* to be followed by FBOs to minimize risk of infection of COVID-19. This course was later integrated with the main curriculum of FoSTaC. The Training Division also provides training programmes for regulatory staff of Centre and States and food laboratory personnel of Centre and States.

8.9 EAT RIGHT INDIA: A NOVEL APPROACH TOWARD ENSURING FOOD SAFETY, HEALTH AND SUSTAINABILITY

One of FSSAI's initiatives to support its standardization activities, the 'Eat Right India' movement aims to promote food safety, health, and sustainability across the food ecosystem.[75] The program envisions a future where all Indians will exercise the choice to access and consume food that is safer, healthier and more sustainable.

Eat Right India focuses on building capacity and providing hygiene ratings to medium and small businesses and food establishments, and aims to reap large benefits via incremental improvements made by a large number of small businesses.[76] For petty food businesses, the approach is to raise the quality, hygiene, and safety of their food by basic training and cluster approach.

This initiative supports both the demand and supply of safe and healthy food while also ensuring sustainability. While the supply-side interventions are aimed at building capacities of food businesses to promote self-compliance, the demand-side initiatives work toward motivating consumers to demand safe and healthy food.[77] The initiatives for the production and consumption of food in a sustainable way are aimed at promoting environment-friendly food practices and habits.

Figure 8.11 summarizes the activities undertaken as part of the Eat Right Initiative.

73. *Food Safety Training and Certification (FoSTaC)*, Food Safety and Standards Authority of India, https://fostac.fssai.gov.in/fostac/index.
74. *Ibid.*
75. *Eat Right India*, Eat Right India, https://eatrightindia.gov.in/eatrightindia.jsp.
76. *Ibid.*
77. *ERI Initiatives*, Eat Right India, https://eatrightindia.gov.in/eri-initiatives.jsp.

Figure 8.11 Eat Right India Initiative on Demand-Side, Supply-Side, and Sustainability Initiatives

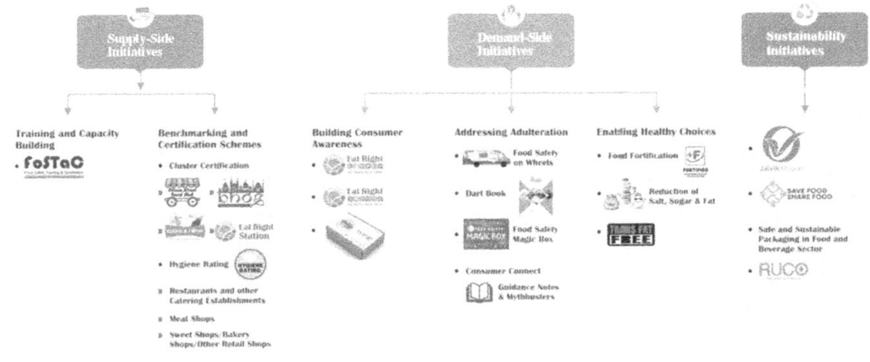

Source: ERI Initiatives, Eat Right India, https://eatrightindia.gov.in/eri-initiatives.jsp.

A collaborative system approach has been adopted to operationalize the vision which involves using a mix of regulation, capacity building, collaboration and empowerment approaches. *Eat Right India* has a unique approach which builds on the collective action of all stakeholders - the government, food businesses, civil society organizations, experts and professionals, development agencies and citizens at large. It is an integrative or 'whole of the government' approach since the movement brings together food-related mandates of the agriculture, health, environment and other ministries.

Eat Right India is also aligned to the National Health Policy 2017 with its focus on preventive and promotive healthcare and flagship programs such as Ayushman Bharat, POSHAN Abhiyaan, Anemia Mukt Bharat, and Swachh Bharat Mission.[78]

In the year 2020, FSSAI has been awarded Food Safety Vision prize by the Rockefeller Foundation for its collaborative approach and vision for the future.[79] The foundation appreciated FSSAI and noted that FSSAI's vision behind Eat Right India 'looks to create a national movement towards healthier diets through a systems-based approach of reducing food waste; improving hygiene and sanitation across the value chain, and increasing access to and affordability of healthy foods.'

The World Bank has also published a case study on *Eat Right India* and validated the program.[80] Figure 8.12 provides an overview of the various projects accomplished under the Eat Right Initiative.

78. *Eat Right Society*, Eat Right India https://eatrightindia.gov.in/eatrightindia.jsp.
79. Ministry of Health and Family Welfare, *FSSAI awarded the Food Systems Vision Prize for its 'Eat Right India' movement*, Press Information Bureau (7 August 2020). https://pib.gov.in/PressReleaseIframePage.aspx?PRID=1644130.
80. *Eat Right India: A Case Study*, World Bank (2020) http://documents1.worldbank.org/curated/en/949431599153256236/pdf/Eat-Right-India-A-Case-Study.pdf.

Figure 8.12 Eat Right India Scorecard (as on 31 January 2021)

Clusters

1. **Project Clean Street Food Hub**
   Completed: 39
   Pipeline: 18
2. **Eat Right Campus**
   Completed: 39
   In Pipeline: 44
3. **Eat Right Station**
   Completed: 3
4. **Blissful Hygienic Offering to God (BHOG)**
   Completed: 18

Stand-Alone/Special

1. **Hygiene Rating Scheme**
   Awarded: 10,000
   In-process: 2,200
2. **Eat Right School**
   Schools Registered: 52,998
   Schools Activity Completed: 47,990
3. **Repurpose Used Cooking Oil (RUCO)**
   Biodiesel Mfg Reg: 29
   States Covered: 14

Sources: Author's representation based on institutional data

8.10 CONCLUSION

India is a diverse nation with several specific challenges and complexities in the enforcement of national regulations governing subjects as critical as food safety. No single approach toward the implementation of the food safety system can perhaps be successful in the country. It, therefore, requires a multifaceted approach with the convergence of different ministries and stakeholders to make an actionable and visible shift in the food safety ecosystem. The FSSAI, as the food safety regulator responsible for ensuring safe and wholesome food for citizens, has taken the lead in galvanizing India's effort of reform in this sector.

In the past decade, the FSSAI has laid down science-based standards for regulation, manufacturing, storage, distribution, sale and import of foods. The legislative framework for the regulation of food safety has already been institutionalized and the focus has now shifted toward implementation and ensuring compliance.

The food safety ecosystem in India has steadily transitioned to match the global scenario and emerging food safety trends. Strengthening the laboratory capacity to meet global benchmarks, creating an operative network of professionals and scientists working in the area of food and nutrition, robust training mechanism for officers, technologists, as well as industry, are some of the crucial steps taken up to build on this effort. This multifaceted approach clubbed with technology has helped the FSSAI in scaling up the outreach of various programs, increasing food safety compliance and supporting ease of doing business.

Consolidating its standardization activities with its *Eat Right India* Movement, the FSSAI has been successful in bringing together all stakeholders to work collectively toward a common wholesome objective of food safety and health for every citizen.

CHAPTER 9

Understanding the SPS Regulatory Framework in the Indian Context

Ashish Chandra & Anupal Dasgupta[*]

The World Trade Organization's (WTO's) Agreement on Sanitary and Phytosanitary Measures (SPS Agreement) sets out the fundamentals for food safety, animal health and plant health and helps standardize and regulate global agricultural trade. SPS standards are vital tools through which various countries ensure that agricultural imports meet certain minimum requirements so as to ensure safety of the product and its citizens. With increasing health awareness among consumers in both developing and developed countries, safe and scientific SPS practices are vital for suppliers of all agricultural products. Hence, Indian SPS standards need to be harmonized with global standards both for import and export, which will increase India's export competitiveness while ensuring that sub-quality products do not enter the Indian markets.

The present chapter was conceived to unravel the myriad regulations and complexities around the adoption, implementation and enforcement of SPS measures in India. The chapter starts with a discourse on the architecture of the SPS Agreement. The authors then examine the regulatory landscape of SPS measures in India and in particular explore the role of various entities including government agencies and standard-setting bodies that have a role in the regulation of SPS measures, in the country. The authors also highlight the systemic concerns arising out of proliferation of standard-setting bodies, laws and regulations and regulatory concerns arising out of lack of coordination among them. The chapter later undertakes a brief sector-wise analyses of certain key sectors which have remained areas of concern for India. Finally, the authors dwell on the apparent issues in India's SPS regulatory regime and suggest certain reorientations. This chapter is also a primer of sorts on SPS regulation in India for global businesses looking to enter the Indian market.

* The authors would like to thank Ms Indumugi C., a penultimate year student at Tamil Nadu National Law University, for assisting in the research for this chapter.

9.1 INTRODUCTION

India has consistently been a net exporter of agricultural products in the past three decades.[1] According to India's Economic Survey (2019-20) India's agricultural exports amounted to USD 34.4 billion against imports of USD 20.1 billion.[2] This increase defied the 15.5% year-on-year fall in overall merchandise exports on account of the COVID-19 gloom. Indian farm exports registered a notable 9.77% growth in April–December 2020, with a simultaneous contraction of 5.5% in agricultural imports[3] thereby increasing the agricultural trade surplus by 36.58% when compared to 2019.[4] While the recent statistics on agricultural exports present a positive outlook, it is our understanding that the potential for agricultural exports is much higher. In this respect, one of the obstacles faced by Indian exporters for agricultural products is the inability to meet the requirements of standards as prescribed by certain importing countries. In many instances, these applicable standards in the importing country mirror the relevant international standards.

Speaking at the 6th National Standards Conclave, India's Commerce Minister Piyush Goyal, expressed the concern that Indian businesses are unable to achieve the full potential of our free trade agreements ('FTA'), despite India having signed a number of them.[5] The minister stated that this is largely on account of the poor quality of Indian production which do not meet the non-tariff barriers ('NTB') of its FTA partners.[6] This is also true for agricultural trade including processed food – which still remains largely underdeveloped. With increasing health awareness among consumers in both developing and developed countries, safe and scientific sanitary and phytosanitary (SPS) practices are vital for the suppliers of all agricultural products.

Thus, if Indian agricultural products have to realize their true potential in the export market, it is the need of the hour to standardize Indian agricultural products in accordance with international standards. Moreover, standardization of Indian agricultural products accomplishes two objectives – (i) India's exports gain global acceptance for fulfilling international standards, and (ii) the standards regime prevents the Indian market from being flooded with substandard imports.

To augment the standardization processes, the WTO agreements on Sanitary and Phytosanitary Measures ('SPS Agreement') and Technical Barriers to Trade ('TBT Agreement') provide a robust framework. The SPS Agreement sets out the

1. *India's agricultural export grows: Economic Survey*, Economic Times (29 January 2021), https://economictimes.indiatimes.com/news/economy/agriculture/indias-agricultural-export-grows-economic-survey/articleshow/80585995.cms?from=mdr.
2. Ministry of Finance, *Economic Survey 2019-20*, 237, https://www.indiabudget.gov.in/economicsurvey/doc/echapter_vol2.pdf.
3. Harish Damodaran, *Farm exports defy overall trend in 2020, see 9.8 per cent growth*, Indian Express (5 February 2020), https://indianexpress.com/article/india/farm-exports-india-covid-19-2020-7175200/.
4. *Ibid.*
5. Joe C. Mathew, *Piyush Goyal calls for zero tolerance for substandard products, services*, Business Today (19 September 2020), https://www.businesstoday.in/current/economy-politics/piyush-goyal-calls-for-zero-tolerance-for-substandard-products-services/story/393899.html.
6. *Ibid.*

fundamentals for food safety, animal health and plant health – helping standardize and regulate global agricultural trade. The word 'sanitary' relates to human and animal health, while the word 'phytosanitary' relates to plant safety. The TBT Agreement complements the SPS Agreement by regulating food packaging guidelines including quality and labelling requirements. The focus of this chapter is limited to the SPS Agreement.

SPS standards are vital tools through which various countries ensure that agricultural imports meet certain minimum requirements so as to ensure safety of the product and its citizens. However, India has historically been slow in terms of setting SPS standards. As per available data, India has notified a mere 281 SPS standards as opposed to 4,504 by the United States ('US'), 2,556 by Brazil, 2,521 by Canada, 1,500 by the EU and 1,021 by Japan.[7] While the government has duly recognized the need for standardization across the board both in terms of technical as well as SPS standards, the regulatory landscape and the efforts must be concentrated to streamline the regime which will make standardization efforts hassle free and provide certainty to businesses.

The revamping of the old Bureau of Indian Standards Act, 1986 created an environment for businesses to measure up to international standards. A new Bureau of Indian Standards ('BIS') Act, 2016 was brought into force with effect from 12 October 2017 establishing BIS as the National Standards Body of India. The 2016 Act enables the Government to require compulsory certification of any good or article of any scheduled industry, process, system or service which it considers necessary in the public interest or for the protection of human, animal or plant health, safety of the environment, or prevention of unfair trade practices or national security.[8]

The Indian government's motivations were further reinforced in 2018 with the implementation of the Indian National Strategy for Standardization ('INSS') during the 5th National Standards Conclave – which sets out the blueprint for the journey forward. The INSS seeks to develop a 'Quality Ecosystem' with a harmonized, dynamic and mature standards framework. It has four broad focus areas (pillars), i.e., standards development; conformity assessment; development and harmonization of TBT and SPS measures; and awareness and education regarding standards.[9] The Government has an ambitious timeline to fully implement the INSS and achieve its intended outcomes by 2023.

It is in this very context that the present chapter is conceived. As the discussion progresses – the authors will strive to unravel the myriad regulations and complexities around the adoption, implementation and enforcement of SPS measures in India. This

7. Sanitary and Phytosanitary: Information Management System, WTO, http://spsims.wto.org/en/Notifications/Search (from 'Type of Notification', select 'Regular and Emergency notification') (Last visited 18 March 2021).
8. *Bureau of Indian standards (BIS) Act 2016 brought into force with effect from 12th October 2017*, Business Standard (14 October 2017), https://www.business-standard.com/article/news-cm/bureau-of-indian-standards-bis-act-2016-brought-into-force-with-effect-from-12th-october-2017-117101400236_1.html.
9. Indian National Strategy for Standardization, 6, https://commerce.gov.in/wp-content/uploads/2020/02/MOC_636655449469105249_INSS_Booklet_2018.pdf.

chapter, under Part II discusses the architecture of the SPS Agreement and the core concepts it tries to promote – harmonization of standards, risk assessment, equivalence and transparency requirements. Part III examines the regulatory landscape of SPS measures in India and in particular explores the role of the six entities (outlined below), involving both government agencies and standard-setting bodies that have a role in the regulation of SPS measures. This Part looks at the functions performed by the Food Safety and Standards Authority of India (FSSAI), Agricultural and Processed Food Products Export Development Authority (APEDA), Marine Products Export Development Authority (MPEDA), Export Inspection Council (EIC), AGMARK and the Bureau of Indian Standards (BIS). It also investigates their unique roles and how they regulate distribution, imports, exports, sales, etc. Part IV highlights the systemic concerns arising out of proliferation of standard-setting bodies, laws and regulations, and regulatory concerns arising out of lack of coordination among them. Part V of this chapter undertakes a brief sector-wise analysis of the lack of coordination in SPS regulatory environment faced by India. We offer our conclusions in Part VI with some observations and possible reorientations.

9.2 THE SPS AGREEMENT: AT A GLANCE

SPS measures can be defined as 'measures that are applied to protect human or animal life from risks arising from additives, contaminants, toxins or disease-causing organisms in their food; to protect human life from plant - or animal-carried diseases; to protect animal or plant life from pests, diseases, or disease-causing organisms; to prevent or limit other damage to a country from the entry, establishment or spread of pests; and to protect biodiversity. These include measures taken to protect the health of fish and wild fauna, as well as of forests and wild flora.'[10]

According to *Pauwelyn*, for a specific government action to qualify as an 'SPS measure', one must subjectively determine the objective or purpose of the regulation.[11] In this sense 'SPS measures' are subject to Annex – A(1) of the SPS Agreement which defines such measures. The list in Annex – A(1) is exhaustive.

The Appellate Body in *Australia – Apples* succinctly guides members in their determination of a particular measure at issue, as an 'SPS Measure':

> Whether a measure is 'applied ... to protect' in the sense of Annex A(1)(a) must be ascertained not only from the objectives of the measure as expressed by the responding party, but also from the text and structure of the relevant measure, its surrounding regulatory context, and the way in which it is designed and applied. For any given measure to fall within the scope of Annex A(1)(a), *scrutiny of such*

10. UNCTAD, *Classification of Non-Tariff Measures*, 7, February 2012.
11. Joost Pauwelyn, *WTO Agreement on Sanitary and Phytosanitary (SPS) Measures as Applied in the First Three SPS Disputes EC – Hormones, Australia – Salmon and Japan – Varietals*, 2 J. of Int'l Econ. L. 641 2 (1999).

circumstances must reveal a clear and objective relationship between that measure and the specific purposes enumerated in Annex A(1)(a).[12]

(Emphasis added)

Thus, to determine whether a particular measure is an SPS measure, there will need to be an inquiry into its purpose, which is largely a subjective issue.

Further, Article 2.1 of the SPS Agreement establishes certain 'Basic Rights and Obligations' which include the right to implement SPS measures that are aimed at protecting plants, animals and humans from pests, contaminants and diseases. Article 2.2 further clarifies that such measures must be 'scientific', while Article 2.3 cautions that such measures must be 'non-discriminatory' toward members where similar conditions prevail and must not be a disguised restriction to free trade.

9.2.1 What Is Harmonization?

The preamble to the SPS Agreement lists 'Harmonization' as one of its key desired outcomes. WTO Members are presumed to be complaint with the SPS Agreement disciplines if their domestic SPS measures 'conform to international standards, guidelines or recommendations' under Article 3.2.[13] Alternatively, members can 'base their sanitary or phytosanitary measures on international standards, guidelines or recommendations' under Article 3.1.[14]

As of date, the SPS Agreement in Annex A(3), recognizes three international standard-setting organizations whose standards are used as reference:

1. Codex Alimentarius Commission ('Codex') - relating to food safety.
2. International Office of Epizootics ('OIE') - relating to animal health.
3. International Plant Protection Convention ('IPPC') - relating to plant health.

These organizations referred to as the 'three sisters' encourage participation of all WTO Members to develop, review and promote internationally recognized standards.

Apart from following the above processes, members may also unilaterally enact their own SPS measures to impose a level of protection 'different from that implicit in the international standard, and [to] implement or embody that level of protection in a measure not "based on" the international standard'[15] (Article 3.3). However, for exercising this option, members have to follow the rules on 'risk assessment' set out in Article 5 of the SPS Agreement which is discussed below.

12. Appellate Body Report, *Australia - Measures Affecting the Importation of Apples from New Zealand*, WT/ DS367/AB/R para. 173.
13. The Appellate Body found that this required the international standard to be adopted 'as is' under domestic law. Appellate Body Report, *European Communities – Measures Concerning Meat and Meat Products (Hormones)*, WT/DS26/AB/R and WT/DS48/AB/R, para. 170.
14. The Appellate Body interpreted this to mean that the domestic measure '[...] "stands" or is "founded" or "built" upon or "is supported by" the corresponding internationals standard. The Appellate Body also clarified that such a measure "may adopt some, not necessarily all, of the elements of the international standard"'. *Ibid.* at paras 163 and 171.
15. *EC – Hormones, supra* note 13, para. 172.

9.2.2 What Is 'Risk Assessment' under the SPS Agreement?

When measures undertaken by WTO Members are neither based on nor conform to 'international standards' – Article 5.1 directs members to ensure that the adopted measures are based on an appropriate assessment of the risks to human, animal or plant life or health. Such an assessment must be according to the risk assessment techniques developed by the relevant international organizations.

The definition of 'Risk assessment' under Annex A(4) of the SPS Agreement can be divided into two parts. In the case of risks associated with pests or diseases, it is the evaluation of the *likelihood* of entry, establishment or spread of a pest or disease within the territory of an importing Member [...] and of the associated potential *biological* and *economic* consequences. In the case of food safety concerns, it is the 'the evaluation of the *potential* for adverse effects on human or animal health arising from the presence of additives, contaminants, toxins or disease-causing organisms'.

Article 5.2 identifies the factors to be considered for a 'risk assessment'. Further, Article 5.3 also includes economic considerations behind measures to achieve the 'adequate level of protection for a member. These factors are reproduced in Figure 9.1.[16]

Figure 9.1 Risk Assessment Criteria under the SPS Agreement

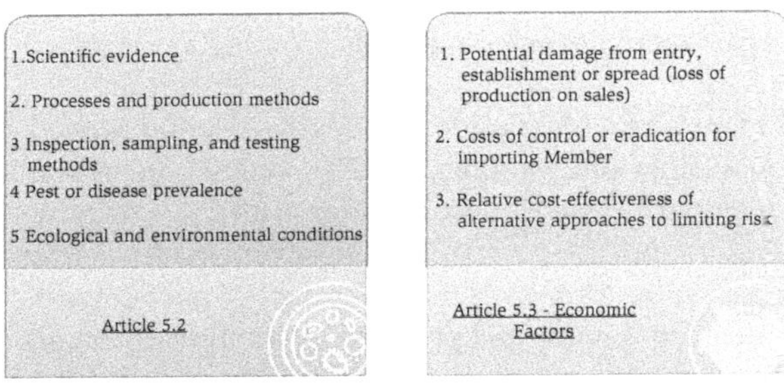

9.2.3 What Is Equivalence?

While harmonizing international standards is a possible solution toward removing trade barriers on account of different technical requirements between trading countries, another alternative to the problem lies in what is known as 'mutual recognition'.[17] This idea is codified under Article 4.1 of the SPS Agreement as 'equivalence'. According to this concept, WTO Members are required to accept other members' SPS measures as equivalent if the exporting Member is able to prove that its own SPS

16. Gretchen Stanton & Christiane Wolff, SPS Secretariat, *Presentation on Risk Analysis in the SPS Agreement and Lessons Learned from Dispute Settlement*, https://www.wto.org/english/tratop_e/sps_e/wkshop_oct14_e/Session1_PPT_SPS_Secretariat.pdf.
17. *Ibid.*

measures achieve the same level of protection as that of the importing member. Article 4.2 encourages members to enter into equivalence agreements for this purpose.

9.2.4 Requirement to Notify SPS Measures

Article 7 requires all members to duly notify the SPS measures that apply in their territories, as also any changes to these measures in accordance with the guidelines provided in Annex-B of the SPS Agreement. All such notifications are freely accessible on the WTO's SPS Information Management System ('SPSIMS') at http://spsims.wto .org in all the WTO official languages.

9.3 SPS STANDARD-SETTING AND IMPLEMENTATION: THE INDIAN REGULATORY LANDSCAPE

Food quality, safety and health-related issues are a major impediment to India's agriculture exports in crucial international markets such as the US and the European Union ('EU'). On the flipside, until recently, there was no regulatory regime to check for low quality imports. Even in cases where there are regulations, these have largely been ineffective due to a myriad of issues like, lack of coordination between various government departments, inherent corruption in the system or inadequate resources for proper implementation.

The data from the United States Food and Drug Administration ('USFDA') alone shows that 22,394 unique shipments pertaining to Human Foods and Animal Feed from India were rejected between the years 2002 and 2021 (Figure 9.2).[18] Such rejections comprise food products including fried and baked snacks, fresh vegetables (such as ladies-finger), fishery products (such as shrimp and prawns), instant noodles, Basmati rice, Indian spices, etc.[19] The reasons for these rejections range from adulteration to insanitary packaging, etc. However, as is evident form the graph below a gradual decline is noticeable starting 2016 – which embodies hope in terms of the 'coming of age' of the Indian processed food industry and other agricultural and allied exports.

18. Compliance Dashboard of the USFDA, https://datadashboard.fda.gov/ora/cd/imprefusals.htm, (from the Interactive World Map, click on India and use the filters 'Human Foods' and 'Animal Feed') (Last visited 23 March 2021).
19. Arpita Mukherjee, *Barriers to India's agri & processed food exports include food quality*, FnBnews (19 December 2016), http://www.fnbnews.com/Top-News/barriers-to-indias-agri--processed-food-exports-include-food-quality-39927.

Figure 9.2 USFDA Data on Indian Shipment Rejections[20]

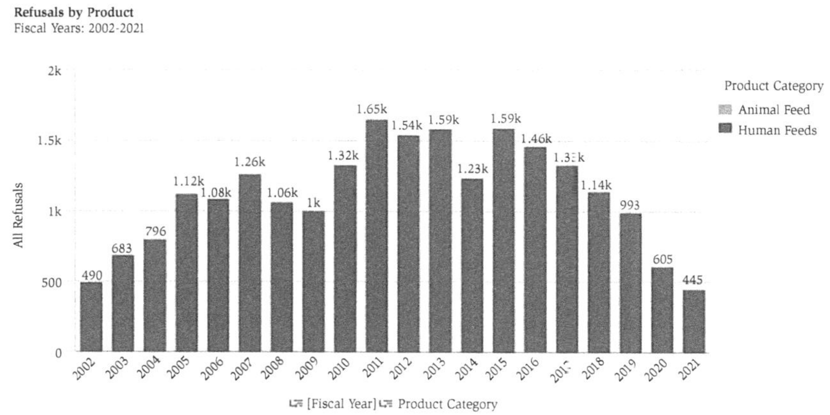

India is also one of the fastest growing markets for imported and processed food in the world. This is largely owed to factors such as a large population base, a rising urban middle-class, growing per-capita income, and an increasing preference for international food products. The rising demand is further bolstered by the lowering of tariffs under various free trade agreements.[21]

The government has introduced various laws and regulators which dictate food safety and trade in plant and animal health. In this light, it is necessary to understand the regulatory environment surrounding SPS standard-setting and compliance in India. In the subsequent paragraphs of this sub-chapter, we hope to identify the key governmental agencies and authorities which govern and facilitate food safety, plant and animal health.

9.3.1 FSSAI

The food safety and quality monitoring system in India underwent an overhaul in 2006 with the enactment of the Food Safety and Standards Act ('FSS Act') which consolidated about nine different legislations governing food safety. This was done to ensure regulatory transparency, consistency and predictability premised on the idea of 'One Nation, One Food Law'. The FSS Act is the parent legislation governing food safety and standards in India. Under this Act, the Food Safety and Standards Authority of India ('FSSAI') was formed in August 2011 – as an autonomous body under the Central Government's Ministry of Health and Family Welfare. The objective was to have a single authority for everything related to food safety and standards. According to its preamble the FSS Act seeks to –

20. Compliance Dashboard of the USFDA, *supra* note 18.
21. Arpita Mukherjee et al., *Food Imports in India: Prospects, Issues and Way Forward*, 2 J. of Econ. Sci. Res., 3 (2019).

> *consolidate the laws* relating to food and to establish the Food Safety and Standards Authority of India for *laying down science-based standards* for articles of food and to *regulate their manufacture, storage, distribution, sale and import,* to *ensure availability of safe and wholesome food* for human consumption.
>
> (Emphasis added)

The FSSAI governs the food safety and import regime under various regulations. A list of all the regulations published by the FSSAI is available at https://fssai.gov.in/cms/food-safety-and-standards-regulations.php. Among these a few key regulations are mentioned below:

- Food Safety Standards ('FSS') (Licensing and Registration) Regulation, 2011
- FSS (Food Product Standards and Food Additives) Regulation, 2011
- FSS (Prohibition and Restriction on Sales) Regulation, 2011
- FSS (Contaminants, Toxins and Residues) Regulation, 2011
- FSS (Laboratory and Sampling Analysis) Regulation, 2011
- Food Safety and Standards (Food Recall Procedure) Regulation, 2017
- FSS (Packaging) Regulation, 2018
- FSS (Labelling and Display) Regulation, 2020.

9.3.1.1 How Does the FSSAI Regulate Food Imports?

Like every other importer - a Food Business Operator in India ('FBO') importing food items needs to register on the DGFT's website to obtain an Importer Exporter Code ('IEC'). Thereafter, the FBO must first obtain a FSSAI Registration/ License through the Food Safety Compliance System ('FoSCoS') website.[22] A central licence is required for imports. These central licences are issued by the FSSAI's regional offices at Delhi, Kolkata, Mumbai and Chennai. The license is granted for a period between one to five years. As a part of the licence condition the importer is required to file an Annual Return in Form D-1 with the concerned regional FSSAI office for each class of food handled during the previous financial year, by 31 May, every year. In addition, for food products which are not standardized as per various FSS Regulations, a product approval must also be obtained from the FSSAI before commencing imports.

Apart from the above the procedure and requirements for import of food articles into India are regulated by the FSS (Import) Regulations, 2017. FSSAI uses an online system for clearance of food imports known as the Food Import Clearance System ('FICS') which is integrated with ICE-GATE (Indian Customs Electronic Commerce/Electronic Data interchange (EC/EDI) Gateway) portal under SWIFT (Single Window Interface for Facilitating Trade) which is a part of an automated Risk Management System ('RMS') implemented by the Indian Customs.[23]

22. The Food Safety Compliance System (FoSCoS) replaced the erstwhile Food Licencing and Registration System ('FLRS') as of June 2020. *See* FLRS to FoSCoS, https://foscos.fssai.gov.in/.
23. FSSAI, *Imports*, https://fssai.gov.in/cms/imports.php.

The Customs authorities may refer food articles to the FSSAI for clearance through the FICS if the RMS finds it necessary. Imports may be referred based on factors like specific intelligence, history or pattern of non-compliance or at random.[24] These imports are then subject to scrutiny of documents, visual inspection, sampling and testing. If sample is found to conforming to all the FSS regulations, a No Objection Certificate ('NOC') is issued and if not, a Non-Conforming Report ('NCR') is generated.[25]

For easing the burden on food importers, food items have been divided into two categories: high risk and low risk. High-risk food items include meat and meat products, fish and fish products, egg and egg products, milk powder, condensed milk, milk-cereal based weaning foods, infant milk food, infant formulae, fats except vegetable fat and cocoa butter equivalent or substitutes. For high-risk items 100% sampling is done for the first five consignments, 25% sampling for the next 20 consignments (if all previous samples are cleared) and 5% in all subsequent consignments (if all previous samples are cleared). In case of low-risk food items 100% sampling is done for the first five consignments, and 5% in all subsequent consignments (if all previous samples are cleared). In case of sample failure at any stage 100% testing is restored.[26]

The Authorized Officer ('AO')[27] first visually inspects the consignment to ensure compliance with packaging and labelling requirements and also checks whether the items have been transported under optimum temperature and hygiene.

Once the AO clears the samples after visual inspection, they are sent for testing to the notified NABL ('National Accreditation Board for Testing and Calibration Laboratories') accredited labs which are randomly chosen through INFOLNET (Integrated Food and Laboratory Network). On conforming to the set safety criteria an NOC is issued clearing the imports.[28]

Animal and Plant Quarantine Departments under the Central Government's Ministry of Agriculture also take samples if the Customs Department has marked the consignment for their NOC. These agencies may reject the consignment regardless of FSSAI's clearance of the same.[29]

9.3.1.2 *What Does the NCC and the NCCP Do?*

FSSAI is the nodal authority that liaises with Codex for India. To this end, NCCP India (National Codex Contact Point of India) has been constituted and designated by FSSAI

24. SO No. 03/2019 – Customs, https://www.punecustoms.nic.in/Standing/Standing_2019/SO-03-2019.pdf.
25. *Ibid.*
26. FSSAI, Manual for Food Imports - 2019, FSSAI, pp. 15-16, https://www.fssai.gov.in/flipbook.php?bookid=327&doc2=0#book2/ (hereinafter, 'Manual for Food Imports').
27. Section 2(b) of the Food Safety and Standards (Import) Regulations 2017 defines an Authorized Officer as a person appointed by the Chief Executive Officer of the FSSAI by an order for the purposes of fulfilling section 25 of the FSSAI Act. Chapter IX of the Food Safety and Standards (Import) Regulations 2017 describes and AO's duty.
28. Manual for Food Imports, *supra* note 26, at p. 20.
29. *Ibid.* at p. 18.

for maintaining liaison with Codex and coordinate Codex activities in consultation with the National Codex Committee ('NCC'). This arrangement facilitates India's participation and inputs to the Codex through an established consultation process.

The NCCP lays down guidelines for national responses on Codex matters and coordinates participation in Codex meetings. It also familiarizes stakeholders with Codex working procedures to enable competent and collective contribution toward domestic standard building and proposes work on new standards.[30]

The NCC advises on the national economic considerations arising out of standardization as per Codex guidelines, so that they are duly considered in discussions. It also assists in ensuring quality and safety of food to the consumers, while maximizing the opportunities the Indian Industry and expansion of international trade. The NCC also appoints Shadow Committees[31] on subject matters related to the corresponding Codex Committees to assist in the study or consideration of technical matters.[32]

Availability of nutritious and safe food is a goal common for all countries and thus the international consensus is emerging toward adopting common global standards. Harmonization of Indian food standards with global standards is critical to achieve this goal. While the FSSAI is working toward harmonizing standards for food safety (additives, etc.) in line with Codex standards it should also do well to adapt harmonization efforts to the local, cultural and geographical origin of the food while adopting or setting standards.[33]

9.3.2 AGMARK

The Directorate of Marketing and Inspection ('DMI') under the Department of Agriculture and Farmers Welfare concerns itself, among other tasks, with the Standardization, Grading and Quality Control agricultural produce and its allied products.[34]

The standards prescribed by the DMI under the Agricultural Produce (Grading & Marking) Act, 1937 are popularly called AGMARK Standards. These standards are essentially quality based with 2-3 grades for each commodity. Grading help farmers to

30. FSSAI, Codex, https://fssai.gov.in/cms/codexfaq.php.
31. For every Codex committee, a shadow committee is constituted. They mirror the Codex committees nationally. There are presently sixteen shadow committees. Under the FSSAI, these are committees mirroring the Codex Alimentarius Commission, Regional Coordinating Committee (including Coordinating Committee for Asia), General Principles, Food labelling, Methods of Analysis and Sampling, Food Hygiene, Food Additives, Contaminants in Foods, Fats and Oils, Processed Fruits and Vegetables, Sugars. Under the Commerce Ministry there is the committee on Food Import and Export Inspection and Certification. Under the Ministry of Agriculture there are three committees – Pesticide Residues, Residues of Veterinary Drugs in Foods and Fresh Food and vegetables. Finally, under the Ministry of Woman and Child Development there is the Committee on Nutrition and Foods for Special Dietary Uses. *See* FSSAI, Codex, https://fssai.gov.in/cms/codexfaq.php.
32. *Ibid.*
33. Siraj Chaudhury, *Food safety needs a collaborative approach*, Live Mint (25 April 2018), https://www.livemint.com/Politics/k0Ph2a8SrkMtFeGu15OWLJ/Food-safety-needs-a-collaborative-approach.html.
34. Directorate of Marking and Inspection, Agmark Certification Scheme, https://dmi.gov.in/Documents/Final%20Text%20Matter%20related%20to%20QC%20Section.pdf (hereinafter, 'Agmark Certification Scheme').

get commensurate prices for agricultural commodities as per the quality produced by them and also acts as a quality assurance for the consumers. As per available information 227 commodities have so far been formulated and notified as AGMARK Standards.[35]

The DMI implements this scheme of certification for both domestic sales and exports. While the AGMARK scheme is voluntary, certification for Blended Edible Vegetable Oils and Fat Spread has been made mandatory under the FSS Act and regulations appurtenant thereto.[36]

The Directorate General of Foreign Trade ('DGFT') has also notified DMI as an inspection and certification body for exports of fruits and vegetables to the EU countries.[37] The European Commission also approves of the procedure of pre-shipment inspection under the AGMARK scheme for exports of fruits and vegetables to the EU.

9.3.3 APEDA

The Agricultural and Processed Food Products Export Development Authority ('APEDA') is a specialized body established by the Agricultural and Processed Food Products Export Development Authority Act, 1986 ('APEDA Act').[38] Initially, its focus remained on assisting exporters in marketing, packaging and training, but later food safety became an important component.[39] It also identified key sectors that are capable of increasing exports such as wheat, fruits and vegetables, and Basmati rice.[40]

Among other functions assigned to it, the APEDA fixes standards and specification for export of agricultural products that are specified in the Schedule to the APEDA Act. Any organic product can be exported only if it is produced, processed and packaged according to the standards laid down in National Programme for Organic Products (NPOP) which is notified by the DGFT as Standards for Organic Production and implemented by APEDA.[41] The NPOP is aimed at harmonization of standards across different countries having been recognized as equivalent standards by European Commission and Switzerland.[42] It is also in the process of achieving bilateral equivalence with South Korea, Taiwan, etc.[43]

---

35. Directorate of Marking and Inspection, Grades & Standards, http://dmi.gov.in/GradesStandard.aspx.
36. Agmark Certification Scheme, *supra* note 34.
37. *Ibid.*
38. Agricultural and Processed Food Products Export Development Authority Act, 1986, https://apeda.gov.in/apedawebsite/corporate_info/APEDA-Act-As-on-date.pdf (hereinafter, 'APEDA Act, 1986').
39. Sandip Das, *Agricultural Products Exports in India*, Agricultural Marketing 339 (2014), https://www.insightsonindia.com/wp-content/uploads/2013/09/agricultural-products-exports-in-india.pdf.
40. *Ibid.*
41. APEDA, About National Programme for Organic Products, http://apeda.gov.in/apedawebsite/organic/PresentStatus.htm.
42. *Ibid.*
43. *Ibid.*

In addition, APEDA carries out inspection of meat and meat products by making regular visits to slaughterhouses, processing plants, storage sites or any other place where such products are handled.[44]

The APEDA Act requires every person exporting any of the scheduled products to register as an exporter for the scheduled product(s), before the expiration of one month from the date on which they seek to export.[45] A Registration-cum-Membership Certificate (RCMC) is issued to any person exporting scheduled products. A registration continues to be in force until it is cancelled by the APEDA.

The APEDA also issues Registration-cum-Allocation Certificates (RCAC) to exporters of Basmati Rice upon registration of contracts with APEDA.[46] As for Peanuts and Peanut products, a Certificate of Exports ('COE') is required to attest for the quantity that qualifies the aflatoxin test based on test reports issued by an authorized laboratory.[47] The COE states that the processing and packaging of the products have been undertaken in a processing unit or warehouse registered by APEDA with a registration number. Almost 128 units have been recognized by APEDA as exporters of peanuts and peanut products.[48]

The entire registration process has been made easier and accessible upon introduction of an online application system.[49] The I-Track system processes new registration, renewal of registration, extension of validity and amendments.[50] There are a host of other activities of APEDA that have been digitalized including the inspection and surveillance of meat houses through a mobile app.[51]

9.3.4 MPEDA

The Marine Products Export Development Authority (MPEDA) was also set up by an Act of Parliament,[52] entrusted with the task of promoting the marine products industry by accelerating exports. It undertakes specific functions with respect to SPS such as fixing standards and specifications for marine products that are suitable for exports and carries out inspection for quality checks of marine products in facilities where they are

44. APEDA, Broad Guidelines for Capacity Assessment of Meat Plants, http://apeda.gov.in/apedawebsite/Announcements/guidelines_assessement_of_meat-plant.pdf.
45. Section 12(1), APEDA Act, 1986; APEDA, Annual Report 2019-20, https://apeda.gov.in/apedawebsite/Annual_Reports/Annual_Report_2019-20_Final_English.pdf (hereinafter, 'APEDA Annual Report 2019').
46. APEDA Annual Report 2019-20; DGFT, Notification No. 18/2015-20 dated August 1, http://apeda.gov.in/apedawebsite/DGFT_notificationfile/01_08_2016_Notification_no_18_reg_term_DA.pdf. The export of Basmati Rice is allowed subject to registration of contracts with the APEDA prior to the shipment. APEDA issues Registration-cum-Allocation Certificates (RCAC) after scrutiny of the applications as per requirements of the Trade Notice dated 16/09/2016 and subsequent amendments issued time to time.
47. APEDA Annual Report 2019-20, p. 36. APEDA has authorized 190 laboratories for sampling and analysing the scheduled products for exports.
48. APEDA Annual Report 2019-20, p. 26.
49. APEDA Annual Report 2019-20, pp. 21-22.
50. *Ibid.*
51. *Ibid.*
52. The Marine Products Export Development Authority Act, 1972, https://mpeda.gov.in/?page_id=472 [hereinafter, 'MPEDA Act, 1972'].

handled. Such facilities may include fishing vessels, processing plants, storage units, or any other place where marine products are stored or handled. It also regulates the exports of marine products by improving their marketing and training.

MPEDA helps exporters gain market access by looking at both tariff and non-tariff barriers, such as anti-dumping duties levied by other countries on India's marine exporters and product standard specifications that hinder market access. It gives recommendations or comments on the relaxation of rules that shrink market access for marine products.

The US is the biggest importer of shrimp from India, but Indian shrimp exports to the US have a chequered history – having come under massive pressure on account of very high anti-dumping duties. However, MPEDA's successful handling of the anti-dumping investigation in the US resulted in the initial duty of 10.17% being subsequently slashed in Administrative Reviews. After thirteen Administrative Reviews of the anti-dumping duties, the present duty incidence is 1.87%.[53]

Registration with the MPEDA is compulsory for any person seeking to export fish and fishery products from India.[54] The registration process has been digitalized and the exporter has to provide MPEDA a completed Form IX along with requisite enclosures.

As regards, standards and specifications MPEDA enforces quality control of seafood is a major concern to public health authorities and consumers.[55] This could involve a host of measures aimed at safety, improvements in product, nutrition, purity, etc. The quality control measure focuses to make seafood exported from India, safer and internationally acceptable in terms of varying SPS standards. MPEDA allows subsidies to registered exporters to establish in-process quality control within their processing units.[56] Any alert or rejection of marine products due to poor quality is notified to MPEDA and the concerned regional division or sub-regional division further investigates and furnishes a report.[57] This ensures that corrective actions can be put in place by the processing unit to prevent further recurrence. The MPEDA has also introduced a Quality Marking scheme to grant a logo as a mark of quality of marine products exported from India that meet a prescribed criterion.

9.3.5 EIC

The Export Inspection Council (EIC) of India is also a body established under section 3 of the Export (Quality Control and Inspection) Act, 1963.[58] Its primary function is to ensure quality export trade by putting in place mechanisms to enforce quality controls

53. MPEDA Annual Report 2019-20, p. 31 https:// https://drive.google.com/file/d/1fxk4LwkETkc8crsUkgT1MpSt70xA7_Lr/view (hereinafter, 'MPEDA Annual report 2019-20').
54. Section 11, MPEDA Act, 1972.
55. MPEDA, Annual Report 2017-18, p. 103 https://mpeda.gov.in/wp-content/uploads/2020/11/1550120514MPEDAAR201718.pdf (hereinafter, 'MPEDA Annual report 2017-18').
56. MPEDA Annual report 2017-18. Subsidies of up to 25% of costs or a maximum of INR 1,50,000 per processing unit will be offered as for registered exporters of seafood.
57. *Ibid.* '37 Rapid Alert Notifications by EU, 50 import refusals by USFDA and 7 violations of Japanese standards'.
58. Section 3, The Export (Quality Control and Inspection) Act, 1963.

and inspections.[59] Functioning as an advisory body to the central government it does the following:

- Notifies commodities that will be subject to quality controls or inspection before exporting;
- Establishes standards for the notified commodities; and
- Detail the type of quality control or inspection each commodity will be subject to.

The Export Inspection Council is located in Delhi and is headed by the Chairman. However, the daily functions of the council are carried out by the Director of Inspection & Quality Control, who is designated as the Executive Head of the Council.[60] All notified commodities are assured quality and safety by a consignment-wise inspection or quality assurance certification. Certifications are provided by field organizations called Export Inspection Agencies (EIA)[61] located at Mumbai, Kolkata, Kochi, Delhi and Chennai with 30 sub-offices hosting NABL accredited laboratories.

EIC requires mandatory certification for some commodities such as fish and fishery products, dairy products, honey, meat and meat products, gelatine, ossein, pre-mixtures, etc. while other food and non-food products are certified on a voluntary basis. For inspection and certification on a voluntary basis, the EIC finds the basis for such an action, on one or more of the following grounds -[62]

- The requirement may be demanded by an international buyer
- The importing countries require such inspection or certification
- If it could be done in accordance with national or international standards of the relevant product
- Contractual specifications.

EIC's certificate of inspection confirms and declares that the product was in an acceptable condition before shipment, acting as an official assurance of quality. The agreements or MOUs signed with import control bodies of other countries, also considers the certificate of inspection as *proof of quality* that it meets their country's requirements.[63] Having more than fifty years of experience, it has received global acceptance and recognition for quality assurances and food safety management.

59. Section 1, The Export (Quality Control and Inspection) Act, 1963.
60. Section 4, The Export (Quality Control and Inspection) Act, 1963.
61. Section 7, The Export (Quality Control and Inspection) Act, 1963.
62. Export Inspection Council of India, Voluntary Certification Scheme on Food Commodities, Document No. EIC/ Vol. Food Certification Scheme / 2007/Issue 3, http://115.112.238.112/eic /voluntary-certification-scheme.pdf.
63. *See* Protocol between the General Administration of Customs of China and Export Inspection Council of the Ministry of Commerce and Industry, India in respect of Hygiene and Inspection requirements for the export of Fish Meal/Fish Oil from India to China (28 November 2018).

9.3.6 BIS

The Bureau of Indian Standards (BIS) was established by the Bureau of Indian Standards Act, 2016.[64] Its main function is to provide product certification schemes for *all products* ranging from agriculture and textiles to electronics. A certification from the BIS allows licensees to use the ISI mark that has become a hallmark symbol to attest for quality in India. While BIS sets voluntary standards for domestic food products, the standards set by BIS for certain products such as bottled drinking water, infant milk and milk powder, has been made mandatory for imports by the FSSAI.[65] The standards generally prescribe permitted raw materials and their quality parameters, hygienic conditions under which the product is manufactured, etc.

One of its central contributions to food safety is the Hazard Analysis and Critical Control Points ('HACCP') certification, qualifying which a product gets IS 15000:2013 certified.[66] This is a process control system designed to identify and prevent any microbial hazards that may cause harm to human health.

During this process, the HACCP will be able to assess the hazard, chances of occurrences during each cycle of manufacturing, raw material procurement, usage of products and prescribe measures to control the hazard.

Under this system, critical control points ('CCPs') are located at various stages where hazards can be either prevented, eliminated, or reduced to acceptable levels. Examples of CCPs include - thermal processing, chilling, testing ingredients for chemical residues and metal contaminants, etc.

9.4 SYSTEMIC ISSUES AND REGULATORY OVERLAPS IN INDIA'S SPS ECOSYSTEM

The SPS regulatory environment in India is plagued by many issues that undermine its efficiency. Proliferation of multiple standard-setting bodies, laws and regulations could destabilize the harmonization process that the SPS Agreement intends to achieve. Some of these issues are discussed below.

9.4.1 Regulatory Overlaps and Conflicts Between State and Central Agencies

With a quasi-federal structure, India shares its powers between the Central and the State Governments depending on the subject-matter, its importance and the need for local knowledge. The 'Preservation, protection and improvement of stock and prevention of animal diseases'[67] and 'protection against pests and prevention of plant

64. Bureau of Indian Standards Act, 2016.
65. Food Safety and Standards (Prohibition and Restriction on Sales) Regulations, 2011.
66. BIS, Hazard analysis and critical control point (HACCP) - Requirements for any organization in the food chain (IS 15000: 2013), https://www.services.bis.gov.in:8071/php/BIS/bisconnect/pow/is_details?IDS = NDg3.
67. INDIA CONST. (1950) Entry 15, List II.

diseases'[68] are both under List II of the Constitution of India, enabling States to regulate these areas. However, 'Establishment of standards of quality for goods to be exported out of India'[69] falls under List I of the Constitution of India, which enables the Central Government to regulate on all matters including plants and animal exports. For example, the FSSAI functions with State Commissioners of Food Safety and other officials who are appointed to enforce the law at the local level and their robust enforcement is key to enhancement of the food safety regime in India. Many states may be unequipped to handle food safety issues owing to scarcity of staff and food testing laboratory infrastructure at the local levels, thereby leading to lack of coordination between the Centre and the State.[70]

9.4.2 Multiple Standard Development Organizations (SDOs)

There is also a proliferation of SDOs with varying duties, with each one of them setting standards for the products that come under their jurisdiction, even though they may have overlapping jurisdictions over the same product. The FSSAI, for example, lays down standards for all 'articles of food' for their 'manufacture, storage, distribution, sale and import'. In contrast, APEDA focuses on exports of agricultural products and standards for organic production systems; MPEDA regulates the export of marine products and its raw materials by fixing standards and specifications for maintaining the quality of sea food that are marketed overseas; the EIC does not, in and of itself, set any standards but ensures that domestic products sought to be exported comply with 'technical regulations or national standards of the importing countries /international standards'. This makes coordination between different agencies a challenging task as exporters might have to comply with varying standards for distribution inside the country and for exporting overseas and may also have to approach different bodies to obtain requisite permissions.

9.4.3 Over or under Regulation in Certain Sectors

As discussed above, some products such as seafood have specialized agencies and general food safety agencies setting standards for distribution, import and export. These sectors seem to have stringent and vast compliances to complete before engaging in commercialization of the products. In contrast, some other products or sectors such

68. INDIA CONST. (1950) Entry 14, List II.
69. INDIA CONST. (1950) Entry 51.
70. Neetu Chandra Sharma, *10 States unequipped to ensure food safety: FSSAI*, Live Mint, (26 November 2019), https://www.livemint.com/news/india/10-states-unequipped-to-ensure-food-safety-fssai-11574708979786.html.

as bakery products like biscuits and breads were largely unregulated until recently.[71] India's pet food and animal feed sector is also completely unregulated.[72]

9.4.4 Lack of Accessible Information

'Transparency' is one of the fundamental principles of the WTO agreements. Through transparency requirements Members aim to achieve a greater degree of clarity, predictability and information about trade policies, rules, and regulations of other Members.[73] Article 7 read with Annex B informs members of transparency obligations under the SPS Agreement.

As a transparency requirement the SPS agreement requires establishment of National Enquiry Points ('NEPs') notified by the Member.[74] Presently, India has three NEPs for SPS measures: (1) food safety related issues fall under Ministry of Health and Family Welfare, (2) animal health and related issues falls under Department of Animal Husbandry, Dairying and Fisheries under the Ministry of Agriculture, and (3) plant health and phytosanitary issues falls under Department of Agriculture, Cooperation and Farmers Welfare under the Ministry of Agriculture.

Another transparency requirement under the SPS Agreement is that of a National Notification Authority ('NNA'). The NNA is responsible for notifying all SPS measures taken by the Member available to the public in a transparent and accessible manner. The Indian NNA comes under the Ministry of Commerce and Industry, only adding more confusion to the legal quandary. The lack of an effective communication inter-se departments dealing with compliance with various aspects of the SPS Agreement is among the key reasons behind delayed notifications, replies and answers.

Furthermore, lack of information in public domain regarding certification and testing procedures is contributing to more uncertainty in the regulatory environment. Given that different agencies certify the same product for different purposes (e.g., distribution, export quality control, equivalent standard of importing country), there is little-to-no uniformity in standardization and regulations.

9.4.5 Lack of Effective Utilization of Mutual Recognition Agreements ('MRAs')

MRAs signed between two countries to adopt equivalent standards for products could prove helpful in streamlining export-import processes. Mutual recognition involves

71. Food Safety and Standards (Food Products Standards and Food Additives) First Amendment Regulations, 2021; Sarath Babu George, Over half of city's eateries lack food safety licence, The Hindu, 13 April 2021, https://www.thehindu.com/news/cities/Thiruvananthapuram/over-half-of-citys-eateries-lack-food-safety-licence/article34312285.ece.
72. India Facing Pet Food Shortages; Govt Urges Industry to Boost Production, Businessworld, 15 April 2021, http://www.businessworld.in/article/India-Facing-Pet-Food-Shortages-Govt-Urges-Industry-To-Boost-Production/15-04-2021-386699/.
73. How to apply the Transparency Provisions of the SPS Agreement, WTO Handbook 2002, p. 31.
74. Indian Standards Portal, National Enquiry Points, http://indiastandardsportal.org/Detail.aspx?MenuId=20.

mutual acceptances of each other's standards as equivalent. It ensures that compliance is faster and easier along with all regulatory requirements being met.

The National Accreditation Board for Certification Bodies (NABCB), the body that accredits other certification and inspection bodies in India has entered into MRAs for Food Safety Management System (FSMS) with the International Accreditation Forum (IAF) and Pacific Accreditation Cooperation (PAC).[75] It is also a full member of the International Laboratory Accreditation Cooperation (ILAC). Auditing agencies that carry food safety audits with recognition from NABCB are directly recognized by FSSAI.[76] However, this does not deal with the main point on having MRAs that mutually recognize the conformity assessment procedure for a given product directly. For example, a country that recognizes APEDA's standards as equivalent to its own standard-setting body in respect of agricultural products can help Indian agricultural exports increase market access in that jurisdiction, in a cost-effective manner. However, the delay is usually caused by the decision-making process itself, for example, Japan took twenty years to decide on the equivalence of standards for Mango.[77]

Additionally, there are some government departments like the Department of Consumer Affairs (Ministry of Consumer Affairs, Food and Public Distribution) which sets standards for weights and measures of products including food (Legal Metrology Division). As seen previously, there is the BIS and other agencies such as the AGMARK, whose standards are applicable for specific food product imports. Thus, there can be issues with multiple agencies, systemic overlaps in regulations and standards and their implementation in a manner which is not discriminatory toward foreign suppliers.

9.5 INSIGHTS INTO SELECT SECTORS AND ISSUES

Let us now look into few specific products and issues which have been contentious for India on account of SPS concerns in domestic and foreign markets. The discussion on Avian Influenza concerns imports restrictions imposed by India on imports of poultry and poultry products, while the discussion on the Foot and Mouth Disease in Bovine Meat and the issue of Maximum Residue Limits (MRLs) are areas of concern for Indian exports.

9.5.1 Avian Influenza and Poultry Products

The European Communities ('EC') in March 2004 had raised a Specific Trade Concern ('STC')[78] in WTO's SPS Committee on certain measures taken by India to restrict

75. India Standards Portal, MLA/MRA, http://indiastandardsportal.org/Detail.aspx?MenuId=21.
76. FSSAI, Gazette Notification No. 328 on Food Safety and Standards (Food Safety Auditing) Regulations, 2018, https://www.fssai.gov.in/upload/notifications/2018/10/5bc198c29f46aGazette_Notification_Food_Safety_Auditing_07_09_2018.pdf.
77. Planning Commission (2007), pp. 225-226, http://niti.gov.in/planningcommission.gov.in/docs/plans/planrel/fiveyr/default.html.
78. A Specific Trade Concern addresses the differences or potential trade-frictions between member countries concerning the conformity of domestic SPS measures.

import of live birds, poultry meat and poultry products due to Avian Influenza ('AI').[79] The US had also shared this concern. Although this issue was subsequently resolved, in June 2007, India imposed a ban on imports of poultry meat, eggs, feathers and seven other poultry products from any country that reported instances of Low Pathogenic Notifiable Avian Influenza ('LPNAI') outbreak in its territory[80] - under the Indian Livestock Importation Act, 1898. The US had reservations regarding the fact that the complete ban imposed by India was disproportionate to the health risks associated with these imports. The US maintained that the imposed restrictions exceeded OIE standards and did not recognize regions in the US with no LPNAI or others with no High Pathogenic Notifiable Avian Influenza ('HPNAI').[81] The ban was also claimed as excessive on account of the fact that it also prohibited imports of products that had been treated against the risks of the AI virus.[82] Such concerns were continually raised before the SPS Committee till mid-2011 and the US was joined by the EU and Australia, who mirrored the US position.

On 19 July 2011 the erstwhile Department of Animal Husbandry, Dairying, and Fisheries ('DAHD') issued an order imposing among other restrictions, an import on a number of poultry-related products from countries reporting AI, including both HPNAI and (importantly) LPNAI.[83] This led to the US requesting consultations with India in March 2012 and subsequently led the Dispute Settlement Body ('DSB') to establish a panel which issued its final report in October 2014.[84]

While India claimed that the import restrictions were consistent with international rules on animal health on OIE guidelines, the WTO panel asserted that India's measures were arbitrarily discriminatory and not in line with the set international standards. In a subsequent appeal, the WTO's Appellate Body ('AB') largely upheld the panel ruling. Without going into the technicalities of the deviations from particular SPS obligations, the crux of the matter in simple terms may be understood as follows:[85]

(i) The AB upheld the Panel's findings under Articles 3.1 and 3.2 that India's AI measures are neither 'based on', nor 'conform to', the relevant international standard (i.e., Chapter 10.4 of the OIE Terrestrial Code).
(ii) The AB upheld the panel's finding that India's AI measures are inconsistent with Articles 5.1 and 5.2 because they are not based on a fair 'risk assessment'.
(iii) The AB upheld the panel's finding that India's AI measures are inconsistent with Articles 5.6 and 2.2 of the SPS Agreement because they are significantly

79. STC Number - 185, http://spsims.wto.org/en/SpecificTradeConcerns/View?ImsId = 185.
80. Chad P. Bown & Jennifer A. Hillman, *Bird Flu, the OIE, and National Regulation: The WTO's India–Agricultural Products Dispute,* 15(2) World Trade Rev. 236 (2016) (hereinafter, 'Chad P. Brown').
81. Chad P. Bown, *supra* note 80 at 239.
82. *Ibid.*
83. AQCS, S.O. 1663(E) issued by India's Department of Animal Husbandry, Dairying, and Fisheries, http://www.aqcsindia.gov.in/pdf/trade-10.pdf.
84. *See* Summary of the dispute to date, *India – Measures Concerning the Importation of Certain Agricultural Products,* DS430, https://www.wto.org/english/tratop_e/dispu_e/cases_e/ds430_e.htm (hereinafter, 'India - Agricultural Products').
85. *Ibid.*

more trade-restrictive than required to achieve India's appropriate level of protection ('ALOP') and are applied beyond the extent necessary to protect human and animal life or health.

(iv) The AB endorsed the Panel's finding that India's AI measures violate Article 6 because they prohibit all imports from any country that has notified AI to the OIE, and thus eliminate the prospect of allowing imports from AI-free areas within such countries.

Following the adoption of the AB report and the panel report as modified by the AB by the DSB, both US and India have been at logger heads over the implementation of the DSB's recommendations. The issue is presently before a compliance panel where India has claimed that it has already complied with the DSB's recommendations by adopting internal measures for this purpose. As per the update on the WTO website the report of the compliance panel is due by the end of November 2021.[86]

India's experience in this dispute was perhaps one of the earliest instances where a developing country was called upon to justify the use of SPS measures against imports. The important takeaways for India from this long-drawn dispute is perhaps the need to develop scientific capacity to back its SPS measures on imports. This would ensure proper risk assessment and satisfy the requirement of having a scientific basis for imposing such measures. This requirement assumes greater significance whenever the restrictions are over and above the international standards set by the recognized standard-setting bodies under the SPS Agreement.

9.5.2 Foot and Mouth Disease in Bovine Meat

Food and Mouth Disease (FMD) in livestock is a contagious viral disease that often causes significant economic impacts to livestock owners. Cattles can often contract the virus easily as there are multiple modes through which FMD can be transmitted. The World Organization for Animal Health (OIE) maintains a FMD disease-free list of countries.[87] In order to export fresh meat from an FMD infested country, Article 2.1.1.22 of the OIE Terrestrial Animal Health code prescribes compliance with OIE Guidelines as a mandatory requirement.[88] The OIE claims that following its international animal health code will sufficiently prevent transboundary transmission of FMD.[89] India has been adopting SPS measures in compliance with OIE Guidelines, and exports only deboned and deglanded frozen Buffalo meat. Additionally, the animals are also required to be raised by purely nourished by natural feeds without any artificial supplements or growth promoters.

86. *See* Communication from the Panel, DS430 (1 September 2021).
87. *See* OIE, List of FMD Free Members, https://www.oie.int/en/animal-health-in-the-world/official-disease-status/fmd/list-of-fmd-free-members/#c156.
88. Article 2.1.1.22, The OIE Terrestrial Animal Health Code.
89. OIE, Foot and Mouth Disease, https://www.oie.int/en/animal-health-in-the-world/animal-diseases/foot-and-mouth-disease/.

The EU banned Indian buffalo meat in 2007 due to increasing FMD cases in India, and the inadequacy of measures taken to confront it.[90] Although India was compliant with OIE standards, the requirements placed by EU based on advice from the European Food Safety Authority (EFSA)[91] were more rigorous and stringent than recognized international standards. In 2014, the EU partially lifted a long-standing embargo on Indian buffalo meat albeit with many conditions.[92] The export norms were now streamlined and all exporters of 'meat products, treated stomachs bladders and intestines prepared from fresh meat of domestic poultry, including meat of farmed and wild game birds' are required to obtain health certificate from the EIC.[93]

India's central plan to combat FMD is being implemented through the Foot and Mouth Disease Control Programme (FMD-CP) which has also been recognized by the OIE.[94] The FMD-CP has been implemented in more than 200 specified districts, with full funding for costs of vaccine, maintenance of cold chain and other logistical support underscoring the importance of controlling FMD in cattle.[95] The Directorate of FMD is located in Mukteshwar, Uttarakhand and collaborates with regional centres across the country, that are involved in continuous survey, monitoring, collection of samples, and managing disease outbreaks that might occur.[96] These regional centres are also responsible for vaccinating eligible cattle at six monthly intervals. Their other functions as regards FMD-CP include awareness campaigns, orientation for the state functionaries involved in its implementation, randomly assigned monitoring and surveillance, mass vaccination, procurement of cold cabinets, assessment of random samples, and virus typing in cases of disease outbreaks.[97] The regional centres assess the effectiveness of the vaccination programme for each round of vaccination through a specific process of random sample collection, screening for antibodies and analysing the results. The regular monitoring or surveillance is done by the State Government. In the event of a disease outbreak, the State Government takes measures to control the

90. European Commission, Commission Decision of 29 November 2007, 2007/777/EC, https://eur-lex.europa.eu/eli/dec/2007/777/oj.
91. *See* Kasturi Das, *Addressing SPS Challenges in India*, CWS (2008). The EC argued that the standards set by EFSA were in consonance with both OIE and WTO Law.
92. APEDA, Lifting of ban on Indian Poultry Meat by EU, http://www apeda.gov.in/apedawebsite/Announcements/Notice.pdf. Dilip Kumar Jha, *EU lifts ban on poultry imports from India*, Business Standard (14 May 2014), https://www.business-standard.com/article/markets/eu-lifts-ban-on-poultry-imports-from-india-114051401154 1.html.
93. *Ibid.*
94. OIE, 83rd General Session – Final Report, May 2015, https://www.oie.int/fileadmin/Home/eng/About_us/docs/pdf/Session/A_FR_2015_public.pdf. (As being compliant with the chapter 8.8.22 of Terrestrial Animal Health Code of OIE.)
95. Department of Animal Husbandry and Dairying, Technical Guidelines to States for Implementation of Various Commitments of Centrally Sponsored Scheme 'Livestock Health and Disease Control', http://dahd.nic.in/sites/default/filess/technical_guidelines_0.pdf (hereinafter, 'Technical Guidelines on FMD').
96. Laboratory diagnosis is done by 31 regional centres that form part of All India Coordinated Research Project (AICRP) for epidemiological research on FMD. Confirmatory diagnosis and detailed research on the virus strain is done by the Directorate of FMD.
97. Technical Guidelines on FMD, *supra* note 95.

transmission rates as per the provisions of the Prevention and Control of Infectious and Contagious Diseases in Animals Act, 2009.[98]

The government has recently expanded the National List of Essential Medicines (NLEM) for human use, to also include a category for animal vaccines. In order to tackle infectious diseases of zoonotic nature effectively, the Union health ministry has issued a gazette notification to include two vaccines – the foot and mouth disease (FMD) (Trivalent) oil adjuvant vaccine and *Brucella abortus* (S19 strain) vaccine, under NLEM for animal use.[99] The advantage of being in NLEM list is that these vaccines will now directly fall under the government's price regulation mechanism thereby making animal vaccines more affordable. The decision to include these animal vaccines in the NLEM list appears to be driven by the fear of zoonotic diseases jumping the species barrier to affect humans – as is the case with COVID-19. Thus, it is only prudent to act in advance, in order to safeguard animal health for long term human health benefits.

The government has also launched the ambitious National Animal Disease Control Programme for FMD and Brucellosis which aims to vaccinate 100% cattle, buffalo, sheep, goat and pig population for FMD and 100% bovine female calves of 4-8 months of age for brucellosis within five years (2019-20 to 2023-24).[100] Other veterinary vaccines such as camelpox vaccine, sheeppox vaccine, PPR vaccine, goatpox vaccine, orf vaccine, buffalo pox vaccine and poultry vaccines are also being considered for being included in the NLEM based on scientific inputs of disease prevalence and objective evidences.[101]

9.5.3 Maximum Residue Limits (MRL) of Insecticides, Pesticides and Preservatives

According to the FAO, 'A Maximum residue limit (MRL) is the maximum concentration of a pesticide residue (expressed as mg/kg), to be legally permitted in or in food commodities and animal feeds.'[102]

Countries importing Indian farm produce are subjecting such imports to rigorous testing for pesticide residues, the benchmarks for which are set way below Codex standards in parts per million ('ppm') levels.

While MRLs should ideally be based on listings maintained by Codex, in recent years there has been a shift toward national standards.[103] Codex standards are fixed after consultations with the countries, and they are pragmatic to a significant extent. As

98. Prevention and Control of Infectious and Contagious Diseases in Animals Act, 2009.
99. Shardul Nautial, *Health ministry brings two vaccines for animal use under NLEM to tackle infectious diseases*, Pharmabiz (19 March 2021), http://www.pharmabiz.com/NewsDetails.aspx?aid=136211&sid=1 (hereinafter, 'Shardul Nautial').
100. *Ibid.*
101. Shardul Nautial, *supra* note 99.
102. *See* FAO, Maximum Residue Limits, http://www.fao.org/pesticide-registration-toolkit/information-sources/maximum-residue-limits/en/.
103. *See* Pulse Pod, The GPC Takes on the Problems with MRLs, https://pulsepod.globalpulses.com/pod-feed/post/the-gpc-takes-on-the-problems-with-mrls.

per established international norms any deviation from Codex standards in setting MRLs need to be based on scientific risk assessment.

In the absence of globally consistent MRLs, complying with varying MRL related constraints on a market-to-market basis, can prove to be both costly and cumbersome and are a huge non-tariff barrier in international trade of agricultural commodities.

In India, the Central Insecticides Board and Registration Committee ('CIB&RC') under the Ministry of Agriculture and Farmers Welfare advises the government regarding risks to human beings or animals involved in the use of insecticides and the safety measures necessary to prevent such risks.[104] The CIB&RC considers factors like good agricultural practices ('GAP'), dose schedule, frequency schedule, pre-harvest interval accounting for acceptable daily intakes ('ADI') based on toxicology data and food consumption patterns in the Indian population.[105] In addition, the Scientific Panel on Pesticide Residues constituted by the FSSAI recommends MRLs of pesticides for agricultural products based on CIB&RC's data.[106] These MRLs are notified under the Food Safety and Standards (Contaminants, Toxins and Residues) Regulations, 2011. As of an FSSAI guidance note from 2020, a total of 213 MRLs had been notified.[107]

With regard to barriers to Indian agricultural exports on account of MRLs set by various member countries, India has faced a spate of rejections and bans for lack of compliance or inability to keep within the prescribed MRL levels. A few of these products which have been contentious in this regard are discussed below.

9.5.3.1 Shrimp (Ethoxyquin)

In 2012 India had raised an STC before the SPS Committee on account of Japan's requirement to mandatorily test Shrimp imports for presence of Ethoxyquin, an antioxidant, which is used as a food additive to prevent browning due to oxidation. In the absence of any Codex standard which would set an MRL for Ethoxyquin in Shrimp, Japan adopted an MRL of 0.01 ppm, pending a full-fledged scientific risk assessment.[108]

India being a major exporter of Shrimp to Japan was aggrieved by this measure and had argued that it was not based on a scientific risk assessment. This was more so since the MRL for Ethoxyquin in Fish was 1 ppm and 3 ppm in Pears. Thus, the limit of 0.01 ppm was excessive, particularly in the absence of any scientific evidence of its toxicity or carcinogenicity. This issue was subsequently resolved in 2014 when Japan raised the prescribed MRL to 0.02 ppm after a scientific study.[109]

---

104. Directorate of Plant Protection, Quarantine, and Storage, Central Insecticides Board, http://ppqs.gov.in/central-insecticides-board.
105. *See* FSSAI, Guidance Note No. 13/2020 on Pesticides: Food Safety Concerns, Precautions and Safety Measures, https://fssai.gov.in/upload/uploadfiles/files/Guidance_Note_Pesticides_04_02_2020.pdf.
106. *Ibid.*
107. *Ibid.*
108. WTO, Sanitary and Phytosanitary Information Management System, STC Number - 342, http://spsims.wto.org/en/SpecificTradeConcerns/View/342.
109. *Ibid.*

9.5.3.2 Basmati Rice (Tricyclazole)

In January 2018, the EU disallowed the imports of any rice having levels of tricyclazole, a common fungicide used for control of neck blast in rice, beyond 0.01 ppm. A reduction of 100% from 1 ppm previously.[110] Rice exporters faced rejection of consignments when traces of the chemical were found beyond the prescribed limits. Comparably, US and Japan allow rice imports with tricyclazole presence up to 3ppm.

9.5.3.3 Banana (Imazalil)

The EU is known to follow a hazard-based approach in determining MRLs in which if a chemical is hazardous, it is not weighed against potential exposure risks. Thus, even very low levels of residue in the produce can lead to rejections. Hence, the EU maintains a strikingly low MRL of 0.01 mg/kg prescribed for 'Imazalil' for bananas against a Codex threshold of 2.0 mg/kg.[111]

In November 2018, India was joined by sixteen other countries in raising an STC before the SPS Committee against lowering of MRLs on pesticides including Imazalil.[112]

9.5.3.4 Grape (Mancozeb)

The EU, on 14 December 2020, issued a notification regarding non-approval of active substance Mancozeb, which is a protective fungicide effective against a wide range of foliar fungal diseases. MRLs for Mancozeb have to be reduced to the default level of 0.01 mg/kg post January 2022.[113] This will push Indian grape cultivators to look for alternatives.

India was also among seventeen countries that jointly raised their concern, before the SPS Committee, against lowering of MRLs for pesticides by the EU, which include buprofezin, diflubenzuron, chlorothalonil, ethoxysulfuron, glufosinate, imazalil, ioxynil, iprodione, molinate, picoxystrobin and tepraloxydim.[114] This issue was raised six times, latest being March 2021, but remains unresolved, as indicated by the

110. Rajju Shroff, How maximum residue levels have become a tool to block our farm produce exports, Indian Express (19 July 2018), https://indianexpress.com/article/india/maximum-residue-levels-farm-produce-exports-5265220/ (hereinafter, 'Rajju Shroff').
111. Ashish Chandra, Non-tariff barriers: What government should do to ensure MSMEs remain competitive globally, Financial Express (3 December 2019), https://www.financialexpress.com/industry/sme/cafe-sme/msme-logi-non-tariff-barriers-what-government-should-do-to-ensure-msmes-remain-competitive-globally/1782873/.
112. Amiti Sen, India, 16 others complain to WTO about EU's residue limits for pesticides, The Hindu BusinessLine (10 November 2019), https://www.thehindubusinessline.com/news/india-16sixteen-others-complain-to-wto-about-eus-residue-limits-for-pesticides/article29937525.ece (hereinafter, 'Amiti Sen').
113. European Commission, Daily News 14/12/2020, https://ec.europa.eu/commission/presscorner/detail/en/MEX_20_2414.
114. Amiti Sen, *supra* note 112.

SPSIMS. Apart from the above, even Saudi Arabia has denied entry of green chillies and cardamom shipments from India on account of exceeding the required MRLs.[115]

While Indian produce is subject to strict checks imposed by the more developed nations, food imports into India are not subject to equivalent standards of SPS measures. India imports large quantities of olive oil, wines, cheese, chocolates and other food products imported from the EU and dates from United Arab Emirates and Saudi Arabia. In this light, India too needs to step up the vigil at its ports of entries, to ensure compliance with MRLs set under Indian law. Efforts should be focused on notifying scientific MRLs to balance the interests of both free trade and SPS concerns.

9.6 CONCLUSION AND RECOMMENDATIONS

In an era where sanitary and phytosanitary measures have supplanted tariffs as barriers to international trade, developing countries like India must find their voice in the global community to avoid being dictated by onerous standards, which unnecessarily encumber India's domestic agricultural practices.

At the domestic level, there is a need for implementing farmer education programs, which would entail implementation of global best practices including cutting down on the indiscriminate use of pesticides and chemical fertilizers. Presently, there appears to be an information asymmetry in this regard. For example, in 2010 an Indian consignment of grapes at the EU port of entry was rejected on the ground of finding higher than approved level of Chlormequat Chloride (ccc).[116] This chemical was not included in the list of chemicals given by APEDA to the exporters and laboratories for laboratory testing, showing that there are no harmonized standards. As a result, exporters and farmers expectedly faced huge financial losses.[117] Such incidences must be avoided at all costs and the government must be proactive in ensuring that chemicals banned or restricted in India's target export markets are also be banned or restricted in India. Efforts must be made to make information on globally acceptable MRLs for various chemicals, available and accessible.

Export control processes must be streamlined and checked for efficiency. Instances of rejections of Indian shipments post export control lays bare the infirmities in the process. Efforts should be concentrated toward creating a single nodal agency for this purpose. Presently various agencies like APEDA, MPEDA, Spices Board, etc. are involved in the process. Having one testing agency would reduce compliance burden and the requirement for multiple levels of laboratory testing.

Efforts must also be driven to ensure the implementation of a world class food safety and management systems even for domestic markets, based on international standards like the HACCP. This would help in aligning our markets to international standards and ensure that all our food products are export ready. The FSSAI has

115. Rajju Shroff, *supra* note 110.
116. Tanu M. Goyal et al., India's Exports of Food Products: Food Safety Related Issues and Way Forward, ICRIER Working Paper No. 345 17 (September 2017), https://think-asia.org/handle/11540/7445.
117. *Ibid.*

mandated implementation of such standards and the same must be duly enforced at the ground level. In this regard, it is necessary to build capacity and technical expertise among small scale food processing units and farmers so that the domestic production is aligned to the global standards. Government efforts must also be targeted at identifying key agricultural exports and provide agriculturalists the relevant infrastructure to make the produce export ready. To this end, it must also strengthen the coordination between Central and State Government mechanisms instituted for the purpose. Absence of robust local mechanisms is one of the serious deficiencies in the current framework which can be resolved by appointing adequate full-time staff and functional laboratories at the State level.

At the multilateral level, efforts must be made to engage meaningfully in the workings of the recognized international standard-setting organizations (Codex, OIE and IPPC) and ensure that recommendations from these standard-setting bodies are in line with the domestic experiences and best practices. This is even more relevant for developing countries like India, which severely lack the institutional capacity and the scientific knowhow to develop risk assessed and science-based standards which deviate from the recommended international standards, as has been our experience in the *Avian Influenza*[118] dispute. While developing countries are expected to be at equal footing in the development of these standards, in reality, standard-setting is oftentimes dominated by developed countries that have the capacity and resources to send staff and meaningfully participate in standard development.[119] One way to circumvent this issue is to identify members with similar interests and share the costs of the exercise. India should also actively invest in improving its pool of scientists, so that it can meaningfully participate in the standard development process. It may be worthwhile to collaborate with top agricultural and allied sciences universities across the country to spearhead this effort in a cost-effective manner. This would achieve both ends of cutting-edge scientific research and meaningful participation in standards development in the global arena.

Alternatively, India could also counter the problem of synchronization of standards between itself and the importing country involved, by negotiating more comprehensive MRAs with the country directly. Although an equivalence agreement for specific products could also be envisaged as a solution, MRAs are more cost-effective and an efficient way of clarifying the mutual recognition of SPS standards across many products.

India must not shy away from raising STCs before the SPS committee in areas where Indian exports are being subjected to standards which are beyond prescribed international standards. Such concerns must be backed with scientific research and data so as to make a strong case against the excesses in the imposed measures. As of

118. India – Agricultural Products, *supra* note 84.
119. Markus Wanger, SPS: International Standards, (July 2020), https://www.researchgate.net/publication/342759937_SPS_International_Standards.

19 April 2021, India has singularly and jointly raised a mere 26 STCs before the SPS committee out of which only three have been marked as resolved on the SPSIMS.[120]

With the Central Government's focus on standardization and its aim to boost Indian exports, efforts must be channelized in a scientific and cohesive manner to achieve a streamlined and transparent ecosystem in keeping with various stake-holder interests. An effort in this direction is already afoot as part of INSS which seeks to develop a 'Quality Ecosystem' with a harmonized, dynamic and mature standards framework – across SPS and TBT measures.

120. *See* WTO, Sanitary and Phytosanitary Information Management System, Search Specific Trade Concerns, http://spsims.wto.org/en/SpecificTradeConcerns/Search. (Use the filter Members: 'India').

CHAPTER 10

India's Initiatives in Addressing Food Safety: The Concerns with Maximum Residue Levels

Murali Kallummal, Malvika Shetty & Hari Maya Gurung

In the decades following the establishment of the World Trade Organization (WTO), the falling tariff rates have correspondingly led to a rise in non-tariff measures/barriers across the membership. These insidious measures are a direct outcome of inadequate transparency provisions in the sanitary and phytosanitary (SPS) and technical barriers to trade (TBT) agreements. Further, it has also led to the deepening of the information asymmetry and has rendered trade policy analysis murkier. This chapter attempts to highlight one such non-tariff barrier known as maximum residue limit (MRL). The chapter addresses the importance of balancing the sovereign rights of the State to institute trade policies that ensures food safety concerns. In addition, the States have international responsibility to establish such policies based on scientific evidence and transparently as agreed under the SPS and TBT agreements.

The authors have highlighted the institutions that develop these MRLs, both globally and within India. They trace the significant concerns that least-developed and developing countries such as India face regarding MRL measures and recommend ways to tackle them within the WTO's framework. Finally, they also raise a critical element of MRL notifications notified by industrial countries for food safety. Such measures are often not in sync with internationally harmonised standards and require newer MRLs that the Codex does not usually use or address.

10.1 INTRODUCTION

Access to any market for agricultural products depends on two key trade policy instruments: applied tariff (a price-based tool), and non-tariff measures ('NTMs' – a non-price-based tool), for example, technical barriers to trade (TBT) or sanitary and phytosanitary (SPS) measures – governed by the provisions of the Agreement on Technical Barriers to Trade and the Agreement on Sanitary and Phytosanitary Measures. The SPS and TBT agreements aim to prevent barriers to trade by harmonising standards across the Member States. However, the agreements balance this obligation on the Member States with the power to set regulations to ensure the health and safety of the consumer and environment.

In the case of the SPS Agreement, Member States are empowered to set regulations that ensure the health and safety of food and feedstuff to be consumed. Amongst these regulations, one can find provisions determining maximum residue limits (MRLs) for various pesticides, additives and contaminants. While pesticides are widely used around the world, their use is not without its fair share of valid concern. Exposure to pesticides can have dire consequences on human health. Pesticides residue in food can have short term adverse or 'acute effects or long term 'chronic' adverse effects that can appear over a long period, sometimes months or years, after the exposure.[1] Maximum Residue Levels/Limits (earlier known as 'tolerances') are therefore determined to ensure that the necessary process of administering pesticides does not, in turn, harm consumers.[2]

MRLs are primarily an SPS-based instrument[3] that are applied when food and feed products are traded internationally. The importing authorities apply legally applicable measures in MRLs, which is the measure for tracing the content of pesticides, agrochemicals and other contaminants in food and feed products. These are mandatory measures that ensure the safety of the consumers.

Internationally, the responsibility for setting an MRL rests with the Codex Alimentarius Commission ('CAC' or 'Codex'). However, the central nodal agencies in each country set MRLs for products traded within their national territory. Therefore, market access to food products depends on the MRLs established by both international and national agencies. Whether they adhere to or exceed the Codex MRLs, these MRLs have to be complied with by exporters looking to participate in the importing market.

While MRLs are essentially policy measures, indispensable in this day and age where pesticides and other chemical products are used more than ever to increase agricultural products' yield, they are often misused as a barrier to market access by the countries to protect their domestic industries from international competition. These measures are a perfect alternative, permitted under the rules of the World Trade

1. Pesticide residues in food, World Health Organization (19 February 2018), https://www.who.int/news-room/fact-sheets/detail/pesticide-residues-in-food; and Food safety: pesticide residue, World Health Organization (16 May 2016), https://www.who.int/news-room/q-a-detail/food-safety-pesticide-residue.
2. Consumers broadly referred here it includes human, animal and environment.
3. Annex A (1) of the WTO Agreement on the Application of Sanitary and Phytosanitary Measures ('SPS Agreement') defines a 'sanitary or phytosanitary measure'. It elaborates the four circumstances under which a measure dealing with human, animal or plant life or health is considered an SPS measure. Since MRLs satisfy the conditions enumerated in this definition, they fall squarely within the SPS agreement's purview. MRLs provisions cannot be dealt with by loose provisions of the TBT Agreement as it pertains to matters of food safety, and it pertains to more rigorous scientific scrutiny as laid out under the SPS agreement.

Organization ('WTO'), especially when the ad valorem tariffs (applied tariffs) have consistently fallen.[4] It becomes difficult for the exporters of primary, semi-processed or processed agricultural products[5] to operate when countries apply SPS measures that are more stringent than those applied by the CAC at the international level. These are introduced by independent national authorities on active ingredient/substances. The MRLs, which are mainly applicable for primary crops and animal products, are also applied to value-added processed food products. Such limits are set on a broad spectrum of contents in the crops, like setting limits on the presence of pesticides, fungicides, weedicides, veterinary drugs, antibiotics, heavy metals, and fertilisers. It is also applied to food and feed additives in processed or value-added agricultural products. The application of the MRL impacts a significant portion of agricultural trade and therefore directly impact India and many other developing countries. Indian exporters are faced with such challenges and concerns.

Therefore, the chapter addresses the various concerns in market access for industry associations, traders and exporters. In addition, to explicitly bring the data-related challenges, it explores the process of MRL setting being practised at the international level. It also traces the relevant bodies for setting the MRLs both internationally (under the SPS Agreement) and within India. Barrett (2017), in an edited series on Studies in Agricultural Economics and Food Policy,[6] highlighted the increasing lack of harmonisation in pesticide MRLs. The lack of harmonisation led to the rejection of consignments based on non-compliance with MRLs notified by the countries; the rejected products are either rerouted or destroyed. In the latter case, there is evidence to suggest that it causes large-scale frittering and is a threat to global food security. To quote from Barret, page 2:

> one of the current and rising impediments to agricultural trade is differing levels from pesticide residues on food production among countries. Given the preponderant use of pesticides in agricultural production globally, trade restrictions arising from lack of harmonisation in pesticide regulation have the potential to lead to wide ranging trade inhibiting effects.[7]

This was blamed on the usages and practices across the European Union (EU) and some East Asian countries such as South Korea, Japan, Hong Kong and Taiwan since 2015. However, to varying extents, all countries use this tactic to protect their domestic industries. By considering the application of such MRLs by the United States (US), the chapter provides an additional nuanced position based on the evidence for

4. Paragraph 4, Page 136, World Trade Report 2012, D. The Trade Effects of Non- Tariff Measures and Services Measures: https://www.wto.org/english/res_e/booksp_e/anrep_e/wtr12-2d_e.pdf.
5. Here after in this Chapter we would be using the term 'agricultural products' to suggest the coverage of a group of products which is inclusive of the various stages of production, like the primary, semi-processed or processed agricultural products.
6. Yeung, M.T., Kerr, W.A., Coomber, B., Lantz, M., McConnell, A., 'Declining International Cooperation on Pesticide Regulation Frittering Away Food Security', Palgrave Studies in Agricultural Economics and Food Policy, Barrett, C. (Ed), ISBN 978-3-319-60552-4.
7. Yeung, M.T., Kerr, W.A., Coomber, B., Lantz, M., McConnell, A., 'Declining International Cooperation on Pesticide Regulation Frittering Away Food Security', Palgrave Studies in Agricultural Economics and Food Policy, Barrett, C. (Ed), ISBN 978-3-319-60552-4.

the lack of harmonisation and its trade impact. At the second level, we would be contextualising India's concerns with increased MRLs usage at the global level. The global practice of applying MRLs is divided between three broad regimes: the Codex (international) and the parallel regimes of two dominant trading nations, the US and the EU. Furthermore, the authors would also be analysing the cost and information asymmetry associated with adopting MRLs by the Indian exporting firms.

10.2 THE HISTORY OF MRL NEGOTIATIONS: SPS AGREEMENT

The discussions in the SPS Committee from 1995 to 2020 have touched on several key concerns. The most important for the developing countries in the context of negotiation on MRLs are discussed in the sections that follow.

10.2.1 Countries Implementing Measures More Stringent Than Codex MRLs

Whilst several WTO Members have implemented regulations on MRLs, most of such issues focused on the measures implemented by the European Union and to some extent against countries such as Japan, China and Mexico. Though the EU has been implementing these measures to protect the EU citizens, these measures have caused significant disruptions to international trade. The role of the EU has been well documented; while the part of the US (being the largest notifier of SPS measures) is not documented sufficiently. There is an indirect reference to such a trend in the WTO documents.[8]

The most controversial aspect is the EU's practice of determining MRLs relying on the hazard-based approach, which has also proved detrimental to exports from developing countries. Chief amongst these are the EU's practice of categorising certain compounds as endocrine disruptors[9,10] and maintaining default MRLs at 0.01 mg/kg for pesticides not explicitly mentioned in the EU Regulation on MRLs.[11]

8. WTO, page 50, '*...the SPS measure notified by G20 economies during the review period were food safety, accounting for 59% of the notifications. Food safety is a particularly important objective in the G20 members' notifications, as the majority of notified measures are related to maximum residue limits (MRLs), food additives or pesticides, and in many notifications several of these keywords were identified.*', *See* 'Report on G20 Trade Measures', Mid-October 2019 to Mid-May 2020 (29 June 2020).
9. Special Trade Concern No. 382. Paragraphs 4.32- 437, G/SPS/R/83 (9 August 2016). The concern raised pertained to Regulation (EC) No 1107/2009, which stated that if a substance is found to be an endocrine disruptor according to the criteria set in this draft regulation, it will not be approved for use in plant protection products unless it is demonstrated that the conditions set in Point 3.6.5.2 of Annex II of Regulation (EC) No 1107/2009 are met.
10. Kallummal Murali and Gurung, Hari Maya, 2017,'***EC's SPS and TBT Notifications on Endocrine Disruptors and Market Access Implications: Case of India's Exports***', CWS Working Paper 34, Centre for WTO Studies, http://wtocentre.iift.ac.in/workingpaper/CWS%20Working%20Paper%20No.33.pdf.
11. Specific Trade Concern No. 306 – Paragraphs 17-19, G/SPS/R/61 (16 February 2011). The concern pertained to the MRLs for a number of chemicals being set at the Limit of Detection (LOD) under EC Regulation 396/2005 established the legislative framework for MRLs of pesticides in or on food and feed of plant and animal origin.

One of the earliest examples of the EU's zealous vigilance can be traced back to September 1998, when several Member States criticised the EC for introducing a proposal for setting new MRLs for aflatoxins in foodstuffs.[12] These countries pointed out that the EC proposal established more stringent levels than the then-existing international standard.[13] Further, it potentially imposed severe trade restrictions and did not seem to be based on a proper risk assessment considering available scientific evidence. In 2001, Côte d'Ivoire raised a concern regarding EC Directive 2000/42, setting MRLs for pesticides in fruits and vegetables.[14] This Directive sets MRLs for several products at the detection threshold.[15] It affected Côte d'Ivoire's exports of tropical fruits, and in most cases, the producers were small farmers who had found export niches in the EU market. As per Côte d'Ivoire, the MRLs were not determined based on pertinent risk analysis. In its response, the EC representative stated that the EC setting the MRLs at the detection level for these chemical products followed the international practice.[16] This was done in cases where older generations of chemical substances for plant protection had been discontinued and forbidden 'either because the industry was unable to or not interested in defending the product, or because safety research showed that there were better substances'.

A Specific Trade Concern[17] raised by Argentina in 2007 highlights some exciting dimensions in the MRL determination by national systems that are more restrictive to trade than the Codex levels. Such MRLs are often applied on old pesticides, and the prices for older pesticides were usually lower than for the newer ones, particularly for those no longer under patent protection. The undertone of MRL fixation and application for rejection is also intended to push the commercial interest of patent-protected agrochemical usages produced by chemical firms in a developed country. It should be noted that, while old chemicals had long series of toxicological data on all aspects of risks (anywhere between 30 to 40 years), the newer alternative is often patent protected and there is very little data to counter the kind of data offered by the old

12. The proposal was made by the Draft Commission Regulation amending Commission Regulation (EC) No. 194/97 of 31st January, 1997 which sought to fix maximum limits for aflatoxin B1 and total aflatoxin in groundnuts, nuts, dried fruit, cereals, milk and processed products thereof. This Draft Regulations was notified at the WTO under the notification G/SPS/N/EEC/51.
13. *Summary of the meeting held on 12-13 March, 1998*, G/SPS/R/10 (30 April 1998), paras 24-31.
14. Summary *of the meeting held on 10-11 July, 2001*, G/SPS/R/22 (5 October 2001) para. 136. Commission Directive 2000/42 sought to make an amendment to the existing Council Directives on the fixing of maximum levels for pesticide residues in and on cereals, foodstuffs of animal origin and certain products of plant origin, including fruit and vegetables respectively.
15. The Detection threshold or the Limit of Detection (LOD) is the minimum concentration of a pesticide/veterinary drug/contaminant in a food sample that 'can just be qualitatively detected, but not quantitatively determined, under a pre-established set of analysis conditions'. LOD defines the minimum amount of pesticide/veterinary drug/contaminant in a food sample below which no finite value can be reported, e.g., not detected at limit of detection of 1gram/kilogram Page 22, FSSAI Manual of Methods of Analysis of Food – Pesticide Residues: https://old.fssai.gov.in/Portals/0/Pdf/Draft_Manuals/PESTICIDE_RESIDUE.pdf. Establishing MRLs at the LOD is the result of relying on the hazard-based assessment of risk. Under EU law, the default LOD is 0.01 mg/kg.
16. *Summary of the meeting held on 10-11 July, 2001*, G/SPS/R/22 (5 October 2001) paras 136 and 137.
17. *Summary of the meeting held on 27-28 June 2007*, G/SPS/R/45 (12 September 2007), paras 12-14 and 170- 173, G/SPS/R/45.

agrochemicals. Further, it is most often driven by the commercial interests of the big agrochemical firms. This could be cited as one of the main drivers for setting such low MRLs for older chemicals. Often it is found that a company that owns an old agrochemical would also have a patent on the newer pesticide, and the requests for data are declined as commercial interest prevails.

In 2016, Belize expressed its concerns regarding the Members' increasing deviations from international standards in applying MRLs as a regulating measure.[18] Belize asked the Committee whether this was due to a gap in the international standard-setting process, which was causing Member Countries to use measures that were far more stringent than the recommendations set by ISSBs. The representative from Belize emphasised that this practice of consistently applying measures by Members that deviated from the recommendations 'called into question not only the efficacy of the international standard-setting processes but even the relevance of the bodies recognised in the SPS Agreement'.

10.2.2 Lack of International Standards

In many of the STCs raised in the SPS Committee meetings, the discussions pertained to measures being implemented that were exceptionally stringent. These issues were exacerbated by the fact that the CAC had not established MRLs for the concerned subjects to which a reference could be made.

For instance, in the aforementioned case of EC's proposal to set stringent MRLs for aflatoxin in nuts, dried fruit, cereals, milk and processed products thereof, the matter was exacerbated by the fact that the CAC had not conclusively determined the MRL for aflatoxin in these foodstuffs at that point of time.[19] In 2003, the USA raised an issue regarding the MRL for Ocratoxin set by Germany. The EC law on the subject had no MRL set for Ocratoxin A in coffee. As per EU law, when this is the case, the Member States of EC have the right to determine the MRL for themselves. Here, the MRL adopted by Germany was far too stringent. However, what indeed exacerbated the situation was that the CAC had set no MRL for Ocratoxin in coffee. The EC subsequently adopted an MRL for Ocratoxin A in coffee which was more flexible than the standard adopted by Germany. Likewise, in 2006, Sri Lanka raised concerns about restrictions on its exports of cinnamon to the EC due to its limit on sulphur dioxide (SO_2). Sri Lanka used SO_2 in the production process as a preservative and browning agent. No Codex MRL[20] existed for cinnamon; therefore, this is an example of trade restrictions compounded by the non-existence of international standards. Ultimately, the CCFAC informed the Committee of work in progress for an MRL to be established for a limit of SO_2 in herbs and spices, particularly cinnamon, through adoption by the CAC.

18. *Summary of the meeting held on 14-16 October, 2015*, G/SPS/R/81 (4 January 2016), para. 11.4.
19. *Summary of the meeting held on 12-13 March 1998*, G/SPS/R/10 (30 April 1998), para. 26.
20. It is also referred to as non-Codex MRLs in this Chapter.

10.2.3 Private Standards

Amongst the responses to a questionnaire circulated by the Secretariat in G/SPS/W/232[21] to take stock of the Member States' experience with SPS-related private standards, a specific issue was highlighted. A common issue pertained to certain private standards that set MRLs for pesticides that were significantly stringent than national requirements in food safety. These national requirements were themselves at times more restrictive than MRLs set by the CAC for the same products. While identifying deviations from Codex standards was more comfortable when they constituted numerical values, it was harder to assess the case of process-based international standards. It was because 'these process-based international standards contained rather general guidelines which were supposed to be given operational effect at the national level'.[22] Most often, they remained non-transparent, and when applied, they did show arbitrariness.

10.2.4 Technical Assistance and Special and Differential Treatment

The SPS Committee has provided a forum for developing countries to seek technical assistance on essential issues. In 2000, Trinidad and Tobago articulated the need to consider the highest SPS standards in any technical assistance programme to permit access to the world's major markets.[23] The representative from Trinidad and Tobago also noted that EC measures were the most stringent and that compliance with them ensures access to every other market.

In several instances, countries were provided technical assistance on a range of issues to help them comply with the provisions of the SPS Agreement and measures that may have been adopted by countries that are more stringent than the SPS Agreement. In case of the issue mentioned above raised by Sri Lanka in 2006 regarding its cinnamon exports to the EC, Sri Lanka had also requested the SPS Committee to consider granting Sri Lanka a time-limited exception, as provided for in Article 10.3 of the SPS Agreement, to export cinnamon to the European Communities with an SO_2 content of 150 ppm until the maximum residue limit for SO_2 in cinnamon were defined at the international level. In response to this request, the European Communities explored the possibility of providing technical assistance to Sri Lanka by assisting in the preparation of the dossier to call for a change in the EC legislation on food additives and contaminants to include a provision for SO_2 in cinnamon.[24] The EC highlighted this issue before the EC Member States and brought their attention to the need to approve SO_2 as an additive in cinnamon. The EC also supported Sri Lanka's formal proposal[25]

21. WTO, '*Questionnaire on SPS-Related Private Standards*', Committee on Sanitary and Phytosanitary Measures (8 December 2008).
22. *Summary of the meeting held on 25-26 February, 2009,* G/SPS/R/54 (28 April 2009), para. 140.
23. *Summary of the meeting held on 15-16 March, 2000,* G/SPS/R/18 (18 April 2000), para. 43.
24. *Summary of the meeting of 24 October, 2005, Resumed on 1-2 February, 2006,* G/SPS/R/39 (21 March 2006), para. 57.
25. *Procedure to Monitor the Process of International Harmonization Submission by Sri Lanka,* G/SPS/W/187 (21 March 2006).

to the CAC to identify cinnamon as a foodstuff where SO_2 could be used and to permit as an interim measure a maximum level of 150 ppm until such time as a standard is established by the CAC. The EC members were encouraged to adapt their import policies to be tolerant in respect to SO_2 in cinnamon in the meantime and pending the modification of the EC legislation.[26]

10.3 DISCUSSIONS ON MAXIMUM RESIDUALS LIMITS UNDER WTO: A BALANCING ACT

10.3.1 Maintaining Market Access in Agriculture and Allied Products

While it has been established that MRLs are an indispensable hallmark of food safety, it must also be acknowledged that these are also used as a protectionist measure by governments to shield the domestic agriculture sector from external competition.[27] For instance, the European Union has time and again been called out for establishing MRLs that are far more stringent than those set by the Codex Alimentarius Commission or, in the absence of Codex MRLs, for determining MRLs relying on the hazard-based approach.[28] India has been one of the countries aggrieved by the EU measures.[29] Two studies looked at the damage caused to Indian agricultural exports to the EU due to their stringent MRL standards.[30] Both the studies found that many of India's agricultural and allied products faced import refusals from EU authorities which harmed India's exports. Chief amongst these exports were those by the statistically significant

26. *Summary of the meeting of 24 October, 2005, Resumed on 1-2 February, 2006,* G/SPS/R/39 (21 March 2006), para. 57 and *Summary of the meeting of 29- 30 March, 2006,* G/SPS/R/40 (26 May 2006), para. 107.
27. Rajju Shroff, How maximum residue levels have become a tool to block out farm produce exports (19 July 2018), https://indianexpress.com/article/india/maximum-residue-levels-farm-produce-exports-5265220/.
28. MRLs can be determined in two ways. These being the risk based approach and the hazard-based approach.

    Risk based approach: This method calculates the probability of the harm that the pesticide or other product could cause based on the extent of exposure to the same (risk × exposure). This approach is used by many countries, including India.

    Hazar- based approach: In this method of assessment, the mere presence of a potentially harmful agent at a detectable level leads to the determination of MRL at the default level of detection (LOD). The LOD is the minimum concentration of a pesticide/veterinary drug/contaminant in a food sample that 'can just be qualitatively detected, but not quantitatively determined, under a pre-established set of analysis conditions'. LOD defines the minimum amount of pesticide/veterinary drug/contaminant in a food sample below which no finite value can be reported, e.g., not detected at limit of detection of 1gram/kilogram. Thus, this method judges the inherent potential of the product to cause harm. This method is used by the European Union. Under EU law, the default LOD is 0.01 mg/kg.
29. Amiti Sen, EU denies India's charge that its pesticide limits create non- tariff barriers (21 February 2020), https://www.thehindubusinessline.com/economy/policy/eu-denies-indias-charge-that-its-pesticide-limits-create-non-tariff-barriers/article3088[illegible]463.ece
30. Kallummal Murali, Aditi Gupta and Poornima Varma, 2012, 'Agricultural Trade from South-Asia and the Impact of SPS Measures: A Case Study European Rapid Alert System for Food and Feed (RASFF)', Journal of Economic Policy and Research vol. 8(2), pp. 40-75, ISSN 0975- 8577; and Jain Disha, Murali Kallummal and Shantanu De Roy, 2017, 'Impact of SPS- Based MRL Standards on Agro Food exports from India to EU', TERI Dissertations, *mimeo*.

small exporters.[31] More specifically, in matters pertaining to MRL measures, many Member Countries do not provide other countries access to the risk assessment reports when they implement more stringent standards than those set by the international standard-setting bodies (ISSBs).

The SPS Agreement was formulated with the hope of harmonising non-tariff measures to eliminate the barriers they often pose to the cross-border trade of agricultural and allied products. Measures such as the stringent MRLs maintained by the EU are counterproductive to this objective. One way to ensure that the countries are abiding by their obligations under the various agreements is through the transparency provisions. Notification obligations can be found across various WTO Agreements. These provisions require Members to notify the WTO Secretariat of the measures adopted. This process helps to eliminate the information asymmetry that causes trade barriers and ensures that trade between Members is open and predictable.[32] Article 7 of the SPS Agreement calls on all Members to notify changes in their sanitary or phytosanitary measures and provide information on the same as per the provisions of Annex B. It then makes comprehensive provisions that spell out the notification procedure under the agreement.

However, there are several instances where Members do not notify other Members about the changes introduced by them. There are also many cases where countries provide notifications with incomplete information. South Centre found that no WTO Member fully complies with their WTO notification obligations. While LDCs find it challenging to comply with the complex and detailed notification requirements due to capacity constraints, all Members fall short in one area or another.[33]

10.3.2 Practical Access to Plant Protection Tools: Recent Harmonisation Efforts

The process of developing plant protection products and getting the same approved before they can be placed on the market is a long and expensive one. Developers are required to submit various kinds of data to multiple authorities to get the plant protection product approved. Often, this process has to be replicated in multiple jurisdictions in order to gain access to different markets.

Efforts are now being taken to boost collaboration between the different national authorities that are involved in the process of approving pesticides that are safe for use in order to shorten the time frame of the approval-seeking process and to reduce the

---

31. Kallummal Murali and Gurung Hari Maya, '***Urgent Need for Market Access Disciplining of Agricultural Trade: Profiling of Stringent and Non- Codex SPS- based Market Standards***', CWS/WP/200/60.
32. Similar notification obligations can be found in the Agreement on Technical Barriers to Trade (Articles 2.9.2, 2.10.1, 5.6.2, 5.7.1 and 10.7) the Agreement on Subsidies and Countervailing Measures (Article 25) and the General Agreement on Trade in Services (Article 3).
33. Page 5, Notification and Transparency Issues in the WTO and the US' November 2018 Communication, Research Paper 92 (March 2019), https://www.southcentre.int/wp-content/uploads/2019/03/RP92_Notification-and-Transparency-Issues-in-the-WTO-and-the-US-November-2018-Communication_EN.pdf

costs that accompany the same. In fact, the national representatives are coordinating this Project under the aegis of the SPS Committee of the WTO by focusing on the menace caused by the pest 'fall armyworm'.

The fall armyworm, a pest native to the Western hemisphere's tropical regions from the United States to Argentina, has wreaked havoc in several continents and is poised to replicate the same in Africa. To address the issue of FAW in Africa, the FAO and the International Center for Maize and Wheat Improvement (CIMMYT) have recommended integrated pest management (IPM) approach at the farm level.

As part of the fifth review of the Operation and Implementation of the SPS Agreement, a proposal had been put forward by Brazil, Kenya, Madagascar, Paraguay, and the United States. This proposal called for the fall armyworm ('FAW') issue to be used as a case study to 'discuss the application of the principles in the SPS Agreement to enable greater access to tools and technologies in integrated pest management strategies'.[34] IPM relies on agronomic management techniques, biological control, and frequent farm field monitoring to avoid and reduce pest infestation. Farmers apply direct control measures only when pest populations exceed economic thresholds to minimise pesticide applications' need.

The follow up to this proposal consisted of a compilation of concepts that support collaboration at the regional and international levels, and that can be employed voluntarily to improve and streamline regulatory processes. The ideas pitched in these concepts include sharing field trial data, common application dossier, joint risk assessments, mutual recognition and familiarity.[35] These and the other concepts mentioned in the proposal aim to enable authorities with capacity constraints to identify regulatory efficiencies that can lead to greater and faster access to safety tools and technologies to manage FAW.

In the case of field trial data, categorising agro-climate zones may allow field trial data to be portable across similar agro-climates that have similar field conditions and where a product may be expected to perform similarly. Several regulatory actions such as seed variety registration, biosafety review and crop protection authorisation require national field trials at multiple sites and multiple planting years. These trials constitute a high cost to the developers of the plant protection product. Allowing field trial data portability would make the repeated field trials under similar conditions redundant, thereby reducing the developers' financial burden and the regulators' bureaucratic workload. Likewise, joint risk assessments conducted collaboratively by two or more regulatory authorities or by a delegated third entity could be used as the basis for each national authority's risk management decisions. It would allow jurisdictions to share resources and capacities.

Further, the concept of familiarity allows for knowledge regarding a product in a jurisdiction to be relied upon for regulatory assessment and registration of the same or similar plant protection product in other jurisdictions. Mutual recognition goes beyond

34. *The Role of the WTO SPS Agreement in Enabling Access to Tools and Technology and Facilitating International Trade- A Case Study On Fall Armyworm*, G/SPS/W/305 (10 September 2018).
35. *Enabling Access to Tools and Technologies- Towards Safer and More Sustainable Agriculture Through Regulatory Collaboration*, G/SPS/W/317 (9 July 2019).

this and allows for national authorities to enter into arrangements wherein they recognise each other's data or regulatory decisions. It may include mutual recognition of each other's standards, data, conformity assessment results, or product approvals and set out conditions or processes that each side must follow to allow for such mutual recognition.[36]

Since FAW is used as a case study here to envisage a framework that helps streamline regulatory processes, the more concepts that may be implemented as a result could also be used to tackle other SPS challenges. The execution of these concepts would also help in the implementation of Article 9 of the SPS Agreement.[37] If brought to fruition, such efforts will significantly lower the cost incurred by companies in launching new and improved pesticides in the market

10.4 GLOBAL INSTITUTIONS FOR FIXATION OF MRLs

10.4.1 Codex Alimentarius Commission (CAC)

As mentioned above, the organisation that determines and monitors MRLs at the international level is the Codex Alimentarius Commission (CAC). Section 3(a) of Annex A (Definitions) of the SPS Agreement states that in the case of food safety, 'the standards, guidelines and recommendations established by the Codex Alimentarius Commission relating to food additives, veterinary drug and pesticide residues, contaminants, methods of analysis and sampling, and codes and guidelines of hygienic practice' are to be considered the relevant international standards, guidelines and recommendations. Likewise, the SPS Agreement refers to the CAC when stating provisions regarding harmonisation of national food safety standards based on international standards, guides and recommendations.

The Codex Alimentarius system is a compilation of food standards and related texts that are internationally adopted. Its objectives are to:

(a) safeguard the health of consumers;
(b) ensure fair practices in the food trade and to guide; and
(c) facilitate trade by establishing definitions and requirements for food and assisting in their harmonisation.

The Codex contains standards for all principal foods and covers raw, semi-processed as well as processed foods. Codex, among other things, includes provisions on residues of pesticides and veterinary drugs, contaminants, food additives, food hygiene, labelling and presentation. While the CAC adopts the draft MRLs, these MRLs

36. *Supra* note 34.
37. Article 9 of the SPS agreement pertains to a Member's obligation to provide technical assistance to other Members, particularly developing country Members. This assistance may be in the form of advice, credit, donations, and grants in furtherance of seeking technical expertise, training and equipment. This is not an exhaustive list. Members may offer any other technical assistance to other Members to enable them to comply with the SPS measures implemented by the importing Members.

are determined by the concerned Codex committees. These are the Codex Committee on Pesticide Residues (CCPR) and the Codex Committee on Residue of Veterinary Drugs in Foods (CCRDF). However, these Committees perform their functions based on the official risk assessors' scientific advice, i.e., the Joint Meeting on Pesticide Residue (JMPR) and the Joint Expert Committee on Food Additives (JECFA).[38] The Codex Committees then use these bodies' expert scientific advice to develop draft MRLs, which the CAC adopts. The JMPR has been meeting annually since 1963. It consists of experts who do not act as representatives of their governments but instead function as independent international experts. These experts conduct scientific evaluations of pesticide residues in food and advice on acceptable pesticide residues in internationally traded food products.

Likewise, the Joint FAO/WHO Expert Committee on Food Additives (JECFA) has been meeting since 1956. An international scientific expert committee evaluates the safety of residues of veterinary drugs, food additives, contaminants and naturally occurring toxins in food. In the case of food additives, the scientific experts that constitute JECFA review all available data, including toxicological, biochemical and chemical data. Based on the evaluation of these data, if the JECFA finds the food additive in question is safe, and then the maximum level of the additive permitted in food is recorded in the Codex General Standard for Food Additives.[39]

New scientific discoveries provide further information on substances and their effect on living beings. Therefore, the Codex system also allows for revision of its standards as may be necessary to ensure that they are consistent with and reflect current scientific knowledge. Such a standard or related text is being revised as per the same procedure which is followed for the development of a new normal. All the CAC Members have been tasked with the responsibility to identify and present any new scientific information to the relevant Codex committee, which may necessitate a revision of any of the prevalent Codex standard or related text.[40]

10.4.2. Institutions Governing MRLs in India

Each country has its institutions to determine MRLs that will be applicable for regulating imports into its territory. These are primarily federal bodies controlled by the central governments. For example, in India, the MRL fixation is carried out by two institutions, namely, (i) the Central Insecticides Board and Registration Committee (CIB-RC) and (ii) the Food Security and Standards Authority of India (FSSAI).

38. Page 8-2, Chapter 8: Maximum Residue Limits for Pesticides and Veterinary Drugs, Principles and Methods for the Risk Assessment of Chemicals in Food, ISBN 978 92 4 157240 8.
39. What do you know about food additives? (28 March 2019), Food and Agriculture Organization of the United Nations, http://www.fao.org/fao-who-codexalimentarius/news-and-events/news-details/en/c/1187310/.
40. Revision of Codex Standards, General Principles of Codex Alimentarius, Codex Procedural Manual (Twelfth Edition), Secretariat of the Joint FAO/WHO Food Standards Programme, FAO, Rome, http://www.fao.org/3/Y2200E/y2200e05.htm.

10.4.2.1 Central Insecticides Board and Registration Committee (CIB-RC), Ministry of Agriculture and Farmers Welfare

The regulation of the import, manufacture, sale, transport, distribution and use of insecticides within India is governed by the Insecticides Act, 1968[41] and the Insecticides Rules 1971. The Insecticides Act endows the national pesticides registration authority, i.e., the Central Insecticides Board and Registration Committee (CIB- RC), with various powers and responsibilities. The Act empowered the Central Government to establish both the Central Insecticides Board and the Registration Committee under section 4[42] (*see* Annexe Box 1) and section 5[43] (*see* Annexe Box 2) of the Act respectfully.

10.4.2.2 FSSAI Scientific Panel on Pesticides Residue

The Food Safety and Standards Authority of India were established in 2011 under the Food Safety and Standards Act, 2006. It is comprehensive legislation on food safety in India (*see also* Chapter 8).

To determine the maximum residue limit of pesticides in food products, the FSSAI has instituted the *Scientific Panel on Pesticides Residue*.[44] Section 13 of the Food Safety and Standards Act empowers the FSSAI to establish scientific panels consisting of independent scientific experts. Section 13(3) (a) to (h) enumerates the issues on which these panels can be established. These include food additive, contaminants in the food chain and pesticides and antibiotic residues.

The Scientific Panel on Pesticide Residues thus recommends the MRLs of pesticides on intended crops based on the CIB- RC data. The RC provides the Panel data on Good Agricultural Practices (GAP), keeping in view the dietary exposure and risk assessment after the Registration Committee approves of the same pesticide. The other data that the Panel utilises for determining MRLs, among other things, include the:

(i) dosing schedule;
(ii) frequency schedule;
(iii) pre-harvest interval;
(iv) active daily intake (ADI)- derived from the various toxicology data and food patterns of the Indian population.

Thus, the Scientific Panel on Pesticides Residue ensures that the MRLs recommended by them are safe for human beings. These MRLs are notified under the Food

41. The Insecticides Act, 1968, Act No. 46 of 1968 (2 September 1968), http://ppqs.gov.in/sites/default/files/insecticides_act_1968_0.pdf.
42. *Ibid.*, 4 (section 4).
43. *Supra* note 28, 6 (section 5).
44. *See* Guidance Note No. 13/2020, Pesticides: Food Safety Concerns, Precautions and Safety Measures, Food Safety and Standards Authority of India, https://fssai.gov.in/upload/uploadfiles/files/Guidance_Note_Pesticides_04_02_2020.pdf.

Safety and Standards (Contaminants, Toxins and Residues) Regulations, 2011.[45] Appropriate punitive action is taken against the concerned food business operators if the pesticide residue exceeds the MRL determined for the products. Currently, the FSSAI seems to be developing standards for the fixation of MRLs for pesticides based on the data received from CIB-RC.[46]

10.4.2.3 Pesticides Management Bill, 2020

On 23 March 2020, the Minister of Agriculture and Farmers Welfare Minister introduced the Pesticide Management Bill 2020 in Rajya Sabha.[47] The Bill seeks to replace the Insecticides Act, 1968 and seeks to regulate the manufacture, import, sale, storage, distribution, use and disposal of pesticides, in order to ensure the availability of safe pesticides and minimise the risk to humans, plant, animals, and environment. However, the Bill has not yet been passed by either Houses of Parliament. Sections 4 (I and II) is discussed in Annexe Box 1 and section 5(1) in Annexe Box 2.

10.5 CONCERNS WITH RISING USAGE OF SPS-BASED MRLS

In simple terms, the SPS-based MRL barrier is a numerical value restricting all imports and all operations of the domestic sector. The MRL, when set at a low level and maintaining them at the same level or lower levels as the technology of detection advances, is costly and often out of reach for many countries. On the other hand, it can have cost enhancing impact on agricultural exporting countries. Therefore, it has a higher cost that can genuinely be a barrier to trade for less-developed countries and small firms. As the Codex Alimentarius is the international reference point for most MRLs, the subsection introduces concepts like information asymmetry, stringency and non-codex MRLs as the core concerns. However, these are increasingly getting overshadowed at the international level by the increased usage of SPS-based MRLs across countries with high per-capita income and value chains in agro-processing sectors. Trading in agricultural products, some of the concerns that emerge from the differences in practices are global versus regional/national practice, commercial interests, technological capability, and developmental differences, primarily when the trade is commercially or otherwise.

Based on the per-capita income, the world is divided into four groups. The WITS database provides trade data regarding reporters' income groups based on the World

45. *See*, Food Safety and Standards (Contaminants, Toxins and Residues) Regulations 2011, Food Safety and Standards Authority of India, https://www.fssai.gov.in/upload/uploadfiles/files/Compendium_Contaminants_Regulations_20_08_2020.pdf.
46. *See*, List of standards in progress, Food Safety and Standards Authority of India, https://www.fssai.gov.in/cms/standards-list-of-standards.php#.
47. Text of the Pesticides Management Bill, 2020 (Bill No. XXII of 2020) as introduced in the Rajya Sabha, https://www.prsindia.org/sites/default/files/bill_files/Pesticide-bill.pdf; Legislative Brief, PRS Legislative Research, https://www.prsindia.org/node/846045/chapters-at-a-glance; Bill Summary, PRS Legislative Research, https://www.prsindia.org/node/845298/chapters-at-a-glance;.

Bank classification of countries.[48,49] A global analysis of agricultural trade reveals only two groups, the 'upper-middle-income and 'others', met the increased demand created by a negative trade balance by the developed countries (imports higher than exports). The lower-middle-income group (India falls in this group) showed a falling trend regarding accessing the expanding developed country market since 2012; *see* Figure 10.1.

Figure 10.1 Global Agricultural Trade Balance (Income Category-Wise) – USD Bn

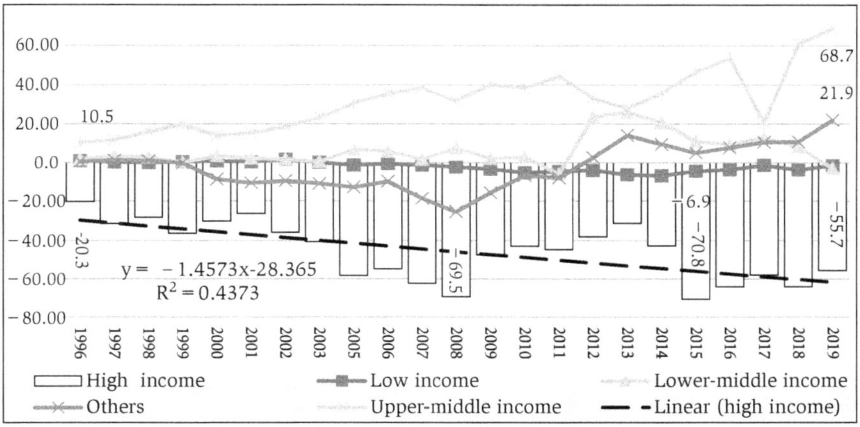

Source: WITS COMTRADE.

Therefore, low per-capita income exporting countries are faced with SPS-based trade barriers when exporting to developed markets. Domestic production suggested an upward movement in food and non-food crops' prices, as suggested by the increase in the FAOs production and yield indices. The falling trade balance could be an outcome of an increase in importing agricultural and allied products or reducing exports as products find it challenging to find an international market. A National Bank for Agriculture and Rural Development (NABARD) survey showed that the average landholding size has marginally decreased by 0.6 hectares, from 1.16 in 2012-13 to 1.1 hectare in 2015-16.[50] From 1998 to 2015 showed evidence of falling exporters from

48. https://wits.worldbank.org/CountryProfile/Metadata/en/Country/All.
49. Kallummal Murali, 2021, 'Import Surge of Agricultural Products under the FTAs: Protection of substitutable products to address livelihoods Concerns', organised by Centre for Development Studies (CDS) national conference on 4th & 5th February 2021, Kerala and the World Economy, Thiruvananthapuram.
50. Average farm landholding size shrinks to 1.1 ha, The Hindu Business Line (17 August 2018), https://www.thehindubusinessline.com/economy/agri-business/average-farm-landholding-size-shrinks-to-11-ha/article24719240.ece.

India's agricultural exports to the US.[51] Some domestic challenges get amplified when there is an increase in SPS-based MRL standards across the global markets. Given that India's average landholding has been shrinking each year, agricultural produce exports face multiple challenges, including traceability. Regulating MRLs in crops for exports has emerged as a significant challenge.

The subsection is divided into five parts: growing challenge of information asymmetry; increased role of private consultancy firms; increase in non-transparency; low tariff and stringent MRLs; and pitfalls of the proposals on MRLs and other related issues.

10.5.1 Growing Challenge of Information Asymmetry

Economies are increasingly driven by data sharing (commercial intelligence), which has been touted as beneficial for societies across agricultural, industrial and services sectors- with an increased role for big data, the internet of things and many other safer, smarter, as more efficient means of transactions. A fundamental element departure is in situations when data is shared freely. Increasingly, countries have seen an increased involvement of private firms' growing presence in data analytics- with corporate firms Google, Apple, Facebook, Amazon web services (AWS) and the like playing an active role in pushing the agenda. However, the WTO, on the other hand, is pushing information asymmetry by making access to data limited to a few big firms. Another dimension is that it limits the firms' potential, allowing access to MRL data to a few commodities and few markets. One of the challenges of any trade agreement is maximising or overcoming the uneven progress in capturing value from data and analytics. Keeping all aspects of market access data transparent and openly available is the key by which this challenge can be overcome.

Until August 2015, the US Department of Agriculture, under its Foreign Agricultural Services (FAS), maintained a database on MRLs on pesticides and veterinary drugs agricultural land processed products for seventy-one countries. It had coverage of 300 *plus* farming products and commodities and 650 pesticide and veterinary drugs exports.[52] The complete database was maintained by a third party, Bryant Christie Incorporated (BCI). The consultancy firms help the US eliminate trade barriers, expand the exports, and provide the information needed to grow in a competitive marketplace. The BCI is considered a suite of regulatory intelligence services providing pesticide and veterinary drug MRLs, contaminant limits, and food additive regulations.[53] The European Union offers details for date MRLs for imposition at the border.[54] However,

51. Kallummal, Murali et al., 'US Import Refusals of Agricultural Products and Their Impact on the Participation of Indian Firms', Agrarian South: Journal of Political Economy. 78, 104 (2018).
52. Maximum Residue Limits (MRL) Database, Foreign Agricultural Service United States Department of Agriculture Foreign Agricultural Service, https://www.fas.usda.gov/maximum-residue-limits-mrl-database.
53. MRL Database, Bryan Christie Inc., https://www.bryantchristie.com/.
54. EU Pesticides Database, https://ec.europa.eu/food/plant/pesticides/eu-pesticides-db_en; https://ec.europa.eu/food/plant/pesticides/eu-pesticides-database/mrls/?event = download. MRL.

for the rest of the markets, the data can only be obtained from the US Global MRLs database that BCI maintains. The access to this is on a payment basis since August 2015. An intergovernmental body such as the WTO would be the ideal body to support such a database. It would allow access to information, which is crucial to assess the importing markets MRLs. In effect, the existing procedure where WTO depends on notifications by the Member States for market access conditions has multiple transparency-related concerns.

10.5.2 Increased Role of Private Consultancy Firms and MRLs

One of the problematic aspects of the unbalanced treatment of market access is the cost implication for users. On the one hand, tariff liberalisation has been relatively harmonised and made predictable by WTO Members committing to their bound tariffs. Three intergovernmental bodies - FAO, WTO and World Bank - provide almost 360-degree information on all aspects of the agricultural sector. On the other hand, the non-tariff measures are loosely committed (with fewer transparency provisions) under the various agreements of Annex 1A of the Marrakesh Agreement. Private firms find innovative ways to fill the gap in market access negotiations in agricultural and allied products. This gap exists because intergovernmental bodies have not taken the necessary steps to make this information available on an open platform. Partly also due to the lack of such freely available information that hinders exports from developing countries to the markets of the developed countries.

Considering the dynamic nature of MRL fixation, one-time consultation would not provide the complete solution. The State would continuously engage the firm for realising market access. Thus, private firms operating and providing this information allows the wealthier countries to gain access to developing country markets. In contrast, exporters from developing countries are discouraged from seeking these services in view of the high costs of acquiring them. The high cost of procuring or consultation services for market access from the BCI deprives many exporters and even some less-developed governments. The minimum cost for *ten* active substances and *ten* agricultural products and *ten* countries is USD 9,000. It has enormous implication as access to the complete database that would cost a fortune for even some of the big companies – *total MRLs database has 1,000 active substances and 875 agricultural products with over 140 markets*. Some of the key features which the BCI has claimed to not be fully available on its website (without paying subscription charges) include:

(1) comparing standards easily between multiple countries;
(2) identifying which MRLs are being revoked;
(3) being alerted if there is a change in MRL standards; and
(4) accessing reports that provide a complete regulatory picture for each country[55]

55. *See*, Pesticides MRLs, Bryant Christie Inc., https://www.bryantchristie.com/BCGlobal-Subscriptions/Pesticide-MRLs.

Some of the above mentioned four possibilities cannot be fully achieved with a USD 9,000 one-time payment – as there needs to be a dynamic approach when addressing the MRLs. Further, the market access challenges are subjected to changing technology and new findings based on risk assessments.

Table 10.1 Introduction of New MRL Notifications by Region – 2013 to 2020

Regions and MRLs	*2013*	*2014*	*2015*	*2016*	*2017*	*2018*	*2019*	*2020*	*2013 -2020*	*Times*
1	2	3	4	5	6	7	8	9	10	11 (times of 10 total)
America	89	439	366	563	401	365	177	131	2531	253
Europe	62	377	264	403	269	197	124	79	1775	178
Asia and Oceania	65	295	180	221	186	169	95	75	1286	129
Africa	–	1	–	1	9	6	12	11	40	4
Codex MRL	–	3	1	2	–	–	4	–	10	1
Regions	**216**	**1115**	**811**	**1190**	**865**	**737**	**412**	**296**	**5642**	

Source: Author based on Bryant Christie.

Tracing the introduction of new MRLs is reflected in Table 10.1. It suggests that the two regions have the highest level of activity regarding MRLs notifications as identified by BCI, and is traced over the years. The total is compared to the ISSB, and the Codex. For the period 2013-2020, the American region dominated with 253 times more MRL notifications than the Codex total, followed by Europe with 178 times, and Asia and Oceania with 129 times. Africa as a region notified the lowest with only four times the Codex international standards. Most developed countries like the US and the EU dominated the MRL notifications. The net result of this overwhelming number of measures (reports) and the existing information asymmetry is that exporters, especially smaller players, from developing countries will be kept out of lucrative markets in the West.

10.5.3 Increase in Non-transparent MRLs

Individual Members have imposed active substances in their national registries of permitted products for purely commercial reasons, without scientific justification. Developing Members often lack the scientific and financial resources to challenge the inconsistency of these trade-restricting measures with the SPS Agreement. In addition, there has been no Codex equivalent MRLs for many of the active substances used by developed Members. Specifically, industrial countries use national standards with loose transparency provisions in the SPS Agreement to their advantage. Some of these national standards are additions to already existing international regulations set by the Codex. Such expansion can also be called non-Codex MRLs, as these are like the unbound tariff lines in tariff negotiations. The Members often set these unbound MRLs at the highest level of detection. With increased technological possibilities, the expressed in terms of stringencies in particles per million (PPM) or particles per billion (PPB) - *from atomic to sub-atomic levels.* The MRL stringency is usually referred to and indicated concerning another value set by a scientific body, expressed either in terms of the *number of times* or the difference in *value itself* in parts per million (PPM/PPB). The MRLs imposed by a nation can be expressed in stock and flow terms: the stock concept in MRLs is the net value of additions and withdrawals that would have happened since the country adopted MRLs to protect its domestic sector from imported food products. Simultaneously, the flow concept is the yearly number of MRLs, which means the annual new MRLs.

Ideally, we must use the 'stock of MRLs' to understand the overall impact on market access across agricultural products. On the other hand, to understand the scope to export a single agricultural product, it is best to look at the latest yearly value of MRLs' across countries and list the comparison. Unfortunately, very few analysis or studies have shed light on the most conducive type of MRLs changes for getting a correct picture of agricultural products' market access.[56] The other dimension of the analysis of the MRLs is the measurement of stringencies. The non-transparency in the MRLs set by nations emerges as a result of the stringency calculations in the context of the internationally harmonised Codex measure. When done in terms of the number of times a national measure is more stringent than the Codex, such a calculation suggest five possibilities.

For this chapter, we have taken the total stock of MRLs of two nations: the US and the EU. Figures 10.2 and 10.3 provides the analysis of the composition of total unique MRLs of active ingredients across all the agricultural and allied products in the EU (33,343) and the US (39,907). These are then compared with unique 10,202 Codex MRLs to arrive at the four categories: (1) *'Only Codex'* - wherein only the Codex has an MRL and country does not maintain; (2) *'Lower than Codex'* - wherein the measure of the country is lower in terms of restrictiveness than the Codex; (3) *'Higher than Codex'* - wherein the country's value is higher in terms of restrictiveness than the Codex MRL; and (4) *Equal to Codex* wherein both have equal MRL values. A fifth category is observed wherein only the country maintains the MRL restriction. Since it cannot be compared with the Codex (International measure), it is termed as *Non-Codex*. It is a non-transparent measure or an unbound measure. Both the US and the EU have a significant share of the total composition of MRLs under this category, with 74 per cent in the US and 67 per cent in the EU, respectively. The large shares of non-transparent

56. Kallummal Murali and Gurung, Hari Maya, 'EC's SPS and TBT Notifications on Endocrine Disruptors and Market Access Implications: case of India's Export, CWS Working paper no 34, (March 2017), http://wtocentre.iift.ac.in/workingpaper/CWS%20Working%20Paper%20No.33.pdf.

MRLs on the active ingredient in both markets suggest the potential barriers that could be used against Indian exports in agricultural products.

Figure 10.2 European Union's Thirty-Three Thousand MRLs and Codex (2015)

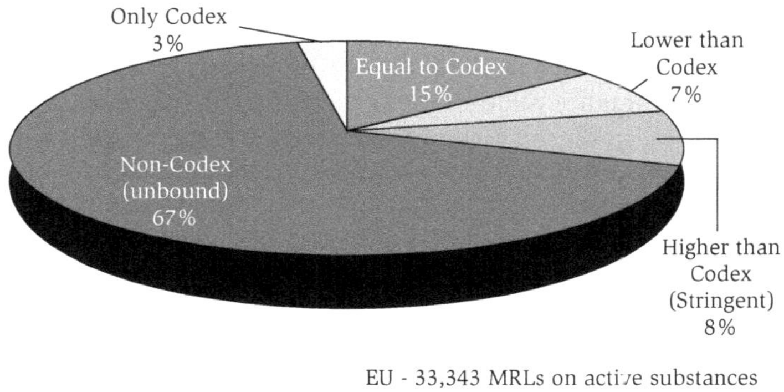

Source: On the basis of the Global MRL Database, United States Department of Agriculture, FAS.

Figure 10.3 United States Thirty-Nine Thousand MRLs and Codex (2019)

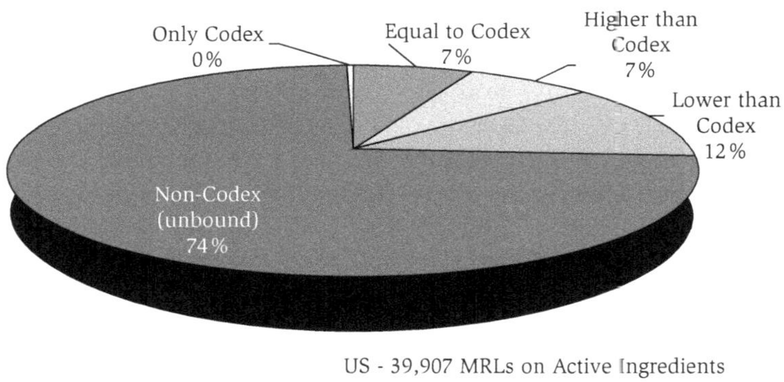

Source: On the basis of the Global MRL Database, United States Department of Agriculture, FAS.

10.5.4 Lower Tariffs Versus Stringent MRLs

There are multiple studies and analysis providing evidence on the decreasing MFN applied tariffs and rising non-tariff measures.[57] For this subsection, we analyse the Uruguay Round bound tariff commitments and MRLs across thirty-five agricultural products - the focus being India's exportable products, *see* Annex Table 1.[58] Figure 10.4 provides a direct comparison of the 26 agricultural product-wise comparisons on two market access variables for imports into the EU. In agricultural products, it is evident that when bound tariffs and stringency in MRLs were applied as trade policy instruments, it was to achieve different goals. The EU had no or low domestic productions in certain products, for which trade policies were so designed that the barriers were kept at relatively low levels. This is observable for products such as gaur,[59] tea,[60] coffee green,[61] peanut[62] and sesame seed.[63] In the rest of the agricultural crops, two possibilities could be observed. The first is substitutability and protection of some domestic productions, observed in the case of wheat and rice.[64] The second possibility is domestic producers' protection in cases such as table grapes, cucumber, wheat gain, apple, milk, cattle meat, rice and beet and sugar root. Across all the eight agricultural and allied products, both the market access barriers were high. Annex: Table 1 of this chapter highlights the EU's most stringent MRL (times) and Bound Rates.

57. Non-Tariff Measures to Trade: Economic and Policy Issues for Developing Countries, Developing Countries in International Trade Studies, UNCTAD (2012); Asia-Pacific Trade and Investment Report: Navigating Non-Tariff Measures towards Sustainable Development, UNESCAP (2019); The Unseen Impact of Non-Tariff Measures: Insights from a new database, United Nations and World Bank (2018).
58. The missing agricultural products are due to the non-availability of ad valorem equivalents for specific duties.
59. *See*, Guar Gum Powder Market Size, Share, Price, Trends, Growth, Analysis, Key Players, Outlook, Report, Forecast 2020-2025 (27 November 2020, 2:39 PM ET), https://reportedtimes.com/guar-gum-powder-market-size-share-price-trends-growth-analysis-key-players-outlook-report-forecast-2020-2025-expertmarketresearch-com/?faodatalab=2020-11-28-1.
60. Chang, Kaison, 2015, 'World tea production and trade Current and future development', Market and Policy Analyses of Raw Materials, Horticulture and Tropical (RAMHOT) Products Team, Trade and Markets Division, Food and Agricultural Organisation (FAO).
61. *See*, Coffee, Sugar tropical beverage crops and foods, Part-II Medium term prospects for agricultural commodities, Projections to the year 2010, Food and Agriculture Organization of the United Nations, http://www.fao.org/3/y5143e/y5143e0v.htm.
62. Nautiyal, P. C. and Mejia, D., 2002, 'Groundnut Post-harvest Operations', National Research Centre for Groundnut (ICAR), Food and Agriculture Organization of the United Nations.
63. *See*, sesame seed, Food and Agriculture Organization of the United Nations, http://www.fao.org/faostat/en/#search/sesame%20seed.
64. Kallummal Murali, 2021, 'Import Surge of Agricultural Products under the FTAs: Protection of substitutable products to address livelihoods Concerns', organised by Centre for Development Studies (CDS) national conference on 4th & 5th February 2021, Kerala and the World Economy, Thiruvananthapuram.

Figure 10.4 Thirty-Five Agricultural Products and the EU Market Access Bound and MRL Stringencies

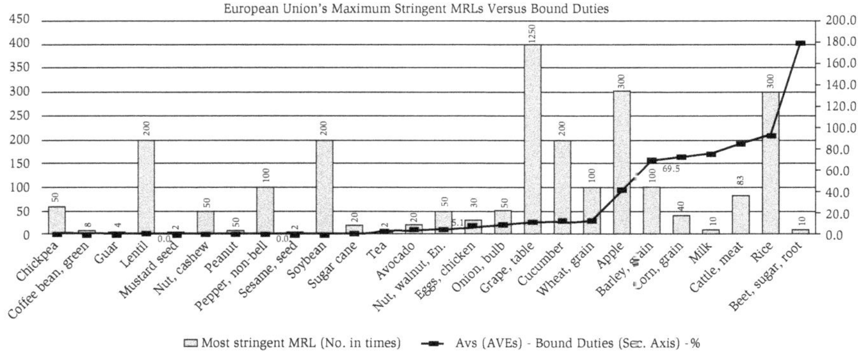

Source: Global MRL Database and WTO, Tariff Analysis Online.

Figure 10.5 Yearly EU's MRL Directives

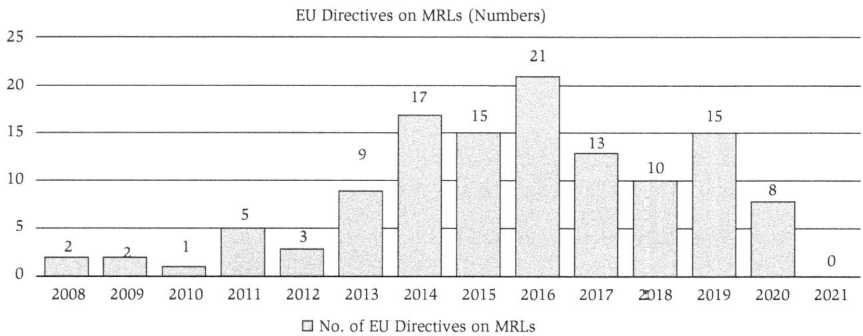

Source: https://ec.europa.eu/food/plant/pesticides/eu-pesticides-database/mrls/.

Further, Figure 10.5 suggests no reversal in MRL usage in the EU market. The analysis of 2008 to 2021 clearly shows that the EU would continue with the default MRLs of 0.01 ppm. A total of 72,493 MRLs[65] were found to be having 0.01 ppm from2008 to 2021. Figure 10.6 depicts the spread in terms of 379 active ingredients and 303 agricultural products. The highlights from the figure, which are in terms of peak coverages, are 2015 and 2019. In both years, the EU notified MRLs with defaults (0.01 ppm) levels with fifty-eight active ingredients and fifty active ingredients in respective years, with above 200 agricultural products covered. As per Figure 10.5, the lowest in

65. The list of EU agricultural products has an 'others' category with 10,784 default MRL of 0.01 ppm.

the year 2010 with no default MRLs with no agricultural products. In 2009, with one active ingredient having a default MRLs for 296 agricultural products.

Figure 10.6 Agricultural and Allied Products and MRLs at the Level of Detection (LOD)

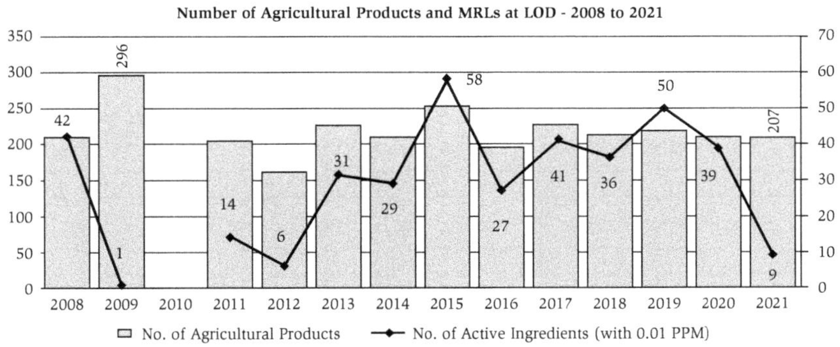

Source: Calculated based on the EU's MRL database, https://ec.europa.eu.

Table 10.2 Agricultural Products with Level of Detection (LOD) MRLs

Range of AIs with Default (0.01 ppm) MRLs	*No. of Agricultural Products*	*% Share of Ag. Products*
1% to 20%	62	20.5
20% to 40%	14	4.6
40% to 60%	39	12.9
60% to 80%	126	41.6
80% to 100%	56	18.5
Above 100%	6	2.0
Total Ag. Products	303	100.0

Source: Calculated based on the EU's MRL database, https://ec.europa.eu.

Table 10.2 shows that almost all of the total 303 EU agricultural products were found to be having one or more active ingredients with 0.01 ppm MRLs - it is also indicated by the EU's Directive, which suggests the continuation of such a possibility (*see* Figure 10.5). The agricultural products with more than 100 per cent coverage are mainly lentils, edible offals (other than liver and kidney), liver, kidney, fat and muscle - these are agricultural and allied products with multiple sub-groups.

In the US, of the thirty-one products which were regulated with tariff and NTMs, a vast majority were held by MRLs (SPS-based standard), with twenty-four products having more than ten times the Codex MRLs. Seven products had more than twice the

Codex MRLs levels (Figure 10.7). The use of Bound duties for imports restriction was limited to less than nine products. Therefore, it establishes that MRLs (SPS-based standards) were used as a means to protect the domestic producers from cheaper imports from third countries; most often, these were the developing countries with very high agricultural GDP shares.

Figure 10.7 Thirty-Five Agricultural Products and the US Market Access Bound and MRL Stringencies

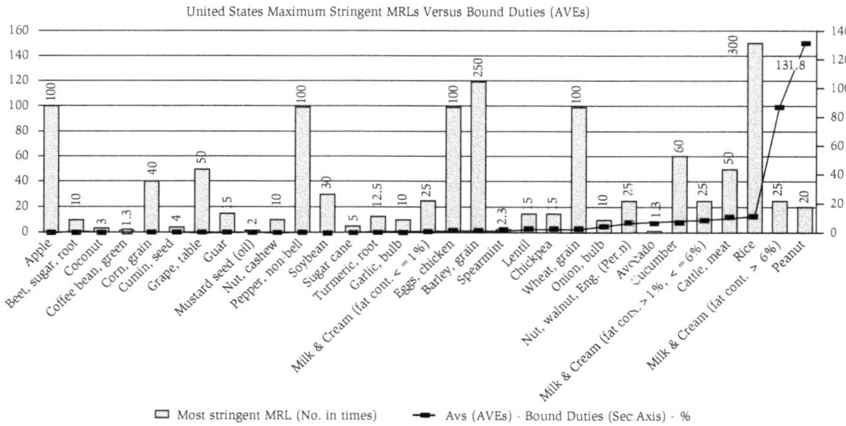

Source: Bryant Christie, Inc. US MRL Database and WTO, Tariff Analysis Online.

Annex: Table 2 of this chapter highlights the US's most stringent MRL (times) and Bound Rates.

10.5.5 Pitfalls of the Proposals on MRLs and Other Related Issues

If the necessary data were available, it should usually take no more than two years for Codex to establish MRLs for a pesticide in various products. Para. 14 of the meeting's summary (27-28 June 2007) also highlighted that the Codex representative mentioned that the Codex Committee on Pesticide Residues had recently adopted new procedures that would allow more rapid development of MRLs.

(1) The Residue Chemistry Expert Group (RCEG) an expert group formed by regulators and industry specialists to propose a new MRL for the OECD countries. The OECD MRL Calculator User Guide indicates the procedure to harmonise such standards across the developed world. Such a harmonised MRL would have a high bearing existing national measures under the

European Union and the United States.[66,67] In a hurry to establish internationally harmonised standards, there is a high possibility the 'OECD MRL calculator' may lead to creating an onerous implication for the developing country exporters.

(2) The application of Special and differential treatment (S&DT) needs to be encouraged in cases wherein there is an absence of risk assessment and the use of the precautionary principle. It should also be noted that the developing countries exporting agricultural and allied products cannot stay away from trading, even for six months. Therefore, there is a need to put some provisions to address it using a milder restriction until a harmonised international MRL is established and accepted.

In addition, small producers in Ecuador who had always produced without the use of any agrochemicals now had to pay some USD 3,000 per year to be certified as organic producers, a very high cost for small growers.[68] All of this puts additional costs on the exporters and can be suggested to equalising the relatively smaller 'tariff advantages' that the developing countries may benefit from in the developed markets.

10.6 CONCLUSION

India's market access for agricultural products in the developed markets, like the US and the EU, is increasingly becoming a matter of concern due to the strategic application of trade policy instruments like tariffs and NTMs. We found evidence for an inverse linkage between tariff liberalisation and the application of SPS measures - this is clear from the analysis of bound rates and stringency measured in times. When the exporters face stringent MRL measures in the external markets, it brings out various concerns. By locating the different standard-setting processes in India and contextualising them against international practices. The chapter finds evidence of considerable gaps in the practice and application of the current global order.

On the one hand, the WTO regulations have overemphasised the role of tariff liberalisation in order to enable market access of goods. On the other hand, the application of non-tariff measures has had a lesser harmonisation impact in global terms. Non-tariff measures are generally in the nature of domestic regulations that have a more significant country-specific influence and therefore a low level of harmonisation. This increases multiple but closely related SPS measures, like use of stringent

66. OECD, 2011, 'OECD MRL Calculator: User Guide', Series on Pesticides, No. 56, Environment Directorate Joint Meeting of the Chemicals Committee and the Working Party on Chemicals, Pesticides and Biotechnology, ENV/JM/MONO(2011)2, 1 March 2011, *see* https://www.oecd.org/env/ehs/pesticides-biocides/oecdmaximumresiduelimitcalculatoruserguide.htm.
67. OECD, 2011, 'OECD MRL Calculator: Statistical White Paper', OECD Environment, Health and Safety Publications Series on Pesticides' No. 57, Environment Directorate, Organisation for Economic Cooperation and Development, Paris 2011, *see* https://www.oecd.org/env/ehs/pesticides-biocides/oecdmaximumresiduelimitcalculatorwhitepaper.htm.
68. WTO, 2007, Summary of the Meeting of 27-28 June 2007, Note by the Secretariat, G/SPS/R/45Corr.1, 31 October 2007.

MRLs which are led by a hazard-based approach, further aided by the information asymmetry.

In the light of the growing information asymmetry as outlined in this chapter, one hopes to see greater attention being paid to the calls for transparency, collaboration and harmonisation that the WTO Agreements have been promoting since its inception. India needs to address some of the concerns of MRLs in the external market and seek a transformation of the global regulatory order by introducing transparency-related measures.

More efforts should be made to establish and maintain a WTO database, providing information on MRLs determined by all WTO Member States. It will go a long way in eliminating the information asymmetry that hinders smaller countries and firms, especially those from developing countries, from participating in global markets. India needs to address some of the concerns of MRLs in the external market access by adopting the following aspects. In the light of the growing information asymmetry as outlined in this chapter, one hopes to see greater attention paid to the calls for transparency, collaboration and harmonisation that the WTO Agreements have been promoting since its inception. These goals can be furthered by championing the smaller players, especially from developing and least-developed Member Countries.

The developed countries ought to acknowledge the information asymmetry that is fuelled by the high cost of acquiring information on established MRLs. Further, a mechanism needs to be envisaged, which allows for cheaper access to this information. For example, it could be in the form of a fund that enables smaller firms from developing and least-developed countries to access such information.

Annexe Box 1:

Section 4(1) mandates the constitution of a Board (known as the 'Central Insecticides Board') by the Central Government. This Board is to –

a. advise the Central and State Governments on technical matters pertaining to the administration of this Act and;
b. carry out such other functions assigned to the Board by or under the Act.

Section 4(2) goes on to enumerate the matters on which the Board may provide advice. These include matters relating to the:

c. the risk to human beings or animals involved in the use of insecticides and the safety measures necessary to prevent such risk;
d. manufacture, sale, storage, transport and distribution of insecticides with a view to ensuring safety to human beings or animals.

Annexe Box 2:

Section5(1) states that the duties of the RC will be to-

a. register insecticides after scrutinising their formulae and verifying claims made by the importer or the manufacturer as regards their efficacy and safety to human beings and animals; and
b. perform such other functions as are assigned to it by or under the Act

Procedure to register an insecticide/pesticide:

The procedure for the registration of insecticides/pesticides has been spelt out under Section 9 of the Insecticides Act, 1968.

- *This registration process* can take place in one of three ways[69]-
  (a) Regular registration under S.9(3)
  Under this process, a person desiring to import or manufacture any insecticide can apply to the Registration Committee for the registration of such insecticide. A separate application needs to be submitted for each such insecticide. The RC then assesses whether the insecticide in question conforms to claims made by the manufacturer with respect to its efficacy and safety (to human beings and animals). If the Committee is thus satisfied, it proceeds to register the insecticide with or without conditions within twelve to eighteen months. Once the applicant pays the prescribed fee, the pesticide is registered, and a registration number is allotted to it. Further, a certificate of registration is also issued within a period of twelve to eighteen months from the date of the receipt of the application.
  (b) *Provisional registration under S. 9(3b),* where the insecticide is being introduced for the first time in India. This is applicable for a period of two years.
  (c) *Me-Too Registration under S. 9(4),* where a person seeks to register an insecticide that has already been registered under S. 9(3) on the application of any other person. In such a case, the grant of the registration number and registration certificate shall take place on the same conditions on which the insecticide was originally registered.
- *Grounds for Refusal*: The RC can refuse to register an insecticide if it believes that the precautions claimed by the applicant cannot be easily observed or they involve serious risk to human beings or animals.
- *Appeal*: An appeal can be made by the applicant to the Central Government within thirty days (or thereafter if the Central Government considers the existence of sufficient cause to prevent the appellant from filing the appeal in time) from the date of the communication of the decision to them. The decision thus obtained from the Central Government shall be final.

69. Process for the registration of insecticides under the Insecticides Act, 1968, http://ppqs.gov.in/divisions/central-insecticides-board-registration-committee/registration-procedure.

- *Grant of License u/S. 13*: A person desiring to manufacture or to sell, stock or exhibit for sale or distribute any insecticide or to undertake commercial pest control operations with the use of any insecticide may make an application to the licensing officer for the grant of a licence.

The Schedule[70] of the Act thus contains a list of insecticides registered under the Act.

The Directorate of Plant Protection and Quarantine, which is structured under the Ministry of Agriculture and Farmer Welfare, has published various guidelines on the registration of pesticides in India.[71] The Directorate also allows for the pesticides to be registered online.[72]

Annex: Table 1 Most Stringent MRL (Times) and Bound Rates – The European Union

S. N.	H S Code (6 Digits)	India's Export	European Union	
			Most stringent MRL (No. in Times)	Bound Rate
1	080810	Apple	300.0	[11.2 + 23.8 €/100 kg/net] [4.8 + 23.8 €/100 kg/net] [6.4 + 23.8 €/100 kg/net] [7.2 MIN 0.36 €/100 kg/net]
2	080440	Avocado	20.0	4.4
3	100300	Barley, grain	100.0	[9.3 €/100 kg/net]
4	121291	Beet, sugar, root	10.0	[23 €/100 kg/net] [6.7 €/100 kg/net]
5	090830	Cardamom	–	0.0
6	020130	Cattle, meat	83.3	[12.8 + 303.4 €/100 kg/net]
7	071320	Chickpea	60.0	0.0
8	080119	Coconut	–	0.0
9	090111	Coffee bean, green	8.0	0.0
10	100510	Corn, grain	40.0	[9.4 €/100 kg/net]
11	070700	Cucumber	200.0	12.8
12	090930	Cumin, seed	–	0.0

70. *See* the schedule, the Insecticides Act, 1968, http://ppqs.gov.in/sites/default/files/insecticides_in_the_schedule_as_on_01.01.2021.pdf; Insecticides in schedule, Department of Plant Protection, Quarantine and Storage, http://ppqs.gov.in/divisions/cib-rc/insecticide-in-schedule.
71. Guidelines for registration, Department of Plant Protection, Quarantine and Storage, http://ppqs.gov.in/divisions/cib-rc/guidelines.
72. Pesticides registration, Central Insecticides Board and Registration Committee, https://pesticides-registrationindia.nic.in/.

S. N.	H S Code (6 Digits)	India's Export	European Union	
			Most stringent MRL (No. in Times)	Bound Rate
13	040700	Eggs, chicken	30.0	7.7
14	070320	Garlic, bulb	–	[9.6 + 120 €/100 kg/net]
15	080610	Grape, table	1250.0	12.4
16	071339	Guar	4.0	0.0
17	071340	Lentil	200.0	0.0
18	080450	Mango	–	0.0
19	**0401**		**Milk**	
	040110	Milk and cream of a fat content by weight of < = 1%, not concentrated nor containing added sugar or other sweetening matter	10.0	[12.9 €/100 kg/net] [13.8 €/100 kg/net]
	040120	Milk and cream of a fat content by weight of > 1% but < = 6%, not concentrated nor containing added sugar or other sweetening matter	10.0	[17.9 €/100 kg/net] [18.8 €/100 kg/net] [21.8 €/100 kg/net] [22.7 €/100 kg/net]
	040130	Milk and cream of a fat content by weight of > 6%, not concentrated nor containing added sugar or other sweetening matter	10.0	[109.1 €/100 kg/net] [110 €/100 kg/net] [182.8 €/100 kg/net] [183.7 €/100 kg/net] [56.6 €/100 kg/net] [57.5 €/100 kg/net]
20	120750	Mustard seed (oilseed)	2.0	0.0
21	080132	Nut, cashew	50.0	0.0
22	080232	Nut, walnut, English (Persian)	50.0	5.1
23	070310	Onion, bulb	50.0	9.6
24	120220	Peanut	10.0	
25	070960	Pepper (spice)	–	3.4

S. N.	H S Code (6 digits)	India's Export	European Union	
			Most stringent MRL (No. in times)	Bound Rate
26	090411	Pepper, non-bell	100.0	0.0
27	100610	Rice	300.0	[17.5 €/100 kg/net]
28	091020	Saffron	-	4.3
29	120740	Sesame, seed	2.0	0.0
30	120100	Soybean	200.0	0.0
31	121190	Spearmint	-	
32	121299	Sugar cane	20.0	0.0
33	**0902**		**Tea, leaves**	
	090210	Green tea in immediate packings of < = 3 kg	2.0	3.2
	090220	Green tea in immediate packings of > 3 kg	2.0	0.0
	090230	Black fermented tea and partly fermented tea, whether or not flavoured, in immediate packings of < = 3 kg	2.0	0.0
	090240	Black fermented tea and partly fermented tea, whether or not flavoured, in immediate packings of > 3 kg	2.0	0.0
34	091030	Turmeric, root	-	0.0
35	100190	Wheat, grain	100.0	12.8

Source: Authors calculation based on Tariff Analysis Online (TAO) WTO and online Global MRL Database (2015).

Annex: Table 2: Most Stringent MRL (Times) and Bound Rates – United States

SN.	HS Code (6 digits)	Product	United States	
			Most stringent MRL (No. in times)	Highest Bound Rate
1	080810	Apple	100.0	0.0
2	080440	Avocado	1.3	[11.2¢/kg]
3	100300	Barley, grain	250.0	[0.15¢/kg] [0.1¢/kg]
4	121291	Beet, sugar, root	10.0	[39.7¢/t]
5	090830	Cardamom	–	0.0
6	020130	Cattle, meat	50.0	10.9
7	071320	Chickpea	15.0	[1.4¢/kg] [1.5¢/kg]
8	080119	Coconut	3.0	0.0
9	090111	Coffee bean, green	1.3	0.0
10	100510	Corn, grain	40.0	0.0
11	070700	Cucumber	60.0	[1.5¢/kg] [4.2¢/kg] [5.6¢/kg]
12	090930	Cumin, seed	4.0	0.0
13	040700	Eggs, chicken	100.0	[2.8¢/doz.]
14	070320	Garlic, bulb	10.0	[0.43¢/kg]
15	080610	Grape, table	50.0	0.0
16	071339	Guar	15.0	0.0
17	071340	Lentil	15.0	[0.15¢/kg] [1.5¢/kg]
18	080450	Mango	–	[1.5¢/kg] [6.6¢/kg]
19	**0401**		**Milk**	
	040110	Milk and cream of a fat content by weight of < = 1%, not con.d nor cont.gad.d sugar or other sweet.g matter	25.0	[0.34¢/litre]
	040120	Milk and cream of a fat content by weight of > 1% but < = 6%, not con.dnorcont.gad.d sugar or oth.sweet.g matter	25.0	[0.43¢/litre] [1.5¢/litre]

SN.	HS Code (6 digits)	Product	United States	
			Most stringent MRL (No. in times)	Highest Bound Rate
	040130	Milk and cream of a fat cont. by weight of > 6%, not condensed nor containing granules added sugar or other sweetening matter	25.0	[USD 1.646/kg] [12.3¢/kg] [3.2¢/litre] [77.2¢/litre]
20	120750	Mustard seed (oilseed)		0.0
21	080132	Nut, cashew	10.0	0.0
22	080232	Nut, walnut, English (Persian)	25.0	[26.5¢/kg]
23	070310	Onion, bulb	10.0	[0.83¢/kg] [0.96¢/kg] [3.1¢/kg]
24	120220	Peanut	20.0	131.8
25	070960	Pepper (spice)	-	[4.4¢/kg] [4.7¢/kg]
26	090411	Pepper, non-bell	100.0	0.0
27	100610	Rice	300.0	11.2
28	091020	Saffron	-	0.0
29	120740	Sesame, seed	-	0.0
30	120100	Soybean	30.0	0.0
31	121190	Spearmint	2.3	1.6
32	121299	Sugar cane	5.0	0.0
33	**0902**		**Tea, leaves**	
	090210	Green tea in immediate packings of < = 3 kg	-	3.2
	090220	Green tea in immediate packings of > 3 kg	-	3.2

SN.	HS Code (6 digits)	Product	United States	
			Most stringent MRL (No. in times)	Highest Bound Rate
	090230	Black fermented tea and partly fermented tea, whether or not flavoured, in immediate packings of < = 3 kg	-	0.0
	090240	Black fermented tea and partly fermented tea, whether or not flavoured, in immediate packings of > 3 kg	-	0.0
34	091030	Turmeric, root	12.5	0.0
35	100190	Wheat, grain	100.0	2.8

Source: Authors calculation based on Tariff Analysis Online (TAO) WTO and online Global MRL Database (2015).

CHAPTER 11

Services Standards: Trends, Gaps and Future Directions

Shiny Pradeep, Trishna Menon & Sreelakshmi S. Kurup

This chapter delves into the regulatory framework of standards in services trade, which are used as tools in international trade to ensure quality, effectiveness and reliability of services. The first part of the chapter provides a brief overview of the international trends in development of services standards. This part highlights the distinct nature of services standards, which stems from the inherent characteristics of services themselves, and explores the resulting challenges and complexities in defining and developing services standards. It then highlights the role of various international organisations in the standardisation of services, including the International Organization for Standardization (ISO). In addition, the role of the World Trade Organization (WTO) is examined briefly, in the context of the discussions under the pertinent agreement – the General Agreement on Trade in Services (GATS).

The second part of the chapter focuses on the development of services standards in India, and highlights the recent trends in this regard, specifically taking into account the evolving nature of services trade. This part then focuses on the specific standards developed in India, and the related ongoing work, in a range of services sectors – including Education, Tourism, Banking and Finance, Accounting, Communication, Information Technology, Environment, Legal, Health-related and Social Services, Logistics, Business, etc. The sectors chosen are based on their underlying potential for growth and development, specifically in light of the Government of India's Champion Services Sector Scheme, approved by the Indian Cabinet in 2018.

The third part concludes. It highlights the potential for standardisation in India's various services sectors, while also outlining the challenges and constraints that are impeding the process of services standardisation in the Indian economy.

11.1 INTRODUCTION

Services are the result generated by activities at the interface between an organisation and a customer and by an organisation's internal activities, to meet customer requirements,[1] and standards are documented agreements containing technical specifications or other precise criteria to be used consistently as rules, guidelines, or definitions of characteristics, to ensure that these services are fit for their purpose.[2]

Of late, the process of standardisation in services has gained increased importance. This is due to the ever-expanding nature of services trade, recent technological developments and integration in global supply chains. Statistics reveal that trade in services is growing at a much faster pace than trade in goods, and is marked by increasing privatisation, deregulation, expansion of digital economy and related developments.[3] The term 'servitisation' has become increasingly popular, with the significant integration and refocus of the traditional manufacturing sector toward services. All these developments underline the need for ensuring interoperability, quality, efficiency, safety and consumer satisfaction in services trade.

In view of this, technical standards in services, like in goods, have become increasingly common and indispensable. The importance of standardisation in services may be better underlined through examples. For those of us attracted to beaches, the standard *ISO 13009:2015* relates to tourism and related services, and provides requirements and recommendations for beach operation.[4] The standard makes specifications to assist travel agents, hotel owners, property developers in better beach management. With respect to core banking services, the *ISO 12812-1:2017* provides a general framework for mobile financial services.[5]

However, owing to the distinct nature of the services trade – marked by characteristics such as non-storability and intangibility, technical standards in services differ from those in goods. While standards for goods typically lay down requirements and specifications pertaining to physical characteristics to ensure quality, specificity of use, etc., for services, standards provide either a description of the service, the terms and conditions to be met by the service-suppliers, or simply specify the qualifications and experience required of a service-supplier.[22] The sectoral specificities and abstract nature of services trade also makes setting standards in services a challenging process. Despite this, the modern-day requirements of enhanced services trade and the integrated nature of global value chains have led to increased standardisation in services, though not to the same extent as in goods. Certain international and regional standardising bodies have published a significant number of standards specifically for

1. BIS Act, 2016, section 2(36).
2. BIS Act, 2016, section 2(39).
3. *See World Trade Report 2019, The Future of Services Trade*, World Trade Organization, https://www.wto.org/english/res_e/booksp_e/03_wtr19_2_e.pdf.
4. *ISO 13009, Beaches, Tourism and related services – Requirements and recommendations for beach operation*, ISO (2015), https://www.iso.org/standard/52329.html.
5. *ISO 12812-1:2017, Core banking – Mobile financial services – Part 1: General framework*, ISO (2017), https://www.iso.org/standard/59844.html.

services.[6] These range from tourism-related standards to standards for waste disposal and management, water treatment and supply, as well as horizontally applicable service standards.

This chapter outlines certain key global trends in services standardisation and how it impacts the domestic framework in India governing services standards.

11.1.1 Standards Development in Services

While there are quite a few international standard-setting organisations engaged in establishing services-specific standards, the number of service standards is far less than product-and-process specific standards. Due to sectoral specificities and the peculiar nature of services trade, standardisation in services is rather fragmented both internationally, as well as domestically within countries. For instance, the sectoral specificities need to be particularly taken into account in certain technical sectors such as telecommunications, postal, transport and financial services, more than in others (such as tourism, education, etc.). For these sectors, specific international standard-setting organisations exist, and standardisation is more prominent. However, the standard-setting process in these sectors requires enhanced capacities and resources for proactive participation, and developing economies often face certain challenges and constraints in international participation.

As regards trade-specific issues concerning standardisation in services, the international trade law regime for technical standards in services is rather rudimentary. As defined by Article VI of the GATS (General Agreement on Trade in Services), it is primarily aimed at ensuring that services trade is not obstructed or impaired due to unfair or unnecessary use of standards and other regulations. However, it is not characterised by substantive provisions aimed at facilitating standards development in services. On the whole, it is governments and businesses that play a key role in standard-setting processes at the international level.

11.1.2 The Role of International Standard-Setting Organisations

At the international level, the International Organization for Standardization (ISO) remains the most important standard-setting organisation in services trade. However, the prominence of ISO in services standardisation is not as significant as in product

6. The ISO has published 700 standards on services so far. *See The ISO Strategy for Service Standardization*, ISO (2016), https://www.iso.org/files/live/sites/isoorg/files/store/en/PUB100393.pdf. The European Committee for Standardization was also mandated in 2013 by the European Commission to formulate service standards, pursuant to which, the European Committee for Standardization identified six possible areas – service terminology, information to the customer, service procurement, service contracts, customer satisfaction measurement and performance measurement. *See Mandate M/517 for the Programming and Development of Horizontal Service Standards Phase I Final Report*, European Committee for Standardization, CEN/BT WG 214 Strategic Advisory Group on Services Ad Hoc Group on Generic Service Standards (February, 2015), https://ftp.cencenelec.eu/CEN/WhatWeDo/Fields/Services/FinalReportPhase1-M517.pdf.

standardisation. The *ISO Strategy for Service Standardization* acknowledges that, while the ISO is famous for its standards in products and processes, the concepts and benefits of international standards for services are not yet well-known.[7] Nevertheless, the ISO has developed and published more than 700 standards in services – mainly in brand evaluation, customer contact centres, tourism, management consultancy, IT services, etc.[8]

Apart from the ISO, there are various other organisations that are engaged in developing and upgrading standards in different services sectors. For instance, the International Telecommunications Union (ITU) is the leading standardisation body for the information and telecommunication services[9]; the International Council of Management Consultants for Management Consultancy; the International Maritime Organization for maritime services; the Basel Committee on Banking Supervision for banking and financial services,[10] etc.

11.1.3 International Trade and Technical Standards in Services

As regards international trade, the World Trade Organization (WTO) framework for standards in services is significantly different from that in goods, and there are no comparable provisions such as the TBT Agreement that govern standards in services. However, the GATS, in addition to providing certain substantive obligations and disciplines, aims at regulating the trade-specific aspects of regulatory barriers in services. The GATS applies to all measures by Members 'affecting trade in services'. While there is no definition of 'technical standards' under the GATS, Article VI of the GATS provides for certain principles governing domestic regulations of WTO Members concerning services trade, and also provides direction for the future development of more concrete disciplines in this regard.

Article VI of the GATS is aimed at disciplining the use of technical standards in services trade, among other regulatory processes and requirements. Article VI:4 calls for development of disciplines by the Council for Trade in Services (CTS) to ensure that

7. *ISO Strategy for Service Standardization*, ISO (2016), https://www.iso.org/files/live/sites/isoorg/files/store/en/PUB100393.pdf. The ISO Strategy also underlines the challenges faced by ISO Members in developing services standards, such as identifying and engaging with stakeholders, etc.
8. *Ibid.*
9. *See ITU-T Recommendation series structure*, ITU, https://www.itu.int/en/ITU-T/publications/Pages/structure.aspx. The ITU's Telecommunication Sector (ITU – T) has well-defined sectoral standards developed by a group of experts by the name ITU-T Recommendations, which are categorised into several letter series.
10. The BCBS is a global standard-setter regulating banking norms across the world. Its 45 members comprise central banks and bank supervisors from 28 jurisdictions. One of its recent standards, SCO, describes the scope and definition of the Basel Framework (effective as of 1 January 2021). *See Basel Framework, Standards*, BIS, https://www.bis.org/basel_framework/index.htm?m=3%7C14%7C697.

measures relating to qualification requirements and procedures, licensing requirements and procedures and technical standards do not constitute unnecessary barriers to trade in services.[11]

Importantly, the GATS Article VI does not provide any guidance for the standard-setting processes in services. Rather, it aims to discipline the application of standards by WTO Members to ensure that the flow of services trade is not restricted. While doing so, the GATS provision recognises the standards set by international organisations, the membership of which is open to all the WTO Members. Pursuant to the mandate provided under Article VI:4 of the GATS, the CTS created the Working Party on Professional Services.[12] The Working Party on Professional Services developed the *Disciplines on Domestic Regulation in the Accountancy Sector*[13] *(the WTO Accountancy Disciplines)* and the non-binding *Guidelines on Mutual Recognition Agreements or Arrangements in the Accountancy Sector.*[14]

The WTO Accountancy Disciplines aim to ensure that measures of WTO Members relating to technical standards, among other domestic regulations, are not 'prepared, adopted or applied' with a view to or with the effect of creating unnecessary barriers to trade in accountancy services.[15] To accomplish this objective, Members are required to ensure that measures are not more trade restrictive than necessary to fulfil a legitimate objective.[16] The definition of 'legitimate objectives' include *inter alia* the protection of consumers, ensuring the quality of the service, professional competence and the integrity of the profession. There are no other provisions on technical standards in the WTO Accountancy Disciplines.[17]

For other sectors, no specific disciplines have been developed so far. However, in 2017, on the sidelines of the WTO Ministerial Conference in Buenos Aires, fifty-nine WTO Members decided to advance discussions on domestic regulations (including technical standards) by issuing a statement entitled *Joint Initiative on Services Domestic Regulation* (JI).[18] While the draft of the envisaged disciplines has reached a definitive shape, at the time of writing, with many JI Members having formulated their indicative

11. Article VI:5 aims at ensuring that until such disciplines are developed by the CTS, the licensing and qualification requirements, and technical standards shall not be applied in a manner that nullifies or impairs the specific commitments of Members.
12. WTO, *Decision on Professional Services*, Council for Trade in Services (1 March 1995), S/L/3.
13. Working Party on Professional Services, Disciplines on Domestic Regulation in the Accountancy Sector (30 November 1998), S/WPPS/W/21; *See also* Decision on Disciplines Relating to the Accountancy Sector, the Council for Trade in Services (14 December 1998), S/L/63. The accountancy disciplines were sought to be adopted formally no later than the conclusion of the forthcoming round of services negotiations. As the round never concluded, the disciplines remain unadopted. However, from the date of the Decision, i.e., 15 December 1998, Members were required 'to the fullest extent consistent with their existing legislation, not take measures which would be inconsistent with these disciplines'.
14. WTO Guidelines for Mutual Recognition Agreements or Arrangements in the Accountancy Sector (28 May 1997), S/L/38.
15. *Ibid.*, ¶ 2.
16. The term 'relevant international organizations' refers to international bodies whose membership is open to the relevant bodies of at least all Members of the WTO. *Ibid.*, ¶ 25 & 26, footnote 2.
17. *Ibid.*, ¶ 25 & 26.
18. Joint Ministerial Statement on Services Domestic Regulation, Ministerial Conference – Eleventh Session, Buenos Aires, 10-13 December 2017 (13 December 2017), WT/MIN(17)/61.

schedules, the available draft of the JI does not contain any substantive provisions on technical standards.[19] It only requires each JI Member to 'encourage its competent authorities' to adopt technical standards developed through 'open and transparent processes', and to 'encourage anybody, including relevant international organizations designated to develop technical standards to use open and transparent processes'.[20]

11.2 THE DEVELOPMENT OF SERVICES STANDARDS IN INDIA

This part of the chapter focuses on the development of services standards in India, and highlights recent trends in this regard, specifically taking into account the evolving nature of services trade. After highlighting the role of the Bureau of Indian Standards (BIS), this part examines the specific standards developed in India, and the related ongoing work, in a range of services sectors – including education, tourism, banking and finance, accounting, communication, information technology (IT), environment, legal, health-related and social services, logistics and business services.

11.2.1 Development of Services Standards by BIS

As a policy, the standards formulation activity of BIS has been harmonised as far as possible with the relevant standards of the ISO or International Electrotechnical Commission (IEC), as applicable. The BIS is a signatory to the Code of Good Practice for the Preparation, Adoption and Application of Standards[21] and has, therefore, aligned its standards formulation procedure with the Code.

Formulation of Indian Standards is one of the core activities of BIS, and is conducted through seventeen 'Division Councils' which represent different areas of economy and technology. Three of these Division Councils oversee the standardisation of services, and they represent the following areas:

- Management and Systems;
- Service Sector I; and
- Service Sector II.

Specialist technical committees called 'Sectional Committees' that function under the Division Councils formulate the Indian Standards. The structure of these committees is designed to bring together all stakeholders with substantial interest in a particular field, so that standards are developed keeping in view the balance of

19. Progress on the JSIs: Communication by the Co-coordinators of the JSIs, https://www.wto.org/english/news_e/news20_e/jsec_18dec20_e.pdf; *see also* Coordinators of joint initiatives cite substantial progress in discussions, WTO (18 December 2020), https://www.wto.org/english/news_e/news20_e/jsec_18dec20_e.htm#: ~ :text = The%20coordinators%20of%20the%20join t,to%20deliver%20concrete%20results%20or.
20. Joint Initiative on Services Domestic Regulation, Note by the Chairperson – Revision (18 December 2020), INF/SDR/W/1/Rev.2.
21. WTO Technical Barriers to Trade Agreement (TBT) Agreement, Annex 3. *See also* TBT Agreement, Article 4.

interests among the relevant stakeholders, and after taking into account all significant viewpoints through a process of wide consultation. Decisions in the BIS's technical committees are reached through consensus.

With respect to the services sector, the BIS's objective is to formulate standards in services sectors including banking and financial services, education services, tourism services, accounting services, legal services, media and entertainment services, health and wellness services, IT and IT-enabled services (ITeS), environmental services, telecommunications services, infrastructure and construction services, transport and logistics services and management and systems.[22]

11.2.1.1 Published Standards

Services standards have been developed and published by the BIS under three technical committees. Table 11.1 shows the number of standards published by each technical committee.

Table 11.1 Published Services Standards

Technical Committee of the BIS	*Number of Published Standards*
Management and Systems Department	394
Service Sector Department I (SSD-I)	71
Service Sector Department II (SSD-II)	3

Source: BIS Website, at https://www.services.bis.gov.in:8071/php/BIS_2.0/dgdashboard/Published_Standards.

The standards published in the Management and Systems Department are based on ISO standards and relate to information and documentation, reference materials, library services, quality management systems, corporate social security requirements, methods for statistical quality control, sampling procedures for inspection, graphic technology, life cycle costing, accuracy of measurement methods and results, human resource management, facility management and asset management.

The majority of the standards published in Service Sector Department I (SSD-I) relate to financial services. Other than these, SSD-I standards relate to information processing, banking, securities, retail financial services, education management systems, tourism and related services, adventure tourism, and recreational diving services. In Service Sector Department II (SSD-II), the published standard relates to Drinking Water Supply Management System – Requirements for Piped Drinking Water Supply Service.

22. *Overview of Standards*, BIS, https://www.services.bis.gov.in:8071/php/BIS_2.0/eBIS/about-standards/.

11.2.1.2 The BIS's Ongoing Work on Services Standardisation

In February 2018, the Union Cabinet approved the Department of Commerce's proposal to provide focused attention to twelve (12) identified 'Champion Services Sectors' to promote their development and realise their full potential. These sectors include IT and ITeS, tourism and hospitality services, medical value travel, transport and logistics services, accounting and finance services, audio-visual services, legal services, communication services, construction and related engineering services, environmental services, financial services and education services. The objective of this scheme is to enhance the competitiveness of India's service sectors to promote GDP growth, create more jobs and promote exports to global markets.

The government agencies (Ministries/Departments) concerned with these sectors are to utilise the available draft sectoral plans to finalise and implement action plans for each identified champion services sector. Each respective line Ministry/Department is to finalise its action plan and implementation timelines along with a monitoring mechanism under the overall guidance of the Committee of Secretaries (CoS) under the Cabinet Secretary.

The BIS' present work on standards is guided by the Indian National Strategy for Standards (INSS) prepared by the Ministry of Commerce and Industry of the Government of India in 2018, and the Standards National Action Plan (SNAP), prepared by the BIS in February 2019, based on the INSS.

The INSS was the result of a broad consensus arrived at over consultations held between 2014 to 2017, through national and regional standards conclaves, involving the participation of experts and stakeholders from central and state governments, industry, regulatory bodies, national and overseas standards and conformity assessment bodies, academics and international forums. One of its professed goals in respect of standards development is to identify sectors where India could pioneer standardisation work, and within those sectors, to develop service standards in a time-bound programme. The INSS notes that India offers many sectors with significant commercial potential that have remained outside the scope of standardisation, and undertaking pioneering standardisation work in these areas would enhance India's contribution to global standardisation efforts. Some of these service areas include the Indian system of alternative medicines, yoga, and ayurvedic traditional healing services.[23]

Given the importance of the services sector to India's and the global economy, the INSS notes that work on standardisation of services needs to be taken in a structured manner, in accordance with a time-bound programme with the simultaneous development of horizontal and vertical standards. The key areas for services standards development are healthcare, tourism, education and skills.[24]

The SNAP positions services standardisation as one of the three key aspects that would define the future national standardisation work of the BIS, and lists certain services sectors as key standardisation areas. *See* Table 11.2 for the key standardisation areas in the service sector.

23. *Indian National Strategy for Standards* 7 (Department of Commerce).
24. *Ibid.*, 8.

Table 11.2 Key Standardisation Areas in Services[25]

Subject Area	*Priority Rank*[26]
Environmental Services	1
Tourism and Hospitality Services	1
Big Data Services	2
Construction and Related Engineering Services	2
IT and ITeS	2
E-commerce	3
Legal Services	3
Medical Value Travel	3
Financial Services	4
Audio-Visual Services	5
Transport and Logistics Services	5
Education Services	5
Health Services	5
Communication Services	6
Retail Services	6

Source: SNAP (February 2019), Annex 2.

11.2.1.3 Cooperation with International Agencies

The BIS is the national enquiry point under the TBT Agreement. As the national standards body of India, it also represents India at the ISO, and is actively involved in development of international standards by acting as either a Participating or an Observer Member on various technical committees, sub-committees, and working groups. It has set up National Mirror Committees to shadow the work of the ISO's Committee on Consumer Assessment (CASCO) and its Committee on Consumer Policy (COPOLCO). At the IEC, the Indian member is the IEC National Committee of India, having its Secretariat at the BIS. The BIS is also a member of the Pacific Area Standards Congress (PASC) and South Asian Regional Standards Organization (SARSO).

The BIS is actively involved in regional and bilateral cooperation programmes pertaining to standardisation, testing, certification, training, etc., and has signed several memoranda of understanding and bilateral cooperation agreements with national standards bodies of various countries.[27]

25. *Standards National Action Plan*, BIS (February 2019), Annex 2, 48.
26. The SNAP accords a priority value to each key standardisation area identified. Here, a rank of 1 indicates a priority value of 1.5, 2 is 1.6, 3 is 2.0, 4 is 2.5, 5 is 2.6, and 6 is 2.8.
27. *Details of Agreement*, BIS, https://www.services.bis.gov.in:8071/php/BIS_2.0/bisconnect/agreement_mou.

11.2.2 Standards Applicable to Selected Important Services Sectors

This section discusses the regulatory bodies and framework for standards in the case of five services sectors, all of which are identified as Champion Services Sectors, *viz.* IT and ITeS, accounting and finance services; banking, financial services and insurance (BFSI); tourism and hospitality; medical value services; education services. These are all sectors where India either already has a strong presence, or where there are factors particularly driving their growth in India.

11.2.2.1 Information Technology and Information Technology-Enabled Services

In the Information and Communications Technology (ICT) sector, the ISO, the IEC and the ITU play a role in ICT standard-setting, with more communications standards than IT standards arising in SDOs for eventual international adoption.[28] The ISO and IEC form a specialised system for worldwide standardisation, and other international organisations also liaise with the ISO and IEC, in this regard. National bodies that are members of the ISO or IEC participate in the development of standards through technical committees established by the respective organisation to deal with particular fields of technical activity. ISO and IEC technical committees also collaborate in fields of their mutual interest.[29]

11.2.2.1.1 ISO/IEC Joint Technical Committee on Information Technology

One such technical committee is the ISO and IEC Joint Technical Committee on Information Technology (JTC 1) which consists of experts from around the world and focuses on the development of international standards for ICT, for business and consumer applications. JTC 1 for information technology, is a consensus-based, voluntary international standards group. JTC 1 experts play a role in recommending baselines and standards for safety features, acceptable quality measures and testing.[30] India is a Participating Member of the JTC 1, and is represented by the BIS.

The areas in which the JTC 1 develops the IT standards required by global markets are indicated in Figure 11.1.

28. Andrew Upgrove, *ICT Standard Setting Today: A System Under Stress,* First Monday (April 2007), https://firstmonday.org/ojs/index.php/fm/article/view/1911/1793.
29. *Part 1: ICT Standards Development Organizations and Their Work,* ITU, https://www.itu.int/en/ITU-T/studygroups/com17/ict/Pages/ict-part01.aspx.
30. *About,* JTC1, https://jtc1info.org/about/.

Figure 11.1 The JTC 1's Scope of Standards Development

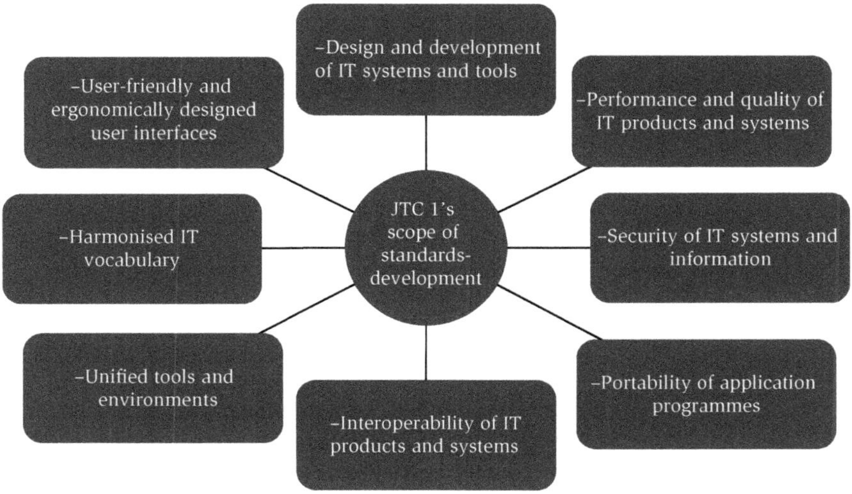

Source: JTC1, About, at https://jtc1info.org/about/.

IT standards are largely created by industry consortia rather than by SDOs. When consortia-developed standards are offered for formal adoption, they are usually submitted to the JTC 1, which was originally formed to consider (and continues to process) SDO-originated IT standards.[31] The JTC 1 follows a voluntary, market-driven process of standards development which involves collaboration and consensus building. Consortia can bring their standards to JTC 1 for globalisation, and consensus building enables the quick development of acceptable standards which can be used globally.[32]

While the JTC 1 consists of various sub-committees that work on standard-setting for information technology goods,[33] the sub-committee JTC 1/SC 40 focuses on the development of standards, tools, frameworks, best practices and related documents for IT Service Management and IT Governance, including areas of IT activity such as audit, digital forensics, governance, risk management, outsourcing, service operations and service maintenance, but excluding subject-matter covered under the scope and existing work programs of JTC 1/SC 27 (Information Security, Cybersecurity and Privacy Protection) and JTC 1/SC 38 (Cloud Computing and Distributed Platforms).[34] These areas of work are indicated in Figure 11.2. This sub-committee was formed in 2013 to bring together standardisation activities in the domain of governance of

31. Andrew Upgrove, *ICT Standard Setting Today: A System Under Stress*, First Monday (April 2007), https://firstmonday.org/ojs/index.php/fm/article/view/1911/1793.
32. *Ibid.*
33. *Subcommittees*, JTC1, https://jtc1info.org/technology/subcommittees/.
34. *ISO/IEC JTC 1/SC 40 – IT service management and IT governance*, ISO (2013), https://www.iso.org/committee/5013818.html.

information technologies, service management and IT-enabled business process outsourcing. There are three key series of standards it has developed: ISO/IEC 38500, ISO/IEC 20000 and ISO/IEC 30105.

Figure 11.2 The Areas of Work of the Sub-committee JTC 1/SC 40

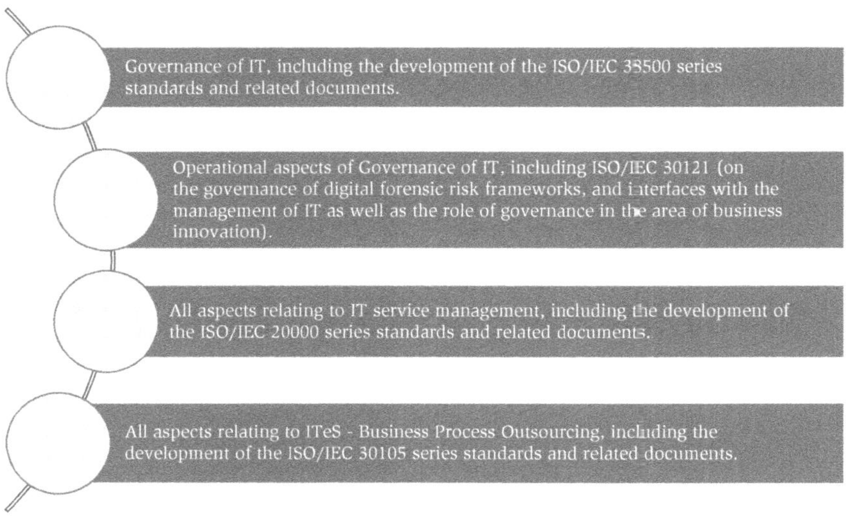

Source: ISO, ISO/IEC JTC 1/SC 40 – IT service management and IT governance, at https://www.iso.org/committee/5013818.html.

11.2.2.1.2 Organization for the Advancement of Structured Information Standards

The international consortium, the 'Organization for the Advancement of Structured Information Standards' (OASIS), is a not-for-profit that focuses on the development, convergence, and adoption of e-business standards. It was founded under the name 'SGML Open' in 1993, and began as a consortium of vendors and users working toward developing guidelines for interoperability among products that support the Standard Generalized Markup Language (which is a standard for defining generalised markup languages for documents). The consortium changed its name to 'OASIS' in 1998 to reflect an expanded scope of technical work.[35]

OASIS is a liaising organisation of the ISO in eleven technical committees and sub-committees, recognised as making an effective contribution to the work of the technical committee or sub-committee for questions dealt with by that technical committee or sub-committee.[36] It produces web services standards, standards for

35. *About us*, OASIS Open, https://www.oasis-open.org/org/.
36. *OASIS*, ISO, https://www.iso.org/organization/306174.html.

security, e-business, along with standardisation efforts in the public sector and for application-specific markets.

OASIS currently has more than 4,000 participants, which represent over 600 organisations and individual members in 100 countries.[37] These include: well-known IT enterprises such as IBM, Adobe Systems, Accenture LLP, Cisco Systems, Dell, Fujitsu, Hewlett Packard Enterprise, Microsoft, Oracle, etc.; and research organisations and universities such as Center for Internet Security, Internet Society, Austrian Institute of Technology, Pence Law Library (Washington College of Law, American University), Carnegie Mellon University, etc.[38] Around 155 of these participants are from India.[39]

11.2.2.1.3 The Electronics and IT Department of the BIS

In India, the BIS is the national standards setting body on IT services. One of the Technical Departments of the BIS is the Electronics and IT Department (LITD) which focuses on standardisation in the field of electronics and telecommunications including information technology. Aside from working on standard-setting in this field, it also participates in international standardisation activity. As a full member of the IEC, it can send its experts to participate actively in any technical committee/sub-committee it wishes to.

11.2.2.1.4 National Association of Software and Service Companies

The National Association of Software and Service Companies (NASSCOM) is a not-for-profit industry association established in 1988, of Indian IT and Business Process Outsourcing (BPO) companies. NASSCOM, in partnership with the National Skill Development Corporation (NSDC), has set up the IT-ITeS Sector Skills Council (IT-ITeS SSC), which has been designated the national standard-setting body for IT skills.

Sector Skill Councils (SSCs) are autonomous, industry-led bodies set up by the NSDC, to create occupational standards, develop competency frameworks, conduct training programmes for trainers, conduct skill gap studies, and assess and certify trainees on the curriculum aligned to National Occupational Standards developed by them.[40] While IT services refer to 'the application of business and technical expertise to enable organizations in the creation, management and optimization of or access to information and business processes',[41] IT skills refers to the technical skills of *individuals* in certain areas of IT. Certification of persons with IT skills would mean

37. *Supra Note 34.*
38. *Members*, OASIS Open, https://www.oasis-open.org/member-roster/.
39. *OASIS Member Locations*, OASIS Open, https://www.google.com/maps/d/u/0/view?mid=1YTu-wmkPXCYO_4XUxOm1-A1tj1c&ll=-3.81666561775622e-14%2C34.26959899999997&z=1.
40. *Sector Skills Councils*, Ministry of Skill Development and Entrepreneurship (MSDE), https://msde.gov.in/en/organizations/ssc.
41. *IT Services*, Gartner Glossary, https://www.gartner.com/en/information-technology/glossary/it-services.

that an individual meets a certain standard of expertise in select areas, such as cybersecurity, or big data and analytics, for example.[42]

The IT-ITeS SSC operates in close cooperation with NASSCOM, as well as under the aegis of NSDC,[43] and aims to set up a robust certification and accreditation process for industry-facing skill development institutes to ensure consistency and acceptability of standards.[44] In partnership with the Indian industry and education sector, the IT-ITeS SSC also aims to improve standards, education and employment within the sector and assist in facilitating the design of a National Qualification Framework (NQF) for India.[45]

11.2.2.2 Accounting and Finance Services

Accounting and Finance Services are a subset of Professional Services, and include accounting, auditing, and bookkeeping services. They cover a wide range of activities such as evaluation of reliability and credibility of financial information, bookkeeping, financial audits and consultancy services on accounting and finance.

11.2.2.2.1 Accounting Standards

Internationally, accounting standards are developed by the International Financial Reporting Standards (IFRS) Foundation, which is a not-for-profit, public interest organisation incorporated in the United States, and established to develop a single set of high-quality, understandable, enforceable and globally accepted accounting standards, and to promote and facilitate their adoption. The origin of the IFRS Foundation began in 1973, with the professional accounting bodies of Australia, Canada, France, Germany, Japan, Mexico, Netherlands, the United Kingdom/Ireland and the United States forming the International Accounting Standards Committee and agreeing to adopt International Accounting Standards for cross-border listings. In 2000, the IFRS Foundation was established, and the International Accounting Standards Committee restructured itself into a full-time International Accounting Standards Board (IASB) under the IFRS Foundation, overseen by independent trustees.[46] As of 2007, more than a hundred countries either required or permitted the use of IFRS', and in 2009, G20 leaders expressed support for the work of the IASB and called for a rapid move toward creating global accounting standards. In 2015, India introduced the Indian Accounting Standards which were based on IFRS'.[47]

IFRS are set by the IFRS Foundation's standard-setting body, the IASB. The IASB is an independent group of experts who are responsible for the development and

42. *Industry-Relevant Courses For You*, Future Skills Prime, https://www.sscnasscom.com/.
43. *Overview*, IT – ITES NASSCOM, https://www.sscnasscom.com/people.
44. *Concept Note Occupational Standards*, NASSCOM, 6, https://nasscom.in/sites/default/files/uploads/Initiatives/Education/Docs/Occupational_Standards_Concept_Note_08June2012.pdf.
45. *Ibid.*, 7.
46. *Who we are: History*, IFRS, https://www.ifrs.org/about-us/who-we-are/#history.
47. *Ibid.*

publication of IFRS Standards, and for approving Interpretations of IFRS Standards as developed by the IFRS Interpretations Committee.[48]

Broadly, the steps in the IASB's standard-setting process are:[49]

(a) *Agenda consultation*: the IASB conducts a comprehensive review and consultation every five years, to define international standard-setting priorities and develop its project work plan.
(b) *Research programme*: It then undertakes research to explore issues, identify possible solutions and decide whether standard-setting is actually required. This usually occurs through the publication of a discussion paper seeking public comment.
(c) *Standard-setting programme*: The IASB reviews the research, including public comments to the discussion paper, and proposes amendments or standards to resolve issues identified through research and consultation. These proposals are published in an 'exposure draft' for public consultation. The IASB and the IFRS Foundation also conducts a process of stakeholder consultation with a range of stakeholders from all over the world.
(d) *Maintenance programme*: Once a standard is issued, the IASB supports its consistent application and maintenance, by consulting on the implementation of a new or amended standard to identify any implementation problems that may need to be addressed. If issues arise with respect to an issued standard, the IFRS Interpretations Committee (IFRIC) may decide to create an IFRIC Interpretation of the Standard or recommend a narrow-scope amendment. After a new standard has been in use for a few years, the IASB carries out research through a post-implementation review to assess whether the standard is achieving its objective and, if not, whether any amendments should be considered.

In India, the Institute of Chartered Accountants of India (ICAI) is recognised as the professional regulator and the standard-setting body in the accounting sector.[50] The ICAI is a statutory body established by the Chartered Accountants Act, 1949 to regulate the profession of Chartered Accountancy in the country. It functions under the administrative control of the Ministry of Corporate Affairs, Government of India.

The ICAI, in consultation with and after examination of the recommendations made by the National Financial Reporting Authority (NFRA) recommends standards of accounting (for corporate entities), called the Indian Accounting Standards (Ind AS), or addenda thereto, to the Central Government, which then notifies these standards by

48. *International Accounting Standards Board*, IFRS, https://www.ifrs.org/groups/international-accounting-standards-board/.
49. *How we set IFRS Standards*, IFRS, https://www.ifrs.org/about-us/how-we-set-standards/#maintenance.
50. Companies Act, 2013, section 133: 'The Central Government prescribes the standards of accounting or any addendum thereto, as recommended by the ICAI, in consultation with and after examination of the recommendations made by the National Financial Reporting Authority (NFRA).'

publication in The Gazette of India. These notified standards are authoritative under Indian law.[51] For non-corporate entities, accounting standards are issued by the ICAI.

The Accounting Standards Board (ASB) of the ICAI, which formulates accounting standards, gives due consideration to the IFRS issued by the IASB, and tries to integrate these, as far as possible, given the conditions and practices prevailing in India.[52] Ind AS are largely based on, and substantially converged with IFRS. The ASB's standard-setting process is depicted in Figure 11.3.

Figure 11.3 The ASB's Standard-Setting Process

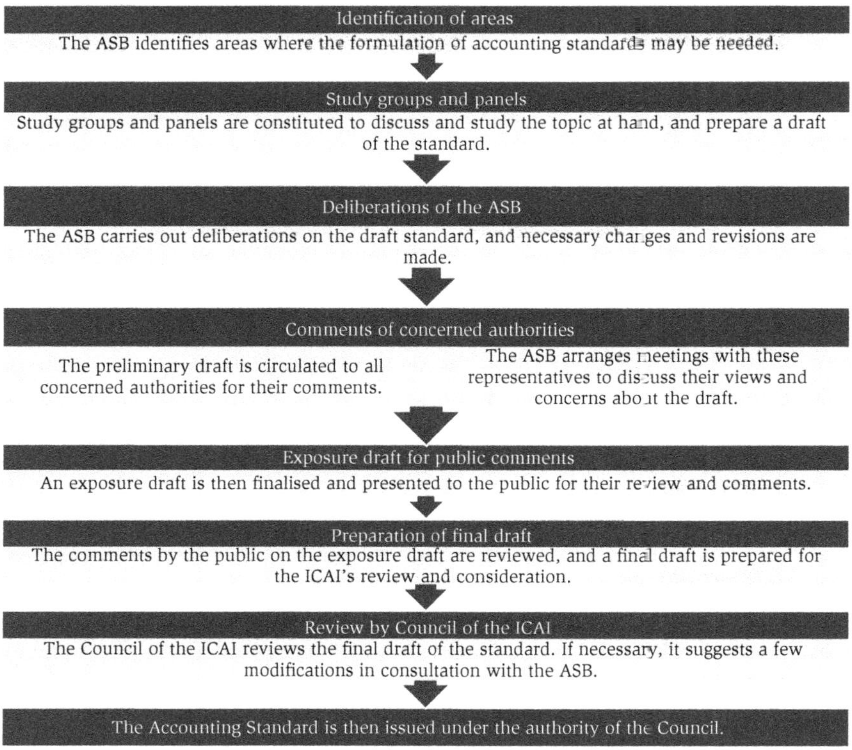

Source: ICAI, Statements of Accounting Standards (revised in 2004), Preface, Section 5, at https://resource.cdn.icai.org/7600acc_bodies_preface_AS_revised04.pdf.

51. Companies (Indian Accounting Standards) Rules, 2015, Rule 4.
52. *Statements of Accounting Standards*, The Institute of Chartered Accountants of India (ICAI), (revised in 2004), Preface, ¶ 2.3.

11.2.2.2.2 Auditing Standards

The International Auditing and Assurance Standards Board (IAASB) is an independent standard-setting body which sets international standards for auditing, assurance, review, quality control and related services. As part of its standard-setting process, the IAASB obtains input from a wide range of stakeholders including the IAASB's Consultative Advisory Group, national auditing standard-setters, member bodies of the International Federation of Accountants (IFAC) and their members, regulatory and oversight bodies, firms, governmental agencies, investors, preparers, and the general public. Exposure Drafts of proposed pronouncements are posted on the website and comments are invited; and final pronouncements are accompanied by a Basis for Conclusions with respect to the comments received by IAASB.

In India, under the Companies Act, 2013, all companies are required to be audited in accordance with Indian Standards on Auditing (SAs) issued by the Auditing and Assurance Standards Board (AASB) of the ICAI. The objectives of the AASB are depicted in Figure 11.4.

Figure 11.4 Objectives of the AASB

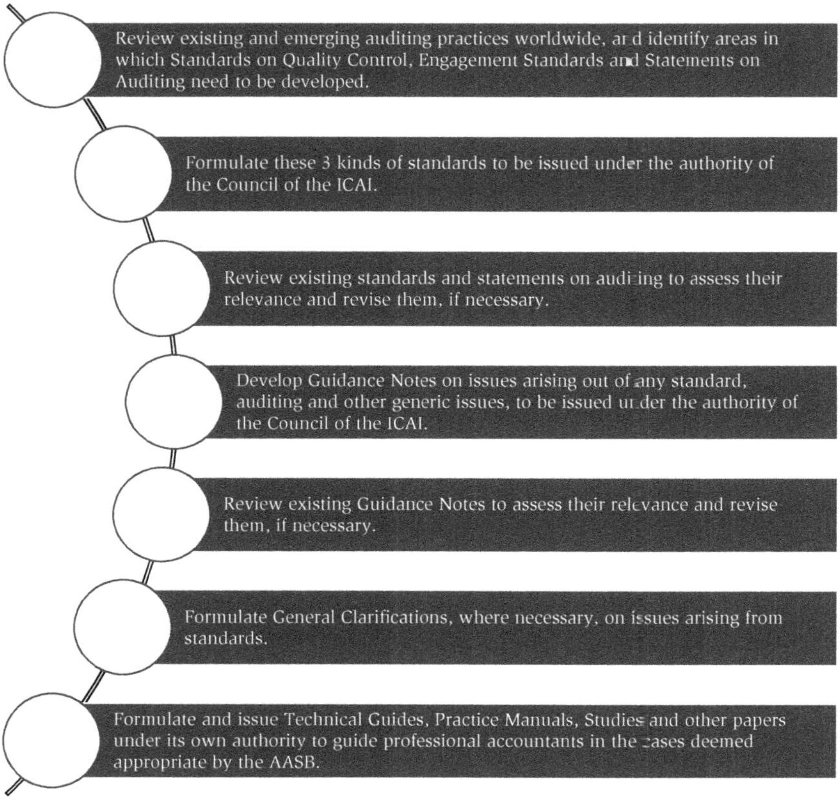

Source: ICAI, Auditing & Assurance Standards Board, at https://www.icai.org/post/objectives-aasb.

The AASB's process for considering new and revised standards developed by the IAASB to be adopted in India includes:

(a) the constitution of a study group to prepare the basic draft of the proposed new/revised standard that corresponds to IAASB's standard;
(b) consideration of the prepared draft by the AASB;
(c) the issuance of an exposure draft to the public including members and regulators;
(d) the consideration of comments and feedback received from the exposure draft and finalisation of the draft;
(e) approval by the ICAI Council; and
(f) the publication of final standards on the main website.

The Central Government must then prescribe the SA or addenda thereto, as recommended by the ICAI, in consultation with, and after examination of the recommendations made by the NFRA.[53] Approved SA are then notified in the Gazette of India, thus becoming authoritative.

11.2.2.2.3 Cost Auditing Standards

The Companies Act, 2013 also provides that the Central Government may require that certain companies conduct cost audits in addition to audits of financial statements.[54] Cost audits may only be performed by Cost and Management Accountants (CMAs) in accordance with Cost Auditing Standards (CAS) issued by the Institute of Cost Accountants of India (ICMAI) subject to approval by the Central Government.

The Cost Accounting Standards Board (CASB) was constituted by the ICMAI with the objective of formulating CAS. The CASB also issues Guidance Notes to explain the requirements of CAS' and provide practical examples and illustrations on technical issues relating to the CAS'. While formulating CAS', the CASB takes into consideration applicable laws, usage and business environment prevailing in India, and gives due consideration to the cost accounting standards, principles and practices being followed by the other countries.

The procedure that the CASB follows to formulate and issue Cost Accounting Standards is depicted in Figure 11.5.

53. Companies Act (2013), section 143(10).
54. Companies Act (2013), section 148.

Figure 11.5 The CASB's Standard-Setting Process for Cost Accounting Standards

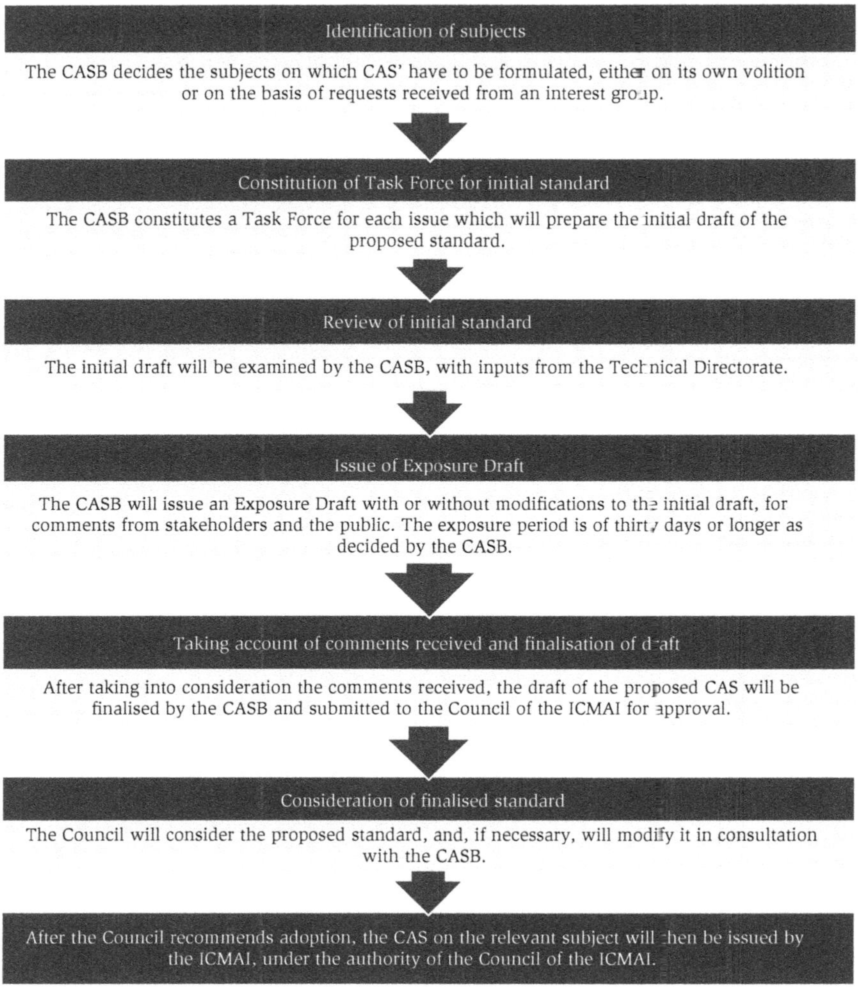

Source: ICMAI, Preface to the Cost Accounting Standards, at https://icmai.in/CASB/casb-preface1.php.

The CASB undertakes revision of Standards and Guidance Notes based on subsequent legal or professional requirements, or any other national or international developments in the field of Cost Accounting. The procedure followed for revision is the same as that followed for formulation of a new Standard or Guidance Note. Limited revision of Standards and Guidance Notes due to changes in reference to legislation is carried out by the Board and with the approval of the Council of the ICMAI. Limited revisions due to the adoption of standardised definitions in any standard is carried out in all the CAS by the CASB with the approval of the Council.

11.2.2.3 Banking, Financial Services and Insurance

BFSI is a services sector that subsumes a large range of services within it, some of which are listed in Table 11.3.

Table 11.3 Kinds of Banking, Financial and Insurance Services

Banking and Financial Services		*Insurance Services*
Deposit-taking	Securities trading	Life insurance
Lending of all types	Securities underwriting	Non-life insurance
Financial leasing	Settlement and clearing services for financial assets and negotiable instruments	Re-insurance
Payment and money transmission services	Financial data processing and related software by suppliers of other financial services	Insurance brokerage and agency
Money broking	Advisory, intermediation and other auxiliary financial services	Actuarial services
Asset management	Investment and portfolio research and advice	Risk assessment
Custodial, depository and trust services	Advice on acquisitions and on corporate restructuring and strategy	Claim settlement services
Provision and transfer of financial information		

Source: WTO, Financial services, at https://www.wto.org/english/tratop_e/serv_e/finance_e/finance_e.htm.

11.2.2.3.1 ISO Technical Committee 68

The ISO's Technical Committee 68 (TC 68) is responsible for creating global standards for the financial services industry. TC 68 is responsible for the development of standards that cover core banking, capital markets including asset management, payments, credit card processing and information security aspects specific to financial services. The committee is organised into three sub-committees: SC2 (Information Security), SC8 (Reference Data) and SC9 (Information Exchange).[55]

11.2.2.3.2 Financial Stability Board

The Financial Stability Board (FSB) is an international body that monitors and makes recommendations about the global financial system.[56] A representative each of the Ministry of Finance, the Reserve Bank of India (RBI), and the Securities and Exchange Board of India (SEBI) are the Indian members of the FSB.[57]

The FSB's objective is to promote international financial stability, which it does by coordinating national financial authorities and international standard-setting bodies as they work toward developing regulatory, supervisory and other financial sector policies. The FSB, working through its members, seeks to strengthen financial systems and increase the stability of international financial markets. The policies developed in the pursuit of this agenda are implemented by jurisdictions and national authorities.

The objectives of the FSB are highlighted in Figure 11.6.

Figure 11.6 Objectives of the FSB

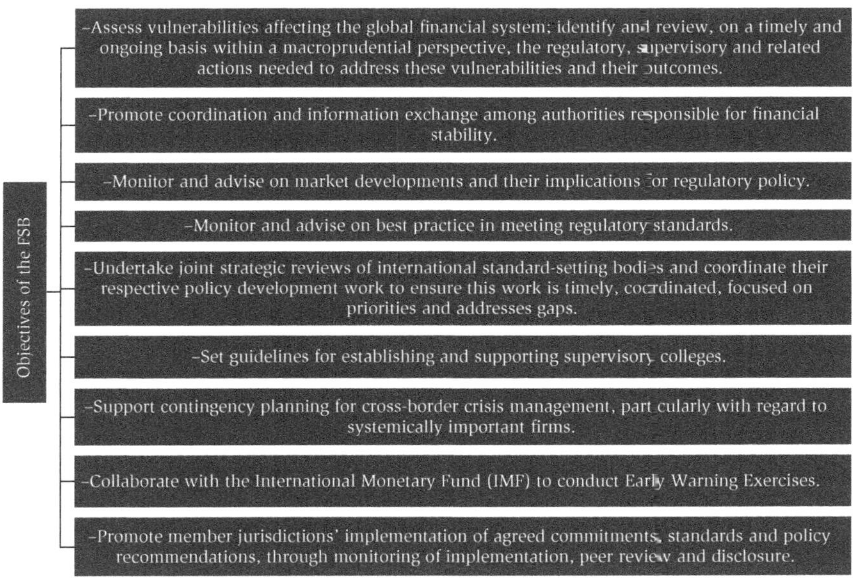

Source: FSB, Mandate of the FSB, at https://www.fsb.org/about/#mandate.

55. *ISO/TC 68 Financial services*, ISO, https://committee.iso.org/home/tc68.
56. *About the FSB*, The Financial Stability Board (FSB), https://www.fsb.org/about/.
57. *Members of the FSB*, FSB, https://www.fsb.org/about/organisation-and-governance/members-of-the-financial-stability-board/.

The FSB's work also includes the maintenance of a Compendium of Standards, which consists of various economic and financial standards, that are internationally accepted as important for sound, stable and well-functioning financial systems. The Compendium of Standards consists of standards which may be classified by their scope:[58]

- *Sectoral*: These cover the economic and institutional sectors such as governments and central banks; banking, securities and insurance industries; and the corporate sector.
- *Functional*: Within each sector, standards cover areas such as governance, accounting, disclosure and transparency, capital adequacy, regulation and supervision, information sharing, risk management, payment and settlement, business ethics, etc.

The Compendium of Standards includes standards set by, *inter alia*, the Basel Committee on Banking Supervision, Committee on the Global Financial System, Committee on Payments and Market Infrastructures, Financial Action Task Force on Money Laundering, the FSB, International Accounting Standards Board, International Auditing and Assurance Standards Board, International Monetary Fund (IMF), Organisation for Economic Co-operation and Development (OECD) and the World Bank. These bodies set standards to recommend best practices and develop regulations in the financial services sector.[59]

11.2.2.3.3 BFSI National Regulators

In India, standard-setting bodies in the BFSI sector are usually national regulators, who have the legal authority to set and implement regulatory rules and procedures in the financial sector. The Reserve Bank of India (RBI) is responsible for regulation and supervision of banks and other financial institutions and money, foreign exchange and Government securities markets. The SEBI (Securities and Exchange Board of India) is the regulator of the securities and commodity market in India. It is tasked with protecting the interests of investors in securities and to promote the development of the securities market. The Insurance Regulatory and Development Authority of India (IRDAI) is an autonomous, statutory body tasked with regulating and promoting the insurance and re-insurance industries in India.

11.2.2.3.4 BIS Technical Committee on Banking and Financial Services

The BIS has a Technical Committee on Banking and Financial Services (SSD-I 3) which mirrors the work of ISO TC/68 on Financial Services and ISO TC/222 on Personal

58. *The Compendium of Standards*, FSB, https://www.fsb.org/work-of-the-fsb/about-the-compendium-of-standards/.
59. *Standard-Setting Bodies in the Compendium*, FSB, https://www.fsb.org/work-of-the-fsb/about-the-compendium-of-standards/wssb/.

Financial Planning and has published thirty-nine standards. Table 11.4 contains the various regulators of non-bank financial entities (NBFEs) in India.

Table 11.4 Regulators of NBFEs in India

Category of Companies	*Regulator*
Non-banking finance companies	RBI
Housing finance companies	National Housing Bank
Merchant banking companies, venture capital fund companies, stock broking, collective investment schemes	SEBI
Nidhi companies, mutual benefit companies	Ministry of Corporate Affairs
Chit fund companies	State governments
Insurance companies	IRDAI

Source: Peer Review of India Review Report by FSB, at https://www.fsb.org/wp-content/uploads/India-peer-review-report.pdf.

11.2.2.3.5 Industry Organisations

Besides these statutory organisations, there are also industry organisations in India, which play a role in developing codes of conduct and setting and maintaining standards for different segments of the financial system.

The Indian Banks' Association (IBA) was formed on 26 September 1946, and as of April 2018 the total membership of the IBA is 249. Its members comprise public sector banks, private sector banks, foreign banks having offices in India, co-operative banks, regional rural banks, and all India financial institutions. Among its objectives are, to promote and develop sound and progressive banking principles, practices and conventions.[60]

The Fixed Income Money Market and Derivatives Association of India (FIMMDA), an association of scheduled commercial banks, public financial institutions, primary dealers and insurance companies is a voluntary market body for the bond, money and derivatives markets. One of its objectives is to recommend and implement healthy business practices, ethical code of conduct, standard principles and practices to be followed by members.[61]

The Association of Investment Bankers of India (AIBI), formerly called the Association of Merchant Bankers of India, was granted recognition by the SEBI as a

60. *Objective*, IBA, https://www.iba.org.in/objective.html.
61. *Mission*, FIMMDA, http://www.fimmda.org/modules/content/?p = 1097.

self-regulatory organisation,[62] to set up professional standards for providing efficient services and establish standard practices in investment banking. It has created a Due Diligence Manual for its members, to establish professional and uniform standards in due diligence and promote best practices among investment banks.

The Association of Mutual Funds of India (AMFI) is an association of all the Asset Management Companies of SEBI-registered mutual funds in India. It was incorporated on 22 August 1995, as a non-profit organisation. The SEBI undertakes regular consultations with members of the AMFI on various issues affecting mutual funds. Its objectives include defining and maintaining high professional and ethical standards in all areas of operation of the mutual fund industry, and recommending and promoting best business practices and code of conduct to be followed by members and others engaged in the activities of mutual fund and asset management including agencies connected or involved in the field of capital markets and financial services.[63]

The Foreign Exchange Dealers' Association of India (FEDAI) was set up in 1958 as an association of banks dealing in foreign exchange in India (typically called Authorised Dealers) as a self-regulatory body. Its major activities include framing rules that govern the conduct of inter-bank foreign exchange business among banks *vis-à-vis* the public and liaising with the RBI for reforms and development of the forex market. Some of its functions include developing guidelines and rules for the forex business, training of bank personnel in the areas of foreign exchange business, and accreditation of forex brokers.

11.2.2.4 Tourism and Hospitality Services

The ISO has a Technical Committee on Tourism and Related Services (ISO/TC 228) which focuses on standardisation of the terminology and specifications of the services offered by tourism service providers, including related activities, touristic destinations and the requirements of facilities and equipment used by them, to provide tourism buyers, providers and consumers with criteria for making informed decisions. There are eight working groups in the technical committee, covering the following areas:

- WG 1 on Diving Services;
- WG 2 on Health Tourism Services;
- WG 7 on Adventure Tourism;
- WG 8 on Yacht Harbours;
- WG 11 on Bareboat Charters;
- WG 13 on Sustainable Tourism;
- WG 14 on Accessible Tourism;
- WG 15 on Accommodation;
- WG 16 on Restaurants.

62. *Promotion and Regulation of Self-Regulatory Organisations*, SEBI, https://www.sebi.gov.in/sebi_data/commondocs/pt3d_h.html.
63. *Know About AMFI*, AMFI, https://www.amfiindia.com/know-about-amfi.

The published standards of the ISO/TC 228 include standards on tourist information and reception services, hotels and other types of tourism accommodation, industrial tourism, environmental specifications and sustainability management systems for accommodation establishments, adventure tourism, recreational diving services, beach operations, yacht harbours, bareboat charters, wellness spas, thalassotherapy, medical spas and medical tourism.

The World Tourism Organization (UNWTO) is the United Nations agency responsible for the promotion of responsible, sustainable and universally accessible tourism. Its first international convention, the UNWTO Framework Convention on Tourism Ethics, was adopted by the UNWTO General Assembly at its 23rd session, in September 2019.

The World Committee on Tourism Ethics (WCTE), an independent and impartial body under the aegis of the UNWTO, is responsible for the promotion of responsible, sustainable and universally accessible tourism. It promotes and disseminates the UNWTO Global Code of Ethics for Tourism (GCET)[64] – a set of principles designed to guide key-players in tourism development.[65]

The Global Sustainable Tourism Council (GSTC), an independent association, manages the GSTC Criteria: global standards for sustainable travel and tourism, and provides international accreditation for sustainable tourism Certification Bodies. It has certified certification bodies, tour operators, transport providers, consultancies, government agencies, hotels and non-profit organisations.[66]

The GSTC Criteria are meant to serve as a global baseline standards for sustainability in travel and tourism, and take into account guidelines and standards for sustainable tourism from each continent. According to the GSTC, wide consultations were held across the world, in both developed and developing countries, in several languages.[67] These criteria are designed to be adapted to local conditions and supplemented by additional criteria for specific locations and activities.[68] There are two sets of GSTC Criteria:

- GSTC Industry Criteria which relate to the sustainable management of private sector travel industry, focusing currently on hotels and tour operators; and
- GSTC Destination Criteria which relate to sustainable management of tourism destinations.

The GSTC Criteria is revised every few years, to comply with the ISEAL Alliance standard-setting code. The revision process includes two public consultations, allowing anyone interested to comment.

Another international organisation, World Travel and Tourism Council (WTTC) is an industry consortium that aims to maximise inclusive and sustainable growth

64. *World Committee on Tourism Ethics* (WCTE), UNWTO, https://www.unwto.org/world-committee-tourism-ethics.
65. *Global Code of Ethics for Tourism,* UNWTO, https://www.unwto.org/global-code-of-ethics-for-tourism.
66. *GSTC Members,* GSTC, https://www.gstcouncil.org/membership/member-search/.
67. *GSTC Criteria Overview,* GSTC, https://www.gstcouncil.org/gstc-criteria/.
68. *GSTC Criteria Overview,* GSTC, https://www.gstcouncil.org/gstc-criteria/.

potential of the travel and tourism sector by partnering with governments, destinations, communities, and other stakeholders. The WTTC, along with its members, governments, health experts and other industry associations, is working on developing recovery protocols for the COVID-19 pandemic-affected world, through an initiative called 'Safe Travels Global Protocols Stamp'.[69] These protocols align the private sector with common standards to ensure the safety of its workforce and travellers as the sector shifts to the 'new normal'. They are living documents which will be updated as new information becomes available about the pandemic.

In India, the BIS' Technical Committee SSD-I 2 on Tourism and Related Services, mirrors the work of the ISO/TC 228. It has published 19 standards that are based on ISO standards.

11.2.2.5 Medical Value Services

Standardisation in the field of health covers many sectors, including dentistry, optics, surgery, medical devices, assistive products, equipment for transfusions, infusions and injections, implants for surgery, sterilisation of healthcare products, health informatics, healthcare organisation management and traditional medicine.

The ISO has a number of technical committees that focus on aspects of health and related services. In this regard, the following committees deal with Medical Value Services:

(a) Standards for quality management and risk management:
  (i) ISO/TC 210, Quality management and corresponding general aspects for medical devices,
  (ii) ISO/TC 212, Clinical laboratory testing and in vitro diagnostic test systems;

(b) Services relating to medical equipment:
  (i) ISO/TC 194, Biological and clinical evaluation of medical devices,
  (ii) ISO/TC 198, Sterilisation of healthcare products,
  (iii) ISO/TC 76, Transfusion, infusion and injection, and blood processing equipment for medical and pharmaceutical use,
  (iv) ISO/TC 168, Prosthetics and orthotics.

(c) Oral health:
  (i) ISO/TC 106, Dentistry;

(d) Healthcare organisation management:
  (i) ISO/TC 304, Healthcare organisation management;

(e) Ehealth technologies:
  (i) ISO/TC 215, Health informatics;

(f) Other safety-related standards:
  (i) ISO/TC 283, Occupational health and safety management

69. *'Safe Travels': Global Protocols & Stamp for the New Normal*, WTTC, https://wttc.org/COVID-19/Safe-Travels-Global-Protocols-Stamp.

(g) Alternative systems of medicine:
 (i) ISO/TC 249, Traditional Chinese medicine.

In India, the practice of the medical, dental, and nursing profession is regulated by law. The National Medical Commission (NMC) was constituted by the National Medical Commission Act, 2019 which came into force on 25 September 2020, superseding the Medical Council of India constituted under the Indian Medical Council Act, 1956. The NMC regulates medical education and practice and lays down policies for maintaining high quality and standards in medical education.[70] The NMC Act, 2019 creates a Medical Advisory Council, whose duty is to advise the NMC on measures to determine and maintain minimum standards in all matters of medical education, training and research.[71]

The Dental Council of India, a statutory body incorporated under the Dentists Act, 1948 regulates dental education and the profession of dentistry. Under the Act, Council is authorised to make regulations, on approval of the Central Government on various matters, including prescribing the standard curricula for the training of dentists and dental hygienists, laying down requirements for admission to various courses and prescribing standards of examinations and other requirements for recognition of qualifications.[72]

The nursing profession is regulated by the Indian Nursing Council Act, 1947 and regulations thereunder. The Act authorises the Indian Nursing Council to prescribe the standard curricula for the training of nurses, midwives and health visitors, teachers of nurses, midwives and health visitors, training in nursing administration and establish standards of examination and other requirements for recognition of qualifications.[73]

The BIS has a Technical Committee on Medical Value Travel Services and Wellness Services (SSD-I 16), which has not published any standards yet.

The National Accreditation Board for Hospitals and Healthcare Providers (NABH), a constituent board of Quality Council of India (QCI), sets standards and provides accreditation for hospitals, small healthcare organisations, blood banks, medical imaging services, dental healthcare, eye-care organisations, entry level hospitals, medical laboratories, emergency departments in hospitals, allopathic clinics, nursing excellence, Ayurveda hospitals, yoga and naturopathy, *unani*, *siddha* and homeopathy hospitals, *panchkarma* clinics and entry level AYUSH centres and hospitals.

70. The National Medical Commission Act, 2019, section 10.
71. The National Medical Commission Act, 2019, section 12.
72. The Dentists Act, 1948, section 20.
73. The Indian Nursing Council Act, 1947, section 16.

11.2.2.5.1 Accreditation Standards: Yoga and Naturopathy

NABH published the second edition of the Accreditation Standards for Yoga and Naturopathy Centres in March 2017.[74] The accreditation standards have been endorsed by the Ministry of AYUSH, Government of India. The 1st Edition of these standards was published in 2009 and was in practice for about six years (2009-15). The 2nd Edition lays down a total of eighty-seven standards (compared to 51 in the 1st Edition). These standards are spread over a total of ten chapters, compliance with all of which is necessary to establish compliance with the accreditation standard.

The Accreditation Standards for Yoga and Naturopathy are aimed at facilitating the centres providing these services to deliver high-quality and safe healthcare services. The standards apply to both government and private centres. These standards include issues regarding access assessment and continuity of care, for instance, whether or not the organisation defines and displays the services it provides - is the first and most fundamental standard. Similarly, there are standards on care of patients (for instance, the existence of documented policies and procedures that guide the care of vulnerable patients - C.O.P. 3); method of treatment (for instance, the existence of documented policies and procedures treatment management - M.O.T. 4), patients' rights and education (for instance, whether the organisation protects patient and family rights and informs them about their responsibilities during care or not - PRE 1), etc.

Similar draft standards were formulated by NABH for Ayurveda hospitals which were endorsed by Ministry of AYUSH.[75] The final standards do not seem to have been published as of date. The NABH standards are applied voluntarily by AYUSH hospitals, as of the date of writing. Among other standards published in the Indian healthcare sector include those on allopathic clinics,[76] Entry Level AYUSH Centres,[77] primary health centres,[78] etc.

11.2.3 Evolving Sectors

These are sectors where standardisation has only started taking root, or where already prevalent, there is a need for upgradation, in line with technological developments and sectoral diversification. These include telehealth services, environmental services, management and consulting services, communication services and education services.

74. *Accreditation Standards for Yoga and Naturopathy Centres 2nd Edition*, National Accreditation Board for Hospitals and Healthcare Providers (NABH) (March 2017), https://nabh.co/Images/PDF/Yoga_Revised_2Edition.pdf.
75. *Accreditation standards for Ayurveda Hospitals*, NABH (July 2015), https://www.nabh.co/Images/PDF/Draft_Ayurveda_Hospital_Issue2.pdf.
76. *See General Information Brochure for NABH Accreditation Programme for CLINICs-Allopathy-Modern Practice of Medicine*, NABH, https://www.nabh.co/Images/PDF/all-gib.pdf.
77. *See Entry Level Standards for AYUSH Centre*, NABH, https://nabh.co/Images/PDF/AYUSH_Centre_Entry_Level_for_print.pdf.
78. *See Accreditation Standards for Primary health centres*, NABH, https://nabh.co/documents_PHC.aspx; *See also Standard Accreditation Agreement between NABH-QCI and Healthcare Organization/ Hospital*, NABH, https://nabh.co/Images/PDF/Agreement_hos.pdf.

11.2.3.1 Telehealth Services

The World Health Organization (WHO) defines telehealth as the 'delivery of health care services, where patients and providers are separated by distance'.[79] It may be noted that the term 'telemedicine' is more specific, and connotes clinical services delivered by registered medical practitioners, whereas telehealth is a broader, encompassing term that subsumes telemedicine.[80] The various specific branches of telehealth and telemedicine include teleradiology, telepathology, remote patient monitoring, telepsychiatry, teledermatology, etc. Supply of telehealth and telemedicine services happens via use of ICT – for diagnosis, treatment of diseases, as well as research and education, etc. These services have become increasingly popular due to increased use of digital technology, enhanced inter-connectivity, and their potential to make medicine and healthcare available to the remotest regions.[81]

The WHO's report on the third global survey on eHealth notes that more than half of WHO Member countries had an ehealth strategy, as of 2016.[82] Countries are also increasingly formulating policies to manage health-related data. The main focus of eHealth Strategies is on achieving interoperability and therefore standardisation process is imminent in ensuring a seamless flow of telehealth services. To ensure the interoperability of such services, key international standards are already being formulated.

In India, there did not exist any specific legal framework governing telehealth and telemedicine services until recently. Presently, while there is no specific statute governing the supply of telemedicine services or one that lays down any related standards, in March 2020, the Ministry of Health and Family Welfare, Government of India, issued the Telemedicine Practice Guidelines, 2020 (Guidelines) under the Indian Medical Council Act, 1956. These Guidelines constitute Appendix 5 of the Indian Medical Council (Professional Conduct, Etiquette and Ethics) Regulations, 2002 and are meant to be used in addition to other applicable standards, protocols or procedures.

The Guidelines lay down the norms for registered medical practitioners to consult patients via telemedicine. However, they exclude the standard-setting process and related aspects, namely, data management systems, standards and interoperability, specifications for hardware and software, infrastructure building and maintenance, etc. Nevertheless, the Guidelines may contribute to development of certain basic standards in this field by providing for ethical and good conduct principles or

79. *See Telehealth, Analysis of third global survey on eHealth based on the reported data by countries*, WHO (2016).
80. *See Telemedicine Practice Guidelines*, Board of Governors in Supersession of the Medical Council of India (25 March 2020), https://www.mohfw.gov.in/pdf/Telemedicine.pdf.
81. *See Global diffusion of eHealth: making universal health coverage achievable, Report of the third global survey on eHealth, Global Observatory for eHealth*, WHO, https://apps.who.int/iris/bitstream/handle/10665/252529/9789241511780-eng.pdf.
82. *Ibid.*

disciplines. For instance, one specific guideline prescribes that telemedicine consultation should not be anonymous and the patient as well as the registered medical practitioner[83] should be aware of each other's identity.[84]

Furthermore, the Guidelines do not emphasise any specific mode for conducting consultations, which may be conducted via any of the three mediums - audio, video or text.[85] The background note to the Guidelines also highlights the risk of abuse or misuse of technology used for telemedicine services, which poses certain challenges or concerns in using such services. Appropriate training and standards enforcement is considered critical to mitigate such risks.[86]

Aside from the above, the All India Institute of Medical Sciences (AIIMS) also has a Telemedicine Facility. The facility currently has four broad programmes - PAN-African e-network with fifty-four countries of the African Union, SAARC Telemedicine Project with 6 SAARC countries, in-house telemedicine link with Rural Hospital at Ballabhgarh, Haryana, and link with fifty-four centres in India and abroad.[87] AIIMS also entertains requests from any governmental hospitals for super specialty consultation, based on the availability of the concerned faculty members. Overall, the standard-setting process in India on telehealth services is still at a very nascent stage.

11.2.3.2 Environmental Services

The standards or regulations in the field of environment are aimed at ensuring and preserving the overall quality of the environment, and are generally referred to as 'environmental quality standards'.[88] They may apply to both industry and services sectors, depending upon the overall implications of such activities on the environment and the desired objective(s) of the standard being set.

While it is the BIS that is the overall standard-setting statutory body in India, for environmental services, it is the Central Pollution Control Board (CPCB) that sets the standards - including for quality of air, water quality criteria, emission norms and sound levels for diesel engines and generator sets. CPCB also prepares and publishes manuals, codes and guidelines relating to various environmental norms and standards, such as treatment of sewage and trade effluents, stack gas cleaning services, etc.

---

83. *Supra Note* 82. Under the Guidelines, a registered medical practitioner is a person who is enrolled in the State medical Register, or the Indian Medical Register under the Indian Medical Council Act, 1956.
84. *Ibid*, ¶ 3.2.1.
85. *Ibid*, ¶ 3.3.
86. *Telemedicine Guidelines, Background*, Ministry of Health and Family Welfare, Government of India, https://www.mohfw.gov.in/pdf/Telemedicine.pdf.
87. *Telemedicine Facility*, All India Institute of Medical Sciences, https://www.aiims.edu/aiimsold_ch01-06-2016/aiims/telemedicine/telepage.htm.
88. *See Glossary of Environment Statistics*, Studies in Methods, Series F, No. 67, United Nations (1997); *see also*, *Environmental Quality Standard definition*, OECD, Glossary of Statistical Terms, https://stats.oecd.org/glossary/detail.asp?ID=838#: ~ :text=An%20environmental%20quality%20standard%20is,allowable%20degradation%20of%20environmental%20media. 'Environmental quality standard' has been defined as a 'limit for environmental disturbances, in particular, from ambient concentration of pollutants and wastes, that determines the maximum allowable degradation of environmental media'.

As regards the statutory standards for environment protection, the Ministry of Environment, Forests and Climate Change formulates rules under the applicable Indian law - the Environment Protection Act, 1986.[89] The Schedules of these rules provide for the industry or services standards with respect to effluent discharge, emissions, etc.

11.2.3.3 Management and Consulting Services

Management and Consulting Services have gained increasing prominence with advancements in industrial and technological development, and the resulting complexities in industry processes and businesses in modern times. At the international level, these are one of the most traded services, with comparative advantage of both developed and developing economies. Accordingly, the need for standards for these services is also widely recognised internationally.

The ISO 20700 standard, developed in 2017, provides the guidelines for effective delivery of management consultancy services. These guidelines focus on deliverables and outcomes of management consulting, and recognise that 'innovation, differentiation and ethical behaviour' are critical parts of these services.[90] They apply to all management consultancy service providers - sole proprietorships, partnership firms, internal departments of corporations, etc. The ISO 20700 standard was developed by active engagement of all Members of the International Council of the Management Consulting Institutes.[91]

In India, the apex body of professionals in the field of management consulting is the Institute of Management Consultants of India (IMCI). It is a registered institute of management consultancy firms and practitioners. The IMCI also is a member of the International Council of Management Consulting Institutes (also called Certified Management Consultant or CMC-Global) since 1989. The International Council of Management Consulting Institutes has authorised the IMCI to carry on the certification process for management consultancy in India - in accordance with international standards - by issuing the designation of Certified Management Consultant (CMC) to members who qualify the assessment process, and fulfil the required/prescribed professional standards of competence and ethics.

The CMC Certificate is recognised as a mark of excellence in management consultancy, and is recognised in about fifty other countries, that are Members of the International Council of Management Consulting Institutes. The qualified consultants use the term CMC™. The use of CMC with a consultant's name indicates that the strict certification requirements as per the Institute of Management Consultant in the country of the Consultant, as well as international standards of competence, ethics and

89. *See* Environment Protection Act, 1986, section 25. There are effluent standards for over 37 industries and emission standards for over 31 industries.
90. *Guidelines for management consultancy services*, ISO 20700:2017, ISO, https://www.iso.org/obp/ui/#iso:std:iso:20700:ed-1:v1:en.
91. *ISO Standards for Consulting*, The International Council of Management Consulting Institutes, https://www.cmc-global.org/content/iso-standards-consulting.

independence, have been fulfilled.[92] These standards incorporate the requirements pertaining to experience (three years in management consulting), education, time spent, independence and qualification process.[93]

In India, all individual Members are required to clear the certification process, which comprises written examination, presentation, viva-voce and two client referrals.[94] The entire certification process is in line with Amsterdam Standard, which has been adopted by the International Council of Management Consulting Institutes.[95]

11.2.3.4 Communication Services

The Telecommunications Standards Development Society, India (TSDSI) is a not-for-profit organisation officially recognised by the Indian telecom authority, the Department of Telecommunications, as the national standard development organisation in the telecommunications sector.[96] The TSDSI is vested with the mandate of engaging at the international level for development of telecom standards, taking into consideration the concerns and interests of India. With this objective, the TSDSI engages with various industry stakeholders, academia and research organisations, government and other regulatory bodies, etc.

TSDSI is a member of the Global Standards Collaboration (GSC) - a voluntary forum of world's twelve leading information and communication technologies standards bodies. TSDSI has also signed memoranda of understanding with many international standard-setting organisations, such as the Association of Radio Industries and Business (ARIB), Japan, Alliance for Telecommunications Industry Solutions (ATIS), U.S., European Telecommunications Standards Institute (ETSI), etc. Certain recently published standards developed by the TSDSI are provided in Table 11.5.

Table 11.5 Recently Published Standards by TSDSI

Standard	*Year of Publication*	*Description*
TSDSI STD 5000 V1.0.0 CPRI Fronthaul Transport	2018	Creates functional block for fronthaul processing for transport of Common Public Radio Interface

92. *What is a CMC?*, IMCI Secretariat, http://www.imcindia.co.in/sites/all/libraries/fckeditor/editor/filemanager/connectors/CMC-Flyer.pdf.
93. *Ibid.*
94. *Eligibility Criteria for Membership*, IMCI, http://www.imcindia.co.in/eligibility-criteria-membership.
95. The Third Annual International CMC Conference (2015), Amsterdam, the Netherlands.
96. *Telecommunications Standards Development Society*, Department of Telecommunications, https://dot.gov.in/telecommunications-standards-development-society-india-tsdsi.

Standard	*Year of Publication*	*Description*
		(CPRI) and/or GE from the Base Band Unit (BBU) or Radio Equipment Control (REC) to the Remote Radio Head (RRH) or Radio Equipment (RE) of a base station. The connection between BBU and RRH is over optical fibre cable (OFC) media.
TSDSI STD T3.9036.104 -15.7.0 V1.0.1 Evolved Universal Terrestrial Radio Access (E-UTRA);Base Station (BS) radio transmission and reception	2020	Sets the minimum RF characteristics and minimum performance requirements of E-UTRA, E-UTRA with NB-IoT or NB-IoT Base Station (BS)

Source: TSDSI, Published Standards, at https://tsdsi.in/published-standards/

TSDSI transposed and established standards have also been recognised by the Telecommunications Engineering Centre, Department of Telecommunications, as national standards. The TSDSI has also developed India Radio Interface Technology (RIT) and qualified Step 7 of an 8-Step ITU00R process, pursuant to which it will be included in the IMT-2020[97] specification of ITU-R, generally referred to as 5G. It is first time that Indian standard of TSDSI RIT as a 5th Generation technology standard has been accepted internationally. The description of this TSDSI developed technology has already been included in the draft IMT-2020 specification document currently under development.

The TSDSI's joint report with the Cloud Computing Innovation Council of India on 'Cloud interoperability and portability (CIP)-Standards' provides for cloud interoperability-Standards Reference Architecture and specifications pertaining to hybrid cloud, smart city, telecom and cloud analytics.[98]

97. The IMT-2020 (5G) Promotion Group was established in February 2013, with the support of three ministries of China (the Ministry of Industry and Information Technology, the National Development and Reform Commission, and the Ministry of Science and Technology), based on the original IMT-Advanced Promotion Group. It is the major platform to promote the research and development of 5G in China. *See* IMT-2020 (5G) Promotion Group and 5G PPP Announce Memorandum of Understanding for 5G (2015), https://5g-ppp.eu/imt-2020-5g-promotion-group-and-5g-ppp-announce-memorandum-of-understanding-for-5g/.
98. *Cloud Interoperability & Portability (CIP) Standard Reference Report*, TSDSI TR 6005 V1.0.0, TSDSI (August 2020), https://members.tsdsi.in/index.php/s/8Z5xMcdf9Z4Ezn7.

The Networks and Technologies Cell of the Department of Telecommunications published the *National Telecom M2M (Machine to Machine) Roadmap*. The Roadmap recognises the futuristic role of M2M in development of new technologies, and ensure affordable and efficient delivery of related services to the public. The Roadmap focuses on communication aspects of M2M technology, with particular emphasis on interoperable standards, policies and regulations, suitable in the Indian context, across different sectors of the economy, and covers both products and services. In addition to the above, the Telecom Engineering Centre of DoT has also published nine technical reports on M2M that provide for sector-specific cases for future action plans with potential models for service delivery.

11.2.3.5 Education Services

Education services can be broadly categorised into four types - primary education, secondary education, higher education and adult education, with other education services categorized separately.[99] The ISO has published many standards on education services. The most recent standard is the ISO 21001:2018 on *Educational organisations – Management systems for educational organisations – Requirements with guidance for use*. It provides requirements applicable to management systems of educational organisations that employ curriculums for developing competence through teaching, learning or research, irrespective of the type, size or mode of delivery. It is also applicable to business organisations with professional training departments. The other standards published by ISO include ISO 29993:2017 on *Learning services outside formal education – Service requirements*, ISO 29994 on *Learning services outside formal education – Additional requirements for distance learning (under development)*, ISO 29992:2018 on *Assessment of outcomes of learning services – Guidance*.

The education services in India constitute one of the largest and most diversified service sectors, given India's youth population. Despite this, standardisation in education services in India has started taking root only lately. There appears to be a perceived lack of standardisation in education services in India, at both school and college/university level in India presently. The BIS is the national standardisation body, whose Program of Work of Services Sector Department I, has a dedicated Sectional Committee (SSD-I 4) on *Higher Education, Skill Development and Related Services*, and another dedicated committee (SSD-I 15) on *School Education and related services*.[100]

SSD-I 4 on *higher education, skill development and related services* covers standardisation regarding integration of information, learning, vocational and professional education, and training for knowledge dissemination, and also envisages coordination with the ISO/TC 232 committee on Learning Services outside formal

99. *See Education Services*, Series M No. 77, ST/ESA/STAT/SER.M/77, United Nations Central Product Classification (1991), https://www.tralac.org/files/2013/12/UN-CPC-Provisional-central-product-classification.pdf.

100. *Committee Wise Position of Work of Service Sector Department I*, BIS, https://www.services.bis.gov.in:8071/php/BIS_2.0/bisconnect/pow/pow_details.

education. Importantly, this Committee is responsible for BIS' adoption of two standards, one Indian standard IS 16533: 2016 on *Education Management System – Quality Requirements for Educational Requirements*, and the second one IS/ISO 21001:2018 on *Educational Organisations – Management systems for educational organisations – Requirements with guidance for use*, which is an ISO standard. Other than this, the standard on *Language-learning services Requirements*, SSD-I 4 (17094) is a draft standard under consideration.[101]

SSD-I 15 focuses on standardisation on services offered by School Education Service providers including accommodation services, canteen services, literacy, coaching and tuition services provided by private persons, etc.[102] No standards have been published or are under consideration concerning these services.

In addition, for quality assurance in higher education, the National Assessment and Accreditation Council (NAAC) created in 1994, is the autonomous institution of the Indian University Grants Commission.[103] NAAC focuses on ensuring that quality assurance is an 'integral part of the functioning of Higher Education Institutions (HEIs)'. Seven key criteria constitute the basis of NAAC's assessment process. These include – curricular aspects; teaching-learning evaluation; research, innovations and extension; infrastructure and learning resources; student support and progression; governance, leadership and management; institutional values and best practices.[104] NAAC has published several books on quality assurance and management, accreditation and related issues as well as Toolkits for Teacher Education Institutions, including *Quality Assurance in Higher Education*,[105] *An Anthology of Best Practices in Teacher Education*,[106] etc.

Furthermore, the Indian Ministry of Human Resource Development launched the National Institutional Ranking Framework (NIRF) in 2015.[107] The NIRF is based on developing a metric system to assess the ranking of a university, based on several parameters. The parameters are broadly categorised into five broad heads – Teaching, Learning and Resources; Research and Professional Practice; Graduation Outcome; Outreach & Inclusivity; and Perception.[108]

---

101. *See Language-learning Services Requirements, SSD-I 4 (17094)*, BIS, https://www.services.bis.gov.in:8071/php/BIS_2.0/bisconnect/pow/pow_details.
102. *See School Education and related Services, SSD-I 15*, BIS, https://www.services.bis.gov.in:8071/php/BIS_2.0/bisconnect/pow/pow_details.
103. The National Policy on Education, 1986 and the Programme of Action, 1992 recommended establishment of an independent national accreditation body to address quality concerns of India's diversifying education sector, leading to the establishment of NAAC.
104. *See Eligibility Criteria*, NAAC, http://naac.gov.in/index.php/assessment-accreditation#accreditation.
105. *Quality Assurance in Higher Education – An Introduction*, NAAC, http://naac.gov.in/images/docs/Resources/Toolkit4Tr_Edctn_Institution/QAHE-Book.pdf.
106. *An Anthology of 'Best Practices' in Teacher Education*, NAAC, http://naac.gov.in/images/docs/Resources/Toolkit4Tr_Edctn_Institution/An-Anthology-of-Best-Practices-in-Teacher-Education.pdf.
107. *See National Institutional Ranking Framework, Overview*, Ministry of Human Resource Development, Government of India, https://www.nirfindia.org/About.
108. *Ibid.*

Under these five broad parameters, there are sub-heads which are subject to revision by the Core Committee. Each parameter head and sub-head has some weight assigned to it, based on which the overall scoring of institutions is done, with a maximum value of 100.[109] While most data is required to be submitted by participating institutions in the format published by NIRF on its portal for each year's ranking, for certain parameters such as research, NIRF may utilise data from international data bases or third-party sources.

On the whole, while standardisation has been prevalent to some extent in higher education services, and has focused on certain fundamental issues with respect to primary and secondary education, it has otherwise remained rather dormant in India. In view of this, the Indian Government has formulated the National Education Policy, 2020, which foresees creation of a world-class education system for India by 2040. The Policy recognises the need for bridging of gap between existing state of learning outcomes and the required outcomes[110] and revamp all aspects of the education structure.[111] The Policy provides specific instructions and directions for standard-setting and accreditation for school education.[112] Similarly, for higher education, a detailed framework has been laid out, with specific roles to be entrusted to professional standard-setting bodies.[113]

Given the modernisation in education sector, and in light of the framework envisaged by the National Educational Policy, 2020, the relevant standard-setting bodies should potentially consider setting updated standards on quality, including on distance learning, use of online platforms, etc.

11.2.3.6 Legal Services

While there is no specific international standard-setting authority for legal services, and no official universal standards been set for legal services, the ISO can be considered as the main standard-setting organisation. The ISO's overarching standards, such as those pertaining to quality management systems, i.e., ISO 9001:2000, apply with respect to legal services also. To ensure application of these standards to legal services, certain countries have formulated specific guidelines. For instance, Standards Australia has formulated a guide - *HB90.6—2000, Legal Profession, The Guide to ISO 9001:2000,* which provides guidance on applying the ISO 9001:2000 specifically for legal professionals.[114]

109. *Methodology for Ranking of Academic Institutions in India, India Rankings 2017,* Ministry of Human Resource Development (2017), https://www.nirfindia.org/Docs/Ranking_Methodology_And_Metrics_2017.pdf.
110. *National Education Policy, 2020,* Introduction, https://www.education.gov.in/sites/upload_files/mhrd/files/NEP_Final_English_0.pdf, 3.
111. *Ibid.*
112. *National Education Policy, 2020,* Standard-setting and Accreditation for School Education, https://www.education.gov.in/sites/upload_files/mhrd/files/NEP_Final_English_0.pdf, 30.
113. *National Education Policy, 2020,* Transforming the Regulatory System of Higher Education https://www.education.gov.in/sites/upload_files/mhrd/files/NEP_Final_English_0.pdf, 47.
114. *The Legal Profession, Guide to ISO 9001:2000,* HB90.6—2000, Standards Australia, https://www.saiglobal.com/PDFTemp/Previews/OSH/as/misc/handbook/HB906.pdf. The standard

In India, the Bar Council of India (BCI) is the apex body to regulate the profession of law. It is a statutory body created under the Advocates Act, 1961.[115] Among its other regulatory functions, the BCI is authorised to prescribe standards of professional conduct and etiquette for advocates, promote legal education and lay down standards of such education, and recognise foreign qualifications (on a reciprocal basis) in law obtained outside India for the purpose of admission as an advocate in India.[116] The BCI Rules, in Part VI, Chapter II provide for 'standards of professional conduct and etiquette'. However, these are not in the nature of standards or requirements that prescribe specifications to be fulfilled for ensuring quality of service supply. The rules prescribe a code of ethics and general disciplinary conduct. With respect to client confidentiality, the Indian Evidence Act, 1872 prohibits advocates from disclosing any communication or information given by the client in the course of their employment.[117]

India's Ministry of Law and Justice, in 2010, had proposed a new statute titled *Legal Practitioners (Regulations and Maintenance of Standards in Professions, Protecting the Interest of Clients and Promoting the Rule of Law) Act, 2010*. The Bill envisaged an approach similar to the UK's system of Legal Services Board, of establishing an ombudsman and a complaints mechanism. However, the draft law did not specifically provide for any rules on the ethics or standards regarding practice of law in India by foreign lawyers. The only reference was for the Board to engage in standards development on legal education and training of legal professionals.

On the whole, while foreign lawyers are permitted to supply services on a fly-in and fly-out basis only, and primarily with respect to diverse matters of international law, or the foreign law of their country, lawyers registered in India, as a matter of fact, would be subject to the same ethical and professional standards laid down under the Advocates Act, 1961 and the rules made thereunder. In case of professional misconduct in connection with law practice in India, they would be subject to disciplinary actions, in accordance with section 36 of the Advocates Act, 1961. The opening of India legal services sector to foreign lawyers is a highly sensitive issue in India presently, and deliberations on this issue have been ongoing for long.

11.3 CONCLUSION

Standardisation of services in India remains at a relatively nascent stage. This chapter provides an overview of the process of standardisation and standards development in services, both internationally and in India. It has attempted to examine and outline the key developments in India in different services sectors, including banking and financial services, telecommunications services, tourism services, management consulting services, education services, telemedicine services, etc. as certain niche and dynamically evolving services sectors. The sectors covered are those in which India has a specific

specifies the minimum requirements for a process-based quality management system that would prove the firm's ability to meet the client requirements.

115. The Advocates Act, 1961, section 4.
116. The Advocates Act, 1961, section 7(1).
117. The Indian Evidence Act, 1872, section 126.

comparative advantage, or which are crucial in the overall economic landscape. Many of these sectors are among the twelve champion services sectors, where the present Government has placed specific emphasis and thrust for development, to realise India's underlying potential and overall competitiveness.

Of the aforementioned sectors, banking and finance, education and telemedicine services appear to be sectors where India could place thrust for future development. With digitalisation of education platforms, developing standards in this sector would be immensely beneficial for Indian education service providers as well as a large segment of the Indian youth population (which often prefers attaining higher education and advanced degrees from the leading international institutions). Similarly, Indian healthcare professionals and service providers are often highly qualified and are well-respected in the developed economies. Development of telehealth standards could be instrumental in giving a greater momentum to the Indian healthcare sector.

Given India's competitiveness in the services sector, the process of standardisation in services is set to significantly reinforce the contribution of services trade to the expansion of the Indian economy. Other than the sectors examined in this chapter, India is competitive in many other professional and business services sectors. However, as with the international standardisation of services, the standardisation of services in India is also confronted with many challenges. One such challenge appears to be lack of intensive research infrastructure - due to unavailability of technological resources, equipment, trained personnel, etc. Another challenge arises due to the sectoral specificities of various services, which makes it cumbersome for one central standardising body to develop standards in multiple niche service sectors. Furthermore, lack of participation and inputs from the industry might be another reason for inadequate standardisation in services. On the whole, proactive industry participation and extensive stakeholder consultations are likely to play an instrumental role in the process of services standardisation, along with increased technological developments.

CHAPTER 12

Standardisation of Digital Economy: An Indian Perspective

Sunanda Tewari, Amandeep Kaur Bajwa & Ridhish Rajvanshi

With every click on the internet, individuals are generating data. This data is being collected by both State and non-State actors for providing better integrated service delivery and user experiences. The rampant digitalisation of all aspects of economy and the growing reliance on the use of data has highlighted the need for its seamless operations, exchange, management, security and privacy – resulting in standardisation of data. In this regard, particularly, the past decade has seen a rise in the adoption of digital standards by various governments across the globe to facilitate e-governance. This includes adopting standards for data interoperability across various platforms, data security and data privacy. It is in this context that the present chapter aims to introduce the readers to the concept of digital standards and data protection laws and related international developments. The focal point of the chapter is the comprehensive examination of development and adoption of standards in India – specifically in the sphere of e-governance, data security and data privacy. The chapter compares and contrasts the Indian regime of data standards vis-à-vis other countries with an aim to give an insightful analysis of the present and future regime of data standardisation in India.

12.1 INTRODUCTION

The rise of digital technology has made it essential to bring in standardisation of the digital regime to ensure uniformity and control. It is essential to develop legal standards that promote and facilitate a coherent, robust and comprehensive system that can function globally. At the same time, there is a need to shield stakeholders from excessive risks involved in the usage of digital technologies while securing data platforms and optimising the digital potential of these platforms and its users.[1]

In a general context, the term 'standard' is often used to refer to a requirement, a compliance measure or a minimum set of qualification criteria that something must meet.[2] For instance, there are set standards for safety of household and similar electrical appliances which prescribe a set voltage for single phase appliances.[3] However, in the digital context, the term standard has a different meaning – it refers to common technical specifications used to ascertain how information or data is described, processed, or transmitted. For instance, HyperText Markup Language (HTML) and Hypertext Transfer Protocol (HTTP) standards describe how web pages are formatted and transmitted so that all web browsers and websites on the internet are working consistently and ensure interoperability.[4] Also, at this stage it is important to distinguish technical standards for digital products *vis-à-vis* digital standards themselves. Generally, the products which facilitate the transfer of data (e.g., Local Area Network cable or a Wi-Fi Router) are governed by traditional standards that regulate their technical aspects, while digital standards govern the flow of data and its sharing and management.

Data is the keystone of the digital technology framework. Data sharing and data management at all times require strong and secure modes of transaction. The growing reliance on data now requires effective framework for the harmonisation and governance of the data standards for effective operation of digital technology. The streamlining of data standards across the globe will help in enabling easier, efficient exchange and processing of data. It will also remove ambiguities and inconsistencies in the use of data. Data standards should further enable the sharing or exchange of information between the multiple users in a way that it guarantees same understanding of what is represented within that information.[5]

The present chapter is divided into four sections. Section 12.1 is the introduction to the chapter where the need for standardisation of the digital economy, specifically operations related to data, is explained. Section 12.2 introduces and explains the concept of digital standards, data security standards and data privacy standards and discusses the important international developments in this regard. Section 12.3 is dedicated to the landscape of digital and data standards in India. The section discusses the evolution of digital standards for e-governance in India. It also traces the trajectory of data security and privacy standards in India and contrasts them with similar development in other countries across the globe. In Section 12.4, the chapter concludes

1. E. L. Sidorenko & Peter von Arx, *Transformation of Law in the Context of Digitalization: Defining the Correct Priorities*, I Digital Law Journal 26-27 (2020).
2. *Data Standards*, A repository of Federal Enterprise Data Resources (1 February 2021), https://resources.data.gov/standards/concepts/ (Data Standards (rep.)).
3. Bureau of Indian Standards, *Indian Standard- Safety of Household and Similar Electronic Appliances* (March 2010), https://law.resource.org/pub/in/bis/S05/is.302.2.7.2010.pdf .(Safety Household Standards).
4. Safety Household Standards, *supra* note 3.
5. STQC Directorate, *Metadata and Data Standard*, e-Governance Standards, Ministry of Electronics & Information Technology, Government of India (01 April 2021), http://egovstandards.gov.in/metadata-and-data-standard.

with the brief commentary on the future of data protection and standardisation regime of India.

12.1.1 Need for Standardising the Data

The significance of data and its role in economy and governance cannot be overlooked. There are numerous benefits incurred from the collection and analysis of personal data. An individual's personal data like healthcare or geographical data can be used to make diagnostics predications or help in traffic monitoring.[6] There is no argument that a pooled dataset allows for quicker detection of trends or target audience. The rapid innovations and increasing reliance on the usage of big data techniques have the immense potential to change our day-to-day lives. For example, big data may be used to detect financial frauds, location tracking for logistics, healthcare emergency response, etc.[7]

Around the world, governments are the largest producers and consumers of information. In their day-to-day activities, they collect, verify, validate and maintain a large number of documents and information which invariably becomes invaluable in nature. Along with governments, private corporates too rely heavily on the personal data, opening the possibilities of its misuse. Hence, emerges the need to regulate the use of collected data, to prevent its arbitrary use and to always maintain data privacy and security. To combat these concerns, data standardisation is required to ensure that there are adequate safeguards in place that protect individuals' data privacy and security by both the state and non-state actors.[8]

In the Indian context, being the second most populous country in the world, coupled with rapid digitisation makes it a huge market for both private companies and the Government. In such burgeoning scenario, data standards are expected to contribute significantly toward e-governance, data security, its privacy and accountability on parts of data collectors and processors. Hence, the very need for regularisation and standardisation of digital India. However, before we discuss the evolution and trajectory of data/digital standards in India, it becomes imperative to study the development of international standards governing data/information and associated laws and regulations.

6. Clemens Suter-Crazzolara, *Big Data and The Journey to Personalized Medicine*, Forbes (17 November 2015, https://www.forbes.com/sites/sap/2015/11/17/big-data-and-the-journey-to-personalized- medicine/#7865d751b0ee.
7. Jacomo Corbo et al., *Applying analytics in financial institutions' fight against fraud*, McKinsey and Company (April 2017), https://www.mckinsey.com/business-functions/mckinsey-analytics /our-insights/applying-analytics-in-financial-institutions-fight-against-fraud. *See also, Big Data, Artificial Intelligence, Machine Learning and Data Protection*, UK Information Commissioner's Office, https://ico.org.uk/for-organisations/guide-to-data-protection/big-data/.
8. *Justice K.S. Puttaswamy v. Union of India*, (2017) 10 SCC 1 (Puttaswamy).

12.2 DIGITAL STANDARDS AND INTERNATIONAL DEVELOPMENTS

For analysing the trajectory of development of digital standards in India, it becomes imperative to study the prevailing international standards. In this section, we discuss international digital standards that cover several aspects of exchange and management of data such as interoperability, architecture, security and privacy along with certain laws/regulations. The section primarily focuses on the General Data Protection Regulation[9] (GDPR) in the European Union (EU) and various international digital standards set by international bodies such as International Organisation for Standardisation/ International Electrotechnical Commission (ISO/IEC), etc. Before, we dive into the specifics of this section, some fundamental concepts of digital standards are discussed.

12.2.1 Digital Standards

As explained, digital standards are gaining significant traction due to evolving technological advancements. Digital standards 'help agencies to follow the same standards and frameworks. It sets a guideline to agree and implement processes for common business processes such as finance, HR and payroll functions to reduce unnecessary difference when operating across different agencies.'[10] Hence, the focus of digital standards is to facilitate interoperability of information across platforms. Under the broad umbrella of digital standards exist data standards. In this regard, the data standards are 'the rules by which data are described and recorded. In order to share, exchange, and understand data, we must standardize the format as well as the meaning.'[11]

Generally, all large data collectors incorporate digital standards to streamline their operations. Digital standards help in building, designing and delivering simple, fast and better services and products. Major developments in adopting digital standards is happening in the sphere of electronic governance (e-governance). These standards are applied by government agencies for providing a consistent platform for interaction and interoperability of data collected by government and its agencies. This will provide faster delivery and simpler services, ensuring data is accessible across the platforms. For example, Australia and Canada identify thirteen best-practice principles for Digital Service Standards (DSS)[12] – requiring the agencies to have understanding of the user, user-friendly process, and more importantly, be consistent and secure (using

9. EU Regulation 2016/679 of the European Parliament and of the Council of 27 April 2016 on the protection of natural persons with regard to the processing of personal data and on the free movement of such data, and repealing Directive 95/46/EC (GDPR).
10. *Ibid.*
11. *Data and digital standards community of practice*, Data.govt.nz, New Zealand Government, https://www.data.govt.nz/toolkit/communities-and-groups/data-and-digital-standards-community-of-practice/.
12. Digital Transformation Agency, *Digital Service Standard Criteria*, Australian Government, https://www.dta.gov.au/help-and-advice/digital-service-standard/digital-service-standard-criteria; *Digital Service Standard, 2021/*.

data security standards). The agencies also need to understand the privacy standards for protection of data, along with ensuring compliance with data protection law and development of digital platforms using open standards. For maintaining interoperability between datasets, it is important to have standards which are based on open standards, service-based architecture and standards related to metadata[13] and schema, among others.[14] This has to be applied by government at federal, state and local levels.[15]

12.2.2 Data Security Standards

Since the inception of World Wide Web, we have seen drastic growth in access to internet over the last three decades - a vast network of information sharing has emerged. This has also left users vulnerable to various cyber-attacks such as phishing, spamming, data breaches, piracy, etc. The vulnerability is primarily for two reasons, *first*, the advancement of technology, and more sophisticated hacking which has led to increase in number of breaches of firewall to access the user's data stored by the companies or the websites, and *second*, the non-compliance, non-willingness to meet the requirement for controller/processor/companies to report the data breaches.

It is evident more than ever that data security and information standard find their relevance because of growing storage of data, especially over cloud, increased sophisticated network and inclusion of more critical sectors into digital world. These standards prescribe the requirements for firewall or certification or security audits or cybersecurity compliances or processes required to be adhered to by companies when handling user information or data.

12.2.3 Data Privacy Standards

Right to privacy has gained importance in the age of internet. The right of privacy is not often enshrined in the basic text but is the result of interpretations of constitutional courts through judgments. At an international level, the OECD Guidelines on Protection of Privacy and Transborder Flows of Personal Data (1980) further inspired the data protection legislations in Australia, New Zealand, Japan and the European Union (then the European Communities).

A new match to the fire was lit by the GDPR. The revised 2013 OECD Guidelines on Privacy along with GDPR redefined the scope and enforcement framework for

13. To facilitate common understanding, a number of characteristics, or attributes, of data are defined. These characteristics of data are known as 'metadata', that is, 'data that describes data.' For any particular datum, the metadata may describe how the datum is represented, ranges of acceptable values, its relationship to other data, and how it should be labelled. Metadata also may provide other relevant information, such as the responsible steward, associated laws and regulations, and access management policy. Each of the types of data described above has a corresponding set of metadata. *Data Standards* (rep), *supra* note 2.
14. *Data Standards* (rep), *supra* note 2.
15. *Government digital standards*, Open Data Institute, https://platformland.github.io/government-service-standards/data/service-standards/.

privacy standards. The stringent compliance led companies to apply similar practices in all other countries, even in jurisdictions which did not have data protection laws in place. This propelled other countries to put in place the adequate level of protection requirements as provided in the GDPR. Broadly speaking, the GDPR has inspired the development of data security and privacy standards across the globe.

In essence, privacy standards set requirements concerning when data can be allowed to flow across border, and the laws applicable to entities involved in cross-border data flow, and storing data locally, especially sensitive, financial and health data. They also establish the concept of consent, right to delete user's data, how long data can be stored, notification and procedures for data breaches, and limited use or specific purpose use of data. Thus, under the privacy standards we identify these privacy norms which act as compliance requirements for anyone processing or storing data.

12.2.4 Digital Standards Issued by International Platforms/Organisations

The following discussion looks at the various standards frequently issued by the international platforms or international organisations, such as ISO/ IEC/World Wide Web Consortium (W3C), etc. Figure 12.1 highlights some digital standards issued by the ISO. The relevant and frequently used standards for data security and privacy around the globe both by governments and body corporates alike are discussed below.

Figure 12.1 Digital Standards Issued by ISO

1.1. ISO 19115-1:2014 on geographic information – metadata

- This standard discusses the description of geographical information and services by means of metadata, widely applicable on 'all types of resources, clearing house activities, and the full description of datasets and services' including 'geographic services, geographic datasets, dataset series, and individual geographic features and feature properties'.

2. ISO 15836-1:2017 and ISO 15836-2:2019 on information and documentation - The Dublin Core metadata element set

- This is a set of 15 core elements describing resources in a cross-disciplinary information environment, originally developed as web resources in 1995. This is also the most widely used metadata element set and describes various physical and digital resources. Most frequently endorsed by the ISO, IETF, RFC, NISO.

3. Standards by ISO/IEC JTC 1/SC 27 on information security, cybersecurity and privacy protection

- The standard provides for the technical reports, specifications in information security along with addressing the requirements in information security, cybersecurity and privacy concerning general methods, management systems requirements, techniques and guidelines.

4. ISO/IEC 27000 on information security management

- This set of standards provides requirements concerning the information security management system which provides organisations for management of various assets security in the financial, intellectual property, sector and 'employee information entrusted by third parties'.

5. Standards by ISO/IEC JTC 1/SC 38 on cloud computing and distributed platforms

- The standards set out certain foundational concepts, application of technologies, operational issues and interactions between the cloud computing (CC) systems and other distributed platform/system. For instance, ISO 19086 establishes a common set for cloud service level agreement building blocks, such as concepts, terms, definitions, and contexts. The interoperability and portability between CC and interaction between two-CC is discussed in ISO/IEC 19941.

6. Standards by ISO/IEC JTC 1/SC 37 on biometrics

- The ISO has published standards relating to biometrics. These are relating to the Common Biometric Exchange Formats Frame work (19785 family), Biometric data interchange formats (19794 family), Biometric performance testing and reporting (19795 family), Biometric profiles for interoperability and data interchange (24713 family), Extensible biometric data interchange formats (39794 family).

7. Encryption and encoding standards for languages

- In the digital world, language is in the form of binary codes such as zeros and ones, and stored as such. These binary codes (machine language) form is defined for each character (that is comprehensible to human). These characters are combined together to form a large character set. The technique for representation in large of multiple character sets within a single character encoding and to large character sets is found in ISO/IEC 2022 (equivalent to ECMA-35, ANSI X3.41, JIS X 0202). The ISO/IEC 10646 family concerns standard related to universal character set (UCS) covering 120,585 characters from the world's scripts applicable on languages of the world in written form and symbols there of. Lastly, ISO 10303-21:2016 concerns product data representation and exchange from one computer to another in an archive, digital signatures and UTF-8 character encoding.

Source: Author's own representation.

12.2.5 Laws/Regulations of Different Countries Acting as De Facto Digital Standards

12.2.5.1 European Union

The EU has been a pioneer in setting standards at an international level. It has consistently worked with international standard-setting bodies toward standardisation of goods, food products, services, best practices in market competition, sustainable energy and now towards the digital trade. The standards setting body in the EU are European Committee for Standardization (CEN), European Committee for Electrotechnical Standardisation (CENELEC), and European Telecommunications Standards Institute (ETSI).[16] EU has an extensive governance interoperability framework (GIF). Under the framework, Digital Service Standards covers approximately 10-15 standards for different aspects such as metadata and schema, based on ISO/IEC standards.[17] The CEN issued *CEN-CLC/JTC 13 'Cybersecurity and Data Protection'* which is identical to *ISO/IEC JTC 1/SC 38*,[18] a cloud computing security related standard. Digital signature in the EU is regulated by the EU Regulation 910/2014 of 23 July 2014 *'eIDAS (electronic IDentification, Authentication and trust Services)* on electronic identification' which repealed *1999/93/EC* from 13 December 1999.[19] While it deals with electronic signature, it also goes beyond in providing authentication, trust services and a secured environment for digital transactions within EU.[20]

EU's privacy standards are set out in the EU GDPR which came into effect on 25 May 2018. This regulation is considered one of the highest standards of privacy and data protection in the world. The GDPR sets uniform regulation of data protection across the EU and brings under its regulatory and enforcement framework, any company (not limited to an EU company) which is processing or storing personal data of the EU citizens.[21] Figure 12.2 highlights types of data standards covered under the GDPR.

16. Internal Market, Industry, Entrepreneurship and SMEs, *European Standards* (europa.eu), https://ec.europa.eu/growth/single-market/european-standards_en#:~:text=Standards%20are%20technical%20specifications%20defining,%2C%20services%20or%20test%2Dmethods.&text=European%20Standards%20are%20under%20the,support%20EU%20legislation%20and%20policies.
17. European Committee for Electrotechnical Standardisation (CENELEC), *Advanced search – Publications and Work in Progress on standards related to Schema*, https://www.cenelec.eu/dyn/www/f?p=104:105:0; European Committee for Electrotechnical Standardisation (CENELEC), *Advanced search – Publications and Work in Progress on standards related to Metadata*, https://www.cenelec.eu/dyn/www/f?p=104:105:0.
18. *Rolling Plan for ICT*, Cloud Computing (RP2020), https://joinup.ec.europa.eu/collection/rolling-plan-ict-standardisation/cloud-computing-rp2020.
19. Regulation (EU), 910/2014 of the European Parliament and of the Council of 23 July 2014 on electronic identification and trust services for electronic transactions in the internal market and repealing Directive 1999/93/EC.
20. Euro Commission, *Trust services and electronic identification* (10 March 2021), https://digital-strategy.ec.europa.eu/en/policies/trust-services-and-eid.
21. Article 3, GDPR.

GDPR does not cover business, aggregated or anonymised data but only personal data, the transfer of which is allowed within the EU.[22] This includes processing of the personal data by either digital or analogue means while exempting the processing of personal data on activities which fall outside the EU law or on personal or household activity by a natural person or by competent authorities against public security and criminal or civil investigations, etc.[23]

Figure 12.2 Data Standards Covered under GDPR

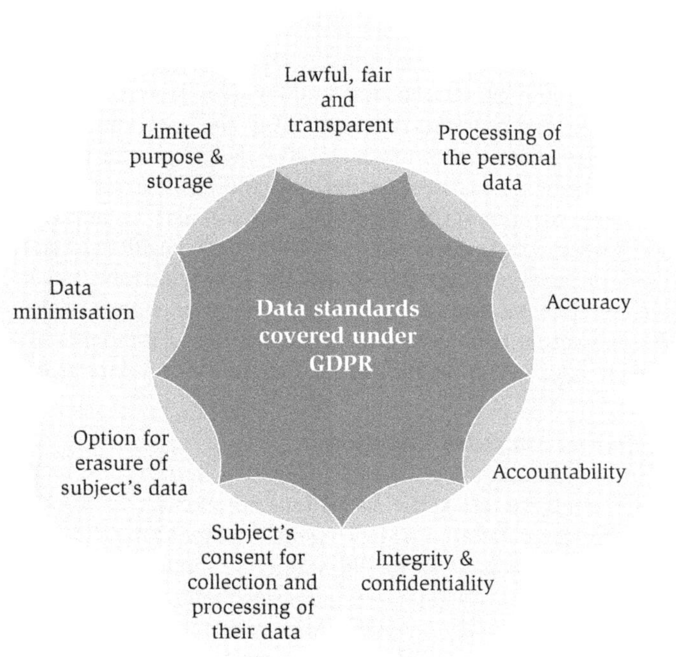

Source: Author's own representation.

The GDPR does not allow cross-border transfer of personal data undergoing processing or intended for processing purpose except 'where the Commission has decided that the third country, a territory or one or more specified sectors within that third country, or the international organisation in question ensures an adequate level of protection.'[24]

Furthermore, for Data Protection of payments and financial information, the GDPR is applicable generally, but additional legal requirements are also required to be met, such as data segregation requirements (for instance, strict separation of payments

22. Article 1, GDPR.
23. Article 2, GDPR.
24. Article 45, GDPR.

data from other business data, and implementation of a Data Access Control Policy and a Data Sharing Policy); banking secrecy requirements; and Payment Card Industry Data Security Standard ('PCI-DSS'). The latest legal requirement for companies here is the ePrivacy Directive (from 2002 and 2009) replacing the proposed Regulation on Privacy and Electronic Communications.[25] The directive proposes to update the current rule to include Voice over Internet Protocol (VoIP) platforms, and machine-to-machine communication, and internet-messaging services; and protection of information on the data subject devices (consent should be sought before information such as photos, calendar, contacts, etc. are accessed or cookies are stored for tracking and monitoring online behaviour of the data subject).[26]

GDPR is generally applicable to all sectors collecting, managing or exchanging data related to the EU citizens and residents. It sets out legal requirement with regard to consent, national data protection and employment laws of EU member States (monitoring, surveillance, investigations, etc.) and the corporations. Thus, to summarise, GDPR enforces data protection requirements and greater privacy for its data subjects such as consent requirement for data processing of subjects; for protection of privacy requirement to anonymise the data; requirement to publish data breach notification and secure, safe transfer of cross-border data. GDPR is often termed as the authority in data protection. Since GDPR was the first regulation to set enormously comprehensive and high data standards coupled with its adequacy requirement, it has indirectly influenced other countries to adopt similar set of standards. In some cases, propelling States to adopt even higher degree of standards on data protection.

12.2.5.2 Development in Other Countries

Akin to the GDPR, similar data regulation regimes are seen across the globe. Australia has built a comprehensive data protection regime. Similar to the EU's GIF, Australia's interoperability framework is built on international standards which are used for defining metadata, data security data description, delivery, etc. The privacy standards in Australia are set by the Privacy Act 1988 (as amended in 2014 and 2017), governing the 'collection, use, storage and disclosure of personal information in the federal public sector and in the private sector'.[27] The Act also lays down thirteen privacy principles applicable to government agencies. Further, exemption from cross-border data transfer is available, if the entity believes that recipient entity is bound by similar law (adequate

25. *E-Privacy Regulation: EU Council Finally Adopts Its Position, and Trilogue begins*, The National Law Review (2 April 2021), https://www.natlawreview.com/article/e-privacy-regulation-eu-council-finally-adopts-its-position-and-trilogue-begins.
26. EU Commission, *Stronger privacy rules for electronic communications* (10 January 2017), https://digital-strategy.ec.europa.eu/en/library/stronger-privacy-rules-electronic-communications.
27. *Privacy Act 1988* (Cth), https://www.ag.gov.au/rights-and-protections/privacy#:~:text=The%20Privacy%20Act%201988%20(Privacy,and%20in%20the%20private%20sector.

level of protection) and there is enforcement mechanism in place to hold the recipient responsible if found in breach.[28] A requirement that is also found in the GDPR.

The United States surprisingly does not have a comprehensive privacy regulation or data protection legislature. The processing of data by government is done by various legislations, depicted in Figure 12.3. Recently, the State of California passed California Consumer Privacy Act, 2018 (CCPA)[29] which is applied to the residents of California. The Act provides similar rights and legal requirements to be met as under the GDPR, such as territorial scope, rights and compliance procedure of controller/data processors, and right to: delete, be informed, opt out, access to one's own data, transfer of data, etc.[30] This is first of its kind in United States, where privacy law is enacted for protection of personal data of the users.

Figure 12.3 Laws Governing Data Privacy in US

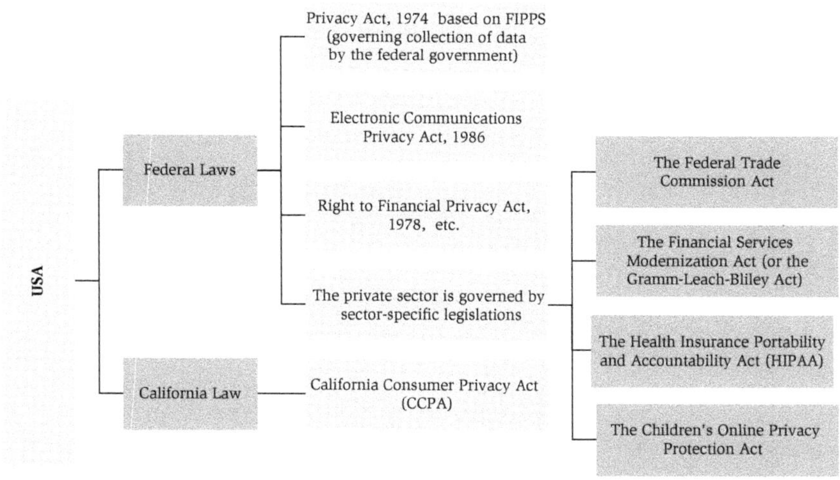

Source: Author's own representation.

28. Use or disclosure of personal information, Australian Privacy Principle 6, https://www.oaic.gov.au/agencies-and-organisations/app-guidelines/chapter-6-app-6-use-or-disclosure-ofpersonal-information.
29. California Consumer Privacy Act of 2018, CAL. CIV. CODE § 1798.140 (t), (2018) (effective 1 January 2020), https://leginfo.legislature.ca.gov/faces/codes_displayText.xhtml?division = 3.& part = 4.&lawCode = CIV&title = 1.81.5.
30. Alice Marini, Alexis Kateifides & Joel Bates, *Comparing privacy laws: GDPR v. CCPA*, Data Guidance, Future of Privacy Forum, 14, https://fpf.org/wp-content/uploads/2018/11/GDPR_CCPA_Comparison-Guide.pdf.

China on 01 June 2017 implemented the Cybersecurity Law of the People's Republic of China (Cybersecurity law).[31] The Act, in the interest of national security, aimed at increasing security requirements concerning data protection, data localisation and cybersecurity. This Act imposes stringent rules regarding cross-border data flows when compared with the GDPR. Also, China has introduced multiple rules setting stringent digital standards. Three national standards were introduced in 2019, collectively called as the cybersecurity multi-level protection system 2.0 which require further compliance by companies (depending on their nature of business) in fulfilling their cybersecurity obligations ensuring 'their networks are free from interference, damage, or unauthorized access, and prevent network data from being divulged, stolen or falsified.'[32] An overview of the requirements set by these national standards are depicted in Figure 12.4.

Figure 12.4 Requirements under China's Cybersecurity Law and Standards

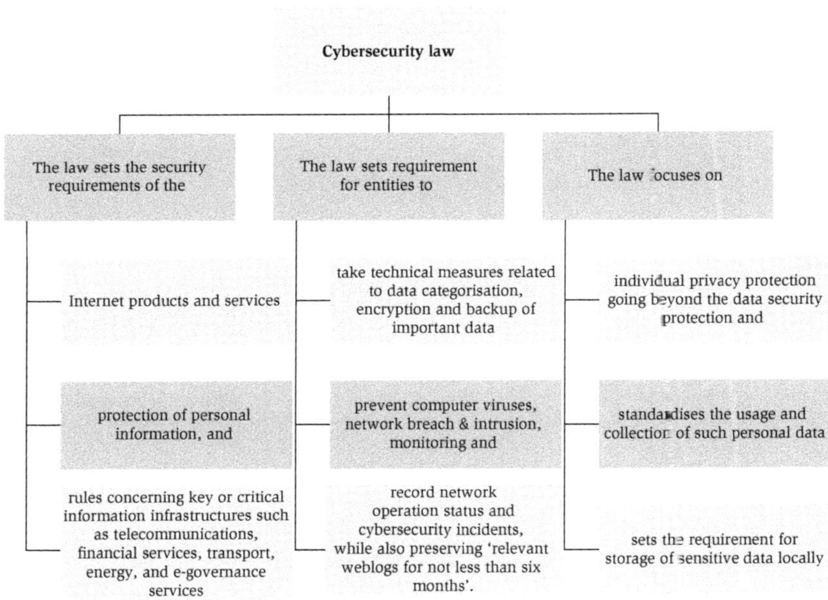

31. Rogier Creemers, Paul Triolo & Graham Webster, *Translation: Cybersecurity Law of the People's Republic of China (Effective 01 June 2017)*, New America (29 June 2018), https://www.newamerica.org/cybersecurity-initiative/digichina/blog/translation-cybersecurity-law-peoples-republic-china/.
32. Jones Day, *New Chinese Cybersecurity and Data Privacy Requirements* (December 2020), https://www.jonesday.com/en/insights/2020/12/new-chinese-cybersecurity-and-data-privacy-requirements; King & Wood Mallesons, *A Brief Introduction to China's Cybersecurity Law*, China Law Insight (16 June 2017), https://www.chinalawinsight.com/2017/06/articles/corporate-ma/a-brief-introduction-to-chinas-cybersecurity-law/.

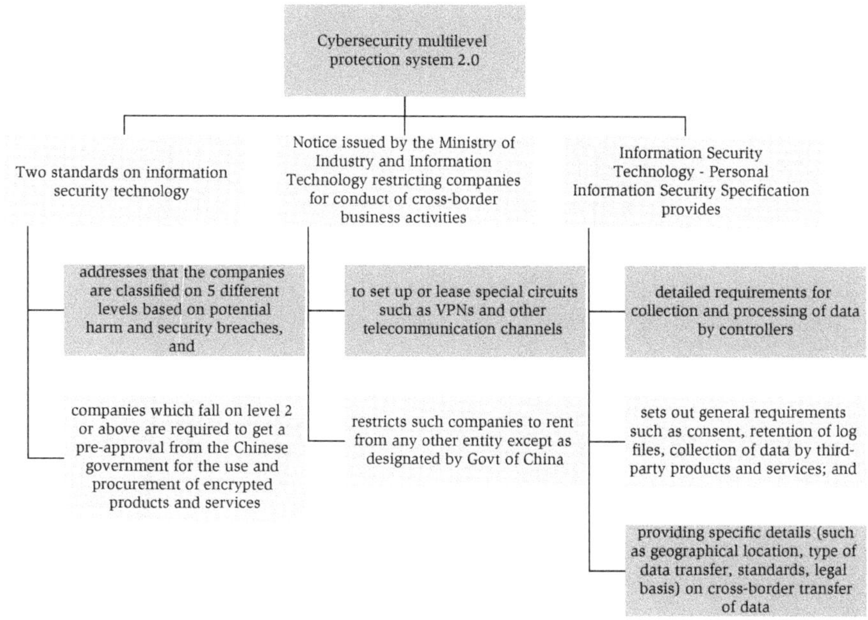

Source: Author's own representation.

Brazil implemented Law No. 13.709/2018, the General Data Protection Law (LGPD) similar to GDPR and is applicable on data processing, individuals (either located in Brazil or whose data is collected in Brazil), extending to any category (online or offline environment) with exceptions. As a developing economy, unlike China, Brazil does not have a comprehensive cybersecurity regulation in place. However, it has approved the National Strategy of Cybersecurity (E-Ciber), focusing on government's intention of cybersecurity measure applicable nationally and internationally. Brazil does have sector-specific regulations, such as for banking/financial data Resolution No. 4,658/2018 of Central Bank of Brazil (BACEN), sets cybersecurity policy and requirements for hiring of data processing, storage and cloud computing services; for health-related data – Ordinance 271/2017, and Ordinance 1,966/18 define and set information security standards and communications policy. This scenario of development of data privacy and security standards is similar to landscape of data standards in India (discussed in detail in Section 12.3). Other relevant legislations setting legal requirements in digital sphere are depicted in Figure 12.5.

Figure 12.5 Regulations and Ordinance in Brazil Governing Data Privacy

- Electronic Commerce Decree (Decree No. 7,962/13) governs
  - contracting on the Internet and provide rules applicable on products and services available online.

- Brazilian Internet Act (Law 12,965/2014) governs
  - contracting on the Internet,
  - liability for website content,
  - dealing with online personal data, and
  - also requires that stability, security and functionality of the network is preserved through technical measures based on international standards and authentication, data records and their logs, and usage of encryption or equivalent record management systems.

- Presidential Decree (8,771/2016) provides
  - for mandatory technical requirement for ISPs to 'shut down a website,
  - remove content, or
  - disable linking due to the website's content and without permission' either when the security of the network matters such as anti-spam, denial of service attacks or when there is congestion on the network and load needs to be distributed.

Source: Author's own representation

To facilitate e-governance, South Africa has also adopted an interoperability framework providing standards for data exchange and operations. Their GIF also provides for open standards, service-based architecture and standards for metadata and schema, among others. Similar to Brazil, borrowing from the GDPR, South Africa has the Protection of Personal Information Act, 2013 (POPIA), its principal data protection legislation.[33] The POPIA is applicable to all personal data processed in South Africa, and the controller/data processor cannot process personal information without the knowledge of data subject, personal information to be treated as confidential, and not to be shared with other parties unless required by law or for implementation of its duties, and finally, any such breach or unauthorised access of the personal information should be notified. Some of the key features of POPIA is represented in Figure 12.6.

33. Protection of Personal Information Act 4 of 2013, https://www.gov.za/documents/protection-personal-information-act#.

Figure 12.6 Key Features of South Africa's Data Privacy Laws

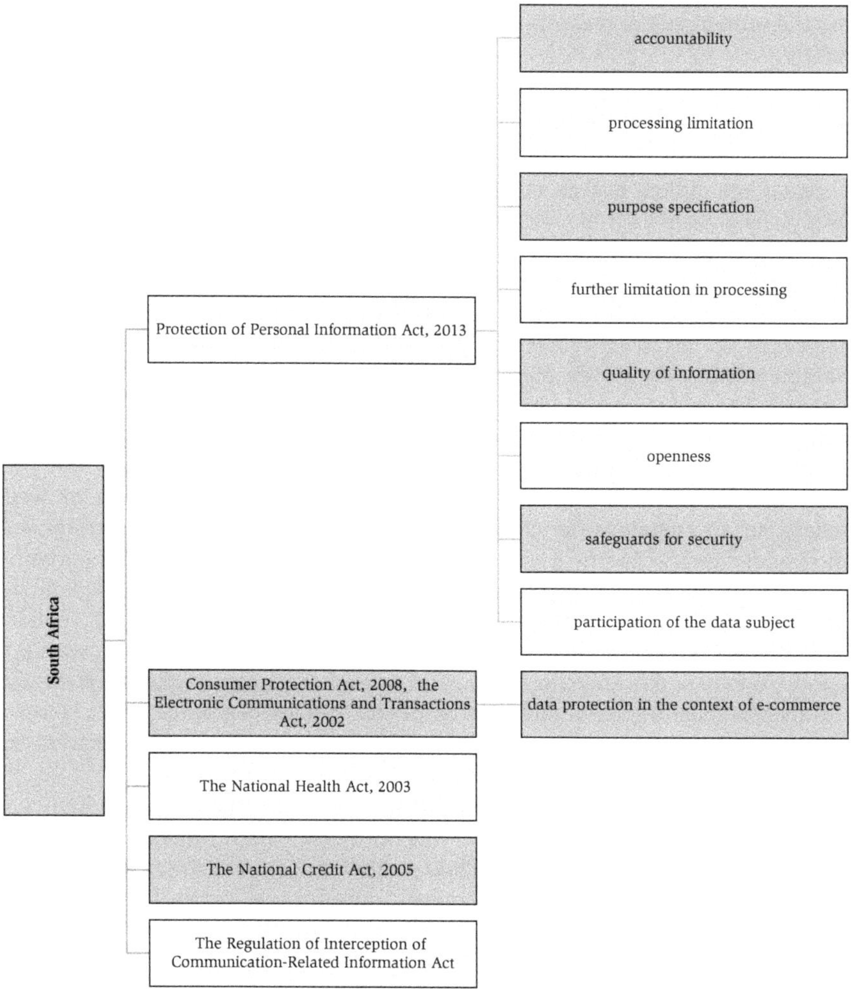

Source: Author's own representation.

From the above analysis, it is clear that most countries are facilitating standardisation in e-governance by adopting widely recognised international standards for data, such as *Dublin Core Metadata Elements set* for defining metadata; *ISO 27000* family for maintaining information security and management; *ISO/IEC JTC 1/SC 38* for standards in cybersecurity - cloud computing. It is evident that most of the data privacy laws implemented by countries across the globe are modelled after GDPR. Resultantly, similar standards for the rights and obligations of data owners and data processors are emerging worldwide. As far as the Indian scenario is considered, it would certainly be important to pass a legislation that safeguards personal and sensitive data and provides for rights and obligation of data owners and processor as seen at the global level. The next section discusses the progression of digital standards in e-governance in India and assess the Indian regime regarding data security and privacy standards *vis-à-vis* other countries.

12.3 DIGITAL AND DATA STANDARDS IN INDIA

The digital revolution has exceedingly permeated India. Currently, there are 450 million internet users in India with an estimated growth rate of 7%–8%.[34] There is no denying that India is becoming a large market in digital sphere for the global players. It is expected that this digital economy is going to generate new market growth opportunities and jobs in the coming forty–fifty years.[35] Hence the urgent need to capitalise on the growing digital economy of India. In order to facilitate the digital revolution in India, the Government of India (GoI) has implemented the 'Digital India' initiative.[36] The initiative recognises the incorporation of digitisation in governance; healthcare, banking and educational services primarily.[37] Other facets that require digital update include creating infrastructure for a cashless economy and digital transactions; transparency in bureaucracy; fair and quick distribution of welfare schemes, etc. to empower the citizens.[38] While, development of infrastructure and promotion of digital economy is one aspect, another is to mandate digital standards for the facilitation of a digital India. As already discussed, and emphasised in other chapters of this handbook, 'Standardisation' supports economic growth, enhances competitiveness and fosters technological developments. It is indeed a powerful tool that protects consumers and supports public policies for promoting trade on one hand and addressing health, safety, and environmental concerns on other. Thus, standardisation facilitates the use of products and services that are available in the market today and those that will arrive tomorrow.[39]

In this regard, to facilitate a digital economy and the Digital India initiative, the National Standards Action Plan of 2019 was set by Bureau of Indian Standards (BIS) recognising the need for standards in digital technology (artificial intelligence, big data, blockchain and distributed ledger technology), information technology (IT) security

34. *Data Protection in India*, Ministry of Electronics and Information Technology, 2, https://digitalindia.gov.in/writereaddata/files/6.Data%20Protection%20in%20India.pdf.
35. Ranjan Guha, *Digital Evolution in India*, Business Today (29 August 2017), http://www.businesstoday.in/opinion/columns/digital-evolution-in-india/story/259227 html. *See also*, MeitY, White Paper of the Committee of Experts on a Data Protection Framework for India, 1 (27 November 2017), https://www.MEITY.gov.in/writereaddata/files/white_paper_on_data_protection_in_india_171127_final_v2.pdf. (White Paper on Data Protection)
36. Digital India, *Digital India Programme*, Ministry of Electronics & Information Technology, Government of India, https://www.digitalindia.gov.in/.
37. White Paper on Data Protection, *supra* note 35, 2.
38. Press Information Bureau, *Digital India – A programme to transform India into digital empowered society and knowledge economy* (20 August 2014), http://pib.nic.in/newsite/PrintRelease.aspx?relid=108926. *See also*, White Paper on Data Protection, *supra* note 35, 2.
39. Bureau of Indian Standards, *Standards National Action Plan 2019*, https://bis.gov.in/index.php/standards-national-action-plan/. (Standards National Action Plan 2019).

(data privacy, security, mobile device security) and software and systems.[40] These standards have been kept at a high priority with score of 1.60, addressing the ambitious Digital India initiative.[41]

12.3.1 Digital Standards in India

E-governance is adoption of information and communication technology by the government to provide better integrated and simplified services to their citizens. In 1993, the United States National Performance Review first coined the term 'e-government'. Subsequently, in the year 2001, the United Nations (UN) defined e-government as a form of government *'utilizing the Internet and the world-wide-web for delivering government information and services to the citizens'*.[42] The backbone of e-governance is interoperability, which allows seamless operations and exchange of data across various platforms, i.e., government to government; government to citizens or government to business or enterprise. It fosters data transparency and accountability in the public system. Aligned with a similar outlook many countries such as the EU, Canada, Brazil, New Zealand, etc. have already adopted digital standards to ensure interoperability for facilitating e-governance.

The task of developing and adopting standards in India is done by BIS. It has been working extensively for developing and adopting standards for services such as travel, tourism and hospitality services, financial services, higher education, skill development services, etc. The standards developed by BIS includes both the physical and digital/electronic aspect of services. However, in recent times, MeitY has become the driving force behind India's transformation into a digital economy and this is reflected in the handover of power for standard-setting from BIS to MeitY. Now with the implementation of national e-governance plan, Ministry of Electronic and Information Technology (MeitY) has been adopting and notifying digital standards to promote e-governance.

12.3.1.1 National e-Governance Plan

In May 2006, the MeitY, GoI (formerly known as the Department of Electronics and Information Technology, now the nodal ministry governing the standards in e-governance space) approved the National e-Governance Plan (NeGP) consisting of thirty-two mission mode projects for e-governance in areas like banking, taxation, insurance, unique identification project at both Central and State level.[43]

One of the key aspects of NeGP is approving standards related to metadata, interoperability, enterprise architecture, information security, etc. and a framework

40. Standards National Action Plan 2019, *supra* note 39.
41. Standards National Action Plan 2019, *supra* note 39.
42. E-Government Toolkit for Developing Countries, https://docplayer.net/8675438-Index-about-this-toolkit-preface.html.
43. MeitY, *Mission Mode Projects | Ministry of Electronics and Information Technology*, Government of India, https://www.MEITY.gov.in/content/mission-mode-projects.

that regulates electronic authentication, mobile and cloud services and other technologies in India.[44] In continuation with developing the standards under the NeGP, the GoI unveiled the Policy on Open Standards for e-Governance. The aim of this policy is to identify open standards for consistent, standardised and reliable implementation of e-governance solutions. This is aligned with the international practice of promotion of open standards in e-governance.

Under the Policy, 'Open Standard' is not defined, but lists the criteria for such standard. This includes - available with or without nominal fee; the patent claims necessary to implement the identified standard is made available on Royalty-fee basis; identified standard is adopted and maintained by non-profit organisation wherein all stakeholders can opt to participate in a transparent, collaborative and consensual manner; the standard is recursively open as far as possible and has technology neutral specification.[45] Overall, the Policy provides a basic framework for the selection of standards. And will aid in facilitating interoperable systems, specifications available in public domain, quality of information and services with human centric design of systems; common terminology and common framework for technology used across the globe and reducing costs and fees.[46]

12.3.1.2 Institutional Mechanism for Standards Formulation

MeitY defines formulation of digital standard as 'evolution and documentation process of a standard in compliance with Open Standard e-Governance Policy, which may consist of an existing national/global standard adopted as is or adapted on need basis (customisation/extension) or formulation of a new standards based on best practice/global solutions.'[47]

The institutional mechanism for the development of standards set up under NeGP is governed by MeitY. The mechanism states technical specifications and requirements of the process, practices and methods for the development of standards in the concerned area. Under the mechanism the apex body is chaired by the Secretary of MeitY. The adoption of standards is a collaborative effort on behalf of strategic members belonging to MeitY, Planning Commission, field of law, scientific experts, National e-governance division, BIS, Standardisation Testing and Quality Certification (STQC) and industry bodies such as NASSCOM, etc. The pictorial representation of standard formulation is provided below (Figure 12.7).

---

44. MeitY, *National e-Governance Plan | Ministry of Electronics and Information Technology*, Government of India, https://www.MEITY.gov.in/divisions/national-e-governance-plan.
45. STQC Directorate, *Policy on Open Standards for e-Governance*, Ministry of Electronics and Information Technology, Government of India, 2, http://egovstandards.gov.in/sites/default/files/Policy%20on%20Open%20Standards%20for%20e-Governance.pdf.
46. MeitY, *Institutional Mechanism for e-Governance Standards Formulation*, 7, http://egovstandards.gov.in/sites/default/files/Institutional%20Mechanism%20for%20e-Governance%20Standards%20Formulation%20Ver1.1.pdf (Institutional Mechanism for e-Governance Standards Formulation).
47. Institutional Mechanism for e-Governance Standards Formulation, *supra* note 46, 2.

Figure 12.7 Institutional Mechanism for Standard Formulation by National e-Governance Standards Division

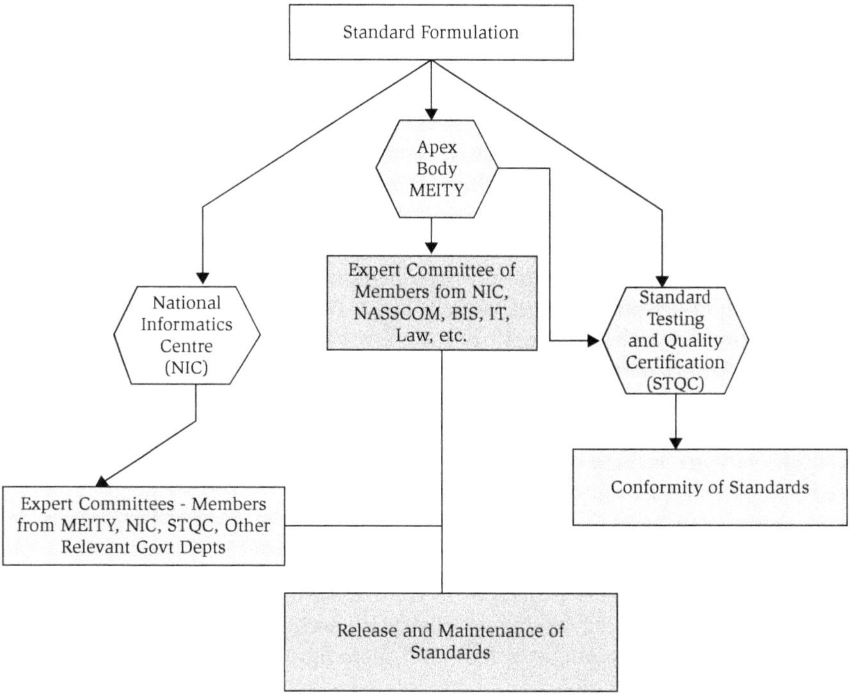

Source: Authors' own representation.

12.3.1.3 Technical Standards for Interoperability Framework

In India, the e-governance platforms operate in silos which inhibits integrated services delivery, logical distribution of data across platforms, seamless and secure exchange of information.[48] An interoperability framework, thus, becomes a necessity to support the flow of information, through which two or more e-governance applications can interoperate.[49] It must be noted that most of the countries such as the EU, New Zealand, Canada developed their government interoperability frameworks in the early 2000s. Even developing economies such as Brazil and South Africa had a minimum standard for interoperability issued by late 2007.

48. MeitY, *Technical Standards for Interoperability Framework for E-Governance in India*, 6, http://egovstandards.gov.in/sites/default/files/Technical%20Standards%20for%20IFEG%20 Ver1.0.pdf. (Technical Standards for Interoperability).
49. Technical Standards for Interoperability, *supra* note 48, 6.

In India, the Interoperability Framework of E-Governance (IFEG) was formulated considerably late, somewhere in late 2010. This framework addresses three kinds of interoperability – organisation, semantic and technical – to facilitate e-governance in India. For the purpose of this chapter, we will be focusing on technical interoperability requirements.

In year 2012, the GoI issued the first version of 'Technical Standards for Interoperability Framework for E-Governance in India'. Akin to other global GIFs, this document lists seven areas for setting standards used by e-governance applications. These areas are presentation and archival; process; data integration; metadata; data interchange; network access; application and security. The standards prescribed for these seven areas are the commonly used international standards prescribed by ISO, IEC, IETF and W3C.

Some of the important standards prescribed under the IFEG, includes – *ISO 15836* as the standard of metadata elements for content; Domain Services Nomenclature for naming resources which are usable in different hosts, networks, protocol families, internet and administrative organisations; *Cascading Style Sheets (CCS), Level 2 (CCS2)* by W3C for presentation of documents and related elements like layout, colours and fonts; June 2009 Digital Signature Algorithms (*DSA) (FIPS 186-3)*; *ISO/IEC 15445:2000* and *HTML 4.01* prescribing document type for Simple Hypertext Web Content, etc.

12.3.1.4 India Enterprise Architecture Framework

The seamless interoperability envisaged by GoI between two different digital platforms cannot be achieved without having an enterprise architecture framework. An enterprise architecture framework is a tool that is required for delivering high-quality government services in complex and heterogeneous environments.[50] This framework allows organisations to standardise their information technology infrastructure and align it with their business goals. This approach has been endorsed by international agencies like the United Nations, World Health Organization, World Bank, etc.

In this regard, MeitY, through the working group constituted by STQC Directorate, conceptualised the India Enterprise Architecture Framework or IndEA Framework. The IndEA Framework provides a generic framework which comprises of reference models which are derived from already established international frameworks, i.e., The Open Group Architecture Framework[51] or the Security Reference Model which provides a framework for dispensing information of the entire ecosystem of IT networks enabling data integrity, privacy, confidentiality and availability of information/IT systems.[52]

50. MeitY, *IndEA Framework*, xi, Ministry of Electronics and Information Technology, Government of India (October 2018), https://www.MEITY.gov.in/writereaddata/files/IndEA_Framework_1.0.pdf (*IndEA Framework*).
51. IndEA Framework (India Enterprise Architecture Framework, *supra* note 50, 79.
52. IndEA Framework (India Enterprise Architecture Framework, *supra* note 50, 98.

12.3.1.5 Metadata and Data Standards

Metadata is structured information that describes, explains, locates or otherwise makes it easier to retrieve, use or manage an information resource.[53] Metadata gives user the access to raw data, which can help the user to comprehend the actual data better. In the context of e-governance, exchange of information across various platforms often leads to redundancy/ambiguity or duplication. Thus, the need for standardising the requirement for defining data. Open Standard Policy provides for the use of *ISO 15836:2009 (Dublin Core Metadata Element Set)* one of the most widely accepted international standard as the Indian standard for metadata and data.

In April 2012, MeitY notified the Metadata and Data Standards (MDDS) under the 'Institutional Mechanism for Formulation of Domain Specific - Metadata and Data Standards in e-Governance'.[54] This document provides for a hybrid approach that may be adopted for standardisation of metadata and data of generic information elements pertaining to various domains or areas by formulating domain/areas specific Expert committees for domain data elements, while MeitY shall be responsible for the common generic data elements.[55]

In this regard, *MDDS - Demographic (Person Identification and Land Region Codification)*, developed by MeitY identifies and standardises the generic data elements (such as date, units of measurement, language code, etc.) used in defining personal identification and regional location and are common to all domain applications.[56] Examples of other domain specific MDDS that have been notified are Drinking water - *Metadata & Data Standards for Rural Drinking Water and Sanitation (September 2016)* by Ministry of Drinking Water and Sanitation; and *Metadata and Data Standards For Panchayati Raj Domain (July 2017)* by Ministry of Panchayati Raj, etc.

12.3.1.6 Standards for Data Preservation

The e-Governance standard for Preservation Information Documentation version 1 (eGOV-PID) of Electronic Records provides standard for metadata dictionary and schema when describing an electronic record. Preservation of information and documentation is necessary not only for maintaining records that are stored for longer durations (e.g., ten years, twenty-five years, etc.) but are also necessary for records required to be preserved permanently.[57]

53. MeitY, *Institutional Mechanism for Formulation of Domain Specific Metadata and Data Standards in e-governance*, 1, http://egovstandards.gov.in/sites/default/files/Institutional_Mechanism_for_Domain_MDDS.pdf. (Domain Specific Metadata and Data Standards).
54. Domain Specific Metadata and Data Standards, *supra* note 53, i.
55. Domain Specific Metadata and Data Standards, *supra* note 53, 1.
56. MeitY, *MDDS - Demographic (Person Identification and Land Region Codification), 6,* http://egovstandards.gov.in/sites/default/files/MDDS%20Demographic%20Ver%201.1.pdf.
57. MeitY, *e-GOV-PID: Preservation Metadata & Schema*, iv, http://egovstandards.gov.in/sites/default/files/e-Governance%20Standards%20for%20Preservation%20Information%20Documentation%20of%20e-Records%20Ver1.0%20%28Metadata%20%26%20Schema%29.pdf (Preservation Metadata & Schema).

The eGOV-PID sets the standards as per the requirements set out in *ISO 14721:2012 Open Archival Information Systems (OAIS) Reference Model* for the preservation of e-records. The implementation of this standard will help in producing valid Submission Information Package (SIP) for archival and preservation of the e-records. The information preserved can be categorised in terms of cataloguing, enclosures, provenance, representation, fixity, authenticity and access rights.[58] The framework provides for *Extensible Markup Language (XML)* by W3C, *ISO/TR 15489-1 and 2 – Information and Documentation – Records Management; ISO 1472:2012 Open Archival Information Systems (OAIS) Reference Model* and *ISO 16363:2012 – Audit & Certification of Trustworthy Digital Repositories* and *InterPARES 2* – International Research on Permanent Authentic Records, A Framework of Principles for the Development of Policies, Strategies and Standards for the Long-term Preservation of Digital Records, 2008.

12.3.1.7 Digital Service Standards

The idea behind developing DSS is to create a new breed of digital services with a high 'speed-to-market' propelled by a robust institutional mechanism, policy instruments and implementation methods to promote effective delivery of digital services.[59] Before we proceed, it is essential to distinguish electronic service from digital services. As already discussed in Section 12.1 of the chapter, e-services are inherently different as they cover electronic aspect of service request and delivery and are generally web or internet based. Whereas under the digital services the complete interaction is digital from end-to-end. Digital services are available across all digital platforms such as the web, mobile application, etc. and incorporates all kinds of technologies such as social, mobile, analytics, cloud and Internet of Things (IoT).

Now, in the Indian context, the DSS will set effective standards for defining, designing, developing, delivering and measuring the value created by the digital services for effective digital governance. Furthermore, the DSS will ensure that there is uniformity and consistency in digital services across organisations both government to government and corporation to government. Hence, ensuring inclusivity and accessibility of digital services.[60]

The Working Group on DSS has suggested that over 170 standards, principles and guidelines are required for a rational taxonomy and to create an easily comprehendible and implementable digital ecosystem across all e-governance platforms.[61] The DSS highlights the need for setting standards for defining, designing, developing, delivering and measuring the value created by digital services. Some of the upcoming and already

58. Preservation Metadata & Schema, *supra* note 57, ii.
59. MeitY, *Digital Service Standard*, 5, http://egovstandards.gov.in/sites/default/files/Digital%20Service%20Standard%20Version%201.0.pdf (Digital Service Standard).
60. Digital Service Standard, *supra* note 59, 9.
61. Digital Service Standard, *supra* note 59, 5.

becoming mainstream technologies targeted for setting standards under the DSS include, cloud services, data analytics, IoT, blockchain and artificial intelligence.[62]

This development of DSS in India is aligned with similar developments seen in other countries across the globe. Australian DSS are concentrated over thirteen areas for developing standards which include user experience, use of open standards, ensuring data security and privacy. Similar overarching requirements are seen in the DSS of Singapore and Canada.

Under the Indian DSS reliance is on providing architectural goals that are consistent with sustainable development goals of the United Nations. The DSS is envisaged as a complimentary architecture to IndEA framework ensuing interoperability of different back-end process. It provides for defining a digital service, realising a digital service, measuring a digital service and governance of such Digital Service Standards.[63] The standards under the DSS are similar to those notified by MeitY, e.g., MDDS standards such as *Dublin Core Metadata Standards*, biometric standards or usage of *e-Pramaan* for a Single-Sign-On Framework, user experience and interaction based on the Accessibility Policy of India and list of standards provided under the IndEA network.[64]

12.3.1.8 Standard and Specifications for e-Authentication

In 2015, the GoI approved the standards and specifications for e-Authentication called 'e-Pramaan: Framework for e-Authentication' providing guidelines for all Central and State ministries, departments and government agencies towards adopting an appropriate authentication model for online and mobile delivery of public services.[65] E-Pramaan Framework prescribes different levels of authentication like - Password; One Time Password (OTP); Digital Certificate; and Biometric - based authentication.[66] These authentication levels represent usage of Single/Multi-factor. The choice of using these levels of factor(s) for authentication is determined by the requirements as deemed fit by the service provider.[67]

12.3.1.9 Localisation and Language Technology Standards

There is no denying that the basic hardware systems and software applications designed and developed today are mostly in English language. In this regard, to proliferate the acceptance and usage of Indian languages in the growing ecosystem of hardware and software there is a requirement to set a standard for the information

62. Digital Service Standard, *supra* note 59, 8.
63. Digital Service Standard, *supra* note 59, 14.
64. Digital Service Standard, *supra* note 59, 27.
65. Ministry of Communications and Information Technology, Government of India, *Standards and Specifications for e-Pramaan: Framework for e-Authentication, 11*, http://egovstandards.gov.in/sites/default/files/Standards%20and%20Specifications%20For%20e-Pramaan-%20Framework%20for%20e-Authentication.pdf (Standards and Specifications for e-Pramaan).
66. Standards and Specifications for e-Pramaan, *supra* note 65, 11.
67. Standards and Specifications for e-Pramaan, *supra* note 65, 12.

interchange which provides encoding for all 22 official languages. The BIS adopted the Indian Standard Code for Information Interchange (ISCII) for Indian languages that originated in Brahmi Script.[68] The ISCII documents follow ISIS 3194:1991 standard. To facilitate Indian scripts in graphical media, the Indian Standard Font Code (ISFOC) has been developed. These code charts are different for each script and are represented in 8 bits only. Further, standards for Indian language keyboard has also been developed. The INdian SCRIPT (INSCRIPT) keyboard layout is the standard for data entry in Indian languages (using QWERTY 101 keyboard, the most common keyboard format, in effect becoming a default option).[69]

In furtherance of international standards like Unicode, W3C,[70] IETF, the 'Character Encoding Standards for Indian Languages' has been issued by MeitY, which provides or BIS's ISCII and *ISO/IEC 10646 (JTC 1/SC 2/WG 2)* and UNICODE as the standard for coding multilingual text.[71] Also, the Best Practises for Localisation of e-governance Applications in Indian Languages suggest the standards *ISO 639 Language Codes*[72] for languages which may be used by mobile application platforms.[73]

Another guideline issued by GoI in 2014 specifies 'Best Practices for Localization of Mobile web application in Indian Languages (Ver. 2.6)'.[74] The purpose of this document is to discuss localisation in Indian language perspective for mobile devices and the concepts associated with localisation like, inputting, storage, display, communication protocols, Common Locale Data Repository (CLDR), etc.[75] This document is predominantly intended for application developers, quality assurance and handset manufacturers and other related stakeholders for seamless interoperability.

Finally, MeitY has also issued Font Standard for Indian languages which prescribes the use of *ISO/IEC 14496-OFF (Open Font Format)* for all twenty-two constitutionally recognised languages.[76] This mitigates the issue of incompatibility of fonts used across different platforms. Further, facilitating the data portability and its access across various applications and platforms.

---

68. Centre for Development of Advanced Computing, MeitY, Government of India, *Standards for Indian Languages*, https://cdac.in/index.aspx?id=mlc_gist_standard#:~:text=Indian%20Standard%20FOnt%20Code%20(ISFOC,represented%20in%208%2Dbits%20only (Standards for Indian Languages).
69. Standards for Indian Languages, *supra* note 68.
70. W3C provides that best practices for delivering web content to mobile devices. The principle objective is to improve the user experience of the Web when accessed from such devices. https://www.w3.org/TR/2008/REC-mobile-bp-20080729/.
71. Ministry of Communication and Information Technology, *Best Practices for Localization of e-Governance applications in Indian Languages*, Government of India, 5 (January 2014), http://egovstandards.gov.in/sites/default/files/Best%20Practices%20for%20Localisation%20of%20e-Governance%20Applications%20in%20Indian%20Languages%20Ver5.7.pdf. (Best Practices for Localization of e-Governance applications in Indian Languages).
72. ISO 639 is standard which provides codes which can be used to refer language names.
73. Best Practices for Localization of e-Governance applications in Indian Languages, *supra* note 71, ii.
74. Best Practices for Localization of e-Governance applications in Indian Languages, *supra* note 71, i.
75. Best Practices for Localization of e-Governance applications in Indian Languages, *supra* note 71, ii.
76. http://egovstandards.gov.in/sites/default/files/Fonts-%20Standard%20Ver.1.0.pdf.

12.3.2 Standards for Data Security in India

While the previous section discussed the data standards adopted by India to facilitate interoperability between various platforms and applications by ensuring seamless exchange and management of data. The present section deals with standards adopted in e-governance for the maintaining the security of the data which is exchanged.

Around the globe, the *ISO/IEC 27001* is the recognised standard for information security management.[77] There are around thirty specific standards under the 27000 family of standards. The standard *ISO/IEC 27001:2013* specifies the requirements for establishing, implementing, maintaining and continually improving an information security management system within the context of the organisation. It also includes requirements for the assessment and treatment of information security risks tailored to the needs of the organisation.[78] This is one of the most consistently adopted standard by various countries such as Australia, Canada, the US and the EU for ensuring data security when implementing e-governance policies.

Similarly, in India, information security standards are prescribed by *ISO 2007*.[79] This is the mandatory standard for all large digital services projects and overall e-governance. The Information Technology Act 2000 (Reasonable Security Practices and Sensitive Personal Data or Information) Rules, 2011 (SPDI Rules) lays down the reasonable security processes and procedures that may be implemented by corporates in India. The SPDI Rules states that corporations in India should adhere to *IS/ISO/IEC 27001*[80] for maintaining information security.

As already noted above standards (both for purposes of e-governance and regulating corporations) for various domains/sectors are under development. Certain important domains like health, finance or biometrics have already adopted data security standards. An in-depth insight of these adopted standards for maintaining data security is discussed below.

12.3.2.1 Biometrics

According to ISO, biometrics is defined as an 'automated recognition of individuals based on their behavioural and biological characteristics'.[81] The *ISO/IEC JTC 1/SC/37* provides for the standardisation of generic biometrics technologies pertaining to human beings to support interoperability and data interchange among applications and systems.[82] The *ISO/IEC 19794-1:2006 – Information Technology – Biometric Data Interchange Formats* is the governing standard for biometrics.

77. Also known as the 'ISMS Family of Standards or ISO27K' comprised of information security standards that have been jointly published by ISO and the IEC.
78. Information technology – *Security techniques – Information Security Management Systems* – Requirements, ISO/IEC 27001:2013, https://www.iso.org/standard/54534.html (Information Security Management Systems).
79. Information Security Management Systems, *supra* note 78.
80. Rule 8, SPDI Rules.
81. Biometrics, ISO/IEC JTC 1/SC 37, https://www.iso.org/committee/313770.html (Biometrics).
82. Biometrics, *supra* note 81.

In India, the GoI is the largest collector of biometrics for the purpose of identification and verification of individuals in e-governance applications.[83] The biometric data collected includes data related to fingerprint image, minutiae, face and iris image. The standards on fingerprint image and minutiae; face and iris image (discussed below) incorporates Common Biometric Exchange Formats Framework of *ISO/IEC/19785* Family – structures and data elements for biometric records[84]; Biometric Data Interchange Formats of *ISO/IEC/19794* Family – data interchange formats for signature/sign behavioural data captured in the form of a multidimensional time series using devices such as digitised tablets or advanced pen systems[85]; Biometric Performance Testing and Reporting of *ISO/IEC/19795* Family provides evaluation of biometric systems in terms of error rates and throughput rates.[86]

12.3.2.1.1 Fingerprint Image and Minutiae Data Standard for e-Governance Application in India (November 2010)[87]

To facilitate the security and interoperability of fingerprint and minutiae data, the GoI has set *ISO/IEC 19794-4:2005(E) – Biometric data Interchange Formats – Finger image data* as the standard for Fingerprint Image Data.[88] Further, to ensure the interoperability of fingerprint images, these images are required to be stored in the format *of Common Biometric Exchange Formats Framework (CBEFF)* according to *ISO 19785-1*. In case of minutiae data, *ISO 19794-2:2005(E)* has been adopted as the Minutiae data format standard. These standards apply to all e-governance projects of Central and State Government of India or any other organisation that uses such data. It must be noted that the latest amendments to these standards are still being deliberated for adoption.

---

83. Ministry of Communications and Information Technology, Government of India, *Fingerprint Image and Minutiae Data Standard for e-Governance Applications in India*, 1 (November 2010), http://egovstandards.gov.in/sites/default/files/Fingerprint%20Image%20Data%20Standard%20Ver1.0.pdf. (Fingerprint Image and Minutiae Data Standard for e-Governance Applications).
84. Information technology – Common Biometric Exchange Formats Framework – Part 1: Data element specification, ISO/IEC 19785-1:2015, https://www.iso.org/standard/66179.html.
85. Information technology – Biometric data interchange formats – Part 7: Signature/sign time series data, ISO/IEC 19794-7:2014, https://www.iso.org/standard/55938.html.
86. Information technology – Biometric performance testing and reporting – Part 1: Principles and framework, ISO/IEC 19795-1:2006, https://www.iso.org/standard/41447.html.
87. Fingerprint Image and Minutiae Data Standard for e-Governance Applications, *supra* note 83.
88. Information Technology – Biometric data interchange formats – Part 4: Finger image data has been revised by ISO/IEC/19794-4:2011, ISO/IEC 19794-4:2005, https://www.iso.org/standard/38748.html.

12.3.2.1.2 Face Image Data Standard for e-Governance Applications in India (November 2010)[89]

To facilitate the interoperability of the face image data among the various e-governance applications, *ISO/IEC 19794-5:2005(E)* has been adopted as the key standard for face image data used for human visual inspection and verification. This standard is required to be used in conjunction with CBEFF, given in *ISO 19785-1* to ensure that face image data is stored in the specific format.

12.3.2.1.3 Iris Image Data Standard for e-Governance Applications in India (March 2011)[90]

For ensuring security and interoperability of Iris image data for e-governance, the GoI has set *ISO 19794-6:2005(E)* as the key standard for Iris Image Data. This standard provides for image data specification, acquisition, storage and transmission formats, however, excluded from its scope is features extraction and matching specifications.

12.3.2.2 Health Services and Documents

The Electronic Health Records (EHR) are digital collection of various medical records that are generated during any clinical encounter or events.[91] Standards are necessary for the lifelong preservation of these electronic health records and to regulate the information collected, stored, retrieved, exchanged and analysis of any images captured, clinical codes or any other data for the purposed of medical examination.

In India, the EHR Standards, 2016[92] provides comprehensive standards for interoperability and data security of EHRs. It provides standards for areas like health record IT standards, where *ISO/TS 2222:2011 Health Informatics – Identification of Subjects of Health Care, MDDS version 1.1 from E-Governance standards, GoI* is prescribed for identifying demographic information including unique identifiers necessary for health record system; *ISO 18308:2011 Health Informatics – Requirements for an EHR Architecture* and *ISO/HL7 10781:2015 Health Informatics - HL7 EHR-Systems Functional Model Release 2(EHR EM)*is provided for health record systems' architectural requirements; *IHTSDO-SNOMED Clinical Terms (SNOMED CT)* is prescribed to maintain a common terminology and coding system standards to express unambiguous

89. MeitY, *Face Image Data Standard for e-Governance Applications in India* (November 2010), http://egovstandards.gov.in/face-image-data-0.
90. MeitY, *Iris Image Data Standard for e-Governance Applications in India*, Government of India, 5 (March 2011), http://egovstandards.gov.in/sites/default/files/Iris%20Image%20Data%20Standard%20Ver1.0.pdf.
91. The Electronic Health Standard, 2016 have replaced the Electronic Health Record Standards of 2013. *See*, Notification of Electronic Health Record (EHR) Standards – 2016 for India, Ministry of Health and Family Welfare, Government of India (30 December 2016), 1, https://www.nhp.gov.in/NHPfiles/EHR-Standards-2016-MoHFW.pdf (The Electronic Health Standard, 2016).
92. The Electronic Health Standard, 2016, *supra* note 91.

meaning of data captured, stored, transmitted and analysed.[93] Where health records are to be used on mobile devices, the mobile application shall adhere to the 'Framework for Mobile Governance 2012' issued by MeitY.[94]

In case of electronic prescriptions or e-prescriptions there are no specific standards to follow but the applicable standards for medical records apply. In this regard, the Pharmacy Council of India, under the regulation of Pharmacy Practice Regulations, 2015 provides that the term 'prescription' also includes the term 'electronic direction' within its ambit.[95] E-prescriptions have to satisfy the requirements of the regular medical prescription as prescribed by the Pharmacy Council of India. It is required to be digitally signed by the registered medical practitioner. And upon being printed, it should appear in the required format along with relevant digital authentication details.[96]

Lastly, where standards have not been provided specifically, as a general rule, standards created or ratified by Standard Development Organisations (SDO) such as BIS or *ISO TC 215 set of standards* or *IEE/NEMA/CE standards for physical systems and interface* maybe used.

12.3.2.3 Financial Services and Documents

In India, Reserve Bank of India (RBI) is the authority that has been issuing guidelines for information security in Banks. Predominantly, all major banks in India adhere to ISO/IEC 27001 for security certification. In year 2011, RBI provided guidelines on information security, electronic banking, technology risk management and cyber frauds (based on G. Gopalakrishna Committee Report).[97] These guidelines suggest that information security cannot be static for banks and they need to proactively update/create/fine-tune/modify their policies, procedures and technologies based on the new developments and emerging concerns.[98] Subsequently, these Guidelines were updated under the Cyber Security Framework in banks issued in June 2016.[99]

The Cyber Security Framework in Banks[100] issued by RBI provides that banks operating in India should immediately have in place a cybersecurity policy that elucidates strategy and approach to combat threats depending upon the level of

93. The Electronic Health Standard, 2016, *supra* note 92, 12.
94. Department of Information Technology, Ministry of Communications & Information, Technology, *Framework for Mobile Governance* Government of India, 8 (01 January 2012), https://mgov.gov.in/doc/Framework%20for%20Mobile%20Governance.pdf.
95. Section 2(j) Pharmacy Practice Regulation, 2015.
96. The Electronic Health Record Standards, 2016, *supra* note 91, 14.
97. *Credit to MSME Entrepreneurs*, Reserve Bank of India (19 April 2011), Circular DBS.CO/CSITE/BC.11/33.01.001/2015-16, https://www.rbi.org.in/Scripts/NotificationUser.aspx?Id=12084&Mode=0.
98. *Cyber Security Framework in Bank*, Reserve Bank of India (2 June 2016), Circular DBS.CO.ITC.BC.No.6/31.02.008/2010-11, https://m.rbi.org.in/scripts/BS_CircularIndexDisplay.aspx?Id=10435 (Cyber Security Framework in Bank).
99. Cyber Security Framework in Bank, *supra* note 98.
100. Cyber Security Framework in Bank, *supra* note 98.

complexity of business and risks involved.[101] In situations where the bank offers mobile payments service, such mobile payments must be secure and should ensure confidentiality, integrity, authenticity and non-repudiability.[102] Further, to ensure interoperability between banks and their mobile payment services, the format for the messages sent by mobile payments service providers, should conform to formats developed by Mobile Payments Forum of India (MPFI)[103] which includes messages in format of ISO 8583 (currently being used by banks for switching of ATM Transactions).

In this regard, on advice of Ministry of Finance, BIS has adopted data standards for Banking and Financial Services. These standards mostly govern the exchange and management of data and not necessarily its security. Some of these adopted standards includes *ISO/TR 13569:2005* which provides guidelines on the development of an information security programme for financial services institutions; *ISO 13616-1:2007 Financial Services – International Bank Number (IBAN) – Part 1: Structure of IBAN* provides the standard for facilitating the processing of data internationally in data interchange in financial environments or within and between other industries; *ISO 9564-1:2011 Part 1* for Personal Identification Number (PIN) management and security, among others.

12.3.2.4 Mobile Applications

Most recent standards adopted by the GoI pertains to mobile application security. MeitY has issued 'Adoption of Mobile AppSec Verification Standard (MASVS) Ver.1 of Open Web Application Security Project (OWASP)'. One of the main aims of the OWASP project is to standardise and disseminate the mobile application testing technologies. The Project concentrates on general mobile threat model.[104] By using this project guidelines, the mobile application developers are ensuring there are no security flaws in their application. Similarly, for cloud services, *ISO/IEC 27017* certification is required.[105] Digital applications providing e-services are required to be audited for security, periodically.

12.3.3 Standards for Data Privacy in India

In India, the Information Technology Act, 2000 (was amended in 2008) (ITA 2000), the Aadhar Act, 2016 and the regulations (discussed below) under them govern the standards for the privacy of Personally Identifiable Information (PII) and Sensitive Information. Currently, there is no central law in India that prescribes standards for

---

101. Cyber Security Framework in Bank, *supra* note 98.
102. Cyber Security Framework in Bank, *supra* note 98.
103. Reserve Bank of India, *Mobile Payment in India – Operative Guidelines for Banks*, 3, https://rbidocs.rbi.org.in/rdocs/Content/PDFs/84978.pdf.
104. Milan Singh Thakur, *The OWASP Mobile Security Project – Data Security Council of India (DSCI) Blog* (13 August 2015), https://www.dsci.in/blogs/the-owasp-mobile-security-project/.
105. Information technology – Security techniques – Code of practice for information security controls based on ISO/IEC 27002 for cloud services, ISO/IEC 27017:2015, https://www.iso.org/standard/43757.html.

data privacy and security. As seen above, the standardisation of privacy and security of the data in different sectors is an evolving situation in India.

The Supreme Court of India in its landmark judgment of *Puttaswamy v. Union of India*,[106] has recognised that 'right to privacy is protected as an intrinsic part the right to life and personal liberty under Article 21 of the Constitution and as part of the freedoms guaranteed by Part III of the Constitution of India'. This judgment acknowledged that the right to data/informational privacy is an intrinsic part of right to privacy and directed the Union Government to put in place a robust legislation/mechanism that shall govern the data privacy and security in India.

Unlike other emerging economies such as Brazil or South Africa, India currently does not have a data protection legislation. To bridge this gap between the law and data protection, in 2019 the Personal Data Protection Bill (PDP Bill) was tabled before the Indian Parliament.[107] The PDP Bill seeks to bring a comprehensive data protection regime in India – similar to EU's GDPR. The PDP Bill prescribes requirements for both personal and sensitive data. It defines and establishes the right of data owners, data processors and data fiduciaries. It introduces a central data protection regulator/authority for effective redressal. The PDP Bill like the GDPR has extra-territorial application in cases where non-Indian organisations are dealing with data generated in India or data having nexus with India. However, it departs from GDPR in a key aspect by providing the requirements of data localisation where enterprises operating in India deal with sensitive information. This requirement is similar to the one found in the Cybersecurity Law of China – where data localisation is permitted in interest of national security.[108]

For non-personal data (NPD) the MeitY unveiled the 'Non-Personal Data Governance Framework', revised in January 2021. The revised NPD framework limits the scope only to 'anonymised' data (devoid of any personal identifiable markers). It provides details for collection of data, rights associated with it and data sharing mechanism between private entities.[109] Lastly, it provides for a separate regulator to oversee the exchange and operations related to such non-personal data.[110]

12.3.3.1 Information Technology Act, 2000

Section 43A of the ITA 2000 provides for 'Compensation for Failure to Protect Data' and enables the enactment of 'reasonable security practices and procedures' for the protection of sensitive personal data by body corporates. While, Section 72

106. Puttaswamy, *supra* note 8.
107. Lok Sabha, Government of India, *The Personal Data Protection Bill, 2019 (Bill No. 373 of 2019)*, http://164.100.47.4/BillsTexts/LSBillTexts/Asintroduced/373_2019_LS_Eng.pdf.
108. Rogier Creemers, Paul Triolo & Graham Webster, Translation: Cybersecurity Law of the People's Republic of China (Effective 1 June 2017), New America (29 June 2018), https://www.newamerica.org/cybersecurity-initiative/digichina/blog/translation-cybersecurity-law-peoples-republic-china/.
109. *Privacy and Data Protection – India Wrap 2020*, The National Law Review (15 January 2021), https://www.natlawreview.com/article/privacy-and-data-protection-india-wrap-2020 (India Wrap 2020).
110. India Wrap 2020, *supra* n. 109.

provides for criminal punishment, when a service supplier discloses personal information without the consent of person in course of performing contract or in breach of such contract.

Appended to Section 43A of the IT Act are Information Technology (Reasonable Security Practices and Procedure and Sensitive Personal Data or Information) Rules, 2011 (SPDI). The SPDI Rules incorporate the OECD guidelines on 'Protection of Privacy and Transborder Flows of Personal Data.'[111] They set forward requirements for the collection of personal information[112] for lawful purposes only and connected with the purpose for which it is collected.[113] The SPDI Rules clearly lay down the duration of period for retaining the data/information collected; and provides the data owners to correct their information.

The SPDI rules currently apply to corporate/private sector entities, and not to the government institutions or agencies. Another issue with SPDI rules is that it is applicable to the 'sensitive data', i.e., sexual orientation, bank account details, medical records, biometric information, physical, physiological, mental health condition or any preceding information received by body corporate for processing, storage under lawful contract. However, it excludes other kinds of personal data such as user online preferences, religious beliefs, political opinion, ethnicity, etc.

12.3.3.2 Aadhar (Targeted Delivery of Financial and Other Subsidies, Benefits and Services Act, 2016 (Aadhar Act, 2016)

The Aadhar Act, 2016 was enacted by the GoI for the collection of personal information of citizens of India,[114] mainly including individual's biometrics. This data is used to provide for targeted delivery of subsides, benefits and other services to citizens. The Act provides for an Aadhar based authentication services wherein both Government and Private entities can ask Unique Identification Authority of India (UIDAI) (a body established under the Aadhar Act, responsible for the administration of the Act[115]) to validate the correctness of the identity of the individual.[116]

The Aadhar Act and its regulations recognise[117] the various principles of data protection and privacy to ensure the information of Aadhar card holders is secure. Under the Aadhar Act, there is a requirement to ensure security and confidentiality of the identifiable information of the record holder.[118] It stipulates necessary steps required for the protection of record holder's information against any unlawful access,

111. The Organisation for Economic Co-operation and Development, *OECD Guidelines Governing the Protection of Privacy and Transborder Flows of Personal Data* (13 July 2013), https://www.oecd.org/sti/ieconomy/2013-oecd-privacy-guidelines.pdf.
112. Rule 5(4), SPDI Rules.
113. Rule 5(2), SPDI Rules.
114. Section 30, Aadhar Act, 2016.
115. Section 11, Aadhar Act, 2016.
116. White Paper on Data Protection.
117. Such as Aadhar (Data Security) Regulations, 2016.
118. Section 28, Aadhar Act, 2016.

use or disclosure and destruction, loss or damage.[119] The information recorded under the Aadhar Act, is allowed to be used only for the purpose of generation of Aadhar number and authentication.[120] This information can be requested from UIDAI barring the core biometric information.[121] The record holder may edit, change or seek rectification for demographic information or if the biometric information is lost or changed.[122] Lastly, the information collected by UIDAI is without the knowledge of the purpose for such authentication.[123]

These are broadly the overarching privacy laws existing in India. Further, in the sub-section we discuss, individual laws/regulation governing data/information privacy in key sectors.

12.3.3.3 Privacy Standards: A Collation of Key Sectors in India

12.3.3.3.1 Financial Sector

The primary legal instruments that address the data protection in the financial sector are Credit Information Companies (Regulations) Act, 2005 (CIC Act), the Credit Information Companies Regulation, 2006 and the regular circulars published by RBI. Also, as mentioned above, the SPDI Rules governs regulation, collection and disclosure of certain aspects of sensitive information which is financial information in nature (such as includes information relating to credit cards, debit cards and other payment instruments).[124]

The CIC Act, along with its Regulation of 2006 embodies the core data privacy principles, such as limitation on the use of data, accuracy of data, data retention, right to forget and data modification.[125] The CIC Act ensures that credit card companies operating in India adhere to basic norms pertaining to data privacy. Any information collected by the companies is for the purpose of credit information and such information should be at all times protected against unauthorised use, access or disclosure.[126]

(1) RBI Circulars or Guidelines

RBI is the governing body for banks and other financial institutions in India. RBI has been issuing circulars that provide guidelines, procedures and modalities to be adopted

119. Section 28, Aadhar Act, 2016.
120. Section 29, Aadhar Act, 2016.
121. Section 28(5), Aadhar Act, 2016.
122. Section 31, Aadhar Act, 2016.
123. Section 32, Aadhar Act, 2016.
124. Rule 3(ii), SPDI Rules.
125. The Credit Information Companies (Regulation) Act, 2005, https://legislative.gov.in/sites/default/files/A2005-30.pdf.
126. Sections 19 and 20, CIC Act.

by banking/financial institutions, such as, the Know Your Customer (KYC) specifications where user information collected by banks/financial institutions remains confidential at all times.[127] Other instruments/guidelines such as Circular on Credit Card, Debit Card and Rupee Denominated Co-branded Prepaid Card Operations of Banks and Credit Card issuing Non-Banking Financial Corporations; Master Circular on Customer Services, 2009 and the Code of Banks Commitment to Customers, etc. all provide for privacy and protection of customer's information and to treat such information as confidential at all times.

(2) Banking Codes and Standards Board of India (BCSBI)

BCSBI is an independent and autonomous body that sets the rules of code of conduct for banking operations in India.[128] While these codes are voluntary in nature, majority of the banks in India adopt them. The Code of Bank's Commitment to Customers code focuses on confidentiality and privacy of customer information. It requires the confidentiality of the user information be maintained even after severed relationship with bank; information collected should be required by the law or the banking regulator; the bank should have customer's authentication to reveal customer's information, etc. Similarly other codes operating in financial sector are Indian Banks Association Fair Practice Code for Credit Card Operations, etc.

NITI Aayog (a policy think-tank of GoI) in 2020 released the draft framework for 'Data Empowerment and Protection Architecture' (DEPA), for financial sector. Through this framework, the NITI Aayog aims to create a secure mechanism based on consent-based data sharing for the fintech sector. Under this framework, RBI's 'Account Aggregator' model shall be replicated. This will allow individuals to share their data across banks, insurer, lenders, mutual fund operators, etc., therefore achieving seamless interoperability.[129] A similar framework is being developed for health and telecom sector.

12.3.3.3.2 Telecommunication Sector

In India various laws/regulations are in operation to regulate this sector. The primary law in this sector is Telecom Regulatory Authority of India (TRAI) Act, 1997 (TRAI Act). In absence of umbrella privacy law in India, the data privacy of consumers in this sector is maintained by Unified License Agreement that are issued to Telecom Service Providers by the Department of Telecommunications.[130]

127. RBI, *RBI Master Direction on Know Your Customer (KYC) Direction*, 2016 (25 February 2016, updated as on 8 July 2016), https://www.rbi.org.in/Scripts/NotificationUser.aspx?Id = 10292 &Mode = 0.This Master Direction was amended by RBI Amendment to Master Direction dated 8 December 2016, available at https://rbi.org.in/scripts/NotificationUser.aspx?Mode = 0&Id = 10770.
128. Huzefa Tavawalla and Kartik Maheshwari, *Data Protection in Financial Sector*, Data Guidance (8 July 2014) https://nishithdesai.com/fileadmin/user_upload/pdfs/Research%20Articles/DataGuidance_Guidance_Note__India.pdf.
129. India Wrap 2020, *supra* note 109.
130. White Paper on Data Protection, *supra* note 35, 2.

Telecom Service Providers are obliged to maintain detailed call records of users including exchange and IP details for at least one year.[131] Any such customer information collected by the service providers shall not be disclosed without the consent of the customer as per terms of consent.[132] Further, the TRAI is empowered to frame other regulations like the Telecomm Commercial Communication Preference Regulations, 2010 which provide for protection against spam or unsolicited commercial communications and stipulates setting up Customer Preference Registration Facility, through which customers can opt out to receive such communication.[133] However, the application of this regulation is limited only to messages received through phone

The data privacy in telecommunication sector in India is inadequate. In year 2018, TRAI released its 'Recommendations on Privacy, Security and Ownership of Data'[134] in the context of telecommunication domain. Under this recommendation, TRAI conceptualises the telecommunication environment as a digital ecosystem that covers telecom service providers, communication network browsers, operating systems, applications, Over the Top Platforms, etc. The recommendation states that ownership of such personal data lies with the data owner or individual and entities processing such data are mere custodians and do not have any primary rights over the data. However, this recommendation only covers personal data and refrains from covering sensitive data.

12.3.3.3.3 Health Sector

In the absence of an overarching privacy law, currently ITA 2000 and SPDI Rules recognises the health records as 'sensitive personal data' and regulates its collection, use and disclosure. However, the application of SPDI Rules is restricted only to private sector, and there is nothing in effect that governs the collection or transfer of medical data in public sector.

The Indian Medical Council (Professional Conduct, Etiquette and Ethics) Regulations, 2002 (IMC Regulation) issued within the ambit of Indian Medical Council Act, 1956 requires the doctor-patient confidentiality to be maintained at all times. However, there are instances of breach where patient information is provided to the patient's relative or parents or friends.[135] With limited privacy safeguards and complex nature of EHRs, the IMC Regulation is not sufficient to govern data privacy in health sector.

To ensure data privacy in health sector, the Ministry of Health and Welfare has proposed the Health Data Management Policy (HDM).[136] It is largely based on the PDP

---

131. Clause 39.20, Unified License Agreement.
132. Clause 37.2, Unified License Agreement.
133. Regulation 3, TRAI Regulations.
134. Telecom Regulatory Authority of India, *Recommendations on Privacy, Security and Ownership of Data* (16 July 2018), https://www.trai.gov.in/sites/default/files/Recommendation DataPrivacy16072018_0.pdf.
135. Section 2.3. IMC Regulation.
136. Ministry of Health and Family Welfare, Government of India, *National Digital Health Mission: Health Data Management Policy – Chapter I: Preliminary* (February 2012), https://ndhm.gov.in/documents/HealthDataManagementPolicy.

Bill. The HDM Policy recognises three entities, i.e., data controller, processors and fiduciaries. It requires the data fiduciaries to abide by the basic data protection principles and establish certain compliance requirements such as security practices and impact assessments. The HDM Policy also allows for consent-based sharing of data and establishes a grievance redressal procedure through the National Health Authority.

12.3.3.3.4 E-Commerce Sector

In India, there is no express law governing the e-commerce sector. Currently, the ITA 2000 along with SPDI rule govern the standards for data privacy in e-commerce sector. A new e-commerce policy is being developed by MeitY. The draft of new policy available suggests rules for sharing source codes, algorithms and data used by e-commerce operators/retailers with the government. It includes provisions for NPD, anti-piracy, cross-border data flows. It also envisages an investigative body to look into the violation committed by e-commerce entities.

Recently, the Ministry Road Transport and Highways has amended the Motor Vehicle Aggregator Guidelines[137] to regulate the business of transport of cab aggregators. The new amended guidelines of 2020 provide for their licensing, regulation of fares, compliances with regard to vehicles, apps and websites, etc. Most importantly, the new guidelines suggest that data generated on an aggregator's website or app should be stored in India for a minimum of three months and a maximum of twenty-four months.[138] It also stipulates that data should not be disclosed or shared without the customer's written consent. However, the guidelines do not define the scope of the kind of data covered under the guidelines and its application is left with the respective State Governments, thus creating uncertainty in its effective implementation.[139]

Lastly, the most recent regulation enacted by the Government of India to regulate data privacy in e-commerce sector is the Consumer Protection (E-Commerce) Rules, 2020. Under these rules, the operating marketplace entities are required to provide information related to activities performed by customers such as return, refund, exchange warrantee, delivery, etc. and maintain security of payment transaction done by consumers.

12.4 CONCLUSION

India like other countries worldwide is shifting towards e-governance. In this regard, India adopted a broad-based strategic approach to e-governance through its NeGP,

137. Noti. CG-DL-E-26112020-223348 (Gazette of India), Ministry of Road Transport and Highways, *Motor Vehicle Aggregator Guidelines 2020*, New Delhi, 26 November 2020, https://morth.nic.in/sites/default/files/notifications_document/Motor%20Vehicle%20Aggregators27112020150046.pdf.
138. Rules 5, 8, 9, 10, 13 and 20, Motor Vehicle Aggregator Guidelines 2020.
139. India Wrap 2020, *supra* note 109.

back in 2006. And under the Digital India initiative, India has actively been implementing laws and regulations to standardise its digital economy. From the above discussion, it is clear that India has been incorporating all important international standards for regulating digital governance and security of data. The data standardisation of 'personal identification and land region codification' is a major achievement – considering the diversity of demographic in India. The IFEG with open standards polices is in tandem with interoperability polices of other countries. The adoption of same has also resulted in the reduction of cost of intellectual property rents for software leading to a considerable reduction in price of final services delivered by the government and promotes access to simplified services across all demographics.

India which was ranked 100 on the UN e-Government Development Index in 2020,[140] a considerable demotion considering the fact, back in year 2018, India had jumped 22 places to achieve a rank of 98.[141] The foremost reason for this ineffective application of digital standards in India is delay in approval of necessary legislation for regulation of the data; other factors include rapidly evolving new technologies, divergence of opinion on 'how to regulate', and lack of effective implementation as well as compliance by the regulatory authority. Moreover, due to infrastructural issues, majority of e-governance services and applications in India are developed and operated in silos. Even after having a robust Open Standards e-Governance Policy, the interoperability of these applications across various e-governance platforms is inoperative.[142] Further, due to the federal structure of India, effective implementation is fragmented.

While there is no doubt that India has made considerable leeway in setting and implementing standards for data security. The most debilitating aspect still remains the lack of a standalone legislation governing data privacy. The PDP Bill of India is modelled after the GDPR. In essence companies already compliant with GDPR would face less challenges when adopting Indian data protection regime. However, this Bill is still under consideration in the Indian Parliament. Moreover, the clauses relating to data localisation and cross-border data sharing under the Bill are major sources of concern for businesses operating in India and for potential investments. As already evidenced from China's Cyber Security Law, any imposition of data-localisation laws is inherently seen as trade restrictive, adding to the cost of business operations. Meanwhile, in the absence of umbrella data protection regime, sector-specific regulations are being implemented to govern the data. This in future may lead to conflict with the overarching PDP Bill. Some of these issues would probably include jurisdictional conflicts between sector-specific regulatory authority, cybersecurity and disclosures to the government.

---

140. Gonewsindia, *India Slips To 100 in UN E-Government Development Index Rankings* (July 2020), https://www.gonewsindia.com/latest-news/technology/india-slips-to-100-in-un-e-government-survey-2020-rankings-16168#:~:text=India%20Slips%20To%20100%20in%20UN%20E%2DGovernment%20Development%20Index%20Rankings,-by%20GoNews%20Desk&text=India%20has%20slipped%204%20places,)%20and%20Iran%20(89)(India E-Government Development Index Rankings).
141. India E-Government Development Index Rankings, *supra* note 141.
142. Civilsdaily, *Challenges to e-governance and requirements for successful implementation* (22 September 2017), https://www.civilsdaily.com/challenges-to-e-governance-and-requirements-for-successful-implementation/.

Comparable economies such as South Africa, Brazil and more recently Egypt have already established data protection laws. In this case, India clearly is lagging behind. However, the steps taken by the GoI are in the right direction. The National e-governance plan with its mandate of setting standards to facilitate e-governance, digital services and other platforms when coupled with PDP Bill will result in a complete re-designing or overhaul of the existing data protection regime in India. Henceforth, resulting in an adequate and robust mechanism for data security, privacy and protection in India.

Index

GLOBAL TRADE LAW SERIES

1. Emmanuel T. Laryea, *Paperless Trade: Opportunities, Challenges and Solutions,* 2002 (ISBN 90-411-9897-0).
2. Xiang Gao, *The Fraud Rule in the Law of Letters of Credit: A Comparative Study,* 2002 (ISBN 90-411-9898-9).
3. Yuwa Wei, *Comparative Corporate Governance: A Chinese Perspective,* 2003 (ISBN 90-411-9908-X).
4. Ross P. Buckley (ed.), *The WTO and the Doha Round: The Changing Face of World Trade,* 2003 (ISBN 90-411-9947-0).
5. Bradley J. Condon, Joyce C. Sadka & Tapen Sinha (eds), *Insurance Regulation in North America: Integrating American, Canadian and Mexican Markets,* 2003 (ISBN 90-411-2301-6).
6. Jan Hoogmartens, *EC Trade Law Following China's Accession to the WTO,* 2004 (ISBN 90-411-2301-6).
7. Yang Guohua, Bryan Mercurio & Li Yongjie, *WTO Dispute Settlement Understanding: A Detailed Interpretation,* 2005 (ISBN 90-411-2361-X).
8. Jan Job de Vries Robbé, Paul U. Ali, *Securitisation of Derivatives and Alternative Asset Classes, Yearbook,* 2005 (ISBN 90-411-2375-X).
9. Markus W. Gehring, Marie-Claire Cordonier Segger, *Sustainable Development in World Trade Law,* 2005 (ISBN 90-411-2366-0).
10. Yann Aubin & Arnaud Idiart, *Export Control Law and Regulations Handbook: A Practical Guide to Military and Dual-Use Goods Trade Restrictions and Compliance,* 2007 (ISBN 90-411-2601-5).
11. Henry Kibet Mutai, *Compliance with International Trade Obligations: The Common Market for Eastern and Southern Africa,* 2007 (ISBN 978-90-411-2664-1).
12. Yong-Shik Lee, *Economic Development through World Trade: A Developing World Perspective,* 2007 (ISBN 978-90-411-2681-8).
13. Yanning Yu, *Circumvention and Anti-Circumvention Measures: The Impact on Anti-Dumping Practice in International Trade,* 2007 (ISBN 978-90-411-2686-3).
14. Ross Buckley, Vai Io Lo & Laurence Boulle, *Challenges to Multilateral Trade: The Impact of Bilateral, Preferential and Regional Agreements,* 2008 (ISBN 978-90-411-2711-2).
15. K.D. Raju, *World Trade Organization Agreement on Anti-dumping: A GATT/ WTO and Indian Jurisprudence,* 2008 (ISBN 978-90-411-2780-8).
16. Xiaochen Wu, *Anti-dumping Law and Practice in China,* 2008 (ISBN 978-90-411-2790-7).
17. Amin Alavi, *Legalization of Development in the WTO: Between Law and Politics,* 2008 (ISBN 978-90-411-2795-2).
18. Henrik Andersen, *EU Dumping Determinations and WTO Law,* 2009 (ISBN 978-90-411-2827-0).

19. Sherzod Shadikhodjaev, *Retaliation in the WTO Dispute Settlement System*, 2009 (ISBN 978-90-411-2811-9).
20. Yi Shin Tang, *The International Trade Policy for Technology Transfers: Legal and Economic Dilemmas on Multilateralism versus Bilateralism*, 2009 (ISBN 978-90-411-2825-6).
21. Reem Anwar Ahmed Raslan, *Antidumping: A Developing Country Perspective*, 2009 (ISBN 978-90-411-3128-7).
22. Pietro Poretti, *The Regulation of Subsidies within the General Agreement on Trade in Services of the WTO: Problems and Prospects*, 2009 (ISBN 978-90-411-3162-1).
23. Esther Lam, *China and the WTO: A Long March towards the Rule of Law*, 2009 (ISBN 978-90-411-3144-7).
24. Jorge Alberto Huerta-Goldman, *Mexico in the WTO and NAFTA: Litigating International Trade Disputes*, 2009 (ISBN 978-90-411-3169-0).
25. Laurence Boulle, *The Law of Globalization: An Introduction*, 2009 (ISBN 978-90-411-2828-7).
26. Daniel Lovric, *Deference to the Legislature in WTO Challenges to Legislation*, 2010 (ISBN 978-90-411-3145-4).
27. Gregory W. Bowman, Nick Covelli, David A. Gantz & Ihn Ho Uhm, *Trade Remedies in North America*, 2010 (ISBN 978-90-411-2840-9).
28. Madalina Diaconu, *International Trade in Gambling Services*, 2010 (ISBN 978-90-411-3248-2).
29. Mohamed Ramadan Hassanien, *United States Bilateral Free Trade Agreements: Consistencies or Conflicts with Norms in the Middle East?*, 2010 (ISBN 978-90-411-3281-9).
30. Marie-Claire Cordonier Segger, Markus W Gehring & Andrew Newcombe, *Sustainable Development in World Investment Law*, 2011 (ISBN 978-90-411-3166-9).
31. Nellie Munin, *Legal Guide to GATS*, 2010 (ISBN 978-90-411-2824-9).
32. Thomas G. Kelch, *Globalization and Animal Law: Comparative Law, International Law and International Trade*, 2011 (ISBN 978-90-411-3338-0).
33. Yann Aubin & Arnaud Idiart (eds), *Export Control Law and Regulations Handbook: A Practical Guide to Military and Dual-Use Goods Trade Restrictions and Compliance*, Third Edition, 2016 (ISBN 978-90-411-5443-9).
34. Yulia Selivanova (ed.), *Regulation of Energy in International Trade Law: WTO, NAFTA and Energy Charter*, 2011 (ISBN 978-90-411-3264-2).
35. Germano Franceschin & Francesco Misuraca, *India: Commercial Law, Customs and Taxation*, 2011 (ISBN 978-90-411-2836-2).
36. Humberto Zúñiga Schroder, *Harmonization, Equivalence and Mutual Recognition of Standards in WTO Law*, 2011 (ISBN 978-90-411-3657-2).
37. Kati Kulovesi, *The WTO Dispute Settlement System: Challenges of the Environment, Legitimacy and Fragmentation*, 2011 (ISBN 978-90-411-3406-6).

38. Martín Molinuevo, *Protecting Investment in Services: Investor-State Arbitration versus WTO Dispute Settlement*, 2012 (ISBN 978-90-411-3827-9).
39. Joachim Åhman, *Trade, Health, and the Burden of Proof in WTO Law*, 2012 (ISBN 978-90-411-3825-5).
40. Umair Hafeez Ghori, *Global Textiles and Clothing Trade: Trade Policy Perspectives*, 2012 (ISBN 978-90-411-3875-0).
41. Yenkong Ngangjoh Hodu, *Theories and Practices of Compliance with WTO Law*, 2012 (ISBN 978-90-411-3228-4).
42. Dan Wei & Fernando M. Furlan, *Brazil in World Trade: Contingent Protection Measures*, 2012 (ISBN 978-90-411-3335-9).
43. Jorge A. Huerta-Goldman, Antoine Romanetti & Franz X. Stirnimann (eds), *WTO Litigation, Investment Arbitration, and Commercial Arbitration*, 2013 (ISBN 978-90-411-4686-1).
44. Gilles Muller, *Liberalization of Trade in Legal Services*, 2013 (ISBN 978-90-411-4853-7).
45. Christian Struck, *Product Regulations and Standards in WTO Law*, 2014 (ISBN 978-90-411-4950-3).
46. Gonzalo Villalta Puig, *Economic Relations between Australia and the European Union: Law and Policy*, 2014 (ISBN 978-90-411-3405-9).
47. Maurizio Gambardella, Davide Rovetta & Simon van Cutsem, *Remission and Repayment of Customs Duties in the EU*, 2014 (ISBN 978-90-411-4764-6).
48. Lisa Spagnolo, *CISG Exclusion and Legal Efficiency*, 2014 (ISBN 978-90-411-5407-1).
49. Dennis Ndonga, *Single Windows and Trade Facilitation: A Tool for Development*, 2015 (ISBN 978-90-411-5834-5).
50. Malebakeng Agnes Forere, *The Relationship of WTO Law and Regional Trade Agreements in Dispute Settlement: From Fragmentation to Coherence*, 2015 (ISBN 978-90-411-6274-8).
51. Julien Chaisse & Jiaxiang Hu (eds), *International Economic Law and the Challenges of the Free Zones*, 2019 (ISBN 978-94-035-0893-1).
52. Boris Praštalo, *Uniformity in the Application of the CISG: Analysis of the Problem and Recommendations for the Future*, 2020 (ISBN 978-94-035-2072-8).
53. Manuel A.J. Teehankee, *Trade and Environment Governance at the World Trade Organization Committee on Trade and Environment*, 2020 (ISBN 978-94-035-2202-9).
54. Marco Tulio Molina Tejeda (ed.), *Practical Aspects of WTO Litigation*, 2020 (ISBN 978-90-411-8596-9).
55. James J. Nedumpara, Satwik Shekhar & Akshaya Venkataraman (eds), *Handbook on Product Standards and International Trade: Navigating the Regulatory Landscape in India*, 2022 (978-94-035-3413-8).

www.ingramcontent.com/pod-product-compliance
Ingram Content Group UK Ltd.
Pitfield, Milton Keynes, MK11 3LW, UK
UKHW020229290926
15470UKWH00002B/437

9 789403 534138